EASTERN EUROPE IN THE TWENTIETH CENTURY – AND AFTER

The first edition of *Eastern Europe in the Twentieth Century* took the story to the fall of the communist régimes in 1989–91. In 1989, the collapse of communism and Soviet power transformed the world order. In this new edition, *Eastern Europe in the Twentieth Century – and After*, R. J. Crampton includes a consideration of the evolution of the region since 1991. Focusing on the attempt to create and maintain a functioning democracy, the author also surveys the development of a market economy.

R. J. Crampton places the revolutions of 1989–91 within the context of each country's historical tradition. The author includes discussion of Albania, Bulgaria, Croatia, the Czech Republic, Estonia, Hungary, Latvia, Lithuania, Macedonia, Poland, Romania, Slovakia, Slovenia, and the Yugoslav federation. This revised edition contains an up-to-date bibliography and extended examination of the breakdown of stability in Bosnia and Hercegovina. The author also analyses the realignment of Eastern Europe towards the west and details key themes such as the emergence of organised crime.

Eastern Europe has been the crucible of the modern world and has now evolved into a post-totalitarian era. R. J. Crampton argues that the collapse of communist-dominated states means, in effect, the end of the twentieth century. He provides an accessible introduction to this key area which is invaluable to students of modern and contemporary political history.

R. J. Crampton is Professor of East European History and a Fellow of St Edmund Hall, Oxford. His publications include *Bulgaria 1878–1918: A History, A Short History of Modern Bulgaria, The Hollow Detente: Anglo-German Relations in the Balkans, 1911–1914* and, with Ben Crampton, *Atlas of Eastern Europe in the Twentieth Century.*

EASTERN EUROPE IN THE TWENTIETH CENTURY – AND AFTER

Second edition

R. J. Crampton

London and New York

TO DES AND JOA
for the peg-bag
and
much else besides

First published 1994
by Routledge
11 New Fetter Lane, London EC4P 4EE

Simultaneously published in the USA and Canada
by Routledge
29 West 35th Street, New York, NY 10001

Second edition 1997
Reprinted 2000, 2001

Routledge is an imprint of the Taylor & Francis Group

© 1994, 1997 R. J. Crampton

Phototypeset in Bembo by
Intype London Limited
Printed and bound in Great Britain by
Clays Ltd, St Ives plc

British Library Cataloguing in Publication Data
A catalogue record for this book is available from the British Library

Library of Congress Cataloguing in Publication Data
Crampton, R. J.
Eastern Europe in the twentieth century and after / R. J. Crampton.
p.   cm.
Originally published: Eastern Europe in the twentieth century.
London ; New York : Routledge, 1997.
Includes bibliographical references and index.
1. Europe, Eastern–History–20th century.   I. Title.
DJK38.C73   1997
947.084–dc21   97–665
ISBN 0–415–16422–2 (hbk)
0–415–16423–0 (pbk)

CONTENTS

CONTENTS

Part II Totalitarianism

Part III Revisionism

Part IV The decline of socialism

Part V The death of socialism

Part VI After the twentieth century – and after eastern Europe?

MAPS AND TABLES

MAPS

TABLES

EASTERN EUROPE, 1914

0 — 250 km

Line dividing the Hungarian
– – – Kingdom from the remainder
of the Habsburg Empire

SWEDEN

DENMARK

Copenhagen

Baltic Sea

Königsberg

Danzig

RUSSIAN EMPIRE

River Vistula

Berlin

Warsaw

River Bug

GERMAN EMPIRE

Lemberg
(Lvov)

GALICIA

BUKOVINA

River Dniester

AUSTRO-HUNGARIAN
EMPIRE

River Danube

Carpathians

River Pruth

Munich

Vienna

Budapest

TRANSYLVANIA

SWITZ

CROATIA

Carpathians

ROMANIA

Agram
(Zagreb)

BANAT

Bucharest

DOBRUDJA

Belgrade

ITALY

Adriatic Sea

BOSNIA-
HERCEGOVINA

Dinaric Alps

DALMATIA

SERBIA

BULGARIA

Sofia

Rome

MONTENEGRO

MACE-
DONIA

Constantinople

Tirana

ALBANIA

THRACE

OTTOMAN

GREECE

EMPIRE

PREFACE TO THE FIRST EDITION

Winston Churchill described how in July 1914, after a long and tedious discussion on the minutiae of local government boundaries in the north of Ireland, the cabinet heard the terms of the Austro-Hungarian ultimatum to Serbia. 'The parishes of Fermanagh and Tyrone', he wrote, 'faded back into the mists and squalls of Ireland, and a strange light began immediately, but by perceptible gradations, to fall and grow upon the map of Europe'.[1] The parishes of Fermanagh and Tyrone are still, alas, in our headlines but with the light again on eastern Europe it appears to be an opportune time to examine the modern history of this area. Some recent events have brought back distant, exotic names last encountered in school history text-books: Temesvar (Timişoara), Macedonia, and, tragically, Bosnia-Hercegovina. There are also names which few text-books would have contained: who or what, for example, are the Gagauze or the Vlachs?

In addition to bringing to light strange or forgotten names the upheavals in eastern Europe have presented the west with new opportunites for trade and business, but at the same time have posed awesome problems. To take better advantage of the new opportunities and to make a start at understanding and solving these problems some knowledge of the area's recent history is essential. That this is so was brought home forcibly to me and three British colleagues in Romania in 1990 when three or four young men, all of them excellent journalists with reputable newspapers, took us to dinner on condition that we gave them a seminar on recent Romanian and Balkan history.

Before 1989 'recent' eastern European history would probably have been taken to mean the period since the communists took power after the second world war. Up to the 1970s at least that takeover appeared to be a huge historical 'Berlin Wall' dividing the contemporary world from a dead past. Yet, as we move further away from the wall, it becomes easier to see over the top of it, and so we perceive more and more the continuities of history rather than its divisions, the more we realise that paths and tracks which seemed to begin at or near the wall are in fact continuations of ones leading to it, that the wall is an interruption not a break. As the distinguished American historian, István Déak, has asked:

Is there any need, then, to emphasize the scholarly importance of the history of the 1920s and 1930s, or that all studies of the region's recent history must now begin, not in 1945, as they have for the last few decades, but at least in 1918?[2]

These are the main justifications for writing this history of eastern Europe in the twentieth century. What, however, is to be understood by 'eastern Europe' and by 'the twentieth century'?

All definitions in history are, of course, contentious and transitory because they are determined by the vantage point of those who make them. Anyone with a rudimentary knowledge of nineteenth and twentieth century history will recognise the chronological limits of F. R. Bridge's excellent analysis of Austro-Hungarian foreign policy, *From Sadowa to Sarajevo*.[3] How many would be as confident in pinpointing the beginning and end of a work whose subtitle was *From Sadowa to Kirk Kilisse*?[4] It is in fact a study of international politics from the defeat of Austria by Prussia in 1866 to the destruction of Ottoman military power in Europe by the Bulgarians in the autumn of 1912. When the book was published, in 1913, the end of Ottoman power in Europe seemed to be a significant turning point, as indeed it was, and would still be widely recognised as such had not another and more dramatic one been reached in June–July 1914 at Sarajevo.

Yet dividing lines must be drawn and for our purposes the twentieth century begins and ends with the break-up of multi-national empires; from those of the hierarchical monarchies which collapsed at the end of the first world war to the dissolution of the ideologically based communist imperium at the end of the 1980s. If the twentieth century has a dominant characteristic it is surely that of a collectivist ideology seizing control of and determining the nature of the state. The ideology presumes a knowledge of historical inevitability; it alone knows where 'progress' must take humanity. The ruling ideologues, acting through a party created for the purpose, shape society and the state according to the dictates of the historical process that they have defined, usually in the interests of a particular race or class, rather than using it to allow individual liberties to flower in the manner in which the individuals chose, as was the case in the era after the English, American and French revolutions. In this sense history may not have ended in 1989 but the twentieth century in eastern Europe seems to have done so.

If this provides us with a clear end-date, the Young Turk revolution of July 1908 could be taken as a possible beginning. The Young Turks' aspirations contained much that was later to be seen in the twentieth century, but also much that had its roots in nineteenth century individualism. The Young Turks wanted to create a state based on a new, collective Ottoman national consciousness. The conscription of nationalism in the cause of the state was not new; the same card had been played with particular enthusiasm by the rulers of imperial Germany and tsarist Russia but they had wished to use nationalism to conserve an existing order, whereas the Young Turks used nationalism as a 'progressive' force. Their problem was that they did not have a nation to work upon.

If the Young Turk revolution may be regarded as the conception of the twentieth century, its birth was in 1917–19. But, Russia and the Soviet Union apart, the century was still in its infancy; ideological nationalism was growing in strength but its western, liberal parents still guided it at least until 1929–31. From then the twentieth century entered its adolesence; ideological nationalism became assertive, crude, and eventually uncontrollable. The adulthood of the twentieth century, when national and class-based ideologies were at their height in eastern Europe, was from the onset of the second world war to the remoulding of the stalinist system between 1953 and 1956. From 1956 to 1968 was middle age, with the passions of ideology not forgotten but tempered by pragmatism and occasionally by wisdom. From 1968 to 1980 old age became more and more apparent; the powers of the body political declined whilst in mental or ideological affairs the follies of youth, above all nationalism, reappeared. If the bodily analogy may be continued, then the Solidarity revolution of 1980 was the cardiac arrest from which the twentieth century in eastern Europe never fully recovered; thereafter all was senility, despite the attempts at resuscitation practised by the young Kremlin doctor after 1985.

These six, rather than seven, ages of the twentieth century in eastern Europe give this book its general framework. The period from the end of the first world war to the beginning of the second is, however, treated as one, as a combined childhood and adolescence. In this period the most rational approach to the area is to treat each country individually, though the Baltic states are placed in one chapter. When ideology has seized complete control such an approach becomes more difficult; although the second world war saw new divisions, the old ones were by and large re-established after 1945 and so a very brief outline of developments in each of the former states is provided. After 1945 the communist system is described and then each of its major crises, 1956, 1968, 1980, and 1989, are analysed, though there are also linking passages which attempt to provide some continuity of development in individual states.

Eastern Europe is defined in political rather than geographic terms. In English usage 'Eastern Europe' has come in recent decades to mean those countries which were under Soviet domination after 1945. In American usage the area covered would be 'East Central Europe and South-Eastern Europe'. Perhaps, as is often the case, the Germans have the most precise phraseology: *Zwischeneuropa* (the regions between) surely sums up best the notion of those areas which were excluded from west European developments but were not fully incorporated in the USSR;[5] thus after 1945 the *Zwischeneuropa* can include eastern Germany and Czechoslovakia but exclude Austria, Finland, and Greece. Although Vienna is further east than Prague or Berlin, democratic, federal Austria is as patently part of the western world as is the Republic of Ireland or Switzerland. Finland was always Scandinavian rather than east European in its orientation and after the second world war acquired a unique status in which it moulded its foreign policy in conformity with Moscow's wishes but was left free to conduct its own internal affairs. The Greek case is more complex. Greece is without doubt a Balkan country; it is also an integral part of the eastern Orthodox community. On both counts it shares much with eastern Europe, yet it is more than an east European state. Not only has it become part of NATO and the European (Economic) Community, it also has long historical ties with Asia Minor and its huge diaspora has linked it more closely than any other east European state or nation with the wider world; Greece is the only state in eastern Europe in its wider definition which has a greater proportion of its frontier on the sea than on land and it has therefore developed extensive, extrovert links with western Europe and beyond.

This history is primarily a political one. It says relatively little on international relations, economics, or culture. The author takes no pride in these omissions but in a work covering such a vast and diverse area there are inevitably some constraints on what can be included. Some of the omitted areas have been well-covered in previous histories.[6] The intention here is to provide a narrative introduction to the domestic politics of states and nations which are again the focus of much attention and whose evolution could once more have great influence upon that of the wider world.

Any author writing on eastern Europe faces the problem of nomenclature. In this work established English names have been used where they are available: Warsaw rather than Warszawa, Prague instead of Praha, etc. At times a German name is more easily memorised in the English-speaking mind than is a Slav, Magyar, Albanian, or Romanian one, and for this reason I have used, to take one example, Teschen rather than Cieszyn or Tešín. In most cases where a settlement or region has a variety of names and where a convenient anglicised or German name is not available, I have taken the form used by the nation which is now the predominant element in the state concerned, hence Braşov rather than Brassó or Kronstadt, and Vilnius rather than Wilno. However, sometimes history dictates that different usage be employed at different times: one talks of Danzig in the 1930s but in the communist period, and especially at the height of the Solidarity movement, it would be absurd to call the city anything other than Gdańsk. There is only one certainty in using names in east European history: whatever the system used it will offend someone; I have not set out with the intention of causing offence, but if offence is taken I apologise for it.

The problem of initials is as intractable as that of names. In general I have used the first letters of the English translation of east European organisations, hence HWP for the Hungarian Workers' Party rather than the Magyar initials MDP. Yet there are some initials, for example KOR for the Polish Committee for Workers' Defence or SED for the Socialist Unity Party of Germany, which have become common usage in English; in a few other instances I have used the original initials to avoid duplication.

Because this book is intended primarily for the interested general reader rather than the specialist scholar notes have been kept to a minimum and are given mainly for direct quotations; where extracts from public speeches or cited documents have been used notes have been omitted as the text should explain the source of the quotation.

PREFACE TO THE SECOND EDITION

By the terms of the definitions used in the first edition of this book neither the twentieth century nor eastern Europe exist any longer. The totalitarian parties determined to shape state, society, and soul in their ideological image have almost all collapsed, the USSR has dissolved, and it has become an expressed objective of both east European states and western governments that the former socialist countries should become integrated into the European system.

Nevertheless, the states of what was once eastern Europe retain some common features and face common problems, albeit in varying degrees of intensity. It is the object of the concluding chapter of the second edition to outline the political development of the area since the collapse of communism.

The first edition defined eastern Europe as 'those countries which were under Soviet domination after 1945' but indicated that the German *Zwischeneuropa* better incorporated the notion of 'those areas which were excluded from west European developments but were not fully incorporated in the USSR'. The collapse of the Soviet Union and the disappearance of a bipolarised Europe have made definition even more arbitrary and precarious. The areas to which the concluding chapter addresses itself are in fact the same as those in part one of the first edition. The Baltic states, having reappeared as independent entities, are included, but the former GDR is excluded. Also excluded are those former Soviet territories which had previously had little or no experience of independence in modern times and which did not therefore feature significantly in the first edition. In effect this means the exclusion of Moldova, Belarus and Ukraine.

Equal treatment has not been given to each separate entity. Where developments have been steady and smooth the story is more quickly told; where the drama, or rather the tragedy, has been more intense and more complex a lengthier examination has been considered advisable.

The preparation of a second edition has also provided an opportunity to make minor adjustments to the existing text and to add to the bibliography the most significant of recent publications.

ACKNOWLEDGEMENTS

The origins of this book are in a course on east European history since 1918 which I taught at the University of Kent at Canterbury between 1981 and 1990. Since then I have taught the same subject in somewhat different guise in the University of Oxford. In both places the enormous joy of teaching this subject has been due in no small measure to the enthusiasm and dedication of the students concerned. I thank them for the intellectual stimulus they have provided. I have also to thank a number of colleagues, former and present, in particular David Turley who persuaded me to concentrate my teaching on the twentieth century. There are also those who have taught with me and I thank them for their inspiration and sometimes their indulgence; they are Leslie Holmes, now of the University of Melbourne, Katy Pickvance in Kent, and in Oxford Timothy Garton Ash, Alex Pravda, and Michael Hurst. Other friends and colleagues whose conversation and friendship I have benefited from include Zbyněk Zeman, Jim Naughton, John Dunbabin, Dmitri Obolensky, Charles King, Michael Kaser, and Archie Brown. I should also like to give especial thanks to a number of friends whose company continues to enrich my personal life as well as my scholarship: they are Colin Seymour-Ure, Antony Copley, Alfred P. Smyth, Blair Worden, Ian Gregor, Chris Taylor, Richard Langhorne, Sasho Shûrbanov, Stefan Troebst, David Mendel, Stevan K. Pavlowitch, and Richard Clogg, the last named of whom is perhaps the most exhausting and therefore the most rewarding of travelling companions.

In the process of publication Claire L'Enfant and Heather McCallum of Routledge have shown superb, unobtrusive efficiency. No author could ask for more sympathetic or more helpful guides. I would also like to thank Jayne Lewin for drawing the maps.

Scholarship is a great joy but it pales in significance beside the comforts of home life. My sons, Will and Ben, are now old enough to provide constructive comment on my work and for this I thank them, and I thank Ben, too, for his invaluable help in finding the cover illustration. But, in all I do, my debt to one person overshadows all other obligations. My wife, Celia, is the one who not only makes everything possible but also makes it worthwhile.

St Edmund Hall, Oxford

ABBREVIATIONS

ACC	Allied Control Commission; established in defeated states after the second world war and usually including representatives of Britain, the USA, and the USSR.
AFD	Alliance of Free Democrats; Hungarian initials, SzDSz.
AIC	Agro-Industrial Complex (Bulgarian); Bulgarian initials, SPK.
AK	*Armia Krajowa*, The Home Army; the non-communist Polish resistance during, and after, the second world war.
APL	Albanian Party of Labour; Albanian initials, PPS.
AVH	Security Police, Hungarian; until 1949 AVO.
AVNOJ	Anti-Fascist Council for the Liberation of Yugoslavia; formed November 1942 by Tito and the partisans.
AVO	Security police, Hungarian; reformed and renamed as AVH in 1949.
BANU	Bulgarian Agrarian National Union; Bulgarian initials, BZNS.
BCP	Bulgarian Communist Party; Bulgarian initials, BKP.
BK	*Balli Kombëtar*, National Union; Albanian non-communist resistance movement in second world war.
BSDP	Bulgarian Social Democratic Party; Bulgarian initials the same.
BSP	Bulgarian Socialist Party; formed April 1990 from the former BCP; Bulgarian initials the same.
BWP	Bulgarian Workers' Party; guise under which BCP was allowed to function 1926–34; Bulgarian initials, BRP.
CDP	Civil Democratic Party; formed when the Czech Civic Forum split in 1991; Czech initials, ODS.
CDU	Christian Democratic Union (German).
CGP	Camp for a Great Poland; loose right-wing coalition formed by Dmowski in December 1926 to oppose the *sanacja*; Polish initials, OWP.
CLS	Compulsory Labour Service (Bulgarian); Bulgarian initials, TP.
CM	Civic Movement; formed when the Czech Civic Forum split in 1991; Czech initials, OH.

CnDU	Croatian Democratic Union; formed 1989; Croatian initials, HDS.
CPCS	Communist Party of Czechoslovakia; established May 1921; Czech and Slovak initials, KSČ.
CPPP	Croat People's Peasant Party; the dominant Croat party in the years 1918–29, led by Stjepan Radić; Croatian initials, HPSS.
CPS	Communist Party of Slovakia; established March 1939; Slovak initials, KSS.
CPSU	Communist Party of the Soviet Union.
CPY	Communist Party of Yugoslavia; Serbo-Croat initials, KPJ.
CSCE	Conference on Security and Cooperation in Europe; later OSCE.
CSDP	Czech Social Democratic Party; Czech initials, CSSD.
ČSSR	Czechoslovak Socialist Republic.
DCR	Democratic Convention of Romania; Romanian initials, CDR.
DEMOS	Commonly used abbreviation for the Democratic Opposition in Slovenia. It later became a coalition of six parties.
DISz	Federation of Working Youth (Hungarian).
DLA	Democratic Left Alliance; dominated by the former Polish communist party; Polish initials, SLD.
DNSF	Democratic National Salvation Front; Romanian initials, FSND.
DP	Democratic Party (Yugoslav); based mainly amongst the Serbs outside Serbia; Serbo-Croat initials, DS.
DPA	Democratic Party of Albania; formed December 1990; Albanian initials, PDS.
DS	State Security; the Bulgarian communist secret police.
DU	Democratic Union; the successor as a political formation to Solidarity; Polish initials, UD.
EC	European Community; later European Union.
ECCI	Executive Committee of the Communist International; the ruling body of Comintern.
EPC	Environmental Protection Club; Latvian, formed June 1988; Latvian initials, VAK.
EU	European Union.
FF	Fatherland Front; Bulgarian resistance coalition which included the communists; later the name of the umbrella front organisation during communist rule; Bulgarian initials, OF.
FIDESz	Alliance of Young Democrats; Hungarian, formed 1989.
FRG	Federal Republic of Germany; German initials, BRD.
FYROM	Former Yugoslav Republic of Macedonia.
GATT	General Agreement on Tariffs and Trade.
GDP	Gross Domestic Product.
GDR	German Democratic Republic; German initials, DDR.
GNA	Grand National Assembly; Bulgarian; elected assembly twice as

large as a normal parliament and the only body which could legally enact alterations to the constitution; Bulgarian initials, VNS.

GRP	Greater Romania Party; Romanian initials, RM.
HCP	Hungarian Communist Party; Hungarian initials, MKP.
HDF	Hungarian Democratic Forum; Hungarian initials, MDF.
HDUR	Hungarian Democratic Union of Romania; Romanian initials, UDMR.
HSP	Hungarian Socialist Party; Hungarian initials, MSzP.
HSPP	Hlinka's Slovak People's Party; Slovak initials, HSLS; until 1925 the Slovak People's Party.
HSWP	Hungarian Socialist Workers' Party; formed at the end of the 1956 revolt as a replacement for the dissolved HWP; Hungarian initials, MSzMP.
HWP	Hungarian Workers' Party; formed after fusion of communists and other leftist groups, June 1948; Hungarian initials, MDP.
IFIs	International financial institutions.
IFOR	United Nations Implementation Force in Bosnia.
IFSC	Inter-factory strike committee; the basic organisation within Solidarity in Poland, 1980–1; Polish initials, MKS.
IMF	International Monetary Fund.
IMRO	Internal Macedonian Revolutionary Organisation, founded in 1893. It was for a time the Internal Macedonian and Adrianople Revolutionary Organisation; Bulgarian/Macedonian initials VMRO or VMORO.
JNA	Yugoslav National Army.
KGB	Commission for State Security; the Soviet secret police.
KOR	Committee for Workers' Defence; formed in Poland in 1976.
KPD	Communist Party of Germany.
KSS/KOR	Committee for Social Self-Defence; formed in Poland in 1977.
LCY	Yugoslav League of Communists; name assumed by the Yugoslav Communist Party in 1952; Serbo-Croat initials, SKJ.
LDLP	Lithuanian Democratic Labour Party; Lithuanian initials the same.
LIO	Large Industrial Organisation; part of the Polish economic reform package of the 1970s; Polish initials, WOG.
LPD	Liberal Democratic Party of Slovenia; Slovene initials, LDS. Also Liberal Democratic Party of Germany; German initials the same.
LW	Latvian Way; Latvian initials, LC.
MAMA	Movement for All Macedonian Action; Macedonian initials, MAAK.
MDS	Movement for Democratic Slovakia; Slovak initials, HZDS.
MEFESz	Association of Hungarian University and College Youth; defunct students' organisation reinvigorated in Hungary in October 1956.

MOVE Hungarian Association for National Defence.

MRF Movement for Rights and Freedom; Bulgarian, formed early 1990 to protect interests of minorities, especially the Turks; Bulgarian initials, DPS.

NATO North Atlantic Treaty Organisation.

ND National Democrats (endeks); original name for followers of Dmowski and one retained despite official changes in nomenclature.

NDF National Democratic Front; Romanian, established October 1944 as one of four front organisations set up by the communists.

NDH Independent State of Croatia.

NEM New Economic Mechanism; Hungarian, introduced in 1968; similar name used for Bulgarian reforms of the early 1980s.

NEP New Economic Policy, adopted by Bolshevik Party in Russia in 1921; Russian initials, NIP.

NKVD People's Commissariat for Internal Affairs; the Soviet secret police and forerunner of the KGB.

NLC National Liberation Committee; Albanian, established during the second world war; Albanian initials, NC.

NLP National Liberal Party; Romanian initials, NPL.

NP National Peasant Party (Hungarian); Hungarian initials, NPP.

NPBSG (Polish) Non-Party Block for the Support of the Government; formed to coordinate backing for the *sanacja* régime in the elections of March 1929; Polish initials, BBWR.

NPP National Peasant Party (Romanian); formed from merger of Transylvanian Nationalist Party and Peasant Party, 1926.

NRP National Radical Party; the dominant party in Serbia after 1903 and in Yugoslavia between 1918 and 1929; Serbian initials, NRS.

NSF National Salvation Front; Romanian, formed after December 1989 revolution; Romanian initials, FSN.

NSM National Social Movement; a Bulgarian fascist organisation led by professor Tsankov; Bulgarian initials, NSD.

OECD Organisation for European Cooperation and Development.

OSCE Organisation for Security and Cooperation in Europe.

OUN Ukrainian Military Organisation; established Vienna 1930.

OZON Camp of National Unity (Polish); formed by *sanacja* government in late 1930s in an attempt to rally popular support.

PAV Public Against Violence; Slovak, formed November 1989; Slovak initials, VPN.

PDA Party of Democratic Action; Bosnian initials, SDA.

PDP Party of Democratic Prosperity; Macedonian initials the same; ethnically Albanian party sometimes known as the Albanian Party of Democratic Prosperity and not to be confused with the

	Party of the Democratic Prosperity of the Albanians which split from the PDP in 1994.
PDSM	Party of Democratic Socialists in Montenegro; name assumed after 1990 by the Montenegrin Community Party; Serbian initials, SDPCG.
PNC	Polish National Committee; established by Dmowski in Russian Poland in November 1914; Polish initials, KNP.
POW	Polish Military Organisation, or Polish Legion; formed by Piłsudski during the first world war.
PP	Peasant Party (Polish); formed in 1931 from the three separate peasant parties; Polish initials, SL.
PPF	Patriotic People's Front (Hungarian); front organisation used by Imre Nagy as potential power base; Hungarian initials, HNF.
PPP	Polish Peasants' Party; formed by Mikołajczyk in 1945 to prevent communist subversion of SL; Polish initials, PSL.
PR	Proportional representation.
PRNU	Party of Romanian National Unity; Romanian initials, PUNR.
PSDR	Party of Social Democracy in Romania; Romanian initials the same.
PSP	Polish Socialist Party; traditional socialist party, formed in the nineteenth century to which Piłsudski had belonged; Polish initials PPS.
PU	Peasant Union (Yugoslav); Serbo-Croat initials, SZ.
PUWP	Polish United Workers' Party; formed December 1948 by fusion of various socialist parties; the ruling party of Poland from 1948 to 1989; Polish initials, PZPR.
PWP	Polish Workers' Party; established in January 1942; Polish initials, PPR.
RCP	Romanian Communist Party; Romanian initials, PCR.
RS	Serbian Republic (*Republika Srbska* in Serbian); the Serbian-dominated entity of Bosnia-Hercegovina.
RSDP	Romanian Social Democratic Party.
RUWP	Romanian United Workers' Party; formed September 1947 from a merger of the RCP and other leftist parties.
RWP	Romanian Workers' Party; Romanian initials, PMR.
SBZ	Soviet Zone of Occupation (in Germany).
SdHF	*Sudetendevtsche Heimatsfront*, Sudeten German Home Front; association of German nationalist groups in Czechoslovakia formed in the early 1930s; later became Sudeten German Party (SdP).
SdP	*Sudetendeutschpartei*, Sudeten German Party; political organisation formed in early 1930s from the Sudeten German Home Front.
SDP	Social Democratic Party; initials used for Hungarian and Czechoslovak parties of this name.

SDPR	Social Democracy of the Polish Republic; the name assumed by the Polish United Workers' Party in 1990; Polish initials the same.
SED	*Sozialistische Einheitspartei Deutschlands*, Socialist Unity Party of Germany; established April 1946; it became the ruling party of the GDR.
SHP	Smallholders' Party; Hungarian initials, FOG.
SLP	Socialist Labour Party; a post-1989 extra-parliamentary manifestation of the Romanian Communist Party; Romanian initials, PSM.
SLS	Slovene Populist Party; sometimes translated as Slovene People's Party; Slovene initials the same.
SMAD	*Sowjetische Militäradministration in Deutschland*, Soviet Military Administration in Germany.
SNC	Slovak National Council; established December 1943 and instrumental in preparing the uprising of August 1944; Slovak initials, SNR.
SNP	Slovak National Party; Slovak initials, SNS.
SPA	Socialist Party of Albania; formed April 1991 from the former APL; Albanian initials, PSS.
SPD	*Sozialdemokratische Partei Deutschlands*, The German Social Democratic Party.
SPP	Slovak People's Party; became Hlinka's Slovak People's Party (HSPP) in 1925; Slovak initials, SLS.
SPS	Socialist Party of Serbia (Milošević's party); Serbian initials the same.
SRP	Serbian Radical Party; Serbian initials, SRS.
StB	State Security; the Czechoslovak communist secret police.
UB	Security Office; the Polish communist secret police.
UDBa	Yugoslav communist secret police.
UDF	Union of Democratic Forces (Bulgarian); formed December 1989; Bulgarian initials, SDS.
UN	United Nations.
UNPA	UN protected area, Croatia.
UNPROFOR	UN Protection Force in Croatia.
USSR	Union of Soviet Socialist Republics.
WEU	Western European Union.
WTO	Warsaw Treaty Organisation; the 'Warsaw pact' or east European military alliance established in 1955.
YC	Yugoslav Committee; founded in Florence, November 1914 by protagonists of Serb-Croat cooperation; Serbo-Croat initials, JO.
YMO	Yugoslav Muslim Organisation; Yugoslav initials, JMO.
YRU	Yugoslav Radical Union; formed by Stojadinović in 1935 to provide nation-wide support for his government; Serbo-Croat initials, JRZ.

1

BEFORE THE TWENTIETH CENTURY

The division between eastern and western Europe may be traced back to Constantine's splitting of the Roman empire in 395, or to the great schism of 1054 which separated the eastern or Orthodox church from western Christendom. The divisions were deepened by the Crusaders' assault on Constantinople in 1204 and much more so by the fall of that city to the Ottoman armies in 1453. Thereafter the west became absorbed with exploration beyond Europe and by the intellectual and political upheavals of the Reformation. The stimulating and invigorating effects of the latter were not entirely absent in the east but that area was inevitably more preoccupied with the advance of the Ottomans. After this had been halted at Vienna in 1683 the Habsburg, Russian, and Prussian empires expanded until, after the third partition of Poland in 1795, they, together with the Ottoman, covered the entire area. Whilst towns were developing in the west, in the east the land retained or regained much of its former economic and social power; the nobility reasserted their authority over the peasants who were tied more closely to the land, leaving urban activities more in the hands of Germans, Jews, Armenians, and other minority groups. This ethnic division limited the strength of the east European bourgeoisie which was further weakened because it coincided less frequently than in the west with vibrant, assertive Protestantism. Economic progress was therefore slow. Outside Bohemia manufacturing was little developed; agricultural improvement, where it occurred, retained the inefficiencies of a system which tied the peasants to the land as a source of cheap, conscript labour.

The wars of the French revolution brought little immediate change in eastern Europe. After 1815 the old boundaries were more or less restored. A kingdom of Poland, with the tsar of Russia as its king, was created and an autonomous Serbia appeared, though this embryonic nation state was not the creation of a nationalist intelligentsia but had arisen from a revolt led by Karadjeordj Petrović who, along with other local chieftains, had been angered by the failure of Ottoman central government to control its local representatives. The intellectual legacy of 1789 was, however, to be seen in the Greek revolt of 1821 and in the eventual setting up of an independent Greek state in 1830.

The years of upheaval did bring about social readjustments. Prussia, seeing the

1

advantages of modern organisation, restructured its administration and abolished serfdom. Soon after the Napoleonic wars this reform also came to Russia's Baltic areas, Lithuania excepted, and in 1839 the Ottoman empire began to refashion its egregious system.

The French revolution had done much to promote the doctrine of popular sovereignty but in eastern Europe the mixture of races did not mean that popular and national sovereignty were the same thing. In eastern Europe perhaps the most profound effect of the intellectual excitements of the late eighteenth century was the impulse to explore cultural and ethnic identity, an impulse promoted above all by Johann Gottfried von Herder who suggested that language and custom were the clues to identification and who regarded the Slav races as being ideally placed to discover and develop their ethnic individuality. Herder was the intellectual progenitor of a generation of scholars who sought to establish or clarify their nations' identity. For nations with a well-documented past, the Hungarians, the Poles, and to a lesser degree the Czechs, identity could be asserted through the claim to 'historic rights', for others it was to be revealed in folklore, language, and ethnic traditions. Apart from the Greek revolution, the abortive Polish revolts of 1830–1 and 1846, and demands inside the Hungarian kingdom for greater autonomy from Vienna, nationalism in the years between 1815 and 1848 was primarily a cultural phenomenon. Its advocates wielded not the sword but the pen; they conducted their battles in books rather than on barricades.

The revolutions of 1848 were essentially the result of the chance coincidence of an old-style food crisis, a new-style manufacturing and financial recession, and a loss of nerve by the Habsburg government, but the revolutions also highlighted the fact that claims for popular sovereignty could lead to territorial problems. At the earliest stage of the revolution in the German states the great Czech historian František Palacký had amazed German liberals by declining an invitation to become a member of the pre-parliament in Frankfurt on the grounds that he was not a German but 'a Bohemian of the Slav race'. He also insisted that the Habsburg empire should be reconstructed on a federal basis so that this 'Austro-Slav' unit could protect central Europe from German and Russian domination. The Hungarians, guided by figures such as Lajos Kossuth, moved a long way towards federation by securing full-scale autonomy under the April laws of 1848, and the Slavs staged revolts in Cracow and Lwów and convened a congress in Prague in June. But they had little immediate effect. There was as much division as unity and this the proponents of the old order exploited ruthlessly. The final, prolonged battle was between the Hungarians and the Habsburg authorities, the latter using many of Hungary's non-Hungarian subjects against the Magyars. Eventually, at the request of Vienna, Russia moved its army over the Carpathians and at Világos in August 1849 delivered the *coup de grâce* to the Hungarian army.

After a decade of absolutism Austria enacted a series of constitutional reforms which produced an imperial parliament, the Reichsrat, elected through a complicated system of chambers or *curiae*. In 1867, a year after Austria's defeat in the Austro-Prussia war, the Ausgleich (compromise) provided the Hungarian kingdom with autonomy in all but foreign and military affairs. The Habsburg empire had become Austria-Hungary.

The Ausgleich initiated a period of stability in the northern half of eastern Europe. Polish nationalism had suffered a crushing defeat with the suppression of a revolt in 1863, and after 1867 the Magyars had a vested interest in maintaining the status quo. Political and territorial change did take place, however, in the south of eastern Europe. The principalities of Moldavia and Wallachia had united under a single prince in 1859 to form what was soon to become Romania. In 1867 Ottoman troops finally left Serbia and in 1875 the Bosnians revolted against the imposition of a tithe in kind. From this developed the great eastern crisis which ended with the wholesale revision of Balkan boundaries in the treaty of Berlin in July 1878. The treaty recognised the full independence of Serbia, Romania, and the small mountain prince-bishopric of Montenegro. The Romanians, who had provided significant military help to the Russians, lost Bessarabia, receiving the southern Dobrudja as compensation, whilst the Ottoman territories of Bosnia and Hercegovina were placed under Habsburg administration. A new Bulgarian state, still technically a vassal of the Ottoman sultan, was created between the Danube and the Balkan mountains, but this was much smaller than either the Russians or the Bulgarian nationalists had intended or hoped. Their version, defined in the treaty of San Stefano in March 1878, had included Macedonia, which Berlin returned to Ottoman rule, and Eastern Rumelia, the territory between the Balkan mountains and Thrace which was to be united with Bulgaria in 1885.

The unification of Bulgaria and Rumelia redressed one grievance created at Berlin but others lingered and festered throughout the peninsula. When they eventually exploded they were to destroy the European balance of power. A significant reason for these grievances was the growth of nationalism. It would be as well, therefore, to cast a brief glance at the evolution of this phenomenon.

Social changes and the emergence of nationalism in the nineteenth century

Between 1848 and 1914 profound social changes had taken place in eastern Europe. Although in most areas, except principally Serbia and Bulgaria, the latifundia (large estates) still existed, they had been subjected to many changes. Serfdom was abolished in the Habsburg empire in 1848 and was to end in Russia in 1861 and in Romania in 1864. Its disappearance meant that without the cushion of free, albeit frequently inefficient labour many marginal economic units could not survive and their owners, although members of the nobility, became tenants or left for the towns. These urbanised nobles had lost their estates and needed to find a role. Petty trading and manufacturing were regarded as German or Jewish occupations so the nobles drifted into the intelligentsia or the bureaucracy. Bureaucratic posts were becoming more numerous as the state expanded both to fill the vacuum left by the abolition of landlord responsibility for local administration and justice, and to assume responsibilities in the postal services, railways, public health, and other new areas of governmental activity. For the impoverished amongst the Polish gentry, the *szlachta*, many of whom had lost their estates after 1830–1 or 1863, entry into the Russian bureaucracy was neither possible nor desirable, but this was not a problem faced by their equivalents in Hungary; after the Ausgleich they would at least be serving their own, Magyar kingdom. The Hungarian bureaucracy thus became a form of outdoor relief for indigent Magyar gentry, civil service employment rising from 25,000 in 1870 to 230,000 in 1918.

In the Czech lands there was no surviving nobility to say yea or nay to a bureaucratic career, but here too trade and manufacturing, until the final quarter of the century, were primarily German and Jewish preserves. The Czech cultural world could not absorb the increasing number of young Czechs emerging from Bohemian and Moravian educational institutions and many therefore entered the ranks of the administration. That administration, however, was dominated by Germans and by the end of the century ethnic tensions both within and with regard to the bureaucracy had become acute, presenting the Austrian section of the monarchy with a problem unknown in the Hungarian kingdom.

The evolution of the intelligentsia was one of the most important of nineteenth century developments. Though difficult to define precisely the intelligentsia may be loosely designated as those whose livelihood was derived not from physical labour, the production of things, or, perhaps, the ownership of property, but from the application of intelligence and training. The *intelligenti* staffed the free professions, the secular cultural institutions, the creative arts, and, to some degree, the bureaucracy; in some instances priests and high-ranking clergymen could also be included. The intelligentsia was crucial in the process of nation-forming. It was also very much a product of urbanisation. Urban growth produced ethnic change. The indigenous German or Jewish populations could not or did not wish to meet the demand for labour which the expansion of industries and urban services created; that was fulfilled by peasants moving in from surrounding or more distant areas, most of those peasants being Slav or, in central Hungary, Magyar. In the Balkans urban development meant the dilution of the existing Greek, Armenian, and Turkish elements in the towns. The changes in urban ethnic balance stimulated the social changes on which the intelligentsia thrived. It was the *intelligenti* who argued the need for the use of non–dominant languages, they who defended the Slav peasant in court or pleaded his case with government officials, they who argued that a tram- or railway-line should be built so that it served Slavs as well as Germans, they who founded libraries or theatres, and they, in so far as they were allowed, who provided the teachers and journalists who educated, defended, and entertained the new town dwellers. And it was these battles which preoccupied nineteenth century nationalist activists, not,

4

outside the Balkans, the demand for the dismemberment of the multi-national empires and the creation of new nation states.

Although national consciousness is associated with urbanisation there are no valid generalisations as to its origins. Language separated Slav from German, but it often united German and Jew. Serbs and Croats spoke the same language, and came from a common ethnic stock, but this did not produce unity because here, as in many other areas, religion was the most important cultural identifier, the Croats being Catholic, and the Serbs mostly Orthodox; the Bosnian Muslims also spoke Serbo-Croat. In Transylvania before 1918 the cause of the Romanian nationalists was complicated because many local Romanians, unlike most of their co-nationals in the Romanian state, were not Orthodox but adherents of the Uniate church which had emerged at the end of the sixteenth century. The Uniates, though practising Orthodox ritual, recognised the pope as the head of the church, and were therefore part of the Catholic world.

The correlation of ethnic identity and religion at times helped in the formulation of national consciousness. Most Balkan Orthodox Christian peasants could be persuaded, by their intelligentsia, that they did not wish to be ruled by Muslims; Catholic Poles could find common cause against Russian Orthodox or German Protestant rulers, and Protestant Estonians or Latvians could resent domination by Orthodox Russians. But it would be dangerous to generalise. The first serious assertion of modern Bulgarian individuality was not against their Ottoman, Muslim, temporal rulers, but against the Greek ecclesiastical hierarchy which had developed in the Bulgarian lands since the mid-eighteenth century. A common religion did not prevent Croat nationalists from resenting Magyar domination, or Czechs questioning Austrian supremacy; nor, conversely, did Protestant Hungarians or Poles feel any lesser loyalty to their nation than their Catholic brothers and sisters.

Religion was of little use in the formation of national consciousness without a sense of a national past. Most nations which demanded recognition of their existence had some past state which, to them, legitimised their claim to a separate identity. After 1848 few Hungarians would be satisfied with anything less than the rights granted in the April laws of that year, whilst the Poles had to look back only to 1795 for their separate state. For others the perspective was longer but the vision hardly less bright; Czechs recalled the Bohemian kingdom destroyed at the battle of the White Mountain in 1620, whilst Serbs, Croats, Bulgarians, Romanians, and Albanians manufactured modern myths from medieval history. On the other hand, ethnic groups without a past state seldom developed a modern national consciousness; the Vlach shepherds of Macedonia, the Sorbs of Prussia, the Kachubs of central Poland, the ubiquitous Gypsies, and the simple peasants of the Pripet Marshes are five examples; the last of these were reported by an article in the *Spectator* as late as the spring of 1992 as having no concept of an ethnic identity, describing themselves simply as *tutejszi*, 'the people who live here'.[1]

Nationalism inevitably posed political difficulties but the major problem with nationalism was not its effect on the subject peoples of the multi-national empires, who would inevitably find some vehicle for their protest, but its impact on the ruling groups, ethnic and/or social. Russian nationalism was an arm of Tsar Alexander III's reactionary policies, magyarisation was a feature of Hungarian politics at the same period and beyond, and in the late 1890s the reaction of the Germans of the Austrian part of the Dual Monarchy to concessions to Czech speakers in the Bohemian bureaucracy showed how strong centripetal nationalism had become amongst Austro-Germans. In the Ottoman empire the attempt to impose a state nationalism from above was to have dramatic consequences for all of Europe.

The gestation of the twentieth century, 1908–18

In July 1908 the Young Turks seized power in Constantinople. The Young Turks were ideologues; they believed that their state and society had to be refashioned according to their own beliefs, that they were the bearers of 'progress'. Their mission was the quintessential twentieth century desire to modernise the state and create a new national consciousness and identity, in their case an Ottoman one. Vienna feared a reimposition of Ottoman authority in Bosnia and Hercegovina and annexed the two provinces; Bulgaria, likewise frightened of a reassertion of Ottoman power in the areas of southern Bulgaria acquired in 1885, declared full independence. The diplomatic tensions thus generated were eventually contained but in the Balkans themselves a more profound danger was emerging. The Albanians realised that modernisation meant centralisation together with conscription and increased taxation. The series of revolts which the Albanians then staged caused the Balkan states to fear that if an independent Albania were created, or if the great powers intervened to restructure the Ottoman administration, the régimes in Athens, Sofia, Belgrade, and Cetinje would not be able to partition Turkey-in-Europe. From this fear came the dismemberment of Ottoman Europe in 1912–13 by the Balkan alliance of Bulgaria, Greece, Serbia, and Montenegro, an alliance which immediately fell out over the division of the spoils and thus precipitated the second Balkan war of 1913 in which Greece and Serbia, now abetted by Romania and Turkey, deprived Bulgaria of most of its recent conquests. In the summer of 1914 factions within the Serbian military, angry at various features of civilian rule in the newly acquired 'Old Serbia' (Macedonia), and seeking therefore to embarrass the government in Belgrade, aided a group of young Serbian Bosnian extremists in a plot to kill the heir to the Habsburg throne. Few in the Serbian army believed the mission to Sarajevo would succeed. How its success developed into the first world war is not the purpose of this book to explain; but war, the midwife of all modern epochs, had arrived to deliver the twentieth century.

The years 1848–1914 had shown that nationalism itself was not a powerful enough force to bring about territorial change. It could, and did, precipitate instability which, if exploited by established military forces, could bring war and territorial revision, but without external military intervention nationalism could not create a nation-state, as the Poles and the Irish knew; of all the new states born in Europe between 1815 and 1914 only two, Belgium and Norway, had appeared without war. The first world war made possible the emergence of national states which had previously been considered impracticable, even by nationalist leaders. The demand for such states, however, was not the cause but the consequence of the war.

The great powers had in fact expected a short war and had not worked out in any great detail the political solution which they wished to see emerge at the end of it. Both sides made promises to the enemies' minorities but however much support for those minorities might have been aimed at weakening the enemy, they were not derived from any pre-existing belief in the need to restructure Europe along nation lines. On 23 March 1916 the Russian ambassador in London noted that, 'During the war, the principle of nationalities took roots so deep here, that it is today considered almost as a reason for England's entry into the war'.[2]

After the horrendous bloodletting of the Dardanelles, Verdun, the Somme, and the Brusilov offensive, a readiness for major concessions to territorial restructuring did appear. The new Habsburg emperor, Karl, announced at the end of 1916 that he was prepared to agree to the creation of a predominantly south-Slav kingdom consisting of Bosnia-Hercegovina, Serbia, Montenegro, and Albania; he would also accept a Polish kingdom with a Habsburg prince on its throne. In France and Britain pressure had been growing for a radical redrawing of European boundaries; this had been exerted particularly in Paris by Louis Eisenmann, and in London by R. W. Seton Watson and the former foreign editor of *The Times*, Henry Wickham Steed. Some of their ideas found their way into the note of 12 January 1917 in which the western powers informed President Woodrow Wilson that they wished to see the 'liberation of the Italians, as also of the Slavs, Roumanes, and Czechoslovaks from foreign rule'.

Although this was far from being a policy commitment on the part of the western powers, it appeared that Austria-Hungary had become the first of the multi-national empires to be sentenced to death. In the following month the second seemed to commit suicide. The Russian revolution had a profound effect upon eastern Europe. In the first place, the non-Russian peoples of the empire saw the revolution and the liberal reforms it produced as their chance to escape from Russian domination. As a consequence, the fall of tsardom terrified the German and Habsburg emperors who met in Bad Homburg in April full of fears that their turn was soon to come. The entry of the United States into the war that month had made this more likely; with a democratic Russia and the backing of the United States, the allies' claim that they were fighting for liberal democracy against old-fashioned, conservative, militarist monarchism had greater plausibility.

In fact the immediate effects of the Russian revolution outside the tsar's empire were less than the German and Austrian emperors feared. Discipline within the Habsburg armies was threatened but it did not collapse; the Czechs boycotted the reconvened Reichsrat and some Slavs who did attend demanded autonomy, but there was no uprising. The most important consequences of the Russian revolution came with the bolshevik seizure of power in November. Before then, liberal, nationalist-based democracy was generally seen as the only available alternative to the pre-war status quo in eastern Europe. Now there was a second option. And it was much more terrifying. The governments of Vienna, Budapest, and Berlin were mesmerised by the bolshevik danger, as well they might be, because bolshevism could exploit social unrest and thereby, perhaps give mass backing to the nationalist demands of the liberal intelligentsias.

At the beginning of 1918 President Wilson pronounced his fourteen points which gave further impetus to nationalist claims. And social discontent was rising rapidly as tensions were generated by the war and especially by the allied blockade, tensions which at last broke surface early in 1918. Food shortages, overcrowding in the cities, inflation, dejection and demoralisation amongst armies short of supplies, together with an exultant bolshevik propaganda, combined to weaken the social and political fabric, especially in the Dual Monarchy and in Bulgaria. Strikes, the formation of soviets, and two serious mutinies amongst Habsburg forces testified to the growing crisis and presaged the collapse of the central powers.

The first to crack in Europe was Bulgaria which sued for peace at the end of September. Austria-Hungary was now much enfeebled and when the emperor offered a number of concessions to discontented groups within the Austrian part of the monarchy it had little effect. On 24 October, when news reached Budapest of a revolt amongst Croat troops in Fiume (Rijeka), Hungarian officers demonstrated in favour of peace. A new government was formed within hours. The Dual Monarchy had ceased to function and within days its head was chased out of Vienna.

When the allies began consideration of the final peace settlement they were inevitably guided by the political evolution of eastern Europe's various and varied constituent elements and by the disposition of forces in the area at the end of the war. Since many of the issues which were pertinent in 1918 have remained so until the present, an understanding of eastern Europe in the twentieth century is impossible without a brief survey of the most important of those elements and forces.

The Poles

After the defeat of the revolution of 1863 there was little sign of political activity amongst Poles until the emergence in the 1880s of the two strains of thinking which were to dominate Polish politics at least until 1939. In 1886 the Polish League was founded in Switzerland. It was later to evolve into the National Democratic Party, the chief figure in which was to be Roman Dmowski. Of relatively humble origin, Dmowski had struggled up the educational ladder and qualified as a biologist, though he soon forsook science for politics, organising a series of very effective school strikes and then becoming a member of the Russian Duma. Dmowski saw Germany as the chief threat to Polish nationhood, arguing that Prussia had risen over the body of Poland and that only a strong and healthy Poland could contain further German expansion. A healthy Poland needed a developed, Polish, middle class, and for this reason Dmowski pressed for industrialisation and the division of the large landed estates amongst the peasantry. He was prepared to allot the state a part in the processes of industrialisation and modernisation and therefore his views were centralist. They were also polonocentric. He wanted a 'Poland for the Poles' and was not an advocate of expansion eastward into the non-Polish lands held by the Polish commonwealth of old; if any minorities were included in it they would have to submit to polonisation if they wished to be accepted as equals in his ideal Poland. Dmowski also believed that it was the Jews who, by taking control of commercial and professional life in Poland, had hindered the development of a strong, native bourgeoisie; in 1911 he organised a boycott of Jewish shops in Warsaw to press home this point and his policies were never devoid of anti-semitism. Nor did he have much sympathy for the traditional aristocracy which he also held responsible for the distortions of Polish history; it was the *szlachta* which had:

> oppressed and exploited the peasantry, it ruined the towns, it made use of and favoured the Jews. The state became helpless *vis-à-vis* its neighbours. Expanding eastward and diluting 'Polishness' in multi-ethnic and multi-religious eastern borderlands, the nobles neglected the western core of the Polish lands, the cradle of the Piast dynasty where the masses were ethnically Polish.[3]

The second main theme of Polish politics emerged from the socialist movement. There had been stirrings of socialism in the 1870s although it was not until 1892 that the Polish Socialist Party was founded in Paris. It had two distinct tendencies. The internationalists, most famously represented by Rosa Luxemburg, regarded national liberation as a secondary objective which would be achieved automatically when Europe was reconstructed on a socialist basis. The other wing was dominated by Józef Piłsudski who came to personify this second main strand of Polish political life. The scion of a minor Polish-Lithuanian noble family he had been expelled from Harkov university, imprisoned, and then released after feigning madness. He joined the socialist movement, insisting that there could be no independence without socialism and no socialism without independence, but he later admitted that he alighted from the socialist tram-car at the stop marked nationalism. Unlike Dmowski he regarded Russia rather than Germany as the chief threat to the Polish nation. Events in Russia from 1905 to 1907 convinced him that armed force was the only means by which Polish independence could be secured and in that year he founded his 'Sharpshooters', who were basically a terrorist organisation fighting against tsarist autocracy. Piłsudski's idealised Poland was more extensive than that of Dmowski, Piłsudski dreaming of a huge Polish-Lithuanian-Ukrainian federation which would cordon off Russia from the rest of Europe. Because it was more extensive and diverse than that of Dmowski, Piłsudski's Poland would be less centralised and more indulgent to its non-Polish minorities.

Both Piłsudski and Dmowski were active in the Russian partition. In the Prussian partition there was mounting pressure on Polish schools, cultural activities, and even on Polish property rights, though Polish deputies were still returned to the Reichstag in Berlin where they could at least attempt to defend Polish interests. The Austrian partition was by far the least oppressive of the three, in part, no doubt, because Austria was the only Catholic power involved in the partitions; in 1914 there were fifteen Poles in the Russian Duma, seventeen in the German Reichstag and 106 in the Austrian Reichsrat.

The Austrian partition was also the main centre of Polish agrarianism. The Polish peasants had no national bourgeoisie to lead them, and cooperation with the gentry was difficult because many peasants still suspected the nobility of using nationalism as a cover for the perpetuation or reimposition of landlord power. Organised agrarianism appeared in the 1880s and despite rapid fragmentation a dominant figure emerged in Wincenty Witos, a Galician peasant of extremely humble origin who became head of the Piast agrarian faction. This was so named after an ancient Polish dynasty, a naming indicative of the group's distaste for concessions to the Ukrainians who made up a considerable proportion of the population of Galicia. In later years, when occupying some of the highest posts in independent Poland, Witos still insisted on tilling his own small plot of land and on retaining his peasant costume; he would never wear a tie.

At the beginning of the first world war Piłsudski put his forces, now known as the Polish Military Organisation, or Polish Legion (POW), at the disposal of the Austrian high command; they immediately proved their worth by capturing Kielce in Russian Poland for a few days. A political body, the Supreme National Committee, emerged alongside the Polish military forces in Galicia. In Russian Poland the tsarist authorities announced that they would reconstitute a Polish kingdom, as a result of which, in November 1914, a number of members of the Russian Duma, led by Dmowski, had established a Polish National Committee (PNC) with the slogan, 'Germany's defeat is our victory'. The PNC later transferred its headquarters to Paris.

There was little sign of a German defeat in August 1915 when the Germans took Warsaw. Their main objective was now to raise a Polish army to which the Poles responded by insisting, 'no government, no army'. By November 1916 the central powers had agreed to establish an interim council of state. With the collapse of tsardom the Germans became concerned at the dangers of Polish independence; in July 1917 they arrested a number of leading Polish military men, including Piłsudski, and in August the POW was dissolved. To contain Polish anger the Germans and Austrians agreed to set up a Polish national kingdom headed by an interim regency council.

The regency council remained in existence till the end of the war but it earned little respect. The Poles were enraged that the negotiations at Brest

Litovsk, to which they were not invited, allowed the Ukraine possession of Chełm, a sizeable chunk of eastern Galicia. At the end of the war a Polish republic was declared in Warsaw whilst in Lublin, in a strange foreshadowing of events at the end of the second world war, the socialist Ignacy Daszyński declared a 'People's', i.e. workers', republic. On 11 November Piłsudski, recently released from Magdeburg prison, arrived back in Poland and three days later power was transferred to him pending the formation of a national government. On 19 November Dmowski returned from the United States insisting that he alone had the right to negotiate with the allies. This could have caused severe difficulties but some form of order was eventually found when the pianist Ignacy Paderewski returned to Poland and formed a government on 17 January 1919.

Hungary and the Hungarians

The Hungarian and Austrian crowns had been united in 1526 after the defeat of the Hungarian armies by the Turks at the battle of Mohács. Thereafter the relationship between Budapest and Vienna had been a question of periodic dispute until the Ausgleich of 1867 granted internal autonomy to the Hungarian kingdom. Included in that kingdom were Transylvania, Slovakia, Ruthenia, Croatia, and the former military frontier along the border with the Ottoman empire. By the early 1870s Hungarian assertiveness was increasing in the form of pressures on non-Magyar education and the reservation of state posts for Magyar-speakers. This was in part to provide a safe haven for landowners impoverished by the abolition of serfdom and by the agrarian crisis of the 1870s, but at this stage Hungarian nationalism was cultural rather than ethnic and those willing to adopt Magyar language and customs were accepted as members of the dominant group.

Magyarisation intensified after the turn of the century. A constitutional confrontation with Austria had ended with the emperor threatening to impose universal and equal suffrage on his Hungarian kingdom. The Magyars capitulated; they could not afford to risk a diet in which a coalition of non-Magyars might form a majority. As an insurance against any recurrence of this threat the Magyar diehards determined that any future universal suffrage system, if it could not be avoided, would return mostly magyarone deputies. A language law enacted in 1907 was amongst the most draconian seen in eastern Europe at any time, not least because of the critical clause which insisted that teachers would be dismissed after a set period if they or their pupils were deficient in spoken or written Magyar.

At the same time the Magyars continued their established policy of electoral management, though the methods used were little different from those in other states:

It was no uncommon trick for the local authorities to declare roads and bridges unsafe for traffic on the day of the election, or for all the horses in non-Magyar districts to be placed under veterinary supervision and forbidden to move outside the commune. As soon as the elections were safely over, these restrictions were removed. There was no fixed time for the closing of the poll; this was left to the discretion of the returning officer, who was always an official of safe Magyar views. . . . It was the endeavour of the officials in charge of the registers to manipulate them in such a way that even when the opposition voter reached the polling booth he more often than not discovered that he was disqualified. The voting lists were drawn up exclusively in Magyar, which made it easy to insert false particulars without the knowledge of the voters of subject nationalities. For instance, the voter's age, address or calling might be incorrectly entered, so that when he appeared he did not answer to the description entered on the list. Further, there was no secret ballot; voters were compelled to declare aloud before the returning officer, and incidentally before various other officials seated with him in the booth, the name of the candidate for whom they wished to vote. . . . The voter could not even be sure that the returning officer would record his vote correctly. A nominee of each candidate was present in the polling booth, but the returning officer had power to eject any of these representatives on the most trivial excuse. In such cases, while a substitute was being procured the returning officer had ample leisure to transfer votes from the candidate he represented to the one officially favoured.[4]

With such control over the electoral process, politics within the Hungarian diet was mainly the prerogative of the Magyars. With almost complete agreement on the national issue, and with no great social divide amongst the political practitioners and power-holders, parties tended to be personal alliances more than groups united by policy or principle. In these circumstances parties proliferated and changed both in internal composition and external alliances. Such fluidity was a legacy handed by the Hungarian kingdom to its successor.

The Czechs

In the fourteenth century Bohemia had been at the centre of European intellectual life. At the end of that century it produced one of the great religious reformers in the person of Jan Hus, burnt at the stake in 1415, but leaving behind him a strong tradition of toleration and moderation. In 1526 Bohemia became part of the Habsburg crown but it was not until the battle of the White Mountain in 1620 that Bohemian independence was liquidated and the native, Czech aristocracy dispossessed. National revival began amongst scholars in the late eighteenth century and was encouraged by figures such as Palacký in 1848.

The Ausgleich of 1867 bitterly disappointed the Czechs who asked why they were not allowed their own compromise. Some leading Czechs took refuge in pan-Slavism, appearing in the 1868 pan-Slav congress in Moscow whilst refusing to attend the Reichsrat in Vienna. This 'Old Czech' faction soon came under criticism from younger elements within the intelligentsia and the growing commercial and industrial bourgeoisie. After franchise reforms in 1873 had made representation in Vienna more direct these 'Young Czechs' wanted a return to the Reichsrat. In 1879 they had their way. Czech deputies reappeared in the imperial parliament and joined the group supporting Count Taaffe's administration. Their rewards included the setting up of a Czech university in Prague in 1882, further franchise reforms in the same year, and a number of concessions on the use of Czech in the outer administration, i.e. in dealings between civil servants and individual members of the public. But these concessions did not mean an end to tension between Czechs and Germans.

In the late nineteenth century the Czech population of the towns and cities was growing rapidly. Organisations such as the sokols, gymnastic societies which appeared first in the 1860s, promoted Czech national identity, whilst *Matice Školská* provided funds for and promoted the growth of Czech schools and cultural institutions. The educated Czechs were soon demanding their place in the administrative sun and during the 1880s, whilst Taaffe was in office, fierce rivalry developed over the nature of the bureaucracy in Bohemia and, to a lesser degree, Moravia. It was the beginning of a long and bitter struggle.

In 1897 enactment of the Badeni language laws seemed to have given the Czechs all they wanted, but the prize was snatched from their hands by the fierce German reaction which convulsed the Germans of Bohemia and of much of Austria. An agreement was reached in Moravia in 1905 but no such solution for Bohemia appeared before 1914, by which time the dispute had paralysed the Reichsrat.

The Czechs had aspired to privileges similar to those of the Magyars inside Hungary, but the Czechs were not as united as the Hungarians. More importantly, the Czechs were opposed not by disunited, weak, and relatively backward national groups but by the Germans. The Magyars had absolute control over their bureaucracy; the Germans were deeply entrenched in that of Bohemia and Moravia, and German confidence had been bolstered by the relentless rise of German power in Europe; the best the Czechs could realistically hope for was a power-sharing arrangement on the Moravian lines. The struggle for administrative rights had, however, taught the Czechs the art of political organisation and as a consequence they had developed a viable party system, backed by their own industrial and commercial middle class.

By 1914 the Young Czechs, now the National Democrats led by Karel Kramář, no longer dominated the Czech political scene. Other parties and other leaders were already making themselves felt. They included Tomáš Masaryk, a blacksmith's apprentice who had risen to the austere heights of a Viennese professorship and was leader of the Realist Party, and Eduard Beneš, who was later to become a dominant figure in the Czech National Socialist Party, which was not to be confused in any way with its later German namesake. The Agrarian Party had enormous influence in the Czech villages, where together with the cooperative

13

organisations, it dominated the lives of most peasants. The Agrarian leader, ¹ Antonín Švehla, was to be less prominent in international affairs than Masaryk or Beneš, but in domestic politics he was to exercise more power than any of the other Czech party leaders.

Slovaks and Czechoslovaks

By the beginning of the twentieth century the Slovaks, who spoke a language very close to Czech, had been part of Hungary for longer than Wales had been associated with the English crown. Although cultural ties with the Czechs were never entirely dissolved there were few political links. Palacký had insisted in 1848 that these should be forged but others, notably L'udovit Štúr, disagreed and called for a separate Slovak existence. By the 1870s neither prescription seemed real in the face of magyarising pressures in the Hungarian kingdom.

A small Slovak National Party did survive, however, arguing that Russian patronage could bring greater freedom. At the same time a Catholic priest, Andrej Hlinka, was also agitating for greater national self-expression, an activity which soon acquainted him with the inside of a Hungarian gaol. The call for closer ties with the Czechs was at this stage muted and voiced mainly by the small Protestant intelligentsia grouped around the periodical *Hlas* (Voice).

'Czechoslovakism' was mainly a product of the first world war. In 1914 Masaryk left Austria and made his way to Paris where he was joined by Beneš and Milan Štefánik, a Slovak astronomer who had long lived in France. These three founded the Czechoslovak National Council which pledged itself to work for complete independence from rather than greater autonomy within the Habsburg empire. The Czechoslovak cause was much assisted when it acquired a military force, the Czechoslovak Legion, formed after February 1917 from Czech and Slovak prisoners of war in Russia. At home, support for the separatists grew slowly until 1917. The bungling incompetence of the authorities in detaining a number of Czech activists, growing German domination, and above all mounting social deprivation brought about by the war and the allied blockade, gradually increased the appeal of the nationalists. On 6 January 1918 Czech deputies in the Reichsrat issued the 'Twelfth Night Declaration' demanding self-determination for the Czechoslovaks; these demands were echoed two days later in President's Wilson's fourteen points. In July, amidst rising social dislocation, Czech political groups in Prague came together to form an internal National Council under the leadership of Kramář. In America Masaryk had secured the support of both Czech and Slovak exile organisations in the Pittsburgh Declaration of June 1918, whilst in London he had the backing of Seton Watson and Wickham Steed. In June the allies recognised his National Council.

In October this body proclaimed itself the provisional government of the Czechoslovak republic in whose name the Prague National Committee seized power on 28 October. Habsburg authority had collapsed and the experienced Czech bureaucracy stepped into its place in Bohemia and Moravia, where the revolution of 1918 seldom involved anything more violent or strenuous than a few telephone calls and the removal of Habsburg insignia from uniforms, buildings, and stationery. On 30 October a number of Slovak intellectuals met in Turčanský Svätý Martin and acknowledged the existence of the Czechoslovak nation.

The Yugoslav lands: Serbia

Serbia's evolution from the rising of 1804 to full statehood was violent and painful. A second revolt under Miloš Obrenović in 1814 meant that Serbia was to have two rival dynasties; of the nine Serbian monarchs between 1804 and 1945 four were assassinated and four driven into exile. The constitution was changed almost as frequently, a tradition which continued into communist days. Political and economic evolution were slow. Full autonomy was secured in the early 1830s but Serbia was still by no means a modern state, having no currency and little infrastructure; when Prince Miloš acquired a bed in 1834 it was only the second in the country. In 1844 a civil code was introduced and in the same year Ilija Garašanin, an advisor to Prince Alexander Karadjeordjević, drew up the *Načertanije*, a document which described how the Serbian lands might one day be united; Garašanin's concept of a greater Serbia was a predominantly Orthodox and Muslim union of Bosnia, Hercegovina, Kosovo, Montenegro, the Vojvodina, and northern Albania; Catholic Croatia was excluded.

There was no immediate prospect of such dreams being fulfilled. The Serbs derived little satisfaction from the great eastern crisis of 1875–8. The new Bulgarian state would henceforth be a competitor for 'Old Serbia', or Macedonia, and no progress had been made in moving Serbian borders nearer the sea. In 1881 Prince Milan Obrenović sought protection and patronage in an alliance with Austria, and in the following year declared himself king. It did little to increase his power. At home he could not prevent the rise of the Serbian Radical Party. Initially much influenced by narodnik ideals the well-organised radicals enjoyed widespread support. In later years they were to shed many of their radical ideas but they remained pro-Russian and they were to become the party which more than any other helped to restore constitutional liberties and to extend Serbia's borders.

After Milan abdicated in 1889 his son and successor, Alexander, restored the more restricted constitution of 1869 and further blotted his political copybook by concluding a disastrous marriage with a Bohemian widow and former lady-in-waiting ten years older than himself. On 10 June 1903 a coup organised by army officers and carried out with exceptional brutality removed Alexander, his wife and the Obrenović dynasty. Despite its violence the coup was popular in Serbia, not least because it brought political relaxation and the re-election of the radicals. Peter Karadjeordjević became king and moved Serbia to a pro-Russian rather than a pro-Austrian foreign policy. At home his major achievement was to ensure that the army did not play a dominating role, and by 1906 the last of the regicides had been removed from ministerial office. However, civilian-military relations were to be a vital factor in Serbian politics until 1917 when the civilian authorities tried and executed a number of prominent soldiers, including Colonel Apis, a leader of the 1903 coup.

The Austrians had been the losers in 1903 but they regained some of their authority with the annexation of Bosnia and Hercegovina in 1908. Nevertheless, Serbian prestige was enormously enhanced, first by the Agram and Friedjung trials in which Habsburg officials attempted to discredit Serb activists with evidence easily shown to be fabricated, and then by the Balkan wars when the Serbs took the lion's share of Macedonia and retrieved Kosovo, the heartland of the great Serbian empire of medieval times. Those who had been boasting that Serbia would play the role of Piedmont in the unification of the southern Slavs were much encouraged and openly spoke of Austria-Hungary being their next victim now that Ottoman power had been smashed.

Despite continuing disagreement between the military and civilian arms of the state, Serbia managed to repel the Austro-Hungarian attack of 1914. In the autumn of the following year, however, they were overwhelmed by Austro-Hungarian, German, and Bulgarian forces. The government and court went into exile on Corfu.

The Yugoslav lands: Montenegro

Montenegro was what remained after the Ottomans had taken the towns and the Venetians the coastline of the middle Adriatic area. Its inhabitants were Orthodox Serbs. By the early sixteenth century it had become a theocracy which was soon under the domination of the Petrović family. In 1799 its independence was recognised by Constantinople. In 1860 Prince Nicholas, or Nikita, became head of state, a position he was to retain until 1918.

During Nikita's rule Montenegro doubled in size, mainly as a result of the treaty of Berlin; in 1910 Nikita was acknowledged as king. Nikita, as king or prince, was reluctant to share power and the few concessions he did make were chiefly designed to ease the securement of foreign loans. Inevitably opposition to his rule appeared, most notably amongst the small intelligentsia which was mainly Serbian-educated. To a large degree Nikita neutralised this opposition by following a foreign policy very much in line with that of Belgrade.

The Yugoslav lands: the Sanjak of Novi Pazar

The Sanjak of Novi Pazar separated Serbia and Montenegro. Until 1878 it was part of Bosnia but thereafter it remained under Ottoman administration but was garrisoned by Austro-Hungarian troops in order to prevent a merger between the two neighbouring South Slav states. Austria-Hungary also had the right to develop roads and communications in the area. Habsburg forces left after the Balkan wars when the Sanjak was partitioned between Serbia and Montenegro.

The population consisted mainly of Serbs, many of whom were Muslim, as were the Turkish minority. The presence of a large number of Muslims in the Sanjak remained a significant fact throughout the existence of a Yugoslav state and after its collapse.

The Yugoslav lands: Croatia and the Croats

The Croat kingdom had been absorbed into Hungary early in the twelfth century and had thus become part of the Habsburg empire in 1526. After 1867 the Nagodba, or agreement between the Hungarian kingdom and Croatia, allowed the latter its own assembly, or sabor, and the use of Serbo-Croat in local administration. Despite these concessions real power in the Hungarian province of Croatia-Slavonia lay with the *ban* or governor appointed by Budapest. The politics of Croatia were immeasurably complicated by the presence of large communities of Serbs whose predecessors had been imported by the Habsburg authorities in the early eighteenth century to defend the military frontier against the Ottomans.

Despite the constraints imposed by Magyar rule the Croats developed their own political groups. Initially the most prominent was the Party of Right, led by Ante Starčević, which rejected the Nagodba and demanded a restoration of autonomy for Croatia-Slavonia and for the Austrian province of Dalmatia. The party rejected cooperation with Vienna or Budapest and was outspokenly anti-Serb. In 1894 it split. Josip Frank's new Party of Pure Right was even more anti-Serb but it was more prepared to cooperate with Habsburg power, and was ready to include Bosnia in an autonomous Croatia. The status of Bosnia was one of a number of issues separating Croat and Serb in Croatia, another being the fact that the Hungarians favoured the Serbs in order to divide them from the Croats.

The year 1903 brought significant changes. The *ban* who had ruled Croatia for twenty years moved to Budapest, whilst the coup in Serbia brought more open government and less pro-Habsburg attitudes to Belgrade. A number of young Croats, some of them former pupils of Masaryk and much influenced by his ideas of closer union between the Slavs, moved towards greater cooperation with the Serbs of Croatia.

In 1905 Croats meeting in Fiume had demanded civil liberties, franchise reform, and the union of Dalmatia with Croatia, a demand endorsed by a subsequent meeting in Zadar of Croatian Serbs. An effective alliance of Serb and Croat parties, with the exception of the Frankists and the recently established Croat Peasant Party, was soon offering support to the Magyars in their constitutional contest with Vienna in return for changes in the Nagodba. This offer was rejected by Budapest but the Croat-Serb alliance in Croatia survived and in the election of 1906 won a majority of seats in the sabor. The Serbs of Croatia were angered by the annexation of Bosnia and Hercegovina in 1908 and in the

17

following years by the Agram and Friedjung trials. The Balkan wars naturally excited Serb passions even further.

When the first world war began there were three trends in Croat politics. The first was that of the Frankists with their conservative, constitutional notions of a greater Croatia. The second was for eventual union with the Serbs in a greater Serbia, and finally there was the idea of a large Yugoslav unit including not only the Serbs and Croats but also the Slovenes and Bulgarians, an idea which had some support amongst the Croats of Dalmatia and the Serbs of southern Hungary. There were still many Croats, however, who did not want union with the Serbs and who, having staged anti-Serb demonstrations in Croatia and Bosnia after the assassination of Franz Ferdinand, remained loyal to the monarchy throughout the war.

The Yugoslav lands: Bosnia and Hercegovina

The origin of the Slav Muslims of Bosnia is not entirely clear. Conversion seems to have occurred gradually after the Ottoman conquest, with various non-Catholic and non-Orthodox groups being more likely to join Islam than those who remained within one of the two main churches. For the Bosnian aristocracy conversion to Islam also ensured continued possession of their estates.

When the Dual Monarchy had taken over the administration of Bosnia and Hercegovina from the Ottoman empire in 1878 a Habsburg official had quipped that the mainly Muslim Bosnians and the Catholic Hercegovinians could be occupied by 'a platoon headed by a military band'. He was wrong. It took over 150,000 troops, 5,000 of whom died owing to resistance from the Muslims. Further action was needed in 1882 to contain a serious revolt which resulted from the attempt by the new authorities to impose conscription upon the area.

After calm had been restored, order prevailed through the long, authoritarian, but basically benign stewardship of Benjamin Kállay, who was effectively in charge of the area from 1882 to 1903. As a Hungarian Kállay knew about Croats and as a former Habsburg consul in Belgrade he had some feeling for the Serbs; in fact he had written a history of Serbia which was so favourable to the Serbs that he himself banned it in Bosnia and Hercegovina. Kállay died in 1903 and was succeeded by count Stephan Burian who relaxed some of the controls imposed by Kállay. After the annexation of 1908 the provinces were each given a diet with four electoral *curiae*, or colleges, based on religious affiliation. The Serbs had little to do with this, preferring to spread greater Serbian propaganda via the sokols, and via unlikely institutions such as literary, temperance, and choral societies. By the eve of the first world war Habsburg control had brought a good deal of modernisation and, it seemed, relative political order and stability, even if little had been done to reconcile the Serbs, Croats, and Muslims.

The Yugoslav lands: Slovenia

The Slovenes were the most politically quiescent of the south Slav peoples both before and after 1918. They had fallen under Habsburg domination in the fourteenth and fifteenth centuries without ever having had a state of their own.

The Slovenes were intensely Catholic. They were also largely owners of their own land. Slovene political activity before the first world war was concentrated, therefore, in the clerical Slovene People's Party, led by Mgr Anton Korošec. Their maximalist programme was for the reconstruction of the monarchy on a trialist, i.e. Austro-Hungarian-Slav, basis but in the meantime they pushed for more use of Slovene in the administration, the judiciary, and education. The other major force in Slovene life was the cooperative movement which, as in other areas, did much to make small-scale individual farming a profitable affair.

With the exception of the tiny *Preporod* (renaissance) group the Slovenes showed little enthusiasm for Yugoslavism before, during, or after the first world war. But if the Slovenes were loyal to the empire this was at least in part because they saw it as their best defence against Italian designs on their territory.

The Yugoslav lands: Dalmatia

Dalmatia had come into Habsburg hands through the treaty of Vienna in 1815, having previously been Venetian and then part of Napoleon's Illyrian experiment.

By 1910 the population was 82 per cent Croat, 16 per cent Serb and 2 per cent Italian. The Serbs' main political force was the Serbian National Party which had been founded in 1879 and which supported the long-established Autonomy Party in the call for a separate Dalmatian administration. The Croats, on the other hand, called for the restoration, within the monarchy, of the ancient triune kingdom of Croatia, Slavonia, and Dalmatia, together with Bosnia-Hercegovina. The Serbs could not allow that the latter might not go to Serbia. Like Slovenia, however, Dalmatia did not produce a strong movement towards Yugoslavism, at least not until threatened with Italian aggrandisement.

The Yugoslav lands: Macedonia

Before 1912 Macedonia was generally understood to comprise the three Ottoman vilayets of Salonika, Kosovo, and Bitolja. It was a byword for racial and religious mixture; it was also an area of grinding poverty.

Although it was the core of the Ottoman empire's European possessions, Macedonia was coveted by the surrounding Christian states, Greece, Bulgaria, and Serbia; the Romanians also showed some interest in the Vlachs, a mainly nomadic people who spoke a language related to Romanian and who some believe to be descendants of Pompey's legions defeated at Pharsalia.

After Ottoman sovereignty over Macedonia was reconfirmed in 1878 the Greeks, Bulgarians, and Serbs were anxious to persuade the local inhabitants that they were a part of the Greek, Bulgarian, or Serb nation. The means for doing this were initially cultural, and primarily ecclesiastical, since the Ottoman authorities still divided their empire by religious affiliation rather than by ethnic identity. Each national church competed in a variety of ways for the support of the Macedonian Christians; a Bulgarian church at Resen in western Macedonia became extremely popular, for example, because of the excellence of its cantor; the son of that cantor achieved even greater recognition later on as the opera star Boris Christoff. By the turn of the century armed bands, *cheti*, had appeared, some of them operating under the auspices of the Internal Macedonian Revolutionary Organisation (IMRO), which aimed at establishing an autonomous Macedonia which would eventually become part of a Balkan federation. This was not what the neighbouring states wanted and they sponsored bands of their own. In 1903 the Bulgarians gave unofficial support to a full-scale rebellion in Macedonia. The failure of the 'Ilinden' rising prompted the great powers to impose administrative reforms in the area but these did little to suppress the appetite of the surrounding states for expansion.

The Young Turk revolution brought hopes for internal reconstruction but by 1911 these had been dashed. In 1912, with the Constantinople government seriously weakened by an Albanian revolt which had spread into the centre of Macedonia, the Balkan alliance was born and by the end of the year the Ottoman forces had been chased out of Macedonia. The second Balkan war left Greece with Salonika and the Aegean coast, Bulgaria with the small mountainous area of Pirin Macedonia, and Serbia in control of most of the heartland of the area, the Vardar valley. The Serbs, in their area, immediately imposed serbianisation upon those Macedonians who had until then not considered themselves Serbs.

Yugoslavism and the foundation of the Yugoslav state

The areas which eventually came together to form the Yugoslav state were as diverse in ethnic composition as they were in historical experience. Serbia and Montenegro were predominantly Serbian, as were Bosnia and Hercegovina, though Bosnia had a large Muslim community. Approximately a fifth of the population of Croatia was Serbian; Slovenes made up the majority of the population of Slovenia, though there was a sizeable German minority; Dalmatia boasted a mixture of Croats, Italians, Serbs, Jews, and others; the Vojvodina had, in addition to Serbs, a large number of Magyars, Croats, Slovaks, Germans, and Romanians; Kosovo's Albanian Muslims made up the largest element in that area, whilst Macedonia had self-confessed Macedonians as well as Bulgarians, Serbs, Greeks, Turks, Jews, Albanians, Vlachs, Gypsies and others.

The nineteenth century had heard plans for south Slav unity, though the definition of south Slav varied. Some, like Garašanin's *Načertanije*, were plans for Serbian aggrandisement. Others, including those of Bishop Josip Strossmayer of

Djakovo in the second half of the century, were attempts to establish union upon the basis of what was considered a common culture and history.

During the first world war support for both concepts grew. The war aims of the Serbian government under Radical Party leader Nikola Pašić, which were declared in December 1914, were undisguised Serbian expansionism. A month earlier in Florence a number of anti-Habsburg protagonists of Croat-Serb cooperation formed the Yugoslav Committee (YC) whose main objective was the formation of a Yugoslav federation. In May 1915 the YC moved to London where it enjoyed the patronage of Seton Watson and Wickham Steed. Efforts by the YC to cooperate with Pašić did not always succeed, and attempts to form a separate Yugoslav military unit in Russia were frustrated by constant friction between the YC leaders and Pašić's government-in-exile in Corfu. Even when serious negotiations at last began it took four months before agreement could be reached in the shape of the fourteen-point Corfu Declaration of 20 July 1917. The Serbs, Croats, and Slovenes were to form a united and independent state which was to be a constitutional monarchy under a Karadjeordjević king. The three separate Yugoslav 'tribes' were recognised, since the new state was to have three flags, three religions, and two alphabets, though the Declaration was ominously silent on the future relations between the three 'tribes' and on the distribution of power between the central government and the constituent regions.

The YC had become convinced that an imprecise agreement was better than no agreement at all because of its fears of Italian ambitions. Such fears were justified because the Italian government, although it allowed Yugoslav representation at the Rome conference of oppressed minorities in April 1918, prevented the Yugoslavs from receiving the recognition given in the summer of 1918 to the Poles and the Czechs.

In the autumn Habsburg authority in the south Slav lands collapsed as the central powers faced inevitable military defeat. In the midst of growing chaos and disorder the Serbian government and the Habsburg south Slavs edged closer together. The latter had become more cohesive in early October with the formation of the National Council of the Slovenes, Croats, and Serbs, which at the end of the month became a *de facto* provisional government of the Habsburg south Slavs. By November the allies had persuaded Pašić to drop his plans for making Serbia the sole representative of the south Slavs and to agree to recognise the National Council as the representative authority for the south Slavs of the former Habsburg lands; it was also agreed that the National Council and the Serbian government were to coexist as equal partners until a constituent assembly had been convened.

Representative groups from Montenegro, the Vojvodina, and Bosnia-Hercegovina agreed to join Belgrade rather than Zagreb. Serbian authority was maintained in Macedonia and Kosovo, although in Kosovo this met with resistance from Albanian guerilla bands, one of which was led by Azam Behta and his wife

Shota, 'an amazon shepherdess who hid her sex by assuming a male name and attire so as not to offend the patriarchal mores of her people'.[5]

The National Council did not concern itself with these violent events to the south and on 24 November voted for unification with Serbia, electing a 28-man delegation to go to Belgrade to represent its interests. On 1 December 1918 the new state was proclaimed. It was called the Triune Kingdom of the Serbs, Croats, and Slovenes, but was rapidly and widely known by the less cumbersome title of Yugoslavia. The head of state was the Regent Alexander Karadjeordjević whose father was too ill to reign.

The new state had been created by the exigencies of war. 'Yugoslavism' had always been the preserve of a few intellectuals and politicians. It had never been a mass force capable on its own of destroying Habsburg power. With the exception of the two mutinies in the spring of 1918, Slovenes, Croats, and even some Serbs continued to fight with the Habsburg army against the Serbs. And when Yugoslavism was applied it was based on a new dualism, a coalescence of the old Serbian kingdom and of the south Slavs of the former Habsburg lands. They had never been easy allies.

Albania

The Albanians are an Indo-European race speaking a language frequently believed to be the oldest in Europe, though there is a wide divergence between the Gheg dialect of the north and that of the Tosks in the south. At the beginning of the twentieth century the clan, or tribe, remained the strongest social unit, particularly in the north, and there was almost nothing which could be identified as modern economic development; one of the area's few profitable exports was tortoises.

After heroic resistance by Gjergj Kastrioti, or Skënderbeg, in the mid-fifteenth century Albania had fallen under Ottoman domination and a majority of Albanians had accepted Islam. This was in part defiance against the Slavs, most of whom remained Christian, and in part to ensure the continued possession of land. In the north some of the Albanian tribes remained Catholic, and the Orthodox church retained its hold on some areas in the south, but religion, of whatever variety, never weighed heavily upon the Albanians.

As long as they were left to indulge their traditional ways of life the Albanians remained faithful subjects of the Sublime Porte. It was the threat of Christian annexation in 1878 which prompted the formation of the first real Albanian political organisation, the 'Albanian League for the Defence of the Rights of the Albanian Nation', more usually known as the League of Prizren. The League was suppressed in 1881 and in 1886 the Porte reimposed its pre-1878 ban on education in Albanian; the Albanians, divided by religion, might be united by language and that had to be prevented.

Mounting Christian pressure on Macedonia increased the Albanians' need to preserve the Ottoman empire as their best defence against absorption. The Young

Turk revolution brought hopes that the empire would be regenerated and would allow some movement towards Albanian autonomy. Albanians meeting in Bitolja at the end of 1908 agreed to adopt the latin script as the official alphabet and a congress at Elbasan in August of the following year established a national board of education. Now the Young Turks were alarmed. After Albanian troops had been prominent in an attempted counter-coup in 1909 the Young Turks reimposed the old restrictions on Albanian education and moved towards rigid centralisation.

The Albanians, acting from a mixture of defensive, conservative nationalism, a desire to have education in their own language, and a fear of domination by the surrounding states, revolted in 1910, 1911, and 1912. The last rising was so successful that it forced the Young Turks out of office, but before the Albanians could capitalise on this gain the great powers began to intervene diplomatically in an attempt to restore order. This in turn provoked the Balkan states to action lest the path to the partition of Albania be closed. The Balkan alliance attacked the Ottoman empire in October. Albanian leaders, realising that the Turks could no longer protect them, met in Vlorë and declared independence on 28 November 1912.

The great powers defined Albania's borders, leaving some Albanians in Greece and many more in Serbia which now ruled Kosovo. The great powers did what they could to make the new state viable but they could achieve little before the outbreak of the great war. Their nominee as prince, Wilhelm zu Wied, arrived in March 1914 but never established his authority, not least because of the machinations of the clan chiefs. He left the country in September. In 1916 it was partitioned by Austrian, Italian, French, and Serbian troops.

Romania and the Romanians

Romania's existence as a modern state began with the union of the principalities of Wallachia and Moldavia in 1859. The first prince, Alexander Cuza, introduced many reforms but he alienated the powerful boyars or landowners. In 1866 they replaced him with Charles of Hohenzollern who was made king in 1881 and who was to remain ruler until his death in 1914.

With Charles came a new constitution which also lasted until the first world war. It was founded on a complicated system of electoral colleges, or *curiae*, based on social class, a system which gave effective power to the boyars and the small urban *haute bourgeoisie*. Political life in Romania developed into a two party, or rather two clique system, with the boyars being prominent in both. The liberals and conservatives, who had little in common with their British namesakes, divided over economic strategy and partially over foreign policy, the conservatives being pro-German and the majority of the liberals being, initially at least, pro-French. In economic policy the conservatives generally supported agricultural and landed interests but the liberals based their approach on the notion of *Prin noi Înşine* (ourselves alone). As with the similarly named Sinn Féin at the other end of Europe the liberal objective was the industrialisation of an agrarian economy without reliance upon foreign capital. The Romanian liberals recognised that their society lacked the traditional western industrialising element, a native entrepreneurial bourgeoisie, and argued that the state had to perform the role of this missing group. Romanian liberalism, therefore, came to represent almost the precise opposite of the traditional, Manchester-school in its attitude to the role of the state in the economy. In a peasant, agrarian economy the cost of this internal industrialisation could be borne by no one but the peasantry and liberal policy was thus designed so that taxation, tariffs, and other arms of the state's financial machinery should take wealth from the countryside and direct it into the industrialising towns.

In the mid–1870s foreign rather than domestic affairs dominated public life. The treaty of Berlin was much resented because of the loss of eastern Moldavia, or Bessarabia, for which neither possession of southern Dobrudja nor the recognition of full independence could compensate. In any case, for many Romanian nationalists the treaty contradicted its own acceptance of full Romanian independence by insisting that the country should allow all its inhabitants, irrespective of race or religion, equal political rights and equal access to jobs. The Romanian constitution allowed such rights only to Romanian citizens and further stipulated that anyone wishing to become a Romanian citizen had to be Christian. This was intended to discriminate against the Jews, many of whom had moved from Russia into Romania during the nineteenth century, their total number rising from around 127,000 in 1859 to approximately 278,000 in 1899.

The liberals were in office for a decade after 1878 and introduced a number of economic measures which made possible the beginnings of modern industry, most notably the extraction of oil from the Ploeşti fields. New customs regulations in 1886 precipitated a tariff war with Austria-Hungary, an ironic development in that in 1883 King Charles had signed a secret treaty with the monarchy. The treaty remained known to only a handful of Romanians.

Despite the treaty obligation to Austria-Hungary, Romania attempted to keep out of the great war. One reason for its reluctance to become involved in the fighting was the questionable reliability of its peasant conscripts. In 1907 a massive *jacquerie* had broken out in Romania. It had required 100,000 troops to suppress it and had cost the lives of some 10,000 peasants. It had prompted laws to improve peasant conditions but much of this legislation had remained inoperative because those responsible for enforcing it were those who would have lost most from its implementation.

Romania finally entered the first world war on 27 August 1916, after the Russian victories in Galicia and when it was assumed Bulgaria was tied down in Macedonia. The Romanians had miscalculated. The Bulgarians, strengthened by Turkish units, invaded and shortly afterwards a massive German onslaught was launched from the west. In December Bucharest fell and the Romanian government moved to Iaşi. The disintegration of Russia made it impossible for Romania to continue fighting and in May 1918 the treaty of Bucharest was signed by which Romania gained Bessarabia but lost the Dobrudja to Bulgaria; the Germans assumed total control over the oil fields. On 9 November 1918 Romania re-entered the war on the allied side.

Transylvania

The Romanians claim that they were the original inhabitants of Transylvania whilst the Magyars insist that the area was depopulated when their ancestors arrived in the eleventh century. Between 1526 and 1699 the area was autonomous within the Ottoman empire, after which it became part of the Hungarian kingdom, though in the eighteenth century the emperor in Vienna also had great influence. The ethnic mix of the area was complicated by the introduction of German settlers: the Saxons, who had arrived in the twelfth century and the Swabians who came in the eighteenth century. A further complication arose in that religious diversity was added to ethnic differences. Transylvania was deeply affected by the Reformation yet escaped the worst excesses of the counter-Reformation; various Protestant sects therefore flourished alongside Catholicism, Judaism, Islam, and after 1698, Uniatism. The latter had been introduced by the Habsburgs to dilute the power of Orthodoxy. Nor did ethnic divisions always coincide with religious ones; amongst the Germans the Swabians remained Catholic whilst the Saxons adopted Lutheranism.

In the early nineteenth century the Romanians took some fright at the tendency towards the magyarisation of the Hungarian kingdom and in 1848 they resisted attempts by Transylvanian Magyars to create an independent Transylvanian state. After 1867 it was much more difficult for Romanians to resist magyarising pressures, though the Romanian Orthodox church, and particularly metropolitan Andreiu Saguna, attempted to do so.

The most important political organisation to emerge in the late nineteenth century was the Romanian National Party, founded in Sibiu in 1881. It demanded autonomy for Transylvania, a radical reform of the electoral system, more freedom for the churches together with state subsidies for their schools, and the use of Romanian in the region's administration and law courts. The party was suppressed in 1894.

For most of the period from 1867 to 1914 the Romanians of Transylvania looked less to Bucharest than to Vienna for help. They could not have expressed a desire to join the Romanian kingdom even if they had wanted to and they therefore asked Vienna for the same rights as those enjoyed by minorities in the Austrian section of the monarchy. Meanwhile the Romanian state showed little sign that it would have responded to appeals for help. The king of Romania, after 1883, was constrained by the secret treaty with Austria-Hungary and in all cases Romanians were conscious, after the loss of Bessarabia in 1878, that Russia would probably limit if it did not veto any extension of Romanian influence or territory. For these reasons, in the pre-first world war period, the Romanian government seemed to be almost as concerned for the Vlachs of Macedonia as for the Romanians of Transylvania.

The Bukovina

In the Bukovina the Romanian proportion of the population was declining as a result of Jewish and Ukrainian immigration. The area, which had become a Habsburg possession in 1775, had been separated from Galicia in 1853 and given its own administration and diet; in 1867 it remained in the Austrian part of the monarchy. It was, however, an area of intense poverty and one so ethnically mixed that no one group could claim ascendency. This, together with its economic backwardness, made it politically inert, its deputies to the Reichsrat being amongst the most faithful of government supporters, whatever the composition of that government might be.

Bulgaria

The treaty of Berlin made Bulgaria a vassal state of the sultan and required it to guarantee religious and political liberties. This it did in the constitution drawn up by an assembly meeting in the medieval capital, Tûrnovo, in 1879.

The Tûrnovo constitution, which was to remain in force at least nominally until 1947, was amongst the most liberal in Europe. Unfortunately it was soon subverted. The first prince of Bulgaria, Alexander of Battenberg, could not cooperate with the liberals who dominated the unicameral assembly. In 1886 he was chased from his throne not by the liberals but by the Russians and their agents who were furious that Alexander had accepted the union of Bulgaria and Eastern Rumelia; at that time the Russians wanted stability in the Balkans whilst they pursued their central Asian objectives.

His successor, elected in 1887, was Ferdinand of Saxe-Coburg-Gotha. He was no more to the liking of the tsar than Alexander had been; Russia refused to recognise him as the legitimate prince and sent its agents to destabilise his régime. These plots were frustrated by the new strong man of Bulgaria, Stefan Stambolov. By 1894 Ferdinand had come to fear that Stambolov was too mighty a subject. He was removed from office, to be brutally murdered a year later by Macedonians whose brother he had executed after one of the numerous plots of the early 1890s. Macedonia had already begun to exercise its baleful influence on Bulgarian politics.

Stambolov's successor, Konstantin Stoilov, enacted laws for the encouragement of industry and helped to negotiate the settlement which finally secured Ferdinand's recognition as prince in 1896; as part of the settlement Ferdinand had to agree that his son and the heir to the throne, Prince Boris, be baptised into the Orthodox church. After recognition Ferdinand moved rapidly and skilfully to consolidate his personal power. This he did through exploiting *partisanstvo*, the Bulgarian variant of Balkan political jobbery, clientism, and corruption. By 1900

Ferdinand could make and break ministries almost at will, leaving it to the corrupt politicians to manufacture parliamentary or electoral support for the new government.

Ferdinand's main concern was to be a major figure in European affairs and he therefore kept a tight rein on foreign policy. In the early 1900s he played the dangerous game of giving secret support to pro-Bulgarian bands operating in Macedonia, despite warnings from St Petersburg and Vienna against such a policy. After 1903 and the failure of the Ilinden rising, Ferdinand had to retract his horns, and his freedom of manoeuvre was further restricted by a serious financial crisis, but he continued to exploit with some skill the divisions between the great powers.

After the declaration of full independence in 1908 Bulgaria continued to press its cause in Macedonia but decided in 1912 that it could make no progress on its own; the dream of absorbing all of the area was given up and partition with Serbia and Greece accepted as inevitable if it were not to fall under the patronage of the great powers. The Bulgarian armies bore the brunt of the fighting in the battles of the first Balkan war but by the summer of 1913 disagreements between Bulgaria and its erstwhile allies had reached such intensity that the Bulgarians used evidence of a Greek-Serbian agreement to launch what was intended to be a pre-emptive strike against these two former allies. It had disastrous results and led to Bulgaria's humiliation in the second Balkan war. In September 1915 came the chance to redeem the losses, but once again the gods of war showed neither favour nor mercy. By the summer of 1918 the home population faced desperate shortages of food whilst at the front the army was equally short of ammunition. When an allied attack was launched from Salonika in September 1918 the Bulgarians were too enfeebled to resist and became the first of the European members of the central powers to leave the war.

The determining events in Bulgarian political development had revolved around the quest for Macedonia, but internal changes had also taken place. Bulgaria was primarily a land of small, independent, peasant farmers. In 1900 the peasants, already hard pressed by falling prices, natural disasters, and the depredations of the usurers, reacted violently against a government plan to replace the tithe in kind with a cash payment. The ensuing crisis produced the Bulgarian Agrarian National Union which became one of the most organised and powerful of eastern Europe's agrarian parties. It was to play a major role in national affairs immediately after the first world war. A small socialist movement also appeared in Bulgaria at the turn of the century and it too was to be at centre stage in the post-war period.

Part I

THE INTER-WAR
PERIOD

EASTERN EUROPE, 1918 – 38

SWEDEN

DENMARK

Copenhagen

Baltic Sea

Tallinn

ESTONIA

LATVIA

Riga

LITHUANIA

Memel

Kaunas

Wilno
(Vilnius)

SOVIET UNION

Danzig

EAST
PRUSSIA

KRESY

River Vistula

River Bug

Berlin

Warsaw

Kiev

GERMANY

P O L A N D

VOLHYNIA

Lvov

SILESIA

SUDETEN AREA

Prague

Teschen

CZECHOSLOVAKIA

GALICIA

RUTHENIA

River Dniester

River Danube

SLOVAKIA

BESSARABIA

River Pruth

Vienna

Bratislava

Budapest

ROMANIA

AUSTRIA

HUNGARY

TRANSYLVANIA

SWITZ

Zagreb

VOJVODINA

BANAT

Belgrade

Bucharest

ITALY

Adriatic Sea

YUGOSLAVIA

BULGARIA

KOSOVO

Sofia

Rome

ALBANIA

TURKEY

Tirana

GREECE

0   250
km

2

THE INTER-WAR YEARS

An introductory survey

Peace treaties were concluded with the defeated powers in 1919 and 1920: Versailles with Germany; St Germain with Austria, Neuilly-sur-Seine with Bulgaria; Trianon with Hungary and Sèvres with the Ottoman empire. From these treaties emerged the new states of Poland, Czechoslovakia, and Yugoslavia; Lithuania, Latvia, and Estonia appeared from other agreements. Serbia and Montenegro were merged into the new Yugoslavia, Romania was greatly enlarged, and Bulgaria shorn of most but not all of its acquisitions since 1912. A number of territorial issues could not be settled immediately; in some cases resort was made to plebiscites, in others international or ambassadorial conferences settled the day, as when the disputed Italo-Yugoslav border was delimited at Rapallo in 1920, or when the ambassadors of the great powers pronounced their judgement of Solomon on Teschen, an area disputed between Poland and Czechoslovakia. In some regions, particularly after the mass armies had been demobilised, the allies had no leverage and the final solution was left to the arbitration of arms.

The post-war settlement was based supposedly on the principle of national self-determination. Because it was believed the nationalism of the subject peoples had been such a disruptive force in the past, nation states were considered the best future guarantors of the status quo. Yet there were many compromises. Czechoslovakia was by no stretch of anyone's imagination a nation state; it emerged because the Czechs persuaded the victorious allies that they were the best safeguard against German, Hungarian, and Austrian revanchism and against German, Hungarian, and Russian bolshevism. For strategic reasons the Czechs were given control over Ruthenia, just as the Yugoslavs took the Hungarian-dominated Bačka which they believed essential to the defence of Belgrade. The Versailles settlement was unable, and did not attempt, to allow every European to live in his or her own national state, but the post-war treaties 'still freed three times as many people from nationally alien rule as they subjected to it'.[1] Furthermore, the victors knew that the pure nation state could not be created in an area where there were so few clear-cut divisions between different ethnic groups. It was a mark of the civilisation of the men of Versailles that, realising this, they strove to provide protection for the minority groups which would inevitably be

31

created; such protection was given in the series of minority protection treaties which each east European state was required to sign.

The post-war treaties transformed the map of Europe but in so doing created many problems; there were, for example, 1,700 extra miles of tariff-affected borders to be controlled. The settlement lasted no longer than twenty years and began to crumble when Hitler occupied the Rhineland in March 1936. Yet it was not the settlement in eastern Europe which caused the collapse. That settlement had many anomalies and created serious tensions, but after 1921 no east European state went to war against another. War, when it came, was not caused by east European instability; as in 1914 it was caused by great powers taking advantage of east European political fragility for their own purposes.

Problems of adjustment: territorial

It had been the peacemakers in Paris who had decided which states should survive and which new ones should emerge from the war. The detailed application of the general settlement was a long and frequently painful process. In the north east, apart from along the Baltic coast, the allies had no real means to enforce their decisions and the frontiers were eventually determined by military force; most of Poland's eastern boundary was so decided, as was the Czechoslovak presence in Teschen. Plebiscites in Sopron (Ödenburg), Silesia, east Prussia, and Carinthia settled the question of which state they were to be in. This was a convenient conjunction of two of the basic principles of the 1918–19 settlement; plebiscites were a devolved form of open covenants openly arrived at, and, because it was assumed that people would vote essentially on ethnic considerations, plebiscites were also a shining example of local national self-determination. It was Wilsonian liberalism in action amongst the people. Unfortunately, people seldom vote in accordance with the precepts of political theoreticians. Jews in Silesia, for example, voted for inclusion in Germany because they feared Polish anti-semitism, whilst many bourgeois German-speakers in Sopron voted for inclusion in Hungary because Austria seemed at that time likely to fall under socialist rule whereas Hungary had recently overthrown its bolshevik régime. Whatever means were chosen to determine final boundary lines the territorial settlement was not finally reached until 1924, with agreements such as the Memel (Klaipeda) convention, an Italo-Yugoslav accommodation over Fiume, and general international acceptance of Poland's eastern boundary.

Problems of adjustment: political

For three to four years after the end of the first world war the political situation in eastern Europe remained fragile; the authorities lived in fear of insurgent activity, primarily from the left. The defeat of the Red Army in the Russo-Polish war of 1919–21 was to lessen the possibility of outright bolshevik conquest, but the danger of internal subversion remained. A rash of bitter strikes with heavy political overtones affected most of the new states between 1919 and 1923. There were also a number of attempted communist coups, all of which failed and precipitated tighter controls on trade unions, labour organisations, and left-wing parties. But the violence was not always from the left. It was a right-wing fanatic who murdered the first president of Poland and a right-wing alliance which deposed the radical agrarian government of Bulgaria in 1923.

In addition to the problem of containing subversion, presumed and actual, the new states had to define their political systems and to regulate conditions of citizenship, to tackle the questions of inheritance rights, pensions entitlements, and a myriad of other issues arising from the creation of new states and societies out of the old order. In many cases the new authorities would probably have liked to take radical measures, usually against a previously ruling minority, but such steps could well have caused the allies to fear that some new variant of bolshevism was afoot; the state in question might then face international isolation and, most crucially, might be unable to secure loans.

In general, political systems had been decided upon and constitutions had been defined by 1922 or 1923. The entirely new states, Czechoslovakia, Estonia, Latvia, Lithuania, and Poland all became republics; Bulgaria and Romania remained monarchies, as did Yugoslavia under the Serbian dynasty; Hungary retained its crown but not its monarch; and Albania became a monarchy in 1928. Few generalisations are valid as to what type of constitution was adopted but in the early twenties there was a clear preference for proportional representation whilst bicameral legislatures were not universally favoured. The problems of centralism versus regionalism were particularly complex in areas of such ethnic diversity, and they were additionally complicated in most states by the need to integrate territories which had previously belonged to entirely different legal and political structures. This was an obvious difficulty for entirely new constructions such as Poland, Yugoslavia, and Czechoslovakia. It was equally a problem in the greatly expanded Romania, though less so in the Baltic states, whilst in defeated Hungary and Bulgaria it did not apply at all.

With the exception of the Czechoslovak, the political systems which emerged in the first half of the 1920s did not last long. Coups in Poland and Lithuania in 1926 increased executive power, Romania instituted an Italian-style 'bonus' system whereby a party securing 40 per cent of the votes received at least 50 per cent of the seats in the lower chamber, Yugoslavia experienced a royal coup in 1929, and in 1934 Bulgaria and Estonia saw authoritarian forces assume control. These changes did not always bring stability, but they all marked a turn away from the representative democratic ideas of the founders of the new European order.

Problems of adjustment: economic and social

Economic stability was won at much the same time as political stability. After 1918 pre-war trading patterns were frequently difficult to re-establish and the new states were ravaged by inflation, only Czechoslovakia managing to keep this particular plague at bay. After the great central European crisis of 1923 had been surmounted, tranquillity returned which in turn made loans easier to procure. By the mid-1920s some states which had suffered severely from inflation were able to signal their return to confidence and stability by introducing a new currency, the Polish złoty in 1925 and the Hungarian pengö in 1926 being two examples. Peasant suspicion of new paper currencies, which during and after the war had slowed down the selling of agricultural produce, had by now been largely overcome.

The major adjustment affecting most peasants in eastern Europe immediately after the first world war was the process of land redistribution. The extent to which real redistribution was achieved varied; in Hungary and Poland the large landowners were less affected than those in Czechoslovakia, northern Yugoslavia, and Romania. The purpose of the reform was to achieve social stability, to redeem promises, explicit or implied, made to peasants during the war, and to deprive the bolsheviks of effective propaganda amongst the peasant masses. Land reform was an enormously complex process, ridden with difficult questions both of principle and of application: what were to be the minimum and maximum holdings? was compensation to be paid to former owners and, if so, over what period and in what form, cash or government bonds? what government agency was to be responsible for this social revolution from above? and how was capital to be provided to the new peasant owners to buy implements, stock, and seed? These and many other problems were generally surmounted with ingenuity and good sense, and the land redistribution process is one of the greatest, if least remarked successes of the east European states in the inter-war period.

This is not to say that the process did not give rise to complaint. The dispossession of aristocrats frequently had the added political advantage of taking property and therefore social power from members of a former dominant minority, to the benefit of the masses of the ethnic majority: it was mainly Hungarians who lost estates in Transylvania, Croatia, Ruthenia, the Vojvodina, and Slovakia, whilst the Germans were the losers in Bohemia, Moravia, and Slovenia as well as in some parts of Poland and the Baltic states. In the very successful Czechoslovak land redistributions the Germans complained, with justification, that there were no ethnic Germans in the land office which administered the reforms. A more frequent complaint was that land redistribution was often taken as an excuse for population redistribution. Thus Ukrainians and Belorussians grumbled that land redistributed in their areas was given in disproportionate amounts to Poles, many of them veterans of Piłsudski's POW. In southern Slovakia Magyar estates were divided up to be given, in many cases, not to the local Magyar peasants but to Czechs and Slovaks, some of them émigrés returning from north

34

America. The Romanian authorities encouraged Vlachs to settle in the Dobrudja to dilute the local Turkish, Tatar, and Bulgarian population; and complaints from Germans in western Poland on land redistribution were as loud and as frequent as they were on many other issues.

The land reforms in general pleased the majority elements in eastern Europe, but if they solved some political and social problems they had economic and social disadvantages. The move towards peasant proprietorship meant a step backward from the large holdings considered appropriate for development with modern machinery. Commercialisation and capitalisation in peasant agriculture could be achieved to some degree, however, through the cooperative movement which was strong in many parts of eastern Europe. With the backing of their own banks the cooperatives frequently enabled the square peg of peasant proprietorship to fit into the round hole of modern, commercialised farming.

The cooperatives could be no defence against population growth and the consequent increased pressure on the land. Population growth was caused by a combination of natural increase and the almost total closure of the traditional safety valve for central and east European population surplus: emigration, particularly to north America. After the onset of the great depression a further escape route was closed as local industry contracted and could not absorb any more labour. An additional problem affecting peasant agriculture, particularly in the more backward areas, was the division of individual holdings into a number of small, and geographically separate strips. This problem of parcellisation was particularly acute in areas where land was inherited by more than one child. Most governments tackled this problem in the 1920s. There were schemes to promote commassation, or bringing the separate strips together in compact holdings; education in agricultural improvement was provided – in Hungary there were broadcasts on the subject which peasants were required to listen to in the village hall – and in the 1920s loans were readily available. It was not always clear for what purposes these loans were used, because a further problem in east European peasant life was that surplus money was traditionally used not for investment in agricultural improvement but for family, religious, or community festivals.

The great depression and its consequences

The taking out of loans, at both a national and an individual level, was not a problem in the second half of the 1920s when capital was plentiful and economies were improving. All was transformed by the Wall Street crash of October 1929 and by the ruination of the central European banking system after the collapse of the Vienna Creditanstaltverein in 1931. Exports of primary produce fell sharply, depriving peasants of markets; at the same time, loans were called in just when repayment of them was becoming impossible. For many peasant families it meant ruin, though those in the most backward areas, for example Albania, were more remote from the world market and therefore less affected (Table 2.1).

Table 2.1 Percentage decline in trade, 1929–33

	Imports	*Exports*
Albania	58.7	40.4
Bulgaria	73.5	55.4
Czechoslovakia	71.0	71.5
Hungary	70.8	62.6
Poland	73.3	65.8
Romania	60.2	50.9
Yugoslavia	70.4	66.8

Source: M. C. Kaser (ed.) *The Economic History of Eastern Europe, 1919–1975*, Oxford, Clarendon Press, 1985, vol. 1, p. 433.

Governments reacted with varying speed to the economic catastrophe. A conference held in Warsaw in August 1930 was attended by all east European states except Lithuania, but it could do nothing against the economic blizzard then blowing. Each state was in effect left to its own devices. This frequently meant a retreat to protectionism, often with dire consequences for former trading partners. Foreign exchange controls were imposed but these had little impact on the individual peasant family. For them marginal help came with debt moratoria, introduced by most states, and even, in some cases, the remission of debts to local banks; in some countries effective state purchasing agencies were set up for specified products. The promotion of crop diversification, particularly into industrial or high value commodities, was another device to escape from economic stagnation. In Bulgaria the government encouraged the planting of strawberries and vines, one prescient British traveller to the country in 1934 noting that 'more will be heard of Bulgarian wine'.[2]

These measures could be little more than palliatives. Salvation for most east European economies only came with the revival of the German economy and the introduction, shortly before the Nazis came to power, of the system of blocked-mark or exchange clearings. After 1933 use of this method of trading expanded rapidly.

> The method was simple at the beginning. Instead of sending to Germany Reichsmark in payment for his imports from Germany, the Hungarian importer had simply to pay *in pengoes* to the Hungarian Central bank the equivalent of these Reichsmark. The German importers of Hungarian goods did exactly the same, in Germany, paying *in Reichsmark* the equivalent of the pengoes he owed. As the Reichsmark paid in this way accumulated in Berlin, and the pengoes in Budapest, the *German* Central bank was able to use the *Reichsmark* funds for paying *German* exporters to Hungary, as the *Hungarian* Central bank was able to use the *pengoe* funds so accumulated for paying *Hungarian* exporters to Germany.[3]

The exchange clearing system greatly increased German economic influence in eastern Europe, giving the Reich easy access to commodities such as Yugoslav chromium ore, Bulgarian tobacco, and Hungarian grain. It allowed the east European states to import German machinery and arms. For those states the system had the overriding advantage that it provided a market for their agricultural goods when no one else seemed prepared to buy them; there was therefore no choice but to trade with Germany. These close economic ties did not mean that Germany thereby acquired control of local policy-making. Yugoslavia, Hungary, and Bulgaria, amongst others, were tightly bound to Germany by exchange clearing agreements but in none did native fascists take power before 1939 and all three played hard to get when the Nazis wanted allies in the second world war.

International alignments in the inter-war years

The objective of international alignments drawn up in the early 1920s was naturally to defend the post-war settlement against any revisionist threats from the defeated powers. This division between revisionist and non-revisionist states was to be a fundamental weakness of the new order, but the League of Nations was available as a mechanism to settle disputes and the states of eastern Europe were rapidly admitted to it. In the 1920s the League did settle a number of such disputes, most notably that arising between Bulgaria and Greece in 1925–6 after frontier incursions in Macedonia.

Underpinning the whole system was dependence on France which concluded alliances with Poland, Czechoslovakia, Romania, and Yugoslavia. The three latter states came together in 1922 to form their own union, which rapidly became known as the 'little entente'.

The primary function of the little entente was to contain Hungarian revisionism; it could also restrict Bulgarian attempts to alter the Versailles settlement. Doubts about the French commitment to eastern Europe were felt immediately after Locarno in 1925. The German-Soviet friendship pact of April 1926 cast another long shadow and awakened fears of what might befall eastern Europe should Germany and Russia cooperate. By the early 1930s France was more and more committed to the Maginot mentality which would leave the east European states to their own devices. They had to make their own dispositions.

Regional agreements were explored but few materialised or were lasting, not least because of the *sauve qui peut* attitudes produced by the great depression. Furthermore, attempts at regional agreements were almost always frustrated by insoluble local rivalries; efforts to create a sustainable and effective Baltic pact were stymied by Polish-Lithuanian hostility, and the Balkan entente of 1934 could never become effective as an international instrument because Bulgaria, its eyes still set on Macedonia and the Dobrudja, would not recognise existing frontiers as permanent whilst the other states would not accept Bulgaria into the pact until it did. In the same year the murder of King Alexander of Yugoslavia, by a Macedonian fanatic acting in collaboration with Croat extremists, gravely weakened attempts to secure a Balkan détente and a wider security pact in Europe.

In 1933 the beast appeared at the end of the corridor. He made his first major move forward in 1936 into the Rhineland. The final wrecking of the Versailles system and the little entente came with the Czechoslovak crisis of 1938. When it became obvious that Hitler's territorial ambitions were not satisfied there were attempts to create a 'third Europe', which in its most grandiose form entailed an anti-German and anti-Soviet bloc stretching from the Baltic to the Balkans. Hungary and Poland were to be its main constituents and were to be joined by the Baltic states, Romania, and Yugoslavia, and if France would not back it there was the remote possibility that Mussolini might cut loose from Hitler and provide great-power support. It was too late. Hitler's star had risen too high for Mussolini to disengage; Poland was reluctant to compromise the non-aggression pacts it had concluded with both Germany and the USSR, whilst it and Lithuania were no nearer cooperation than before and in 1938 even stood on the brink of war; furthermore, no attempts to bring Hungary and Romania together could overcome the Transylvanian dispute.

Beneš had argued in 1918 that Czechoslovakia was the key to stability in central and eastern Europe. In many ways he was right. It had been created by allied backing; when Franco-British support was withdrawn in 1938 it collapsed, and with it the Versailles settlement. The chaos of war and destruction in which the new eastern Europe had been conceived and born would return. Yet, except for the three Baltic republics, the nation states created by the Versailles settlement would re-emerge, some of them in different shape, at the end of the second great twentieth century European war. Before that process is described the internal developments in those states between the wars and three of the main political forces affecting them will be examined.

3

POLAND, 1918–39

Defining the frontiers

The major preoccupations of Paderewski's new government in January 1919 were in the east where chaos enveloped many areas which the Poles regarded as rightfully theirs. Lwów, threatened by Ukrainians, was the first objective. This was soon secured and by April Piłsudski's men had taken Vilnius, a town redolent with meaning for Polish nationalists and in which, one day, Piłsudski's own heart was to be buried. In the meantime, Poland's *Drang nach Osten* had brought it into conflict with Lenin's Soviet régime. The Russo-Polish war of 1919–21 was to be decisive for Poland and for the rest of the continent; it stopped that westward expansion of bolshevism which the statesmen of Europe feared so much.

The war began fitfully as Polish and bolshevik forces moved into the vacuum left by the collapse of German military power. By August 1919 Minsk was in Polish hands. In the following year Piłsudski joined with Petliura, a Ukrainian ex-socialist romantic nationalist and military leader, to advance into the Ukraine but although Kiev was taken the offensive collapsed and by July 1920 the bolsheviks were racing into Poland; soon the Red Army was threatening Warsaw itself. Piłsudski then carried out a brilliant regrouping operation which enabled him to defeat the invaders in the battle of Warsaw in August. In the autumn the Poles chased the bolsheviks eastwards through Belorussia and the Ukraine until an armistice was agreed in October. The definitive peace was signed at Riga on 18 March 1921. Poland was left in possession of large areas of Belorussia and eastern Galicia, her border with Russia thus running far to the east of that originally suggested by Lord Curzon during the peace negotiations in Paris.

In October 1920, after the victory at Warsaw, Polish troops under the command of general Lucjan Żeligowski reoccupied Vilnius and the surrounding district. The Lithuanians, who regarded the city as their natural capital, brought the matter before the League of Nations, but to little avail. Polish troops refused to budge and on 1 February 1922 an assembly elected in the city declared the area 'without reserve or condition an integral part of the Polish republic'. The city and its surrounding district were to remain a bone of contention between

Poland and Lithuania throughout the inter-war years. After March 1921 there followed a series of intrigues and minor adjustments on the eastern border before the frontiers were settled in 1922 and finally recognised by the western powers in March 1923.

Though the League and a series of ambassadorial conferences had proved ineffective over Vilnius, in the west the views of the victorious allies had more weight. Poland was awarded Poznania and some of Silesia and Pomerania. Danzig was to be made into a free city in which the Poles had access to wharves and other facilities and whose foreign policy they could control. The settlement of the western borders, however, could not but be influenced by events in the east. The Czechs had taken the disputed territory of Teschen early in the Russo-Polish war and at the height of Poland's mortal danger the western allies, meeting in the Spa conference in July 1920, were not anxious to return it to a state which appeared to be about to succumb to bolshevism. Trans-Olza, together with its valuable minerals and its 140,000 mainly Protestant Poles, was thus incorporated into Czechoslovakia.

Plebiscites held in eastern Prussia were also influenced by the fear of the advancing Red Army, though here the Polish elements were in a clear minority. Upper Silesia was a more complex issue, and control of the area could give economic domination in central Europe. Two Polish risings had already taken place by the time the western allies organised a plebiscite on 20 March 1921. In it many Jews, terrified of Polish anti-semitism, voted for inclusion in Germany; others, Poles as well as Germans, opted for Germany because they feared that without a railway between the new state and Upper Silesia the Polish government would not be able to feed them, an understandable preoccupation in a central Europe which was only just beginning to escape the fearful effects of the allied war-time blockade. In the event 700,000 Silesians voted for Germany and 450,000 for Poland; the Poles complained that the Germans had brought in 150,000 'out-voters' and a third Polish revolt was staged under the leadership of Wojciech Korfanty. The allies decided that partition was the only solution; by it the Poles received Katowice but lost Oppeln. The settlement increased both the German minority in Poland and the Polish minority in Germany.

Building a new state: Poland's diversity

The new Poland was a coat of many colours. It had inherited territory from Austria-Hungary, Germany, and Russia but even within these partitions there were differences. From Russia came not only the congress kingdom but the kresy, the lands to the east with their Belorussian or Ukrainian peasants and their largely Jewish towns; the German partition included the industrial areas of Silesia as well as the farmlands of Poznania and Pomerania; and within the former Habsburg lands western Galicia was much different in social structure and political outlook from eastern Galicia or, as it is sometimes called, the western Ukraine. This divided inheritance left Poland with three railway systems and economic infrastructures, no less than six currencies, varying educational practices, legal systems which were not completely standardised even by 1939, and a multitude of military legacies:

> The apocryphal story of the ex-Austrian officer who had to consult his French army manual before telling his ex-Russian infantrymen how to load their ex-English ammunition into their ex-German rifles had more than a grain of reality.[1]

Differences of social and economic development were equally marked. In the west the Junkers had generated a taste for efficiency and industriousness which their Polish neighbours and tenants could not escape, and so larger, market-oriented farms were common, whereas in the kresy there were quasi-feudal survivals in tenurial relationships; in the west holdings were generally large enough to warrant capitalisation whereas in the east and south they were small and usually divided into separated strips.

Added to this were ethnic differences. In 1921 the new state had an estimated population of twenty-seven million, 69.2 per cent of whom were Polish, 14.3 per cent Ukrainian or Ruthenian, 3.9 per cent Belorussian, 7.8 per cent Jewish, and 3.9 per cent German; the remainder were Lithuanians, Russians, Czechs, and others. In the east Belorussians or Ukrainians formed the majority of the peasantry, whose landlords were usually Polish, whilst in the west the majority of peasants were Polish. Poland was also the largest Jewish state in the world, containing approximately a third of all Jews. They were predominantly urban, although there were a few Jewish landowners in western Galicia. The urban Jews were primarily engaged in small-workshop manufacturing and trading: 62.9 per cent of those engaged in trading in 1921 were Jewish. Jews were also prominent in the intelligentsia and the professions; as Poland's native commercial and industrial bourgeoisie was relatively small the intelligentsia played a correspondingly larger role in the nation's political life. This facet of Polish social life Dmowski had been exploiting since before the war; tension and contest between Pole and Jew was therefore woven into the fabric of political life.

Polish politics, 1921–6

During the war with Russia Piłsudski had been accepted as president and commander in chief – he was made first marshal of Poland in March 1920 – and from July 1920 to September 1921 the agrarian leader Witos had been prime minister in a cabinet of national defence, but the political divisions which the war had concealed were open again by the time the treaty of Riga had been signed. Despite a plethora of parties the two main tendencies were that which backed Piłsudski and that which aligned with Dmowski.

After the first world war Piłsudski did not join the party political fray but retained enormous influence based primarily on the army which he was determined to keep free from political interference and which, in return, idolised him, as did many civilian Poles for whom he would always remain the man who had saved the nation in 1920. Dmowski, on the other hand, did initially immerse himself into party politics. His National Democratic Party joined with a number of other groups to form the Popular National Union, but its supporters retained their former name of 'endeks', coined from the initials ND. The movement which propagated Dmowski's ideas and policies was known as the *endecja*.

In addition to the Piłsudski and Dmowski factions there were a number of leftist groups, the strongest of which was the Polish Socialist Party, the PSP, to which Piłsudski had once belonged. The communists were weak because they had rejected the idea of national independence and had argued for incorporation into the bolsheviks' brave new, but Russian, world. There were also the agrarian parties. Witos' Piast group remained the largest of these. Its hostility towards the Ukrainian peasants meant that it was closer to Dmowski's polonocentric attitudes than to Piłsudski's latitudinarian concepts, and this alignment was strengthened by the fact that Piast represented the middle peasants rather than the landless agricultural labourers or the dwarf-holders, and therefore it was suspicious, as were the endeks, of extreme agrarian reformers. The more radical agrarians, with the encouragement of Piłsudski, broke away to form Wyzwolenie (liberation). There was also a third peasant group, the National Peasant Party. Christian Democracy was also present, especially in Silesia where it was ably led by Korfanty, and the ethnic minorities had their own nationalist organisations and frequently also had separate socialist and agrarian parties as well.

At the end of the Russo-Polish war the endeks believed that they had the upper hand, not least because they were convinced that Piłsudski's former links with imperial Germany had made him unacceptable in the eyes of the allies. The endeks were also the largest group within the constituent assembly elected in February 1920 before the incorporation of the eastern lands with their non-Polish majorities. The constitution was enacted on 17 March 1921, the day before the treaty of Riga, and was a monument to anti-Piłsudskiism. On the assumption that only the marshal could be president, presidential powers were cut to a minimum, and the president, though the highest army officer, was not allowed to become commander in chief in wartime. The strongest organ in the new body politic was the sejm or lower house of parliament, elected by universal suffrage and proportional representation; the sejm, sitting with the senate, was to elect the president. The cabinet and all individual cabinet members were to be directly responsible to the sejm. The multiplicity of parties meant that in order to form ministries they had to combine in clubs or blocs which would then barter over posts to form a cabinet: government was therefore by coalitions of coalitions.

The first elections under the new constitution were not held until 1922. No group dominated the new assembly and immediately the shortcomings of the system became apparent. A cabinet could be formed from a centre-right alliance, from a centre-left combination, or from an all party coalition. The latter was acceptable only in the case of dire national emergency such as that of 1920, but a centre-right government was impossible because Piast and the endeks had not yet agreed upon land reform, from which the endeks wished to shelter the Roman Catholic church. The formation of a centre-left grouping faced two major obstacles. The first was the rivalry between Piast and the more radical agrarians of Wyzwolenie; the second was the fact that a centre-left combination could be kept in office only if it had the votes of the ethnic minorities in the sejm, a position which Witos would not relish. Finally, a non-party cabinet of pacification under the distinguished soldier, Władisław Sikorski, was formed on 16 December 1922, but its formation had been precipitated by an ominous development.

The new assembly's first task had been to elect a president. Piłsudski refused to touch the job and only on the fifth ballot did a winner emerge in Gabriel Narutowicz, a friend of Piłsudski and a nominee of Wyzwolenie, but a man who had been absent from Poland for many years. The right were enraged. They had done reasonably well at the election and they now felt that an opponent had been foisted upon them by the votes of the non-Polish deputies. On 16 December Poland's first elected president attended an art exhibition, refusing pressing advice to take a body-guard with him. He was assassinated by a right-wing fanatic whose grave, after his execution, became a place of pilgrimage for extreme right-wing supporters. Stanisław Wojciechowski, a Piast nominee, stepped into Narutowicz's place.

Sikorski's government remained in office until May 1923 when it was replaced by a centre-right coalition under Witos. Piast had by then settled its differences with the endeks in the Lanckorona pact, so called from the house at which it was concluded, but the coalition was to have little time to savour power. Ever since the end of the war a variety of factors had caused inflation in Poland. The state had no gold reserves; trade had been totally dislocated; state budgets could not be balanced because successive governments were faced with the vast and varied costs of repairing war damage, of promoting a new economic infrastructure, of paying a 'liberation tax' to the allies, of discharging indemnities on Austrian and German properties and on public debts, of meeting the expenses of the frontier delimitations and the plebiscites, and of purchasing arms for use in the war of 1919–21; and all this without foreign loans or reparations. And then in 1923 the Polish mark was pulled down by its German namesake and plummeted from 53,375 to the dollar in May to over six million in December. The Witos-endek coalition did not care to adopt policies which would harm either the peasants or the industrialists so what deflation there was came at the expense of the urban workforce. The inevitable labour unrest culminated in a general strike when the government ordered the army to take over from striking railwaymen; clashes in Cracow in November resulted in the death of fourteen workers and the resignation of the government in December.

Władisław Grabski, who formed the next cabinet, had no party affiliations and had already showed acumen in tackling inflation when he was a member of Sikorski's government. The sejm gave him extraordinary powers to continue his good work, the next manifestation of which was the introduction of a new national bank, the Bank Polski, and in April 1925 of a new currency, the złoty, fixed at par with the Swiss franc. He also introduced a land reform act, which set maximum holdings at 180 hectares (300 hectares in the east), and in February 1925 concluded a concordat under which a number of issues outstanding between the state and the Catholic church were settled: in essence the church submitted to land reform in return for a say in the appointment of those who were to teach religion in state schools.

Grabski's proved to be the longest-lasting of Poland's pre-1926 cabinets but by the second half of 1925 it too was in difficulties. The problem lay again in Germany. The Upper Silesia convention of 1922 had obliged the Germans to purchase six million tons of Silesian coal per annum until 1925 and this had been a lifeline for the Poles many of whose previous export markets had been cut off by new political boundaries. After the expiry of the 1922 obligation the Germans refused to buy any Polish goods at all until the Poles had granted concessions to their German minority. This boycott was devastating since it directly affected over a quarter of Poland's exports; unemployment rose sharply and only with difficulty did Grabski prevent a collapse of the złoty. Even so, the public was alarmed and the directors of the Bank Polski expressed their fears as to the future of the currency. Grabski resigned in November. His career told a depressing tale; his achievements had come about because he had been given extra-parliamentary powers, and his political demise was decided upon less by the sejm than by the Bank and public opinion. The 1921 constitution was patently ineffective.

The *coup d'état* of May 1926

Grabski's successor was a former Austro-Hungarian diplomat, Aleksander Skrzyński, also without party affiliation. Nevertheless, his short-lived administration could not override party political affiliations. His cabinet included a number of socialists who were not prepared to tolerate the severe deflationary policies he advocated, and who therefore left the government with the assertion that they would not endorse 'a rich man's budget'. Skrzyński resigned on 5 May 1926. Witos again agreed to form a government, despite warnings that to do so would enrage the left to a dangerous degree. In fact the key to Poland's future was not Witos or the sejm but Piłsudski who was then lowering in his estate at Sulejówek.

When Witos formed a coalition of Piast and endeks on 10 May, Piłsudski put into operation a well-prepared plan. Troops were moved towards Warsaw, Piłsudski expecting that in this hour of crisis his prestige would still all opposition. On the morning of the crucial day, 12 May, he left home after ordering lunch for 2.30 p.m.; he obviously anticipated no resistance. But resistance there was, and it was not until 15 May, and after the loss of some five hundred Polish lives, that his victory was assured. It was a victory which owed much to his old socialist allies in the railways who had prevented the movement of troops loyal to president Wojciechowski and the government.

Piłsudski's coup of May 1926 had many causes. Government had been hopelessly weak in the face of mounting social and economic difficulties, above all inflation, and this weakness was in no small measure the result of the political system which by 1925 could boast ninety-two registered political parties, thirty-two of them represented in the sejm, and eighteen separate clubs. The variegated composition of the cabinets and their dependence for survival on votes from various factions in the sejm inhibited forceful action: the socialists prevented wage control, the agrarians vetoed food-price regulation, the endeks shielded industry, and the Polish nationalist factions blocked radical land reform for fear it might harm the interests of Polish landlords in the eastern lands. The political system was further discredited by the public trafficking in office which became a characteristic of the sejm: clubs could be held together and coalitions maintained only by the offering of favours such as government contracts, licences to cut forests, or exemptions from land reforms, but all of this was conducted in the open. Polish political laundry was no dirtier than that of most other states, but the fact that it was washed in public brought the system into disrepute, particularly amongst the committed young nationalists of the intelligentsia who had expected more from their new national state. Piłsudski, whose personal honesty was above reproach – he donated his pension to the Stefan Batory university in Vilnius – recruited many supporters in this constituency, though many were soon to desert him.

By 1926 the national minorities were also disaffected. They had been promised local government concessions in September 1922 but little had been done: only the Silesians had their own assembly and autonomy, and that had been granted in 1920 when Warsaw was hard pressed by bolshevik troops and allied diplomats. The Ukrainians were particularly disaffected and in 1925 violence had broken out following the formation of the Ukrainian National Democratic Organisation. In Poznania, Pomerania, and Upper Silesia the Germans were angered by land reforms which they feared might destroy the power of local German landlords. Piłsudski, whose attitude towards the ethnic minorities in the east had always been considered generous, would not be opposed by them, whilst the Germans in the west had not forgotten his war-time allegiance.

The small working class had expected an improvement in their living conditions after the end of the Russian war but instead suffered continually from inflation and unemployment; by April 1926, when the złoty had fallen to half its value of two years before, the unemployment rate was edging towards one third of the industrial labour force. Pilsudski's old allies on the left would not oppose him. The peasants were not natural or established allies of Piłsudski but, on the other hand, their expectations of land reform had not been fulfilled. A radical bill in 1920 had been forced through under the pressure of the bolshevik advance, on the assumption that if Poland's government would not give the peasants the land Lenin might. After the emergency, however, reform was delayed by the landlords and to a lesser extent by the Catholic church and though some redistribution was achieved it could not keep pace with a rising population. If the peasants were unlikely to support Piłsudski they had little cause to take up arms to help his opponents. The communists also welcomed the coup until Moscow told them that they were mistaken.

Foreign affairs also played their part in bringing about the coup. Since 1921 the basis of Polish foreign policy had been treaties with Romania and France and the maintenance of the Versailles system. Locarno in October 1925 had disturbed the Poles because, despite the guarantees which followed, it hinted that western commitment to Poland might be suspect. Even more alarming was the Soviet-German neutrality pact of April 1926. If Poland's two mighty neighbours were on good terms, could the country afford the weak and divisive system it had endured since 1922?

For Piłsudski himself the army was as important as any of the issues impelling him towards his decisive step. After resigning the presidency in 1922 he relinquished his post of chief of the general staff and during the 1923 Witos cabinet withdrew to his estate at Sulejówek. His opponents meanwhile wished to increase the authority of the minister of war and thus place the army firmly under civilian control, and a number of bitterly fought bills attempting to settle the relationship between the army and the civilian power were presented to the sejm between 1921 and 1926: the prospect that Witos might scrap one such bill, which gave Piłsudski much of what he wanted, was a factor of great importance in prompting the May coup.

The *sanacja*: the *Bartelowanie*, 1926–30

Upon taking power Piłsudski insisted that he did not wish to introduce a dictatorship. Poland, he said, could not be ruled 'with the whip'. Nor had he a political programme, or a party; his purpose, he maintained, was not to change Poland's political system but to cleanse it. The post May-1926 system came to be known, therefore, as the *sanacja*, the 'cleansing'. In addition to cleansing the system Piłsudski was also determined to keep his beloved army out of the politicians' hands, to stabilise the economy, to limit social injustice, to unite all Polish citizens in respect for their state, and to make Poland a major European power.

For the first four years of the *sanacja* the government was dominated by moderate elements of the intelligentsia led by Kazimierz Bartel, a self-educated professor of mathematics. Bartel served as prime minister for the majority of the period 1926–30, which therefore bears his name, the *Bartelowanie*.

The *Bartelowanie* achieved considerable success. The economy staged a remarkable recovery symbolised by the Poznań national exhibition which opened in May 1929 and closed at the end of September, a few weeks before the Wall Street crash. The British miners' strike in 1926 had allowed Polish exporters into the Scandinavian markets and in the following year a stabilisation loan of

$62,000,000 had steadied the złoty enough to put it on the gold standard. Inflation was also contained by ending the index linking of official salaries, and the balancing of the government's books was helped by separating railway expenditure from the general budget; railway costs were enormous not least because the German trade embargo of 1925 and the growth in coal exports to Scandinavia had necessitated the building of a line from Silesia to the new port under construction at Gdynia. Increases in industrial production between 1926 and 1928 reduced unemployment by two-thirds. In the countryside the *Bartelowanie* managed to partition more land per year than the 1925 act obliged them to, and agriculture was further aided by the encouragement of commassation, especially in the east, and by the extension of rural credit facilities.

A streamlining of the administration was brought about by the use of commissions of apolitical experts whilst at the centre the power of the prime minister was augmented; Bartel required each incoming cabinet minister to provide him with an undated but signed letter of resignation. Central authority was increased over that of local government, a factor which helped to eliminate the excesses of regionalism which had been apparent, especially in the west, since 1921.

The minorities benefited from the curbing of the local officials and this helped to bring about an improvement in relations between the minorities and the state. So too did the government's announcement that it would guarantee equal treatment and would no longer pursue the policy of assimilation adopted by the pre-1926 administrations. There were also modifications to the school law which eased pressure on the minorities, and the Jews welcomed a series of measures which included positive steps to encourage the revival of Jewish trade. Where the government did not succeed, however, was in satisfying Ukrainian demands for a university of their own in Lwów and in trying to persuade universities to abolish the *numerus clausus* for Jews.[2]

Piłsudski was never on close terms with the Catholic hierarchy, which disapproved of some aspects of his private life. Yet for the sake of national unity Piłsudski secured good relations with the church by recognising its domination of religious education and also by giving concessions on clerical immunity and on the church's property rights.

Piłsudski was entirely successful in shielding the army from political interference. The marshal himself became inspector general of the army and minister of war, a post which he retained until his death. He also removed a number of politically dubious officers from senior commands and others were bypassed for promotion. Those who enjoyed Piłsudski's favour were mostly former comrades in his wartime legion; the graduates of the Austro-Hungarian, German, or Russian staff colleges were discriminated against, with the result that the Polish army was left under the control of largely unschooled men whose knowledge and appreciation of recent military thinking was slight. Piłsudski and his 'colonels' could envisage military action only in the form and in the places they had experienced it, primarily in the eastern marches between 1919 and 1921. Thus the Polish cavalry was not mechanised, the air force was neglected – Piłsudski believed that it could be used only for reconnaissance – and there was almost no provision of anti-aircraft guns. A high price was to be paid for this in 1939.

Piłsudski achieved little success in his search for domestic political unity and for a satisfactory relationship with the sejm. When the assembly reopened in the autumn of 1926 Piłsudski made himself ridiculous by demanding that as a mark of respect the deputies should stand during his opening address – they refused and the opening was delayed until it was agreed to stage it in a hall from which the chairs had been removed. The incident was symptomatic of Piłsudski's contemptuous attitude towards the sejm, which he once described as 'a sterile, jabbering thing that engendered such boredom as made the very flies die of sheer disgust'.[3] More serious than the squabble about the chairs was Piłsudski's refusal to accept the presidency when it was offered to him. This was a major error of judgement. It needlessly offended the sejm and the senate, and it belied his repeated assertions that he wished to impart dignity and purpose to the nation's institutions. The new president was Ignacy Mościcki, a dependable Piłsudskiite.

Not surprisingly, opposition to the *sanacja* crystallised around Dmowski, who brought certain right-wing factions together in December 1926 to form the Camp for a Great Poland, CGP, which struck a particularly resonant chord amongst Polish university students. Whilst Piłsudski could not win over the raucous right of Dmowski he established much better relations with the old right, as represented by the large landowners of the east who were offended by the vulgarity and populism of the CGP. Piast, on the other hand, refused to be reconciled to the May 1926 régime and called for a restoration of democracy, albeit with an amended constitution. The other centre parties were generally more favourably disposed and only Korfanty's Silesian Christian Democrats joined Witos in dogged opposition to the new rulers. On the left the PSP and Wyzwolenie preferred Piłsudski to Dmowski, as did the ethnic minority groups.

During 1927 these political divisions were muted, as Piłsudski and his colleagues successfully tackled the country's economic difficulties. By March 1928, however, the government was ready for a general election, which was a virtual referendum on the May coup. During the campaign there emerged the NPBSG, the Non-Party Block for the Support of the Government. Its origins were in the kresy but it helped to coordinate the government's campaign throughout the country. It included members from almost all segments of Polish life and most of the parties which were not inveterate foes of the *sanacja*, the diversity of its following being a reflection of the widespread disillusion with the pre-1926 system. The NPBSG's efforts, together with some government influence and encouragement, produced a sizeable but not an overwhelming vote in support of the *sanacja* parties, which received 25.7 per cent of the votes cast compared to 8.8 per cent for the right, 10.2 per cent for the centre, 26.8 per cent for the non-communist left, a surprisingly high 6.9 per cent for the communists, 18.1 per cent for the ethnic minority parties, and 3.5 per cent for ethnic minority socialists and radicals. All the indications were that the pro-government vote was to a large extent genuine and that, given that the non-revolutionary left included Piłsudski's allies in the PSP and Wyzwolenie, the election was a popular endorsement of the new régime.

The *sanacja*: the crisis of 1930

The period between the election of 1928 and that of 1930 saw fundamental change in the nature of the *sanacja*, and interwoven with its political decline were a drastic turn of the economic tide and rising militancy amongst the Ukrainians.

Piłsudski's relations with the sejm again began badly. His speech at the opening of the 1928 session was interrupted by rowdies, most of them communists, and then the assembly elected as its marshal, or speaker, the veteran socialist leader, Daszyński, rather than Bartel who was Piłsudski's nominee. There followed disagreements over taxation and the abrogation of a press law but the major clash was on the issue of constitutional change. After the coup most groups were ready for substantial constitutional revision but little had been enacted beyond some increase in the powers of the president and the prime minister. In 1928 there was talk of more radical change, but the NPBSG could not be sure of its support in the assembly and towards the end of the year fear of a *dirigiste* solution brought the three main peasant parties closer to each other than at any time since 1921.

In February 1929 a Wyzwolenie deputy demanded the impeachment of the finance minister, Gabriel Czechowicz, for failing to submit supplementary budgets to the sejm for ratification. In fact it had been Piłsudski who had forbidden the presentation of such accounts because they showed that eight million złoties had been funnelled into the NPBSG electoral coffers. Czechowicz resigned but only after Piłsudski had lashed the sejm with more barrack-room language, at one point referring to the deputies as those who 'cover themselves with their own excrement'. In June 1929 Czechowicz was tried and found guilty on technical charges. The affair had caused the resignation of Bartel in April. His successor was Kazimierz Świtalski whose fourteen-man cabinet included six soldiers, a foreshadowing of the reign of 'the colonels' which was to come after 1930.

Throughout the summer of 1929 the government worked hard and with conspicuous success at making enemies. The socialists, already fidgeting at rumours of constitutional change, were angered when they were deprived of control of the funds through which the state medical scheme was administered, and in September the six main parties of the centre and the left – the three peasant parties, the PSP, the Christian Democrats, and the National Workers' Party – issued a joint refusal to a government invitation to discuss common problems. The basis for the centre-left, or centrolew, alliance had been laid. The consummation of the alliance was prompted later in the year by heavy-handed government attempts to intimidate the sejm, attempts which Daszyński repelled, though he could not prevent the prorogation of the assembly until the new year. By the time it was open for business again Piłsudski's hopes of securing agreement for an increase in the powers of the executive had vanished. The marshal decided that the time for firmer action had arrived.

He was not the only one to make such a decision. Early in 1930 a Vienna congress of Ukrainian nationalists had established the Ukrainian Military Organisation (OUN) under the leadership of Ievhen Konovalets. The OUN's tactics were to use sabotage and terrorism to provoke the government into reprisals so fierce that they would compromise the more moderate Ukrainian groups which were prepared to negotiate with Warsaw. The sabotage campaign was at its height during the second half of 1930.

In June the government had been forced into its first major cut in the budget. The world economic crisis was also making itself felt in other ways. Unemployment was rising and was to reach 25 per cent of the industrial workforce by 1931; national income had entered upon the steady decline that saw it drop by a quarter between 1929 and 1933, years which also saw a fall of 22 per cent in the real income of industrial workers and a steep reduction in agricultural prices which left peasants unable to pay taxes or the interest on their loans.

This was the background to the profound political crisis which afflicted Poland in the summer of 1930. Yet another change of prime minister did nothing to appease the centrolew which formed a new organisation, 'For the Defence of the Law and of the People's Freedom'. Agitation continued, with the PSP organising a series of meetings culminating on 29 June in a huge gathering in Cracow attended by supporters of all centrolew factions. The meetings attacked the government's failure to stop the economic rot and demanded an extraordinary session of the sejm and an end to the Piłsudskiite 'dictatorship'. In response to this and to the mounting Ukrainian campaign Piłsudski himself became prime minister in August. He accepted the demand for an extraordinary session of the sejm but as soon as it met it was suspended. On the night of 9/10 September eleven centrolew leaders were arrested, and by the middle of the following month several thousand opponents of the government, including sixty-four sejm deputies, were in prison, many of them in the military fortress of Brześć (Brest Litovsk).

Shortly after the September arrests the sejm had been dissolved and elections called for November. The centrolew, deprived of its leaders and facing considerable government 'intervention' in the campaign, polled 22.1 per cent against a government vote of 47.4 per cent; the right secured 12.7 per cent, the ethnic minorities 14.5 per cent, the communists only 2.1 per cent, and 1.2 per cent were spoilt or given for other groups. Once again, however, there were many who voted for the *sanacja* not because of government influence or because of bribes but because they saw it as the best government for Poland.

Many who thought this in November ceased to do so in the following month. During December a number of the Brześć detainees, many of them heroes of the national liberation struggle, were released. Their descriptions of the treatment to which they had been subjected appalled a large number of Poles, including many moderate Piłsudskiites. All of the arrested leaders had been savagely beaten, some had had to face mock executions, and others, including Witos, had been forced to clean latrines with their bare hands; now they had covered themselves with their own excrement. The Brześć prisoners were tried in October 1931 and found guilty. Most appealed, only to have their sentences increased. Rather than face a return to prison they went into exile.

The *sanacja:* the rule of the colonels, 1930–5

Within Poland the Brześć affair wrecked any hopes Piłsudski had of welding his subjects into a united nation which would stand equal with the great powers of Europe. The treatment of the prisoners, who had committed no crime, disgusted and repelled both the intelligentsia and the old right whilst it frightened the minorities and the socialists lest they be in line for similar treatment, not least because in 1931 the 'pacification' of the Ukraine began. Even the moderate members of the *sanacja* leadership were alienated, Bartel himself complaining to President Mościcki that Brześć had 'isolated Piłsudski from all the better elements of the country'.[4] All that remained of the *sanacja* leadership was the praetorian guard, Piłsudski's cronies of the POW: the 'colonels' and their hangers-on. The colonels themselves took cabinet posts and leading positions in industry whilst the lesser officers, who seldom had the quality and dedication of those who had fought with Piłsudski, found posts in local government and the crucial middle ranks of the bureaucracy: as Piłsudski himself put it, 'The lice crawled all over me.'[5]

The events of 1930 had destroyed the centrolew as an effective political force and in 1931 the three peasant parties at last came together to form a united Peasant Party, the PP. The role of Piast in the formation of the PP was vital. Before 1930 Witos had refused to join with Wyzwolenie because its more radical agrarian policies would benefit the Orthodox Ukrainians in eastern Galicia and endanger Catholic Polish political supremacy in the region. Yet in 1930 his fellow Catholics in the *endecja* had proved powerless; also he had shared a prison cell with a Ukrainian and had come to see that sectional peasant interests could override ethnic and religious differences and that solidarity with the other peasant groups would be at least as effective as cooperation with the Catholic endeks. Whilst the peasant parties moved closer together the PSP distanced itself from the *sanacja*, though it refused communist overtures to join a popular front.

The government, seeing the weakening of the 1926 alliance, took steps to increase its own powers. Because of its growing strength the CGP was dissolved, only to be succeeded by an even more right-wing body, the National Radical Camp, though this openly fascist organisation never had a large membership and soon conformed to the general practice of Polish politics by splitting into a number of separate groups. Other measures taken by the government to bolster its authority included a bill of November 1931 which provided for the conscription of railway workers in times of war or national emergency; in May 1932 the government increased its power to enact decrees, placed restrictions on the right of assembly, and reduced the autonomy of the universities, albeit after anti-semitic excesses in these seats of learning. The administration also made consistent and not entirely unsuccessful efforts to win trade unionists away from the socialist or Christian trade unions into those run by the *sanacja*.

Piłsudski himself took little interest in domestic affairs outside the army, but he did partake in the running of Polish foreign policy, appointing his close associate, colonel Józef Beck, foreign minister in November 1932. The prevailing ideology in the Polish foreign ministry was Piłsudski's 'doctrine of the two enemies' which required good relations but not alliances with Germany and Russia. The doctrine did not, however, exclude non-aggression pacts; in 1932 Beck concluded such an agreement with Stalin. Much more controversial was a similar pact with Nazi Germany in January 1934. It has been asserted that soon after Hitler came to power Piłsudski approached the French with a suggestion that the two states should remove the new German chancellor. It is unlikely that this was a serious suggestion. Piłsudski initially regarded the Nazis as windbags and much less of a threat than the old Prussians, but he did already sense that French guarantees to Poland might not be honoured. In such circumstances Warsaw had little choice but to establish good relations with Berlin, and the approach to France was probably little more than an exercise to provide justification for a policy already decided upon. In the event the pact with Hitler provided short-term benefits. It enabled a number of disputes between the two states to be settled, it lessened for a while the likelihood of German pressure on Danzig and the Polish corridor, and it suspended covert German assistance to the Ukrainian malcontents. The disadvantages of the agreement were to become clear a little later.

Despite the apparent diplomatic accomplishments of the *sanacja* it could not retrieve the ground it had lost since 1930 in terms of popular support. One reason for its poor performance, and it was one which the government did not dare to admit in public, was that Piłsudski was grievously ill. The need to secure a political system which would keep the *sanacja* in power after its architect had departed brought about a new constitution which, although drafted in 1934, could not be pushed through the sejm until March 1935. The president, who was to be directly elected by universal suffrage every seven years, was now to be the dominant figure; indeed he was to be responsible not to the sejm but only 'to God and to History', a daunting prospect. The president was to nominate the supreme commander of the armed forces, who was to be responsible directly to him. The sejm was reduced in authority and in size and though universal suffrage was retained proportional representation was not. On 12 May 1935, within a few weeks of the enactment of the new constitution and on the anniversary of the 1926 coup, Piłsudski died.

The *sanacja*: from Piłsudski's death to the second world war, 1935–9

From 1935 until the cataclysm of 1939 the *sanacja* remained weak. In September 1935, in the first election held under the new constitution, the principal opposition parties had called for a boycott of the polls and only 46.5 per cent of the electorate had turned out to vote. In the final pre-war election, in November 1938, the government, despite a repeat of the opposition call for a boycott, managed to increase participation to 67.3 per cent, mainly because of an upturn in the economy brought about by the state's promotion of industrial development in the 'central industrial zone', centred in the triangle formed by the confluence of the Vistula and the San.

Despite these successes the weaknesses of the régime were profound. There were fundamental differences of policy and personality within the *sanacja*. Piłsudski had officially nominated Walery Sławek as his political heir, but Mościcki emerged from his self-effacement to demand a return to a more open system and a diminution of the colonels' power. This was not to the taste of marshal Śmigły-Rydz who, as Piłsudski had wished, succeeded him as inspector general of the army. In October 1935 a compromise candidate for prime minister was found in Marian Zyndram-Kościałkowski who angered the colonels by attempting to placate the left, a not unwise move after serious rioting in the spring of 1936 in Częstochowa and in Lwów where eight deaths were reported. Kościałkowski resigned in May to be replaced by general Felicjan Sławoj-Składkowski who was seen as a temporary appointee but who remained in office until September 1939. His major contribution to the politics of Poland was to inform ministers and provincial governors that the inspector general of the army was 'the first citizen of the country after the president' and should be respected and obeyed by all. Śmigły-Rydz had disposed of Mościcki; the army had prevailed over the civilian sector.

Simultaneously with Sławoj-Składkowski's becoming premier a new opposition group was formed at Morges in Switzerland. General Haller, the leader of the Polish army on the western front in 1918, Ignacy Paderewsky, and Witos were seeking a middle way between the obstinacy of the *sanacja* and the extremism of the *endecja* and they called for a centre-right coalition which would swing Poland around to a pro-French foreign policy and restore democracy at home.

The government's reply was to form a new group of its own, the Camp of National Unity, OZON. This last ditch effort to mobilise support offered, according to one Warsaw newspaper, '40 per cent nationalism, 30 per cent social radicalism, 20 per cent agrarianism, 10 per cent anti-semitism'.[6] OZON failed to attract any group which had been outside the *sanacja* and, in expropriating the Dmowskiite ideas which Piłsudski had deplored and in attempting to be all things to all men, it was more reviled than respected.

The government was particularly unsuccessful in its efforts to win Polish youth to its side. In this sector of society fascist and extreme right-wing sentiments were common. Italy, similar in population to Poland, was a Catholic nation which had suffered crippling internal political divisions but which had, it seemed, been rescued and made into a great power by fascism; there were many Poles who wished to follow this example. The young intelligentsia had poor employment prospects which made competition from the vibrant Jewish intelligentsia all the more difficult to bear. At the same time, left extremism had little to recommend it. It was inevitably associated with Poland's Russian enemy, whose anti-religious and anti-peasant policies were anathema to most Poles, even without the gathering cloud of the stalinist terror. Yet despite its attractions fascism never completely dominated the main right-wing group in Poland, the *endecja*. Despite Dmowski's rapid move to the right, his fulminations against what he called 'judaic-masonic liberalism', and his appeals for a national revolution on Italian lines, this group was too steeped in francophilia, cultural and political, and too loyal to the Roman Catholic church to be properly fascist, though it remained unutterably opposed to the *sanacja*.

Social unrest accumulated throughout the 1930s. The large agricultural sector had suffered badly from the decline in world prices for primary goods, and it was not until 1933 that the government had made any moves to alleviate the increasing problem of peasant indebtedness. By the end of the 1930s visitors to the villages spoke of the peasants being without sugar and having no more than one set of clothes, the others having been cut up to dress the children. Peasant reaction, encouraged by the PP, included a number of strikes in Galicia in 1932 and 1933, and for a week in September 1932 peasants refused to sell their produce in Warsaw. In the summer of 1936 there were violent clashes between striking peasants and blacklegs in Zamość and Volhynia. In the following year another peasant strike, prompted by Witos and his Morges associates, produced 'probably the most serious outbreak of social unrest in Poland in the whole of the inter-war period'.[7] In the towns meanwhile the socialists garnered support as unemployment stayed high and wages low, and, following the disturbances in Lwów and Częstochowa, the PSP secured a notable success in the Łódź municipal elections of September 1936.

The minority races seldom supported the *sanacja*. All were disturbed by local government reforms in 1933, which made Polish the official language in all local government bodies, and by the abrogation of the national minority protection treaties in September 1934. The pacification of the Ukraine left a legacy of bitterness which was intensified by the suffering of the Ukrainian peasants during the depression, and which also hit very hard at the Jews who played such a large part in trading, small-manufacturing, and money-lending. There was some improvement for the Ukrainians in 1935 when a number of their leaders were released from the detention camp at Bereza Kartuska but by 1939 relations between Poles and Ukrainians were as bad as ever.

The position of the Jews was worse. The virulent anti-semitism of sections of Polish youth, especially in the intelligentsia, took great encouragement from the Nazis who were persecuting with impunity one of Europe's richest and most assimilated Jewish communities. The authorities continued to pander to such prejudice; on the eve of the second world war some officials believed that the only solution to the Jewish problem was massive emigration; Dmowski and his allies insisted that the Jews should be expelled. And yet, despite these pressures no one contemplated what was eventually to happen and meanwhile Jewish cultural life flourished in Poland as never before.

The Germans, on the other hand, enjoyed increasing security and self-confidence. After the pact of 1934 and Hitler's international successes from the Rhineland onwards, the Warsaw government trod carefully when dealing with the German minority among whom Nazism soon established enormous influence, though no separate Hitlerite party emerged.

By the late 1930s foreign policy in general and relations with Berlin in particular had become the most vital issue in political life. Beck, who retained control of this area after Piłsudski's death, kept the 1934 pact with Germany in good repair, believing that Hitler, an Austrian, was interested above all in expansion southwards into Austria, the Czech lands, and the Balkans. This could suit Poland well. Nazi preoccupation with Austria, Bohemia, and Moravia would make much less likely embarrassing disputes over Danzig, Silesia, and the Polish corridor; and in the long run Germany might welcome Polish help in her struggle with Russia with whom Hitler could never be reconciled. In the meantime the disappearance of Czechoslovakia would allow Poland to take Teschen, and to bind the emergent independent Slovakia into the 'third Europe', which, under Polish and Hungarian domination, would defend central and eastern Europe from domination by either Germany or the Soviet Union.

Given the reluctance of the western powers to act against Hitler, Beck had few real alternatives to this policy. And initially it worked. Poland was exempted from pressure on Danzig, German links with the Ukrainian dissidents were severed, Beck was able to force Lithuania to establish diplomatic relations with Poland in 1938, and Munich provided the opportunity to take possession of Teschen in much the same fashion as the Czechs had originally seized it in 1920.

But Beck had made a number of crucial miscalculations. The 'third Europe' was not a viable prospect; Hitler was not prepared to allow Slovakia to be independent as well as separate; the Führer was ready to use Stalin against Poland and not vice versa, and his gaze was not fixed solely upon the south. This became increasingly clear after Munich. Pressure on Danzig and the corridor, the strip of Polish territory separating east Prussia from the rest of the Reich, began immediately, and Berlin called upon Poland to join the anti-comintern pact. After the occupation of Prague in March 1939 Germany seized Memel, an obvious precedent for Danzig, and at the same time increasing numbers of Germans fled from Poland with cries of persecution, cries which were grist to Goebbels' propaganda mill.

Beck maintained that the British guarantee of March and April 1939 would save Poland because he believed that Hitler, despite all the bluster, would not fight for the corridor. There were, however, disturbing debates on the fact that Britain had guaranteed Polish independence but not her territorial integrity, a distinction that was to become critical in 1944. In the meantime the international emergency of 1939 brought some moves towards domestic consolidation and reconciliation. In March an internal loan to provide the army with much needed anti-aircraft guns was doubly over subscribed and early in 1939 it was announced that the Brześć exiles were free to return. Yet even now the *sanacja* would not open its doors to its former opponents and Śmigły-Rydz refused to include Witos and the other exiles in a national coalition government.

When the Nazi war machine was unleashed on Poland on 1 September 1939 the Poles had 313 tanks to face the Germans' 3,200; they had a tiny air force totally unsuited to modern warfare; they had few anti-aircraft guns, and they had a régime 'jealously guarding its political monopoly'.[8] On 17 September the unexpected, unprovoked, and undeclared Soviet invasion of eastern Poland hastened the collapse of the Polish forces; in the argument as to which power, Germany or Russia, presented the greater danger to Poland, it seemed that both Piłsudski and Dmowski had been right. The government fled to Romania, hoping in vain to be allowed passage to France. The *sanacja* was destroyed beyond all recall and the government in exile formed under Sikorski was a combination of the Morges front and the PSP.

Despite all of the weaknesses of the Polish state and the defects of its government the Polish nation fought its invaders with adamantine ferocity. Polish forces accounted for eight months of German war production and inflicted more casualties than did the French in 1940; of all of the losses suffered by the Wehrmacht between September 1939 and June 1941, half were incurred in Poland. Nor did the fighting cease with the defeat of the army.

4

CZECHOSLOVAKIA, 1918–38

The composition of Czechoslovakia

The new state of Czechoslovakia consisted of four main territories. In the west were the former Austrian provinces of Bohemia, Moravia, and parts of southern Silesia; to the east were Slovakia and Ruthenia, both formerly part of the Hungarian kingdom but different in social and ethnic composition; and, following the bitter dispute with Poland, Czechoslovakia was awarded the area around Teschen.

The new leaders in Prague moved rapidly towards building a political system. They convened a national assembly whose Czech members reflected the distribution of votes in the 1911 Reichsrat elections and whose Slovak representatives were nominated by the most prominent Slovak leader then in Prague, Vavro Šrobár; the Germans in the new state refused an invitation to attend. By the middle of November the national assembly had declared itself a constituent assembly, Masaryk had been elected president with Kramář as prime minister, and a provisional constitution had been published.

The rapidity and smoothness with which the Czechs could move at this early stage owed much to their own political experience and sophistication at home and to their diplomatic skill with the allies abroad. The core of the new state was the association of Czech and Slovak in a single Czechoslovak nation. Despite unequal levels of political development and differing attitudes to the Catholic church the first world war had driven Slovak political activists towards closer cooperation with the Czechs, especially after the collapse of tsarism had left both Czechs and Slovaks without any potential patron in central Europe. On 24 May 1918 Hlinka told a secret meeting of the Slovak National Party in Turčanský Svätý Martin that 'The thousand years of marriage to the Magyars has failed. We must part.'[1] A few days later the Pittsburgh declaration showed that Slovak émigrés agreed.

Union with the Czechs posed serious problems for the Slovaks. They had no administrative experience or cadre; their agriculture was primitive and the countryside bedevilled with problems of share-cropping, emigration, and alcoholism; Slovak industry was not as advanced as that of the Czech lands and had depended greatly upon help from the Hungarian government; and above all Slovakia had suffered from the magyarisation policies followed by the Budapest government. By 1914 there was one school for every 26.25 Magyar-speaking pupils but for Slovak-speakers only one for every 701.42 pupils and most of these Slovak schools were Protestant. By 1918 so complete was the Magyar domination of the Slovak counties that of the 12,447 civil servants working in them only thirty-five volunteered to remain behind and work for the new state, as did only one of the 464 judges. The gaps had to be filled by Czechs.

Before that could happen Slovakia had to be safeguarded against a new form of Hungarian expansionism. In November 1918 Hungarian troops had moved into Slovakia to prevent its occupation by the small units of legionnaires – the force originally recruited from prisoners of war in Russia – and sokols sent from Prague, but Budapest's initiative was frustrated by allied intervention and in January 1919 Hungarian troops had evacuated Slovakia. In the spring of 1919 a more serious incursion took place. The Soviet régime of Béla Kun, anxious to link its territory to that occupied by the Red Army, moved Hungarian troops into both Slovakia and Ruthenia. Kun also hoped to take advantage of the Magyar minority which accounted for about a sixth of Slovakia's total population and for a higher percentage of its working class and urban poor. On 16 June a Slovak Soviet Republic was proclaimed in Prešov. It immediately began the expropriatory and confiscatory policies of the Hungarian Soviet régime as well as introducing the intensely unpopular military draft, and the equally unwelcome prohibition. The Slovak Soviet lasted little more than a fortnight. The Hungarians' supply lines were hopelessly extended and Kun therefore agreed to evacuate Slovakia and Ruthenia in return for Clemenceau's promise, dishonoured in the event, to secure a Romanian withdrawal from Hungary.

The Hungarian incursions strengthened Czech claims in Paris that Czechoslovakia was the sole reliable bastion of the new order in central Europe. They also helped to paper over the cracks which had already begun to appear between Czech and Slovak. Partially to resist the domination of Prague, Hlinka formed the Slovak People's Party which consisted mainly of Slovak Catholics, many of them priests who had already associated together to defend the interests of those Slovak Catholics whose bishops or archbishop remained outside the new state. Although in later years this was to become the strongest opposition party in Slovakia many peasants were initially attracted to the new régime because of its promise to grant land reform and because of its opposition to the Hungarian armies in 1919. Furthermore, Hlinka overstepped the bounds of prudence. In September 1919 he slipped into Poland whence he made his way to Paris to plead that Slovakia be given 'a controlled international status within the new state'.[2] The French turned him out and the Czechs locked him up until the general election of April 1920. In the short term the escapade scuppered any chance that the constitution then being defined would allow Slovakia devolution, but Hlinka had now been imprisoned by both the Hungarians and the Czechs;

this was to help to make his standing amongst the Slovak decentralists all but unassailable.

If the Slovaks needed the Czechs the converse was also true. One in three of the population of the Czech lands was German. The Czechs could not be confident of defending the new state against a German minority which constituted approximately a third of the population; association with the Slovaks would decrease the minority to just under a quarter and thus make it much more manageable.

Ruthenia was even more backward than Slovakia. When Hungarian troops left in May 1919 the education system in the area amounted to nothing more than twenty-two primary schools; there were only twenty-one Ruthene-speaking public servants and over half the population was illiterate. The dominant influence was the Uniate clergy who provided spiritual guidance, if little else, for over 90 per cent of the population. Yet the allies could not allow that Ruthenia should be given to the Ukraine or to Russia, since this would be vehemently opposed by the Poles, not least on the grounds that it would constitute a gratuitous extension to bolshevism. The same reasoning ruled out its return to Hungary which was in any case a defeated power, whilst to hand the area to Poland might make the latter over-mighty. To include it in Czechoslovakia, however, would not disturb the territorial balance. For their part the Czech negotiators in Paris made it known that were they to assume responsibility for Ruthenia it would be only as trustees for a liberal Russia. In all of this the Ruthenians had little say or interest. The majority of politically conscious Ruthenians were in exile, and in November 1918 at a meeting in Scranton, Pennsylvania, they had already voted that their homeland should become a province of Czechoslovakia. In May 1919 the tiny resident intelligentsia of Ruthenia agreed. Alone of the constituent elements of the new republic the backward Ruthenians were guaranteed autonomy under the Czechoslovak constitution.

If the backward Ruthenes were incorporated without difficulty the opposite was true of the Germans of the Czech lands. The German settlements of Bohemia, Moravia, and Silesia, known to history as the Sudeten Germans, did not form a compact whole but were spread along the northern and western borders of the new state. In the days of the Habsburg empire the Sudeten Germans had achieved much. A disproportionately large number of the empire's school and university teachers had been Sudeten Germans, many of them keen Pan-Germans. They had also formed the core of the imperial army's crack régiments, had suffered disproportionately high casualties during the recent war, and in relative terms had contributed to Austrian war loans with greater enthusiasm than any other part of the empire. Inevitably they regarded the intrigues of Czech politicians and the unreliability of the imperial army's Czech soldiers as treachery. Much in the fashion of the Ulster Protestant landowners the Sudeten Germans saw themselves as stalwart defenders of the dominant culture of the old state at its periphery.

The Sudeten Germans were 'the most powerful German minority in the central and eastern European states'[3] and they did not tarry in making known their feelings towards the new Czechoslovak state. On 29 October 1918 German deputies in the Austrian Reichsrat who represented Bohemian and Moravian constituencies met in Vienna and declared an independent republic of German Bohemia with its capital in Reichenberg (Liberec). They were doomed. To the allies, Germans everywhere were suspect both as former enemies and as present revolutionaries, in addition to which there was the argument that the inclusion of the Sudeten Germans in Czechoslovakia was essential for strategic reasons; without the areas along its mountain frontiers Czechoslovakia would be unable to defend itself. Czechoslovak troops occupied the Sudeten areas in December 1918 and an uneasy peace was maintained until 4 March 1919 when fifty-two Germans were killed during demonstrations against the prohibition on Germans voting in Austrian parliamentary elections. In June the Germans showed their solidarity in local elections which saw 90 per cent of the German ethnic vote cast for nationalist German parties. In the general election held in April 1920 seventy-five German deputies were returned to the parliament in Prague; they attended merely to register their refusal to participate in the politics of the new state. 'Negativism', the refusal to accept the Czechoslovak state, had triumphed.

The western allies had welcomed Czechoslovak action against the Sudeten Germans but were less happy with Czechoslovak policy towards Teschen. This industrial and coal-mining area was inhabited by Germans, Poles, Czechs, and Jews, and through it ran the main railway linking Bohemia with Slovakia. The Czechs seized it during the Russo-Polish war, much to the fury of the Poles. A European commission then assumed responsibility for the area until the ambassadors of the powers decided in July 1920 that the city should be included in Poland and that the surrounding area with its coal mines and the vital railway should be incorporated into Czechoslovakia.

The Czechoslovak political system

By the time that the Teschen decision had finally settled Czechoslovakia's borders its internal political system had already been defined. The constitution, which was to last until the end of the first republic, had been adumbrated in Masaryk's Washington Declaration of October 1918, and the provisional constitution introduced on 13 November was little different from the final version enacted in February 1928. The head of state was to be a president elected every seven years by both houses of parliament, the chamber of deputies of three hundred members and the senate which was half that size. Both bodies were to be elected by proportional representation, with a universal, direct, secret, and compulsory ballot, though the voting age for the senate was higher than that for the chamber. Local government was to be based on twenty-three župy, or counties, though Czechoslovakia remained a strongly centralised state. This meant the break-up of the historic provinces of Bohemia and Moravia but the measure was intended to provide the Germans and other minority groups with units in which they would form the majority. The constitution guaranteed that a language would be accepted as official in any area where two-thirds of the population spoke it; four languages – Czechoslovak, German, Ruthene (Ukrainian), and Hungarian – were recognised as state languages though the first was to have special status. The constitution continued the Austrian system whereby separate schools had to be provided for any linguistic group which made up a fifth of the local population. Furthermore, minority language schools were to be provided where forty children wished to avail of them, all ethnic groups were to be allowed freedom to publish their own newspapers, and broadcasting was not to be confined to Czech and Slovak services. Nor did the constitution place any restriction upon political parties based upon ethnic affiliation, unless such parties broke the law, endangered public order, or threatened the safety of the state. The constitution in fact actively aided the representation of the minority groups as the complicated system of proportional representation provided for the redistribution of votes according to ethnic as well as party political preferences.

That each ethnic group had the freedom to form political associations inevitably encouraged the proliferation of parties. In the elections of April 1920 twenty-three of them took part, seventeen returning delegates to the chamber of deputies; in 1925 there were twenty-nine parties, sixteen of which secured seats in the parliament. The most important were: the Czechoslovak Social Democrats, formed by a merger of the Czech and Slovak parties in 1919; the Czechoslovak Agrarian Party, again the result of a merger, this time in 1922; the Communist Party of Czechoslovakia, formed in 1921; the National Democrats under Kramář; the Czechoslovak National Socialists, a small group which Beneš joined in 1922; the Czech People's Party, a largely Catholic group; and Hlinka's Slovak People's Party. Others included the Tradesmen's Party, the German Christian Socials, the German and the Hungarian Agrarians, the German National Socialists, and a number of small and extreme groups on the right.

Despite the large number of parties Czechoslovakia enjoyed political stability, although government was inevitably by coalition. From 1922 to 1926 there was a 'red-green' combination of socialists and agrarians, from 1926 to 1929 a 'black-green' coalition of agrarians and bourgeois/conservative groups, and from 1929 to 1938 a broad combination which included at times representatives of all three main groupings: green, red, and black. The relative stability of these coalitions was in part the result of the willingness of participating parties to placate each other with items of legislation. A further cause was that the parties enjoyed so much power that Czechoslovakia became 'a state of political parties'.[4] This power rested to some extent upon the fact that the political parties were the employers of deputies in the chamber, a condition which naturally strengthened party discipline. Also the electoral system meant that votes were cast not for individual candidates but for parties which then distributed seats amongst their own candidates, a process which bestowed enormous power upon the party machines because candidates were as anxious to please the party bosses as the electorate. Furthermore, there was a tendency for government departments to be awarded to the same party in successive coalitions, and thus the ministry of foreign affairs, for example, was usually in the hands of a Czech national socialist, the ministry of agriculture in those of an agrarian, and the ministry of transport in those of a social democrat. Continuous tenure in a ministry enabled a party to build up patronage and this operated at all levels throughout the ministry, thus ensuring that a party's power was exercised at provincial and local levels as well as at the centre.

The most important reason for political stability, however, was the emergence of the Hrad and the pětka, two unofficial, semi-constitutional mechanisms to cope with political difficulties. The Hrad derived its name from the presidential palace, the Hradčany, whilst pětka is the Czech word for five. These unofficial or semi-official institutions could exist because the cabinet, unlike that in Poland, did not have to conduct all its affairs in parliament and was therefore open to unobtrusive influence by the other sections of the political establishment, particularly the president and his associates. Prominent amongst the latter were Beneš and the agrarian leader, Antonín Švehla. This small group dominated the formulation of Czechoslovak foreign policy before September 1938, but it was a testament to Czech political sophistication that the power of the Hrad was exercised only when necessary and never to the immediate detriment of the functioning of the democratic system. Nevertheless, its shadowy existence ensured that it became a favourite bogey of the disaffected, particularly those on the extreme right.

The pětka, described both as 'a brain's trust under Masaryk's leadership'[5] and as 'the real government of the country',[6] emerged in September 1920. Tensions in that month made a coalition difficult and therefore a non-political administration was formed under Jan Černý, a bureaucrat. His cabinet 'resembled a ventriloquist's dummy: it had no political will or voice of its own'[7] and to provide these missing factors the leaders of the five major parties met regularly to give advice and at times direction to the prime minister. The five were Švehla, Alois Rašín from the national democrats, Rudolf Bechyne of the social democrats, Jiří Stříbrný for the national socialists, and the Czech populist leader Mgr Jan Šrámek. The pětka, which was based upon the admirable principle of 'We have agreed that we will agree', ensured that the non-party administration steered a moderate course acceptable to a majority of the chamber of deputies and thus prevented a cabinet crisis at a time of grave social unrest. These unofficial meetings of 1920 were so successful that thereafter it became common practice for leaders of the dominant parties, both within and sometimes outside a coalition, to meet unofficially to pre-arrange cabinet and government business. Whether this persisting tradition of unofficial and unpublicised guidance of the commonwealth served Czechoslovakia well in its moments of great crisis – 1938, 1948, 1968 – may be debated.

The founding father of the pětka was Švehla, whose importance in the Hrad, in the pětka, and at the head of what was to become the largest and most influential party in the land, made him almost the equal of Masaryk in shaping the history of the first years of the Czechoslovak republic.

The social and political crisis of 1918–21

The pětka had emerged from crisis. Many Slovaks were still suspicious of Prague, most Germans were openly hostile to it, and all ethnic groups were affected by the social problems afflicting all of Czechoslovakia. The return of hundreds of thousands of soldiers and ex-prisoners of war, the switch back to peacetime production, and the total disruption of economic exchange which followed the dissolution of the pre-war state system in central and eastern Europe placed enormous strains upon the housing stock, the labour market, and food reserves. In Czechoslovakia industrial real wages fell by 60 per cent and industrial unemployment reached 350,000 or 8 per cent of the labour force, then considered a high level. If the workers wanted work the peasants wanted land. A tenth of the land in Czechoslovakia in 1918 was held by some 150 families whilst one in two Czech farmers had no more than half a hectare, and in Slovakia two out of every three peasant families were landless. No government could afford to disregard this problem, not least because it was being tackled by other régimes, including Lenin's.

The provisional government established under Kramář in November 1918 took immediate action. The land control act of April 1919 limited arable holdings to a maximum of 150 hectares, with the excess being compulsorily purchased and redistributed to dwarf-holders and the landless agricultual labourers, with legionnaires receiving priority. The process of redistribution was slow and was incomplete in 1938 but, despite these shortcomings, the land control act dissipated tensions in the countryside and encouraged the evolution of a stable and contented peasantry; Masaryk called the land reform 'the greatest act of the new republic'.[8]

There was also reform in the industrial sector. The nostrification act of December 1918 required all companies and financial institutions operating in Czechoslovakia to register as Czechoslovak companies and to include Czechoslovak citizens on their boards of directors. For the workers the main reforms were the introduction of the eight-hour day, sickness and unemployment schemes, and a tightening of the restrictions on child and female labour. There was a series of other lesser reforms, the ministry of social welfare issuing 157 reforming decrees between 1918 and 1923.

Few of these social reforms would have been of much benefit without the action taken by the finance minister, Rašín, to check inflation. Because de la Rue and other firms could not cope with the rush of orders for new currencies, after 1919 most central European states were still using Habsburg notes but other governments, having no scruples about inflation, were printing these with abandon. In February 1919 Rašín sealed the Czechoslovak borders, called in all notes in circulation and had them stamped with the Czechoslovak emblem; until the Czechoslovak crown was introduced in April only stamped notes were accepted as legal tender. These and other tough deflationary measures ensured that Czechoslovakia continued to be spared the inflation which raged unchecked in most neighbouring states.

Despite the reforms which his cabinet initiated Kramář was out of tune with the mood of his people. With the achievement of national independence his National Democratic Party had lost much of its *raison d'être*. Bourgeois in composition and conservative in social outlook, it was ill-equipped to respond to the social pressures of the post-war months. The personal political standing of Kramář also suffered because he was absent for months in Paris; much of the credit for reforms such as the land control act was therefore quite justly taken by Švehla who, with Rašín, dominated domestic affairs in the absence of Kramář. After local elections in June 1919 had reflected the popular mood, a new administration was formed under the social democratic leader, Vlastimil Tusar. His authority was confirmed by the republic's first general election, held in April 1920.

Tusar seemed admirably placed to satisfy radical opinion but he could not suppress divisions within his own party. A left-wing faction, 'the marxist left', had emerged as an organised group late in 1919 and pressed for a seizure of power through workers' councils and affiliation with the Third International. The majority of the Czechoslovak social democrats, like those in Germany, rejected such notions and were determined that socialism should be achieved through the ballot box rather than revolutionary action on the streets. By mid-September Tusar's position within his own party was so embattled that the leading political figures no longer considered him capable of governing the country and therefore, in the discussions which gave birth to the pětka, engineered the appointment of the non-party government led by Černý.

It was Černý who had to weather the revolutionary storm which hit Czechoslovakia in the second half of 1920. There had been industrial action on the railways to frustrate military aid for the Poles, and after mounting unrest a general strike was declared in December. In the mining district of Kladno it assumed violent form, with thirteen people losing their lives, but the general populace remained deaf to calls for revolution. The peasantry had no wish to disturb a system which had given them land reform, whilst the majority of the proletariat was unwilling to jeopardise newly found democratic freedoms for a bolshevik escapade which could lead to civil war.

The Kladno episode hastened a formal division in the Social Democratic Party. The moderates remained loyal to the political democracy of the new republic whilst the marxist left seceded in May 1921 to form the Communist Party of Czechoslovakia, which was joined by the German, Ruthene, and Magyar left in October.

The departure of the left confirmed the social democrats as defenders of constitutional rule and legality but it also deprived them of the status of the country's largest party. That mantle fell upon the agrarians when the Czech and Slovak parties merged in 1922. Even before the war the agrarians had had extensive and efficient organisations closely linked to the powerful cooperative societies. Above all, however, the authority of the agrarian party rested upon its initiation and control of the process of land reform and on the fact that its moderate policies were acceptable to a peasantry which was essentially conservative. The social democrats, meanwhile, did much to destroy what support they had in the countryside by opposing the redistribution of large estates which they wanted to keep as state or collective farms.

By the late summer of 1921 the pĕtka considered that the country was sufficiently stable for it to be returned to a government dominated by politicians rather than civil servants. In September Beneš became prime minister. He was to remain in office until October 1922. His experience and expertise were primarily in diplomacy, which he had dominated almost since independence, and in office he engineered the little entente and prepared the ground for the Czechoslovak-French treaty of 1924, the twin bases of Czechoslovak foreign policy until 1938.

When Beneš resigned as prime minister in October 1922 the pĕtka chose Švehla as his successor. This was the first time that a prime ministerial change had taken place without an immediate crisis and it seemed, therefore, that political stability had been achieved. The change also registered the national strength of the Czechoslovak Agrarian Party, since that party was to fill the prime ministerial seat for almost all of the remaining life of the republic.

Švehla's cabinet included luminaries from the five parties which had formed the pĕtka and was known popularly as 'the ministry of all the talents'. Much of its activity was intended to continue and consolidate the work of previous administrations. Partly to conciliate the strong trade union lobby within the Social Democratic Party, unemployment benefits were to be organised according to the 'Ghent scheme' whereby the unions were made responsible for distributing unemployment payments, the government contributing half of the cost. The scheme, introduced in 1921, became operative in 1925 when sufficient funds had been accumulated. Unfortunately only a third of Czechoslovak wage-earners belonged to unions, which were strongest amongst the skilled workers employed in the large industrial units found primarily in Bohemia and Moravia. Non-unionised and unskilled labour predominated in Slovakia and Ruthenia whilst amongst the Sudeten Germans manufacturing tended to be in very small craft workshops or mills where the workforce, though highly skilled, was non-unionised. Even social welfare legislation was ensnared in the complications of ethnic politics.

Švehla's minister of finance was Rašín, who once again staged an uncompromising, stern, and successful campaign against the inflation which beset Czechoslovakia's neighbours. So successful was he that in 1922 and 1923 capital flowed into Czechoslovakia, which became, for a short period, 'the savings bank of central Europe'.[9] This was not an entirely unmixed blessing. The inflow of capital raised the value of the Czechoslovak crown but when capital later returned to the now stabilised economies of the surrounding states the Czechoslovak currency was not readjusted downwards, a failing which harmed exports and led to an unnecessary rash of bank failures and a needless if temporary increase in unemployment in 1923. By that time, however, Rašín was no longer responsible, as he had been murdered early in the year by a crazed ex-communist student. He was the only prominent victim of political assassination in Czechoslovakia during the inter-war period.

The Slovak question in the first half of the 1920s

Immediately after the declaration of independence, Slovak frustrations over union with the Czechs had been contained by fear of Hungarian incursion and by the expectation of land reform. By 1922 neither of these conditions applied, in addition to which the most forceful and attractive Slovak advocate of Prague's centralist domination, general Milan Štefánik, had been killed in an air-crash in May 1919.

The leading anti-centralist party, the Slovak People's Party (SPP), after 1925 renamed Hlinka's Slovak People's Party (HSPP), rapidly recovered from the embarrassments of Hlinka's precipitous descent upon Paris in 1919. Hlinka's party, pointing out that the 1920 constitution had not included that provision for Slovak autonomy alluded to in the Pittsburgh Declaration, introduced a Slovak autonomy bill into the chamber of deputies in 1922. It was rejected but the SPS had established that autonomy was the core of its programme, and in Slovakia itself opinion was drifting towards the decentralists.

The Slovaks resented the fact that the Czechs could refer to 'Czech' schools but that the Slovaks could describe theirs only as 'Czechoslovak', not 'Slovak'. There was also growing complaint over Czech domination of the Slovak civil service. Hlinka and his allies made constant propaganda from figures showing that the Slovaks, though around 17 per cent of the total population, had only 1.7 per cent of posts in the central administration; not even the Slovaks' admitted educational backwardness could explain such disparities, they said. Nor were Slovak dispositions sweetened by the knowledge that Slovak salaries were lower than in the Czech lands although taxes, until 1929, were higher. Slovakia was also suffering economically. Retreating Hungarian troops had taken some industrial plant with them in 1919 but much greater harm was caused when the Slovak economy, which had been nurtured in the Hungarian hothouse of subsidy and protection, was exposed to open competition from the Czech lands. Many Slovak concerns were taken over by Czech companies or banks but when Rašín's deflationary policies were introduced the new owners disposed first of their least viable assets; usually they were Slovak. By 1922 some five hundred plants, representing approximately one-third of Slovakia's productive capacity, had ceased to function. In the countryside land reform had brought great benefit to many but there were still a large number, Magyar as well as Slovak, who had not enough land. The traditional method for making ends meet had been wage-labouring, seasonal or yearly, in the large estates or forests which abounded near at hand or across the Danube in Hungary. Now the new border cut them off from the latter and at home land reform had broken up the labour-absorbing estates. These grievances helped to produce a number of serious outbursts of agrarian unrest in one of which, in 1920, two protesting farm workers were killed by gendarmes.

Perhaps the most widespread source of Slovak discontent was religion. A new 'national church', which conducted its services in Czech and spared its priests the rigours of celibacy, had been introduced into Bohemia and Moravia. It eventually found about four million adherents, far fewer than the Roman Catholic church, but it puzzled and sometimes angered the Slovak Catholics. They were also offended by Masaryk's individual style of protestantism, by the pulling down of a statue to the Blessed Virgin Mary in Prague, by the decline in religious instruction in schools, by the introduction of divorce, by the conscription of priests, and by a series of other minor grievances. Matters came to a head in 1925 when the central government decided to abolish or replace a number of religious holidays. One of the new national holidays was to be 6 July, the day on which the Czech reformer Jan Hus had been martyred in 1415; good Catholics did not wish to honour such a person.

That the populist and clerical parties were the beneficiaries of rising Catholic concern was proved in the general election of November 1925 when the HSPP almost doubled its share of the vote, 34.4 per cent as opposed to 17.6 per cent in 1920, and the clerical parties throughout the republic received 21 per cent as opposed to 14.8 per cent.

The German question in the first half of the 1920s

Whilst the Slovaks drifted towards anti-centralism, the Sudeten Germans moved in the opposite direction.

At the beginning of the 1920s the Germans had many grievances. They hated conscription, they saw land reform as a device to dispossess and enfeeble them, they fumed against a foreign policy which aligned them with the despised Serbs who had killed the heir to their throne, and in Rašín's deflationary crusade they perceived little beyond the depressing effect it had upon Sudeten German manufacturers and exporters.

Even the constitution's generous language laws did not escape German censure. The compulsory use of Czech in commercial documentation, it was argued, delayed and increased the costs of business and had a particularly deleterious effect on tourism in Karlsbad, Marienbad, and other resorts. Postal and railway services, though state owned, were declared to be 'commercialised undertakings' and therefore exempt from the provisions of the language regulations. The language laws were meant to be a measure of linguistic rather than ethnic affiliation but, for purposes of calculating the two-thirds necessary to make a language official or to produce the 20 per cent needed to establish schools teaching in a specific tongue, magyarone or German-speaking Jews were counted as Jews not Hungarians or Germans. In the ever-sensitive area of education the Germans complained that all new schools built in mixed areas were Czech, that their university had lost its historic name, and that the Germans who formed just under a quarter of the population received only 5 per cent of the money disbursed in state scholarships.

Despite these grievances 'activism', the willingness to take a constructive part in the politics of the Czechoslovak state, increased. In the elections of November 1925 900,000 Sudeten Germans voted for activist parties whilst only 250,000 supported the negativist groups. This shift in opinion had been brought about partly because Czechoslovakia, albeit at some cost to the Sudeten Germans, had achieved a fiscal stability much in contrast to most of central Europe, and partly because the Germans came to accept that the state did intend to honour its promises to the minority groups. Most important, however, was the realisation that negativism had achieved nothing and that its prospects for the future were even worse. Austria was too weak to help the Sudeten Germans; so too was Weimar Germany, at least until 1923, and after 1925 it was unlikely to compromise the Locarno spirit for the sake of the German minority in a state which enjoyed allied favour. The Sudeten Germans would have to look after themselves and the easiest way of doing so was to become part of Czechoslovakia's functioning democracy.

The supra-national coalition, 1926–9

By 1925 the cohesion of the red-green coalition was weakening under the impact of rows over the Hus celebration and over the social democrats' demands for a reduction in agricultural tariffs, to which the agrarians would never agree. In March Černý was brought back as prime minister to oversee the elections due in November.

Those elections brought significant gains to the populists and the clericals, and also to the communists who gained 13.2 per cent of the total vote and were the second largest party in the chamber of deputies, thanks mostly to their appeal to the poor and discontented of the non-Czech areas. Švehla returned as prime minister in December but it was not until October 1926 that he had finally constructed a cabinet which had the confidence of the assembly. Absent from the new government were the social democrats who remained out of office until 1929, the only period throughout the first republic when they were not part of the administration. The main parties within the cabinet were the agrarians, the HSPP and, most surprisingly, two German parties, the agrarians and the Christian socials. The national democrats joined it in 1928. This 'green-black coalition', or 'the gentlemen's coalition' as it was sometimes known after the adhesion of the national democrats, was clearly a conservative alliance, but its most striking feature was that Czechoslovak, Czech, Slovak, and German parties were all represented. Little wonder that the new coalition was greeted as 'an internal Locarno'.

The policies of the green-black coalition, like those of all governments of the first Czechoslovak republic, were determined by its composition. The absence of the social democrats meant that the pace of social reform was slackened and the agrarians were granted their long-voiced demand for fixed agricultural tariffs. The two most significant items of legislation, however, were those made at the behest of Hlinka's Slovak People's Party.

The first was that the state make its peace with the Catholic church. In December 1927 it was agreed that the state was to allow the Vatican to nominate bishops to Czechoslovak sees, though Prague was to vet each nomination, and episcopal boundaries were to be redrawn so that no Czechoslovak Catholics should be placed under the jurisdiction of bishops whose seats were in a foreign country. The state was gradually to retreat from its earlier anti-clerical legislation, especially with regard to education, and was in future to pay the salaries of Catholic priests. In return the church was to end its hostile attitude towards Prague. The second act was for local government reform. In 1927 the *župy* were abolished and the country divided into the four provinces of Bohemia, Moravia, Slovakia, and Ruthenia. The strong centralism of the 1920 constitution was not much diluted but for the first time in modern history Slovakia had been given a corporate identity; it was, said the HSPP, 'the first spark of autonomy'[10] and it did make it easier for the Slovaks to prepare their own bureaucratic cadres.

Despite these concessions there was still unease in Slovakia. In 1928 this assumed major proportions following the arrest of Vojtěch Tuka. Tuka, founder of Rodobrana (home defence), a para-military organisation to police HSPP meetings, was a former mathematics professor and editor of the HSPP newspaper, *Slovák*. On 1 January 1928 he published an article alleging that there had been a secret annex to the Turčanský Svätý Martin declaration of 1918 limiting its validity to ten years, in which case Prague's writ would no longer run in Slovakia after 28 October 1928. The government was faced with a dilemma. To act against Tuka would anger the HSPP and might destabilise the coalition; to leave him untouched could raise passions in Slovakia to a dangerous level. The government dithered, partly because Švehla was out of action through illness, and partly because provincial elections were to be held in December. After the elections, which showed a swing to the left, further inaction was caused by Švehla's resignation in February and his replacement by František Udržal, and by tensions between the agrarians and the rest of the coalition which became so destructive that the agrarian boss, Milan Hodža, was dismissed from the cabinet. He had been opposed to action against Tuka and after his departure the government at last moved. In May Tuka was in court, charged with espionage on behalf of Hungary; the trial substantiated the charge and proved that the annex to the Turčanský declaration did not exist. In October Tuka was sentenced to fifteen years' imprisonment.

The discrediting of Tuka came too late either to save the green-black coalition, which was falling apart through internal wranglings and jealousies, or greatly to help the government parties at the general election which Udržal had called for

27 October. Two days after the election sixteen million shares changed hands on the Wall Street stock exchange.

The great depression and Czechoslovak politics, 1929–35

The election of 27 October 1929 confirmed that the black-green coalition had lost public favour. In Bohemia and Moravia the moderate left made noticeable gains whilst in Slovakia the HSPP vote declined because the ardent anti-centralists wished to protest against the party's participation in the government and the moderate autonomists were disturbed by the revelations of the Tuka trial. The new cabinet formed by Udržal on 7 December was a broad coalition ranging from the national democrats on the right to the agrarians in the centre and social democrats on the moderate left. It was therefore a coalition of bourgeois and moderate socialist groups. It was also basically a Czech-Czechoslovak-German rather than a Czech-Czechoslovak-Slovak-German coalition, the HSPP leaving the government never to enter it again.

The premiership of Udržal, which lasted until 24 October 1932, was dominated by the effects of the depression. Between 1928 and 1934 the sale of agricultural produce increased but earnings from it declined by a third and indebtedness almost doubled. The index of industrial production dropped by 40 per cent between 1929 and 1933 and exports fell by over 70 per cent; the balance of trade, which had shown a surplus of 500 million crowns in 1928, registered a deficit of 200 million in 1933, a year in which unemployment rose to 750,000, or 16.6 per cent of the labour force.

The government took a number of steps to alleviate the suffering caused. As the Ghent system brought unemployment relief only to a minority of the unemployed, direct payments were instituted and welfare cards were introduced which provided the needy with food, clothing, and other necessities. In 1932 the state grain purchasing agency, Centrokooperativ, had been founded, and in March 1933 a 'work loan' was floated to pay for labour-creating public works, whilst in June of the same year a bill was passed extending the government's power within the economy; over two hundred decrees were eventually passed under the terms of this act. In February 1934 the crown was devalued by 16.6 per cent to help exporters. Trading agreements were concluded with a number of states, including Britain, the United States, and South Africa. Further assistance to industry came from an increase in arms production after Hitler came to power in Germany and from conscious efforts to encourage diversification; Škoda and Tatra cars and Bata shoes were amongst the products to receive government encouragement and by 1936 industrial production was at 96 per cent of its 1929 level.

These reforms put some strain on the coalition, Udržal resigning in October 1932 to give way to Jan Malypetr. In party terms the social democrats had grave misgivings over the grain agency but were reconciled by reforms in the system of collective bargaining. The national democrats, however, could not accept the humiliation of devaluation and left the cabinet.

The reforms of the first half of the 1930s did not exempt Czechoslovakia from social unrest; at least twenty-nine people died in strikes, demonstrations, and other disorders. Despite the distress and unrest, however, there was no strong fascist movement in Czechoslovakia. For this there were two main reasons. First, the potential fascist leader, general Radola Gajda, displayed almost total incompetence when staging attempted coups in 1926 and 1933. Second, there was not a strong enough sense of Czechoslovak nationhood to produce a Czechoslovak fascist movement; on the other hand, fascism and its near equivalents were to find fertile soil in the German and Slovak communities which did have a strong sense of nationhood.

Before that was to happen there were important developments in foreign policy. Under the terms of the Czechoslovak-Soviet treaty of May 1935 the Soviet Union agreed to come to Czechoslovakia's assistance in time of war if the French also stood by their obligation to do likewise. The treaty was a reflection of Czechoslovakia's increasing sense of insecurity in the face of the threats presented by growing Hungarian, German, and perhaps Polish revanchism. However, if the treaty increased external security it also promoted internal tension in that it was unpopular amongst the Slovaks and the Germans, nor was it much to the liking of the agrarians, who did not relish close association with the aggressively atheist power which had liquidated peasant ownership.

The elections of May 1935 produced surprisingly little change in the distribution of votes in the Czech and Slovak communities but a massive increase in the strength of the German nationalists. In November Malypetr gave way to Milan Hodža as prime minister and Masaryk resigned as president, nominating Beneš as his successor. In the vote of 18 December the election of Beneš was contested, his victory being assured only when Hlinka, after consultations with the Vatican, committed the HSPP to his cause, a favour for which Beneš was to show remarkably little gratitude.

Though the elections and changes in ruling personnel in 1935 commanded much attention they could not for long obliterate the overwhelming question of Czechoslovak politics in the second half of the 1930s: the challenge to centralism from the Slovak and German extremists.

The Slovak question in the 1930s

Slovakia's economic and social suffering in the 1930s was profound. The effects of the depression were considerable but they were compounded by a trade war which developed after 1930 with Hungary, a traditional market for Slovak timber, and were not much alleviated by efforts to relocate sections of the arms industry in Slovakia; in the mid-1930s 91.5 per cent of industrial employment was still in the Czech lands.

Hlinka made little use of the economic crisis, perhaps because it was by no means merely a Slovak phenomenon but more probably because he had little interest in economics. In 1930 he had introduced a second autonomy bill; after it failed he concentrated primarily on cultural affairs. In May 1932 he pushed his own nominees into controlling positions in *Matica Slovenská*, the most important and long-standing of Slovak cultural organisations. Later in the same summer he staged a similar takeover at a convention of Young Slovak Intelligentsia called to discuss the economic and social plight of the region, telling Hlinka at this meeting that he was prepared to carry through his autonomy programme, 'even at the price of the republic'.[11] In August of the following year he made a dramatic incursion into the celebrations to mark the 1,100th anniversary of the founding of the Christian church in Slovakia, a celebration to which he had not been invited. He and his supporters burst into the meeting and invaded the platform, from which Hlinka proceeded to deliver a speech which included the ominous words, 'There are no Czechoslovaks. We want to remain just Slovaks – out with the Czechs.'[12]

This concentration upon cultural affairs was an accurate reflection of Slovak anti-centralist opinion. During the 1920s the Slovaks had rapidly become more literate and they tended to see national self-expression primarily in cultural terms. In the 1920s the Slovaks had gone a good way to creating their own cultural infrastructure and it was this, rather than any economic distinctiveness, which they were anxious to emphasise in the subsequent decade. They were particularly determined to stress their individuality in view of the assertion of some Czechs that the best solution to the problem was to let Slovak quietly die as a literary language.

These assertions of cultural separateness by the HSPP garnered an adequate but not an abundant electoral harvest. In the elections of May 1935 the HSPP was the most successful party in Slovakia, taking 30.68 per cent of the Slovak vote, an improvement on 1929 but not equal to that of 1925. Despite its lacklustre electoral performance the HSPP pressed ahead with demands for legal recognition for the Slovak as opposed to the Czechoslovak nation, for making Slovak the official language in Slovakia, for a legislative diet in Bratislava, and for a ministry of Slovak affairs in Prague. Prague was not to be moved. Fearing similar decentralising demands from the other minorities, above all from the Germans, the Hrad refused any political concessions. Beneš, always a trenchant opponent of concession, argued that Czechoslovakia, surrounded as it was by Nazi, fascist, and authoritarian régimes, could survive only as a united Czechoslovak nation based upon and held together by a united Czechoslovak culture.

Beneš was helped by the fact that the HSPP leader, Hlinka, was old and ill and therefore less able than a younger person to cover up the divisions in his party. There had always been a gap between the clericalists around Mgr Jozef Tiso and the lay faction of Karol Sidor who toyed with the idea of a Slovak-Polish federation; there had also been arguments over whether the Slovaks should be content with autonomy or press for all-out independence; and in the late 1930s there was serious division on the powerful right of the party between

Rodobrana, the Nastup (step forward) faction led by the Ďurčanský brothers, and a small fascist group Of the three the Nastup group was the most powerful. It attracted the young who had never known Magyar domination and who looked admiringly at the new, virile, and totalitarian régimes of Italy and Germany.

Hlinka made his final public appearance at a party rally in Whitsun 1938 to mark the twentieth anniversary of the Pittsburgh agreement. American Slovaks, ostentatiously travelling via Poland rather than set foot in the Czech lands, brought with them the original text of the agreement complete with Masaryk's signature. This was an important as well as an emotional occasion. It produced the Whitsun programme which called for a Slovak legislative assembly, a widening of the powers of Slovak officials, full legislative and judicial powers for self-governing Slovak associations, the immediate setting up of an independent provincial council for education, the slovakisation of Bratislava university, an end to censorship, the recall of Czech bureaucrats from Slovakia, and more posts for Slovaks in the central administration. These demands formed the substance of the third Slovak autonomy bill presented to the chamber of deputies in August 1938 by which time international developments had made parliamentary discussion almost irrelevant.

On 22 September, under all but intolerable international pressure over the Sudeten question, Beneš agreed to recognise the Slovaks as a separate nation, though even now he attempted to dilute the Slovak victory by suggesting that there be three distinct nations, Czech, Slovak, and Czechoslovak. At this point, with the state on the verge of dismemberment, disintegration, or war, the Slovaks suddenly veered back towards the central government when they realised that the drastic weakening of the Prague régime would, as Beneš had always warned, stimulate both separatist aspirations amongst Slovakia's own minorities and the territorial appetites of their Hungarian and Polish patrons. But by then it was too late.

The German question in the 1930s

The rise of destructive anti-centralist sentiment amongst the Sudeten Germans had two main sources: the effects of the depression in Czechoslovakia and the growing aggressiveness of the Nazi régime in Germany. It was the backing of a strong foreign government which gave the anti-centralists in the Sudetenland a strength to which their Slovak comrades could never aspire; it also ensured that the Sudeten question became an international rather than a purely Czechoslovak problem.

The economy of the German areas of Czechoslovakia was severely hit by the depression. Exports to traditional markets in Germany, together with tourism focused on centres such as Karlsbad, suffered from new German currency regulations which also froze the assets of two Sudeten German banks which, for reasons of national sentiment, had lodged their deposits in the Reich. That they were baled out by the Živnostenská Bank of Prague produced more resentment than gratitude because Sudeten German financial dependence upon the Czechs had been made embarrassingly clear. The result of these economic difficulties was vast unemployment; half of the total of the country's unemployed was to be found amongst the Sudeten Germans and the number of unemployed in the Sudetenland was greater than the total number of unemployed in France.

The Germans made far more political capital out of their economic difficulties than did the Slovaks. By 1930 Nazi organisations such as the National Socialist Student League and Volkssport, the German equivalent of the sokols, had appeared and had been addressed by leading Nazis such as Goebbels and von Schirach. By the time Hitler came to power the Prague government had become sufficiently alarmed to ban all Nazi groups. This merely forced a realignment of extreme nationalist forces in the Sudetenland. From the former organisations emerged the SdHF, the Sudeten German Home Front, led by a former gym teacher, Konrad Henlein. The emergence of the SdHF frightened a number of established politicians but Masaryk rejected pressure to suppress it, insisting instead that it must be allowed freedom to develop within the law; at the same time it was suggested that its structure be changed and that it should function as a political party. To this Henlein agreed, and thus SdHF metamorphosed into the Sudetendeutschpartei, SdP. The butterfly was no more attractive than the caterpillar.

Henlein denied any connection with the Nazi party in Germany. He did, however, paint life in the Reich as superior to that in Czechoslovakia and he called for boycotts of Jewish and Czech shops, doctors, and other services. He also demanded a reorientation of Czechoslovak foreign policy. The law of the land forbade any advocacy of the break-up of the state and Henlein therefore argued for its federalisation.

These arguments, against the background of the depression and of Hitler's government in Germany, brought Henlein spectacular success in the May 1935 elections, with the SdP taking 63 per cent of Sudeten German votes and 15.2 per cent of votes in the republic as a whole. On the day after the elections Henlein telegraphed his loyalty to Masaryk, but he also made it clear that he would never take part in government. Despite Henlein's assertions of loyalty, the régime in Prague nevertheless had to take some defensive measures against the growing anti-centralist threat both in the Sudetenland and to a lesser degree in Slovakia. In the spring of 1936 the defence of the state act was passed, for which the SdP deputies voted. The act provided for measures to be taken on the outbreak of war and allowed the government to declare martial law in areas where the state or its democratic and republican character were threatened.

Henlein was not restrained. At a rally in Eger on 12 June 1936 he produced a new rabbit from his capacious hat. The nationality laws were inadequate, he said, because they protected individuals rather than racial groups. Henlein's demand for group rather than individual rights was in conformity with his party's corporatist, collectivist outlook, but for Prague it represented the gravest threat since the declaration of a German-Bohemian republic in 1918. In addition to the Eger speech Henlein also nominated three Sudeten German deputies to the German Reichstag. This was done with the help of Berlin and 1936 saw significant increases in links, organisational and financial, between the SdP and the German Nazis. The government responded with the February agreements of 1937. These important concessions promised ethnic proportionality in the civil service, the distribution of public expenditure on a regional basis, a just allocation of public money to German welfare and cultural needs, government contracts for German firms in German areas, greater use of German as an official language, and stricter central control over local officials. These concessions merely provoked fresh demands from Henlein. On 27 April he proposed in the chamber of deputies that members of the different racial groups should be enrolled in national organisations which would constitute separate legal entities and would direct all the internal affairs of that nation. All persons over eighteen would be obliged to register and once registered would not be able to change their national affiliation. The deputies of each nation would elect a 'spokesman' who would not sit in parliament but would be the official representative of the nation in the state. Henlein was asking for a series of corporate states within the state and if, in 1937, this was an unrealistic demand it served its immediate political purpose of vitiating the concessions made in the February agreements. Meanwhile the Nazi press whipped up opinion with stories of atrocities committed on Sudeten Germans by Czech policemen.

In an attempt to contain these growing pressures prime minister Hodža announced that government spending in German areas was far in excess of the 23 per cent which the principle of proportionality required, and that subsidies to German cultural institutions were higher than for other minorities.

Neither the SdP nor the Nazis were impressed. On 20 February 1938 Hitler claimed to be the protector of all *Volksdeutsche* (Germans living outside the German state) and in the following month he incorporated Austria into his Reich. Czechoslovakia was now surrounded on three sides by Nazi Germany, had a virtually undefended southern border, and had lost its land links with the west. As gloom spread in the Prague establishment the Henleinists exalted and were increased in strength when the German Agrarian and Clerical Parties abandoned their independence and merged with the SdP. Hodža responded on 28 March with an announcement that a 'minority statute' codifying all legislation on minority rights would be drawn up. It was a meaningless gesture and could in no way quieten the rampaging SdP.

The buoyant morale of the SdP was apparent at its congress in Karlsbad on 23–4 April when, in an eagerly awaited speech, Henlein put forward eight demands: full equality with the Czechs; recognition of the Germans as a legal corporate entity; recognition of a German settlement area into which only Germans could move; complete self-government; legal protection for Germans living outside the German areas; an end to the injustices suffered by the Germans since 1918; recognition of the principle of German officials in German territories; and complete freedom to express Nazi ideology.

The Karlsbad demands were enthusiastically endorsed by the Sudeten Germans in local elections in May. The government reacted with some firmness. In the same month it staged an impressive mobilisation in response to rumours of German troop movements and Beneš came forward with his 'Third Plan' under which twenty or more cantons would be created, with the Germans enjoying a large measure of autonomy in those in which they formed a majority. This was a great advance but nothing short of virtual separation from Prague could now satisfy Henlein. In September, with diplomatic pressure mounting and Hitler becoming ever more frenetic, Beneš agreed to accept the Karlsbad demands. Czechoslovakia was in effect to be federalised.

Beneš doubted whether the SdP would accept even this concession, and in this he was correct. After widespread rioting on 12 September Henlein decamped to Berlin where he declared three days later that the Sudeten Germans would be satisfied with nothing less than incorporation into the Reich. On the same day Chamberlain took a plane for Berchtesgarten.

Munich and the Second Republic, September 1938 to March 1939

The diplomatic details of the last chapter of the Czechoslovak tragedy are too well known to be repeated here. In its final hours the first Czechoslovak republic was not well served by the practice, evolved since 1918, of leaving major decisions to unofficial groups. Beneš, who had always been in the Hrad and had dominated foreign policy formulation, was convinced that he knew best and that those arguing for resistance to Hitler were naïve adventurers. The large body of public and political opinion which believed him to be wrong was not only too constrained by the dangers of the situation but also too conditioned to accepting decisions made behind closed doors to press its objections to the point of rebellion. Nevertheless, when Beneš urged acceptance of British and French advice to surrender the Sudetenland to Germany, and to grant autonomy to the Slovaks, there was fierce opposition in cabinet, from the military, and from up to half a million citizens who marched through Prague calling for 'no surrender'. In the face of such popular anguish Hodža's cabinet resigned, to be replaced by a government of officials under the non-political soldier, general Jan Syrový. Beneš resigned and went into exile. He was replaced by Emil Hácha, an aged jurist. In the same month, in Vienna, southern Slovakia and southern Ruthenia were ceded to Hungary. Poland took Teschen.

Meanwhile, on 6 October 1938 representatives of all Slovak parties, except the communists had joined an executive meeting of the HSPP at Žilina, where they agreed to declare autonomy for Slovakia; Ruthenia did the same a few days later. On 19 November parliament in Prague formally recognised these changes. The first Czechoslovak republic was dead; the second, or Czecho-Slovak, republic had begun its short life.

In Prague Syrový soon made way for Rudolf Beran whose policies were tailored almost entirely to Germany's cloth. The communist party was dissolved and the remaining parties merged into two new groups, the Party of National Unity for right and centre-right factions, and the Party of National Labour for those on the left. Real power, however, lay in Berlin. It was from here that restrictions upon Jews, together with a host of measures limiting individual and corporate liberties, were dictated. At the same time, foreign policy was aligned with that of Germany, forcing the second republic to leave the League of Nations and to limit its contacts with the western powers. Czecho-Slovakia was *de facto* a dependency of Nazi Germany.

In Slovakia Mgr Tiso was made prime minister and Karol Sidor was sent to Prague to become minister in charge of Slovak affairs. Slovakia itself became in effect a one-party state ruled by the HSPP, under its new guise of the Slovak Party of National Unity. In November 1938 it absorbed the Slovak sections of the Party of National Labour and in December staged a general election in which it received 97.5 per cent of the votes. All non-party organisations, even the sokols, were dissolved and absorbed into the Hlinka Guard, an armed body formed shortly after Hlinka's death in 1938. The Hlinka Guard rapidly became the most powerful organ of the party, eagerly enforcing the régime's anti-Jewish and anti-Czech decrees.

Yet the party leadership was still far from united. Separatism had triumphed over autonomism but there were still disagreements about how rapidly Slovakia should move. Tiso and the other moderates argued that an independent Slovakia should evolve gradually but this was not the view of radicals such as Tuka, who had recently been released from prison, the Ďurčanský brothers, the arch anti-semite Alexander 'Sano' Mach, and the powerful leader of Slovakia's Germans, Volksgruppenführer Franz Karmasin, all of whom intrigued actively with the Germans.

Eventually Prague decided to counter these intrigues. On 9 March 1939 Czech troops moved into Slovakia, Tiso was dismissed, and a number of politicians and Hlinka Guardists were arrested. Hitler decided to use this emergency to activate his plans for the incorporation of the Czech lands into the Reich. Tiso was called to Berlin on 13 March and told to declare Slovak independence; if he did not, he was warned, the country would be given to Hungary. Tiso immediately agreed to summon the Slovak diet, which on the following day declared Slovakia an independent state.

At the same time Hácha was ordered to Berlin and informed that the Czech provinces were to become part of the Reich. On 15 March German troops moved across the Munich frontiers and on the following day, in the Hradčany Palace, Hitler proclaimed the Reich Protectorate of Bohemia and Moravia. It was his only visit to the city but during it he broke his dietary habits to partake of Bohemian beer and Prague ham.

5

HUNGARY, 1918–41

Between 1918 and 1920 Hungary experienced three revolutions, the first two of which were based in Budapest and the third of which was nation-wide.

Revolution 1: Károlyi and the democratic revolution

As early as June 1918 workers' councils had been formed in Budapest but it was not until the central powers' military failures of September and October that Habsburg authority was destroyed. By the end of October the historic kingdom of Hungary was gradually falling to foreign occupiers or indigenous malcontents whilst the armed forces disintegrated under the impact of defeat, mutiny, and the widespread formation of 'councils' or 'soviets' in the ranks. Terrified of foreign occupation and social revolution, the right, the centre, and the moderate left grouped around a national council under count Mihály Károlyi who was accepted as minister president by King-Emperor Karl on 31 October. The cabinet was made up of members of Károlyi's own Independence Party, the social democrats, the radicals under Oszkár Jászi, and members of a number of interest groups, including one feminist.

Károlyi himself was a member of an old and extremely wealthy Hungarian family but his social conscience had been roused through his association with the cooperative movement and so great had been his outrage at the political shenanigans of the old rulers that in 1910 he had fought a duel with count Tisza who was then speaker of the Hungarian parliament. It was hoped that Károlyi's long-standing support of the west would help Hungary in its dealings with the allies, and that his favourable standing with the radicals at home would help to preserve internal order. Károlyi began well. He offered the non-Hungarian peoples self-determination, hoping that they would prefer inclusion in a democratic, Hungarian federation to independence. He appointed Jászi minister for national minorities. The Hungarian government recognised the new states of German Austria, Poland, Czechoslovakia, and the Ukraine. Károlyi also announced that he would hold an election based on universal and secret suffrage and as a gesture of intent for his social policies parcelled out his own estates amongst his former tenants.

78

Despite the encouraging start Károlyi was not the man for the hour. His generous attitudes carried little weight with the western allies, the minority peoples, Hungary's new neighbours, or the revolutionary extremists, all of whom were to play a part in his downfall. Above all, Károlyi and his government were faced with insoluble social problems. The allied blockade grievously aggravated the food shortages which the chaos of the final months of the war had produced; by the end of the fighting some 400,000 deserters were hiding in the forests and mountains and as soon as the armistice was signed they descended into the food-producing areas to seize food and in some cases land; the rapid demobilisation of some 1,200,000 soldiers immediately after the end of the conflict deluged the job markets with men just when factories were closing because their raw materials and/or their established outlets were lost to foreign occupiers or nationalist rebels; by the end of 1918 the Czechs were occupying Slovakia, the Yugoslavs had taken Pécs, Hungary's only major coal-producing area, the Romanians were advancing into Transylvania, and an allied army under general Franchet d'Esperey was encamped near the southern border. The alienation of Hungarian territory worsened the supply problem and produced a flood of refugees, many of them landowners or members of the bureaucracy or the teaching profession. These representatives of the former ruling élite were not entirely welcome in the new democratic Hungary, some of whose rulers resented having to provide relief for what they regarded as former class enemies. The refugees were concentrated in Budapest, where they competed with residents for two of the scarcest commodities in the city: jobs and living space. The many who were unsuccessful in their search for the latter had to spend months or even longer living in the railway wagons in which they had arrived.

That Hungary did not experience full-scale social revolution was in large measure because of the foreign invasions which initially consolidated Magyar support behind the Károlyi government; even the *enragé* elements of the urban left were persuaded that internal calm was necessary to ensure territorial integrity together with such meagre food and coal imports as the allies would allow. This argument grew thinner in the early months of 1919, a year in which Hungary, in the words of Herbert Hoover, 'presented a sort of unending, formless procession of tragedies, with occasional comic relief'.[1]

There was no comic relief on the social front as inflation, unemployment, shortages, and over-crowding intensified, placing the national consensus under increasing strain. To allay the mounting unrest Károlyi reconstructed his cabinet in January, giving greater authority to the social democrats who now dominated the government; they alone, it was believed, could control the urban masses. But even their ability to do this was increasingly called into question as strikes, takeovers of factories and estates, demonstrations, and acts of violence and insubordination multiplied. The political beneficiary of these disorders was the extreme left, now gathering under the flag of 'bolshevism'.

The communists promised everything to everyone – work for the unemployed, higher wages for those in work, greater benefits for the wounded and the widow, accommodation for the homeless, bread for the hungry, lower rents for the tenant, and, for those who feared foreign invasion, protection by Trotsky's Red Army which, they said, was advancing through Galicia and the Ukraine. Their strength grew rapidly, not least in the trade unions and in political organisations within the army.

The government's response was late and ineffective. The communist leader, Béla Kun, was imprisoned in February after a massive demonstration on behalf of the unemployed in which a number of policemen were killed and injured. Kun was placed in a prison separated by a low wall from the police barracks, whence on the night of his imprisonment appeared a party of burly officers to take their revenge. Kun survived the rough-handling with his prestige much enhanced. In Moscow Lenin arrested three Hungarians in the city to negotiate the return of prisoners of war, his move suggesting both that Red Russia cared about Kun and that it was prepared to take action on his behalf. By the middle of March the communists seemed invincible. There was a general fear that bolshevism represented the future and that its success was therefore inevitable, and this feeling weakened even able social democrats such as prime minister Zsigmond Kunfi who now seemed paralysed in the face of the bolsheviks' Hungarian acolytes. The use of repressive methods was also disliked because it smacked too much of the old régime. Some of Károlyi's supporters feared that his action against Kun might precipitate a civil war from which the hated neighbours would profit territorially, whilst others worried that the same tough methods might be used against the régime itself by its opponents on the right.

The only hope for Károlyi lay in intervention by his political mentors in the west. Such intervention came and was decisive; but it was in a form opposite to that which the prime minister wanted. On 20 March, with disorder and communist strength mounting by the minute, colonel Vyx, an officer in general Franchet d'Esperey's army, addressed a note to the Hungarian government. The Hungarians were ordered to withdraw their forces thirty miles to the west, the Romanians were to advance forty miles in the same direction, and the two armies were to be separated by a neutral zone under allied control. The new dispositions gave the Romanians the lion's share of Transylvania, whilst the allied zone included towns such as Debrecen and Szeged in the heartland of Hungary. Worst of all, Budapest was told that the lines of demarcation were political as well as military; the implication was that they were to be permanent. The note destroyed the moderate revolution and was a clear 'emotional break with the west'.[2] Károlyi knew that only a coalition government could persuade the Hungarians to accept such terms but the leader of the rightist factions, count István Bethlen, refused to be implicated in such a savage settlement. Károlyi was lost, and within twenty-four hours had been deposed by the extreme left under Béla Kun. It was one of the many paradoxes of Hungarian history that a government of the extreme left had been brought to office on a wave of intense national outrage.

Revolution 2: Béla Kun and the soviet republic

Acting under pressure from their followers, the new masters of Hungary, or more accurately of Budapest, established a soviet régime headed by people's commissars sitting in a council of people's commissars. The official head of the cabinet was a social democrat, Sándor Garbai, but the most influential figure was Kun, who became commissar for foreign affairs so that he might establish a close rapport with Lenin and Trotsky whose international armies were to save Hungary's national territory. Although in these frenetic days the fine distinction between communist and socialist was seldom drawn, Kun was in fact the only communist amongst the full commissars and throughout the Hungarian soviet republic the socialists were numerically dominant in the government and in the various elected bodies convened during that short period.

Kun set about reforming Hungary with great energy. His government's first act was to seize all land in holdings larger than one hundred *holds*.[3] On 22 March came a stream of decrees confiscating bank deposits, abolishing tithes, separating state and church, setting up revolutionary tribunals, preparing for the election of workers', soldiers' and peasants' councils, nationalising all industrial concerns with more than twenty workers, giving the authorities power to requisition accommodation and other scarce commodities, allying Hungary with Russia, and declaring Hungary's determination to fight to the end in defence of the soviet régime. Further reforms included the eight-hour day for factory workers and a series of welfare measures, one of which was the setting up of summer camps for the children of Budapest's proletariat.

Yet, despite this zeal for internal restructuring, the preoccupations of Kun's régime were perforce with external affairs. The western allies were appalled by his advent to power. Hungary lay in the rear of the line at which they intended to hold bolshevism and from which they hoped to launch their counter-offensive against it; Hungary was at the centre of the zone of client states which the French wished to build; bolshevism might well spread from Budapest to the sizeable Magyar minorities in Romania, Czechoslovakia, and Yugoslavia; and were Hungarian and Russian bolsheviks to link they could easily create a communist Ukraine which could ruin Poland. In such circumstances central Europe would be out of the allies' control, communism could reach through the Ukraine and Hungary into Austria and Germany and make the international proletarian revolution irresistible. Yet the allies, busily demobilising their armies, had few troops with which to discipline the Hungarians and could do little more than reimpose the blockade in its most severe form.

By April the allies were prepared to talk to Kun. From 4–5 April general Smuts was in Budapest to offer a new armistice line between the Hungarians and the Romanians. The terms were better than those handed down by Vyx but Kun, despite his personal wishes, could not agree to them. A government which had come to power because of the threat to national territorial integrity could not be seen to accept such terms; furthermore, most of his officers were from the old régime and would have deserted him had he signed away any Hungarian lands, whilst agreement with the western powers who were intervening in Russia would endanger his alliance with Moscow.

The failure of the Smuts mission removed the allied prohibition on a continued Romanian advance. Within days Romanian troops were crossing the Tisza whilst in the north the Czechs moved further into southern Slovakia. By May Day Kun was in a state of moral and physical collapse. By the second half of the month a recovery had been staged. Helped by supplies of food and arms from Italy, Kun's Red Guard had burst through Czech lines, retaken a sizeable chunk of southern Slovakia, and driven a wedge between the Czech and Romanian forces. In a note from Clemenceau on 11 June the allies ordered a stop. The note charged the Hungarian forces to withdraw behind the original line, in return for which Romanian troops would be required to retire to their former positions. The debate which followed was the most intense ever conducted by the Hungarian soviet régime and ended with a victory for Kun. He argued that the terms should be accepted because it would give a breathing space during which Hungarian forces could be regrouped and strengthened, the allies could fall out amongst themselves, and, most importantly, revolutionary situations could develop in the German states. By the middle of July Kun could report to Paris that the Hungarian evacuation of southern Slovakia was complete and that therefore the Romanian withdrawal should begin. It did not. The allies were not prepared to help Kun and so, by the end of July, the Romanians were again advancing into Hungary. Kun could no longer defend the country from the despised Romanians and his régime collapsed. By then Kunfi, his representative in Vienna, had begun negotiations with the allies, rightists had stolen most of his régime's cash reserves from a Viennese bank, and his own army had melted away. On 2 August Kun left Budapest and two days later the Romanians entered the city. Kun fled to Moscow. There he remained until Stalin packed him off to the gulag where he died in 1941.

By the time the Romanians reached Budapest the population was too weakened and disillusioned to resist them. Kun's government had failed not only in its external policy but also at home where it had built up a powerful phalanx of opponents and displayed critical weaknesses.

In the first place Kun lacked any party machine with which to impose his policies. The Hungarian communist party had been set up in Moscow and then in Budapest only in November 1918; it had no organisation or apparatus, a factor which increased the importance of Tibor Szamuely's security forces. The socialists and communists joined to form the Hungarian Socialist Party but a merger at the head did not create a body, nor did Kun even enjoy undisputed ascendency at the top. His 'communist centre' group had to face criticism from the former social democrats on the right and from the extreme left represented primarily by Szamuely. Kun, moreover, was himself not an effective organiser or leader and remained 'an agitator and nothing more.'[4]

Long before it agreed to evacuate Slavakia and inadvertently opened Hungary to further Romanian advances, Kun's régime, despite the nationalist origins of its rule, had offended national sentiment in many ways. Statues of national heroes had been pulled down, soldiers were forbidden to wear the national emblem next to the red star, and it became an offence to sing the national anthem or to hoist the national flag. The régime also excited anti-semitic feelings. Kun was Jewish. So too were Szamuely and the minister of war, Vilmós Böhm, together with a large proportion of the political commissars in the army and the judges and prosecutors in the revolutionary tribunals; the cutting edge of the revolution therefore had a notably Jewish profile. Resentment towards the 'Red Terror' was easily associated with anti-Jewish feelings.

Nor could the soviet régime effectively combat the social problems of Hungary. A new currency was decreed and the government printed notes to cover expenditure. Inflation was therefore virtually unchecked whilst the new notes were treated with enormous suspicion, especially by the peasantry. All attempts to deal with this problem merely provoked further opposition.

So, too, did the régime's efforts to reconstruct Hungarian society. In the cities the expropriation of wealth inevitably roused great resentment amongst the bourgeoisie, whose jewellery was 'nationalised', whose bathrooms were frequently 'socialised', and whose cafés and restaurants were frequented by Red Guards carrying nationalised hat-stands on which owner and patrons were 'invited' to hang presents for the needy proletariat. More sinister was the 'Red Terror' organised by Szamuely and implemented by his hated 'flying squads'. The squads were particularly active in the villages, where they forced peasants to sell grain and accept the new notes as payment.

The villages had other grievances. The peasants could not accept attacks upon traditional features of their life such as the turning of churches into cinemas. They also much disliked mobilisation into Kun's forces, but above all they rejected the régime's agrarian policy which did not divide up large estates but merely nationalised them, frequently turning the former owner or bailiff into the manager. Kun's policy was dictated by his determination to avoid creating a rural petty bourgeoisie but it left the counter-revolution with massive potential support.

Not even the proletariat, in whose name the revolution was made, felt a great debt of gratitude to the government. The rural proletariat was denied its wish for land, whilst in the factories the activists resented the fact that, as on the estates, former owners were retained as managers because of the lack of trained replacements. For the urban working masses the reality of life under Kun was continued inflation and food shortages, especially as peasant discontent was translated into non-cooperation. Added to this was enforced enlistment in the revolutionary army, not least because Kun's promised deliverance by Trotsky's Red Army failed to materialise.

Revolution 3; the counter-revolution

The first and second of Hungary's three revolutions had destroyed the liberal centre and the socialist left. Only the right remained. In Hungary, however, capitalism was but little developed and the small bourgeoisie which had evolved was to a large degree non-Magyar. The right in Hungary was therefore either the old right of the conservative magnates or the new right which had emerged rapidly in response to the events of 1918–19. The right had mobilised in 1919, particularly in the 'Hungarian Vendée' to the west of the Danube, though its headquarters became the city of Szeged to the east of the river. Here, under French protection, a counter-revolutionary force, the National Army, was assembled under admiral Miklós Horthy, a former commander of the Habsburg navy and aide to the emperor. Horthy represented the old military caste which was one of the three constituent elements of the 'Szeged Idea' which was to dominate Hungary from November 1919 to March 1944. The other elements were the old right made up of the conservative aristocracy, which in Hungary was not as closely associated with the military caste as elsewhere in Europe, and the radical new right. The latter was drawn from the peasantry, the Magyar petit bourgeoisie, and the ranks of the war-time armies; it called for anti-semitic legislation and land reform, both of which the old right rejected. The leading personality of the new right was Gjula Gömbös, a soldier and leader of one of the most important of the new patriotic associations, the Magyar Association for National Defence (MOVE). From November 1919 until December 1921 the new right and its military forces dominated Hungary.

The National Army entered Budapest in November 1919 after the Romanian evacuation, and the city, like the rest of the country, was subjected to a 'White Terror' administered by 'order detachments' whose prime victims were partisans of the Kun régime, Jews, and anyone considered a threat to public order. The terror was in full swing when new elections were held in January 1920, the socialists refusing to enter a competition which was so clearly not a free one. The dominance of the new right was registered also in the passing of a land reform act, promising to redistribute 900,000 acres, and by the introduction of a *numerus clausus* for Jews entering universities. However, after the old right had established its supremacy in 1922, the latter was largely ignored whilst the land reform legislation was used primarily for political rather than social purposes.

After Horthy's entry into Budapest he had been declared regent, the crown being retained because it was the symbol of the historic Hungary now so clearly under threat from the peace treaty.

The treaty of Trianon, 4 June 1920

The severity of the peace treaty imposed upon the Hungarians shocked them all. Trianon Hungary was but 32.6 per cent of the area of the historic kingdom. Lost were Transylvania, regarded by many Magyars as the intellectual cradle of the nation, Slovakia, Croatia, the Vojvodina, the Banat, the Bačka, and Ruthenia. Although the new state was 89.8 per cent Magyar, one-third of all Magyars were now outside Hungary. The economy of the state had been shattered, since much of the industrial development and the trade of pre-war Hungary had been linked with other parts of the historic kingdom; now industries were deprived of their raw materials and their markets, and Hungary no longer had access to the sea. Many railways had lost their economic rationale and the new frontiers cut across no less than twenty-four flood-control authorities. There were also strict limits upon the Hungarian armed forces. Plebiscites, which had been granted to the Germans in various disputed areas, were not permitted in Transylvania, Ruthenia, the Banat, or Slovakia.

The severity of the settlement was in part a punishment for the Magyar's past record with regard to national minorities, as well as for its recent flirtation with bolshevism, but it also owed much to the fact that the Czechs, Romanians, and Yugoslavs had been allowed to state their demands on Hungary to separate committees and therefore no single body in Paris had seen the total effect these claims would have upon Hungary. Furthermore, the allied leaders were bored and dispirited and, as the future Lord Beveridge told Károlyi, 'had more important things to worry about than the fate of ten million people in Hungary'.[5]

For the Hungarians themselves the peace settlement caused a great bitterness which was constantly in the public mind: the national flag was never raised above half-mast during the inter-war years, in remembrance of the lost territories. Furthermore, because the peace settlement was supposedly the work of the democratic powers of the west, democracy was discredited in the eyes of many Hungarians. This benefited the right, old and new, and inevitably placed Hungary in the ranks of the revisionist powers.

Acceptance of the peace treaty did little to stabilise the political situation in Hungary and in April and October 1921 King Karl attempted to return to the country, the second attempt ending in a clash with troops led by Gömbös. The expulsion of the king was necessary because his presence alarmed the allies, but the use of force angered many officers. After Karl's second expulsion, however, the army, like the rest of the nation, saw no alternative but to accept the domination of the old right, personified in the prime minister who was to dominate the 1920s, István Bethlen.

The Bethlen system, 1921–31

Bethlen, a calvinist from Transylvania, was appointed prime minister in April 1921. He had been prominent in the counter-revolution but had not been associated with its most bloody excesses. His political objectives were to liquidate the revolution and defend Hungary from any further bolshevik visitations. This would require the restoration of the previous political system, first at home and then, if possible, abroad. And there would also have to be a programme of industrialisation to make good the economic damage caused by Trianon.

Bethlen's 'régime of consolidation' was intended to place Hungary once more in the hands of its gentry with their 'Christian-national ideology'. The social power of the magnates and the gentry rested upon their domination of the land and of the bureaucracy, whilst their political supremacy was vested in the traditional Hungarian form of parliamentary rule. The latter demanded the domination of the assembly by the government party. Here there was a problem. The 1920 elections, the first in Hungary held with a secret ballot, had produced a parliament in which the largest party was the smallholders rather than Bethlen's Christian National Party. The answer was a merger of the two, through which the much more experienced and sophisticated Bethlen formed the Unified or, as it was generally known, the Government Party, which was completely under his domination.

Before achieving this he had made sure that at least one mistake of 1920 was not repeated. In February 1922 a franchise bill was passed restoring open voting to all non-urban constituencies, a definition which left a number of towns and industrial suburbs in the rural category. There were also educational and rigorous residential qualifications which discriminated against the labourers of town and countryside. The bill faced considerable opposition and the speaker of the assembly had to stop the clocks to avoid the operation of a parliamentary guillotine. The effect of the bill was 'to eliminate the electorate altogether as a real determining factor in public life'.[6] In April 1922 Bethlen hastened to use the new system to secure a more pliable parliament.

The power of the Government Party was bolstered by governmental influence over the press and the police. Even more important was the fact that the prime minister appointed all of the *főispáns*, or lord lieutenants of the counties, figures who wielded enormous local power. Bethlen's parliamentary authority rested upon his use of the Government Party, but his power in the country at large was much more dependent upon his control of the local government machine via the *főispáns*.

Bethlen's dominance of parliament was helped by the nature of Hungarian parties which in the 1920s were, with the exception of the social democrats, small and extremely fluid parliamentary groups which had little or nothing in the way of national organisations; many were hardly more than 'coffee-house' parties. Alliances between these many groups changed frequently and it was relatively easy for the government to play one off against another and so keep them all weak. Furthermore, the small liberal and social democratic forces in the first half of the 1920s still believed that Horthy and Bethlen were temporary phenomena and that when they had disappeared the western powers would assume a more understanding and benevolent attitude to the democratic Hungary which would then emerge. This illusion was dispelled in 1926 when it was discovered that French francs were being forged in Budapest with the knowledge of a former prime minister and perhaps of Bethlen himself. French attitudes would clearly not soften for some time.

If liberal opposition was weak so too was that from the left. The communists, and to a lesser degree the social democrats, had been severely discredited by the experience of Kun and the Romanian occupation. To ensure their continued weakness they were bought off in the Bethlen-Peyer pact of December 1921. Under this agreement the government promised to restore confiscated property to the trade unions, the cooperatives, and the Social Democratic Party, to release left-wing activists detained without trial, to allow socialists the same freedom as other Hungarians, and to permit economic strikes. For their part Peyer and the other social democratic leaders agreed that they would cut all links with the leftist émigrés, that they would behave as 'patriotic' Hungarians, and that they would not agitate amongst the miners, transport workers, and, most important of all, public employees and agricultural labourers; the social power of the ruling élite was to be sacrosanct. Nevertheless, the urban workers derived some gain from the compromise with Bethlen's system which encouraged industrial expansion and in later years extended welfare benefits.

Bethlen also concluded an agreement with the Catholic church. The church was to retain wide powers in the education of Catholic children, to have a virtual veto over who was made minister of education, and to have a considerable voice in the appointment of judges and other officials in Catholic areas. In return the church gave open support to the government.

The army was less easy to win over. For historic reasons the relationship between army and government in Hungary was unusual. Before 1918 all senior officers had been trained in imperial military colleges where the language was German. For that reason the most nationalistic of Magyars had preferred the Honvéd, or territorial reserve, whilst those choosing the professional army and attending staff colleges included many ethnic Germans, Croats, Serbs, and other non-Magyars. After 1918, therefore, a high proportion of senior officers were non-Magyar and even as late as 1941 all but six of the twenty-seven generals on the active list were from Hungary's German minority. The old school of officers resented the acceptance of the treaty of Trianon and the use of force against the king in 1921, whilst their younger colleagues tended towards the right-radical views of Gömbös. Bethlen managed to contain the discontent of both groups by distributing office amongst them and, in the later 1920s, by beginning a silent evasion of the most restrictive clauses of the treaty of Trianon.

The corner-stone of the Bethlen system, however, was the landed magnate and his property. Bethlen would have no truck with right-radical notions of land reform. Land did not, he insisted, belong to the people or to those who tilled it, but simply 'to those under whose name it appears in the land register'[7]. As he told parliament, 'In this state, where private property is sacred, to ask for land reform is like asking for my pants.'[8] Bethlen could also point out that the small farm was far less efficient than the large. If Hungary were to accumulate capital for modernisation or to finance loans for the same purpose, then the large farm must be retained; modernised societies such as Britain and the USA had not divided large estates, whereas states such as the despised Romania, which had done so, had diminished or destroyed their exportable surpluses. It is true that some land was redistributed under the terms of the 1920 act but few recipients were left with enough to become fully independent proprietors and thus land reform did not destroy the magnates' greatest social and political weapon: their position as employers of agricultural labour. Work, which remained essential for survival, was made dependent upon good political behaviour; this could be observed not only by means of the open ballot but also by many recipients of land under the 1920 act who were told that their retention of that land was conditional upon their reporting subversives to the authorities. For their part the magnates kept labour-saving machinery off their estates; this was a *de facto* concession to a work-dependent rural proletariat but even this helped to perpetuate magnate political power. The magnates were also helped by the fact that the Bethlen régime did not manage to contain inflation until it had wiped out the debts of many landholders.

Support for the magnate was not much to the taste of the new right. Nor was Bethlen's refusal to condone anti-semitism. In pre-war Hungary the aristocracy had shielded the Jews. The latter had proved good tenants and had also shown a remarkable ability to assimilate and adopt Magyar culture, and, furthermore, the magyarone Jews had been extremely helpful in ensuring that Hungary's Magyar-speakers were a majority of the population of the kingdom. After Trianon this did not apply, but Bethlen wished to see the traditional attitude continue. This was not solely for moral reasons. He was aware that if the lower orders were allowed to pillage Jewish property this would set an unfortunate precedent, in addition to which it would harm Hungary's image abroad, not least amongst the financiers of London and New York. Bethlen therefore allowed the anti-semitic legislation of 1920 to fall into disuse and he refused all appeals from the new right for further discriminatory acts.

Bethlen did, however, continue to limit very strictly the number of Jews in the civil service. The bureaucracy, once the place of refuge for the lesser gentry, was now to be used to provide jobs for the refugees, many of whom had in any case worked as government employees in the lost territories. This was a costly project but Bethlen financed it by selling gold and foreign currency reserves, by loans, and by a series of government monopolies. By 1924 he had been so successful that the office of refugees was abolished, and the new right had been denied a potentially vast pool of recruits.

The decay of the Bethlen system

The depression wrecked Bethlen's system. By 1932 agricultural production was only 44.8 per cent of its 1929 level, wheat prices were falling despite government purchasing and subsidies, and exports had collapsed following the general contraction of world trade and the particular blows delivered by both Czechoslovakia and Austria's abrogation of their trade treaties with Hungary. The financial crisis of the summer of 1931 made matters infinitely worse because short-term loans were called in. The larger estates were badly hit but the effect on the smallholder, whose debts were far higher a proportion of total assets, was devastating. Unrest inevitably followed. Strikes and demonstrations increased, reaching their high point in a massive protest meeting in Budapest on 1 September 1931 in which a number of people were injured; more serious and sinister were acts of terrorism, the most notable being the blowing up of a Vienna-Budapest express. In party politics the first crack in the Bethlen system came in October 1930 when Gaszton Gáal led a group out of the Government Party to form the Independent Smallholders Party. The revolt of the petty bourgeoisie had begun; the new right was mobilising.

Bethlen soon threw in the towel, resigning on 19 August 1931. He was replaced by Gyula Károlyi, a crony and a relation by marriage of the regent, but such a change could not stem the rise of the rightist tide. The absence of an organised or an acceptable left-wing alternative to the existing system channelled mounting discontent to the right. The hard-pressed smallholders naturally favoured the new right's radical proposals for land redistribution whilst many younger army officers welcomed its assertive nationalism, but it found its major support in the 'frayed white collar' group. During the 1920s Bethlen had recruited the refugees and then the young graduates into the bureaucracy, paying their salaries with foreign loans. The collapse of the international credit system in 1931 made this impossible. There were no more bureaucratic jobs to be had yet the universities continued to turn out as many graduates for Trianon Hungary as they had formerly produced for the whole of the historic kingdom, and this 'intellectual proletariat' looked to the new right for salvation.

The new right also fed on increasing anti-semitism. Only 1.7 per cent of posts in the bureaucracy were held by Jews but in the professions it was different, particularly in the leading positions of those professions. The middle classes ruined by the depression and the young graduates unable to find jobs held the Jews responsible for their plight and anti-semitism became 'a generally understood codeword for the dismantling of the existing system and substituting a radically reorganised Hungarian society'.[9] The association of Jews with the Kun régime and the steadfast refusal of the social democrats to have any truck with anti-semitism reinforced the role of the Jewish question as a propellant, driving the socially and economically frustrated to the extreme right.

Gömbös as prime minister, October 1932 to October 1936

The growth of social tensions and of anti-semitism led in October 1932 to the appointment as prime minister of 'the man who was considered most likely to pacify the masses'[10] – Gyula Gömbös. Gömbös, 'one of those musical-comedy buffoons Hungarian political life produces from time to time',[11] came of mixed Armenian and Swabian parentage – his mother hardly spoke Hungarian – and had risen to prominence as a leading spokesman of the radical and military elements at Szeged. His position in MOVE had given him considerable power and in 1928 Bethlen had taken him into the governmental tent, making him minister of war and entrusting him with the unwholesome and unpopular task of cleaning up a number of cases of corruption. Gömbös had called himself a 'national socialist' as early as 1919 and had actually assisted the Nazis in the Munich Beer Hall *putsch* in 1923, but thereafter he became more an admirer of Mussolini than of Hitler, his aping of the Duce's style earning him the nickname 'Gömbölini'.

Gömbös was a true *Rechtsradikal*. He had no time for the gentry; his cabinet was the first, Kun's excepted, not to contain a single count, and he insisted that he was not concerned where a man came from but only where he was going; he held the magnates in contempt for their association with the Habsburg system and for their protection of the Jews. He wanted to build a corporate state and attempted to persuade working class leaders to accept inclusion in one. They refused, though they gladly took the welfare benefits, including the eight-hour day, abolished in 1919, and the forty-eight hour week which he also offered. Gömbös was not an enthusiast of industrialisation and arguments that land redistribution would hinder this process were of no consequence to him; he advocated the breaking up of the large estates. Nor would he have been keen to accept foreign capital if that had any longer been available. What capital the state needed could come from a third source, which was 'to tax and expropriate the ethnic entrepreneur, whose functions would be, theoretically at least, rendered superfluous by the gradual expansion of the economic functions of the state apparatus';[12] a fifth of the large estates in Hungary were Jewish-owned and in order to nationalise this wealth the right to property would have to be subordinate to national priorities and duties, a proposition which the old right with its dedication to the sacredness of property viewed with abhorrence. Nevertheless, Gömbös' ideas had a wide appeal for the distressed and threatened Magyar because their implementation would not only accumulate wealth but create jobs.

When he came to power Gömbös issued a new programme promising radical reform but little was in fact achieved. Even after the elections of 1935, when he had a parliament more to his own liking, Gömbös' major enactments – the entails reform bill and the land settlement bill – precipitated little real change. His most important success was the conclusion in February 1934 of a trade treaty with Germany by which the Germans agreed to buy Hungarian agricultural produce and bauxite. This agreement played a considerable part in helping Hungary to pull away from the depths of the depression. Non-Jewish farmers, workers, merchants, and manufacturers became increasingly pro-German whilst the large number of Hungarian agricultural labourers who went to the Reich as seasonal workers and came back with such symbols of wealth and distinction as a bicycle, became ardent pro-Nazis. Gömbös and his ilk happily spread the word that Germany was helping ordinary Hungarians to shake free of the Jewish middleman.

The major reason for Gömbös' lack of radicalism in office was that on coming to power he had accepted certain conditions dictated by Horthy: there was to be no dissolution of parliament, so that until 1935 Gömbös had to work with an assembly tailored to Bethlen's requirements; the land question was not to be tackled until economic health had been restored; and the Jewish issue was not to be made a matter of legislation.

Gömbös did make some efforts to solidify his political authority. He insisted that Bethlen pass to him the leadership of the Government Party which he renamed the Party of National Unity. He also refused to defend Government Party deputies against attacks from Gáal's Independent Smallholders Party, a natural ally for one such as Gömbös, and in 1935 he formed an electoral pact with that faction. True to his fascist inclinations Gömbös also tried to fuse party and government, most notably in his decision that the *föispáns* should be presidents of the local branch of the Government Party; he also replaced all *föispáns* whom he deemed unreliable. Governmental control over the press was intensified and private communications were subjected to monitoring by the security forces. In the army Gömbös' radicalism was popular amongst the junior officers who also welcomed his plans for replacing the long-service army insisted upon by the treaty of Trianon with a short-term conscript force; such an army would train more men and would enhance promotion prospects for younger professional officers. His plans to replace senior officers with his own nominees were initially vetoed by the regent, but early in 1935, when twenty-two senior officers resigned following a League of Nations report into the assassination of King Alexander of Yugoslavia, Gömbös immediately installed his own nominees in their place. Horthy was furious and relations between the two, never close, remained distant until Gömbös died in Germany in October 1936.

The old versus the new right, 1936-9

Gömbös' successors until the embroilment of Hungary in the second world war were count Kálmán Darányi (October 1936 to May 1938), count Béla Imrédy (May 1938 to February 1939), count Pál Teleki (February 1939 to April 1941), and László Bárdossy (April 1941 to March 1942).

The main feature of Hungarian politics remained the contest between the old and the new right. The latter continued to grow in strength and activity with the leading mass organisation, the Arrow Cross, claiming up to 200,000 members in 1939, a year in which it secured a quarter of the vote in the national election. This was held under the electoral law of 1938 which had restored the secret ballot and made voting compulsory, though the residential qualifications still excluded large numbers of itinerant and semi-itinerant workers. The reacquisition of southern Slovakia in 1938 and Ruthenia in March 1939 aided the new right because the deputies who were co-opted to represent these areas were generally of that persuasion.

Three important concessions in 1938, the electoral law, the rearmament programme, and the first Jewish law, showed that the government sensed the growing strength of the radical right. These concessions followed pressure from the army and from Germany, whilst the cloud gathering over Czechoslovakia also pushed

91

Horthy and Darányi towards concession, since Hungary could not afford to be left out of any partition. In 1938 Imrédy, attempting to repair his régime after losing a vote of confidence because of his failure to secure all of Slovakia and Ruthenia, prepared a second Jewish bill which extended the definition of 'Jew', imposed a *numerus clausus* of 6 per cent for the professions and 12 per cent for business, and removed some previous exemptions. The bill became law in January 1939. In the following month Imrédy's opponents discovered that one of his great-grandmothers had been baptised at the age of seven. When shown evidence of his presumably Jewish ancestry Imrédy fainted and, on recovering, resigned. Shortly after the second Jewish law came the second land reform bill which promised to redistribute some 1.2 million *holds*; the land acquired was to come, in succession, from unused land, land in Jewish ownership, and the land of the magnates. In the event the confusion of the following years prevented systematic application of the act.

Despite these concessions the new right had made little real progress. The anti-Jewish legislation was mild in comparison both to that of some other states and to what was demanded by Hungarian anti-semites, and the land reform did not satisfy the smallholders or the landless. Moreover, Horthy steadfastly refused all efforts to introduce a more authoritarian political system.

The relative failure of the new right had many causes. In the first place it was not unified. Although the Arrow Cross could boast a substantial following there were other groups with whom it did not always cooperate. Nor, after the death of Gömbös, was there a clear leader. The most obvious candidate was Ferenc Szálasi, but his revolutionary credentials were compromised by his absolute insistence that he would take power only if offered it constitutionally by the regent. This the regent was unlikely to do, not least because his advisers convinced him that Szálasi intended to depose him and murder his son; in August 1938 Szálasi was imprisoned by the Imrédy government. Imrédy himself, before the disclosure of his ancestry, flirted with the ideology of the new right but few in his social circle followed him, and if the Arrow Cross was a body without a head, Imrédy's gentlemanly group was a head without a body.

Its lack of unity and the poor quality of its leadership meant that the new right could never really break the hold of the old right on the instruments of power. Although Gömbös had appointed his own *főispáns* and had placed a number of his supporters in the civil service he could not end security of tenure in the bureaucracy, and the nominees of Bethlen continued to dominate most ministries. At the apex of the system Horthy, even if his power was by no means unlimited, retained enormous influence, and he continued to regard the new right with patrician disdain and distaste.

The new right and the fascists also lacked a clear or a unified ideology. Most groups were 'hankering after distorted medieval ideas such as privileged "estates", economic autarky and a pseudo-tribal organisation of social life';[13] meanwhile Szálasi's thinking revolved around the concept of 'Hungarianism', a rambling concept which involved a 'Carpatho-Danubian Great Fatherland' as a third force in a world whose other great powers would be a German-dominated Reich to the west and a massive Japanese empire to the east.

Even the main strengthening factor of the new right, the close association with German revisionism which had secured the return of Slovakia and Ruthenia, was also a cause of weakness. German domination could threaten Hungarian national independence, particularly if Hitler made a strong bid to exploit the Swabian *Volksdeutsch* minority.

When Hitler launched his next major attack upon the Versailles system in September 1939 the new right was little stronger within the Hungarian political establishment than it had been when Gömbös died. The contest with the old right was, however, by no means over.

Non-belligerent Hungary, September 1939 to June 1941

At the outbreak of the German-Polish war the Hungarian government declared the country a 'non-belligerent', the Germans having expressed the hope that it would not opt for complete neutrality. Despite this concession to Berlin, German forces were not allowed to use Hungarian railways or to overfly Hungarian territory, whilst Polish refugees, civilian and military, were allowed into the country. In later months the Hungarian government also allowed large numbers of Polish soldiers to leave in order to join the Polish army in the west, and it let a number of prominent Poles, including Śmigły-Rydz, pass secretly through Hungary to Poland.

As well as declaring for non-belligerency in September 1939 Horthy called for an internal truce. All forces except the rabid right and the small far-left groups agreed. The prime minister, Teleki, could not resist the temptation to use this opportunity to place further restrictions upon the trade unions, to cut back on welfare benefits already conceded, and to extend government control over the press and the media. Externally, however, Hungary still refused to commit itself entirely to the German camp.

Yet the growth of German power and influence was irresistible. The fall of France and the territorial readjustments in the east brought northern Transylvania back under Hungarian control in August 1940 and if nationalist appetites for the historic kingdom had not been satiated, then it could be argued that half a territorial loaf was better than no bread. Understandably, the Germans and their Hungarian acolytes manoeuvred with increasing confidence. A series of realignments of the multifarious right-wing parties, engineered in part by the Germans, brought them a bank of thirty-three absolutely dependable MPs in the Hungarian diet, and in October 1940 Szálasi had been released from prison; he soon had 300,000 supporters. On the international front the enhanced power of Germany was seen in Hungary's accession to the tripartite pact on 20 November 1940. In 1941 it was seen internally when Hungary at last joined the rest of the continent in driving on the right-hand side of the road.

In December 1940 Teleki's government signed a pact of eternal friendship with Yugoslavia. The pact was ratified in February 1941. When the Germans decided to move against Yugoslavia in March they demanded right of passage for their troops through Hungary. Teleki argued that this would be a dishonourable breach of the February treaty but he was outweighed by a combination of his cabinet colleagues, the regent, and the general staff. On the night of 2–3 April he committed suicide. On 11 April Hungary joined in the attack upon its erstwhile treaty partner, its reward being Prekomurje, Medjimurje, and the Bačka. Hungary's association with revisionist Germany had now brought it 52.9 per cent of the territories lost at Trianon, but even these gains did not mean that Hungary's rulers joined immediately in the war against the Soviet Union. That commitment was made on 27 June after aircraft without markings had bombed Kassa (Košice) and Munkács.

6

THE BALTIC STATES, 1918–40

The emergence of the Baltic states

That the three Baltic states appeared together after the first world war, disappeared simultaneously into the Soviet Union in 1940, and reappeared with the collapse of Soviet power in 1991, was more the product of external factors than the result of internal similarities. Estonian is a member of the Finno-Ugric linguistic group rather than the Indo-European to which Latvian and Lithuanian belong. Latvia has a more divided recent past than the other two states, since its component parts, southern Livonia, Courland, and Letgale, had separate administrative lives under the tsars. Lithuania differs in that Catholicism is the creed of the majority whereas in Latvia and Estonia Lutheranism predominates. In Lithuania the pre-revolutionary landholders had been Polish or Russian, whilst in Estonia and Latvia they had been predominantly German; and in Lithuania the emancipation of the serfs did not take place until 1861 whereas in the other areas it had been enacted shortly after the Napoleonic wars.

The nationalists within the Baltic states had been encouraged by the revolution of 1905 and the reforms which followed it but it was not until after the fall of tsardom that they could take any serious steps towards self-government. Subsequently the rise of bolshevism presented a new threat, which led to the German occupation of the entire area and which, after November 1918, the allies were willing to contain by any means, including the sending of the British fleet to the Baltic and the keeping of White Russian and even German forces in the area. By 1920 these means had secured the defeat of the bolsheviks, but Lenin was prepared to acknowledge this only when the war with Poland forced him to look for security on his army's northern flank.

In sum, the bolsheviks, who wished to end Baltic independence, were too weak to do so; the White Russians, with similar ambitions, were too disorganised; the allied powers, whose actions had encouraged the idea of independence, preferred not to think too deeply about it.

It was therefore imperative for the Baltic peoples themselves to seize the initiative.[1]

95

Estonian nationalists met in the ancient university town of Tartu on 4 March 1917 to call for autonomy. The provisional government in Petrograd responded sympathetically, agreeing on 30 March to establish a single Estonian administrative unit under a commissar advised by an elected council, the Maapäev. The bolshevik revolution increased the Estonians' desire for complete separation from Russia and on 24 February 1918 the Maapäev declared full independence, electing a three-man liberation committee in which it placed executive authority. A successful propaganda campaign against both the bolsheviks and the Germans led to allied recognition of Estonia on 3 May. At the end of the war the allies were anxious that the Germans should not withdraw immediately and leave the Baltic open to the bolsheviks who had already launched a campaign to 'liberate' the area from German imperialism. The Estonians formed their own army and in the first few months of 1919, much helped by a British squadron which steamed into Tallinn, they drove out the bolsheviks. By this time the western allies were tiring of their widespread responsibilities and the Russo–Polish war had mobilised bolshevik power, so that it was not until 2 February 1920 that the Estonians were able to negotiate a final peace treaty in which Lenin's government recognised their full independence. *De jure* allied recognition followed on 21 January 1921 and in September 1922 Estonia was admitted to the League of Nations.

March 1917 saw the establishment of a Latvian provisional council representing southern Livonia, Courland, and Letgale. This was recognised by the provisional government in Petrograd but not by rival left-wing groups in Latvia itself. Latvia's internal political spectrum was much more fragmented than those in Estonia or Lithuania because Latvia's administrative history was more divided, because there was a much larger Russian minority in the Latvian areas, and because there was a stronger industrial element in the economy and therefore a more numerous working class and a much more powerful socialist lobby which was still dazzled by bolshevik success; the Latvian riflemen formed an élite section of the revolutionary armies. An all-Latvian conference in Riga in August 1917 decided to declare independence as soon as the Germans took the city, which they did early in the following month. Splits continued, however, with rival Latvian organisations in Petrograd and Riga, until in November 1918, a new, unified Latvian people's council was established in the Latvian capital. The council declared independence on 18 November 1918 and appointed Kārlis Ulmanis as president. This in turn signalled a bolshevik assault and the declaration in Moscow on 14 December of a Soviet Republic of Latvia. A further complication in Latvia was that it had been a major theatre of operations for the German army and, given the allied desire for a defensive force against the bolsheviks, a German military presence was maintained, but primarily in the form of a number of Freikorps rather than the regular army. The Freikorps joined with and dominated the White Russian forces also operating in Latvia against the bolsheviks. The Freikorps were aided by the Landwehr, or home defence force, formed by the local German population. Given the number and variety of political and military forces in the area, there was a danger of complete disintegration in Latvia and for this reason the allies again used the British fleet, this time to chase the White Russians out of Riga in the autumn of 1919. By August 1920 sufficient order had been restored for a peace between the Latvians and the bolsheviks to be signed in Riga. Allied recognition and admittance to the League of Nations were simultaneous with those of Estonia.

Because Lithuania had been under German occupation since 1915 it was unable to respond to the Russian revolution as rapidly or as effectively as Estonia or Latvia. But the effect of that revolution was felt. In June 1917 a Lithuanian council was established and in September a conference in Vilnius of delegates from all over Lithuania elected a Lithuanian provisional council, or Taryba, and chose as its president a prominent lawyer, Antanas Smetona. In March 1918 the German emperor accepted the notion of an independent Lithuanian state and with Germany's defeat in November the Taryba declared itself a constituent assembly, devised an extremely liberal constitution, and nominated as president Augustinas Voldemaras, a former lecturer at Perm university in Russia. In fact regular political life in Lithuania, as in the other Baltic states, could not begin until the country had been cleared of bolshevik and White Russian forces. This was achieved in the spring of 1920 and by June of that year a constituent assembly had agreed a provisional constitution. It was confirmed in 1922 when the Taryba was replaced by an elected parliament. In July 1920 a peace treaty with the bolsheviks had been signed in Moscow. The treaty recognised Lithuania's independence and territorial integrity and it accepted Lithuania's claim upon Vilnius. The Poles, of course, did not. After their forces had seized the city in October 1920, Lithuania declared a 'state of war' with Poland and sealed the borders so effectively that even the postal services had to take a roundabout route. The Lithuanian capital was moved to Kaunus. Lithuania itself made an adjustment to its borders on 10 January 1923; when French forces began their occupation of the Ruhr, the Lithuanians took possession of the port and surrounding district of Memel (Klaipeda) which until then had been administered as an allied condominium. Lithuanian sovereignty over the area was recognised under a convention of 8 May 1924.

Domestic political affairs: Estonia

Together with the other two Baltic states Estonia gave itself an exceedingly democratic franchise based upon universal, equal, secret, and proportional voting. Again in conformity with Latvia and Lithuania, Estonia's was a unicameral legislature but Estonia went even further along this path by vesting all power in its parliament, the Riigikogu; the head of the cabinet was also to be the head of state.

The first major legislation enacted by this egalitarian assembly, as in Latvia and Lithuania, was a far reaching programme of land redistribution. As elsewhere in eastern Europe this process served three purposes. It moved towards greater social justice, it deprived pro-bolsheviks of useful propaganda, and it destroyed the former landowning political élite which in this case had been German and Russian. Before the revolution 58 per cent of land in Estonia had been the property of large estate-owners but the expropriation law of 10 October 1919 transformed this picture. Over a thousand estates, 96.6 per cent of the total number, were broken up and the land redistributed to small farmers or the landless agricultural labourers. The latter fell from 65 per cent of the population before liberation to only 13 per cent in 1939, whilst the reform more than doubled the number of land-holders from 51,000 to 107,000. Most of the holdings created by the reform were under twenty hectares and were scarcely viable. Compensation of about 3 per cent of the value of confiscated estates was eventually agreed in 1926 but it was to be paid in government bonds rather than in cash and there was to be no payment for expropriated forest land. Priority in the redistribution of property was to go, as in most other states in eastern Europe, to army veterans.

The importance of the land reform as a piece of social engineering helped the agrarian party, the Farmers' Union, to become the dominant political force and its leader, Konstantin Päts, the most prominent of national figures. The open franchise, proportional representation, and a paucity of restrictions on the formation of political associations led to a multiplicity of parties and this, together with the vast powers vested in parliament, caused instability in government. Between 1919 and 1934 Estonia had twenty-one different administrations, the average life of a cabinet being eight months and twenty days. The agrarians led ten of those cabinets. Amongst the other parties, national liberal groups held the centre ground and the non-marxist socialists commanded the left; in 1925 the social democrats and the independent socialists joined to form the Socialist Workers' Party.

Despite the general freedom of political association, the Communist Party was banned because it was asserted, rightly, that the party took orders from the Moscow-dominated Comintern. In January 1924, in the wake of communist activities in Bulgaria and Germany, the Estonian government clamped down on known communist cells but to little effect; the party remained active, especially amongst the dock workers of Tallinn and in the Russian ethnic minority near the border. In November 1924 an attempt to spring some communist detainees from gaol led to their being tried, convicted, and in some cases sentenced to death; one trade union leader was executed on 15 November. This provoked an attempted seizure of power by the communists on 1 December. The *putsch* lasted only a few hours, cost twenty-one lives, and evoked almost no support amongst the workers or soldiers.

The *putsch* encouraged a drift to the right, already begun as a result of doubts about the liberal constitution. In 1926 some restriction was placed on the right to form political parties through a law which required them to put down a deposit during a general election and which made that deposit forfeit if the party failed to gain more than two seats. This did cause some decrease in the number of factions contesting for political power but the total still remained high enough to deprive them of almost any ideological significance. This was a further impetus to move to the right, where the demand for a much stronger executive fitted well with the fascist notions popular in Europe since 1923. In Estonia two national referenda were called by the established parties but neither produced the requisite majority for constitutional change. The Freedom Fighters, an extreme right-wing group, took up the cause with relish. In October 1933, after foreign economic influence had forced Estonia into a 35 per cent devaluation, a third referendum, held amidst much violence, produced a majority for change. A new constitution was drawn up, creating the office of president; it became effective in January 1934. The presidential, parliamentary, and local elections, which were held in the same month, again amidst great violence, made Päts president but also produced significant gains for the Freedom Fighters who now had control of the three most important towns, Tallinn, Tartu, and Narva. On 12 March 1934 Päts, fearing a fascist takeover, appointed general Johan Laidoner, a hero of the war against the bolsheviks, commander in chief of the army with a brief to maintain order. The Freedom Fighters were disbanded and parliament was prorogued, and in February 1935 existing political parties were dissolved and a new corporate body, the National Association (*Isamaaliit*), was formed. Constitutional amendments to align political procedures with authoritarian principles were introduced and in February 1936 Päts staged a plebiscite to confirm the changes and his own assumption of power. Further constitutional reform in 1938 introduced a bicameral parliament but there was little dilution of the tough régime which Päts and Laidoner had established in their pre-emptive coup. Their rule was not one of terror but they governed by decree, enjoyed the support of a para-military organisation, the *Kaitseliit* (defence league), had an efficient secret police, and took tough action against opponents such as the leader of the centrist People's Party, Jaan Tõnisson.

The 1930s also saw a step back from the admirably tolerant policies that the Estonian republic had adopted towards its minorities. The largest minority was the Russian, forming 12.4 per cent of the population in 1922 and 11.9 per cent in 1934; the other important groups were the Germans, 1.7 per cent and 1.5 per cent in the same years, and the Jews, 0.4 per cent in both 1922 and 1934. Three-quarters of the population were Lutheran Protestants, 19 per cent were Orthodox. The constitution of 1920 allowed the minorities generous rights and a law of 1925, which was in some measure an effort to preserve unity after the *putsch* of the preceding December, gave them the right to virtual autonomy in cultural affairs. The Germans took immediate advantage of the new law and the Jewish community followed suit in 1926. With the 1925 legislation, 'the Estonian government was able to claim, with every justification, that it had found an exemplary solution to the problem of the minorities'.[2] The fact that the minorities did not form a large parliamentary presence in the pre-coup years may suggest that they did not feel any great threat to their established way of life. On the other hand, the docility of the Germans may have indicated more resignation than contentment, since they did have some cause for complaint. In 1927 the Estonian government in effect nationalised the German cathedral in Tallinn and in the 1930s the pressures grew appreciably, despite, or perhaps because of, the rise of strident nationalism in Germany. English was made the first foreign language in Estonian schools, German names could no longer be used for streets, and legislation in 1935 requiring the use of Estonian for the transaction of government business made it much more difficult for Estonian Germans to follow careers in the civil service or the army. Despite these restrictions, however, Estonia's record in the treatment of minorities is generally regarded as one of the best in eastern Europe in the inter-war period.

Domestic political affairs: Latvia

Latvia's constitution created an electoral system as liberal as that in Estonia and the similarities continued when the Latvian assembly made agrarian reform its first major item of legislation. Here the former landowners were allowed to retain up to fifty hectares of land but, by a parliamentary decision of 1924, they were not to be given compensation. Some 1,300 estates were broken up and redistributed; a total of 1.7 million hectares changed hands, creating approximately a quarter of a million new holdings, none of which was larger than twenty-five hectares. As in Estonia veterans were given priority in the allocation of redistributed land.

In political terms there was considerable instability. Between 1919 and 1934 Latvia had eighteen separate governments and thirty-nine different parties were represented at one time or another in the all-powerful saeima or parliament. There was in fact one political party for every 45,000 of the population, this proliferation of political groupings being much helped by the regulation that only one hundred signatures were needed for a political party to be registered and therefore entitled to some government financial support. The most powerful party in the 1920s was the agrarian and essentially conservative Peasants' League; the three most important centre parties came together in 1922 to form the Democratic Centre, whilst on the left the Social Democratic Party retained its marxist ideology without adopting the leninist, totalitarian methods of its sister party to the east.

The rise of the political right in Latvia was simultaneous with that in Estonia. Its main representative body was more strident than the Freedom Fighters. The Thunder Cross, a reborn version of the outlawed Fire Cross, adopted overt Nazi methods and policies but managed to add even to their catalogue of antipathies by being anti-German too. In October 1933 the agrarians proposed a series of constitutional reforms which, as in Estonia, were intended to strengthen the executive. Despite agrarian assurances that destabilisation would be resisted, no matter from which quarter it threatened, the socialists feared that they would be the prime target of any such move. Their fears seemed confirmed in November when seven communist deputies were arrested for revolutionary intentions, whereas the equally subversive Thunder Cross remained untouched. By the spring of the following year political unrest, combined with and to a degree resultant upon the world economic crisis, forced President Ulmanis to take action. On 15–16 May he staged a *coup d'état*. He banned both the Communist Party and the Thunder Cross before deciding to clear the slate completely, proscribing all parties, including his own. Thereafter Ulmanis ruled through the bureaucracy, the army, and the para-military *Aizsargi* (defence league). He did not trouble himself to secure the endorsement of a plebiscite.

In Latvia the right made much of the minority question. Of the minority groups the Russians were again the largest, forming 7.8 per cent of the population in 1920 and 10.6 per cent in 1935. In the same years the Germans accounted for 3.6 per cent and 3.2 per cent of the total, the Belorussians constituted 3.4 per cent and 2.5 per cent of the population, other Slavs made up 4.7 per cent and 1.4 per cent, the Lithuanians 1.6 per cent and 1.2 per cent, and the Jews 5.2 per cent and 4.8 per cent. A minority which was religious rather than ethnic was to be found in the Catholics of Letgale who made up 22.6 per cent of the population in 1925 and 24.5 per cent in 1935.

Minorities did not have the right to form autonomous cultural communities but they did have control over their own schools. By the late 1920s, however, they were the object of growing right-wing hostility. A number of German and other churches were taken over by the Latvians; the German agrarian association was closed, its funds being merged into those of the Latvian chamber of agriculture, and in 1935 the guilds, many of which were of medieval origin, were closed down and their property, which included many ancient churches and historic buildings, was nationalised under the so-called new year laws. These laws also made it obligatory to use Latvian names for streets and within the bureaucracy.

Domestic political affairs: Lithuania

Lithuania's constitution and its land legislation were delayed by the emergency over Vilnius but the political system, when established firmly, conformed to the general Baltic pattern of open franchises and over-powerful parliaments.

The land law of 29 March 1922 appeared less radical than those of Estonia and Latvia. The maximum holding allowed was 150 hectares, rather than the 80 contained in the original proposal. Some compensation was to be paid, though not to Russian landowners, most of whom had come into possession of their property when it was confiscated from local noblemen after the rising of 1863. The land reform also broke up the village commune system which had been another Russian importation. Many peasant beneficiaries of the redistribution, however, failed to make a living from their land and left for the towns or, if they could squeeze in under the quota regulations, for north America.

The relative moderation of the land act was a reflection of Lithuania's Catholicism; it had been the christian democrats who had rejected the more radical, original bill and it was they, the political arm of the Peasants' League, who dominated the Lithuanian parliament, the seimas, in the early 1920s. The main group on the left was the Social Democratic Party, whilst the populist Party of the People's Socialists was the chief centre party. A distinct feature of the Lithuanian political scene in the early 1920s was that there were always ministers who took special responsibility for the Belorussian and the Jewish minorities. The Jews formed 7.3 per cent of the population, the Russians c. 9 per cent and the Poles 3.2 per cent.

Lithuania enjoyed little more governmental stability than its Baltic companions to the north or its Polish enemy to the south, having eleven cabinets between November 1918 and December 1926. In 1925 the Polish concordat with the Vatican included a clause by which the latter recognised Polish sovereignty over Vilnius. This severely damaged the prestige of the christian democrats, who lost their parliamentary majority in the May of the following year, as a result of which a coalition government of the Party of the People's Socialists and the Social Democrats was formed. The new government agreed in September 1926 to establish diplomatic relations and to sign a non-aggression pact with the USSR, and to release a number of communist prisoners. This frightened the right, especially the vociferous Nationalist Party which joined with discontented elements in the army to stage a coup on 16–17 December 1926. Smetona was installed as president and Voldemaras as prime minister.

The new government dissolved parliament and in May 1928 introduced a new constitution. The presidency was given much more extensive powers, whilst those of the parliament were so reduced that the assembly never convened. The government preferred instead to enact decrees which it enforced through the army, the bureaucracy, and its own Nationalist Party organisations.

Authoritarianism did not bring stability. The growing power of the Nationalist Party worried many Lithuanians, not least the christian democrats, whilst Smetona found it increasingly difficult to work with Voldemaras who was moving steadily to the right and becoming increasingly closely associated with the Iron Wolves, an organisation with a very close resemblance to fascism. In April 1929 Voldemaras took a heavy hand to the social democrats on account of the activity of their exiled supporters in Vilnius, and his actions became more extreme after an attempt on his own life in May. In September Smetona sacked him and instituted a virtual personal rule. He enacted further constitutional reforms to bolster his own power and imprisoned a number of his opponents, including Voldemaras who was sent to gaol in 1934. In 1935 Smetona banned all political parties except his own, the nationalists, and in 1938 introduced yet another constitution, Lithuania's sixth, which separated church and state, repealed minority legislation passed in 1920, and enhanced yet more his own powers.

Smetona had made his political career as the creator and defender of the Lithuanian nation state. In the late 1930s he suffered a series of very damaging reverses. In March 1938, after a minor frontier incident, the Poles issued a forty-eight hour ultimatum that Lithuania end the 'state of war' with Poland, establish diplomatic relations, and open the border. Lithuania had no choice but to accept.

In March 1939 came a much more serious blow. Hitler, immediately after his success in annexing Bohemia and Moravia, demanded that Lithuania relinquish Memel. A state which could not resist Poland could not withstand Hitler and on 22 March the German fleet steamed into Memel with the Führer aboard its flagship. Smetona was forced to reconstruct the government and to bring back into it representatives of the christian democrats and the populists; he also reinstated Voldemaras whom he had to release from gaol. Smetona was to remain at the helm until the liquidation of Baltic independence in June 1940.

The Baltic states in the international context

It was a considerable achievement of the Baltic states that despite their political difficulties and disappointments they managed to secure a degree of economic independence and viability. The first world war and the war against the bolsheviks had wreaked havoc but even more difficult to overcome was the dissolution of existing institutions, especially the banks, and the disruption of established patterns of economic activity, above all trade with Russia. The Germans stepped into the banking void but nothing could save the many huge factories which in pre-liberation days had served the Russian market. By the late 1920s some trade with Russia had been re-established. The Soviet Union signed commercial agreements with Estonia and Latvia in 1927 and Lithuania in 1931. Trade with other states, particularly Britain and Germany, grew more rapidly. Britain pressed the Baltic states to buy defined proportions of their coal imports from the United Kingdom and in return imported furs and agricultural produce, particularly butter, flax, and bacon. For Germany too the Baltic states were a source of food and agricultural products and after 1935 up to half of the output of Estonia's developing oil-shale fields was bought for the German navy.

Partly because they were not heavily encumbered by debt, the Baltic states weathered the world depression of the early 1930s with less pain than many other areas. Whilst world industrial output declined by 7 per cent between 1929 and 1938, that in Estonia increased by 45 per cent; in Latvia industrial enterprises grew in number from 1,430 in 1920 to 5,717 in 1937, the workers in them increasing from 61,000 to 205,000 in the same period, with a 27.7 per cent increase from 1935 to 1939 when labour was so scarce that it had to be imported from Poland. Many of the enterprises in Latvia, as in Estonia and Lithuania, processed primary products: sugar-beet refineries, distilleries making alcohol from potatoes, and furniture manufactories formed a substantial part of industrial activity.

Industrial and agricultural activities were helped by the cooperatives which were widespread and efficient in all three states. In 1939 Latvia had 225 consumer cooperatives and 244 for dairy farmers. In Lithuania *Maistas*, a huge, modern packing combine, was an important factor in promoting the production and export of meat. The cooperatives were largely responsible for the fact that

Lithuania produced 10 per cent more food than it needed; Denmark's excess was only 6 per cent.

Another contribution to economic success and social stability was the widely developed system of social welfare found in the Baltic states, and more particularly in Estonia and Latvia. In labour legislation the Baltic states were the equal of the Scandinavian. The eight-hour day for factory workers was widely respected, as were laws forbidding the employment of children. Estonia had one university student for every 332 inhabitants, the highest ratio in the world, whilst the Latvians insisted their social insurance schemes were second only to those of New Zealand.

Social security did not provide international security. When the Baltic states first emerged most would have preferred a security system based upon a Baltic-Scandinavian axis. In the very early 1920s there were efforts to build such a bloc. A conference in Helsinki in the first month of the decade was attended by the three Baltic states together with Finland and Poland. But after the Polish seizure of Vilnius any combination including both Poland and Lithuania was impossible, whilst Estonia and Latvia did not wish to become too involved with Lithuania lest they be forced to accept obligations which would make it imposs-ible for them to look towards Poland as a balance to any threat from the east. The Scandinavian states, meanwhile, made plain their reluctance to join any grouping which might bring entanglement with a great power, as a Baltic-Scandinavian alliance surely would. A non-aggression pact was signed in 1922 by Poland, Finland, Latvia, and Estonia but it had little effect and by 1925 was moribund. A more encouraging development was the Latvian-Estonian agree-ment of 1923 which settled disputes over the border town of Valga, provided for increased trade, and committed the two states to a ten-year defence pact.

In December 1927 the Vilnius problem became acute. The new right-wing administration in Lithuania had closed a number of Polish schools, to which the Poles replied with equal vigour by dismantling the Lithuanian school system in Poland. The matter was taken to the council of the League of Nations, where Piłsudski browbeat Voldemaras into agreeing a 'truce' with Poland, though the state of war was not ended; conferences at Königsberg in May and November 1928 likewise did little to settle this and other issues still outstanding between the two countries.

In the late 1920s and early 1930s diplomatic activity was dominated by the Soviet Union's search for a series of bilateral agreements which would guarantee its western borders and leave it free to meet any Japanese encroachment in the far east. The trade agreements with the Baltic states helped in this direction. So too did the Litvinov protocol of 9 February 1929, which was signed by the USSR, the Baltic states, and Romania, and the Soviet-Finnish and Soviet-Polish non-aggression pacts which were signed in July 1932. Similar agreements had been signed with Latvia and Estonia in February and May of the same year and, together with the Soviet-Lithuanian accord of 1926, provided the Soviets with links with all of their western neighbours.

This *pax sovietica* was wrecked by the Polish-German non-aggression treaty of January 1934. Poland, it seemed, had a free hand in the east. In September 1934 an agreement between the Baltic states was signed in Geneva providing for regular consultative meetings over the next ten years. The so-called Baltic *entente* did not have much real effect. It could seldom overcome internal dissonances. Estonia and Latvia abandoned plans for a customs union after an Estonian-Finnish trade treaty in 1937 caused serious commercial disagreements between Tallinn and Riga; and plans for a joint academy of sciences were dropped after a furious row between the same countries over an Estonian professor's publications on Latvian folklore. Relations between Lithuania and the other two states were even more distant, and neither Estonia nor Latvia reacted to the Polish ultimatum to Kaunus in 1938. This lack of cohesion was a tragedy in that the Baltic states could together muster armies of about half a million which, even if poorly equipped could still 'present quite an obstacle to an aggressor, especially if they were supported by a great power'.[3]

The Soviet Union had reacted to the German-Polish pact and to the advent of Hitler by trying to renew its agreements with its western neighbours and by signing treaties with France and Czechoslovakia in 1935. The Baltic states would have preferred a multi-lateral agreement and in any case they did not welcome Soviet approaches to Paris and Prague; the Baltic states were developing economic links with Germany which they did not want to jeopardise by alignment with Germany's presumed enemies.

Meanwhile, it was assumed that, since there was no mention of the Baltic states either in the Anglo-German naval agreement of 1935 or in the British announcement on 18 April 1939 of guarantees to Romania, the region had been left to Moscow and Berlin to do with as they wished. Since the German seizure of Memel the USSR had been pressing upon the Baltic states that it had a special interest in their independence, but for Latvia and Estonia there was more comfort in the non-aggression pacts offered by Germany and signed in June 1939. The pacts were designed to strengthen those states' neutrality, to keep them out of any western-Soviet bid to encircle Germany, and to provide a barrier against any attempted Soviet intervention in the war Berlin was planning against Poland.

These agreements were superseded by the Nazi-Soviet pact of August 1939 and the secret division of the Baltic into German and Soviet spheres of interest. In the short run the partition of Poland brought Vilnius back to Lithuania but Soviet pressure was being brought to bear further north. On 18 September 1939 a Polish submarine which had sought sanctuary in Tallinn and which had been impounded according to international law, escaped and made its way to Britain. The Soviets declared that Estonia could not control its coastline and that the Soviet navy must therefore do the job for it. Soviet ships entered Estonian territorial waters and Soviet planes its airspace. By 28 September the Estonians had been bludgeoned into signing an alliance with Moscow which allowed the

Soviets to man Estonian military bases and to establish separate Soviet garrisons in Estonia.

Their Baltic bases served the Soviets well in the war they launched against Finland in November. The Baltic states now did not even dare to do anything but abstain in the League of Nations when it voted to expel the USSR for the attack on Finland. The changes in the international scene after September 1939 had forced the Baltic states into diplomatic servility to the USSR; these changes also brought about unprecedented cooperation between the Baltic states, which at the same time increased their trading links with Germany in an attempt to escape growing Soviet aggression. It was in vain. They had been allotted to Stalin under the Nazi-Soviet pact's secret protocol and after Hitler had eliminated France Stalin took his share of the loot.

In June 1940 Moscow exerted enormous pressure on Lithuania over the arrest of a Red Army soldier by the Lithuanians and over an alleged secret treaty between Lithuania and Latvia. On 15 June the Soviets demanded the reconstruction of the Lithuanian government under the virtual supervision of the Soviet envoy, and the occupation by the Red Army of all points of strategic importance. Smetona fled; on 16 June the Red Army moved into Lithuania and on the following day into Latvia and Estonia which had been presented with similar demands. The troops and communist officials arrived in time to prepare what Tass was pleased to call the 'spontaneous uprising of the working peoples' which took place on 21 June and led in July to the formation of new governments on a popular front basis; each one had a communist as the minister of the interior. Elections were then held on franchises unconstitutionally decreed by the new governments and with all candidates being vetted by the communists. After the elections communist-inspired demonstrations were staged, economic installations were nationalised, and on 1 August Baltic parliamentary delegates begged a meeting of the Supreme Soviet to admit their states to the Soviet Union.

Treaties of incorporation, implicit in the enforced military agreements of the previous year, were signed by Estonia on 28 September, by Latvia on 5 October, and by Lithuania on 10 October. The Baltic states had ceased to exist and were not to reappear for almost half a century.

7

ROMANIA, 1918–41

The new Romania: problems of integration

That victorious Romania was bordered by two defeated states, Hungary and Bulgaria, and two untouchables, Hungary and Russia, meant that in territorial terms it was amongst the most favoured of the post-war states. By means of the peace treaties it doubled in size and population, acquiring the Banat and Transylvania from Hungary, northern Bukovina from Austria, and Bessarabia (eastern Moldavia or Moldova) from Russia, whilst Romanian possession of the southern Dobrudja, acquired from Bulgaria in 1913, was confirmed: greater Romania was the second largest state in eastern Europe.

This vast increase in size inevitably affected the political life of Romania between the wars. There were the familiar problems of integration. The economic systems of the new territories had evolved in different conditions to those of the original kingdom, the regat. Their railway networks were focused upon the former Hungarian, Austrian and Russian systems; their trading links were with areas not connected commercially to the regat; their monetary systems and legal codes were different, as were their tax structures. Romania tackled these difficulties in much the same way as Poland, Czechoslovakia, and Yugoslavia. By 1923 all railways in greater Romania were using the same gauge; a common currency, the Romanian *lei*, had been imposed; and measures were in hand to harmonise the various legal systems. Forceful steps had also been taken to break old trading relationships and channel exports from the new territories in the direction required by the rulers in Bucharest.

It was much less easy to integrate the populations of the new territories. The regat had been a Romanian nation state in which the Romanians comprised 92 per cent of the population. Greater Romania was a state of nationalities in which the Romanians formed only 70 per cent of the total. Each of the new territories contained sizeable numbers of non-Romanians. In the Dobrudja there were Bulgarians, Tatars, Turks, and Gypsies; Bessarabia had large numbers of Ukrainians as well as communities of Bulgarians, Gypsies, Jews, and Gagauze or Turkish-speaking Christians; Jews, Germans, Ukrainians, and Gypsies were also to be found in the Bukovina; Transylvania was populated by Hungarians, the Hun-

107

garian-speaking but distinct Szekelers, Jews, Germans, and Gypsies; and in the Banat was to be found a mix of nationalities as confusing and varied as anywhere in Europe; here a traveller in the 1930s recorded even French-speaking communities. All of the new territories also contained large Romanian elements but this did not mean that they were ready to accept unconditionally their inclusion in the Romanian state. The Romanians of Transylvania were culturally sophisticated and politically experienced, having cut their political teeth on the extremely tough nut of Magyar parliamentary politics. The Transylvanian Romanians were also accustomed, as were those of the Bukovina, to standards of political behaviour and levels of administrative efficiency which were not traditionally part of public life in the regat. Tension between Romanian and non-Romanian was to be expected and was constant, but at times clashes between the Romanians of the regat and those of the new territories were of equal if not of greater political importance.

The fears of the new Romanians had been clearly expressed in 1918. In December the Transylvanian Romanians, in congress at Alba Iulia, had accepted union with the regat on condition that they be allowed civil liberties, universal suffrage, and a sizeable measure of local autonomy. Similar demands had already been made by the Romanian activists in Bessarabia who in December 1917 had declared their region an autonomous component of Romania; they had also added land redistribution to their list of demands.

The allies were alive to the dangers of Romania's political record and insisted that greater Romania have 'a purely democratic régime in all branches of public life'. The rulers of the regat were not so keen. Romania's firm tradition of francophilia dictated a strongly centralised system and the political brokers of Bucharest, long acclimatised to using the administrative machine for paying for services rendered, were not anxious to forgo the large opportunities for patronage and influence which the new territories offered. Besides, they argued, Romania must be compensated for the losses and sufferings of the war; the new lands, Bessarabia excluded, had been enemy territory and must therefore contribute towards this compensation. If this went against allied inclinations the Romanians were in the fortunate position of being able to plead the need for a strong, centralised Romania to meet the bolshevist challenges from Russia and Hungary. Many diplomatic blind eyes were thus turned towards Romania in the immediate post-war period with the result that the Romanians in general, and the regateani in particular, established privileged positions in public administration, the banks, and so on. This was another cause of tension between the centre and the periphery within the ranks of the dominant ethnic group. It also meant that, with the exception of the Germans who were relatively well-treated, the non-Romanians, or 'foreigners' as they were frequently and contemptuously called, lived in a state of permanent alienation. In 1940 this was an important, though not the only, cause for the dismemberment of greater Romania.

The political crisis of 1918–22

The pre-1914 political duopoly of the conservative and liberal parties had been shattered by the first world war. The conservatives, pro-German and pro-landlord, lost their *raison d'être* with the defeat of Germany and the enactment of land reform in 1919. At the same time, the liberals were discredited as far as the peasant mass of the population was concerned by their anti-peasant fiscal policies. The political faction wishing to articulate peasant feelings was the Peasant Party, founded immediately after the first world war. A small number of extremists argued that industrialisation in Romania was pointless because it could never catch up with states already geared to industrial production, and that Romania should therefore concentrate on home-based, peasant craft industries which could satisfy the limited demands of a simple, peasant society. The Peasant Party leader, Ion Mihalache, did not go this far. Romania, he urged, with its grain and oil exports, could not cut itself off from the world and should concentrate on even more equality in the distribution of land, on strengthening the weak cooperative movement in the countryside, and on such industrialisation as benefited the peasant. The Peasant Party, however, suffered from a certain degree of doctrinal instability. It never lived up to the radicalism of its 1921 programme; its willing-ness to encourage the efficient producer verged on support for the unpopular kulak; and its nebulous notions such as 'the Romanian spirit' or 'the Romanian genius', meant that in times of great instability or upheaval it was near the precipice dividing a nationalist from a fascist party.

Nationalism remained the main platform of the Transylvanian Nationalist Party which also became a strong force in the immediate post-war political arena. Led by Alexandru Vaida Voevod and Iuliu Maniu, the nationalists were a mature, organised and skilful force steeled in the tough crucible of Magyar politics, and important in that they united in one party the peasantry, the merchants, and the intelligentsia.

Other Romanian parties were numerous and fluid, frequently changing their composition, their names, their leaders, and their allegiances. The People's Party of general Alexandru Averescu provided a refuge for many of those who had previously felt most at home in the conservative camp. Nicolae Iorga's National Democratic Party claimed to be a non-class party dedicated to recompensing those who had suffered during the war, though it was also held together by a strong tinge of anti-semitism. An off-shoot of Iorga's party, the National Christian Defence League, concentrated upon anti-semitism and was led by professor Cuza of Iaşi whose main concern was the alleged Jewish threat to the purity of Christian virgins. It was in Cuza's ranks that Corneliu Zelia Codreanu began his egregious career.

In Romania the left was weak. The bolshevik threat, associated as it was with Romania's chief national enemies, was a major cause for this weakness, which was exhibited starkly in 1919–20 when an attempted general strike was suppressed with relative ease.

The first general election held in post-war Romania produced a majority in favour of the Peasant Party and the Transylvanian nationalists. A government was formed by the Peasant Party, but this was not to the liking of the Romanian political establishment headed by King Ferdinand. He, like his liberal friends, feared that the victorious parties would be too indulgent of the non-Romanians and would comply too readily with the dictates of the minority protection treaties. This latter factor could lead to too much foreign meddling in Romania, as, perhaps, could the two parties' readiness to admit foreign capital into the country. It was not in this way that a powerful greater Romania, capable of keeping the bolsheviks in check, would be fashioned and preserved. In May 1920, the peasants were elbowed aside in what was essentially a royal *coup d'état* with the reins of government being handed to general Averescu. Ferdinand was unable to appoint the purely liberal cabinet which he would have preferred; the election results could not be quite so cavalierly disregarded and in any case the liberals had had serious confrontations with the allies over the peace terms. Furthermore, Averescu could be asked to perform a necessary task ideologically unpalatable to the liberals: the redistribution of landed estates in the new territories. Averescu was also entrusted with the containment of the leftist agitation which was manifested in the attempted general strike of 1919–20 and in the Red Army's advance into Poland in the spring of 1920. In December 1920 a bomb in the Romanian senate showed that the threat had not been entirely dispersed, and throughout 1921 Averescu remained at the helm, to be replaced in January 1922 by the liberal leader, Ion Brătianu. Romania, it seemed, had returned to its traditional political life.

Romania in the 1920s

The liberals set about devising a new constitution which, they said, was made necessary by the acquisition of the new territories. It was introduced in 1923 and reaffirmed the centralist tradition of the regat, declaring Romania to be a 'unitary and indivisible state'. Centralisation was intensified in 1925 when the country was divided into seventy-one *préfectures*, each one headed by an official appointed in Bucharest rather than elected locally. The 1923 constitution retained the bicameral legislature but the powers of the crown were strengthened and the upper house was made more responsible to influence by the bureaucracy. Direct male suffrage was introduced but individual liberties, particularly the right of association in trade unions, were hedged; in 1924 the Romanian Communist Party was banned and many of its activists arrested. In 1923 the political system had been moved more to the right by a constitutional amendment according to which any party receiving 40 per cent of the votes in a general election was to have half the seats in the lower house of parliament, the other half being distributed according to the number of votes cast for all parties, including that which had achieved the 40 per cent premium. This change was copied from Italy and did something to contain the dangers of party parcellisation which afflicted Poland, but, given the ease with which voting could be fixed, this placed a powerful weapon in the hands of an administration and it continued to be the usual practice for a government to go to the country after it had been appointed rather than before; in what has been described as 'mimic democracy',[1] elections, as in many other countries, were thus devices by which governments were confirmed in power rather than a means for deciding whom the electorate wished to see in office.

In deciding the latter the crown still played an influential role and in 1926 fears that the heir to the throne, Prince Carol, was anti-liberal led to an arrangement by which he renounced his right to the succession. The pretext for this was his liaison with Madame Elena Lupescu, but as public morality in Romania was notoriously relaxed, few were deceived into believing that the exclusion bill was anything but a political manoeuvre.

In economic terms the constitution of 1923 had reflected liberal attitudes to foreign influences, since it ruled that only Romanian citizens were to own land in Romania and that the subsoil and therefore the mineral wealth of the country were to be nationalised. In office the liberals instituted a policy of severe financial retrenchment in order to stabilise the currency because, despite their distaste for foreign capital, a British loan was essential if the government were to balance its books. With the exception of the loan, however, the liberals stuck to their strategy of using internal resources to finance industrialisation. Export levies or even prohibitions were imposed. Their purpose was in part to break the established trading patterns of the new territories but also to provide home manufacturers with abundant supplies of cheap food and raw materials. Where export levies were imposed they had to be paid in convertible currency and this extra source of taxation was intended to finance Romanian industrialisation. Tariffs were raised to protect home producers and to stimulate domestic manufacturing; by 1927 Romania was one of the most protectionist states in Europe. Foreign influences within the economy were limited by legislation which restricted the share of foreign capital in any Romanian concern to 40 per cent of the total invested, whilst three-quarters of the employees and two-thirds of the directors had to be Romanian.

The pressures which export levies, tariffs, and other economic measures placed upon the peasants did nothing to increase the popularity of the liberals in the Romanian countryside, and in March 1926 Brătianu stepped aside to allow Averescu to lead the government. He in turn was replaced in January 1927 by Vintile Brătianu. But the liberals' eight-year domination of Romanian politics was coming to an end and not even the usual means of electoral control could contain rising resentment. The peasants complained not only of tariffs and taxation but also of poor credit facilities, ineffective representation of peasant interests in the new chambers of agriculture established in 1926, and corrupt administration; their grievances were sharpened by poor harvests in 1927 and 1928.

Most of these complaints were familiar ones, but after 1926 the peasants had a new and much more powerful political vehicle for the expression of such complaints. In 1926 the Romanian Peasant Party had joined with the Transylvanian Nationalist Party to form the National Peasant Party (NPP) under the leadership of Maniu. By May 1928 the NPP could attract 60–100,000 supporters to a rally in Alba Iulia, a rally which ended with calls for a national peasant parliament and attempts to stage a Mussolini-style march on Bucharest; and although the rally ended with a touch of farce – the march on Bucharest fizzled out and the organisers had to ask the government to provide free rail transport to take many of the peasants home – the ability of the NPP to ignite peasant passions was no longer in doubt.

As the NPP increased in strength the liberals weakened. The fear of bolshevism which had sustained their rule early in the 1920s had dissipated and in 1927 death robbed them of both King Ferdinand and the party leader, Ion Brătianu. Romania seemed to be becoming less stable and when the liberals had to swallow their economic-nationalist pride and seek another European loan they found that creditors were seriously concerned at Romania's condition. Such concern was encouraged by NPP delegates who toured the European financial capitals urging that no more money should be lent to Romania as long as the liberals remained in office.

On 3 November 1928 Vintile Brătianu submitted his resignation. It was intended as a tactical move and he was astounded when it was accepted and, a week later, Maniu was made premier. The NPP programme reflected the party's dualistic origins and promised redress of peasant grievances together with decentralisation, a more accommodating attitude to foreign capital, and respect for the constitution and for individual liberties. The latter was seen in the abolition of the state of siege imposed by the liberals, in the ending of censorship, and in the general election of December 1928, one of the few genuinely free votes held in Romania. The NPP had no reason to fear an open vote and received a massive 78 per cent of the poll. The NPP did not, however, abandon the 40 per cent premium.

Maniu's administration brought about a certain degree of *sanacja*, insisting that state monopolies be more autonomous and financially responsible, and that the role of the government in mines, cooperatives, and public industries should be reduced, both measures which limited the patronage at the disposal of an administration. On the other hand, excessive force was used to counter any sign of industrial unrest. Over twenty workers were killed in 1929 during a strike in the Jiu valley coal mines; the police showed great brutality in dealing with those accused, wrongly, of conspiring to assassinate Vaida Voevod; and the party went as far as to set up its own armed force. When the liberals walked out of parliament, however, it was not these tough measures to which they objected but government plans to decentralise the administration and to rig economic policies to the mast of peasant interests. In order to help the peasants the NPP government abolished duties on agricultural exports, gave more assistance to rural cooperatives, made credit easier to obtain both through the cooperatives and through the banks, and relaxed the restrictions on land sales which had been imposed as part of the post-war land reforms; the previous provision that no purchaser of such land should have more than twenty-five hectares was disregarded and this enactment aided the emergence of a small kulak element in the Romanian countryside. In 1941 16 per cent of holdings were over one hundred hectares in extent, a fact which was later to furnish the NPP's communist enemies with useful propaganda material. The liberals criticised these measures and were equally unhappy with the steps taken to attract foreign capital, steps which included the abolition of the 1924 act nationalising mineral assets, and the dilution of other legislation limiting the scope and power of the foreign investor.

Maniu's government had come to office with great potential for radical change in Romania. It had soon acquired a massive public endorsement of its programme, its party organisation was strong, and, the king being still a minor, there was no opposition from the crown. That these great expectations remained for the most part unfulfilled was primarily the fault of the great depression. The NPP's economic strategy, with its reliance upon foreign loans paid for by Romanian agricultural exports, could not work in a world which did not want to buy primary produce and which no longer had capital to lend. But even discounting the global economic catastrophe the NPP did not do many things which it ought to have done, and which it had said it would do. No measures were taken to force the breaking up of the remaining estates over one hundred hectares, not enough was done to encourage commassation, and the party itself lost much of its peasant character as former peasant activists eased themselves into the comfortable ways of the city-bound party bureaucrat. The party was further debilitated by tensions between the two constituent organisations, the Peasant Party of the regat and the nationalists from Transylvania. When Carol returned from exile in June 1930 another weight was thrown on to the anti-government scale. In October Madame Lupescu also returned whereupon Maniu resigned.

The rise of the new right

By the early 1930s both the liberals and the NPP had failed in office. The left had been insignificant since the early 1920s and what remained in the contest for real power was the crown, the army, the new right, and the influence of foreign powers. Initially the crown gained at the expense of the other factors. Carol and his advisers carefully exploited divisions amongst their opponents, widening the rift between the peasants and the nationalists in the NPP, and between the Brătianu and the Ion Duca factions of the Liberal Party. Many peasants were disillusioned with the NPP; many of them moved towards Duca but with his murder in December 1933 the most obvious focus for peasant loyalties became the new right.

Romania's fascist movement was the strongest in eastern Europe. It is chiefly associated with the bizarre figure of Codreanu. Born of a German mother and a Polish/Ukrainian father in the predominantly Jewish town of Huşi in northern Moldavia, Codreanu had become an enthusiastic member of Cuza's National Christian Defence League and had hurried back to Romania from Jena in December 1922 to lead a student strike against the liberals' new constitution which would grant Romanian citizenship to Jews. In 1924 Codreanu murdered the police chief of Iaşi who had maltreated some of Cuza's followers and who had then been decorated for his actions. Codreanu's crime added enormously to his already considerable popularity and it went unpunished:

> In the Romania of the 1920s, murder was not considered a crime if not committed for personal gain, and the murder of a prefect of the corrupt, arbitrary police, the right arm of an unpopular government, was an act of heroism.[2]

Any doubts as to Codreanu's standing with the masses were dispelled when he married shortly after the murder; nearly three thousand ox-carts formed a four-mile procession of admiring and rejoicing peasants.

As yet Codreanu had no organisational power base. Cuza's League had collapsed in 1923 and Codreanu had to wait until a spell in prison in 1927 before revelation came to him. It came in the form of a vision of the Archangel Michael who urged Codreanu to lead the Romanian people to a new age of harmony and purity. On release Codreanu therefore set up the League of the Archangel Michael. After 1930 the movement was generally known by the name of the youth movement set up in that year: the Iron Guard.

The guardists were predictably nationalist, anti-semitic, authoritarian, and anti-marxist, though they did not evolve a developed concept of the corporate state. The Iron Guard was characterised by an extreme and often macabre ritualism; meetings frequently involved song and dance, guardists wore tiny bags of Romanian soil round their necks, and the cults of death and self-sacrifice were assiduously cultivated – the police killed far more guardists than the guardists killed policemen.

The 'movement', so called because Codreanu shunned words such as 'party' which smacked of the old system, was organised into 'nests', sometimes known as 'chapels', which were to be no more than thirteen in number and which were to emphasise concepts such as duty, discipline, and honour. The movement was close to the Orthodox church and constituted a twentieth-century version of tsarism's 'Orthodoxy, Autocracy and Nationalism'. The strength of the guardist movement lay partly in the weakness of the other political factions, and to a considerable degree in the failure of the NPP régime of 1928–30. This drove many peasants, especially the more intelligent younger ones, into the ranks of the Iron Guard, the more so as the NPP's talk of the Romanian genius had already schooled many peasants in chauvinistic patterns of thought. The Guard also won peasant support by providing volunteer gangs who repaired roads, built bridges, and helped with irrigation; one group constructed a dam. The guardists also established and ran guardist restaurants and shops.

As elsewhere in Europe, the intellectual proletariat were attracted to fascism. Romanian lawyers and university teachers had always been closely associated with party politics and when the depression cut back the number of lucrative posts available for the educated, fascism seemed the only hope for a non-socialist future. With more lawyers in Bucharest than in Paris and with 2.0 students per thousand of the population compared to 1.7 per thousand in Germany, fascism had a rich recruiting ground in Romania's unemployed intelligentsia. Many within the intelligentsia, unemployed or with jobs, found the fascists attractive for deeper reasons. The francophile intelligentsia of the nineteenth century, typified by the Liberal Party, had hoped to industrialise Romania but by 1930 this strategy seemed to have failed; in rejecting the ambitions of their fathers and grandfathers the young Romanian intelligentsia identified truculently with Romanian traditions and customs. They too found 'the Romanian genius' in the peasant ethos and in extreme, exclusive, and assertive Romanian nationalism.

Finally, existing political parties and the political police, at least in the early stages of the Guard's evolution, welcomed a movement so energetic in its persecution of the extreme left.

The crown versus the Iron Guard and the rise of 'Guided Democracy'

In the mid-1930s the king was still able to keep the Iron Guard at bay. Shortly after the murder of Duca in December 1933 he made Gheorghe Tătărescu prime minister, a post which he retained until 1937, an exceptionally long period in office when one considers that between 1930 and 1940 there were eighteen changes of premier. The economy had recovered somewhat from the worst stages of the depression and its growth was further stimulated by more state intervention in the form of subsidies to heavy industry, increased tariffs, guaranteed prices for agricultural produce and, much in contrast to liberal policies a decade before, export bounties for wheat. On the political front the power of the state was also increased, primarily in an effort to check the Iron Guard. The Guard itself was banned, though it reappeared under a different name; police surveillance was stepped up; the king established his own youth movement, and in 1936 a compulsory labour brigade was introduced.

In 1937 a general election was held because Tătărescu's administration had run its full constitutional term. The election was remarkable on three counts. It was relatively free from official interference, there was an uncharacteristically low turn-out, and no party received 40 per cent of the votes cast and therefore the premium did not apply. For the NPP the chief objective seemed to be to prevent Tătărescu from securing another term of office and to this end it allied with the Iron Guard, a tactic which led some senior NPP figures to resign from the party.

The 1937 election, despite its relatively open nature, was the swan song of Romania's 'mimic democracy'. After a few interim cabinets Carol, much influenced by his advisor, Armand Calinescu, suspended the constitution and formed a ministry headed by patriarch Miron Christea, the head of the Romanian

Orthodox church, and which included a number of prominent politicians such as Vaida Voevod, Averescu, Iorga, and Tătărescu. This was the beginning of Carol's 'Guided Democracy', a form of royal dictatorship instituted to keep the extreme right at bay. Carol's reasoning was that there was no longer any point in sticking by the old constitutional rules because the NPP's readiness to align with the extreme right could always prevent a government nominated by the king from securing the 40 per cent of votes necessary for a dependable parliament. Carol's commitment to parliamentary and constitutional rule had always been shallow but he was genuinely alarmed by the Iron Guard, not least because Codreanu had promised the Nazis that, should he form a government, Romania's foreign policy would be realigned on a pro-German basis. Foreign policy was a royal preserve and Carol meant to keep it so.

In a further effort to curtail the antics of the Guard, Carol introduced a new constitution, adopted after a plebiscite in February 1938. Romania became a corporatist state. Carol insisted that democracy was a foreign importation not suitable for Romania and therefore all existing political parties were abolished; the Front of National Rebirth, established in December 1937 with Carol at its head, was to be the only legal political party. The powers of parliament were much reduced and the administrative system made yet more centralised, with ten regions replacing the seventy-one *préfectures*.

The new constitution was aimed primarily at the Iron Guard, an impressive display of guardist power at the funeral of two of its members killed in Spain having done much to persuade Carol to move against the fascists. He could scarcely have imagined that they would capitulate so easily. Codreanu weakly acquiesced in the dissolution of his organisation, which in turn did not contest the arrest of its leading figures, Codreanu included. On 29–30 November 1938, *Walpurgisnacht*, Codreanu and thirteen other leading guardists were 'shot whilst trying to escape', a euphemism for their real fate: garrotting. Carol, it seemed, had, like Horthy, won the contest with the new right. He had created a guardist state without the Guard.

The Germans did not contest the suppression of their ideological allies and German-Romanian relations remained good. The German minority in Romania was well-treated and Romania was a vital area of economic interest to the Germans, primarily on account of its oil. In March 1939 the Wohltat pact between Berlin and Bucharest gave the Germans considerable influence in Romania's domestic economy as well as a preponderant place in its external trade; under the pact the Germans agreed to aid the development of Romanian agriculture, especially the cultivation of industrial and oleaginous plants, but Romanian industry was to remain dependent on Germany: 'In effect, Romania was to become an economic satellite of the Reich.'[3] For that reason the Germans wanted peace and stability in Romania. Yet that peace and stability were eventually to be undermined by Germany and its military successes.

The defeat of King Carol

The guardists reasserted themselves in vociferous and active fashion after the defeat of Poland. They killed the king's adviser, Calinescu, in revenge for the death of Codreanu, but the real blow to the anti-guardists was the defeat not of Poland but of France. This destroyed the morale of what remained of Romania's traditional francophile establishment, thus leaving the revived Guard even stronger. Carol bent to their wishes somewhat, tightening police controls and refashioning his corporate state into a totalitarian one based upon a new National Unity Party which included the Guard. This could not save Carol because the chief danger to him now came not from within but from outside Romania.

Carol had boasted to his people that his astute diplomacy would save them from involvement in the brewing European conflict, and that he would keep the country intact and safe by building a massive defensive wall: the 'Imaginot line' as it became known. This was hubris. In the one area which he insisted was his own preserve, foreign affairs, Carol suffered his most stunning defeats with the reconstruction of eastern Europe in the summer of 1940. When Stalin demanded the cession of Bessarabia and northern Bukovina, although the latter had never been Russian territory, Hitler advised Romania to give way without a struggle. Carol did so on 28 June; the dismemberment of greater Romania had begun. On 30 August the second Vienna award gave the Hungarians northern Transylvania, the terms of the award being so horrifying that the Romanian delegate fainted at the conference table. On 7 September came the treaty of Craiova and the return of the southern Dobrudja to Bulgaria. In a few weeks Romania had lost one-third of its territory, two-fifths of its arable area, and one-third of its population; of this third one half, six million, were Romanians.

By now popular anger and resentment had reached boiling point and after an attempted guardist *putsch* on 3 September 1940 Carol abdicated. He fled the country in some danger of his life, taking with him Madame Lupescu, a motley gang of hangers-on, and most of what Romania had in the way of art treasures.

Before fleeing Carol had handed power to general Antonescu, an able soldier who had shown sensitivity as well as firmness in suppressing the *jacquerie* of 1907 and who in recent years had been in disgrace on account of his pro-guardist activities. The territorial losses of 1940 had vindicated all the Iron Guard's anti-royalist propaganda and Antonescu moved rapidly to reconstitute and realign the state. Romania was declared a National Legionary State and the Iron Guard, now led by Horia Sima, became the only legal party.

The defeat of the Iron Guard

The new system was of short duration basically because the elemental fury of the Guard clashed with Antonescu's soldierly inclinations towards order.

The economy was already impaired because the king had salted away many of the state's financial assets in foreign bank accounts, most if not all of which were now blocked. This made it even more difficult for Antonescu to condone guardist attempts to attack Jewish or even liberal economic enterprises; he disapproved of the imprisonment of Jewish or liberal managers and owners, often the only people capable of running the factories, and he disliked the romanianisation decree of November 1940 which allowed for the confiscation of non-Romanian factories, farms, ships, and dwelling places. Even more distasteful was the disruption of economic and political life which followed the exhumation of dead guardists and their reburial in elaborate ceremonies, attendance at which was vital for leading public figures. Guardist passions were rising apace, fed by anger whipped up during the reburials and augmented by the tragic consequences of an earthquake in November 1940. At the end of that month order seemed to collapse entirely; anti-guardist prisoners were massacred, the prominent NPP economic theorist Virgil Madgearu and the venerable Iorga being amongst the victims. In December the guardists turned their rage fully upon the Jews.

The hot-heads in the Iron Guard were emboldened enough to attempt a full-scale revolution and the deposition of Antonescu on 21 January 1941. It was the culmination of months of tension in which Antonescu and the army had grown increasingly concerned at the apparent collapse of order. Their fears were shared by the Nazis with whom Romania was now officially allied. Hitler had already determined upon Operation Barbarossa; he wanted only stability in Romania upon whose oil his conquest of the Soviet Union would largely depend. Berlin therefore gave full approval to Antonescu's decision to crack down upon the Guard. The attempted coup of 21 January gave him the pretext he needed and after three days of violent civil conflict the Guard was crushed.

After the fighting Antonescu removed the guardists from office, abolished the guardist state, and established full-scale military rule. Nazi Germany had given its assent to the first deposition of a European fascist régime. In June Antonescu's government gladly joined the war against the USSR.

8

BULGARIA, 1918–41

Bulgaria was the last state to join the central powers in the first world war and the first to leave them. It was also the only defeated state to retain the political system with which it went to war, namely that devised at Tûrnovo in 1879. But Bulgarian politics in the inter-war years, at least until 1934, was to display a turbulence and a violence much in contrast with constitutional continuity.

The social and political crisis of 1918–20

In late September 1918 the allied forces in northern Greece, the long-derided 'Gardeners of Salonika', lunged into the Bulgarian army in Macedonia and drove it back into Bulgaria. By 29 September the demoralised Bulgarian régime had both concluded an armistice and released a number of political detainees, including the powerful leader of the Bulgarian Agrarian National Union (BANU), Aleksandûr Stamboliiski. This had been done in the hope that the agrarian leader would be able to contain growing unrest in the army but this he proved unable, and perhaps unwilling, to do. A rebellion centred upon the town of Radomir to the west of Sofia threatened to develop into a nation-wide revolution. In the event social collapse was prevented by a combination of German units moved in from the Ukraine, a number of die-hard Macedonians under general Aleksandûr Protogerov, the mass desertions which even the radicalised army experienced, and the refusal of the extreme left to cooperate with BANU. The Radomir rebellion fizzled out in a bungled attempt to take Sofia.

It had been widely assumed that the allied armies which were then advancing into the country would not welcome a Bulgarian variant of bolshevism but no-one objected to the one major and immediate political demand made by the allies: the removal of King Ferdinand. He left Bulgaria immediately, to be succeeded by his son, Boris III.

The king was as yet too young and inexperienced to play a key role in Bulgarian politics. After the disasters of 1913 and 1918 the army was discredited, as were the old parties of the sûbranie (parliament). The factions contending for power were therefore the agrarians, the socialists, and the Macedonians. The agrarians enjoyed extensive popular support and had the advantages of an efficient, nation-wide organisation as well as a respected and able leader, Stamboliiski. The socialists had been divided since 1903. The 'broads', who became the social democrats, had been prepared to compromise with non-socialist parties in the sûbranie, whilst the 'narrows' stuck rigidly to the marxist canon, even rejecting the leninist doctrine of cooperation with the peasantry. In 1919 the narrows became the Bulgarian Communist Party. Immediately after the war the Macedonians were a negligible factor; they were discredited by their association with the central powers, they were regarded with suspicion by the allies, and they were demoralised by defeat and disarmament. They were to make a remarkable recovery.

From September 1918 until March 1920 the major conflict in Bulgaria was between the agrarians and the communists. In the general election of August 1919 the agrarians had polled 31 per cent and the communists 18.2 per cent but the leader of the communists, Dimitûr Blagoev, had refused to cooperate with the petty-bourgeois peasants. Stamboliiski had therefore been forced to form a coalition of agrarians and left-wing parliamentary parties such as the democrats, but his government had to face a constant threat from the left. The communists were spoiling for a proletarian revolution. There was much combustible material in Bulgaria's towns. Food was still scarce and most townsfolk were kept alive initially only by American aid; refugees had crowded into the urban centres; work was difficult to find as demobilised soldiers sought jobs in industries that had collapsed during the war or were now trying desperately and ineffectively to switch to peace-time production. Morale was further depressed by the severe influenza epidemic which ravaged an urban population debilitated by the privations of war.

By November 1919 tension was high and in Plovdiv four demonstrators were killed during clashes with police; at the end of the following month the communists and the broad socialists had come together in committees which precipitated a week-long general strike. It was a vital test for Stamboliiski and for Bulgaria's fragile political structure. Both survived, thanks largely to Stamboliiski's uncompromisingly tough attitude towards the strikers. For this he took his reward and in March 1920 went to the country in what proved to be the conclusive round in the agrarian-communist confrontation. The poll did not give him an absolute majority, so he resorted to the traditions of Bulgarian parliamentary politics and declared invalid the election of thirteen opponents, nine of them communists; dependable agrarians replaced these thirteen and Stamboliiski was able to form a solely BANU government. It was to remain in power until 9 June 1923.

Agrarian rule, 1920–3

Stamboliiski's objectives were to make Bulgaria a peasant-dominated state in which all members of the dominant group would be offered a rich and fulfilling life. This would involve an equitable distribution of property and the provision of cultural and welfare facilities in all villages. The BANU organisations, closely linked to the cooperatives, would play a vital role in village life and in linking the peasant economy efficiently to the national and international markets. In foreign policy Stamboliiski rejected territorial chauvinism and looked forward to a Balkan federation of agrarian states.

In terms of the equitable distribution of landed property the BANU régime did not have a great task to perform because Bulgaria was already overwhelmingly a society of small peasant proprietors. Nevertheless, an act of April 1921 set a maximum of thirty hectares for all families, with an extra five hectares for every family member after the fourth. Land confiscated under this act was to go to a state land fund which would redistribute the property to the few landless agricultural labourers and dwarf-holder families; the main 'victims' of this redistribution would be the church, the state, and the local authorities. By 1923 only 82,000 of a projected 230,000 hectares had been redistributed, although the programme was continued by succeeding governments, and by 1929 the state land fund had provided land for 64,000 indigenous Bulgarians and 28,500 refugees, most of them from Macedonia.

The agrarian government did much to strengthen the cooperatives and to increase the vocational element in education, especially in the rural areas. Attempts to establish a state grain-purchasing monopoly were wrecked by the allies who feared unfair competition, although a tobacco monopoly did function until 1923.

The notion of maximum property holding was applied also to the towns where each family was allotted two rooms and a kitchen with extra space for larger families. This act, not surprisingly, proved intensely unpopular amongst the small urban bourgeoisie. Another innovation which discomfited this group was the compulsory labour service (CLS) introduced in June 1920. Men aged between 20 and 60 were to serve for a year and women of 16 years and above for six months. The CLS battalions were mainly employed in building roads, schools, and other items of social overhead capital, but they were also intended both to absorb excess labour and to inculcate a sense of social commitment and agrarian patriotism. That the CLS was organised in units with military names and headed by a former general made the allies suspect, incorrectly, that it was being used as a means for evading the military restrictions placed upon Bulgaria by the peace treaty, and in November 1921 the allied governments intervened to enforce certain modifications of the scheme, including the introduction of the right to purchase exemption. After 1923 women were no longer conscripted but the CLS remained a feature of Bulgarian life notwithstanding subsequent changes of government.

Stamboliiski's foreign policy was determined first by the terms of the peace treaty signed at Neuilly-sur-Seine in November 1919 and, second, by his desire to bring about cooperation between the Balkan and east European states, preferably upon the basis of a common, peasant ideology. For a defeated power Bulgaria was dealt with relatively leniently by the peace treaty, at least in its territorial clauses. The country was required to surrender small enclaves on its western border to Yugoslavia; the loss of the southern Dobrudja to Romania was confirmed; and Bulgarian Thrace was to be ceded to Greece, with the provision (article 48) that Bulgaria should be allowed economic access to the Aegean. The reparations clauses, however, were more severe, with Bulgaria being required to deliver to its former enemies specified quantities of coal, livestock, railway equipment, etc., and to pay some 2,250 million gold francs over a period of thirty-seven years. The military terms of the treaty limited the Bulgarian army to 20,000 men who were all to be volunteers serving over a long period.

Stamboliiski had no choice but to accept the terms dictated by the allies but he did manage to lessen the reparations burden in 1923. Acceptance of the treaty was inevitably exploited by the extreme right, which found even greater cause for complaint in other items of Stamboliiski's foreign policy. These included his willingness, noticeable particularly after Lenin's policies towards the peasants softened in March 1921, to establish better relations with Russia, but most important was Stamboliiski's accommodating attitude towards Bulgaria's neighbours, above all to Yugoslavia. The Macedonian extremists could not abandon the notion of a Macedonia either autonomous or incorporated into Bulgaria and for this reason they hated Stamboliiski's efforts to achieve a détente with a Yugoslav régime which was subjecting Macedonia to rigid Serbian domination. Stamboliiski's policy towards Yugoslavia was made more difficult because the Macedonians of IMRO had established a state within the state at Petrich, from where they mounted raids into Yugoslav and Greek Macedonia. Nor did Stamboliiski's ideas of a federation of peasant states have much appeal in Belgrade where the Croat agrarian leader, Radić, was regarded as the chief internal enemy. Yugoslav minds changed somewhat when Mussolini came to power and reactivated the Italian threat to Dalmatia. Stamboliiski visited Belgrade in 1922 – in retaliation for which IMRO seized and held the west Bulgarian town of Kiustendil for three days – and in March 1923 the Bulgarian and Yugoslav governments signed the Niš convention. This promised close cooperation on border security and precipitated in Bulgaria a drive to suppress all terrorist organisations, though the government's authority could still not reach into the Petrich enclave or prevent further acts of Macedonian terrorism against government ministers and supporters.

The *coup d'état* of 9 June 1923

By the spring of 1923 IMRO was only one, albeit one of the most powerful, of the many factions chafing under agrarian rule. Another prominent group on the extreme right was the 15,000 White Russian refugees under the command of general Wrangel, a force which, given Stamboliiski's neglect of the army, was one of the best-armed and most disciplined in the country. The former Bulgarian officer corps resented Stamboliiski's disregard for its army but hated still more the lowly status to which demilitarisation had reduced its members, many of whom were serving as waiters or lowly paid bureaucrats and many more of whom were unemployed. The formation of the Military League provided this disgruntled group with a focus for its discontent. The clergy had long been appalled at Stamboliiski's personal godlessness; churchmen were further angered by the government's land redistribution policy which involved the alienation of monastic property, and by decrees which reduced the religious content in school education. The lay intelligentsia also had cause for complaint. Stamboliiski ended the established practice of professors holding other posts, primarily in government service, and the nationalist intelligentsia resented plans to abolish the two letters which most easily distinguished the Bulgarian alphabet from the Russian, a change which was not in fact made until after the second world war. The bureaucrats disliked the decreases in salary they had suffered and also the tendency to use party rather than official organisations to implement policy; this was seen in, for example, the use of the BANU Orange Guard rather than the police to control meetings and even street parades organised by the party, and in the use of BANU cells, the *druzhbi*, rather than the relevant local government bodies to supervise the election of teachers.

By the spring of 1923 the established political parties were also in a somewhat fevered state. In 1922 a number of them formed the National Alliance to campaign against what they saw as increasing agrarian arrogance. Their activities had been frustrated and a number of their leaders imprisoned, so that by the end of the year they were more than ever convinced that legal opposition to BANU rule was useless. When Stamboliiski won a massive majority in the general election of April 1923 leaders of the established parties began to fear that one-party rule, a republic, and a new round of radical social reconstruction were imminent. The communists, meanwhile, were also on the receiving end of agrarian power; many were incarcerated and Stamboliiski spoke of isolating them in camps 'like lepers'.

Whilst opposition intensified, the agrarians overestimated their own strength. All sections of the population had become concerned at the widespread corruption of BANU rule, though this was probably exaggerated by the government's foes. BANU was also deluded by its electoral victory in 1923 because, despite the landside vote in its favour, it lacked an armed force capable of countering those of Wrangel, the Military League, or the Macedonians. There were also divisions in the leadership of BANU; the party had no patron abroad; and Stamboliiski had failed to smash, take over, or completely bypass the official state machine as represented by the bureaucracy, the army, the monarchy, and the constitution. Stamboliiski believed, incorrectly, that in a predominantly agrarian society the countryside would prevail over the town and that under continuous BANU rule opposing factions and institutions would atrophy.

The fallacy of these thoughts was shown on 9 June 1923. On that day a carefully organised conspiracy composed of the Military League, the National Alliance, and the Macedonians, acting with the knowledge if not the encouragement of the king, deposed the agrarian government. The operation took only a few hours but it took days to hunt down and eliminate some agrarian leaders. Stamboliiski was unearthed on 14 June. His Macedonian captors tortured him, slicing off 'the hands that signed the Niš convention' and then sending his severed head to Sofia in a biscuit tin. A new government was established under Aleksandûr Tsankov, a professor of economics and leader of a newly formed coalition of parliamentary parties, the Democratic Alliance.

Communist insurgency and the rule of terror, 1923–6

The communists had stood idly by during the June coup, interpreting it as a struggle between the rural and the urban bourgeoisie. In Moscow the Comintern had doubts about this strategy and in mid-summer ordered a reversal of policy and a rising against the new government. This took place in September. Given such a short time for preparation and the rapid switch in attitudes towards the defeated agrarians, the rising was doomed to disastrous failure. It provided Tsankov's régime, which until then had been relatively mild, with every excuse to launch a fierce campaign against the left. When, in April 1925, communist activists attempted to kill the king by detonating a bomb placed in the roof of the Sveta Nedelya cathedral in Sofia, the anti-leftist campaign became frenetic. Bulgaria was subjected to months of terror in which schools became detention centres, public executions were held, and, it was rumoured, detainees were fed into the central-heating furnaces of Sofia's police headquarters.

The events of 1923 and 1925 had brought about the elimination of the left in Bulgarian politics. The old centre, as seen in the moderate parliamentary parties, and the old right, represented primarily by the Macedonians, were to contend for domination during the next decade, but whilst they did so the army and the crown were also preparing for their entry on to the political stage.

Fragile parliamentary rule, 1926–34

Tsankov remained in office until January 1926, when foreign distaste for his methods forced his resignation as a condition for the granting of a loan to the Bulgarian government. His successor was Andrei Liapchev, a leader of the Democratic Party. Liapchev reduced government controls, granting amnesties, relaxing censorship, and allowing the communists to become active again as the Bulgarian Workers' Party (BWP). As a Macedonian, however, Liapchev either could not or would not impose controls upon the Macedonian extremists who became a major source of embarrassment to his government. Internecine strife between the various Macedonian factions led to frequent public murders in Sofia and other towns, whilst operations from the IMRO base in Petrich brought about serious difficulties with Bulgaria's neighbours. In October 1925 the Greeks had occupied areas of southern Bulgaria in retaliation for a frontier incident and in 1927 the Yugoslavs sealed the border. At home, in 1930, Bulgaria endured its own 'Dreyfus affair' when it was revealed that the evidence which had condemned a colonel Marionopolski to death as a spy had been false and had been extracted by IMRO torturers. The incident enraged the army.

Liapchev was weakened further by the progressive disintegration of the parliamentary parties, a process which made government through the sûbranie increasingly ineffective and unattractive. A weak government was in no position to make an effective response to the economic blizzards which blew after October 1929. In the election of June 1931, one of the few open elections held in Bulgaria, the Democratic Alliance received only 30.7 per cent of the votes and 78 seats compared to figures of 47 per cent and 150 seats for the People's Bloc. Like the victory of Maniu and the NPP in Romania in 1928, the advent of the People's Bloc provided a distressed Balkan nation with a turning point at which it was unable or unwilling to turn.

The People's Bloc included a number of left-of-centre bourgeois parties and some agrarians. Since 1923 BANU had been split into a number of factions but inclusion in the 1931 cabinet offered hope that these divisions might heal and that central government might once more be reconciled to the majority of the peasant nation.

The new government did introduce a number of measures designed to alleviate the worst effects of the depression. Peasant debts were cut by 40 per cent; loan periods were extended; subsidies were granted to those willing to grow export crops; families were guaranteed five hectares of land which could not be taken in restraint of debt; and Hranoiznos, a government grain-purchasing monopoly introduced in 1930, was given extended powers over a variety of crops. These measures did not, however, save the People's Bloc from increasing pressure from the right and the left of national politics. In February 1932 urban distress gave the BWP a majority of seats on Sofia's municipal council – it was dissolved in the following year – whilst on the right Tsankov, now divorced from his former parliamentary colleagues, had established a fascist National Social Movement (NSM) which was attracting increasing attention.

The agrarians themselves bore much of the responsibility for this in that they had used their return to office as the occasion for grotesque squabbling over office and patronage, a process which alienated many of their natural supporters in the rural areas and amongst the non-socialist intelligentsia. Neither bolshevism nor agrarianism was to the taste of a small group within the civilian and military intelligentsia. Their gaze was turning increasingly to Zveno (link), a small but vocal supra-party pressure group founded in 1927 and having close connections with anti-royalist army officers. Zveno saw party politics as the root of Bulgaria's public ills and, in a Bulgarian variant of *sanacja*, urged their suppression and the creation of a political morality which put country before party. Zveno also called for the containment of the Macedonians and for a foreign policy based on a pro-western and pro-Yugoslav orientation rather than, as was then the case, one leaning towards Italy.

The *coup d'état* of 19 May 1934

On 19 May 1934 Zveno sympathisers in the army, led by colonels Damian Velchev and Kimon Gheorghiev, seized power in a smooth and efficient coup. They had been motivated by the decline in the effectiveness and popularity of the People's Bloc government and by increasing fears of isolation abroad. In 1933 the London convention on terrorism had defined a terrorist state as one which indulged in or allowed acts of terrorism against other states, a definition which could be used against Bulgaria as long as IMRO continued its operations from Petrich. In February 1934 the signature of the Balkan entente of Yugoslavia, Romania, Turkey, and Greece heightened these feelings of insecurity; it was a recreation of the alliance of 1913 which had inflicted disastrous defeat upon the Bulgarians. The precise timing of the coup was determined by more local and immediate factors. A cabinet reshuffle had not only provoked yet another unseemly squabble as ministerial snouts thrust deep into the trough of patronage but also raised the possibility of a purge of republican officers by the new minister of war; furthermore, Tsankov was planning a huge rally for 21 May when Reichsmarschall Goering would be in Bulgaria on a private visit. The coincidence was suspicious and might excite NSM passions to a dangerous pitch.

The new government was headed by Gheorghiev, though Velchev exercised enormous influence from behind the scenes. A great deal was accomplished in the short life of the 19 May régime. Diplomatic relations were established with the Soviet Union and those with Yugoslavia improved greatly, primarily because Gheorghiev and Velchev grasped the Macedonian nettle. In what was a surprisingly easy and immensely popular action the army was sent into Petrich and the IMRO organisation broken up; IMRO was not eliminated and other Macedonian factions had not yet been touched, but from 1934 onwards Macedonians of whatever hue were less of an embarrassment to the authorities in Sofia. Almost as popular as the containment of the Macedonians was the disbandment of the political parties, together with their presses and ancillary organisations. The sûbranie was dissolved.

The 19 May régime intended to create a new Bulgaria which was étatist and élitist. Local government was subjected to central control and the administrative machine and the banks were rationalised to eliminate inefficiency and political jobbery. The state was allotted a much more prominent role in the economy, whilst the political structure was to be redesigned on a corporatist basis which would represent the estates into which society was now to be divided: workers, peasants, craft-workers, merchants, the intelligentsia, bureaucrats, and the free professions. Only one trade union was to be permitted, and the government's ideas were to be propagated through a new body, the directorate for social renewal, which would exercise great power in education, the press, and in the general cultural sphere.

Although rich in contemporary ideas the new régime was insecure. The directorate for social renewal was not an ideal vehicle for the propagation of the new ideology; there was some indecision as to whether or not a new government party on fascist lines should be established; the power of the king had not been defined; and the new rulers were too intent on implementing their ideas to see the political dangers under their noses. In January 1935 Gheorghiev was pushed aside by general Pencho Zlatev, who was much closer to the king and who was, in April, himself replaced by a civilian, Andrei Toshev. In November Toshev gave way to Gheorghi Kioseivanov, who was entirely the king's man. He was to retain his post until 1940.

The rule of King Boris, 1935–41

Between 1918 and 1935 the successive convulsions of Bulgarian politics had seen the elimination of the agrarians and the extreme socialist left, the withering away of the moderate left, socialist and non-socialist, the suppression of the Macedonians, and the failure of the non-political, anti-royalist Zveno. Only the king and the army remained. As the king's man, Kioseivanov's first task was therefore to neutralise the army. In this he was greatly helped by Velchev who, having left the country early in 1935, returned clandestinely in the autumn. His arrest followed so rapidly upon his crossing the border that suspicions that he was enticed to return by government agents cannot be entirely discounted. The government certainly made full use of the escapade. Velchev was tried and condemned to death, his life being saved only by the exercise of the very royal prerogative of mercy which he had wished to abolish; with his reprieve came the dissolution of the Military League, and after some assiduous courting of the garrisons by the king, the army too was all but removed from the political arena. With that accomplished Kioseivanov settled into his second task, that of drawing up a new constitution.

This proved more difficult than the subjugation of the army. The king and his advisors were anxious to avoid the clutches of the new right, as represented by Tsankov's NSM, which grew more fascist and more self-confident with every success of Hitler's Germany. At the same time there was still a danger from the left. The communists gained much prestige from the Reichstag fire trial in Leipzig in 1933 in which their leader, Gheorghi Dimitrov, was acquitted after making a fool of Goering and the Nazi prosecuting counsel. The danger from the left was also manifested in the founding of the Popular Front in 1935, in violent industrial unrest in neighbouring Greece, and in signs of sympathy for the strikers amongst Bulgarian tobacco workers and even amongst the military. To find a political mechanism which would allow some representation of popular opinion without opening the gates to the extremists of right and left was in the end an impossible mission. Instead of devising a new constitution, therefore, Boris and Kioseivanov opted for 'slow though steady progress', by which they meant piecemeal tinkering with the Tûrnovo system, and in which they were resisted by the petorka (five), a loose association of leaders of a number of recently abolished parties who were later joined in the People's Constitutional

Bloc by some agrarians and, in conformity with the doctrine of the Popular Front, the communists.

'Slow but steady progress', said its proponents, brought Bulgaria nearer to a 'tidy but disciplined democracy'. This in fact meant: alterations in the franchise which was opened to unmarried women and widows but was also made subject to educational qualifications; the staggering of voting during general elections so that police could be concentrated more than once in the appropriate place; and the introduction of laws requiring candidates to attest in writing that they were not communists. Party organisations remained under interdict but, on the other hand, the government was not yet prepared to form a large official party on the totalitarian pattern and the sûbranie, weakened though it was, was never entirely docile.

Whilst Boris and Kioseivanov were searching for an appropriate constitutional system their attention was increasingly diverted from domestic to foreign affairs. After the fall of Stamboliiski Bulgaria's foreign policy had been based loosely upon cooperation with Italy, with whom antipathy to Yugoslavia formed a common bond. Revision of the treaty of Neuilly had not been lost sight of, but it was not a major or an immediate demand, Bulgarian objectives being concentrated upon the rights of access to the Aegean offered by article 48 of the treaty; change was to come via 'peaceful revisionism' effected through the League of Nations with the help of Italy. By 1935 this policy was no longer tenable. Relations with Italy, despite Boris' marriage to an Italian princess in 1930, were cooler and the League of Nations was of diminishing value at a time when the Balkan entente had made the need for foreign support all the more necessary. Boris' answer was to avoid connections with and obligations to the great powers and to concentrate on building bridges towards Yugoslavia which had never been entirely happy at the exclusion of Bulgaria from the Balkan entente. This was eventually successful. In January 1937 the two states signed a pact of eternal friendship which was followed in July 1938 by the Salonika agreements under which Bulgaria and the states of the Balkan entente swore never to use force against one another.

With the great changes of September 1938 it became more difficult than ever for King Boris and his ministers to pursue their preferred policy of avoiding involvement in great power politics. Germany had by then become a major trading partner and the chief provider of weapons for the Bulgarian army. After the first Vienna award of November 1938 Bulgaria was the only revisionist power not to have retrieved any of its lost territory and this inevitably made the axis camp more attractive to Bulgarian revisionists. Britain meanwhile was attempting to enlist Bulgaria and other states in anti-German alliances but Boris continued to stand firm against alignment with either camp, declaring once: 'My army is pro-German, my wife is Italian, my people are pro-Russian. I alone am pro-Bulgarian.'[1]

When significant territorial changes first occurred in the eastern Balkans in the summer of 1940, Bulgaria could no longer refuse to be involved. In September, with German help and Soviet acquiescence, Bulgaria recovered the southern Dobrudja by the treaty of Craiova. That still did not involve a definite commitment to the axis side but in the autumn of 1940 German pressure increased. It became clear that Berlin was not prepared to countenance Soviet domination of the eastern Balkans and with France destroyed and Britain standing alone Boris had to choose between forcible subjection to or cooperation with Hitler. At the least the latter alternative offered, it was believed, a chance of preserving some national independence whilst furthering Bulgarian territorial aims in Macedonia and Thrace. The final straw was Hitler's need for right of passage through Bulgaria to Greece in the early spring of 1941. On 1 March 1941 Bogdan Filov, recently appointed prime minister to usher in these major changes in foreign policy, signed the tripartite pact. German troops were soon pouring into the country *en route* to Greece.

Whilst Boris' freedom of manoeuvre in international affairs was being restricted there was also a tightening of internal controls, many of them introduced to palliate the Germans. Amongst the latter were some restrictions upon the Jews and the prohibition of freemasonry, a phenomenon widespread in Bulgarian political circles. The defence of the realm act of 1940, however, was more of the king's designing and could be used to contain all political extremes, including that on the right. Boris was to continue playing his skilful game of retaining some independence despite his now firm and open commitment to the German side.

9

YUGOSLAVIA, 1918–41

The beginnings of the new state and its constituent elements

The new Kingdom of the Serbs, Croats and Slovenes, like all states in 1918, faced enormous problems. In the short term the most daunting problem and the one first tackled was that of preserving the fragile social fabric. The central issue was land. In February 1917 the Serbian government had offered land to south Slav volunteers from the Habsburg Monarchy; fighting men were to be given five hectares and non-combatants three hectares. In November 1918, in the face of widespread disorders, the national council in Zagreb had given a promise of land reform which was confirmed in the first public declaration of policy by the regent, Prince Alexander, who insisted that, 'In our free state there can and will be only free landowners.' On 25 February 1919 came the interim decree on the preparation of the agrarian reform which applied to all the kingdom except pre-1912 Serbia and which provided for the redistribution of estates in excess of one hundred cadastral *yokes*, though in some less favoured areas the figure was five hundred *yokes*.[1] Priority in the redistribution was to be given to volunteers and to victims of the war; compensation was to be paid to all except the Habsburgs and members of other enemy dynasties. Over two million hectares, excluding forest land, were to be redistributed to some half a million households, over a quarter of the national total. On the other hand, the reform was a preliminary enactment and its implementation was frequently delayed, in some cases by as much as fifteen years, though it served its immediate purpose of containing radical passions.

In addition to this immediate and essential service the reform served other political functions. In Bosnia-Hercegovina and in Macedonia the dispossessed landowners were predominantly Muslim and therefore the redistribution increased the relative social and political power of the Christians, whilst in Slovenia, Croatia, the Vojvodina, and Macedonia those who lost property were frequently non-Slav and those who received it were Slav. The land reform therefore benefited the Christian Slavs who dominated the new state.

This did not mean that there was unity amongst those Christian Slavs. The Serbs found it difficult to think of the new state as anything other than an extended and unified Serbia. There was even a tendency to see an expanded Serbia as no more than the just rewards of victory. Half of the 370,000 Yugoslav casualties during the first world war had been suffered by the Serbian army, whose proportionate losses had been three times higher than the British and two-and-a-half times as high as the French; military action and typhus had killed one in five Serbs even before the losses of the Balkan wars were taken into account. Some Habsburg south Slavs, on the other hand, had fought to the very last under the Habsburg colours. If past sacrifices were not enough to justify Serb dominance, then the Serbs could point to the present function of their army which, it was frequently and not altogether unjustly argued, was the only force disciplined enough to contain the multiple threats from Italian expansionism, Hungarian political radicalism, and internal disintegration. The Serbs, and more especially the dominant National Radical Party (NRP) led by Pašić, also laid great emphasis upon the role of the Serbian state as an instrument of national unification. For the NRP serbianism was less the product of language, culture, or religion than of the Serbian state, and in the new combination of territories which made up the Triune kingdom only Serbia had experience of a state administration; in such circumstances many Serbs were puzzled as to why they should be asked to consider equality for areas which previously had been merely provinces. The makers of the new state believed that a new consciousness would replace former 'tribal' loyalties: in the words of an architect of the constitution of 1921, 'Racial consciousness was to disappear before the "State idea" – a much higher political conception and a much stronger political force.'[2]

Expansion of Serbian practices in administration began immediately after the formation of the new state, often because there was no alternative. Early in 1919 Serbian legislation concerning the property of those in states formerly at war with Serbia and concerning military and judicial administration were extended throughout the new state; by February 1919 the gendarmerie, a Serbian military force employed to carry out civilian police duties, had some 12,000 men throughout Yugoslavia. The Serbian army, which had generally been welcomed as a liberating force, was also used to maintain law and order. Unfortunately, neither the civil nor the military arm of the Serbian state conformed to the standards expected of such institutions in the former Habsburg lands where administration, if cumbersome, had been fundamentally honest. Serbian bureaucracy was corrupt, inefficient, and riddled with political clientism. The army, too, gave offence, often unintentionally. It was customary for the Serbian army to mete out beatings both to its own men and to civilian offenders, but corporal punishment had been abolished in Croatia in 1869 and its return seemed to many Croats to be a regression to semi-feudal practices. In Macedonia and Bosnia-Hercegovina things were worse, because many of the ex-POWs and volunteers sent to these areas had been promised land and did not wait for implementation of the February 1919 decree to take it, usually from Muslims. In this process not a few personal scores were settled against the Muslims, especially in Bosnia where, during the war, the predominantly Muslim Schutzkorps had been fierce in its persecution of Serbian guerillas.

A much more serious problem arose with the army in Croatia. Croat units of the old Habsburg army had been disbanded in December 1918 and Croat professionals who wished to join the new Yugoslav army faced humiliating difficulties. In the first place they had to apply to join the new army, whereas officers from the former Serbian army did not. The Serbian officer corps was still besotted with its indubitably glorious feats in the Balkan and the first world wars. But those victories had been gained at a price. The high casualty rates had meant rapid promotion, even for the less well-educated, in an army which already had a relatively rapid promotion system. For Croat officers serving in the Austro-Hungarian army educational standards had been more exacting and promotion had been slower, with the result that those who did enter the Yugoslav forces frequently found themselves serving under younger and less well-trained Serbian superiors. This was one factor which drove Croats to abandon a military career. Others were what the Croats regarded as discriminatory practices such as the posting of Croats to distant and troubled regions, the use of the cyrillic rather than the latin alphabet, the observance of Serbian as opposed to Croat customs, and the celebration of Orthodox rather than Catholic festivals. By 1939 only one tenth of Yugoslavia's officer corps was Croat.

The frustrations occasioned by the spread of Serbian practices were most effectively articulated in but were by no means confined to Croatia. Other areas were less able or less willing to express their discontent. In Macedonia centralisation was as unpopular after 1918 as it had been after 1913 when Serbia first took control of the area, but political consciousness and organisation were not well developed; Pašić confidently predicted the absorption of the Macedonian Slavs into the Serb race within five to ten years. Most importantly, however, in the critical formative years of the new state, the Macedonian Slavs could expect no help from their natural sponsors in Bulgaria, where Stamboliiski was anxious to cultivate good relations with Yugoslavia.

The Albanians of Kosovo were as backward and underdeveloped as the Macedonian Slavs. In Bosnia-Hercegovina the Muslims found it hard to support Orthodox Serbia, the more so as many Muslim landlords had suffered dispossession, legal or otherwise. However, if the Bosnians were to oppose Belgrade the government might then break up Bosnia and redistribute it amongst other areas, in which case there would be no unit within the new state in which the Muslims enjoyed a majority. The Muslims were trapped into keeping a hold of the Yugoslav nurse for fear of something worse; it was primarily for this reason that the Yugoslav Muslim Organisation (YMO) was to be a reliable supporter of the Belgrade government in the 1920s. In the Vojvodina the Slavs felt threatened by the Magyars and Germans, and this provided sufficient fear to guarantee obedience to Belgrade.

The Slovenes, as the most economically and politically developed of the Yugoslav 'tribes', might have been expected to suffer most from the expansion of the Serbian state, yet in 1939 one observer went as far as to comment that, 'of all the three races which comprise Yugoslavia, the Slovenes have probably benefited most from the Union'.[3] The Slovenes were linguistically more distinct from the Serbs than were the Croats and the lack of bilingual bureaucrats enabled them to preserve some local control over the administrative machine. Slovene political and social organisations were well-developed, with the Slovene Populist Party (SLS) under Korošec having played a sophisticated role both at a local level and in the Reichsrat in Vienna. After 1918 the Slovenes continued their political sophistication at the national level by judiciously ensuring that each cabinet contained at least one of their number, whilst Korošec was the only non-Serb to become prime minister in inter-war Yugoslavia. Yet the Slovenes' relative contentment was a product of deeper factors than linguistic individuality or political *savoir-faire*. Before 1918 the Slovenes' political preoccupations had been directed to defending Slovene culture against germanisation. They demanded a university of their own, they fought for more Slovene secondary schools, and they wanted to see Slovene as an official language. All of these desires were granted by the Triune kingdom.

If the Slovenes could feel that union had brought the achievement of their political desires, the opposite was true of the Croats. Before 1918 they already had an extensive school system, a university, an official language, albeit one under siege after the Hungarian language laws of 1907, and their own assembly meeting in their own capital. Yet the Croats were not satisfied: they wanted proper implementation of the 1869 Nagodba; in effect, the Croats wanted their own version of dualism within one section of the Dual Monarchy. The Croat political psychology thus became steeped in dualism to such a degree that, by 1918, whilst 'the Serbian vision focused strictly on centralism, the Croatian knew only of dualism, and envisaged the new state as a better dualistic system which would improve Croatia's old position'.[4] When the new system turned out to be not an improvement in Croatia's position but rather a worsening of it, the Croats could find no response within that system. They could think only of its radical restructuring on a dualistic basis. In that lay the fundamental political conundrum of inter-war Yugoslavia.

Political parties and the constituent assembly

The provisional government formed after the declaration of 1 December 1918 announced its intention to convene a constituent assembly, but not until the boundaries of the new state had been defined, a process which was not complete until the signature of the treaty of Trianon on 4 June 1920. By then Yugoslavia had experienced yet more upheaval.

There had been murmurings of unrest in the summer of 1919 when some sympathy was expressed for the revolutionists in Hungary. The whole country resented the heavy-handed tactics of the Serbian army whilst many honest peasants saw their savings decrease in value through bungled attempts by the

Belgrade government to contain inflation. The Croats felt provoked by the appointment of an unpopular *ban* and, in the spring of 1920, by the arrest of Stjepan Radić, leader of the Croat People's Peasant Party (CPPP). Predictably, the Croats reacted strongly. In early September areas around Zagreb were in open revolt and discontent was endemic until the elections to the constituent assembly were held on 28 November. But even here the non-Serbs found reason to complain. Although the voting was direct, secret, and conducted according to a form of proportional representation, the registers were based on the 1910 census. This meant that the Serbs were over-represented because their enormous casualties between 1912 and 1918 were disregarded; in Belgrade it required 2,737 votes to elect one deputy but in Zagreb the number was 4,954.

The parties which competed for representation in the constituent assembly inevitably reflected their geographic origins. These parties remained prominent in Yugoslav political life until the suppression of the parliamentary system in 1929. Pašić's NRP had long since lost its original radical impulses and had become the party of the Serbian establishment. It was to remain in office for almost the entire period of constitutional rule between 1921 and 1929. Until 1926 the prestige of Pašić himself was one reason for the NRP's hold on office but equally important, and more lasting, was its control of state patronage. This gave it considerable power in that it had in its gift large numbers of jobs not only in the government monopolies over tobacco, matches, cigarette papers, salt, and kerosene, but also in the numerous state-owned concerns which included railways, mills, docks, mines, and steel mills, as well as forests, hotels, hospitals, banks, publishing houses, theatres, and opera houses. The NRP's base was in Serbia but it also enjoyed strong support amongst the Serbs of the Vojvodina where governmental control was particularly effective. The party supported a centralist policy but was willing to accept federalism if it were based on ethnic divisions and not upon the historic boundaries so beloved of the Croats.

The Democratic Party (DP), formed in 1921 under the leadership of Svetozar Pribičević, was dedicated to centralism. Pribičević had justified his centralist reputation in the provisional government when he insisted upon the abolition of existing regional governments. The party's main appeal was to Serbs living across the border in Croatia or Bosnia, the so-called *prečani* Serbs, but it also had considerable support amongst the Serbs of Metohja, the Sandjak of Novi Pazar, and Kosovo, most of whom preferred the DP to the NRP.

The Slovene Populist Party had earned its spurs in the Vienna Reichsrat and had an efficient organisation closely tied to the Catholic church. From the latter it derived the paternalistic social policies of Leo XIII's *De Rerum Novarum*. Its main aim was to secure *de facto* autonomy for Slovenia, in which endeavour it was largely successful.

The quiet success of the SLS was much in contrast to the extravagant failures of the Croat People's Peasant Party. Founded in 1904 by the Radić brothers the CPPP had by 1918 made Croat state rights the main plank in its platform. Its ideologue, Antun Radić, had died in 1919 but his brother, Stjepan, had always been its dominant personality. Half-blind, a demagogue who spoke in a whisper, a fervent Catholic but a staunch anti-clerical, a nationalist Croat married to a Czech with whom he corresponded in cyrillic, Stjepan Radić was a man of many contradictions, the greatest of which was his inability to translate the support he enjoyed into any kind of lasting success. Radić believed that power lay in the peasantry who dominated Croatia numerically, culturally, and economically, and who had guarded the national traditions in times of oppression. The state which he wished to see created for his peasant followers would be one which respected historic Croat rights, eschewed militarism, and guaranteed individual liberties. When universal manhood suffrage was applied in the elections of 1920 the peasantry responded by giving Radić and the CPPP an absolute majority of the votes cast in Croatia, a feat unequalled by any other party in any of Yugoslavia's regions.

In addition to the CPPP there was the all-Yugoslav Peasant Union (PU). This alliance of Croat, Serb, and Slovene peasants crystallised around the Serbian Agrarian Party and polled the fifth largest vote in 1920. It was closely linked to the cooperative movement which meant that in Slovenia, where that movement was well-developed, it was the second largest party. It also had strong support in Bosnia-Hercegovina. Its national policies were centralist rather than federalist.

Of the urban, sectional parties the social democrats were of the traditional reformist mode and were overshadowed in 1920 by the newly formed Communist Party of Yugoslavia (CPY). The CPY's most rewarding polling grounds were the backward regions of Montenegro and Macedonia, whilst in Croatia, though not in Slovenia, it was initially stronger than the Social Democratic Party; in Serbia the CPY and the social democrats merged. The communists were, of course, the fashionable party in urban radical circles but in the non-Serb areas they dissipated their support by taking a centralist line, by underestimating national or regional sensitivities, and by neglecting agrarian problems. In 1921, following the assassination of the minister of the interior, the CPY was declared illegal and thereafter its strength and its internal cohesion declined rapidly. The Comintern's insistence, until 1935, that the CPY abandon its centralist line did little to help. The party's fortunes revived only in 1937 when it received a new secretary general, Josip Broz, and when the combination of continuing economic stagnation and political sterility encouraged a movement towards the left.

Muslim interests were represented in the Yugoslav Muslim Organisation (YMO) led by Mehmed Spaho. The Muslims had resisted centralisation to the extent of refusing to allow their religious headquarters to be transferred from Sarajevo to Belgrade but in later years fear of the division of Bosnia restricted the YMO's anti-centralism almost to the point of nullity.

All these parties, as well as a number of other groupings, were represented in the constituent assembly; of the 419 seats the DP took 92, the NRP 91, the CPY 58, the CPPP 50, the PU 39, the YMO 24 and the non-Serb social democrats 10.

The assembly convened in December 1920 and debated four separate drafts of the constitution before the final version was sanctioned on 28 June 1921.[5] The Vidovdan constitution enacted that the Triune kingdom should have a unicameral legislature, the skupshtina, elected by universal, equal, and direct male suffrage. Its official language was to be Serbo-Croat-Slovene, a political convenience but a linguistic nonsense. The state was to be unitary but divided into thirty-three centralised departments; dualism and federalism alike were rejected outright.

This was clearly not to the liking of the Croats but they had foreseen such an outcome and had expressed their dissatisfaction in a manner which was both dramatic and disastrous. They boycotted the assembly. Other anti-centralist groups followed their example but however impressive this might have been as a political gesture it removed any resistance to Pašić, Pribičević, and the other centralisers; had the dissenters remained, Pašić might have been forced to include them in a coalition to enact the constitution. As it was, even with the absence of 163 anti-centralists, Pašić had to make concessions on the land issue in order to secure the support of the basically anti-centralist YMO.

Shortly after the enactment of the new constitution the regent Alexander became king following the death of his father King Peter.

Political instability, 1921–29

Between 1921 and the royal *coup d'état* of 6 January 1929 Yugoslavia was offered the benefits of parliamentary government. Political freedoms were respected for all but the communists and, intermittently, the CPPP, whilst both the king and the army remained outside the political arena. Yet freedom could not bring stability. At the base of the system the vast majority of the peasant population were increasingly discontented as politicians perfected and perpetuated the dubious arts of clientism and corruption, whilst at the apex parliamentary government was ruined by the seemingly irreconcilable gap between Belgrade and Zagreb.

Radić had allowed the CPPP to take part in the elections held in March 1923 but the party boycotted the assembly and left Pašić and the centralists to form an administration. Pašić, from his position of strength, was prepared to conciliate, but Radić refused. His tactics were difficult to understand and much of the confusion in the next few years followed from his maverick conduct which became 'the despair of all those Serbs who honestly desired cooperation with Croatia'.[6] The CPPP found a natural ally in Mussolini's anti-Yugoslav régime and in IMRO. Contact was established with both. Yet, despite this affinity to right-wing extremism, Radić in June 1924 made a sudden and initially secret journey to Moscow where he forged links with Krestintern, the communist-sponsored peasant international. This was but an ephemeral association which, Radić admitted, brought him nothing because, as he admitted, 'The communists do not want allies, only servants.'[7] Yet this transitory and profitless association enabled the opponents of Radić to brand him a communist sympathiser. By 1924 the ficklness of Radić meant that Pašić could pose as Yugoslavia's defender against terrorism, Italian aggrandisement, and bolshevism; Radić was a powerful bonding agent for disparate elements in a divided country. The Croat leader was unabashed and reacted with even more extreme outbursts, demanding a reduction of the army and hinting at Croat secession. For that he spent a brief spell in prison.

Radić's lack of success did not dent his popularity in Croatia, as the elections of February 1925 showed. After this poll Pašić, acting again from a position of strength, once more offered the CPPP a compromise. This time Radić was ready to listen. He agreed to accept the Vidovdan constitution and to drop his call for a republic, in return for which he and other peasant leaders were released from gaol and a grand coalition was formed around the NRP and the CPPP with Pašić remaining prime minister and Radić becoming minister of education. The Croats were also given greater control of administration in Croatia, and fiscal, economic, and judicial reforms were granted to both Croatia and Slovenia. By August 1925 tension had subsided sufficiently for King Alexander to make his first visit to Zagreb.

The grand coalition did not work. Radić had scant respect for his Serbian cabinet colleagues, Pašić excepted, whilst in Croatia itself there was some disenchantment with the CPPP leader whose entry into government did little for the peasantry and whose new relationship with the Serbian establishment gave rise to anxiety in some Catholic circles. Furthermore, the CPPP showed every sign of becoming an establishment party, having little rapport with and even less concern for the majority of the population. The coalition was wrecked in April 1926 when its main architect, Pašić, resigned after accusations of corruption had been levelled against his son; in December Pašić *père* died. After the collapse of the coalition the NRP stitched together a weak alliance with the SLS, the YMO, and the DP which was now led by Ljubomir Davidović; in 1924 Pribičević had split with the main party to form the Independent Democratic Party. The new coalition survived until the elections of September 1927 after which an anti-Croat pact of the NRP, the YMO, the SPP, and the DP took office.

The important development at this point was not in the government but on the opposition benches, since Pribičević, the arch–centralist, now formed an unholy alliance with Radić to demand federalisation and the abandonment of a proposed economic agreement with Italy. It seemed that Croat sectoral interests could override the religious/ethnic divide between Catholic Croats and Orthodox *prečani* Serbs and the new entente was to last until 1929. It caused considerable embarrassment in Belgrade. The government had no one capable of imposing its authority upon the skupshtina, which rapidly dissolved into a bear garden. The nadir was reached on 20 June 1928 when a Montenegrin radical produced a revolver to kill two deputies and wound Radić, who died seven weeks later. Those shots signalled the end of Yugoslavia's parliamentary system.

King Alexander's dictatorship, January 1929 to October 1934

The death of Radić precipitated six months of crisis so intense that Alexander mused on the 'amputation' of Croatia, which he would have preferred to federalism. In an attempt to lessen non-Serb hostility to rule from Belgrade he appointed the SLS leader, Korošec, as prime minister, but the gesture had little effect. Some Croats and Slovenes were now so disaffected that they set up anti-parliaments in Zagreb and Ljubljana, claiming that political and financial power was so concentrated in the hands of venous Belgrade politicians that even the state banks were 'virtually useless to the territories of the former Habsburg Monarchy'.[8] To make matters worse, the country was facing severe financial problems and the harvest was poor. When the government held ill-advised celebrations to commemorate the tenth anniversary of the foundation of the state the rioting in Zagreb cost one life for each of the years being 'celebrated'.

If the state were to survive something had to fill the intensifying political vacuum. The political parties were too discredited and too regionalised; the trade unions and the peasant organisations were too weak; the bureaucracy was too unpopular and too serbianised; and there was no religious body with country-wide allegiance. There remained the army but this, since the execution of colonel Apis in 1917, had been a pliant instrument in the hands of Alexander. Only the king could act. He did so on 6 January 1929, the Orthodox Christmas Day. He abolished the Vidovdan constitution and with it all political parties, the skupsht-ina, the trade unions, and all organisations with a regional or a religious basis; all locally elected bodies were to hand their authority to royal appointees. In Belgrade the chief of the palace guard, general Petar Živković, was made prime minister. The king became the source of all legislative and political power.

The immediate purpose of the coup had been to prevent political collapse. Its long-term function was to create a new Yugoslav consciousness which would end the regional affiliations which had undermined the Vidovdan constitution. To this end the Triune became the Yugoslav kingdom and a single, Yugoslav flag replaced regional ones. A new legal code, applicable throughout the country, was enacted; regional differences in taxation were reduced; and a new Yugoslav Agrarian Bank was established, the existing regional banks being regarded as centres of particularism. The coup was followed by a purge of the bureaucracy, which had shed one-third, supposedly the most corrupt and unpopular third, of its number by May 1929. In October the country's thirty-three departments were replaced by nine new administrative units, the *banovine*, with topographical rather than historic names. Each unit was to be administered by a *ban*, whose powers inside his *banovina* and whose accountability to the central authorities were akin to those of the governor of a tsarist *guberniya*. Of the new *banovine* two had Croat majorities, one was overwhelmingly Slovene, and in the remainder the Serbs were predominant. The Croats suffered most from the new arrange-ments, since their historic units had been more mutilated than others, but the reform also angered the Muslims because in none of the new and very centralised units did they constitute a majority; their grudging obedience to Belgrade had not served its purpose. The imposition of royal authority was accompanied by a significant augmentation of police and military powers.

Alexander did not regard his naked royal dictatorship as permanent. In 1931 it was clothed with a constitution. A new, and this time bicameral legislature was introduced along with universal, equal, and direct, though not secret, manhood suffrage. However, the political parties remained under interdict; in addition, the process by which candidates were to be nominated, together with the restrictions placed upon individual liberties, were such that the new system commanded even less support than the Vidovdan constitution. In the elections held in December 1931 and January 1932 opposition calls for abstention were heeded far more widely than the government was prepared to admit.

Alexander's attempt to build a new Yugoslav system and to formulate a Yugoslav consciousness failed. The Croats were hostile from the start and Korošec's initial approval was soon withdrawn, with the result that Alexander's Yugoslavia was as Serb-dominated as its predecessor. Individual liberties and the restraints upon police power declined simultaneously with a number of sensational murders, all of which, especially that of the historian professor Milan Šufflay in February 1931, brought discredit upon the system. The increase in state power and arbitrariness provoked counter-reaction. IMRO had never ceased its disruptive activities but there was a more worrying development in the growth of the Croat terrorist movement, the Ustaša, which was linked both to IMRO and to fascist Italy. Most serious of all, perhaps, was the effect of the coup on Serbia. If the Croats and Slovenes had not been won over, the Serbs, who had previously been relatively united in support of the state, were now divided. Some of them were alienated by the attempt, albeit unsuccessful, to lessen the Serbian domination on which, to add insult to injury, many of the faults of the previous system were blamed. Alexander had implicitly made the Serbs, the most reliable proponents of centralism, the villains of the Vidovdan piece.

Whilst these political difficulties were mounting the economy of the country was being swept into disaster by events far beyond Belgrade's control. By 1934 Alexander had realised that his system was failing and had decided upon further changes. He did not live to implement them because on 9 October 1934, at the beginning of a visit to France, he was assassinated in Marseilles by a Macedonian terrorist who had links with IMRO and the Ustaša.

The regency, 1934–41

The heir to the throne, Peter, was a minor and therefore his cousin, Prince Paul, became regent. Paul saw the need to reconcile Serb and Croat but would undertake no major constitutional change, insisting that he must hand the kingdom unchanged to King Peter when he came of age in 1941. This made Yugoslavia 'a dictatorship without a dictator',[9] but this was not entirely disadvantageous. In the first place it suspended the vicious and debilitating struggle to find an acceptable political system and, second, the political stasis allowed more attention to be paid to the desperate social problems which beset the country.

The economic and financial disasters of 1929 and 1931 hit Yugoslavia every bit as hard as other countries and the responses were basically similar. The right of every peasant family to a minimum holding immune to restraint for debt was confirmed and in 1932 debt payments were suspended for six months and foreclosures in train were cancelled. Banks which feared difficulties could ask for a moratorium. In 1936 a 'final' scheme for the regulation of the debt question was introduced, halving pre-1932 debts and easing repayment terms on the remainder, but by 1939 even this solution was in need of reform. The basic problem was that alleviation of existing debts eased the symptoms but the disease afflicting peasant agriculture could not be cured without industrialisation and, on the farms themselves, modernisation and the improvement of agricultural techniques. For a class without capital reserves this would have meant more borrowing but the suspension or slowing down of previous debt-payments had inevitably produced a shortage of credit, since few would lend when repayment seemed so insecure. The government attempted to help by investing what it could in social overhead capital and there was also a certain degree of 'self-help' amongst the peasants, particularly in Croatia where the depression reactivated the peasant ideology of the now-banned CPPP. Under the guidance of the *gospodarska sloga* (economic union) a number of Croat peasants organised themselves to control the selling of commodities such as wine and pigs, with the result that prices were increased, the richer peasants in the meantime subsidising the less fortunate. More important in reviving the Yugoslav economy, however, were the good harvests of 1935 and 1936 and, above all, the 1933 and 1934 trade agreements with Germany which, by the second half of the decade, were providing valuable markets for Yugoslav agricultural produce, iron-ore, bauxite, and manganese.

The political affairs of Yugoslavia in the second half of the 1930s were dominated by Milan Stojadinović who was appointed prime minister in June 1935, a position he was to hold until February 1939. He began his premiership by reducing political controls. Censorship was greatly relaxed and 10,000 political detainees were released. To bolster his political authority Stojadinović formed a new political movement, the Yugoslav Radical Union (YRU). However, this combination of NRP, SLS, and YMO elements, though it guaranteed Stojadinović a pliant skupshtina, never became the popular force which its creator had intended it to be. Power under Stojadinović depended as before not on popular approval but on political jobbery, whilst he also benefited substantially from the gradual improvement in the national economy in the second half of the 1930s.

Stojadinović in office had two main and interlinked objectives. He had to ensure Yugoslavia's safety in a worsening international situation and to do this he needed to strengthen internal cohesion by solving the Serb-Croat problem.

Foreign security had been an increasing preoccupation of King Alexander. The foundation of Yugoslav foreign policy in the early 1920s had been the little entente, which was an effective guarantee against Hungary. It offered little security, however, against an aggressive Italy and to meet this danger Alexander in 1927 had signed an alliance with France. Fear of Italy was also the main motivation for Alexander's participation in the Balkan alliance of 1934 and for his desire to bring the Bulgarians into this grouping, to achieve which he was even prepared to make minor territorial adjustments in Bulgaria's favour.

After the assassination of Alexander Yugoslavia's relative weakness became more apparent. Belgrade's attempt to have Italy and Hungary disciplined by the League of Nations for their part in the Marseilles outrage ended with nothing more than a mild rebuke to Budapest; France, and to a lesser extent Britain, shielded Italy whose cooperation against Germany they were seeking. The great powers were of little value to Yugoslavia. At the same time the little entente was a wasting asset. The Yugoslavs feared Italy, the Czechoslovaks feared, or should have feared, Germany, whilst Romania feared neither. Yugoslavia was forced to look to new arrangements for its security and so in March 1937, two months after the conclusion of the pact with Bulgaria, signed a neutrality agreement with Italy.

Whilst Stojadinović was seeking security abroad he also tried to improve relations at home between the Serbs and the Croats. On taking office he showed his good intentions towards the latter by allowing them to erect a statue to the martyred Radić and by 1936 he was attempting to negotiate with the successor to Radić, Vladko Maček. Maček was not yet ready for compromise and Stojadinović therefore made further concessions. The exiled son-in-law of Radić was allowed to return to Yugoslavia and Stojadinović also initiated attempts to secure Serbian acceptance of an agreement that he had negotiated with the Vatican in 1935. On this issue an intense debate raged in the skupshtina throughout the summer of 1937. At its conclusion fate played a cruel trick. On the very night on which the bill accepting the agreement was passed, the Serbian Orthodox patriarch died. This wrecked the deal. The Serbian Orthodox church penalised all its adherents who had voted for ratification and Stojadinović was forced to withdraw the concordat. Maček would not now negotiate with a prime minister who had lost so much of his support in Orthodox Serbia. In the December 1938 elections the government used all its power to influence the result but, despite this, the YRU did badly, especially in Croatia. In February 1939 Stojadinović resigned, to be replaced by Dragiša Cvetković.

Cvetković's objectives were much the same as those of Stojadinović, though the international situation was becoming ever more tense. The Anschluss of 1938 had brought the German frontier down to Slovenia, whilst the Munich settlement, and even more so the German occupation of Prague in March 1939, made some Slovenes and Croats jealous of the fact that the Slovaks had managed to escape a centralist régime they disliked. Hitler's every advance increased both the pressure on Belgrade and the secessionist inclinations of the Slovenes and Croats. Under such pressure Cvetković was encouraged to resume negotiations with Maček, and his ardour was reinforced by the Italian occupation of Albania in April. A solution was found in the *sporazum* (agreement) signed on 20 August and ratified by the skupshtina six days later. The *sporazum* created a much larger and single Croatian *banovina* from the two existing Croatian *banovine* and sections of four others. The new unit covered one-third of the national land area and contained one-third of the national population; over three-quarters of its population were Croats. The new *banovina* was to have a sabor and a *ban* who was to be responsible not to the government or to the parliament in Belgrade but directly to the king. The sabor was to determine policy for Croatia on most matters, the main exceptions being defence, internal state security, foreign affairs, and external trade. For the first time since 1928 the Croats acknowledged the central government, of which Maček and four other Croats now became members.

If the *sporazum* placated the Croats it angered the Slovenes and the Serbs; in addition the *prečani* Serbs, abandoned in the new *banovina*, felt resentful and threatened, particularly when the new authorities in Zagreb allowed a number of Croat extremist exiles to return. Yet these same extremists and those in the Ustaša were equally dissatisfied with the *sporazum*; even though it had allowed them to come home, the *sporazum* was for them the beginning rather than the end of the process of redefining relations between Croatia and the rest of Yugoslavia. To underline the point they expressed their ire in acts of terrorism in Zagreb and other centres. Even the more moderate Croats found continued reason for complaint. The extreme right joined with the illegal CPY to spread rumours that the central government intended to join the war and that as a consequence Croat régiments would be sent to the front line in France. Defensive measures along Croatia's border with Hungary also proved unpopular because they took valuable agricultural land out of use to little apparent purpose.

The coup of March and the invasion of April 1941

The internal compromise of August 1939 did not solve the increasing dilemma facing Yugoslavia in foreign affairs, a dilemma which became greater after the outbreak of European war in the following month. Prince Paul was by sentiment pro-British, and the pro-French tradition in Serbia had, with a few hiccups, survived since the first world war. Yet Germany could not be offended. Yugoslav economic dependence on the Reich was established and it would be foolish to oppose Berlin when France and Britain seemed so weak, so distant, and, given their diplomatic record in the 1930s, so unreliable. The fall of France made the position infinitely worse and then, in the spring of 1941, Hitler's attentions turned towards the Balkans from where he would be able to harry the British lines of communication in the eastern Mediterranean. Pressure was placed upon Belgrade to join the tripartite pact. This provoked pro-British factions in the military, especially the air force, to warn the government against such a move. By March 1941 German troops were passing into Bulgaria *en route* to Greece to rescue the Italians trapped there since the previous autumn. By the second half of the month Cvetković felt that he could resist no longer and on 25 March went to Vienna with his foreign minister to sign the treaty.

Yugoslavia was not explicitly committed to a pro-German foreign policy but this was what was assumed by the pro-British faction which implemented its previous threats by removing, on the night of 26–7 March, both Cvetković and Prince Paul. King Peter assumed full powers. The coup was bloodless and, in Belgrade at least, immensely popular. Opposition to a pro-German orientation was not the only reason for this popularity. Many Serbs saw the coup as a chance to reassert the Serbian domination that had been compromised in the *sporazum*; many Croats also welcomed the Serbian basis of the *putsch*, believing that it provided them with the excuse they had so long been looking for to cut all links with Belgrade and to set up a completely independent Croatian state on the Slovak model.

The new government in Belgrade was headed by a leading *putschist*, air force general Dušan Simović, and was openly pro-British; it also signed a treaty of friendship with the Soviet Union. But by now Hitler had lost patience and on the day the Yugoslav-Soviet treaty was signed, Sunday 6 April 1941, he unleashed a savage attack upon Yugoslavia, Belgrade being subjected to horrendous bombing on that Sunday. Meanwhile the Bulgarian, Italian, and Hungarian armies joined the Wehrmacht in the dismemberment of the country.

The invasion showed up the weakness of inter-war Yugoslavia. Where armies were largely recruited from local inhabitants who had a commitment to the political structure, as in Slovenia and Serbia, the invasion was contested, but in Croatia resistance was minimal or non-existent; in one case Croatian officers left a party to surrender to the advancing enemy and then returned to their junketings 'as if nothing had happened'.[10] In the march on Zagreb the Germans took 15,000 prisoners, including twenty-two generals.

10

ALBANIA, 1918–39

The search for stability, 1920–8

Albania was the only European state with a Muslim majority; 70 per cent of Albanians were Muslim, 20 per cent Orthodox and 10 per cent Catholic. The population after the first world war was 92 per cent Albanian. But if Albania was one of the most ethnically homogeneous of states in eastern Europe, it was also the most backward. Four-fifths of the population were illiterate; in 1919 the only working motorised vehicles in the country were three dilapidated Ford trucks left behind by allied troops; in 1927 the country had one hundred trained doctors, twenty-one dentists, and fifty-nine pharmacists, whilst the districts of Dibër and Kosovë had hospitals but no doctors; in 1939 only 1.5 per cent of the population were engaged primarily in manufacturing industry.

At the end of the first world war Albania was partitioned and occupied by Serbian, Greek, French, British, and Italian troops; the only functioning Albanian government was that based in Durrës under Italian protection. This was not to the taste of the northern tribal chiefs, southern landowners, and those few members of the intelligentsia who wished to reassert their independence. They convened a congress which met at Lushnjë from 21 January to 9 February 1920. Its purpose was to secure the withdrawal of foreign forces, to protect Albania against further foreign domination, and to establish political institutions. The contrast between these modernist aspirations and the conditions in which they had to be sought was illustrated by the fact that the congress could only meet after a general *besa*, or suspension of blood feuds, had been declared.

The statute produced by the Lushnjë congress was the first constitutional document promulgated in Albania without foreign dictation. It provided for the calling of an assembly of seventy-nine members to be elected on a wide franchise, but given the backwardness of Albanian society this made those who organised the voting the decisive element in any poll; the statute also set up an executive in the form of a four-man supreme council which was to consist of one Catholic, one Orthodox and two Muslims, one of whom would be a Bektashi and one a Sunni.

After the Lushnjë congress the Durres government dissolved itself but other

144

obstacles to national reunification were not overcome with such delicacy. Outside the Hotel Continental in Paris on 13 June 1920 Avni Rustem Bey gunned down Esad Pasha Toptani, *frondeur par excellence* and the man who in the Balkan wars had sold Shkodër to the Montenegrins. Although Esad represented much that was backward in Albanian political culture, the fact that an alleged reformer and moderniser such as Avni Rustem should remove him in this fashion did not augur well for Albania's political evolution. After Esad had been eliminated his political power base, Durrës, was taken by the Lushnjë Albanians who then set about driving out what was left of the Yugoslav forces occupying the country. Even the Italians had now had enough. In August they signed the protocol of Tiranë and left the country.

From 1920 to 1925 the Albanians sought in vain for political order and stability; up until December 1922 there were seven different governments. Political groupings, which were based more on personal relationships and enmities than on ideology or principle, remained inchoate and shifting. Nevertheless, tendencies and strands of opinion were discernible. A progressive party had been formed in 1920 amongst those who were anxious to press ahead with modernisation. They regarded Avni Rustem as their hero and he told a founding conference of the Grand Fatherland Federation in April 1921 that they must strive for national unity, education, and the introduction of cooperatives to help the peasant farmers and the handicraft producers. Within a year the federation was in disarray and was dissolved by the government. A second tendency was that associated with the National People's or Populist Party founded in 1920. The title was a misnomer because the party, though it counted reformers such as bishop Fan Noli amongst its original members, represented primarily the aspirations of the tribal chiefs and landowners. They argued that the Lushnjë statute should be adapted to accommodate national traditions.

Another original member of the Populist Party had been Ahmed Zogolli, the leader of the Mati tribe in north central Albania. Educated in Constantinople, he had spent much of the war in Vienna but on returning to Albania had quickly marked himself out as one of the most audacious and effective of the defenders of Albanian independence. Between December 1921 and February 1924 Zogolli dominated, if he did not lead, Albania's multitude of ministries. His methods were at times unscrupulous even in the context of Albanian politics, but he was a genuine and passionate defender of Albanian interests. His authoritarian disposition meant he wished to establish a strong, centralised state in place of the anarchic, tribal, oligarchic parliamentarianism which had operated before partition in 1916 and since the Lushnjë statute had come into operation. He wanted to see modernisation and knew that this could not come about without the import of western capital and expertise; at the same time he did not wish to see the complete abandonment of traditional methods of production in manufacturing, nor did he wish to see foreign influences become predominant. To these ideas, which were forming in the early 1920s, Zogolli remained true throughout his period in Albanian politics.

Zogolli became prime minister and minister of the interior in December 1922 at the age of twenty-seven; in doing so he changed his name to Zogu, the deleted suffix being considered too Turkish for a modern Albanian patriot. In the same month the supreme council was renamed the supreme council of the regency. In the following year the progressive Noli tested the waters with an agrarian reform bill but such interference with property was rejected as opening the doors to bolshevism. With Noli and his associates defeated, Zogu decided in September to dissolve the assembly and to call a constituent assembly to revise the Lushnjë statute. His opponents believed that any constitution produced under Zogu's auspices would be nothing other than a vehicle for his own dictatorship and a rash of plots and conspiracies swept the country. Zogu compromised. On condition that the elections would be held and that he could remain prime minister, he agreed to give up the ministry of the interior, which was to rotate on a weekly basis.

The elections of November/December 1923 produced a stalemate, with twenty independents holding the balance between the Noli faction and the Zogists. There was soon resort to more traditional Albanian methods and violence became widespread. On 24 February 1924 it reached the parliament building when Beqir Walter, a supporter of Avni Rustem and an associate of Fan Noli, shot at Zogu, wounding him three times.

> The prime minister, wounded in the hand, the thigh and the middle abdomen, staggered into parliament with his gun in his hand and managed to reach the government bench. He was immediately surrounded by his supporters who quickly procured a doctor, although Zogu at first did not want to see him because he did not know him.
>
> The scene in parliament was understandably tense, most of the deputies seemed to recognise the danger of an open gunfight since everyone present was armed. The president of the parliament, Eshref Frashëri, and his staff had crowded into the corner of the hall while shooting continued in the forehall between Walter and the followers of Zogu. Walter, who had locked himself in the bathroom, commenced singing patriotic songs as he shot through the doors. After the assailant had been subdued ... Zogu from his bench announced in a loud voice, 'Gentlemen, this is not the first time this sort of thing has happened. I ask my friends to leave it alone and deal with it afterwards.'[1]

They did. On 20 April Avni Rustem was murdered in Tiranë and 'it was absolutely clear that Zog was behind the attack'.[2] In retaliation, on 1 May, twenty-six deputies who supported Noli set up an anti-parliament in Vlorë. The country was on the edge of disintegration.

The immediate escape came with a *coup d'état* by Noli who, with Italian support, seized power in June. He immediately imposed censorship of the press and refused to call elections or to hold a referendum to sanction the coup. He pursued his opponents with some vigour, setting up special courts to confiscate the property of those of them who had fled abroad. He received support from the tiny Albanian bourgeoisie and from the intelligentsia, a group which was not much larger but which had clear and defined aspirations for a modernised, westernised state whose citizens were economically and socially emancipated.

Noli's government published a twenty-point programme which called for a complete disarming of the population, the extirpation of feudalism, a democratic political system, the economic liberation of the peasantry, nation-wide provision of education and health-care, and friendly relations with all foreign states. The most important and controversial of the reform proposals was that concerning the land. The government responded to pressure from the peasantry for an immediate end to tithe farming; henceforth the levy was to be collected by the villages themselves, if they so wished. But further than this Noli did not go. In fact he disappointed peasant hopes both by failing to introduce a radical redistribution of property and by bending, despite a food shortage, to landlord pressure to reimpose the import tariffs on wheat he had just abolished. Noli had had time to frighten the landowners without being able to win over the peasantry, but his adventurism was no doubt restrained by the fear that too much zeal might bring down upon him and his followers the fate which Stamboliiski and the Bulgarian agrarians had suffered in the previous year. Noli was also cautious in dealing with the Soviets, but even the most careful of approaches to that quarter was regarded with deep suspicion by the Albanian traditionalists; Noli agreed to consider recognition and was much embarrassed when a Soviet delegation arrived in Tiranë unannounced late in 1924.

By the end of that year Noli had alarmed so many elements inside and outside the country that his government fell to Zogist forces on 24 December. Between December 1924 and 1928 Zogu strove to build a new, stable political order. His first step was to quieten national fears. He had had Yugoslav assistance in preparing his forces for this operation, but, in order to assure the Albanians that he was not a stooge of Belgrade, he circulated a forged letter from the anti-Yugoslav Mussolini in which the Duce allegedly wished Zogu well. In December he promulgated a series of constitutional amendments which replaced the supreme council with a president, appointed for seven years, who had wide-ranging powers including the right to veto legislation and to dissolve the assembly. On 25 January 1925 a constituent assembly confirmed these changes to the Lushnjë statutes and nominated Zogu president. Zogu represented his resumption of power as the restitution of legality but his return to Tiranë was essentially a restoration of the old order, even if it was less bloody than that in Bulgaria in June 1923.

Zogu's aims were to restore order and stability, to strengthen national solidarity, and to secure the foreign backing which would bring both international protection and capital for investment. Internal order and external backing were interlinked. At home Zogu used tough methods against those unwilling to accept his rule; a new gendarmerie, advised by a British expert, was introduced and a new civil code implemented to put a stop to such customs as the automatic shooting of adulterous wives. This inevitably provoked retaliation by the traditionalists. The revolt which broke out in northern Albania in November 1926 proved to be the most serious internal threat to his authority that he was to face, and it was a major stimulus to the signing of the pact of Tiranë with Italy on 27 November 1926. By this time Zogu's firm policies had involved him in probably as many as six hundred blood feuds, some with powerful clans, and Zogu led a beleaguered life, seldom leaving his office in his palace and eating only meals brought to him by his mother. A second Tiranë pact was signed with Italy in November 1927 after Belgrade had severed diplomatic relations following the arrest of a Yugoslav citizen on charges of spying.

The reign of King Zog

The association with Italy brought security against Yugoslav or Greek aggression and lessened the dangers of foreign incitement of revolt amongst the discontented or bored Albanians. Sensing that order had been restored, in September 1928 Zogu introduced another major constitutional change, declaring himself king. He also changed his name again; Ahmed was not a fitting name for a European monarch, so he became King Zog of the Albanians. A monarchy was not alien to a nation accustomed to sultans, pashas and tribal chieftains, and the possibility of reversion to one had been much discussed since the introduction of the 1925 constitution. The new constitution of 1928 made the parliament unicameral and gave the king virtually unlimited powers.

By 1929 Zog had achieved stability and order. He could tax and conscript the whole country without incessant local rebellion. A notion of Albanian identity was spreading through all classes, not least because Zog assiduously stressed the comparison between himself and Skënderbeg, the great national hero of the fifteenth century who had defied the Ottomans. Having secured stabilisation Zog could now devote more time to centralisation and the gradual modernisation of Albania. Those who opposed the reforms were faced with the alternatives of repression at home or an exile abroad in which they would be pursued by government assassins. There were few opponents. For the bureaucrats and the intelligentsia, who were not financially independent, there was little choice because only conformity would bring employment.

Zog's reforms began with the introduction of the civil code of 1929, based on the Napoleonic model. This, together with the new gendarmerie, began to contain brigandage. In 1930 a new penal code strengthened the modernising impulses in the legal sector, as did a commercial code decreed in 1931. National law, centrally determined, was replacing local, tribal custom. Centralisation was seen again in the nationalisation of education in 1933 which was part of a systematic but only partially successful programme to overcome illiteracy. The education of females made considerable progress, albeit from a very low base, but in general education suffered because the supply of teachers did not increase at the same rate as did the number of pupils. Nor was there any institute of higher education in the country, though Zog was generous in his provision of scholarships for bright children to study at foreign universities. Another sign of westernisation was the abandonment of the veil, pioneered by Zog's sisters in the 1920s; it was finally banned by decree in 1937. The same decree proscribed combinations of western and oriental dress – the fez was not to mix with the *frack*. In 1937 Zog at last succeeded in persuading the Orthodox hierarchy to establish an autocephalous Albanian church, though its leading officials were of dubious background. The Muslims of Albania had left the caliphate in 1922.

The major reform issue was land, tackled by the land law of May 1930. Each family was to be allowed forty hectares of arable land with an additional five hectares for the fifth and every subsequent member of the family. Existing landowners were to be allowed to keep two-thirds of their estates on condition that they promised to adopt modern production techniques and did not leave land fallow. Redistributed property was to be purchased by the recipients at a price of twenty Albanian francs per hectare which was to be paid into the newly established Land Bank. The measure was well-intentioned. It would also have the advantage of weakening the social base of the large landowners who could have posed a threat to Zog's authority. Unfortunately, the law had little impact. Land registration had begun only in 1927 and was not sufficiently advanced to make such a whole-scale redistribution of property feasible; nor was the Land Bank adequately developed to cope with the burdens which it was supposed to bear. In the end only about 8 per cent of state and 3 per cent of privately-owned land changed hands, in all some 1,200 hectares, most of which was given free to refugees from Kosovo.

Whilst pressing ahead with his reforms Zog was finding the close ties with Italy established in the mid-1920s increasingly irksome. By the early 1930s, 'From Zog down to the most lowly local official there was no one over whom the Italians could not exercise influence in one way or another.'[3] This influence was exercised through diplomatic channels and even more so through the numerous financial, economic, military, and cultural advisers the Italians had in Albania. To Zog it posed the threat that they could engineer a coup to remove him. Relations between Tiranë and Rome therefore deteriorated sharply in the early 1930s. In 1931 the Italians, who had in the past been rather generous lenders, insisted for the first time that a loan be given from government to government rather than privately or through third parties. Rome seemed to want to emphasise the Albanian régime's dependence on it, the open admission of which Zog was determined to resist. Rumours, encouraged by the Yugoslavs, that Italy intended to demand the signature of an Albanian-Italian customs union, which would have killed off most if not all of Albania's few manufacturing enterprises, persuaded Zog to refuse renewal of the pact of Tiranë. In 1933 the Italians complained bitterly at the nationalisation of education because it deprived the Catholic church of many of its schools in Albania, nor did Rome much welcome either Zog's signing of a commercial agreement with Yugoslavia in December

149

1933, or the establishment of diplomatic relations with the USSR in September 1934.

Defiance of Italy was popular at home but in the long term it inflicted real damage on Albania's fragile finances. The depression had hit what little export earning capacity the country had and the cessation of Italian loans and subsidies dealt an even harder blow. Government revenues fell and, because the head-quarters of the Bank of Albania were in Rome, printing extra money was not an available option. Zog was forced to cut official salaries and make some bureaucrats redundant; almost all public works had been suspended by the begin-ning of 1934 and, with so little money in circulation, trade virtually ceased. The dangers to Zog were obvious and were underlined by a rebellion in Fier in August 1935.

By then Zog had already begun to moderate his stance. In October 1935 he refused to support the League of Nations' sanctions against Italy over Abyssinia and a settlement of the schools issue in 1936 made it easier to restore the old working relationship between Tiranë and Rome. Italy received further con-cessions in that year and in return Albania was allowed its much-needed loans. Zog therefore continued his gradual modernising programme and if he could not offer the Albanians much in the way of bread at least he could give them circuses, or at least one. In April 1938 he married the Hungarian beauty Geraldine Apponyi; Hitler sent a Mercedes, Mussolini promised a yacht, and Horthy, ever the gentleman, sent a coach and pair. The Catholic church did not approve of the match and the vice-president of the assembly therefore officiated at the ceremony.

A dynasty is much more difficult to dislodge than a single, parvenu prince, and Zog's marriage had this obvious political purpose. The dangers to Albania had grown in March 1937 with the signature of the Yugoslav-Italian pact of friendship; Albania had always been relatively safe as long as Italy and Yugoslavia were not on good terms but should they agree then Albania could no longer rely on one to save it from the other; with no likelihood of an incursion by a Yugoslavia riven by internal disputes, the danger from Italy, once it had escaped from its Abyssinian and Spanish entanglements, was clear. In the summer of 1938 the Italians told Hitler that Albania was to them what Austria was to Germany. The replacement of Stojadinović by Cvetković in February 1939 was seen by both Berlin and Rome as an anti-fascist move and Mussolini, with the Spanish civil war nearing its end, decided that delay must be kept to the minimum. When Hitler marched into Prague without informing him the Duce pressed ahead, his ultimatum to Tiranë on 25 March demanding that Albania be made an Italian protectorate garrisoned by the Italian army. Zog appealed to Berlin, there were demonstrations in Tiranë calling for the people to be armed, and in the middle of it all Queen Geraldine gave birth to a son, Leka. It was too late to save the dynasty. Zog scuttled out of his country with unseemly haste shortly after Italian troops arrived on Good Friday, 7 April. His credibility was totally destroyed.

A confused and dispirited nation found only one person, Abas Kupi, willing to resist the invaders, but he and his few followers could do little against a modern army, even if it was Italian. It was Kupi's first but not his last taste of defeat.

11

IDEOLOGICAL CURRENTS IN
THE INTER-WAR PERIOD

COMMUNISM

Communist strategy, 1918–28

In 1919 the left-wing socialists of eastern Europe believed that the bolsheviks had provided an infallible guide to the art and practice of revolution in an underdeveloped society. Their faith was absolute and simple: 'They need only chant the magic incantation "All power to the Soviets", and the walls of the capitalist Jericho would fall down.'[1] The walls did not come tumbling down. Eastern Europe in 1919 was not analogous to Russia in 1917. Generally speaking there was peace, there were few communal tenures, and the large estates were in most places earmarked for redistribution to the peasants; there was in eastern Europe, outside the minority of the extreme left, a sense of revolution achieved rather than revolution pending. Furthermore, in eastern Europe the agrarians were better organised and more effective than the Russian social revolutionaries; the association of the extreme left with Russia was frequently a hindrance; and amongst the two peoples who showed considerable goodwill to the Russians, the Czechs and the Bulgarians, agrarianism was particularly well developed.

The failure immediately to bring about a soviet-style revolution did not mean the end of the association of the extreme left with the bolsheviks. Indeed, failure in the early years forced the left into greater reliance on the Russians for moral, physical, and financial support. But that support commanded a price. Moscow insisted upon obedience to a centrally-determined policy. And association with the bolsheviks meant also that the communist parties of eastern Europe were deeply affected by the twists and turns of Soviet policy and by the personal rivalries which accompanied or underlay them.

From the very beginning Lenin had insisted that the failure of the Second International had proved that any successor organisation must consist only of true revolutionaries who would submit to central discipline. Such an organisation appeared with the Third International, or Comintern (Communist International), established in Moscow in 1919. Leninist notions, concerning the need both for central control and for cooperation with the peasants, were seen in the twenty-one conditions for membership laid down by Comintern's second congress in 1920: constituent parties were to combat reformism, moderation, and pacifism in their ranks; they were to form cells in and eventually seize control of trade unions and similar organisations; they were to make a special effort to win peasant backing; they were to support the oppressed and colonial peoples' struggles for emancipation; in states where the communist party was legal and could send deputies to parliament a secret, parallel organisation was to be set up which would be 'capable at the decisive moment of fulfilling its duty to the revolution',[2] and all communist deputies were to be unflinchingly obedient to the decisions of the party central committee; communist parties were to do all that they could to support any soviet régime in conflict with the forces of counter-revolution; all communist parties were to be organised on the basis of democratic centralism and were to conduct periodic purges to cleanse their ranks of petty-bourgeois or careerist elements; and all parties were to abide by decisions of the Comintern congress or of the Comintern executive committee (ECCI).

Initially Comintern was uncompromisingly revolutionary in its policies but in 1921 attempts to foment insurrection amongst German miners proved disastrous. This, together with the internal Russian crises of 1921, enforced some moderation of Comintern policy. At the third Comintern congress in December 1921 'left-wing infantilism' was condemned. But this did not mean that an aggressive or forward policy had been abandoned. The means of promoting the revolution was now to be the united front, which called for cooperation with other radicals and their parties. In this willingness to work more closely with groups such as the agrarians can be seen a reflection of the bolsheviks' desire to cooperate with the Russian peasantry through the New Economic Policy (NEP). In later years there was a clear distinction between a united front 'from below' and a united front 'from above'. By the former was meant cooperation with the rank and file of peasant, social democratic, or other radical parties with the object of separating the leaders from the led and placing the latter securely under communist domination. A united front from above was more of a loose coalition in which the communists joined with other parties, acting through and with their official leaders. In the early 1920s this distinction was not elaborated and the united front of those years could be of either description. In fact little progress was made from above or below, since the conditions which the Comintern imposed on parties cooperating with it were extensive and usually crippling.

In fact the December 1921 decisions did not remain long in force. The agrarians had stolen much of the communists' reforming thunder and in 1923 the prospects for socialist revolution had receded, partly because of the collapse of the communists in Germany but chiefly because of the failure of the Bulgarian comrades to come to Stamboliiski's help during the coup of June; to talk of a united front in such circumstances was ludicrous. The fiasco of the Comintern-inspired rising by the Bulgarian communists in September 1923 dramatically emphasised the bleakness of revolutionary hopes.

The lesson of Bulgaria was that peasant and worker had to be brought closer together. To this end, in October 1923, the Peasant International (Krestintern) was established in Moscow. Krestintern was to coordinate the activities of workers and peasants but it did little more than reiterate its slogan of 'Peasants and Workers of all Countries, Unite!'. It held only two peasant congresses, theoretically the governing body of the movement, and remained firmly under Soviet domination, its general secretary, I. N. Smirnov, being Soviet commissar for agriculture. The Krestintern had few successes, and the non-communist Green International in Prague was always more influential. Radić did for a short while cooperate with Krestintern but he did so not through a desire for a Lenin-style alliance of worker and peasant but because he hoped to scare Belgrade into granting concessions to Croatia. Meanwhile BANU turned a cold shoulder and the Romanian National Peasant Party rejected Krestintern overtures as an interference in Romania's internal affairs. Krestintern was the poor relation of Comintern.

A somewhat lower and less effective profile in peasant agitation suited the mood of the mid-twenties. In the Soviet Union the heyday of NEP and Bukharin's gradualist road to socialism counselled cooperation with the peasantry, whilst in the rest of Europe the return of economic stability lessened privation, thereby shrinking the communists' recruiting grounds and forcing them into greater material dependence upon Moscow.

This restrained attitude lasted until the sixth Comintern congress of July–September 1928. There had been mounting evidence that the communist movement was in difficulty, and Stalin used every morsel of such evidence in his domestic political intrigues. As early as 1924 a futile rising in Bessarabia had collapsed even more quickly than the Bulgarian rising of 1923; in 1925 in Bulgaria the bombing of Sveta Nedelya cathedral unleashed ferocious repression upon the left. In 1926 the British general strike had illustrated the weakness of non-communist unions whilst in Poland the hope that Piłsudski would remain true to his socialist ancestry proved wildly misplaced. In 1927 war-fever seized some of the Soviet leadership, and this, together with the rapidly spreading conviction that a British-dominated international conspiracy to unleash war against socialism, questioned the utility of the gradualist and cooperative approach to relations with other left-wing organisations.

The sixth Comintern congress ordered a complete about-face. The emphasis was now to be on proletarian revolution. The changes in Comintern policy were closely connected with the coming switch of policies inside the USSR and were justified on the grounds that imperialism was becoming more aggressive and that the class struggle had therefore intensified. In these circumstances there was no effective difference between parliamentary democracy of the bourgeois type and fascism. Both were part of the joint offensive which the bourgeoisie was mounting against socialism, with the parliamentary parties being used to subvert socialism from within and fascism to bludgeon it from without. There could therefore be no cooperation with the parliamentary parties; the social democrats were written off as 'social fascists' and the peasant parties denounced as fascists in all but name. The united front from below, with communists infiltrating and subverting other parties, was to be permitted but everything was to be subordinated to the defence of socialism in the Soviet Union. At the same time the 'bolshevisation' of all communist parties, which had been ordered by the fifth Comintern congress in 1924, was to be accelerated.

From Comintern's sixth congress to the Popular Front, 1928–35

If the period of stabilisation from 1923 to 1928 had seen few gains for the communists outside the USSR, that which followed it saw a series of disasters. The main result of the new policy was, of course, that the great German Social Democratic Party was offered up as a sacrifice to Hitler and his rampaging Nazis. In eastern Europe the Czechoslovak Communist Party (CPCS) suffered severe but not equal tribulation. The CPCS had always been exceptional. Even before the formulation of a communist party Czech socialist prisoners of war in Russia had gravitated towards the mensheviks rather than the bolsheviks and after the foundation of the CPCS in 1921 its leader, Bohumír Šmeral, had insisted, in the face of Comintern opposition, that the Czechs and Slovaks were a single nation. He also argued that in Czechoslovakia the bourgeoisie was much more developed and, unlike that in the rest of eastern Europe, was too strong to be overthrown by an alliance of workers and peasants. The CPCS also enjoyed more freedom of operation than any other party in eastern Europe and its membership was greater; it was a mass party rather than a cadre party on the Soviet model and this encouraged a spirit of independence; in 1925 nine of the twenty-seven communist deputies in the Czechoslovak parliament quit the party in protest at interference on the part of Comintern. In response Moscow backed a group of young extremists headed by Klement Gottwald who criticised Šmeral for failing to see that the Czechoslovak Agrarian Party was 'proto-fascist'. At the CPCS's fifth congress in February 1929 Gottwald's group seized control and brought about the bolshevisation of the Czechoslovak party. The cost, however, was a massive loss of membership and an equally dramatic decline in support in the elections of that year.

Other parties benefited from the tighter discipline imposed after the sixth Comintern congress. In Yugoslavia the CPY had fallen to bitter feuding after it had been banned in 1921 but some order was restored after ECCI, just before the sixth congress, sent the Italian party chief, Palmiro Togliatti, to impose a unified leadership under Djuro Djaković; Comintern support after 1928 considerably bolstered the latter's authority, even if the 1929 rising staged by the CPY against the new royal dictatorship was ineffectual. The Romanian party, which was also in exile and which also had become split, was likewise persuaded into greater unity and discipline.

Despite the restoration of cohesion to some individual parties the policies laid down by the sixth congress produced little success for communism in eastern Europe. The impact of the depression did encourage some gains, for example in the Sofia municipal elections of 1932, but few European peasants could respond

155

enthusiastically whilst the Soviet countryside was being subjected to enforced collectivisation and starvation.

By 1935 this failure to garner support, together with the catastrophe in Germany in 1933 and the storm clouds massing in Spain, had forced a rethink. In its seventh congress in 1935 Comintern ordered yet another about-turn when the Popular Front from above was decreed. It was now accepted that there was a difference between parliamentary democracy and fascism and that all parties of the left needed to combine against the latter. The communist parties, however, were not to forsake their right to criticise other parties and the communists were to retain their organisations and cadres intact, since they had not lost sight of their ultimate goal of a proletarian revolution. According to Gheorghi Dimitrov, the Bulgarian communist appointed general secretary of Comintern in 1935, the Popular Front was not the dictatorship of the proletariat but a form of action appropriate to the eve of a socialist seizure of power. The conditions necessary for the formation of a Popular Front therefore included a disorganised and paralysed bourgeoisie and a working class which was determined to resist fascism but which was not yet sufficiently politically sophisticated to fight under communist party leadership.

The Soviet purges and the Nazi-Soviet pact, 1935–41

After promulgation of the Popular Front doctrine many parties went to work with a will, but they achieved little. The communists' image, despite the boost of Dimitrov's acquittal in the Leipzig trial, was tarnished by collectivisation; more importantly, Stalin's determination to purge and rebuild the CPSU affected foreign parties too. Between 1937 and 1939 the leadership of many eastern European and other parties was torn asunder.

Particular groups were at risk. As in the Soviet Union, association with Lenin and the pre-1917 Bolshevik Party made for especial vulnerability. So too did exile in Moscow, to which many leaders had recourse after their parties were declared illegal. Jews, supporters of Trotsky, and those who had disagreed with Stalin, particularly in the field of nationalities policy in which he was supposed to be an expert, suffered particularly heavily. The party which suffered most grievously was the Polish. It was vulnerable on all of the above accounts and so ravaging was the purge of its ranks that in 1938 the party was disbanded. The Yugoslavs also suffered severely. They had been in exile in Moscow since the early 1920s and had also differed with Stalin on the question, so important in the Yugoslav party, of nationalities policy. Of the Yugoslav exiled leaders the only survivor was Josip Broz, or 'Tito' as he was later to be called, and that was primarily because he spent much of the time in Spain. All parties, however, saw leaders arrested, imprisoned and executed. The Bulgarians and Czechoslovaks suffered less than others; the Bulgarians were shielded to some degree by Dimitrov and after Munich most Czechoslovak leaders sought refuge in France rather than the USSR. Nevertheless, thousands of the rank and file of the CPCS did flee to the Soviet Union only to perish in Stalin's gulag.

The purges disoriented and demoralised the east European communist parties to such a degree that when the shock of the Nazi-Soviet pact came they were too punch-drunk to protest. Indeed, communist influence in most of eastern Europe began to revive only after the German attack upon the USSR in June 1941.

The reasons for the weakness of communism in eastern Europe between the wars

Communist weakness in the inter-war period had many causes. In the first place the communist parties were under considerable pressure from the governments of eastern Europe; the communist party was declared illegal in Hungary and Poland in 1919, in Yugoslavia in 1921, and in Bulgaria, Romania, and Estonia in 1924; in Albania it did not exist until after the Italian occupation of 1939. And, despite help from Moscow and communist skills in underground activity, legal restrictions could not but make life more difficult. Discipline and conformity were less easily enforced in an illegal party and in a number of such parties splinter groups on both the right and the left appeared. The Bulgarian party, for example, had the Lûch (ray) faction on the right and also its 'left sectarians' upon whom such embarrassing excesses as the Sveta Nedelya incident were conveniently but unfairly blamed.

More important in the east European context was the fact that communist doctrine found it difficult to accommodate the independent peasant proprietor who was in many ways the epitome of the petty bourgeois producer. In the 1920s many peasants had already been given what they most wanted: land. The communist response was that they should be given more, that compensation payments should be abolished, and that more should be done to promote agricultural improvement. In the 1920s, when many peasants were enjoying relative prosperity, this had little impact. In the 1930s many of the gains the communists might otherwise have reaped were squandered by the impact of collectivisation. It was not just that the peasants were revolted and frightened by the hideous brutality with which the policy was applied, the very objective of the policy itself was unacceptable to them and alien to their mentality. A British traveller in Romania in the 1930s was told the following story of a communist agitator who had appeared in a Bessarabian village:

> There was a bolshevik who had come to that village. When he told everyone of the fine things that communism would bring the people listened to him. One day there was a crowd with him and he chose an old man from the rest so that he could explain what he meant. 'Now suppose you have two cows,' he said. 'You keep one and give the rest to the community. Do you understand?' 'Yes, that is excellent,' answered old

Naie. 'If you have four horses, you keep two and give two to the community.' 'Yes, that is very good.' 'If you have six pigs, you keep three and give three to the community.' 'That is good too.' 'And if you have eight sheep, you keep four and give four to he community.' Naie shook his head. 'Oh, no, that is not good.' Then the bolshevik became angry and said he was stupid because he had agreed when he had asked him about the horses, the cows, and the pigs. 'That is so,' said Naie, 'since I have no horses, cows, or pigs, but I have many sheep.'[3]

It is one of the paradoxes of east European history, however, that despite the obvious difficulties of recruiting in the countryside the communists fared better there than in the towns. The developed proletariats of Czechoslovakia and Poland were socialist rather than communist and communist strength was concentrated in the less-developed areas to the east, the south, and the south-east. In part this was because the share-croppers were more vulnerable than the self-sufficient peasants to the fluctuations of the international agrarian commodity market, and share-croppers were to be found in Slovakia, Ruthenia, and parts of the Balkans. But the concentration of communist strength in the more backward areas was also connected to the national question. In 1924 the Comintern had pronounced in favour of self-determination, even to the point of separation. This meant that, until the reversal of this policy in 1935, the communists had greater appeal to those who felt nationally disadvantaged. Thus, communist support in Poland was concentrated not amongst the anti-Russian Polish workers but amongst the anti-Polish Ukrainian and Belorussian peasants; in Czechoslovakia it was not so much the proletariat of Bohemia and Moravia who voted for the CPCS as the peasants of Ruthenia and Slovakia. In the latter, communist support was particularly strong amongst the Magyars, partly because they saw themselves as a minority amongst a minority, partly because many of them were poor share-croppers, and partly because a large number of Hungarian communists had taken refuge in Slovakia after the suppression of the Kun régime. In Romania too communist support was to be found primarily amongst the minorities of Bessarabia and the Bukovina, though the Magyars of Transylvania had a prior loyalty to the Magyar state whoever ruled it. In Yugoslavia the communists had some supporters amongst the Belgrade proletariat but Serbs in general, despite their pro-Russian traditions, did not like the Comintern's policy on national minority rights. This policy, however, did have a limited appeal to the aggrieved peasants of Croatia, Bosnia, Macedonia, and Montenegro, but the appeal was more a national than a class one.

The association until 1935 of the communist party with national separatism made it easy for governments to secure general popular support for the containment of communism, and in any case Soviet domestic policies after 1929 lessened the party's appeal in many of its former areas of strength; after the sufferings of the Ukraine between 1929 and 1931 the Ukrainians of Poland looked more to Berlin or Vienna than to Kiev or Moscow.

The communists' association with Russia, even before the purges and the Nazi-Soviet pact, could also be a disadvantage in such traditionally anti-Russian areas as Poland, Romania, and Hungary. In these countries it was significant that the Jewish profile amongst the communist leadership was high. This was in itself not a factor making for communist strength.

That the communists failed to cash in on the devastations of the depression in eastern Europe made easier the advance of the forces of the extreme right.

FASCISM

Fascism as action rather than ideology

Whilst communism, despite its clearly defined doctrine and its highly disciplined and international organisation, prospered little, its most vigorous opponent, fascism, though having none of these apparent advantages, thrived, particularly in the second half of the 1930s. Mass fascist movements emerged in Romania and Hungary, where the fascists were to enjoy brief if frenetic periods in office. And in a number of states where mass movements did not emerge there were nevertheless authoritarian, right-wing leaders and organisations employing many of the methods and policies of fascism. Poland after 1935, Lithuania, Yugoslavia under Stojadinović, Zog's Albania, and Boris' Bulgaria were not fascist states but they had learnt a number of lessons from Mussolini's Italy, whilst in Hungary and Romania the established power-holders fondly believed that they could weaken fascism by adopting some of its policies.

Fascism is not easily defined. It has no corpus of ideology similar to the canons of marxism-leninism. It is a phenomenon of action rather than ideas: a Hungarian who interviewed peasants involved in an early fascist movement reported, ' "We fight for the Idea," they repeated when I questioned them, but were unable to tell what the "Idea" was about.'[4] Milan Hodža urged the fascists to formulate their own ideology and their own concept of the ideal state, as the communists had done, but few heeded him. All that the fascists could really say was that they were for an authoritarian state whose function in most cases was to protect and foster the interests of its dominant nation. In so far as that state was conceptualised it was usually corporate in nature. Gömbös in 1935 announced that he would create a 'one party, corporate state'[5] and such a state was eventually set up by the Arrow Cross in 1944–5, whilst in Slovakia Tiso's system was essentially corporate. Dimitrije Ljotić, who was to found the Yugoslav fascist organisation *Zbor* (rally), resigned from government in 1934 when King Alexander refused to accept his draft constitution which contained provisions for a corporate state. On the other hand, the Croatian Ustaše were not keen on the corporate idea because it had long been part of the ideology of the Slovene People's Party and of a number of Serbian political groups in Croatia.

Like fascist movements in the west, those in eastern Europe demanded control and discipline of society and of themselves. Control was to be exercised through the security forces and through the mass organisations for youth, women, workers, and others. Gömbös established youth and women's movements in Hungary, though they were disbanded immediately after his death, whilst in Slovakia Tiso had to move rapidly to ensure control over the Hlinka Guard into which a number of potentially powerful youth and para-military organisations had been merged in October 1938. In the Iron Guard's six rules for legionary life, the first demanded discipline and subservience to the next in command. Again, as in the west, the *Führerprinzip* was an integral and extremely important part of fascist thinking.

If fascism was a phenomenon of action more than thought it was also at least as strong in its antipathies as in its sympathies; feeding on hatred and fear more readily than on benevolence and magnanimity, the fascists were anti-socialist and anti-communist. These antipathies were intensified by the association of socialism and communism with Russia, whose expansionist ambitions were still feared, a factor of particular importance in strengthening the political right in the Baltic states, Poland, and Romania.

Parliamentary democracy, on the other hand, was more derided than feared. In international terms, in the second half of the 1930s in particular, the western democracies appeared feeble and ineffective alongside or opposed to assertive and successful fascism, whilst at home parliamentary democracy was seen as breeding corruption and inefficiency. Czechoslovak party-political jobbery was called in as evidence for this point of view; in Lithuania the move to the right in the mid-1920s was due in no small measure to rampant political and bureaucratic corruption; and in Romania it was said that only the immoral and the corrupt secured election to parliament and once in place did little more than encourage the further contamination of politics and administration.

In many of the political establishments of eastern Europe corruption was endemic and the fascists' outrage against it was a further indication that they were in general anti-establishment. Amongst the Slovak Catholic masses there was widespread resentment not only at an establishment which was predominantly Czech but also at one in which the Slovak contingent which was mainly Protestant. Similarly in Croatia Croat, Catholic resentment at Serbian, Orthodox centralism fattened the Ustaša movement after its foundation in 1929. In Romania the established bureaucracy fuelled many fascist passions, the more so in the former Habsburg territories whose previous administrations had been much less venal. In Czechoslovakia, or more accurately in the Czech lands, the small fascist groups were united in their condemnation of the Hrad and of the powerful political parties which constituted the Bohemian and Moravian establishments.

The fascists, though fiercely anti-socialist, had little love for capitalism. Capitalism, like socialism, promoted materialist values which conflicted with the national spirit, and frequently capitalists themselves were not members of the sainted nation. Capitalism was also an agent of modernisation, a process which the fascists wanted not to halt but to control and direct. At times, however, fascist behaviour did show traces of anti-modernisation, particularly in a reversion to anti-rational, obscurantist practices. Many rituals harked back to medieval or earlier times and in fascist circles 'there was a revival of astrology and necromancy, discredited since the dawning of the "Age of Reason" '.[6] Arcane and irrational as well as anti-rational practices reached their peak amongst the Iron Guard of Romania, whose cult of sacrifice, blood, and death was epitomised in an incident in 1936 when ten Guardists attacked Mihail Stelescu, a former colleague who had turned against them. Stelescu was in hospital recovering from an appendectomy when his ten assailants surrounded his bed and fired 120 shots into his prostrate body. They then hacked his body to pieces with axes, after which, said an official investigation, they 'danced around the pieces of flesh, prayed, kissed each other and cried with joy'.[7]

Fascism and anti-semitism

The most obvious and most vicious expression of anti-rationalism and irrationality was anti-semitism. Jewish people were frequently associated with capitalism, socialism, modernisation and many of the other evils which enraged or frustrated the fascists; anti-semitism had therefore been an important element in most, though not all, east European fascist movements even before the establishment of Nazi power in Germany. An Italian journalist identified anti-semitism as the only point of 'national cohesion' amongst the Danubian parties of the right, although this did not hold good for Serbia or Bulgaria. Anti-semitism frequently enabled the fascists to appeal to entrenched popular prejudice. This was much more effective than reason as a means of combating established political power; in Romania, for example, in the 1920s anti-semitism enabled the extreme right to attack the NPP which could make a much more credible claim to be the best protector of peasant interests. Also, since Romanians had no dispute with the 1919 peace settlement, the fascists could not use national humiliation by the democratic peacemakers of Versailles as a rallying cry, and so anti-semitism was all the more important as a propaganda weapon; it was internal rather than external chauvinism. At a more sophisticated level some fascists drew a distinction between exploitative and creative capital; it was easy to define exploitative capital as that in foreign or Jewish ownership and creative capital as that in the hands of nationals. By such arguments did the fascists attempt to replace the class struggle with the national struggle.

Action against Jews also had the important function in the second half of the 1930s of serving as a gesture of goodwill or obeisance to the new lords of central Europe, the Nazis. Hungary's first anti-semitic law of 1938 was to a considerable degree motivated by a determination to secure German goodwill during the partition of Czechoslovakia. Later, in Hungary and elsewhere, the fact that former Jewish wealth had been seized and distributed to nationals bound recipients of that wealth to the fascists.

The widespread existence and use of anti-semitism by fascist organisations was reflected in the frequent use of phrases such as 'Christian-National' to describe fascist values or programmes, the adjective 'Christian' being a code-word for anti-semitic.

Fascism and the nation

The 'National' concept was central to fascism. In 1921 the Rome congress of Fascists declared:

> The nation is not merely the sum total of living individuals, nor the instrument of parties for their own ends, but an organism comprising the unlimited series of generations of which individuals are merely transient elements; it is the supreme synthesis of all the material and non-material values of the race.[8]

Codreanu reflected this basic fascist notion in his statement that the nation was more than an aggregation of living individuals, since it also included 'the souls and the bones of the dead and the legacy of future generations',[9] and it was because the nation encompassed the living, the dead, and the yet-to-be-born that parliamentary democracy was denounced; it allowed representation only to the living, who would have consideration only for short-term objectives of a squalid, material, and personal nature. In Hungary Gömbös had spoken of a 'unitary Hungarian nation' and Szálasi was later to propagate notions of mystical communion between Hungarians of present, past, and future generations. In Lithuania the national ideal was again the prime impulse to fascism, which in Lithuania 'consisted mainly of a reaction against what was, or what was considered to be, a threat to Lithuanian nationality – Poland and the Polish cultural influence'.[10] In Czechoslovakia would-be fascist leaders found it necessary to jettison non-Czech sounding given names; Gajda changed his from Rudolf to Radola; with German-sounding names there could be little credibility in a claim to represent a continuum with the previous and future generations of Czechs.

The importance of the national ideal is again apparent in the fact that fascism was weak in both Czechoslovakia and Yugoslavia where a state-national consciousness did not exist and indeed had to compete with dissatisfied constituent minorities amongst whom fascism or something very near it was strong. Fascism was further compromised in Czechoslovakia by an internal paradox in that Czech fascists were fiercely anti-German; the Germans in Czechoslovakia were construed as the major threat to the security of the state, although it was all but impossible to be anti-German and fascist when Hitler was showering fascism with conspicuous victories. Furthermore, in Czechoslovakia fascism was irreconcilable with a national ideal which fed upon the Husite tradition of tolerance and respect for the individual and which had reached its apotheosis in the liberal, generous-minded Tomáš Masaryk, who in 1900 had courageously defended a Jew accused of ritual child murder. Nor could the fascists in Bohemia and Moravia complain that modernisation was the work of foreigners who would exploit the nation, because Czechs had played a significant role in the industriali-sation of the area.

In eastern Europe the drawing of the frontiers in 1919 was in general less important as an explanation of fascist strength than in the west. In Hungary, of course, all functioning parties denounced the Trianon settlement, because not to have done so would have been political suicide. However, if the resentments at national defeat and a sense of national deprivation or injustice were essential ingredients of fascism, why was the latter strong in Romania but weak in Bulgaria?

Fascism and religion in eastern Europe

A further difference between west European and east European fascism was the prominence of the religious factor in the latter. Most east European fascist leaders – Szálasi in Hungary, Codreanu in Romania, Bolesław Piasecki in Poland, Dimitrije Ljotić in Serbia, and the Croat Ante Pavelić – as well as leaders of near-fascist movements such as Tiso in Slovakia, Dmowski in Poland, and Volder-maras in Lithuania, proclaimed their Christian conviction or were even ordained priests. Clerical conservatives had welcomed the fascists as allies in the struggle against godless socialism. In February 1939 the Provincial of the Jesuit Order in Slovakia, Father Rudolf Mikus, said that the Jews must be removed from Slovak public and commercial life, though any solution to this problem must, he said, be just. By 1938 the Slovak autonomists were using the slogan 'One God, One Party, One Nation', even if another favourite slogan had a less than Christian content: 'Slovakia for the Slovaks, Palestine for the Jews, the Danube for the Czechs'.[11] In Croatia close links were established between the Ustaše and some members of the Catholic hierarchy. The connections between fascism and the Orthodox church, though less formalised, were often as strong. Indeed it could be argued that the Orthodox church, with its emphasis on ritual and its penchant for mysticism, was particularly appropriate to fascism. Orthodoxy allowed, even encouraged, the subsumation of the individual into the collective, corporate body; it welcomed the surrender of the individual to the spiritual union of the church; so strong was the faith of Ljotić that the Yugoslav government, when it wanted to arrest him, used a charge of religious mania to detain him. But it is in Romania yet again that the absurdity of fascism reached its full reduction. Codreanu had founded his movement because when in prison he had had a vision in which the Archangel Michael urged him to devote his life to God as revealed in the Romanian Christian tradition. Romanian fascism was 'a "born again" Christian Orthodox movement'[12] in which Codreanu was the earthly representative of the Archangel and 'The Romanian people were God's children, blessed by the Orthodox church'.[13] Every Guardist meeting began and ended with hymns or prayers, and Codreanu spoke of the ultimate goal of the movement as being 'spiritual resurrection! The resurrection of nations in the name of Jesus Christ!'[14] The Orthodox church in Romania had no difficulty in associating

163

with anti-semitism, the patriarch, for example, believed 'almost literally that the Jews had sucked the blood of the Romanians'.[15] For many churchmen, Orthodox and Catholic, the marriage with fascism was one of convenience and one which became an increasing embarrassment, but for many fascists the belief that their movement had a deep Christian foundation was genuine and lasting.

The social bases of east European fascism

Fascism in eastern Europe, as in the west, drew its support from a wide range of professional and social backgrounds. The army was one of the main groups which supported the Arrow Cross whilst a significant proportion of the adherents of the Lithuanian Iron Wolves, an élitist, allegedly secret fascist organisation, were to be found amongst army and air force officers. In general, however, mass support for east European fascism came from the same area as in the west: from the lower ranks of the established, or middle, middle class, and from the upper reaches of the lower middle class, be that middle class bureaucratic, business, or intelligentsia. Fascism could, it was assumed, provide both a defence for those who feared falling down the social ladder and a rapid means of advancement for those who wished to claw their way up it. Movement in either direction would be more likely and more pronounced in times of great social instability, a fact which goes a long way to explain the strength of fascism after the onset of the great economic crisis in 1929. In areas where one ethnic group replaced another, social mobility was even greater and frequently, though not always, produced strong fascist tendencies. In Transylvania the Romanians, formerly discriminated against by the Magyars, were after 1919 the dominant element and were described in the 1930s as:

> bent on creating for themselves a national middle and upper class – an ambition which can be achieved only, or most easily, at the expense of the Magyar, German, and Jewish national aristocracy and bourgeoisie. The acres of the Magyar Council or the Saxon Chapter, the director's fees of the Jewish banker, the magistrate's or panel doctor's or porter's jobs are prizes desirable enough, in any case, to eyes grown sore and belts grown slack with long waiting; how much more desirable when the acquisition of them can be hallowed by the name of national policy.[16]

Once again in eastern Europe social and national causes were inseparable.

Amongst the stalwarts of fascism in Hungary were those of proletarian origin whose jobs had levered them out of that stratum: the concierges, office messengers, and domestic servants. But this is not to imply that working class support for fascism was unknown. Szálasi campaigned vigorously in the proletarian quarters of Hungary's cities and was well rewarded for his efforts, one of the main features of the Arrow Cross being its 'very pronounced plebian social structure'.[17] It was also Arrow Cross men who were prominent in the great miners' strike in Hungary in 1940, though in general terms the Arrow Cross was weaker amongst those sections of the working class which had been unionised. As the latter were primarily the skilled workers in heavy industry, proletarian fascist support was strongest amongst the unemployed, the unskilled, and the workers in the small craft workshops for whom the Arrow Cross provided help in finding jobs as well as recreational and cultural facilities. In Romania the Iron Guard also found support in the urban workers. They, in fact, had few alternatives because they had been leaderless since the strikes of the 1920s. The communists had all but disappeared and the social democrats polled fewer votes than the Jewish parties; the Romanian worker was therefore drawn to the anti-capitalist, anti-banking, anti-bourgeois rhetoric of Codreanu and his Legion; the more so when many employers were Jewish.

The critical factor in eastern Europe, however, was not the worker but the peasant. And for the fascists, with their distorted views of history, the peasant had especial, almost mystical qualities, since in the peasantry were believed to repose the quintessential characteristics of the nation. The peasant had not been touched by, and indeed must be shielded from, modernisation. The traditional peasant did not treat his land as capital, a wealth-producing facility, but as a factor uniting him with the past and future generations who had or were to till it; nor did the peasant exploit his fellow citizens, relying instead on the labour of his immediate family. Continuity, a racially unmixed lineage, mutual cooperation, and immunity from the corruption of modern, materialist values were seen as hallmarks of the peasantry which therefore became the model, in so far as it existed, of *Homo fasciensis*. In Hungary such a peasantry could not exist until land had been redistributed, hence in part the fascist drive for land reform, whilst in Romania the intelligentsia went on a journey of historical rediscovery and found their nationalist souls in native peasant traditions. In the nineteenth century the Romanian élite had tried to create a new Paris in the Balkans but they had failed; they were therefore neither western because of their birth nor Romanian because of their education; and the post-1918 generation reacted against them and looked instead to its own country for its ideal; thus 'The village and the peasant became symbols of honesty, sanity, and primeval purity, the stronghold of national life.'[18] In Hungary too, in the 1930s, many young intellectuals believed that they could pay their debt to their nation by going into the countryside and helping the peasants, these 'village explorers' following in the tradition of the alienated gentry of Russia who went 'to the people' in the 1870s and 1890s.

Attempts to enlist peasant support were not conspicuously successful in the 1920s when, by and large, rural economies were not depressed; Gömbös even dropped land reform from his political programme. The picture changed dramatically in the early 1930s. When the half-crazed Zoltán Böszörményi launched the first and short-lived attempt at a fascist rising in Hungary he chose as his starting point Nagybaros, a region to the east of the Tisza so deprived that it was the breeding ground for strange sects and for the so-called 'arsenic women' who found life so hard that in an attempt to alleviate its burdens they poisoned their menfolk. In areas with an established peasantry, fascist propaganda sought to prove that most of the evils which beset those rural paragons of national virtue were attributable to the arch-enemy, the Jew. It was frequently the Jews, said fascist propagandists, who provided the loans which, after the collapse of agrarian prices, were so difficult to pay off; it was the Jewish merchant who bought crops at artificially low prices, and the Jewish pedlar who sold manufactured items at inflated ones; it was Jewish money which corrupted the bureaucrat and caused him to make life so difficult for the peasant; and it was the Jewish socialist who schemed to take the peasant's land from him and his family and to incorporate it into an anonymous collective or state farm.

Peasant support for fascism varied directly with the strength of peasant control over the land and with the degree of economic self-sufficiency and national independence. In Hungary the rural population was to a large extent still dependent on the landlords; in Romania they had been dependent on the landlords or their frequently Jewish bailiffs until the end of the first world war. On the other hand, in areas where peasant proprietorship had been a reality for a generation or more, for example Slovenia, Bulgaria, and Serbia, fascism made little headway. Furthermore, there seems to be some correlation between the strength of rural fascism and the prevalence of effective agrarian cooperation. In Bohemia, Moravia, Slovenia, Bulgaria, and to some extent western Galicia, agrarian cooperatives had defended peasant interests against 'foreign' landowners, whilst in Slovakia, eastern Galicia, Poznania, and Pomerania the drift of the masses was more to the right. The exception was Croatia, where social factors were submerged by the all-consuming national confrontation with Belgrade.

Amongst active fascists generational divisions were probably more significant than social ones. Fascism was primarily a movement of youth, and particularly the youth of the intelligentsia. Transylvanian and Moldavian students were prominent in the early development of Romanian fascism, with medical students in Cluj, Iaşi, and Bucharest demanding that their Jewish colleagues should not be allowed to dissect non-Jewish cadavers. In Kaunus students had taken a leading part in the demonstrations which led to the military takeover of December 1926; when Piasecki established the Polish Falanga he was a young man of scarcely twenty summers, and it was mainly young intellectuals who joined Zbor, set up by Ljotić. Fascism was attractive to youth because it was a phenomenon of action rather than thought and because it seemed to be the movement of the future. The old order was compromised by the failures of 1914 and 1929; marxism-leninism had by 1930 been subordinated to Stalin's vicious, introspective revolution; social democracy was irredeemably discredited by its main virtue, its willingness to compromise; and keynsianism was not presented as a fully formulated doctrine until 1936. Mussolini, however, had shown how political order could apparently be plucked from social chaos, Hitler was demonstrating the deadly efficiency of militant fascism as a remedy for national grievances, and Franco was to prove that clericalism and militarism were by no means spent forces. Fascism, for many, was the Zeitgeist.

166

It was also the product of new education. In many east European states, particularly those created or enlarged after 1918, education had expanded rapidly in the post-war period and inevitably bore the stamp of those years. By the 1930s the new schools and universities were producing graduates who could not, given the economic exigencies of the time, hope to find work. Their un- or under-employment, combined with an education based on 'an intellectual pap which consists very largely of national self-glorification',[19] was an explosive mixture which a fascist fuse could easily ignite. It was a simple progression to demand that Jews be deprived of their jobs or be limited to a share equal to the proportion of Jews to the total population, and it was the young intellectual proletariat which stood to gain from such discrimination.

The role of west European fascism

The influence of west European fascist régimes inevitably played some role in the development of east European fascism, but it was indirect and not always beneficial. Mussolini and Hitler both acted as exemplars, whether it was in encouraging Gömbös to stage a march on Budapest in 1922 or in determining the design of the uniforms worn by Tsankov's adherents in Bulgaria, and naturally fascist pulses were quickened by every diplomatic victory won by the Palazzo Chigi or the Wilhelmstrasse. Conversely, Hungary's fascists were not alone in being devastated by the signature of the Nazi-Soviet pact in 1939. Nor could east European fascist leaders expect a great deal of sympathy from Berlin. Hitler wanted reliable rather than cognate governments in eastern Europe and he disliked any tendency to instability or even anarchy. Until 1944 Germany gave limited encouragement to the Arrow Cross and for the most part preferred the established and orderly rule of Horthy, just as in 1941 it had preferred Antonescu's disciplined rule to the raging furies of the Iron Guard. Nor did German money flow in vast quantities into east European fascist coffers. Henlein was given Nazi cash but not until at least 1935 and other fascist leaders received little beyond small sums to instigate pogroms against local Jews or to finance high-profile assistance to the Francoists in Spain. In Yugoslavia and Czechoslovakia western fascisms were more of an embarrassment than a help to local fascists, since both Germany and Italy were former or present foes.

The weaknesses of eastern European fascism

Despite the strength of fascism in Romania and Hungary it did not carry all before it. It had weaknesses as well as strengths. If a fascist movement depends much upon the quality of its leader, as by its own *Führerprinzip* it should, then east European fascist leaders were not well chosen. Gömbös' pride and bombast could reach absurd levels, as when he let Berlin know that if Germany regarded Hungary as part of its *Ostraum* then Hungary would look upon Germany as part of its *Nordwestraum*. Szálasi was totally unfitted for dynamic revolutionary leadership; in the climacteric days of October 1944 he spent much of his time writing seven volumes of incomprehensible memoirs and communing with John Campbell, a long dead Scot who was predicting the imminent defeat of the allies. In Czechoslovakia Štříbrný had twice been accused of embezzlement and Gajda, a professional soldier, had during the first world war been charged with lack of discipline and contact with a foreign power. Even in Romania the leading Guardists seemed dazzled by the notion of self-sacrifice and allowed themselves to go to the slaughter without resistance, with the result that when the legionary state was created the most able Guardists were already dead.

Policies as well as personalities were defective. The Romanian government in 1938 talked of implementing one item of guardist policy: the expulsion of Jews who had arrived in Romania since 1918 without proper legal documentation. Their number could have been as high as 800,000. The immediate results were a collapse of the *lei* and a huge increase in the value of the pound sterling on the black market; the consequent crisis proved that the Jews were essential to Romania's financial stability – the very opposite of what the guardist activists were arguing. Similarly, anti-semitic legislation which forced the Orthodox Jews of the Bukovina to keep their shops open on the Jewish sabbath not only offended the Jews but also infuriated Christian shopkeepers who had previously enjoyed competition-free Saturdays. In Slovakia early in 1939 the authorities were allowing Jews to emigrate and to take their capital with them. They were even allowed to sell their property and to convert the proceeds into sterling at a rate of 300 crowns to the pound rather than the normal 400–500 crowns, the reason for this apparent generosity being that without it the terrified Jews would sell their property to Reich Germans; it was one thing for Slovaks to expel Jews, it was another for them to pave the way for German colonisation. When later in its history the Slovak régime began to expel Jews from the professions it had to compromise and dilute its policy lest it deprive its own people of basic medical services.

Despite these contradictions, for many east Europeans fascism retained a strong attraction and one which was naturally intensified when local fascists redistributed Jewish property.

ANTI-SEMITISM

The Jewish communities of eastern Europe

The Jewish communities of inter-war eastern Europe were to be destroyed in what was the *reductio ad horribile* of the twentieth century's linking of the state and militant ideology: the final solution. The few Jews who managed to escape before this demonic policy was adopted were witness to the intellectual power and vivacity of the annihilated communities, since they enriched western art, medicine, literature, music and science. Eastern Europe's history is full of irony, but there is none greater than that Hitler should dismiss atomic physics as 'Jewish science'. As a result of his deranged prejudices many senior scientists working on the atomic bomb were Jewish refugees from eastern and central Europe, particularly from Hungary.

The Jews of eastern and central Europe before 1941 could be divided into three broad categories. The most numerous were the 'eastern' Jews. Mainly Yiddish-speaking, they were orthodox, many of them adhering to the strict Hasidic sect. They were overwhelmingly poor and nearly all belonged to the local proletariat or lower middle class; 'A typical east European Jewish community had a high birthrate and a low rate of intermarriage, and, while it was largely urban in nature, many of its members still lived in the old-style *shtetl* (small Jewish town).'[20] They constituted a relatively large proportion of the urban population and 'played a highly conspicuous role in local economic life, particularly in commerce'.[21] They perceived their Jewishness either through their religion or via a secular form of Jewish nationalism whose most extreme variant was zionism. They were to be found in Galicia, central Poland, the kresy, Lithuania, Ruthenia, the Bukovina, Crisana Maramureş (north-eastern Transylvania), Bessarabia, and Letgale (south-eastern Latvia). The 'western' Jews were to be found in Poznania, Pomorze, Bohemia, Moravia, Hungary, Wallachia, the rest of Latvia, and in Estonia. They were acculturated, that is, they spoke a local language rather than Yiddish, and tended to follow a reformed rather than the orthodox form of Judaism. They were more urbanised than the eastern Jews but were not a large proportion of the total urban population. They had a low birthrate and a high rate of intermarriage, and there was little if any support amongst them for zionism or Jewish-based political movements. They were more affluent than the eastern Jews and had a higher penetration into the professions and the upper echelons of the economy.

Both the eastern and the western Jews were ashkenazim; those of Bulgaria, Serbia, the Dalmatian coast, and Macedonia were sephardic. The latter were descendants of the Jews driven out of Spain in 1492 and *inter se* they spoke neither Yiddish nor the local language but Ladino, a derivative of Spanish. They were again primarily urban and commercial, and in pre-1914 Salonika formed, according to some estimates, 80 per cent of the population; for this reason the Bulgarians, when attempting to beat the Greek army into the city in 1912, made sure that a number of Jewish officers were in the van of their forces.

These categories were general and there were many variations within them; the Jews of Courland, for example, were middle class and though they spoke German they retained their Yiddish and were orthodox rather than reform in religion. In addition there were some Jewish communities which were at an intermediate stage between the eastern and the western. Such communities were those of Slovakia, Slovenia, Moldavia, and central Transylvania. Some Jewish communities were virtually unclassifiable, one example being those of the Karaite sect found near Vilnius and perhaps in parts of Romania.

In almost all areas Jews, of whatever description, had been made the victims of judeophobia and been subjected to occasional pogroms which, even if not necessarily frequent, could be extremely vicious. The origins of these feelings are obscure but the Jews did excite the fear of the outsider and the stranger, they were held collectively responsible for the death of Christ, and they were blamed for natural catastrophes such as the Black Death. In the nineteenth century, however, these primitive, brutal, elemental passions of the past were conscripted, organised, disciplined, and directed for political purposes; they were made into a mass movement. Judeophobia became anti-semitism.

The rise of modern anti-semitism

The reasons for the transformation of judeophobia into anti-semitism are varied. In the first place it has to be noted that in many areas of eastern Europe the Jews were relatively recent arrivals. In the kingdom of Hungary Jews were not allowed to live in towns until the reforms of Joseph II in the later eighteenth century. By 1848–9 almost all restrictions had been removed and full equality before the law came with the Ausgleich of 1867; in 1895 Judaism was granted the status of a 'received religion' which meant that it could even be given government subsidies, a privilege which a number of Protestant churches did not enjoy. These relaxations meant a steady increase in the Jewish population of Hungary throughout the nineteenth century. In some areas of the kingdom which were to be separated from the rest of Hungary at Trianon, for example Ruthenia, a second wave of Jewish immigration occurred after the first world war as Jews fled from the chaos of revolution and war in Russia, the Ukraine, and Poland.

Many Romanian Jews were also recent arrivals. The achievement of relative political stability in the Danubian principalities in the first half of the nineteenth century, together with increasingly anti-Jewish policies in Russia under Nicholas I, encouraged Jewish migration to Moldavia. The largest increase in Romania's Jewish population, however, came with the end of the first world war, not only because of the incorporation into Romania of areas such as Bessarabia and the Bukovina which had sizeable Jewish communities but also because, again, many Jews fled from Russia and Russian-occupied territory during the war.

Many Jewish communities in Poland had been established for centuries, having been given refuge there when they were driven from the German lands in the fourteenth century because of their alleged responsibility for the Black Death. But in the first world war many more arrived. The Russians decided they did not wish to have any more Jews in their empire and therefore the Russian army, when it advanced in 1914 and 1916, drove the Jews out of its newly-occupied territories. When the tsar's armies retreated they left behind a tide-line of refugees who found themselves in Poland, Romania, and Ruthenia.

The Jews were frequently not only relatively new arrivals but also startlingly different from the host nations. They were urban rather than rural and they had strange habits of dress, speech, and religion. Even the westernised Jews could be different, as in Bohemia and Moravia, for example, where most of them were acculturated to German rather than Czech, the former being for most of the nineteenth century the language of high culture, commerce, and administration. The Czechs therefore regarded the Jews as essentially German, and in rural areas the same word was used for German or Jew.[22] After 1918 more and more Jews began to acculturate to Czech but the process was far from complete by 1938 when a Czech Jew could still complain that the Germans hated him because he was Jewish and the Czechs because he spoke German.

To the east the gulf between Jew and gentile was wider than in central Europe. One explanation for this was education, Jewish schools generally being better than the others. In Romania Jewish schools produced a Jewish intelligentsia which was frequently socialist and which looked for its cultural values to France or Germany, and certainly not to the 'unspoiled' Romanian peasant. In Russian Poland after 1863, whilst the Poles were denied all but elementary education in their own language, Jewish schools teaching in Yiddish or even in Hebrew were thriving and the wealthier Jews were sending their children to university in Austria or Germany.

There were also deep social divides between Jews and Christians. These divisions were intensified or created by modernisation. In pre-partition Poland the gentry had relied on agriculture for their wealth and required the peasantry to remain on the land to create it. Commerce, handicraft manufacturing, usury, inn-keeping, and other urban and semi-urban services were left to the Jews. Much the same happened in the Hungarian kingdom. The magnate retained his estate, which the peasant worked, whilst the impoverished gentry staffed the bureaucracy; once again commerce, manufacturing, and the professions became largely the preserve of the Jews. In Hungary, however, there was the vital difference that the Jews adopted the Magyar language and Magyar culture.

In other areas the Jews also performed the functions of all or part of the bourgeoisie. In Romania romanianised Greeks, Armenians, and Germans dominated the administration whilst Jews functioned as middle-men in commerce and also played an important role, especially in Moldavia, as bailiffs to the large landowners. In Bulgaria the Jews were to be found mainly in commerce and manufacturing but they did not exercise a monopoly in these areas.

Jewish domination of commerce and the free professions had not mattered as long as the noble estates remained viable and the peasants remained on the land. But, to an increasing degree, particularly from c. 1870 onwards, they did not. In Russian Poland the growth of industry created a demand for labour, but the low wages and poor working conditions, together with the fact that the profits went to Jewish owners, meant that the Polish peasant was not much attracted to the city. He was, however, frequently driven to it by world market forces, particularly after the agrarian crisis of the mid-1870s had made farming a more precarious occupation. Of these processes he knew little but of the consequences of living in a slum and working for a Jewish employer he knew a great deal.

The development of education and of the rural cooperative movement also increased tension between Christian and Jew. These two forces had the effect of freeing the Christian population from their reliance on Jewish inn-keepers and money-lenders and of asserting their independence in the commercial world; one such Pole, albeit an anti-semite, recalled, 'When schools began to flourish the people got wiser and stopped their drinking. Folk began to waste less time. Agricultural societies were formed, and Catholics went into business.'[23] From being the usurers and publicans who exploited the peasant the Jews were transmogrified into the established business-men who were now to be charged with frustrating his advance towards commercial or professional success.

Under the old order the Jews had been used to carry out social and economic functions which the gentry despised and which they wished to prevent the peasantry, their source of cheap labour, from exercising. To the peasant, therefore, and, more importantly, to the aspiring native middle class which emerged with modernisation and social mobility, the Jewish people were perceived as lackeys of the old order. Dmowski believed that the Jews had run the old Polish Commonwealth for the *szlachta*:

> The old-fashioned patriots and democrats were friendly to the Jews because a Jewish *faktor* (broker) was an indispensable economic counsellor and a source of political news and gossip for an isolated and degenerated squire. For the 'modern Pole', the Jew was either a dangerously strong competitor in the town or an exploiter in the country-side; thus the 'modern Pole' was an anti-semite if only for this economic reason.[24]

The effects of the first world war

The first world war aggravated all the factors making for anti-semitism. The influx of Jews into Poland during and after the fighting was so great that even Polish Jews showed resentment against the 'Litvaks', as they called their newly arrived co-religionists. The role played by the Jews in underpinning the old system inevitably meant resentment towards them in the post-war world; they became 'a focus for the hostility that was felt, basically, toward the politically or economically important élites that survived from Habsburg days in the successor states'.[25] At the same time, the Jews forfeited gentry support because the latter's decline seemed likely to be greater than it would otherwise have been had not the comfortable positions in commerce and the professions already been filled by Jews. Most important of all was the atmosphere of the new and supposedly nation states in which national allegiance and identity were paramount factors. In the insecurity and instability of the immediate post-war period these frustrations frequently found violent expression. There were pogroms in Lwów, Pinsk, Vilnius, and other Polish cities. Czechoslovak troops entering Slovakia in 1919 indulged in excesses at the expense of local Jews, whilst in Romania in the early 1920s there were vigorous protests against plans to allow Jews to become Romanian citizens. Hungary, after the White Terror, imposed its theoretical *numerus clausus* upon Jewish entry into the universities, and in Croatia in 1920

Jews, together with the Germans and Hungarians, were prevented from voting in the general election because the new rulers did not consider them politically reliable.

With the return of relative order in the 1920s there were fewer such outbursts. The *numerus clausus* in Hungarian universities was largely ignored, Piłsudski attempted to extend the autonomy of the *kehilot* or Jewish communal organisations, and in Czechoslovakia Jews were allowed to register themselves as a separate nationality. But if the Jews were spared outright persecution in the 1920s they were still the victims of discrimination. Frequently gentiles were no more prepared to employ Jews than Jewish employers were willing to have gentiles in their workforce, though this was often for the simple economic reason that to employ workers from both communities would necessitate celebrating two sabbaths per week, therefore forcing the enterprise into an uncompetitive position *vis-à-vis* its rivals who could operate for six full days a week. There was also a tendency for new governments to favour their own nationals in the economic sector. Jewish entry into the Hungarian bureaucracy was made difficult and the same policy was adopted in Poland where Jews who had been in post in the Habsburg administration in Galicia before 1918 were dismissed. This was perhaps understandable in new or reborn states whose whole state psychology was rooted in the creation of so-called nation states, but for the Jews of Lithuania and Poland, for example, it meant increasing pressure on them as their new Christian rivals were smiled upon by the new authorities; in 1926 in Lithuania there were few Lithuanian-owned shops in the main cities whereas a decade later they were everywhere.

Jewish attempts to contain these pressures were not aided by the political diversity which characterised most Jewish communities in eastern Europe. The Jewish intelligentsia, more especially its younger members, tended to socialism but ordinary divisions of right and left were immeasurably complicated by differences over issues of religious practice and attitudes to the questions of assimilation and zionism. This weakness was all the more apparent in the second half of the 1930s.

Anti-semitism in the 1930s

The position of the Jews was made infinitely worse by the depression of the early 1930s which compounded many of the anti-semitic forces already strengthened by the first world war. Social tensions were intensified by the large number of young, educated people who could not find work, by the massive increase in peasant indebtedness, with many of the debts being owed to Jewish moneylenders or Jewish-dominated banks, by the fact that many of those banks were unable to pay interest on deposits, and by the desperate mass unemployment in the towns.

The educated youth, whose lack of family and other commitments meant that they could turn more easily than most other groups to radical political action,

were especially embittered by what they saw as a Jewish stranglehold on commerce and the professions. Jewish domination was considerable. In Poland in
1931 56 per cent of doctors, 33.5 per cent of lawyers, and 24.1 per cent of
pharmacists were Jewish; in that year the Jews formed 8.6 per cent of the total
population. In Hungary in 1930, when practising religious Jews were 5.1 per
cent of the total population, 34.4 per cent of doctors, 49.1 per cent of lawyers,
and 45.1 per cent of pharmacists were Jewish, as were 31.7 per cent of journalists,
28.9 per cent of musicians, and 24.1 per cent of actors; in addition to which,
'In industry, banking and commerce alike Jews seemed to be in clear control of
the commanding heights',[26] and had an estimated 20–25 per cent of the national
wealth in their hands; in Budapest 38.2 per cent of the two-storey, 47.2 per cent
of the three-storey, and 47.5 per cent of six or more storey buildings belonged
to Jews. In Romania the figures were similar. Although only 4–5 per cent of
the total population in 1938, Jews constituted 27.4 per cent of lawyers, 67.1 per
cent of employees in commercial enterprises, 51.3 per cent of the doctors in the
army's medical service, and 70 per cent of journalists. In the same year Tiso
estimated that the 4 per cent of Slovakia's population who were Jewish owned
38 per cent of the nation's wealth. In Croatia commerce 'to a great extent was
controlled by Jewish commercial houses'.[27]

The crisis of the early 1930s also restricted governments' economic freedom
of action in that no one seemed to know how to cope with a situation in which
economic and financial resources had seized up. There were exceptions to this
rule of governmental paralysis. One was the Soviet Union but this could not be
emulated because its revolutionary origins terrified the conservatives and its
collectivisation policies alienated the peasantry. Italian fascism suffered less than
the western democracies but the most robust European response to the global
tragedy seemed to have come from Berlin. The Nazis' energetic policies encouraged anti-semites everywhere. Thus mass, virulent anti-semitism came to a head
in the mid- to late 1930s, inspired and encouraged by its evil genius in Berlin.

Hungary's first anti-Jewish law of April 1938 set a quota of 20 per cent on
Jewish participation in selected occupations, but this level was to be achieved
gradually by natural wastage, with the war-wounded, veterans, and holders of
decorations for valour being excluded from its provisions, as were other Jews
nominated by the regent for their service to the Hungarian nation. The law was
intended both to place Hungary on good terms with Berlin and to buy off local
anti-semites. It did not work. Those who were not anti-semites were disgusted
by the very existence of such a law whilst the committed anti-semites were
enraged by its moderation; the bill was 'as satisfying to the zealots of fascism as
a portion of broccoli fed to a tiger'.[28] The following year saw tougher legislation.
The number of exemptions was reduced and the definition of who was a Jew
made stricter: it was now to be anyone with one parent of the Jewish faith.
Three thousand Jews were expelled from government posts and Jews were banned
not only from selling tobacco, liquor, and pharmaceutical products but also from

peddling. The *numerus clausus* was to be reduced from 20 to 6 per cent and the reduction was to be rapidly enforced.

When Slovakia had become an independent state in March 1939 Tiso had stated that his country's Jewish 'problem' would be solved by 'Christian methods'. It was decreed in the same month that Jewish land was to be confiscated and that all Jews aged between 20 and 50 were to serve for sixty days a year in labour gangs. The 1939 law also stated that the Jews, in conformity with their share of the population, should form no more than 4 per cent of the membership of any profession. The *numerus clausus* was to be applied immediately to the bureaucracy and the judiciary, but its enforcement in medicine and pharmacy had to be delayed as Jews accounted for 44 and 36 per cent respectively of those engaged in the latter occupations; immediate enforcement of the new law would have wrecked medical and pharmaceutical provision. Jewish penetration into the ranks of engineers, technicians, and veterinary surgeons was even higher and they remained little affected by the new law until the Nazis took full control in the summer of 1944.

In Romania in 1937 a number of Jews were expelled from merchant and some professional associations and the short-lived government of the Transylvanian poet and fascist, Octavian Goga (December 1937 to February 1938) talked both of imposing a *numerus clausus* in the professions and education and of expelling Jews who had no legal right to citizenship; at the same time a number of Jewish newspapers and libraries were closed. There was some relaxation after the fall of the government but Iron Guard rule brought worse horrors. New laws imposed proportionality on the professions for those who had not been Romanian citizens or resident in Romania before the first world war. This ruling deprived the majority of the Romanian Jews of the right to own property, publish newspapers, join the army, or play any part in public life; nor could they trade in goods over which the state exercised a monopoly, marry Christians, or convert to Christianity, whilst the *kehilot* and other Jewish institutions were closed. In addition to legal persecution Romanian Jews were subjected to systematic plunder and to horrific acts of random terror such as Constanța's 'column of infamy' to which hapless Jews were tied and, according to some reports, publicly castrated.

The situation of the Jews in Poland deteriorated sharply in the mid-1930s. The agreement with Germany in 1934 was a fillip to local anti-semites; Goebbels, for example, came to speak to students at Warsaw university and in 1935 the 'ghetto benches' for Jews were introduced at Lwów Polytechnic and then in Vilnius and other universities. In 1936 came severe restrictions on ritual slaughter and in 1937 some associations of doctors and journalists closed their ranks against Jewish membership. There were occasional pogroms, for example at Grodno in 1935 and Brześć in 1937, and throughout the late 1930s there was a systematic and intensifying boycott of Jewish economic establishments, with the right-wing Christian press publishing the names of gentiles who had bought from Jewish shopkeepers. This boycott devastated many Jewish families and communities. Even worse was tax discrimination. By 1939 Poland's Jews, who made up 10 per cent of the population, paid between 35 and 40 per cent of the taxes; by September 1939 one in three Jewish families had been beggared by the combination of popular prejudice and governmental cynicism; had it not been for overseas charity, principally from the United States, many Polish Jews would have starved to death in these years.

In 1938 a terrified Jew spoke for most of his people when he remarked, 'We would become Turks tomorrow if we could ensure our safety that way.'[29] But for most Jews in eastern Europe there was to be no salvation from any quarter and what was to come was to be beyond the wildest imaginings of horror.

Part II

TOTALITARIANISM

EASTERN EUROPE DURING THE SECOND WORLD WAR

0   250
km

SWEDEN

REICHS-
COMMISARIAT
OSTLAND

SOVIET UNION

DENMARK

Baltic Sea

• Copenhagen   • Memel

• Berlin   River Vistula

GERMANY   • Warsaw   River Bug   REICHSCOMMISARIAT
UKRAINA

GENERAL GOVERNMENT

• Lvov
River Dniester

Prague •   TRANSNISTRIA

BOHEMIA-
MORAVIA   SLOVAKIA   RUTHENIA   BUKOVINA

River Danube   • Bratislava   N.   River Pruth
Vienna •   • Budapest   TRANSYLVANIA

SWITZ   HUNGARY   ROMANIA

• Zagreb   Bucharest •

CROATIA   • Belgrade
To Italy   SERBIA   BULGARIA

Adriatic Sea   • Sofia

ITALY   To
Italy

• Rome

TURKEY

GREECE

12

THE SECOND WORLD WAR IN EASTERN EUROPE

The Nazi territorial restructuring of eastern Europe

Munich meant the end of the Versailles settlement in central and eastern Europe. The little entente had been virtually destroyed and its main prop, France, shown to be enfeebled and ineffective. The road lay open for revisionism and the Poles were the first to tread it. With as little compunction as the Czechs had shown in 1920 they seized Teschen, parrying western criticism with the question as to who Britain and France would prefer to see in control of the area: Poland or Germany? In November 1938 southern Slovakia and southern Ruthenia were handed to Hungary in what became known as the first Vienna award; Czechoslovakia had lost 29 per cent of its territory, 34 per cent of its population, 40 per cent of its national income, and a major proportion of its industrial capacity.

Even greater changes came in 1939. Hitler's seizure of Bohemia and Moravia in March showed that his ambitions were not to be limited to territory inhabited predominantly by Germans. In the same month, by seizing Memel and renouncing the German-Polish non-aggression pact of 1934, he signalled clearly that his next thrust would be to the north east. In the meantime Hungary used the March 1939 emergency to take northern Ruthenia, whilst in April Mussolini celebrated Good Friday by launching his conquest of Albania. Furthermore, the British and French guarantees to Romania and Poland, which had been intended to restrain Hitler, encouraged him to seek a pact with Moscow to deter Britain from going to war for the sake of Poland.

The Nazi-Soviet pact of 25 August sealed the fate of eastern Europe. The German invasion of Poland began on 1 September and on 17 September the Red Army moved into eastern Poland, with Lithuania being given Vilnius and its surrounding area. Eastern Poland, with its important reserves of timber, oil, gas, and potash, as well as its cultural value as the homeland of Kościuszko and Mickiewicz, was absorbed into the Soviet Union. The Germans' original intention had been to establish a satellite Polish state after the western powers had agreed peace terms, but this plan had been foiled both by the unwillingness of the west to negotiate with Hitler and by the failure of the Germans to find any Pole willing to collaborate with them as head of such a state. German-occupied

179

Poland was therefore partitioned, with large areas, including Teschen and the upper Silesian coalfields, being absorbed totally into the Reich. The remainder formed the General Government which was to consist of four districts based on Warsaw, Lublin, Radom, and its capital, Cracow. It was governed by Hans Frank.

For almost a year these boundaries were maintained but when Hitler dropped parachutists into Holland and drove his panzers across the breadth of France the German–Soviet balance of power was disturbed. To redress it Stalin was allowed to absorb the Baltic states and to take Bessarabia and northern Bukovina from Romania. The Hungarians then demanded compensation, arguing that they should have Transylvania and the Banat in order to threaten the flank of any Soviet descent upon the Ploeşti oil-fields; the second Vienna award of August 1940 required them to be content with northern Transylvania. Further Balkan realignments came in September when the treaty of Craiova transferred the southern Dobrudja to Bulgaria.

The Balkans were further destabilised at the end of October when Mussolini launched his ill-fated invasion of Greece. This gave the British an excuse to send forces there, a development which enraged Hitler because any British involvement in the Balkans would complicate his plans to make the peninsula entirely subservient to Germany without having to have recourse to military measures. This was achieved in Romania, whose dominant figure, general Antonescu, was a willing collaborator with the Nazis, and in Bulgaria where King Boris, much less enthusiastically, joined the tripartite pact at the beginning of March 1941.

Yugoslavia seemed about to take the same step when the Belgrade *coup d'état* of 26/27 March wrecked such plans. Hitler decided to obliterate the country and when the conquest was completed the state was dismembered. Croatia had declared its independence as soon as the German attack began and at the end of the fighting this allegedly independent Croat state (the NDH) was recognised by Italy and Germany; its head was Ante Pavelić. Slovenia, meanwhile, was partitioned between the two axis powers; most of Bosnia and Hercegovina fell to Croatia; Hungary took Prekomurje, Medjimurje and the Bačka whilst the Yugoslav Banat remained under German administration; the German army was the main authority in the small rump Serbia, where an administration under general Milan Nedić was made responsible for purely local affairs. Macedonia was partitioned between the Bulgarians who took the main share, the Italians who were given part of western Macedonia, and the Germans who retained control of the coast; Montenegro was annexed by Italy, and Kosovo added to Italian-run Albania. With Yugoslavia dismembered the German army was then able to continue southwards and conquer Greece.

The next major territorial revisions came after the launching of the German attack upon the Soviet Union on 22 June 1941. Galicia was added to the General Government and Białystok to east Prussia whilst the Baltic states and Belorussia were incorporated into a new unit, Reichscommissariat Ostland. A second Reichscommissariat was formed for the Ukraine but, because of the fluidity of the front, this territory was never given definitive boundaries. The two

Reichscommissariats came under the Reich ministry for the occupied eastern territories which was created in July 1941 and headed by the Nazi theoretical expert and Baltic German, Alfred Rosenberg. The capitulation of Italy in September 1943 forced a series of territorial redefinitions which saw the creation of new units, 'zones of operation', including that for the Adriatic littoral which was placed under the Gauleiter of Carinthia.

In an empire acquired so rapidly there was no possibility of a rational administrative division or categorisation of territories. Some, primarily those in the former Polish republic, were fully incorporated into the Reich. Others were in a half-way stage towards incorporation, being appended to existing administrative areas and placed under the authority of the local chief of the civil administration; this was the case with parts of Slovenia and with the Białystok region in 1941. A third category was that of the appended territories which were under German administration and were part of the *Grossdeutsches Reich* but which were not yet slated for full integration into it; the eastern territories, the General Government, and the Protectorate of Bohemia and Moravia fell into this definition though their status differed considerably one from another. Finally, there were some areas which the Germans never intended to incorporate but control of which was essential for strategic reasons and which were therefore placed under direct military control. The Serbian Banat was one such example.

The degree to which the subjected population participated in the administration varied greatly. In the General Government Frank did refer to so-called high committees of Poles and Ukrainians for information and occasionally for advice but these bodies had no power. In the Ukraine there was even less participation, whereas in Ostland, or at least in what had been the Baltic states, the Germans allowed local organisations more responsibility in local affairs. In the Protectorate from September 1939 to January 1942 there was a dual administration with Nazi appointees shadowing Czech ministers.

The conquered territories were every bit as susceptible as the German homeland to the conflicting jurisdictions which characterised Nazi rule. The civil authorities could not intervene in military affairs which were the responsibility of the Wehrmacht or the SS, whilst security was entirely in the hands of Himmler and his multifarious organs of nastiness. In economic affairs there were a host of conflicting and competing bodies such as the Organisation Todt, Sauckel's labour recruitment forces, Speer's armaments industry, Goering's economic administration, and specialised agencies such as that for food procurement; the postal services and the railways were under central control from Berlin.

Germany's 'new order' in Europe

The Nazi propaganda machine declared that Germany was building a new order in Europe. On 6 October 1939 Hitler told the Reichstag that Germany and the Soviet Union had established a 'zone of peaceful development' in the former Polish republic, and between 1939 and 1941 the emphasis remained on the construction of a European community of nations, *Völkergemeinschaft*, stretching from the Baltic to the Mediterranean and living in peace and economic self-sufficiency. The Germans, of course, would play the leading role. It was a time of great self-confidence, with grandiose schemes for the reconstruction of European cities and for projects such as a massive power generation plant to utilise the currents flowing through the Straits of Gibraltar. Following the attack upon the Soviet Union there was much talk of colonisation in the east, but after Stalingrad it was the defence of European civilisation against bolshevism which dominated German propaganda output.

Despite talk of some form of a European 'co-prosperity zone', the occupied territories were ruthlessly exploited by Nazi Germany. The degree of exploitation varied from area to area and intensified as the Reich's military situation deteriorated after the defeat at Stalingrad early in 1943 and the surrender of Italy in September of the same year. Increasing shortages of recruits led in some areas to enforced enlistment in the German war machine; in Estonia, Latvia, and, after the Italians had departed, Albania, SS divisions were formed from the local populace but this was unusual as the SS was reluctant to accept non-German personnel. No one, however, objected to using non-German manpower and resources, and much of German occupied Europe became a vast pool of labour and raw materials for the Reich. Between 1939 and 1941 some 150,000 skilled workers from Bohemia and Moravia were sent to Germany, and when the Protectorate government was reconstructed in January 1942 a *Reichsdeutscher*, Walter Bertsch, was made minister for labour. Bohemia and Moravia were treated relatively favourably. The situation in Poland was very different. On 19 October 1939 Goering decreed that the economy of the General Government was to be entirely subjected to the Reich's requirements; all raw materials, scrap metal, and machinery needed by the Wehrmacht were to be handed over and almost all economic enterprises were to be germanised. The only ones unaffected were those which provided the barest essentials of life for the local population. The General Government was in fact to be little more than a reserve of slave labour and a dumping ground for unwanted racial groups. In the eastern territories Erich Koch, the Reichscommissar for the Ukraine, declared in Kiev in March 1943 that he would 'get the last ounce out of this country. I have not come here to spread bliss. I have come here to help the Führer.'[1] He lived up to his word.

The determination to maximise the economic return on conquest damaged the Nazi war effort. In much of what had been the Soviet Union the non-Jewish local population were prepared to welcome the Germans, not least on the assumption that they would restore land which had been forcibly collectivised. Rosenberg would have liked to do so but the economic lobby feared that such a policy would decrease agricultural yields. In fact yields did decline, primarily because of a shortage of the requisite heavy machinery, and the decline enabled Rosenberg to enact his new agrarian order of 16 February 1942. This provided for the transition from collective to communal farms, with an indication that a return to private farming might be possible in more stable times. Koch, however, insisted that the state farms be exempt from this ruling; they were to become German enterprises. Neither communal nor germanised farms would win the peasants of the eastern territories over to the new order.

Outside areas under direct Nazi control German economic influence was almost as pervasive. The Slovak arms factories were an asset of particular value to the German war machine, not least because for much of the war they were beyond the range of British bombers. German capital participation in Slovakia rose rapidly from 4 per cent in 1938 to 51.6 per cent in 1942, by which time the Germans had extra-territorial rights in many arms manufacturing concerns. The Romanian oil reserves were another vital factor for the German war machine, Hitler telling his generals early in 1941 that 'the life of the axis depends on those oil fields',[2] but this posed no great difficulties because Antonescu's Romania was an eager accomplice in the German drive to the east. Romania also provided considerable quantities of food for Germany. With Hungary and Bulgaria, neither of which had mineral reserves to compare with those of Romania, the Germans drove harder bargains for the food they purchased and frequently did not even live up to their side of those bargains. In 1942 a Bulgarian survey showed that the Germans had delivered only 28 of the 132 commodities they were obliged to supply in return for deliveries of Bulgarian agricultural produce. Deliveries to Hungary were equally unreliable. Inevitably the agrarian states responded in equal terms, prime minister Kállay of Hungary later recording that 'of the various lines along which Hungarian resistance was conducted, our economic resistance was the most successful and the most systematically carried out';[3] at the end of 1944 Hungary had eighteen million quintals of grain in store which should have been delivered to Germany.

The refusal by the Nazi's to sacrifice or dilute their political objectives, together with their ruthless exploitation of their military power, had its inevitable result in the sovereign states of eastern Europe, because

> When it became apparent that the new order meant an economic reorganis-ation of Europe for the exclusive benefit of the Reich, the Balkan countries ceased to identify the 'struggle against bolshevism' as their own, and sought to disengage themselves from the German grip by all possible means.[4]

Inevitably racial policies were an important feature of the new order. Hitler, in his speech to the Reichstag on 6 October 1939, had talked of a resettlement policy which would bring about clearer lines of ethnic division, and on 17 October a new Reich commission for the strengthening of German nationality was established under Himmler's direction. Its first act was to organise the transfer to the confines of the Greater Reich of ethnic Germans from the Baltic states and Soviet-occupied Poland. In the autumn of 1940 agreements with the govern-ments of the USSR and Romania provided for the transfer of *Volksdeutsche* from northern and southern Bukovina, Bessarabia, and the southern Dobrudja; a number of these ethnic Germans were moved to Slovenia.

In the incorporated areas of Poland most non-Germans became victims of summary expulsion; the speaking of Polish was forbidden and all non-German educational facilities were closed. The remainder of the population was presumed to be of at least partial German origin and was divided into one of the categories drawn up in the racial registers, or *Volksliste*, introduced in September 1940. The long-term aspiration for the General Government was that it would gradually lose all its non-German population; for this reason male and female Poles recruited for labour in the Reich were kept apart. It was also planned to resettle *Volksdeutsche* in the General Government in such as way as to split up the resident Poles into pockets which, because of their isolation, would be the more easily cowed and intimidated. A start to this process was made in late 1942 in the Zamość area when Polish families were removed and replaced by Germans from Bessarabia. The policy was carried through with such brutality that the resistance marked out the responsible officials for especial vengeance, and so effective were these reprisals that the plan was abandoned.

So too were schemes to replace the Czechs with Germans from the South Tyrol; the Nazis had had some difficulty placing the Czech nation in their weird ethnic hierarchy, but had eventually decided that they were semi-Aryans, like the Celts, and as such need not be resettled in the east. The Slovenes were less favoured. The Nazis decided here that about one-third of the population, all of them peasants, were former Germans who, in the right circumstances, could regain their German national consciousness and characteristics. The remaining two-thirds were either liquidated or earmarked for resettlement in Croatia or Serbia, a plan which was wrecked by the reluctance of the latter two administrations to accept them.

From the second half of 1943, with the reversal of military fortunes, the chief preoccupation of those involved in the resettlement programme was to find safe havens for the *Volksdeutsche* who were being driven westwards by the advancing Red Army.

In Nazi-occupied lands local nationalisms were attacked with enormous ferocity. All organisations and social groups which had fostered nationalism were to be eradicated, the intelligentsia most of all. In the General Government there was to be nothing other than primary education, and that in German. The Czechs were not so repressed but even in the Protectorate all non-German institutes of higher education were shut; the same fate befell Lithuania in 1943 when Kaunus and Vilnius universities were closed as a punishment for resistance to labour mobilisation. In the Ukraine Rosenberg's original hopes had been for the winning over of the local intelligentsia who would then form the backbone of an anti-Russian, pro-German nation. Koch disagreed. He would not tolerate a Ukrainian intelligentsia. This he would rather shoot than recruit.

In the satellite states the Germans insisted upon special privileges within the administrative structure. Nazi advisers in Slovak ministries represented a form of 'dual power', whilst in Croatia the German army and the SS were as important in the administration as the officials of Pavelić.

In both the satellite and the allied states the local *Volksdeutsch* communities provided the excuse for massive German interference. The Slovak constitutional statute of July 1940 gave the Germans in Slovakia representation in the Slovak state secretariat, and they had already received in May the right to collect their own taxes in addition to those levied by the Slovak state. In Croatia a state law of 21 June 1941 gave resident Germans the rights of a public corporation, and civil servants of German origin took oaths of allegiance to Hitler as well as to Pavelić. In Romania the second Vienna award also called for the granting of corporate status to the German community and after full codification of these rights in November 1940 the Germans could issue their own laws. Hungary was much less indulgent to its German minority. Unlike their *Volksgenossen* (racial comrades) in Romania, Hungary's Germans could not hoist the swastika or make other public display of their pro-Nazi feelings; in fact, less than half of Hungary's Germans were pro-Nazi. Bulgaria, because it had no German minority, was able to escape such pressures.

The persecution of the Jews

Nazi policy towards the Jews in occupied Europe passed through three stages: ghettoisation, culling, and extermination. In the General Government the three stages followed one upon the other; in the eastern territories the culling took place before as well as after ghettoisation.

Soon after the German and Soviet armies crushed Poland Hitler launched his war *à l'outrance* against the Jews. They were dispossessed of all items of real value. They were denigrated by being forced to wear the yellow star and by having their synagogues destroyed or turned into secular buildings, even, in some cases, public lavatories. They were driven out of the villages and smaller towns to compact settlements in the larger cities. They were required to form *Judenräthe*, or Jewish councils, which were to regulate affairs within the Jewish communities and which became transmission levers for the application of Nazi policies.

Concentration was followed by segregation and isolation. The 160,000 Jews crammed into Łódź were formally sealed off from the rest of the town in May 1940 to form the first ghetto in Nazi-dominated eastern Europe. By November of the same year a high brick wall sealed close to half a million Jews into the Warsaw ghetto. With the walls came the cutting off of telephone lines, whilst postal services were at the mercy of the Gestapo who would accept letters written only in German or Polish, not in Yiddish. Only the smaller ghettos remained unsealed. They were ugly. The boundary of that in Warsaw was deliberately drawn so as to exclude an area of parkland; that in Vilnius had but one tree. They were soon also unbearably overcrowded. In Vilnius 25,000 people were crammed into seventy-two buildings on five streets. Under such circumstances not only was the minimum of privacy impossible but also urban services, especially the water supplies and the sewage systems, were placed under intolerable strain and frequently ceased to function. Disease, especially typhus, flourished, its spread aided by the ever-present and intensifying hunger. In the winter the cold was an equal or greater affliction, especially after December 1941 when the Nazis confiscated all fur coats and most other items of warm clothing. Between January and December 1940 there were 94 recorded deaths from hunger in the Warsaw ghetto; between the same months of the following year there were 11,000; a despairing diarist recorded, 'the most fearful sight is that of freezing children [standing] dumbly weeping in the street with bare feet, bare knees and torn clothing'.[5] Hunger, cold, disease, and the random terror of Nazi or other police forces accounted for probably half a million fatalities in the ghettos of eastern Europe.

The ghettos nevertheless managed to produce a social structure, at least in the early days. The *Judenräthe* and other bodies organised welfare services such as hospitals, schools, and soup kitchens. There were also organisations for relaxation. Most ghettos formed choral societies, that in Kaunus had a mandolin orchestra whilst the largest, that in Warsaw, had string quartets and five theatres, three performing in Yiddish and two in Polish. The Warsaw ghetto also had two Catholic churches for those of the Christian faith who were classified as Jews under Nazi racial laws. Many ghettos had newspapers, which frequently carried war news derived from illicit radio receivers in the ghetto and which were at times fiercely critical of the *Judenräthe*.

The ghettos were soon affected by the second stage of the Nazi policies: culling. The chief instruments of this policy were the 'special units' or *Einsatzgruppen*. They became operative in the summer of 1941, killing 70,000 people in Białystok in July, and two-thirds of the 60,000 Jews in Vilnius. The *Einsatzgruppen* worked with hideous, gratuitous cruelty. In Kaunus they fired the hospital where patients and staff alike were burned to death, and at Babi Yar outside Kiev in September 1941 they butchered 33,000 men, women, and children in two days.

The *Einsatzgruppen* were soon at work in the established ghettos of occupied Poland but by 1942 they were being superseded by more efficient and more technological forms of murder. In December 1941 a conference met at Wannsee near Berlin to work out the timetable of the 'final solution', or the total eradication of European Jewry. The main instrument of this hideous plan was the extermination camp. Chełmno (Kulmhof) was the first to function but it was soon overtaken by the even more infamous camps at Auschwitz-Birkenau, Treblinka, Majdanek, Sobibor, and Belzec. The gas chambers at these grim locations consumed their victims with voracious appetite. Into them were fed Jews from all over Europe. In March 1942 15,000 Jews from Lwów were gassed in Belzec, in March and April of the same year double that number walked along what is now Lublin's Street of the Tormented *en route* for the furnaces of Majdanek or Belzec; between July and September 1942 305,000 of Warsaw's surviving 350,000 Jews were consumed in Treblinka, 70,000 from Łódź died in Auschwitz-Birkenau between June and August 1944, and from almost every corner of German-dominated Europe they came in misery to die in terror. Of the deportees approximately one in ten were considered fit for work, a small proportion of whom survived before, to use the macabre argot of the camps, they went 'up the chimney' or were slain in some act of mindless brutality by the guards.

Some Jews managed to escape. At the end of the war there were 10,000 in hiding in the forests and marshes of Poland and a further 15,000 in the Baltic states, whilst 30,000 more had found sanctuary in convents or in the homes of gentiles, some of whom acted out of sympathy and some for profit. There were also acts of defiance and resistance by the Jews themselves.

The most notable of these was the Warsaw ghetto rising of 1943. In general the *Judenräthe* discouraged plans for resistance; the elders had either not heard or did not believe what was really entailed by resettlement, the Nazi euphemism for transportation to the death camps, and therefore did not want action by young fanatics to bring down retribution upon the entire community. By April 1943, however, the Warsaw ghetto had been culled of most of its older inmates, with almost two-thirds of its remaining inhabitants being aged between 20 and 40. Furthermore, the Polish resistance was well organised in Warsaw, and though it could not afford to give extensive assistance, it provided the fighters in the ghetto with one-tenth of their arms and ammunition. The rising began on 19 April when German and Latvian SS units encircled the ghetto intending to deport its remaining inhabitants. By the end of that day they had been forced to withdraw after suffering over 200 dead and wounded. By 22 April they were using electronic listening devices and dogs to locate their enemy, after which they turned to the flame-thrower. Until 10 May, when resistance finally ceased, the ghetto was an inferno in which most of its buildings and occupants were consumed. The flag which had been hoisted over the ghetto was that of Poland.

There was little that native gentiles of the occupied countries could do to save their Jewish neighbours but in states which were under German influence rather than occupation there was more room for manoeuvre. Their rulers frequently did more to frustrate than to further the final solution.

Croatia was perhaps the exception to the rule because here the Ustaša authorities felt no compunction in visiting upon the Jews the fate that they seemed already determined to inflict upon the Serbs. On the other hand, the fact that the Banat and Serbia were the first areas of occupied Europe to be declared *Judenfrei* (cleared of Jews) was as much the result of the small number of Jews living there as of the zeal with which the local population harried them. In Bohemia and Moravia the Nazis insisted in June 1939 that the Jewish question be placed under German control. The definition of 'Jewish', as laid down by the Nuremburg laws, was applied and in 1942 transportation to Theresienstadt began; from there the Czech Jews were sent to be gassed in Poland.

In Slovakia the authorities' failure to apply all of their own anti-Jewish laws frustrated the Germans. On 28 July 1940 Hitler called Slovak leaders to a conference in Salzburg, as a result of which Mach, Tuka, and the radicals increased their power at the expense of Tiso and the moderates. Jews were banned from living in streets named after Hlinka or Hitler, and a year later, in September 1941, the Jewish codex required that they wear the yellow star. The codex also annulled all debts owed to Jews, confiscated Jewish property, and expelled Jews from Bratislava. Twenty thousand Jews were to be deported under the German resettlement scheme, for which the Slovak government was to pay five hundred Reichmarks per deportee; the deported Slovak Jews were later to build the first gas chamber at Auschwitz.

By October 1942 some 60,000 Jews and Gypsies had been deported from Slovakia. Then the deportations stopped. Slovak Jewish leaders knew what was afoot because one Slovak deportee had miraculously escaped from Majdanek to be followed by two others, one from Sobibor and one from Treblinka. Opposition to the deportations had been voiced by the Protestant community, but now the much more influential Catholic church also weighed in against them, no one more forcefully than Bishop Kmet'ko of Nitra. Further pressure to distance Slovakia from the resettlement policies came from Slovak troops who had witnessed Nazi atrocities in the east, and from the BBC and Radio Moscow both of which warned that one day those involved in the persecutions would be held accountable for their actions. Stalingrad and then the surrender of Italy seemed to bring that hour of reckoning nearer by the day. After the suppression of the Slovak uprising in the summer of 1944 the deportations were resumed, with the active and often enthusiastic participation of the extremist elements within the Hlinka Guard. The Nazis and their allies were left time enough to destroy most of Slovakia's Jews.

In Bulgaria the Jews were forced to wear the yellow star, and they suffered loss of civil rights and dispossession before being expelled from the cities where most of them lived and worked. Yet when rumours circulated that the Jews were to be 'resettled' in Poland there was a furious public outcry, with fierce denunciation of such a project in the press, the parliament, and most notably in the pulpits of the Bulgarian Orthodox church. King Boris steadfastly refused pressure from the Nazis to agree to the deportations and the 50,000 Jews of the Bulgarian kingdom survived, though neither throne, parliament, nor church could save those in Bulgarian-occupied Thrace and Macedonia.

Romania, despite its appalling record of anti-semitism, did not deport the Jews of the regat or southern Transylvania. The Jews of Bessarabia and the Bukovina, however, were liquidated with a savagery made more horrendous perhaps because local Romanians were taking revenge for Jewish cooperation with the Soviet occupiers between 1940 and 1941. The Jews of northern Transylvania were deported after the Nazis had occupied Hungary in March 1944.

In Hungary itself anti-semitic legislation continued to be passed but also continued to be met with ingenious means for its evasion. In 1941 intermarriage with Christians was forbidden. In 1942 Jews lost their licences to sell newspapers and henceforth no licence could be passed on from one generation to another; by this measure 61,000 out of 113,000 employed Jews lost their jobs. In the same year came a law expropriating Jewish landholdings and removing Jews from the army; they were to serve instead in labour battalions. But few of the larger Jewish estates or even firms were confiscated and the Hungarian bureaucracy simply did not have the resources to ensure that the second act was fully applied. In addition to this, a perceptible recovery had weakened the economic impulse to seize Jewish wealth and after 1941, and more so after Stalingrad, there was also a desire to gain moral stature with the allies. Some wealthy Jews also employed 'Strohmänner' (straw-men) or Christians who, for a rich reward, took nominal control of a firm leaving its original owners in actual charge. The Protestant churches and the masonic lodges also offered protection and in a number of instances Christians increased their total number of employees in order to dilute the proportion of Jews until it was lowered to the requisite 6 per cent. Furthermore, despite diplomatic pressure from Berlin, until the German occupation of 1944 the Jews of Hungary did not have to wear the yellow star and they were not subjected to restrictions on the right of domicile. Yet, despite these evasions, anti-semitic legislation did have deep, deleterious effects. Many conservatives feared that the weakening of the Jews would increase the political influence of lower middle-class, right-radical elements, whilst the seizure of Jewish property could be taken as a precedent for the confiscation of noble estates. They were correct, in that anti-semitic legislation

> corrupted and undermined the moral resistance of the Hungarian people at large. It whetted the appetite of those whose greed was not satiated by legislative action alone, and confused those law-abiding citizens who otherwise would not have dared to take away the jobs, property, or lives of others.[6]

Nor were there any mitigating factors for those Jews dragooned into the labour battalions. After 1941 they were forced to clear mines or were thrown into battle as ill-armed, untrained cannon fodder. And if they survived the battlefield, as a few did, they were still at the mercy of their officers, many of whom were fascist. One pastime enjoyed by the latter was to force Jews to climb trees and move about in them like squirrels whilst those officers who so desired practised upon them with live ammunition. One man who perished in this form of gratuitous terror was Attila Petschauer who in 1936 had returned proudly from the Berlin olympics with a gold medal for fencing.

As in the case of Bulgaria and Romania the Jews of the areas occupied by Hungary suffered more than those in the home state. In August 1941 around 12,000 Jews were driven out of Ruthenia into the General Government, and others were to follow later in the war. At the beginning of 1942 there was a particularly vile attack upon Jews in the Novi Sad area. This so outraged Hungarian opinion that the government held an enquiry but the guilty parties fled to Nazi Germany which refused to extradite them.

After the occupation of March 1944 the Nazis and their Hungarian sympathisers launched a massive assault upon the Jews, other racial 'undesirables', and the Hungarian intelligentsia. Almost all of the provincial Jews were taken to camps or forced into death marches. A few brave conservatives continued to oppose the deportations and in this they were joined by many others outside Hungary. The Vatican sent an official protest, as did the Swedes and the Swiss; the kings of Britain and Sweden wrote to Horthy, the archbishop of Canterbury appealed to him, and President Roosevelt threatened him by sending swarms of American bombers over Budapest. The admiral acceded and on 26 June 1944 ordered a halt to the deportations, but little notice was taken of his order, especially after the fascist seizure of power in October. It was only a lack of time which allowed half of the 200,000 Jews crowded into the capital's ghetto to escape the raging madness of the Arrow Cross and the SS.

Political considerations no doubt helped Bulgarians, Slovaks, Hungarians, and others to resist the Nazis on the Jewish issue. After the summer of 1943, with the triumphs of the Red Army in the east and the collapse of Italy in the west, the inevitability of an allied victory became ever more apparent. With equal inevitability those in power would be held to account for their actions by the victors. But it would be wrong to imply that many of those who did attempt to frustrate the Nazis did so out of anything other than a sense of human decency. Even Szálasi retained enough of his professed Christianity to be disturbed by the deportations.

Government and resistance

Czechoslovakia: the government in exile

President Beneš had left Czechoslovakia shortly after the Munich settlement but it was not until Britain and France were at war with Nazi Germany that he was able to form a Czechoslovak political organisation in exile, the Czechoslovak National Council established in Paris in October 1939. Beneš insisted that the Munich settlement was unlawful; in such circumstances neither Czechoslovakia's loss of territory nor his own resignation was valid, and therefore the Czechoslovak National Council should be recognised as the Czechoslovak government in exile. This made little impression on the British and French governments and it was not until after the fall of France that Beneš was paid any great heed in London. By that time he had succeeded in bringing some five hundred Czechoslovak airmen and half an infantry division from France; the presence of these men on British soil, Beneš later wrote, was 'my last and most impressive argument'[7] and on 21 July 1940 the Czechoslovak National Council was recognised by Britain as a provisional Czechoslovak government in exile. Until the German invasion of the Soviet Union the desire of Beneš to secure full recognition was frustrated by divisions, most of them fomented by communists, within the Czechoslovak armed forces; even then he had to wait a further year until in August 1942 Britain followed the Soviet Union in declaring the Munich settlement unlawful and invalid.

Beneš' government in exile included both communists and Jews but it had few Slovaks or anti-fascist Germans. Beneš did not budge from his insistence that there was no separate Slovak nation and he had developed a conviction that the Sudeten Germans were collectively responsible for the fate of Czechoslovakia; from this conviction sprang his determination to expel them after the war had been won.

In exile Beneš' preoccupation was with the diplomatic search for security, both Czechoslovak and European. Before June 1941 he concentrated on seeking an alliance with the Poles, a difficult task in that the latter refused to contemplate giving up any territory held in September 1939, Teschen included. Notwith-standing such difficulties an agreement in principle was reached with the Polish government in exile in November 1940 and by January 1942 a detailed text had been worked out and signed. It provided for a post-war confederation of states in central Europe, though Beneš refused to include Slovakia as a full partner in such a confederation. The entry of the Soviet Union into the war, however, brought about a realignment of priorities for Beneš. Emotionally more disposed towards Russians than Poles and politically more at home with the Soviets than with the mainly conservative Poles, Beneš bowed to Moscow's pressure and renounced first the confederation and then even a Czechoslovak-Polish alliance. In December 1943 Beneš went to Moscow and concluded a portentous treaty with Stalin; the Soviet supremo renounced any intention of interfering in Czechoslovak internal affairs. This considerably enhanced the authority of Beneš and with more enthusiasm and self-confidence than ever he pushed the notion that after the war the west would become more socialist and the Soviet Union more western; 'convergence' would be the *leitmotif* of post-war politics, he believed, and therefore the Soviets must be built into a European system in which they would play a major, even a dominating role in containing Germany and in reconstructing the continent's political and social systems.

Czechoslovakia: Bohemia and Moravia

In the Protectorate of Bohemia and Moravia the Czechs retained their own president, Emil Hácha, and their own government under the premiership of Alois Eliáš. The German representative in Prague, the protector, was a career diplomat, Konstantin von Neurath; much more power, however, rested with his deputy, Karl Hermann Frank, an uncompromising Sudeten German.

Isolated and abandoned by the western powers and no less by their own leaders, especially Beneš, the Czechs sought to salvage something from the political wreckage. When the two political parties permitted under the second republic were merged into the National Solidarity Movement in April 1939 the Czechs had little choice but to enlist *en masse*; by May 98.4 per cent of the eligible males had joined and by 1941 its membership was over four million. The National Solidarity Movement had some fascist characteristics, especially in its attempts to reorganise industry along corporatist lines, but it was nevertheless staunchly Czech, so much so indeed that the Nazis always regarded it with more than a modicum of ambivalence.

The outbreak of war in September raised hopes amongst the Czechs that Nazi Germany might soon be brought to book and the Nazis, sensing this, tightened their control in the Protectorate by placing Nazi administrators, usually Sudeten Germans, alongside Czechs. An anti-German demonstration staged on 28 October, the Czechoslovak national day, provided the Germans with another excuse for moving against the Czechs. The demonstrators jostled Frank and slightly injured his driver, as a result of which the police opened fire; Jan Opletal was wounded and died two weeks later. On the night after his funeral the police raided university hostels and arrested 1,800 people, nine of whom were later shot. Czech universities were closed and the Czech intelligentsia effectively silenced for the remainder of the war.

With the intelligentsia neutralised the Czech lands remained stable for almost two years. The appetite of the German war-economy brought a fall in unemployment from over 80,000 in March 1939 to 17,000 in June 1940; and rationing was introduced later and at more generous levels than in the Reich. Resistance groups did emerge, however, and these were loosely united by the Central Committee for Home Resistance which remained in radio contact with London; as the Gestapo knew full well, prime minister Eliáš also maintained links with the government in exile through this medium. But resistance in the Czech lands was difficult. The surrender of 1938 meant that the army's weapons remained locked up in the arsenals and were not hidden for future use, as was the case often in Poland or Yugoslavia, and, since Bohemia and Moravia were not within easy or safe flying distance of British or French airfields, drops of equipment and personnel were hazardous.

The lack of resistance was a political embarrassment for Beneš, but his prestige was re-established in 1941. The attack on the Soviet Union had caused some rebirth of hope amongst the traditionally russophile Czechs. It had also reactivated the communists and there was a noticeable increase in sabotage in Bohemia and Moravia in the summer of 1941. In September von Neurath was sent on extended leave and his powers were handed over to Reinhard Heydrich, an SS Obergruppenführer and one of Hitler's favourites. It was not the increase in Czech resistance activity which brought Heydrich to Prague as much as a confidence that the war in the east would soon be won and therefore it was time to integrate the Protectorate much more fully into the Reich. He began by introducing martial law in September and in the following month arrested Eliáš for treason. In January 1942 he reconstructed the government of the Protectorate, abolishing the collective responsibility of the Prague cabinet and nominating the ministers himself. From March 1942 the Czech economy was to be completely subordinated to the demands of that of Germany. Having cowed the local politicians, Heydrich intended to settle the Jewish 'problem'.

His first assault on what remained of Czech political rights seemed to provoke no response from the local population. This frightened Beneš lest the allies conclude that the Czechs had no capacity for resistance, in which case he and his government in exile would be of little account in allied calculations in the post-war settlement. It was largely at Beneš' instigation, therefore, that it was decided that an attempt should be made on Heydrich's life. After the requisite training two agents, one Czech and one Slovak, were dropped near Prague. On 27 May 1942 they attacked Heydrich as he drove to the city from his country residence; he died on 4 June. He was the first prominent Nazi to be murdered by non-Nazis and no Nazi of higher rank was to be killed by any European resistance force during the war.

The Nazis exacted fearsome revenge. Lidice and Ležáky, two villages chosen apparently at random, were razed to the ground, their menfolk shot, and their women and children sent to concentration camps. The business was carried out with chilling thoroughness; a man in hospital with a broken leg was taken out and executed, and a woman in a maternity ward was separated from her child after its birth and sent to Ravensbrück. The Nazis publicised their actions and even circulated rumours that their retribution was to be even more exacting.

As was intended, the examples of Lidice and Ležáky served to cow the Czechs into passivity. Except for a rising in the very last days of the war, for which the Germans again exacted a heavy price in blood, there was no further conspicuous act of resistance and per capita troop deployment in the Protectorate was little different from that in Germany itself.

Czechoslovakia: Slovakia

After the German-inspired declaration of independence in March 1939 Tiso became president of Slovakia. The prime minister was his rival, the more radical Tuka, who had allies in Sano Mach, the propaganda chief and head of the Hlinka Guard, and in Ferdinand Ďurčanský who was made minister of the interior and minister for foreign affairs.

The new state had been recognised by the western allies and the Soviet Union as well as by the axis powers. From the beginning Slovakia was never as compliant as the Nazi rulers would have wished. Tiso declared that the state's ruling dogma was 'Christian Solidarism'. The Slovak constitution rejected the sovereignty of the people; Slovakia, it declared, had been created by the Lord's will; the separation of church and state, enacted by the Hungarian authorities in the 1890s, was abolished, and the Catholic nature of state and society was reflected in the school curriculum and in regulations such as those requiring army officers to attend religious services or insisting that only people married in church might teach in Slovak schools.

The Germans' most enthusiastic supporters were Tuka, Mach, and the radicals, whose power increased after the Salzburg meeting of July 1940 when Mach was put in charge of internal affairs and more German advisers were introduced into Slovakia. In the long run, however, the Nazis realised that they would never nazify the country; Slovakia, they concluded, was better treated as an even more backward Bavaria where the Catholic majority would always be guided more by their church than by any other institution. Support for Tuka therefore waned and the Nazis reluctantly accepted such acts of Slovak independence as the suspension of the Jewish deportations.

For most non-Jewish or non-Gypsy Slovaks the early years of the war brought few hardships. The annulment of debts to Jews, the redistribution of Jewish property, and the moneys to be made from the trade in *Schutzbriefe*, the letters of exemption from deportation, made a number of Slovaks wealthier than they had ever been. Slovak industry flourished under German sponsorship and, as throughout eastern Europe during the war, peasants were assured of a ready market and a good price for their produce, something which few had enjoyed since the onset of the depression.

Yet it was the war which undermined the popularity of the Slovak régime. The distaste with which Slovak soldiers regarded Nazi conduct in the east had been one reason for suspending the Jewish deportations but the declaration of war on the United States in December 1941 was even more unpopular as so many Slovak families had relatives who had emigrated to that country. After Stalingrad Tiso and his associates were ever more anxious to escape from the alliance with Nazi Germany. The inexorable approach of the Red Army and the allied bomber fleets added to this determination and also encouraged anti-Tiso Slovaks to overthrow what they saw as a Nazi puppet government. From such feelings was born the Slovak rising of August 1944.

Resistance had first been seen in Slovakia in 1939 when 3,500 Slovak troops refused to march against Poland; later, disaffection in the army in the east had been such that the Germans had stiffened many Slovak units with *Volksdeutsche* squads. By 1943 political resistance was coalescing around two points. The first was the bourgeois political groups led by figures such as Vavro Šrobár. They were increasingly concerned at the consequences of Germany's coming military defeat but could not yet formulate a coherent or satisfactory notion of the future relationship between Slovakia and the Czechs; fundamentally they agreed that the Czechoslovak state should be reconstituted but not on what they considered the anti-Slovak basis of the government in exile. Šrobár suggested in January 1943 that a Slovak National Council should be formed which, at the appropriate moment, should depose Tiso, dissolve the Slovak state, and negotiate for the reconstruction, on favourable terms, of Czechoslovakia.

The second point of coalescence was the Slovak Communist Party. In March 1939 a separate Slovak Communist Party (CPS) had been created. It was, of course, illegal under the Tiso régime but after Stalingrad it was not persecuted with the former vigour; a top-level ideological symposium in June 1943, for example, was held in the offices rather than the cells of Bratislava prison. In line with Comintern policy the CPS had been instructed to join with other anti-fascist, patriotic parties in opposing Germany and its allies, but after the dissolution of Comintern in June 1943 the CPS found itself in a difficult position. As the Soviet Union moved towards closer relations with Beneš, the CPS was told to rejoin the united CPCS. The CPS, especially its Davist wing (from Dav, a throng) led by Ladislav Novomeský and Gustáv Husák, was not necessarily keen to do so. It was the Davists who dominated the CPS in 1943 and it was they who eventually came together with the bourgeois opposition groups to sign the 'Christmas agreement' of December 1943 which set up the Slovak National Council (SNC). With Beneš and Stalin finding common ground, the formation of the SNC was a timely reminder of Slovak political concerns.

The SNC chose a board of trustees as its executive authority; it was made up of seven democrats, four communists, including Husák, and two social democrats. The SNC declared its loyalty to a Czechoslovakia in which the Czech and Slovak components would have equal rights and in which the Catholic church would be excluded from political life. It also set about organising a rising in the summer of 1944.

The uprising began on 27 August near Turčanský Svätý Martin. It was timed to coincide with the anticipated arrival of the Red Army in eastern Slovakia and had a notable early success in capturing the head of the recently disbanded German military mission in Romania, general Otto. It had few other triumphs. The Red Army did not force the Carpathians as had been expected, nor would the Soviets allow the western allies to use Soviet air strips to supply the Slovaks. The Slovaks had little chance against the crack divisions which the Germans now rushed into the country. Nor was the rising well served by the divisions amongst its leaders. The communists, anxious to imitate Soviet practices, wanted to place more reliance on partisan units and to reshape the Slovak army on the Soviet model, the army having declared, almost to a man, for the SNC.

After the rising Tiso fled to an Austrian monastery where he eventually surrendered to the Americans. In his place the Germans put Stefan Tiso but it was the SS rather than the Slovak government which now wielded power, as the Jews learnt to their terrible cost.

The rising of 1944 left many bitter legacies, particularly in the CPCS which had had to pretend that it rather than the CPS was in control of events in August. This pretence embarrassed the Czech communists but it angered their Slovak comrades. Nevertheless, the rising did something to rescue Slovak nationalism from its association with clerico-fascism. But association with the national cause, however much it may have helped the communist cause in Slovakia, was to place many Slovak communists in grave danger.

Poland: the government in exile

History has few ironies more painful and cruel than the contrast between Czechoslovak and Polish experiences during the second world war. The Czechs and Slovaks suffered nothing like the horrors imposed upon the Poles, nor could their resistance efforts compare to the prodigious feats of the Poles, yet skilful diplomacy enabled the Czechoslovak government in exile to win the battle that mattered most in the post-war world, that for the support of Hitler's fellow conspirator of 1939, Stalin. Whereas Beneš returned home in triumph, the Polish government in exile was denigrated and forgotten; to Britain's eternal shame there was not even a place for its leaders or their heroic soldiers and airmen in the victory parade in Whitehall in 1945.

The Polish government in exile was based on a combination of the Morges Front and the Polish Socialist Party and was led by general Władisław Sikorski, who also served as commander in chief of the Polish armed forces. The Polish government in exile, which came to London after the fall of France, had the moral authority of being the representative of the state on whose account the allies had gone to war. This authority was augmented by the refusal of any Pole to form an administration under Nazi auspices, and was helped not a little by the fact that the Poles had managed to smuggle out their gold reserves. It was helped above all by the spectacular performance of its armed forces, not least in the battle of Britain.

The major preoccupation of the Polish government in exile was its relations with the Russians. These had been severed when the Soviet Union stabbed Poland in the back on 17 September 1939, after which the Soviet government had deported hundreds of thousands of Poles from its zone of occupation to central Asia; many Poles, particularly members of the intelligentsia and of the officer corps, had been killed; Soviet rule was 'if anything, more ferocious and more costly of human life than that of the Nazis across the dividing line'.[8] The German attack upon the USSR brought about a rapid restoration of relations, though the Sikorski-Maiski agreement, signed between the Polish leader and the Soviet ambassador in London in June 1941, caused divisions within the Polish leadership. Whatever its opponents might argue, however, the agreement did eventually bring about the release from the Soviet Union of many thousands of Polish families who were soon to form the backbone of the army being formed by general Anders.

By early 1943 the Soviets, having regained their military confidence, were insisting that they retain the territories taken from Poland in 1939 and that the future frontier be drawn along the Curzon line. The Poles resisted but in April 1943 it became all too apparent that the Polish-Soviet problem was not one of frontiers alone. The Germans announced in that month that they had discovered some 5,000 bodies in a mass grave in Katyn forest near Smolensk. They were, said Goebbels and his propaganda machine, the remains of Polish officers butchered by the Soviet security forces. The Poles did not accept this claim but they did back efforts by the International Red Cross to mount an enquiry into the crime. In a rage Stalin once more severed relations with the Polish government in exile. In July the Poles suffered a further, and devastating, blow when Sikorski was killed in an air-crash off Gibraltar. He was succeeded as prime minister by the agrarian Stanisław Mikołajczyk and as commander in chief by general Kazimierz Sosnkowski, a fierce opponent of the Russians.

The battle over the frontiers was lost at the end of the year at the Tehran conference where the three allied leaders, playing 'hopscotch amongst the frontiers',[9] decided that the Soviet Union would keep the areas annexed in 1939 and that Poland would be compensated in the west with lands to be taken from a defeated Germany. Soon after the Tehran meeting the Beneš-Stalin treaty of December 1943 meant that Poland was surrounded by suspicious, if not overtly hostile, states. When the three allied leaders next met, at Yalta in February 1945, a pro-communist régime had been installed. Its arrival and consolidation was a function not only of Soviet military power but also of the dynamics of Polish internal affairs.

Poland: resistance and revolt at home

The Polish state and nation suffered to an unparalleled degree in the second world war. Each day of German occupation saw three thousand Polish deaths, a total of six million, of whom approximately half were Jewish; for the Poles themselves casualties were particularly high amongst urban dwellers and the intelligentsia, half the population of Warsaw, for example, is thought to have perished between 1939 and 1945; in all 22 per cent of the Polish population of 1939 died compared with 10.8 per cent in Yugoslavia and 0.4 per cent in the USSR. In addition to this there was wholesale destruction of industrial and social capital. Warsaw was deliberately razed to the ground and throughout the country an estimated one-third of the housing stock was lost together with much of the railway system, the port facilities, and educational establishments. The manner of the killing was as appalling as its extent. In Warsaw there were random shootings, particularly of those who gathered to pray or place flowers at the spot where others had been gunned down.

Yet, despite the bestiality of Nazi rule, the Poles of the General Government were never cowed. The government in exile maintained its authority through a resident government delegacy which organised a virtual parallel state to that run by governor Frank in Cracow. This underground state established an educational system, published newspapers, including English-language papers for British prisoners of war on Polish soil, maintained regular radio contact with London, collected funds, and administered justice, particularly against Germans who had been guilty of particular cruelty, as, for example, at Zamość. It also organised administrative sabotage by ordering Polish employees of the German authorities to mis-file papers, to mis-direct mail, to spread rumours which sapped German morale, and to frustrate the occupying forces in a myriad of ways.

There was also fierce, sustained and effective military resistance. Isolated acts of resistance began as soon as the German army arrived and by the spring of 1940 it was significant enough for Hitler to order 'extraordinary pacification' before the German attack upon the west. By February 1942 all resistance units except those controlled by the small communist groups and the extreme right had come together in the Home Army, the *Armia Krajowa*, (AK). Though the AK could not escape being influenced by the divisions amongst its ultimate political masters, the government in exile, it was nevertheless by August 1944 an essentially united force of some 380,000, making it the fourth largest of the allied armies after the Soviet, American, and British. In an effort to emphasise continuity between pre-1939 and post-occupation rule, the AK was organised in units coterminous with the inter-war local government boundaries, both west and east of the Curzon line.

The AK harassed the Germans in small-scale operations such as the sabotage of rail traffic, and it has been estimated that one in eight of the German transports to the eastern front was destroyed or seriously delayed thanks to the efforts of the AK. It also cooperated in intelligence operations such as that by which a complete V2 rocket was smuggled out of Poland for examination by experts in Britain; together with the invaluable pre-war information on Enigma, this made the Polish contribution to the intelligence war greater than any other.

The long-term strategy of the AK and the government in exile was that the main military effort of the Polish forces should be reserved for when the liberating armies reached Polish soil. Then there would be a general mobilisation in areas immediately behind the German lines in order to cripple the Wehrmacht at this critical moment. Operation 'Tempest', devised late in 1943, modified this. Because of the reprisals which the Germans were taking on Polish civilians and because of the AK's own lack of heavy weapons it was agreed that the AK should not itself attack major cities but should enter them in cooperation with the liberating armies, though sabotage operations were to be intensified as soon as the Red Army crossed the 1939 border. This strategy was called into question soon after the Red Army did cross that border in January 1944 because AK officers and troops were frequently arrested or forced to join the pro-Soviet army under general Berling which had been formed from Poles who had stayed in the USSR. This problem was eased in late March 1944 by arrangments between the Red Army and AK units which placed the latter under Soviet operational command; it was but a fragile truce. In July AK units cooperated with the Red Army in the taking of Vilnius and other cities only to find that soon after the conquest Soviet security personnel were detaining or even liquidating AK troops.

By this stage the Polish communists had once again become a political factor to be reckoned with. The party, dissolved by the Comintern in 1938, had been reconstituted in January 1942 and a number of agents parachuted into Warsaw to recruit and organise support. A year later, after the breach over Katyn, a union of Polish patriots had been formed to sponsor leftist forces and to contest the authority in Poland of the government in exile. This committee was clearly being prepared to take over in liberated Poland, a problem which could be shelved when the Red Army was in disputed areas but which could not be ducked when Soviet forces crossed into what was indisputably Polish territory. When that happened Stalin's allies moved quickly, establishing a committee of national liberation in Lublin in July 1944. The Lublin committee was a virtual provisional government and one which showed no mercy for its domestic opponents. With Lublin being less than a hundred miles from Warsaw and with the Red Army in rapid advance, it seemed that a pro-communist administration might be installed in Warsaw within weeks if not days.

The government in exile was faced with a dilemma. If it did not call Warsaw to arms then the Polish capital would be taken by the Red Army and a pro-communist Polish government installed; any pretence by the government in exile to be the legitimate authority in Poland would then be lost. On the other hand, a rising would take the Germans by surprise and within a few days the Red Army would arrive to be handed the key to the Polish capital by Polish nationalist forces fully aligned with their government in exile. If the Poles were masters of the city the western governments would not be able to ignore Polish claims for support against the Lublin government, and Stalin would be forced to negotiate with the government in exile. The debate was intense and agonising, with the London authorities finally leaving the decision to local commanders. The latter were greatly influenced by calls from the Soviet controlled Radio Kościuszko for a general rising in Warsaw, by indications that the Germans intended to fortify the city, thus making it into a second Stalingrad, and by reports that Soviet tanks had already reached the eastern suburb of Praga.

The Warsaw uprising began at 5 p.m. on 1 August. Only one in ten of the Polish combatants was armed but it was assumed that the remainder could seize weapons from fallen Germans and that these would be sufficient for the three or four days until the city was taken by the Russians. Fighting finally ceased on 2 October, by which time an estimated 200,000 Varsovians had died. When the rising began the Polish premier was in Moscow desperately seeking a political accommodation with Stalin; when Mikołajczyk asked for assistance the general-issimo promised that he would give 'the necessary orders'.[10] No help arrived; Radio Kościuszko went silent; the Soviet aircraft whose presence over the city had been so comforting disappeared; the Red Army stopped in its tracks; and Stalin denounced the leaders of the rising as 'a gang of criminals who embarked on the Warsaw adventure to seize power'.[11] As in Slovakia he refused permission for the western allies to fly supplies from Soviet air-strips, of which there were a hundred within an hour's flying time of Warsaw. When the Soviets did make their one drop to the insurgents, on 13 September, they did not attach parachutes to the canisters of food, medicines, and arms, most of which, not surprisingly, were ruined. The allies, meanwhile, had managed to fly a number of missions from Bari to the Polish capital but it had been a desperately dangerous under-taking across much of occupied Europe in a time of almost maximum daylight.

In mitigation of the Soviets' behaviour it could be said that they were forced to divert attention from the Polish theatre of operations to the Balkans when the Romanians switched sides on 23 August, and that the Poles were unaware that the Germans had regrouped in strength to the east of the Vistula. Yet by the middle of September these factors no longer applied, the Red Army was on the Vistula and in an excellent position to render aid to the Poles in Warsaw. It also has to be said that it was much to Stalin's advantage for the Germans to destroy Warsaw and the AK. This would both eliminate the communists' chief armed rival and show the Poles once more that the west, as in 1939, could do nothing to help them.

The Nazis and their associates went about the suppression of the rising with a savagery surprising even for them. When cleared of insurgents the city was demolished, building by building, street by street, district by district. Hitler and Himmler, exalting in this chance to annihilate a race which, they said, had blocked Germany's eastward expansion for seven hundred years, called for the killing of all participants and civilians; 15,000 were executed on one day alone. Of particular nastiness were 4,000 SS men enlisted from the gaols of eastern Europe, and 6,000 men, most of them brutalised Ukrainians, recruited from prisoner of war camps. So vile was the conduct of the latter that their commander was executed for insubordination and excessive cruelty – a rare distinction in his circle.

Allied warnings that post-war retribution would be taken against those who had committed atrocities eventually secured for the Poles recognition as belligerents, so those who survived were able to march out of the ruins as prisoners of war with banners flying; their commanders ended the war in Colditz. But the AK was broken as a fighting force and the political credibility of the government in exile shattered. Stalin's Lublin Poles had no immediate challengers.

The tragedy of the Warsaw rising was fundamentally the result of faulty intelligence work. The Poles should not have given credence to Radio Kościuszko's calls for an uprising; many such calls had been issued before. The Poles took most of their information from the BBC and other allied networks and had little first-hand intelligence on the latest German dispositions, whilst the sighting of the tank in Praga, to which so much importance was attached, was not followed up; had it been, the Poles would have learnt that it was a lone reconnaissance vehicle. Above all, the Poles committed a massive, if understandable, blunder in not informing the Soviet high command of their intentions. Such sober judgements, however, cannot dim the nobility of the Polish sacrifice in 1944; even more so than in the nineteenth century, the world had cause to take seriously the Polish revolutionaries' slogan: 'For Your Liberty and Ours'.

Yugoslavia: governments

The Yugoslav government in exile exercised little influence during the second world war. Its country was not only dismembered but its constituent parts had entered upon a series of fratricidal wars, and its nominal head, King Peter, commanded little respect either amongst the allies or amongst his own people, the more so when he offended Serbian national tradition by marrying in a time of national crisis. The government's authority declined even further when its original head, the historian Slobodan Jovanović, resigned. His successors, Miša Trifunović and Ivan Šubašić, were not of comparable stature.

In Yugoslavia itself a pretence at independent government survived only in the NDH. Croatia had seen a *coup d'état* before the *état* had been formed, when the Ustaša of Ante Pavelić seized power in Zagreb on 15 April 1941 and set up the NDH even before the Yugoslav surrender. The Germans preferred Pavelić to Maček, who in any case had no desire to work with them and whose Croat People's Peasant Party (CPPP), despite its large popular following, had always maintained that it wanted a solution to Croatia's problems within rather outside a Yugoslav state. The Nazis were not much worried that the chief obsession of Pavelić and the Ustaša was killing Serbs, the Croatian rulers insisting that one-third of the Serbs would be forced into exile, one-third converted to Catholicism, and one-third exterminated; although 'only' half of the latter target was 'achieved', it was reached through a violence so elemental and extreme that at times the Germans had to send tanks and armour to protect the Serbs.

Tribal vengeance against the Serbs was not enough to ensure stability for Croatia's rulers; for that Pavelić had to secure support from the peasants and from their political leaders in the CPPP. The Germans were also anxious to bring more order into Croatian affairs. In January 1942 the Croatian council of state was established with German and CPPP representation, and a Croatian Orthodox church was set up for those Serbs who had survived the initial Ustaša onslaught, though it was still illegal to use the cyrillic script. Pavelić could always rely on extreme nationalist support but many more moderate Croats were shocked at Ustaša behaviour and were angered that an ostensibly nationalist leader could give Dalmatia to the Italians and allow the Germans to run his foreign policy; if such Croats remained loyal to Pavelić it was primarily through fear of his police or of the communist-dominated partisans of the resistance. In early 1943 Pavelić reconstituted his council of state in an attempt to give it wider appeal, and in March he forced all peasants to enlist in the newly created Peasant Association.

These measures had little long term effect. By mid-1943 the partisans were well established in the Bosnian mountains whilst Croatia was becoming more and more a German dependency. The Wehrmacht had assumed control of all military operations in Croatia in late 1942, and in March 1943 the SS became a virtual state within the state when it was made responsible for the enlistment of the Croatian *Volksdeutsche*. German influence increased even more with the surrender of Italy, after which the authority of Pavelić was more or less confined to Zagreb.

Yugoslavia: resistance and revolt

The first acts of resistance in Yugoslavia were performed by the četniks, Serbian royalists operating under the former minister of war, Dragoljub-Draža Mihajlović. Mihajlović was a conservative, royalist, Serbian nationalist whose political objective was to recreate a Yugoslavia ruled by his king and dominated by the Serbs. He had the advantage of operating within the Serbian national tradition of home-based guerilla activity, and he had the support of one of Serbia's traditional allies, Britain. His strategy was to recruit and arm his followers and prepare them for a general rising when the country was on the point of liberation. That liberation would be brought about by the forces of the major powers to which the resistance army must subordinate itself at the appropriate moment. In the meantime there would be every reason to act against any future domestic political rivals if it seemed that they might threaten the restoration of a Serbian-dominated Yugoslav kingdom.

Such a rival soon appeared. After 22 June 1941 the Yugoslav communists rapidly organised resistance forces and made their first attack upon the Germans in July. In Serbia, however, the peasants preferred the traditionalist Mihajlović to the revolutionary communists under the mysterious sounding 'Tito'. In December Tito pulled out of Serbia and moved into Bosnia. In doing so he was forced to abandon the existing partisan structure which had been based on recruitment in defined geographic areas outside which those particular units did not operate. From the dedicated hard corps of those who remained with him he formed, on Stalin's birthday, the first proletarian shock brigade. By the middle of 1942 there were five such units, each of between 800 and 1,000 hardened fighters; Tito had moved from a territorial to a class basis for his army. The brigades were short of ammunition, however, and in mid-1942 set out on their two-hundred mile 'long march' to the mountains of north western Bosnia. Here they found ready support amongst the Serbs who were being harried by the local Ustaša.

In the territories which they controlled the partisans established people's committees. These were under overt or covert communist domination but they were often welcomed because they brought sanity and justice to local affairs, promised reconciliation between the ethnic groups, and instructed local peasants on better methods of agriculture. The partisans organised postal services, education, military training, and an efficient police force; on 1 May 1942 they even staged the so-called partisan Olympic games at Foča. At times the partisans were under severe pressure from the Germans and their allies, no more so than in June 1943 when German forces caught the partisans in the Sutjeska valley. Ingenuity, courage, perseverance, and support from the local population saved them on this and other occasions. The partisans were a well organised insurgent movement with a most efficient political leadership, but they were never an army which could engage the Germans on the battlefield and their lack of heavy weaponry meant that they could not seize major fortified objectives. As Mihajlović had calculated, it was the army of a great power which finally liberated Belgrade in October 1944 and gradually drove the occupiers out of the country. As Mihajlović had feared, and as Tito had hoped, the liberating army was that of the Soviet Union.

By the time that the Red Army reached Yugoslav territory Tito's forces vastly outnumbered those of Mihajlović, though the latter retained the loyalty of most Serbs in Serbia. Tito's appeal lay in his role as liberator from the axis and reconciler of the Yugoslav peoples. For him these were means to an end, and that end was the creation of a socialist republic. He was every bit as willing as

Mihajlović to use the war to liquidate his domestic enemies, even having talks with the Germans in the spring of 1943 and offering not to attack them if they left him free to deal with the četniks; he also expressed a readiness to join with the Germans to expel any western allied forces which might land on Yugoslavia's Adriatic shore. So overt was Tito's socialist ambition that it frightened Stalin. Soviet policy was for broad coalitions and when Tito told Moscow that he intended to form a provisional administration Stalin insisted that it include a variety of political forces. Accordingly, at Bihać in Bosnia in November 1942, Tito formed the Anti-Fascist Council for the Liberation of Yugoslavia (AVNOJ). The second AVNOJ conference, at Jajce a year later, virtually declared AVNOJ the provisional government of Yugoslavia. This further alarmed Stalin who had not been best pleased that the Yugoslavs chose to make this contentious announcement on the eve of the Tehran conference.

The partisans recruited most easily amongst the *prečani* Serbs and amongst the many Bosnians, Croats, and Slovenes who were sickened by local atrocities and by the degree to which their homeland had become dominated by the Germans or the Italians. The surrender of the latter helped Tito considerably in his struggle with Mihajlović. Most Italian troops were in areas in which the partisans rather than the četniks operated so their arms were seized by followers of Tito rather than of Mihajlović. By the end of 1943 the British had become convinced that the partisans were a more effective force against the Germans than Mihajlović and therefore the latter was abandoned and all resources for Yugoslavia concentrated on the partisans. The partisans also profited in the long run from their leaders' willingness to take the casualties which inevitably followed the killing of axis personnel. This Mihajlović was neither willing nor able to do. On 21 October 1941, in Kragujevac, the Germans killed up to 5,000 citizens, many of them school-children, in reprisal for an attack by resistance forces. Had such massacres become regular it would have gravely weakened the Serb nation upon which Mihajlović wished to rebuild his royalist Yugoslavia.

Tito's partisans claimed to be one of the most successful of European resistance forces. Until at least the middle of 1943, however, the Germans still regarded the četniks as their main enemy, particularly in Serbia and along the Belgrade-Zagreb route which was the Germans' chief strategic concern. The Germans continued to dominate the cities and to extract from the country the mineral resources they coveted, and the German forces tied down in Yugoslavia were never their élite; in military terms the partisans were little more than an irritant. Their most important achievement was to create a force which stepped rapidly and ruthlessly into the political vacuum left when the Germans departed. Also, and more importantly, the partisans kept alive and rehabilitated a sense of Yugoslav nationality and a recognition of the value of the concept of Yugoslavdom at a time when both were under fierce attack from without and from within.

Albania

King Zog had fled Albania shortly after the arrival of the Italian army in 1939. In the following year he joined the refugees escaping from France to the United Kingdom, arriving in Liverpool with vast quantities of personal luggage which were promptly destroyed in an air raid. Despite his constant requests the British refused to recognise him as the head of a government in exile.

Resistance in Albania was as fragmented as in Yugoslavia. The only Albanian chief to contest the occupation of 1939 had been Abas Kupi but it was to little effect. Kupi, a royalist, took to the hills. In November 1941 the Albanian Communist Party was established with help from the Yugoslavs and was based in the Albanian-dominated areas of Kosovo and Metohija. In September 1942 the communists and a number of tribal headmen, including Kupi, came together at Peza to found the National Liberation Movement, later to be associated with the National Liberation Committee (NLC). Soon after this a second organisation appeared, the National Union or Balli Kombëtar (BK), a moderate, republican force. Both the NLC and the BK displayed a fierce nationalism and territorial appetites which made it difficult for the British, with their commitments to Greece and Yugoslavia, to help them. British liaison officers did engineer a meeting of all three factions at Mukai near Tiranë in July 1943 but no lasting unity could be achieved. In August, with Italian authority collapsing, Kupi took over much of the country but in the following month the Germans moved in in force, abolished the fascist constitution, and set up a council of regency which included the reformist Mehdi Frashëri. The BK, though it wished to see the back of the Germans, had no real complaint with the political complexion of the council and BK resistance activity therefore slackened. The communist leader, Enver Hoxha, made this his opportunity to denounce his political foe, to step up his own resistance efforts, and to turn his guns on BK forces. By now the communists had come to dominate the NLC and in November 1943 Kupi broke away, declaring for the restoration of Zog.

In the spring of 1944 fighting intensified, with BK units sometimes joining the Germans against the NLC which was now styling itself the National Liberation Army. By July the German-sponsored Albanian régime was dissolving as the partisan forces pushed northwards from their strongholds amongst the southern Tosks. An anti-fascist council and a provisional government on the Yugoslav model had already been formed and when the Germans finally left Albania in October the communists were by far the most dominant political force in the country.

The independent states: Hungary

All Hungarians were attracted to revisionism but not all found the revisionists appealing. The conservative, old right wished in fact to have its territorial cake and eat it, to hunt with the revisionist hounds and run with the allied hares, both because they found the fascists, and more so the Nazis, vulgar and because they feared they might not win. The right radicals, on the other hand, had complete faith in a German victory and hoped that the new order would bring about a social as well as a territorial restructuring. The split between the old and the new right which had dominated most of the 1930s in Hungary therefore continued through the second world war.

The conservatives had delayed full commitment to the Nazi war effort and if Hungary could not resist being drawn into the war against the Soviet Union it did its best to minimise its involvement in the wider conflict; when Hungary eventually found itself at war with Britain and the United States in December 1941, it regarded that war as 'formal' and until March 1944 it did not fire on allied planes passing over Hungary or subject allied personnel who landed in or escaped to the country to anything but the most minimal of restrictions. In return Hungary was not bombed by the allies.

Internally Hungary also refused full conscription into the new order. Until the German occupation of March 1944 the neutral press was available in Budapest; there were no restrictions on listening to foreign broadcasts, the government banned discussion of Nazi ideology, forbade articles arguing that the Germans would win the war, and even permitted a number of nominally left-wing delegates to sit in parliament.

Reluctance to throw Hungary fully behind Germany was in part the result of military developments. The doubts with which Horthy and his colleagues had committed Hungary to the new campaign were confirmed when the Germans failed to take Moscow in December 1941. In February 1942 Horthy's son, István, was made deputy regent, since Horthy feared that if he died without a nominated successor the Germans would put their own man in the regency. In March Horthy replaced his prime minister, Bárdossy, who had, the regent considered, been too compliant with the Germans. His successor, Miklós Kállay, had been agriculture minister under Gömbös so had some credibility on the right, but he was also a magnate from one of Hungary's oldest families and a well-known anglophile; indeed, he had never entirely severed his links with the British.

For magnates such as Kállay cooperation with Germany in the war had been meant to serve two purposes. The first was the obvious wish to recover as much as possible of the historic Hungarian lands. The second was to keep domestic reform at bay. Kállay was determined to defend magnate power against the forces of the radical right, hoping nevertheless to retain the territorial gains secured through diplomatic cooperation with Germany's radical right régime. But his task was made more difficult because the war weakened the magnates vis-à-vis the new right supporters. The revival of demand for industrial products all but wiped out unemployment, for which the radical right was given the credit; support for Szálasi and other rightists rose rapidly amongst the workers of Csepel. On the other hand, from 1942 food became more scarce because the Germans were taking increasing quantities. This inevitably forced up prices. In addition, after 1942 the Germans seldom paid for the produce they were taking from the country and the government had no alternative but to print money to pay the producers. The small farmer was not necessarily harmed by inflation. The black market would always absorb, at rising prices, wine, vegetables, sausages, and other home-produced items, whilst inflation diminished the real value of peasant debts. It was the magnates who suffered. The staple products, especially grain which was the main income of the large estate, were subjected to rigid price controls, and the income which they did provide, unlike that earned in the black market, was heavily taxed. The controlled war economy therefore weakened the social base of the magnates.

The major issues in Hungarian politics, however, were not domestic but external and they revolved around the question of Hungary's commitment to the German cause. During 1941 Hungary had not been required to make a major contribution to the fighting in the east but in 1942 this changed. The Germans demanded more men as a result of which the Hungarian second army was put into the German lines; in January 1943 it was all but destroyed in the fighting around Voronezh. The traditional élite, with its social power being eroded, could not survive an external débâcle but Voronezh suggested that continued association with Germany would bring just such a disaster. The rulers of Hungary therefore tried, in their own phrase, to 'jump out' of the war by concluding a peace with the allies.

Chief amongst the protagonists of 'jumping out' were Kállay and the still influential Bethlen. Links with the British had never been severed and were maintained in neutral capitals such as Lisbon, Stockholm, and Istanbul. The spring of 1943 seemed a good point at which to jump out. The German and Romanian armies were far away and therefore in no position to coerce Hungary back into the axis; furthermore, if Hungary were to defect and bring Italy with it, the western allies would have direct access to the centre of Europe where they could cripple the Germans and keep the Russians at bay. The Hungarians were fond of such geopolitical dreaming. After Italy had dropped out of the war and had been occupied by the Germans, a more sober mood prevailed; even then, however, there was room for *opéra bouffe* incidents such as the signing of a secret surrender document on board the British embassy yacht in Istanbul; so secret was this surrender that the Hungarian government do not seem to have been told about it.

Germany's friends in Hungary knew that the government wished to jump out of the war and they made their dispositions accordingly. The Nazis still had strong support, not least from those who had profited from the anti-Jewish legislation. In March 1944 they acted. Horthy was called to an urgent meeting with the Führer in Klessheim and required to replace Kállay with Döme Sztójay. Two days later, on 19 March, German troops marched into Hungary, allegedly at the request of the Hungarian government. It was the belated victory of the new right over the old.

The real power in Hungary after March 1944 was the Reich plenipotentiary in Budapest, SS Standartenführer Edmund Vessenmayer. At his prompting the

Hungarian economy was tied yet more closely to the demands of the German war machine, anti-Jewish policies were imposed with real fury, and in August all political parties were abolished. Horthy's last effort at resistance came later in that month. Emboldened by widespread opposition to the Jewish deportations, by the liberation of Paris, by the Romanian volte-face, and by the rapid advance of the Red Army, Horthy replaced Sztójay with general Géza Lakotos, a soldier whom he trusted. With the regent's approval Lakotos despatched a delegation to parley with the Russians as soon as their forces crossed the Hungarian border on 23 September. On 11 October an armistice was signed in Moscow which committed the Hungarians to changing sides and fighting with the Red Army against the Germans. Four days later the Hungarian fascists seized power. They had little difficulty in doing so as they had for some time been in possession of most of the strategic points within the capital.

The Arrow Cross government which was formed under Szálasi on 15 October presided over one of the most bizarre and horrific episodes in Hungarian history. The final assault upon the Jews was launched and the Hungarian intelligentsia was also made the object of a wide-ranging and frenetic purge. All Hungarians between the ages of 12 and 70 were mobilised for service with the army or in the economy. It was at this point that Szálasi busied himself with his memoirs and his spiritualist conversations. Meanwhile the Red Army drove on across the Hungarian plain and by the end of December had encircled Budapest. The city was subjected to a horrifying siege which did not end until 13 February 1945, by which time most of historic Buda and Pest were in ruins. By 4 April 1945 the last German soldiers had left Hungary.

The independent states: Bulgaria

By signing the tripartite pact in March 1941 Bulgaria committed itself to the axis side, but did not actually declare war on Britain and the United States until after Pearl Harbour. It never declared war on the Soviet Union. The Germans would naturally have welcomed Bulgarian participation in the war on the eastern front but Boris convinced them that Bulgarian troops would not fight well outside the Balkans, the more so if they were engaged against the Russians whom many peasants, if not the intelligentsia, held in high regard. Boris also argued that the Bulgarian army was not equipped with the modern weapons needed for war on such a mammoth scale, and that it would be of much greater use defending the Balkans against the indigenous partisans and possible intervention by the Turks or the western allies. Bulgaria therefore remained the only country in the axis camp which did not have troops engaged against the Red Army, nor would Boris permit volunteer units to go to the eastern front, not least because he feared that if they were to return in triumph they might depose him and establish a fascist dictatorship. Hitler accepted Boris' arguments over Bulgarian commitment to the eastern campaign but there were fierce disagreements over the number of troops that the king was prepared to send for occupation duties in Yugoslavia and Greece. There was also conflict over Bulgaria's refusal to allow the deportation of Jews from the Bulgarian kingdom.

Boris' assumption had been that cooperation with the Germans was the lesser of two evils, as non-compliance might precipitate intervention on the Yugoslav or Polish pattern; at least his chosen path allowed him to preserve Bulgarian sovereignty and some freedom of action for himself and his government, as his Jewish subjects were to realise. The king also hoped that in the long run he would be able to lead Bulgaria out of the war with its territory intact. Boris, however, did not survive the war. He died suddenly on 28 August 1943 at the age of 49, the official cause of death being coronary thrombosis. His death gravely weakened Bulgaria. The regents who succeeded him, the most powerful of whom was Filov, made Dobri Bozhilov prime minister. Bozhilov had little political will or vision of his own and thus Filov's influence was prolonged. By the beginning of 1944 this was increasingly to Bulgaria's disadvantage because the need to extricate the country from the war became ever greater. In November 1943 Sofia had suffered its first heavy air-raid and in January 1944 even more severe punishment was meted out to the city. Social dislocation followed and exacerbated existing problems of food and fuel distribution. These sufferings added strength to the small partisan movement which was beginning to cause concern to the régime.

The partisans were the military arm of the Fatherland Front (FF), a coalition of communists, left-agrarians, social democrats, and Zveno. The FF had been mooted as early as 1941 but had not emerged as an effective group until July 1942, and it was not until the privations of 1944 that it began to attract reasonably widespread support. By that summer the government was desperate to placate the allies and therefore made a number of political concessions, including promises to repeal the anti-Jewish laws and to relax political controls. As authority crumbled, support for the FF grew and by the beginning of September it was in a position to pose as a valid alternative government.

The decay of governmental authority in Bulgaria was primarily the result of military developments. As the Red Army continued its advance westward, pressure on the Bulgarian régime intensified. In May the Soviet Union delivered a virtual ultimatum demanding that Bulgaria expel all German military and naval personnel and observe strict neutrality. The Bulgarian response was to attempt to negotiate a peace with the western powers, and to replace the incumbent prime minister with one acceptable to London and Washington; failure to secure a peace could mean that the Soviet Union would declare war on Bulgaria and then occupy the country. Events could hardly have turned out worse for the Bulgarian régime. Romania's sudden capitulation in August 1944 brought Soviet forces to the Danube even more rapidly than Bulgaria's rulers had feared. Desperate attempts to negotiate a peace with the western allies continued but made scant progress. On 30 August Stalin announced that the USSR would no longer recognise Bulgarian neutrality and on 5 September declared war. Three days later

Bulgaria declared war on Germany; Bulgaria had become the only country to be simultaneously at war with Britain, Germany, the United States, and the Soviet Union. To add to this confusion the internal opposition, and especially the communists, fomented strikes, demonstrations, and desertions. On the night of 8–9 September a partisan brigade took command of Sofia and on 9 September 1944 a Fatherland Front government was established under Kimon Gheorghiev. The new administration included Velchev and Gheorghiev from Zveno, four agrarians, two social democrats and four communists.

The independent states: Romania

When the great struggle in Russia began, Romania under general Antonescu was a willing partner on the German side. The initial victories returned Bessarabia and the Bukovina to Romanian rule and Romania also took over Transnistria, the area between the Dniestr and the Bug. The early stages of the war also brought prosperity to Romanian industry and agriculture, though there were disagreements with the Germans on payment for some Romanian imports of manufactured goods. For Romania, however, as for Germany, Stalingrad proved to be, as Churchill described it, 'the hinge of fate'. The great battle accounted for 150,000 Romanian lives and destroyed the fighting spirit of the Romanian army. With the power of the army went the political credibility of Antonescu, whose efforts after Stalingrad were concentrated upon escaping from the conflict and ensuring that Anglo-American action in the Balkans prevented total Soviet domination. By August 1944 he had had no success. With the Red Army already having crossed the Pruth, the young King Michael staged a *coup d'état* on 23 August, locking Antonescu in a commodious safe built to house the royal stamp collection. A new government was formed which included one communist. The Romanian army switched sides to fight its way with the Russians towards Germany. That campaign cost a further 111,000 Romanian lives but at least the surrenders of 1940 had been redeemed, as the Iron Guard would have wished, in blood.

EASTERN EUROPE, 1945 – 91

0   250
km

SWEDEN

DENMARK
Copenhagen
Baltic Sea

Wilno
(Vilnius)

SOVIET UNION

Berlin
EAST
GERMANY
POLAND
River Vistula
Warsaw
River Bug

WEST
GERMANY
Prague
Lvov
River Dniester
CZECHOSLOVAKIA
River Pruth
Bratislava
Vienna
Budapest
AUSTRIA
HUNGARY
ROMANIA
SWITZ
Zagreb
Bucharest
Belgrade
River Danube
YUGOSLAVIA
BULGARIA
ITALY
Adriatic Sea
Sofia
Skopje
TURKEY
Rome
ALBANIA
Tirana
GREECE

13

THE COMMUNIST TAKEOVERS

Eastern Europe at the end of the second world war

The communist domination of eastern Europe was not accomplished over-night. The commissars did not simply move in as soon as the Gauleiters had packed their bags and left; the takeovers were complex processes varying in form and timing from country to country. In a classic examination of these processes Hugh Seton Watson discerned three stages: a general coalition of left-wing, anti-fascist forces; a bogus coalition in which the communists neutralised those in other parties who were not willing to accept communist supremacy; and finally, complete communist domination, frequently exercised in a new party formed by the fusion of communist and other leftist groups. During the first and second stages the communists established enormous influence through social organisations under their control, such as trade unions, women's and youth associations, professional bodies, and Soviet friendship societies, all of which were usually grouped in a 'national' or 'popular' front which was directed by the communists or their lackeys. As one young communist was told in eastern Germany: 'Its got to look democratic, but we must have everything in our control.'[1]

At the same time Soviet influence grew. Soviet advisors were placed in govern-ment institutions, especially the army and the police, whilst newly negotiated trade agreements gave the USSR a preponderant influence in the local economy. In the defeated states joint Soviet and local concerns, the so-called joint stock companies, were established through which Soviet officials could exercise direct control over important sectors of the economy.

Historians will no doubt debate for generations whether there was a cold war because of the communist takeovers or whether there were communist take-overs because of the cold war; what they will not dispute is that the takeovers and the cold war were inextricably interwoven. Eastern Europe had been ack-nowledged as the Red Army's responsibility in the Tehran talks of December 1943, and this became clear to the world in June 1944 when the western allies landed in Normandy rather than in the Balkans. In October 1944 in the infamous 'percentage agreements', Churchill, in seemingly cavalier fashion, handed

211

Romania and Bulgaria to Soviet domination, keeping Greece for the west, and agreeing to share Yugoslavia and Hungary. Churchill's embarrassment later led him to claim that such an arrangement had been meant to last only until the end of the war, but it showed that he had sniffed the reality of the distribution of power.

At Tehran the west had agreed that the Soviet Union should take Poland east of the Curzon line because Stalin claimed that this was necessary for the defence of the USSR, nor did the west object when the Soviets offered the same justification for taking Bessarabia, East Prussia, northern Bukovina, and Ruthenia, even though the latter was absorbed before the end of the war in direct contravention of the Atlantic Charter. These territorial adjustments were agreed at Yalta in February 1945 and at Potsdam in July.

The Yalta conference had also produced the declaration on liberated Europe which called for 'free and unfettered' elections in the territories released from German domination; the realists in eastern Europe were not much reassured and were further depressed when the victor powers agreed at Potsdam that the USSR's neighbours should have governments which were 'democratic and friendly' to Moscow.

The western allies did show some concern for non-communist political interests in eastern Europe but it was Soviet conduct in Germany that caused them real alarm. By 1947 the British and American zones had separated almost entirely from the Soviet and in March of that year the division of Europe into two hostile blocs became much more sharply focused. The communists left the governing coalitions of France and Italy, the Truman doctrine warned against communist attempts to expand into Greece, and in the summer the Soviets insisted that the east European states should not take Marshall Aid. In September 1947 the major European communist parties met at Szklarska Poręba in Poland to discuss tactics in the face of what they regarded as growing imperialist aggression; they agreed to set up the Communist Information Bureau, Cominform. In May 1948 the new currency introduced into the three western zones of Germany provoked the Soviet blockade of Berlin and the Berlin airlift. By the time that these ended fifteen months later, communist power was firmly established throughout eastern Europe.

In the immediate post-war months Stalin's priority had been to establish a secure western border for the Soviet Union. A dependable government in Poland was essential for this, not least to ensure unhindered access to the Soviet garrisons in eastern Germany which were the front line of Soviet defences against any further incursion from the west. Whether Stalin intended to establish fully communist governments elsewhere in eastern Europe is not clear. What he would have liked was not necessarily what he was scheming to bring about. With the exception of Poland, it is probable that Stalin merely took advantage of what opportunities came his way; as a recent study has noted, 'Stalinisation was a process, not a plan.'[2]

There was no doubt that the Red Army greatly helped in creating favourable opportunities; Stalin had once told the Yugoslav communist, Milovan Djilas, that 'This war is not as in the past; whoever occupies a territory imposes his own social system as far as his army can reach.'[3] The Soviet forces provided massive material and psychological support to local communists; without the presence of the Red Army it would be difficult to explain why the tiny communist parties of Romania and Hungary succeeded whilst the large ones of France and Italy failed. The Red Army, more especially in the earliest days after the war, could favour local communists by supplying them with vehicles, petrol, paper, type-writers, and other scarce items necessary for the carrying out of political activities. Yet occupation by the Red Army did not always bring communist rule: Austria, Finland, Bornholm, and northern Iran experienced the former without having to endure the latter, and, conversely, there was no significant Red Army presence in Albania, Yugoslavia, Bulgaria, or Czechoslovakia when communist power was established in those countries.

The communist takeovers depended upon a number of factors, internal as well as external. In the first place socialism seemed in 1945 to be 'the future'. The successful consumer capitalism which began to emerge in the 1950s was as yet largely undreamed of, the general image of capitalism being the system which had failed in 1929 and the 1930s, the system from whose debilitation had emerged militant fascism, war, and the horrors of Auschwitz. The Soviet econ-omy, on the other hand, had been spared the rigours of the depression; that it had inflicted the horrors of collectivisation, famine, and terror was conveniently forgotten. Furthermore, the massive destruction brought about by the war demanded coordinated efforts at renewal; many believed that this was a task so vast that it could not be accomplished without the aid of the state and perhaps only under its direction. The communists were regarded by many as proven practitioners of such planned restructuring.

The restructuring of the Soviet Union in the 1930s had of course been achieved at the cost of enormous suffering but since then, it seemed, Stalin had softened the nature of Soviet socialism. In the war he had come to an accom-modation with the Russian Orthodox church; collectivisation was not immedi-ately introduced into the territories acquired as a result of the war; Comintern had been abolished in 1943; and east European communists now talked much less of the dictatorship of the proletariat, class warfare, or the transition to socialism, but rather of the need to build a common front against fascism, to ensure peace, and to reconstruct society, objectives which could be shared by all of goodwill. These developments the optimist could interpret as meaning that socialism did not now have to be an exact copy of the Soviet model. The resistance record of the communists after 1941 also gave them added credibility and many believed that the communists had earned a right to a say in govern-ment. They were no longer, it seemed, the stool pigeons of Moscow; all the signs were that in political terms the individual communist parties had become 'house trained'.

Finally, the communists were usually the best organised political force. In addition to the vital support of the Red Army in supplying ordinary items of everyday necessity, they had the backing of Moscow at an international level, which could be important particularly in the defeated states – Hungary, Bulgaria, Romania, and Germany – where the allied control commissions (ACCs) gave the western powers at least a theoretical right to interest themselves in local politics.

At least as important was the fact that in many countries the communists' enemies had been destroyed or greatly weakened in the 1930s and the war. Most significant in this respect was the social dislocation suffered by the communists' foes. Aristocrats had survived after 1918 in East Prussia, Poland, and Hungary. By 1945 they were ruined. In East Prussia they were decimated after the plot against Hitler on 20 July 1944; in Poland and Hungary, if they did not flee at the end of the fighting, their lands were confiscated through land reform.

The bourgeoisie fared little better. There were relatively few industrial or commercial magnates in 1939 and many of these had been forced to hand over their factories or firms to the Germans or at least to work at their direction. In either case the owners were now liable to charges of collaboration and frequently had to forfeit their property. For those who could still survive on their savings, post-war inflation, currency reforms, and the imposition of maxima on bank deposits soon removed this safety net. The *petit bourgeoisie*, frequently either Jewish or German, suffered even more. The first were usually destroyed during the war, the second were mostly driven out after it.

In many areas it was the peasantry alone who had survived more or less intact, and in the war they had enjoyed relative prosperity. They were naturally suspicious of the communists who had destroyed the peasant proprietor in the Soviet Union, but in the period immediately after the war the communists did much to redress this image. They championed land reform and made sure that it was they who masterminded the process, whilst at a local level they involved themselves in the myriad committees which worked out the details of the reforms. At the same time they subverted the peasant political organisations.

Of the other social or political forces which might have stood in the way of an eventual communist takeover, the intelligentsia had frequently been weakened in the pre-war years of authoritarian rule or, as in the case of Poland particularly, had been decimated by German and Soviet occupation after 1939. Where it did survive the intelligentsia tended more than most elements to sense the *Zeitgeist* and to give the benefit of the doubt to the communists. The trade unions too were frequently well-disposed to the communists, though in many cases trade unionism had been a major casualty of the pre-war repression of left-wing organisations. In those cases where trade unions were not willing accomplices the communists found little difficulty in subverting them and placing their own sympathisers in positions of authority.

This was less easy to do in the churches. Here the communists increasingly deployed force and violence, beginning with the weakest. The Uniate church, with its links to Rome, was banned, and many Protestant organisations lost the right to run schools or charitable institutions before being subjected to direct persecution. As the communists gained in confidence they did not even hold back from grappling with the Catholic church. Again the church lost its rights in education and in the provision of youth clubs and other social or charitable facilities. It could not be allowed to exercise social authority, though in most cases the Catholic church was so powerful an adversary that it was not tackled until all other opposition elements had been neutralised and the communist takeover formalised.

In an area devastated by four years of intense, mobile warfare, where casualty rates had been high and massive sufferings inflicted upon the civilian population, there was little inclination or ability to offer armed resistance to the communists. This did appear, however, in a few instances, mostly in places where the local population had been absorbed unwillingly into the Soviet Union. In Poland's former eastern territories, the Baltic states, Ruthenia, and the Ukraine this unequal struggle went on even into the 1950s.

Although these characteristics could be ascribed to one or more of the states which fell under communist domination the takeover process varied, as a study of each country, in rough order of the takeovers, will illustrate. That order will show that the takeovers took place first in the least industrialised countries and occurred last in the most developed. From its very inception the marxist experience in eastern Europe belied the thinking of its founding father.

Albania

When the Germans withdrew from Albania in the autumn of 1944 the communists under Enver Hoxha were already well established as the dominant political force. In May 1944 the National Liberation Movement had transformed itself into the National Liberation Front and deposed King Zog. In October a congress at Berat established a provisional government, nine of whose eleven members were communists.

There were few obstacles to this rapid communist takeover. The allies had never recognised an Albanian government in exile so there was no one to intervene on behalf of former politicians; the close ideological ties between Hoxha and other communists gave Albanians some hope that Albanian, Greek, and Yugoslav communists might find a post-war settlement of border questions which would be more satisfactory to the Albanians. All other political factions in the country were disorganised and when opposition manifested itself later in the Catholic areas of the north, the well-armed communist army and security forces had no difficulty in suppressing it.

Yugoslavia

The communists in Yugoslavia had established a strong hold in the resistance movement and at Jajce in November 1943 had gone a long way towards turning

AVNOJ into a provisional government. They were also aided by the fact that Yugoslavia was considered a victor power and therefore had neither an occupation force nor an allied control commission. Furthermore, for many Yugoslavs the western powers were compromised by their association with Mihajlović, whose name the communists had systematically blackened, and with King Peter, whose conduct in exile had angered a large number of Yugoslavs. The return to Yugoslavia of many refugees in the spring of 1945 also enabled the communists to liquidate thousands of actual or potential opponents in the most primitive and effective of ways.

Somewhat paradoxically, the chief impediment to communist advance in Yugoslavia was Stalin himself. Anxious lest conspicuous intentions to create communist systems after the war might alarm the allies and drive them to a separate peace, during the war the Soviet leader had persistently advised the Yugoslav communists to tread cautiously. Stalin joined with Churchill to urge Tito to come to an agreement in June 1944 with Šubašić which provided for a post-war coalition of royalist and partisan forces. In September 1944 in Moscow Stalin virtually ordered Tito to bring back the king, parrying Tito's objections with the suggestion that he 'should slip a knife into his back at the appropriate moment'.

Šubašić arrived in Belgrade in November 1944, a month after its liberation. Thereafter he went to Moscow to give substance to the general agreement with Tito. It was decided that the king would not return until after a plebiscite had been held on the future of the monarchy; in the meantime a regency would be appointed. This was much to the fury of King Peter who was of age and who did not like the composition of the regency whose three members, one Croat, one Serb, and one Slovene, though non-communists, were all nominees of Tito. The regents took office in March 1945. At the same time a new cabinet was formed for the 'Democratic Federation of Yugoslavia', with Šubašić as minister for foreign affairs; all but five of the twenty-eight ministers were ex-partisans but the appearance of coalition government was enhanced by the inclusion of a member of the CPPP and of the leader of the Serbian Democratic Party, Milan Grol. In August over a hundred former members of the Yugoslav parliament were added to AVNOJ to form a national provisional parliament whilst the political leadership of the partisan movement, the National Liberation Front, was reshaped and renamed The Popular Front. Further reforms enlarged the franchise, giving the vote to women and to all over 18 years of age, collaborators excepted.

There was little doubt in Yugoslavia that gestures towards coalition were hollow and that the communists, though they might share government, would not share power. In the summer of 1945 three of the non-communists resigned and when elections for a constituent assembly were held in November there was only a single government list which electors could accept or reject. Attempts to publish opposition newspapers were frustrated by strikes held by communist-organised workers, by the denial of paper allocations, by censorship, and by open intimidation. What was left of the demoralised opposition boycotted the elections of 11 November, which then registered a 96 per cent vote for the Popular Front.

It was now but a short step to the formalisation of the communist takeover. On 29 November a republic was proclaimed and the constituent assembly declared itself to be the people's assembly. The new constitution which was adopted on 31 January 1946 created the Federative People's Republic of Yugoslavia. At that time Yugoslavia was the only federal state in eastern Europe, its constituent parts being the republics of Serbia, Croatia, Slovenia, Bosnia-Hercegovina, Montenegro, and Macedonia. Within the bounds of Serbia were Serbia itself, and the provinces of Vojvodina and Kosovo-Metohija. The constitution provided for the socialisation of the economy and it enabled the communist party to exercise a leading role in society.

After the takeover the communists continued their campaign against their enemies, past and present, real and imagined. Mihajlović was captured in March 1946 and, after his trial had been used to attack the western powers, he was executed on 17 July. In September in Zagreb leading members of the Ustaša were placed in the dock in a trial which also led to the imprisonment, albeit in relative comfort, of archbishop Stepinac; it was a double blow against Croat nationalism and the Roman Catholic church. In 1947 the leader of the radical wing of the agrarians, professor Dragoljub Jovanović, was arrested together with a number of other non-communist party leaders. These mopping-up operations, however, were consequent upon rather than preliminary to the takeover.

Poland

In their march to power the Polish communists faced two major enemies: the historic groups which had dominated the country between the wars and, after these had been defeated, the agrarians.

The communists themselves began with a relatively weak organisation. The old Polish communist party had been liquidated in 1938 and no attempt was made to reconstitute it until after the German invasion of the Soviet Union. In the summer of 1941 an 'Initiative Group' had been parachuted into Poland and in the following January the Polish Workers' Party (PWP) was established. Its first leaders were killed and it therefore fell under the domination of Władisław Gomułka whose links with and dependence upon Moscow were less than those of most other east European communist leaders. This, plus the party's commitment to the cause of resistance, helped to some degree to overcome popular suspicion of a party which was inevitably seen as pro-Russian.

By the summer of 1944 communist forces, military and political, were numerous and coordinated. The military were marshalled under general Berling whilst the major political organisation was the Lublin committee. The Lublin committee constituted a virtual provisional government for areas under Soviet military control, and consisted of fifteen members, all of whom were communists or fellow travellers.

The communists were immeasurably strengthened by the Warsaw uprising, with its virtual destruction of the leadership of the historic political forces and their military infrastructure. At the end of December 1944 the Soviets recognised the Lublin committee as the provisional government of Poland and that government established itself in Warsaw on 19 January 1945, two days after the liberation of what remained of the city. The Yalta agreement in February brought an extension of territory westwards to the line of the Oder and the Neisse, together with the promise of 'free and unfettered elections'. But there were growing doubts as to which forces would be able to compete in such elections.

In March 1945 the government delegate, that is, the representative in Poland of the government in exile, plus the commander of the AK, general Okulicki, and fourteen other prominent figures were invited to have discussions with the commander of the first Belorussian front, general Ivanov. To refuse would have been an insult, yet the sixteen knew that the invitations were a trap; as indeed they proved to be. Despite guarantees of their safety, the sixteen were arrested and taken to the USSR where they were accused of plotting joint AK-German operations against the Red Army and subjected to a show trial in June 1945. As general Okulicki said from the dock, this was a political trial whose object was to blacken the name of the AK and the non-communist underground.

The sentences handed down were not long by the unsavoury standards of such trials but they came in the same month as the formation of a new government which the western allies then recognised. The new administration included the PWP, the traditional Polish Socialist Party (PSP), the Democratic Party, the Labour Party, and the Peasant Party (PP) whose leader, Mikołajczyk, had arrived back in Poland in the autumn of 1944. Fourteen of the twenty-two members of the cabinet had been in the Lublin government. The PWP was small and alien, 'having hardly enough native Polish communists to run a factory, let alone a country of some thirty million people'.[4] But it enjoyed Soviet sponsorship. The PSP, though large, was weakened because many of its leaders were in exile, one of them being amongst the sixteen tried in Moscow; it was then further enfeebled by being merged with the Polish Socialist Workers' Party and placed under the leadership of Józef Cyrankiewicz, who had just been released from Auschwitz and who did little to resist communist pressures. The PSP, despite its 200,000 strong membership, was tolerated because it allowed the PWP the leading role in the coalition; in November 1946 many of its more right-wing members were purged and more were to suffer a similar fate in June 1947. Meanwhile the Democratic Party and the Labour Party were small, ineffective, and docile.

The communists' growing political self-confidence was bolstered by their increasing control over the economy. On 3 January 1946 the nationalisation decree had placed in public ownership all enterprises employing more than fifty workers per shift and all but two of the country's banks. Socialists and trade unionists helped to apply the nationalisation decree and in so doing learned to cooperate with the communists. In 1947 a three-year reconstruction plan placed the economy even more firmly in governmental hands. The Nazis had destroyed most of the Polish industrial bourgeoisie; the communists were not going to allow it to reappear.

They could not, however, prevent the continuation of illegal opposition to their growing authority. In the autumn of 1945 a sustained campaign against communist power was launched, precipitating what was in effect a civil war in which as many as 35,000 anti-Soviet activists took to the marshes or the forests. The partisans, some of them linked to the remaining structures of the AK, were strongest in the east where serious clashes took place until July 1946 and minor incidents continued for a decade. The emergency enabled the communists to expand the security services and to extend their control over them. Soviet advisers helped to establish a political police, the Security Office or UB; in April 1946 the Volunteers' Citizen Militia Reserve was set up, its 100,000 members forming a virtual private army of the PWP; and a new Internal Security Corps had to be created, even though at the height of the fighting as much as half of the regular army was already deployed against the underground. All of these organs of repression could be, and were, used in the other great confrontation in Poland: that between the communists and the agrarians.

The communists had from the beginning of their resurgence in 1944 attempted to win over the peasants and so deprive Mikołajczyk of his power base. To that end on 6 September 1944 the Lublin government had decreed that estates of over one hundred hectares were to be redistributed. Brigades of workers and soldiers were sent out to the countryside to explain the reform and to help the peasants to divide up the land; the fact that the land was distributed in very small plots of 2–3 hectares was proof that the communists wished to please as many people as possible. In a concession rare in eastern Europe, even the middle peasants, those owning 5–20 hectares, were to be given a share of the redistributed estates. Even more telling was the fact that the reform had been introduced at the very height of the Warsaw uprising; social, class-based gains were to be used to deflect peasant attention from the titanic national struggle in progress in Warsaw. When the newly acquired territories in the west came into Polish possession the communists were quick to install their own man, Gomułka, as the minister for regained territories. The land, stock, implements, and homes of over eight million Germans were available for distribution amongst Poles and the communists were determined that it should be they who dispensed the patronage.

They also attempted to subvert the agrarians' party organisation. Only Mikoł-ajczyk's return to Poland frustrated communist attempts to reconstitute the Peasant Party. In September 1945, with the agrarians inside the ruling coalition, the communists attempted to pack the agrarians' supreme council whereupon Mikołajczyk split away to form his own Polish Peasants' Party (PPP). By January 1946 the PPP, with 600,000 members, was the largest political grouping in Poland. It called for respect for the law, judicial independence, local self-government, radical social reform, and, in accordance with the Potsdam conference's decisions, a general election before July 1946.

The elections were to be the final battle between the communists and the agrarians. Before that battle commenced the communists proposed that the PPP should join a 'Democratic Bloc', a coalition of parties willing to fight the election on a single list. Mikołajczyk agreed as long as the PPP were guaranteed three-quarters of the seats won by the bloc candidates. This was an unrealistic demand; the communists refused such terms and began a campaign of verbal and physical intimidation of Mikołajczyk and his followers. In the meantime the elections were delayed so that a referendum might be held which would ask voters three questions: did they favour a senate? did they approve of recent social reforms? and did they accept Poland's new borders? Few were likely to disapprove of social reforms such as land redistribution, and, whatever popular feelings were over territorial losses in the east, the new western lands brought considerable wealth to those who settled there and no one was likely to vote against the acquisition of these areas; the senate was a different matter, however, since it seemed to have little contemporary relevance and Mikołajczyk advised his supporters to vote against it. Mikołajczyk had decided to test his ability to mobilise the peasant vote. After a vicious campaign in which the agrarians suffered decreases in paper allocations, the arrest of over 1,000 of their activists, and the closure of a number of party branches, the government announced that 68 per cent of the population had voted in favour of a senate. The PPP maintained that in the 2,805 polling booths where they had insisted upon a count before the police arrived to take possession of the voting urns there had been an 83 per cent vote against the senate.

The referendum was a dress rehearsal for the elections which took place in January 1947. Intimidation was again widespread: there were raids on PPP headquarters; two political trials attempted to blacken Mikołajczyk as a foreign agent; the PPP had limited access to the radio; the western territories, where communist influence was strong, were overrepresented; over 100,000 PPP activists, said their leader, were arrested and 142 candidates were detained by the police. In some constituencies there was an open vote in which bands of organised workers bullied the electorate; and in ten of the fifty-two electoral districts, accounting for almost a quarter of the total electorate, the PPP lists and candidates were disqualified on technical grounds. It was hardly surprising that the Democratic Bloc came away with 80.1 per cent of the vote, the PPP with 10.3 per cent, and the so-called Independents with 9.6 per cent.

The communists could now move swiftly to a full takeover. The dependable socialist leader, Cyrankiewicz, was made prime minister and on 19 February a new constitution was enacted. This 'little constitution' bore many resemblances to that of the USSR, though a fully Soviet-style constitution was not introduced until 1951. By then the political structure of the country had been refashioned on communist lines, though the underground resistance was not entirely defeated. This resistance continued to provide a convenient excuse for increases in the security forces which were then used to intimidate what remained of open political opposition. Mikołajczyk was subjected to intensified abuse and intimidation and his party's journals to increasing censorship. In the autumn of 1947 he heard that he was about to be arrested and, with his eyes on the fate of peasant leaders in Hungary, Bulgaria, and Romania (see pp. 222–5, 225–8, and 228–31), he once again went into exile. It was the end of effective opposition. What remained of the PPP was taken over by pro-communists and in 1949 it was fused with the PP to form the United Peasant Party which was entirely subservient to the ruling communists.

Fusion also took place amongst the socialist parties. On May Day 1947 communist leader Gomułka declared that the working class needed only one party to defend its interests and therefore called for a merger of the PSP and the PWP, the Labour Party having already merged with the PWP. This was not the first time that such a suggestion had been made but in the past it had been resisted by the PSP; now its resistance was weaker and grew ever more so in 1948 as pressure from the Cominform mounted. In March 1948 Cyrankiewicz decided to agree to fusion, though he did not yet tell his party executive and it was not until December of that year that the marriage was consummated with the formation of the Polish United Workers' Party (PUWP). The new force was dedicated to the principles of marxism-leninism and it now had sufficient numbers to dominate the country in accordance with those principles.

In Poland, however, the final stage of the takeover, sovietisation, was not to be as intense as in other east European states. Nazi policies, frontier changes, and the expulsion of the Germans meant that Poland was now 98 per cent Polish. This meant that it was more than ever Catholic, russophobe, and, with its industries smashed by war, predominantly peasant.

This was hardly the most promising territory for Soviet-style socialism, yet for strategic reasons it was also the major priority for Soviet domination. The communists were therefore careful not to tread on too many toes. The Catholic church was treated with great circumspection; although the 1925 concordat was abolished and civil registration of marriages introduced, the church retained its property until 1950 and religion could still be taught in schools; the communist Bolesław Bierut took a religious oath on becoming president and appeared in Corpus Christi Day parades just as his pre-war predecessors had done. Furthermore, the Polish communists had established very close ties with the small peasantry; they had by no means denounced state or collective ownership but they had made a great, if not entirely successful, play for peasant support. Finally, inside the PWP Gomułka had defeated the extremist pro-Soviet faction, those who wanted to make Poland into a constituent republic of the USSR. Unlike many of his colleagues in the other east European states, Gomułka willingly and openly recognised the contribution of the western powers to the victory over Germany, and criticised looters from the Red Army, even ordering Polish troops to shoot them.

Such non-conformity was soon to be punished.

Hungary

When the Red Army first entered Hungary in December 1944 it seemed that the country was heading for a rapid communist takeover. The provisional government established at Debrecen had a distinctly marxist-leninist tinge, and a quarter of the delegates elected to a provisional assembly in November were communists. The results owed much to skilful electoral manipulation; the pro-communist area of Orosháza with its population of 30,000, for example, returned fourteen deputies whereas only half that number came from the moderate Pécs and Baránya regions with a population at least ten times larger.

Even though the Germans had barricaded themselves in Budapest a provisional government was formed. It was a four-party coalition made up of the Hungarian Communist Party (HCP), the Social Democratic Party (SDP), the Smallholders Party (SHP), and the National Peasant Party (NP). The provisional government's major act was radical land reform. Some 35 per cent of Hungary's arable land, over three million hectares, was redistributed to 642,000 families, most of them landless agricultural labourers, dwarf-holders, or domestic servants. It was an enormously popular measure which broke the social and political power of the magnates for ever.

In enacting land reform the Hungarian provisional government was following the pattern set in Poland, but in two fundamental respects the situation in Hungary was different. In the first place, as a defeated enemy state Hungary had an Allied Control Commission to supervise its affairs; much more importantly, Stalin was not ready to risk a communist takeover in Hungary until socialist domination of Poland had been secured. This so-called 'Polish trade-off' required that local communists in Hungary and Czechoslovakia stay their hands, perhaps for as long as ten or even fifteen years. For this reason, until the intensification of the cold war in 1947, the Hungarian communists respected election results, did not contest open debates in the national assembly, put little though increasing pressure on religious organisations, did not interfere with what was a relatively free press, and even tolerated a functioning stock exchange. It seemed that the takeover would.be a gradual one.

In November 1945 a general election was held. The results shocked the communists. The Smallholders Party (SHP) won a clear majority with 57 per cent of the vote. The Social Democratic Party had 17 per cent, the same proportion as the communists, with the National Peasant Party taking 7 per cent. A government was formed under Ferenc Nagy of the SHP whilst the SHP leader, Zoltán Tildy, became president.

The elections were less of a defeat for the communists than it might at first sight appear. Before the elections the major parties had agreed, at the instigation of the Soviet president of the ACC, that whatever the result of the poll the ruling four-party coalition would continue in office. The communists then insisted that they would remain in the coalition only if they were given the ministry of the interior. The Soviet military had handed control of the internal security forces to the Hungarian communists. They rapidly separated the security police from the ordinary police. The former, the AVO, was made directly responsible to the minister of the interior who, from March 1946, was an impatient young communist, László Rajk. From the beginning the AVO, or AVH as it was known after reorganisation in 1949, was a private army of the communists and one which they valued highly; the communist leader Mátyás Rákosi recalled later that the party

> took absolute control of the political police, the AVO . . . It was the only institution of which we kept total control for ourselves and firmly refused to share it with the other parties in the coalition.[5]

The communists were also strengthened by the fact that they had a number of sympathisers or even covert party members in senior positions in other parties. One of the ministers representing the social democrats, Erik Molnár, had been a closet communist since 1928 and in the 1930s had master-minded the communist infiltration of the SDP. The NP was also heavily penetrated; one of its ministers, Ferenc Erdei, had once asked to join the HCP but had been told that he was of more value remaining where he was; of the thirty-two NP deputies elected in 1945, fifteen were secret members of the HCP. It was because the SHP was more or less immune to infiltration that it became the prime political enemy of the communists.

With a secure hold on the police force, with trojan horses placed in most of its opponents' camps, and with the Red Army stationed in the country until, it was presumed, the conclusion of a peace treaty, the Hungarian communists were in a good position to begin that war of political attrition which Rákosi later made famous with the phrase, 'salami tactics'.

The first to be sliced from the body politic were the members of the so-called Sulyok faction within the SHP. The Sulyokists were on the left of the SHP and as such might compete with the communists for support, but the outspoken nationalism of the Sulyokists and their readiness to criticise increasing police powers could well make them more popular in the common constituency. The Sulyokists were attacked in March 1946 as chauvinists, which they may well have been, and as reactionaries, which they most certainly were not. Tildy refused to defend them and thus their twenty-one deputies were forced to withdraw from parliament. In October they formed the Hungarian Independent Party hoping to win working class support by attacking the high living standards of communist and trade union bosses. The Independents made little progress, especially because unionised workers refused to print what they condemned as 'reactionary calumnies'; the communists could not allow competition for support from the working class.

In the summer of 1946 the communists, with the cooperation of their dependent police, had attempted to weaken the main body of the SHP by complicating its relations with the Soviets. Both the SHP and the Catholic church were said to be involved in a series of anti-Russian and anti-semitic outbursts. The Soviets therefore insisted on the closure of Catholic youth organisations. Rajk obligingly suppressed over 1,000 of them. At the same time the Soviets blocked SHP plans to establish peasant trade union organisations; the communists had their own such bodies and once again they would not tolerate competition. Communist attacks became more bitter and more frequent towards the end of the year, the HCP perhaps believing that it had to act before February 1947 and the signature of the peace treaty which, it was assumed, would mean the withdrawal of the Red Army, the disbandment of the ACC, and probably the dissolution of parliament. The peace treaty also dominated SHP thinking and accounted for its apparent tractability. The SHP believed that it could afford to wait and reassert itself when fresh elections were held after, it was presumed, the Red Army had left the country. The gamble did not pay off; the peace treaty included a provision that the Red Army should stay in Hungary in order to guard the supply lines to its occupation forces in Austria.

After the peace treaty communist pressure on the SHP became intense, with its popular secretary general, Béla Kovács, coming under particularly virulent attack. In March 1947 Kovács was seized by the secret police whilst walking home from the parliament in which he had been taking sanctuary for a number of days. In May 1947 prime minister Ferenc Nagy went on holiday to Switzerland. The communists immediately declared in public that he had gone to prepare for their expulsion from government, as had happened in France and Italy; in private they threatened that if he did not remain abroad he would never see his infant son again. Nagy resigned, to be replaced as prime minister by a communist stooge, Lajos Dinnyés. The SHP was shattered; it regrouped, powerless, under István Dobi, a drunkard who had been advocating collaboration with the communists since 1945. In July 1948 Tildy resigned as state president, to be succeeded by Arpád Szakasits, a pro-communist social democrat.

In these circumstances the communists enacted a new law which enabled electoral commissions to exclude many oppositionists when the next elections were held in August 1947. The HCP formed a common list with the SDP and the NP; official returns gave these parties 22 per cent, 15 per cent and 8 per cent respectively, though the communist vote, if not that of its allies, was magnified artificially. For the opposition the Independents polled 14 per cent, the Democratic Peoples' Party 16 per cent, the Catholic Party 5 per cent, and the SHP 15 per cent.

By the autumn of 1947 all pretence at gradualism had gone. The Independent Party was dissolved, as was the Democratic Peoples' Party after it had objected to the secularisation of schools. By the beginning of 1948 only the SDP could offer any real political alternative to the HCP. Since the SDP was too large and too clearly socialist to suppress, the HCP called for fusion, arguing, as in Poland, that the working class needed only one party to defend its interests. In February 1948 those within the SDP who questioned the idea of fusion were expelled and in June 1948 the HCP and the SDP merged to become the Hungarian Workers' Party (HWP). At the same time, the army was purged and sovietised, whilst the economy was subjected to greater degrees of central planning, particularly with the revision of the 1947 three-year plan.

By the end of 1948 the one institution largely outside communist control was the Catholic church. The secularisation of schools in 1947 had provoked intense resentment, as had a whole series of niggling restrictions on the church's activities; a sick person wanting to see a priest, for example, had now to apply in writing. As intended, these measures provoked the senior church dignitary, cardinal József Mindszenty, into ever more outspoken complaint until, on Christmas Day 1948, he was taken into custody. Many other religious activists, by no means all of them Catholics, followed in later months.

Communist domination was now secured. In April 1949 new elections were held, this time without the embarrassment of opposition candidates. The newly elected parliament enacted a soviet-style constitution. Political sovietisation had been completed; next would come the complete sovietisation of the economy and society, a process which was to claim many victims, one of the most prominent of whom, László Rajk, had already been arrested in May 1949.

Bulgaria

The Bulgarian communists had two advantages which few other parties in eastern Europe enjoyed: they had in the past been a strong factor in national politics, and popular suspicion of Russia was less intense than elsewhere. The communists were naturally included in the government formed by Gheorghiev on 9 September 1944, its other component parties being the agrarians, the social democrats and Zveno.

Communist muscle was exercised from the very beginning. The communists controlled the ministries of the interior and of justice, and, at Soviet insistence, a dependable communist had been included in the new three-man regency. The existing police forces were disbanded and an entirely new organisation was created which was totally subservient to the communists. There were also attempts to purge the officer corps, particularly those who were not in combat alongside the Red Army now that Bulgaria had joined the war against Germany; when opposition parties resisted these attempts to create a new, pro-communist officer corps, the local communists both sought and received the help of the Soviet representatives on the ACC.

The contemporaneous communist assault on the civil service, despite its ferocity, went almost unchallenged. Because the administrative machine had been only slightly refashioned by the inter-war governments and because the Nazis had not been allowed to get their hands on it, the local Bulgarian communists had a great deal of purging to do. They did not fail in their task. The new people's militia arrested or simply butchered thousands of employees of the former régime as alleged war criminals. In the country which had seen the fewest war crimes in eastern Europe there were more alleged war criminals per capita than anywhere else; the government admitted to 11,767 victims but the real figure was almost certainly over 50,000 and perhaps as many as twice that number.

At the beginning of 1946 the people's court in Sofia dealt a huge blow to the former régime. After a dubious trial the three war-time regents, 160 parliamentary deputies, and a number of other politicians who were prominent before 9 September 1944 were convicted of various crimes against the people. The prosecution demanded fifty death sentences and was given precisely twice that number, the executions being carried out immediately. The right wing of Bulgarian politics had been destroyed and it had become clear that the battles which lay ahead would be vicious and bloody.

The communists now began their systematic attack upon the centre-left and the left. The dominant force here was the agrarians. Their leader, Gheorghi Dimitrov, known as 'Gemeto' ('The GM') to distinguish him from his namesake who headed the BCP, chose not to join the cabinet, though he remained secretary of his party. Gemeto had spent the war in Cairo and Istanbul and this the communists used to insinuate that he was a British agent who would, if allowed, involve Bulgaria in a civil war similar to that in Greece. The communists also accused him of defaming the Bulgarian army then engaged in massive battles in Hungary. In January 1945, at Soviet insistence, Gemeto was dismissed as leader of the party. He fled to the United States and was replaced as head of BANU by Nikola Petkov, a minister without portfolio.

In the first half of 1945 the communist attack was evident less in the sort of personal assault which had removed Gemeto than in persistent efforts at entrism in both the BANU and the Bulgarian Social Democratic Party (BSDP). In May an agrarian congress was so packed with communist sympathisers or stooges that the pro-communist wing under Aleksandûr Obbov was able to seize control of the party press and a number of party organisations. The methods used in this process were often of the basest; Petkov's secretary, for example, was arrested and died in custody. Many other agrarians were removed, to be replaced by pro-communists. Similar tactics were deployed against the social democrats whose real leader, Kosta Lulchev, found himself outnumbered by thugs of the Dimitûr Neikov faction which favoured closer cooperation or even fusion with the BCP; Neikov's followers took control of the party press and of a number of party buildings and offices. In July both Petkov and Lulchev complained to the Potsdam conference and then resigned from the FF coalition.

The attack on the agrarians and the social democrats had been timed to weaken them just before the first post-war elections which were due to take place in August. The plan misfired temporarily in that the Soviets, in the face of opposition pressure relayed through the western allies on the ACC, agreed to postpone the vote until 18 November. This the Petkovists and Lulchevists treated as a great victory of which they made much in their newspapers, though not on the radio to which they were denied proper access. The incident also gave the anti-communists a false impression of the power and the commitment of the western allies; the latter, for their part, did little to correct this tragically mistaken impression.

Petkov and Lulchev advised their supporters to boycott the November elections. The communists had in the meantime been strengthened by the return to Bulgaria of two of their leaders who had been in Moscow since before the war: Gheorghi Dimitrov and Vasil Kolarov. These two established figures helped the FF to win 86 per cent of the vote in November; there were no oppositionists in the new sûbranie.

For the following six months Bulgarian politics seemed to be in a stalemate. Neither the opposition nor the western powers would accept the elections as fair and representative of national opinion. At the foreign ministers' conference in Moscow in December 1945 the Bulgarian ruling coalition was told to widen its base, but the concession was meaningless because the new members of the government had to be 'suitable' and 'loyal'; when they did enter the cabinet they were virtually ignored. Petkov and Lulchev declined to join the government on such terms, refusing to bow even to the bullying Soviet deputy commissar for foreign affairs, Andrei Vyshinsky, who visited Sofia in January 1946. When the two oppositionists let it be known in March that they would join the government if their nominees were made under-secretaries in the ministry of the interior, with responsibility for the militia and local government, the Soviets vetoed the plan.

The crisis was coming to a head but before the communists could be sure of victory in their confrontation with Petkov and Lulchev they had other obstacles to remove. The army, which had been purged again in the autumn of 1945 as soldiers returned from the war against Germany, was once more attacked, this time with the clear intention of discrediting the minister for war, Velchev, and thus neutralising Zveno. The powers of the war minister were transferred to the cabinet and Velchev himself sent to Switzerland where he went into exile. Others were less lucky; his aide-de-camp was tortured to death. Zveno, however, was eliminated from the political equation and the army removed from politics for the foreseeable future.

On 8 September 1946 a plebiscite was held which resulted in the declaration of a republic and the exile of eleven-year old King Simeon II and his family. This had been timed to impress upon the Paris peace conference, which was about to open, the alleged distinction between the peace-loving FF and the war-mongering monarchy. It was also intended to simplify the elections for the grand national assembly (GNA) to be held on 27 October; the GNA was to draw up a new constitution and a preceding declaration of popular opinion against the monarchy would prevent any centre-right coalition grouped around that institution. In the elections the FF took 78 per cent of the vote; in the GNA it had 364 seats to the opposition's 101. Dimitrov became minister president.

In the early months of 1947 Petkov subjected the Dimitrov government to fierce criticism, making much play, for example, of the fact that its expenditure on the police was much in excess of that of the so-called 'monarcho-fascists'.

But Petkov was on much less secure ground than he believed. Throughout 1947 there was a series of arrests and most of those involved, though they were usually minor figures, confessed to crimes which implicated Petkov in alleged anti-state activities. Petkov had been encouraged by the western powers but their influence in Bulgaria would be much reduced when the peace treaty was signed and the ACC withdrawn. On 4 June 1947 the United States senate ratified the peace treaty; on 5 June Petkov was arrested in the GNA. He was subjected to one of eastern Europe's most disgraceful show trials in August. On 20 September the peace treaty came into force; on 23 September he was executed.

The elimination of Petkov had been the *conditio sine qua non* for the communist takeover. In most of eastern Europe the agrarians, being the natural representatives of the majority of the peasant populations, were the chief obstacles to communist domination. In most other states the communists had been able to woo the peasantry with land reform. In Bulgaria, where most peasants already had their own land, this tactic could not be deployed; Dimitrov once admitted wistfully to Rákosi that he envied him the large estates which he could break up to win peasant favour. If the peasants could not be won over then their leaders had to be destroyed.

After the destruction of Petkov the BCP moved rapidly to a full takeover. In December the 'Dimitrov' constitution, redrafted under Soviet guidance, was passed by the GNA which also endorsed a two-year plan for the economy. The communist takeover had been completed with the enactment of the Dimitrov constitution, but some of the operations usually characteristic of the pre-takeover stages were not carried out until later. In January 1948, despite warnings from Dimitrov, Lulchev voted against the budget; in November, though an old man, he was sentenced to fifteen years in prison. His party had by then ceased to exist, the collaborationists having voted in August to take the BSDP into the BCP; this was absorption rather than fusion.

Romania

The royal coup of 23 August 1944 in Bucharest had preserved the existing state apparatus and had possibly prevented a Soviet occupation together with the immediate imposition of a communist régime. Nevertheless, Romania was irredeemably within the Soviet sphere of influence, as was recognised in the percentage agreements in October when Moscow was given a higher 'share' in Romania than in any of the other Balkan states.

Initially the communists were content to remain within a broad coalition, not least because in August 1944 the party had fewer than 1,000 members. To help to make good this lack of numbers the communists were instrumental in setting up four front organisations, in all of which they exercised considerable influence. The four were: the Society for Friendship with the Soviet Union; the Union of Patriots, for communist sympathisers from the left of the intelligentsia; Patriotic Defence, a welfare organisation which collected funds for the victims of famine and war but which had armed units; and the Ploughman's Front, a body which was originally set up in Transylvania in 1933 for radical peasants and which was now greatly expanded and virtually run by communists. In October 1944 a National Democratic Front (NDF) was created and included the Union of Patriots, the Ploughman's Front, the Social Democratic Party (RSDP), the Communist Party of Romania (RCP), and the trade unions.

The first government established after the coup was led by a soldier, general Constantin Sanatescu, whose cabinet included four representatives from the National Peasant Party (NPP), four liberals, three social democrats, and one communist. Until the end of the year this administration busied itself with the obviously necessary tasks of a post-fascist government: the arrest of guardists, the repeal of anti-semitic legislation, and the purge of fascists from the bureaucracy. The government also sent the Romanian army into battle alongside the Red Army, expelled a number of Germans from Transylvania, campaigned for the return of the lost territories, above all northern Transylvania, and began the task of economic reconstruction.

The Sanatescu government did not enjoy good relations with the Soviets. The latter deliberately remained silent as to the fate of northern Transylvania and also backed communist complaints against the minister of the interior, an NPP man. In December 1944 Soviet complaints were widened to include Sanatescu, who resigned, to be succeeded by another soldier, general Nicolae Radescu.

Radescu remained in office only until March. During his premiership communist aggression became more open, particularly after a visit to Moscow by two prominent RCP leaders, Ana Pauker and Gheorghe Gheorghiu-Dej. The communists' main complaint was that not enough was being done to persecute fascist sympathisers, a complaint which enabled the communists to direct their fire on the prime minister who was also minister of the interior. Organised workers restricted Radescu's right to use the press, thus forcing him to state his case in public speeches which were frequently disrupted, again by organised workers. During one such speech, at the former Iron Guard bastion of the Malaxa metallurgical plant, shots were fired. On 24 February a large demonstration in the centre of Bucharest to protest at the Malaxa violence led to further shootings and fatalities. The communists claimed that the army was responsible but the bullets recovered from the dead were not standard army issue. Radescu, however, dissipated any credit that this might have earned him by saying, in a radio broadcast, that the communists were 'foreigners without God or a nation'. On 27 February Vyshinsky arrived in Bucharest to insist that Radescu be removed and replaced by the leader of the Ploughman's Front, Petru Groza. Vyshinsky hinted to King Michael that refusal might mean the end of Romania as an independent state. Groza became prime minister on 6 March 1945.

Soviet intervention in Romania's internal affairs had been cynical and brutal. The western powers registered their displeasure and, following the foreign ministerial conference on the Balkans in Moscow in December 1945, Groza's cabinet was widened to include a liberal and a member of the NPP. As in Bulgaria, however this had little effect, since the new ministers were required to be 'suitable' and 'loyal' to the government. In reality, Soviet influence could not be gainsaid.

Soviet power was increased by means of its growing economic domination of Romania. The USSR had demanded three hundred million dollars in reparations, with the goods delivered being valued at 1938 prices which were two or three times below the 1945 level. In January 1945 the first joint stock company was established. Under Groza these multiplied until by 1948 they had given the Soviets virtual control over the Romanian oil and timber industries, Danubian shipping, and Romania's Black Sea ports.

Communist power advanced step by step with Soviet influence. The Groza cabinet was a coalition but many of the non-communists were renegades from their own parties or had pasts so compromised that they were easily controlled by the communists who could threaten exposure in the event of non-obedience. Groza himself was 'a poseur and publicity-seeker, a buffoon and a boor'[6] whose vague notions of worker-peasant cooperation and whose lust for office made him the ideal stooge for the Soviets and their Romanian accomplices. In any case the RCP now had its hands on most of the levers of power; communists headed the ministries of the national economy, justice, and the interior.

When Groza took office the Soviets at last agreed that northern Transylvania should return to Romania; only a government of which Moscow approved was to be allowed to take credit for the achievement of this cherished national objective. The communists attempted to increase their popular standing by trying and executing general Antonescu and also by introducing more land reform. A bill of March 1945 confiscated all land owned by Germans, collaborators, war criminals, and absentee landlords, together with estates in excess of fifty hectares; church properties and those of monasteries, the crown, and charitable institutions were to be kept undivided and turned into state farms. Peasants with less than five hectares were to form committees to distribute confiscated land; the small peasants were to be mobilised to enforce the benefits the communists claimed to have brought them. To cash in on these benefits the communists called for elections in November 1946; first, however, they enacted a new electoral law which made registration difficult for anyone opposed to the NDF, and impossible for anyone remotely connected with the fascist régime.

The government bloc won 348 seats, the Hungarian People's Union who were communists from Transylvania, 29, the NPP 33, and the Liberals 3. There was a great deal of manipulation at the polls most of which was probably unnecessary because the NDF, despite the Soviet presence, had a good deal of popular support. Much of this was to evaporate in the following year as the communists eliminated most of their political opponents and allies.

A purge of the civil service, and especially of the diplomatic corps, had been under way since Groza came to power, but with the advent of the cold war the communists began to attack organisations as well as individuals. In June 1947 a number of NPP leaders were arrested and tried, Mihalache and Maniu later being sentenced to solitary confinement for life; in August the NPP and the Liberal Party were dissolved. In the following month the RSDP fell. After the November 1946 elections the communists had packed local social democratic committees with their own trusties and in February 1948 they were able to overcome opposition to fusion; the RSDP merged with the RCP to form the Romanian Workers' Party (RWP) with an avowedly marxist-leninist programme.

By then the king had been neutralised. One who had acted so resolutely against Antonescu could not be tolerated and when he announced his intention to marry, the communists raised an outcry against what they said was the excessive expense this would incur. On 30 December 1947 King Michael abdicated, though he later declared, understandably, that this had been done under duress.

The takeover was all but complete. It was given legal dressing in the spring of 1948. The government bloc was enlarged to include the RWP; the Hungarian People's Union, which was the successor to the Patriotic Union; and the leftwing of the recently dissolved NPP which had joined the Ploughman's Front. The new organisation, which was of course run by the communists, called itself the People's Democratic Front. In elections in March it won a massive majority and immediately enacted a republican, Soviet-style constitution.

The GDR

The territories which were to become the German Democratic Republic (GDR) consisted of those areas west of the Oder-Neisse line under Red Army occupation; some of these had been originally taken by the western armies but had then been exchanged, in accordance with previous agreements, for fourteen of the twenty districts of Berlin.

Unlike their comrades elsewhere the communists in eastern Germany were acting under direct allied, i.e. Soviet, rule. They faced a number of difficulties. Their economy was burdened with reparations payments to the USSR; they were operating in an area which had never constituted a separate, defined political entity, and consequently there was no pre-existing state machinery which they could seize; as the cold war developed, they were operating in increasing competition with what many of their citizens saw as an alternative, accessible, and preferable political model within the same national community; and until the separation of the two Germanies they had to make political calculations which included organisations and factions in the west as well as the east, a fact of great importance in relations between the communists and the social democrats.

In July 1945 the conquering Red Army established the Soviet Military Administration in Germany (SMAD), which included eleven centralised departments of government. Five of these departments, including that of the interior, were headed by communists. Though these departments were originally intended to be all-German institutions, the western powers did not accept their jurisdiction and so they remained confined to the Soviet zone of occupation (SBZ). In the same month the SMAD also allowed both the re-establishing or foundation of four anti-fascist, republican, and democratic political parties: the Communist Party of Germany (KPD), the Social Democratic Party of Germany (SPD), the Christian Democratic Union (CDU) and the Liberal Democratic Party of Germany (LPD). The last two were entirely new parties. All four parties became members of the Anti-Fascist Democratic Front whose decisions could be binding only if taken unanimously: there was to be no anti-communist caballing. A united trade union organisation and a new youth movement were also established in July 1945.

Initially the KPD exercised considerable moderation. Its new programme avoided talk of a transition to socialism; it made no mention of Marx or Engels, the dictatorship of the proletariat or agrarian collectivisation; it wanted the redistribution of large estates, and in industry nationalisation only of the commanding heights of the economy; it called for rigorous measures against dedicated Nazis; but it did not ask for fusion with other left-wing parties.

Though the KDP was moderate it was also increasingly influential within the SBZ. The Soviets inevitably looked upon it as a favoured child when it came to the distribution of paper, office-space, ink, typewriters, vehicles, and so on. The KPD also had a good record in the resistance, which made it popular amongst those who had opposed or forsaken nazism, and which gave it a distinct advantage when the denazification process created huge gaps in the ranks of civil servants, teachers, and other professions. One area in which the KPD had a very prominent presence was the reconstituted police apparatus. The first German police authority set up in the SBZ was the locally based traffic and criminal police, which was established in June 1945, but even here political reliability was important in appointment or promotion. By the end of the year each province and district had its own political police, strictly supervised and controlled by the Soviets, who were also to have considerable influence over the centralised *Volkspolizei* (Vopos) set up in July 1946.

The communists took a prominent part in the expropriation of industrial and commercial enterprises. Many of these were seized in the first days after the end of the fighting, the initiative frequently being taken by *ad hoc* committees dominated by communists recently released from camps or prisons. In later months, and particularly after decrees on dispossession in 1946, the SMAD took possession of enterprises which had no owner or whose owners were shown to have connections with war crimes. In the summer of 1947 the German Economic Commission was established, placing almost all important sectors of the economy in the SBZ under central control. With communist power already well entrenched in the civil service the KPD, under the overall direction of the SMAD, was the dominant political factor in the east German economy even before the introduction of the new currency in the west, in June 1948, led to the Berlin blockade and the complete economic divorce of the SBZ from the other zones.

The communists had also done much to establish their influence in the countryside. The redistribution of large estates began in September 1945. The property of war criminals and prominent Nazis was automatically forfeit, as was land in excess of one hundred hectares. By the end of the redistribution process over three million hectares had been transferred. Landless agricultural labourers and dwarf-holders received land, as did some middle peasants and a number of factory and office workers whose places of work had been destroyed; most of the redistributed land, however, went to the incoming Germans driven out of states to the east, especially Poland. The land reform gave the communists great kudos amongst those who received property and amongst members of the other political organisations with whom the communists had cooperated in implementing the reform; over 10,000 local land reform committees, 'revolutionary organisations of workers and peasants', involving over 50,000 people only a quarter of whom could be considered communist, had proved that the communists were efficient and cooperative, and that, in effect, one could do business with them.

The land reform had been a social necessity. In the first place, the death or flight of large landowners had dislocated the agrarian structure and there was a desperate need to put people on the land to produce food. Moreover, most of the incoming refugees knew no other occupation than agriculture. Even for the non-refugees there was little alternative but to work on the land because the urban centres had been pulverised by bombing and what remained of their industries had been destroyed or dismantled by the occupying forces. That the communists helped to foster the proliferation of a small agrarian bourgeoisie was to cause them embarrassment after the end of the decade but in the meantime the land reform served them well and was easily accomplished.

It was less easy to find a working relationship with the other main left-wing party, the SPD. Immediately after the end of the war the SPD in the east had been in favour of immediate fusion with the KPD, arguing that the creation of a united working class party would be the first step towards, and an essential prerequisite of, reunification. The western powers were suspicious, as were the communists who feared that they would be swamped by the larger and, at that time, much more powerful SPD. In some areas local united committees had been set up by SPD and KPD factions but once the KPD leaders had returned from Moscow and established themselves these committees were dissolved; spontaneity and local initiative were not phenomena with which the Moscow-trained communist of the KPD or SMAD could feel comfortable. Once central party control had been established a softer line appeared. On 19 September 1945 the leader of the KPD, Wilhelm Pieck, spoke of the damage caused by the division of Germany and of its working class. The KPD and the SPD, however, were both inter-zonal parties and no decision on their relationship could be taken without the involvement of party organisations in the western part of Germany.

At a unified SPD conference in Wenningsen near Hannover in October 1945 Kurt Schumacher from the west ruled out fusion with the communists. He was still unconvinced that the KPD's intentions were honourable, besides which, he argued, fusion should be a consequence of, not a preliminary to, unification; until that came about Schumacher would be SPD leader in the western zones and Otto Grotewohl in the SBZ. In November Grotewohl stated his conditions for fusion: it had to be gradual and not brought about by pressure, it had to be democratic, and it had to be effected throughout the four zones and not just in any one of them. Within five months fusion was to take place in a fashion which contravened all of Grotewohl's conditions.

As relations between the Soviets and the western powers worsened over the delivery of reparations and other questions, communist political and social muscle was increasingly exercised in the SBZ. The KPD was not in the least restrained by the fact that the main effect of its actions was to strengthen the anti-fusionist lobby in the SPD. By the end of the year the situation had become yet more complicated by the approach of local elections in the western zones; the communists feared that these polls, like recent votes in Austria and Hungary, would humiliate them by showing the popularity of the social democrats. Fusion would avoid such embarrassments. In December Grotewohl was forced into discussions with the SPD on common action in the forthcoming elections. He would not budge; he rejected the idea of a common list for SPD and KPD candidates, and remained unshaken in his determination that unification must precede fusion; he knew that in a reunited country and a fused party the SPD would vastly outweigh the KPD.

Grotewohl, however, was not master in his own house. In February 1946 the head of the SMAD, marshall Gheorghi Zhukov, began to apply heavy, even brutal pressure. He informed Grotewohl that there was no prospect of a united Germany or a united SPD and that therefore there was no point in delaying fusion. Under central guidance from KPD headquarters, local KPD/SPD committees were established to back the call for union, the anti-fusionist sections of the SPD press were censored, the trade unions were mobilised to add strength to the fusionist cause, and Zhukov even threatened to intern anti-fusionists. This was too much for Grotewohl and his associates. They conceded. On 21–2 April 1946 a joint KPD/SPD congress agreed upon fusion and the setting up of the Socialist Unity Party of Germany (SED).

The SED's 80-member central committee included twenty representatives from the western zones. Its programme called for reunification in a democratic, anti-fascist republic, the participation of the trade unions in the running of industry, the end of capitalist monopolies, and the transition to socialist production, preferably by democratic means but 'with resort to revolutionary methods if the capitalist class abandons the democratic ground'.

The first test of the new party's popularity came in elections held in the SBZ in August 1946. These elections allowed the parties to enter under separate lists and in no province did the SED secure an absolute majority; in greater Berlin, where the presence of the western allies meant that the SPD could compete against the SED, the former gained 48.7 per cent of the vote compared to the SED's 19.8 per cent.

The communists did not experiment with separate lists again and in 1948 the SED itself was reformed into a marxist-leninist party. It was one of the many reflections of the division of Germany which itself was both a cause and a consequence of the intensifying cold war. At the same time the communists extended their control through a series of social organisations. The Free German Trade Union Association, founded in February 1946, had already contributed significantly to growing communist power in society, as did the Free German Youth which was established in the following month. In January 1947 the American and British zones had joined in Bizonia and this, together with the general deterioration of relations between the Soviet Union and the western powers, led to increasingly tight communist control over the SBZ. In the first half of 1947 the establishment of organisations such as the Union of those Persecuted by the Nazis, the Women's Democratic Association of Germany, the German Cultural League, and the German-Soviet Friendship Association, all of which were under communist control, meant that by the summer of 1947 most citizens of the SBZ belonged to an organisation supervised by the communists.

In December 1947 the SED convened a people's congress in Berlin; invitations were sent to west German parties but only the KPD responded. This was the first of three such congresses which were to be 'the vehicle used to transport the SBZ into the German Democratic Republic'.[7] The second congress met in March 1948 and elected a German People's Council. The third congress met in May 1949, after the SED had persuaded the other parties to agree to a single list election. The third congress proclaimed itself to be a people's chamber and approved a new constitution. Shortly afterwards a second chamber was formed from provincial representatives. In October the two chambers formally adopted the new constitution. In effect, the German Democratic Republic had been born; its first president was Pieck and its first prime minister Grotewohl. It was not yet a sovietised state but it was one in which the communists were unquestionably the leading force.

Czechoslovakia

Czechoslovakia differed in various ways from the other states which were to fall under Soviet domination. It had a democratic record which no other could equal; it was a state with more than one national component and one in which the nationalities concerned had differential resistance records in the recent war, though, unlike Yugoslavia, the resistance leaders did not emerge as post-war state leaders; after December 1945 there were no Soviet troops on its territory; and it was a state whose wartime leader in exile, Beneš, had concluded a treaty of friendship with the USSR which placed a high degree of trust in that state.

Beneš returned to his native country in April 1945 to define the nature of the newly restored Czechoslovak state. This was done at Košice in eastern Slovakia, since the Nazis had not yet been expelled from the Protectorate. The Košice programme affirmed that the state would henceforth be one of Czechs and Slovaks; the Germans and Hungarians were to be expelled, though in the event most of the latter were spared this trauma. The Slovaks were to be

235

recognised as a separate nation with their own organs of government, namely the Slovak national council for the legislature and the board of commissioners for the executive. There was no mention of federation. Czechoslovakia's foreign policy was to have a Slav orientation and its army was to be modelled upon that of the USSR; economic policies were to encourage enterprise whilst leaving the commanding heights firmly under state control. Local government was to be restructured, the previous system having been compromised by 'collaborationism'; the new one was to resemble that of the Soviet Union.

The Košice programme also announced the formation of a National, or People's Front consisting of most of the anti-fascist parties. A National Front government was also formed, with Klement Gottwald of the CPCS as prime minister; there were two other Czech communists and a further three from the Slovak Communist Party. The other members of the government came from the Social Democratic Party, the Czech National Socialist Party, the People's Party, a Catholic group in the Czech lands, and from the Slovak Democratic Party. The cabinet also contained a number of non-party experts, at least two of whom were admitted or covert communists. The communists in fact controlled the ministries of the interior, defence, agriculture, education, and information; thirteen of the twenty-six ministers were pro-communist, twelve non-communist, and one neutral; the latter was the foreign minister, Jan Masaryk, son of the founder of the first republic and one of the few commoners allowed to tell dirty jokes to King George VI.

The communists were in a strong position for a seizure of power, but this they avoided partly because it would have rallied anti-communist sentiment around the immensely popular Beneš, partly because of the dictates of the Polish trade-off, and not least because they confidently expected that they would soon be able to win power through the ballot box.

Communist confidence on this point had been strong since the first post-war elections in May 1946. Although over 250,000 potential voters had been disenfranchised by regulations against 'collaborators', the communists secured an impressive 38 per cent of the total votes cast, with shares of 40 per cent in the Czech lands and 30 per cent in Slovakia. The Czech National Socialists took 18 per cent of the vote, the People's Party 16 per cent, the Social Democrats 13 per cent, and the Slovak Democrats 14 per cent, though the latter took 62 per cent of all votes in Slovakia. Gottwald continued as prime minister.

From the elections of May 1946 until the summer of 1947 Czechoslovakia enjoyed a period of relative tranquillity. Gottwald stressed that the communists would find a Czechoslovak road to socialism; there was no pressure on the churches; the opposition exercised its right to criticise the government; and non-socialist social organisations such as the sokols, the boy scouts, and the legionnaires, suffered no restrictions on their activities.

The picture changed in July 1947. The Czechoslovak government, its communist members included, had wanted to accept Marshall Aid. The Kremlin refused, insisting that for Prague to accept American help would be a breach of the December 1943 treaty of friendship; Masaryk, returning from the negotiations in Moscow, likened the decision to a second Munich. The brutal Soviet veto did not help the public image of the Czechoslovak communists, but this was not their only difficulty. They had lost one of their ministerial posts; their proposed 'millionaires tax' had been rejected, the first time since 1945 that a communist-sponsored bill had failed to become law; there were difficulties because of the poor harvest; and in September they came under fierce criticism from other parties at the Szklarska Poręba meeting. In November they did very poorly in open elections within the universities and their plans to fuse with the social democrats received a setback when the fusionist SDP leader, Zdeněk Fierlinger, was replaced by the anti-fusionist Bohumil Laušman. In the same month three ministers received parcel bombs through the post and investigations pointed to communist involvement. A public opinion poll in January 1948 indicated that support for the communists had fallen to only 25 per cent; with general elections due in the summer it seemed that Gottwald's hopes for taking power through the ballot box were decreasing just at the time when Soviet pressure for action was increasing.

Stung by the setbacks at home and by the withering criticism from other European communist parties, the CPCS hit back. It established a special department to organise the infiltration of other parties, the Czech National Socialists being earmarked as the primary target; at the same time, covert communists who were already established in other organisations were made more active. It was in Slovakia, however, that the communists launched their main attack. Ever since the elections of 1946 they had reviled the Slovak Democratic Party; in the spring of 1947 they sought to smear it by establishing links between it and the extremists of the Hlinka Guards. The mechanism for doing so was the trial of Tiso who was to be executed on 18 April. In September the security forces, which were totally under communist control, reported the discovery of an anti-state conspiracy by supporters of the war-time independent Slovakia. The trade unions and other communist-dominated organisations were mobilised against the Slovak Democrats but by November most non-communists had realised that the alleged conspiracy was a canard which was designed to split the Slovak Democrats, to weaken their hold on the board of commissioners and, at the same time, to enfeeble political Catholicism and Slovak nationalism. In fact the communist plot collapsed in on itself. Instead of splitting, with its left wing moving towards the communists, the Slovak Democratic Party closed ranks and became more unified; in Prague the National Socialists, together with the People's Party and the Democratic Party, took fright at the communists' use of the police apparatus.

It was this question which brought about the final crisis in Prague and the communist takeover of February 1948. Ministers from the non-communist parties demanded on 12 February that the communist packing of the provincial police be ended, but the minister of the interior, Václav Nosek, took no heed and his recalcitrance was supported by Gottwald. The communists, fearing that they were facing the danger of a French- or Italian-style expulsion, mobilised support in the trade unions and other groups and set up 'action committees' to bypass the elected local government councils. Nosek ordered civil servants to work with the action committees, which were communist-dominated and which, in total contravention of the law, were also given arms. On 20 February the people's militia was formed, an armed force of some 15,000 which, said the communists, was 'a spontaneous force' recruited from the people. On the same day the twelve non-communist ministers resigned, hoping that Beneš would be forced to form a new administration excluding the communists. He did not. Instead Beneš tarried, whilst popular tensions rose almost to boiling point, especially on 22 February when thousands of armed trade unionists paraded through Prague, attacking offices of the opposition parties and of non-communist organisations such as the sokols. The head of the army, the closet communist general Ludvík Svoboda, without consultating the president, committed his forces to support of 'the people'. The communists were also strengthened by reassurances from the Soviet Union that Moscow would not allow any western interference in Czechoslovakia. This message was delivered by deputy foreign minister Valerian Zorin, who was in Prague ostensibly to arrange the wheat deliveries which had been the Kremlin's sugar to sweeten the pill of turning down Marshall Aid. Units of the Red Army were also concentrated on Czechoslovakia's borders. On 25 February Beneš, fearing civil war and/or Soviet intervention, accepted Gottwald's proposals for a new administration. The non-communist ministers had been hoist by their own petard.

The Czechoslovak experience has been called 'the elegant takeover'[8] but it was hardly a takeover at all. At the end of 1947 the Czechoslovak communists were less coherent in their policies than in 1945; they did not seize power in February 1948, it was handed to them. Beneš made no attempt to mobilise the huge opposition to the communists amongst students, in the sokols, amongst the legionnaires, in the churches, and above all in Slovakia. It was not as if Beneš did not know the nature of the communist threat; he had seen Ruthenia snatched from Czechoslovakia and had hurried back to save Slovakia from a similar fate; he had told his ambassador in Belgrade to report personally because the former's office was so full of agents that everything would be revealed to the Soviets in minutes; he had backed the efforts of the minister of justice to prevent Nosek from packing the police force; he had refused to have the fusionist Fierlinger as foreign minister; and at all times he had kept his contacts with the western powers. On the other hand, he was convinced that the USSR should play a major role in central Europe, and fear of a resurgent Germany and resentment at the supine west of the 1930s were still strong enough for many of his compatriots to agree with him. He still believed that Soviet socialism would moderate and become more European whilst European capitalism would evolve into something more socialist; convergence was the way of the future and Czechoslovakia could and should provide a living example of it. Furthermore, he could not take any illegal action against the communists; if they were expected to behave constitutionally, the rights of the constitution could not be denied to them.

In February 1948 Beneš still commanded enormous respect and authority. The memory and habits of the pětka and the Hrad were still strong enough for many to put their faith in their president. But Beneš was a stricken man, suffering from spinal tuberculosis, arteriosclerosis, and high blood pressure; and he was facing a force which had no time for or patience with the traditions of democratic, inter-war Czechoslovakia.

That tradition ended in February 1948. Shortly after the takeover Jan Masaryk was found dead beneath the window of his office, a symbol of the moral collapse of the old order. All independent opposition to the communists now ceased, as the National Front placed pro-communist stooges in the leading posts of the non-communist parties; in the summer the SDP was subsumed into the CPCS in what was, as in Bulgaria, not so much fusion as absorption. In May 1948 new elections gave the communists an entirely dependent assembly which rapidly drafted and passed a Soviet-style constitution. On 6 June Beneš resigned; three months later he died. Before that Gottwald had become president and Antonín Zápotocký prime minister. By the end of the year Czechoslovakia was firmly embedded in the Soviet camp and the process of sovietisation was under way.

14

THE COMMUNIST SYSTEM

The communist states of eastern Europe remained individual states but their political systems had much in common.

At an international level they were integrated into the Soviet sphere of influence. This was achieved through a network of bilateral treaties, Moscow being suspicious of multi-lateral agreements which might have allowed too much initiative to be shown away from the centre. A multi-lateral military organisation did not come into being until 1955 when the Warsaw Treaty Organisation (WTO) was established. This was partly in response to the inclusion of the Federal Republic of Germany (FRG) in NATO and partly because the Soviets needed an excuse to retain Red Army units in Hungary after the signature of the Austrian state treaty; previously those units had been kept in Hungary officially to guard Soviet supply lines to Austria. The international economic organisation, the Council for Mutual Economic Assistance, Comecon, came into being in 1949 to coordinate eastern economic responses to the Marshall Plan. Until the mid-1950s, however, Comecon had little real effect, employing no more than nine officials in its Moscow headquarters, and after its activation as a living organism its function was not to create an east European equivalent of the common market but rather to coordinate the national economic plans of member states.

Soviet influence was paramount at the domestic as well as the foreign policy level. Albania, Bulgaria, Czechoslovakia, the GDR, Hungary, Poland, and Romania adopted the Soviet economic policies of the rapid promotion of heavy industry and the collectivisation of agriculture. This, as in the Soviet Union, was to be achieved through a series of economic plans, centrally determined and centrally administered. For this reason the new socialist countries reshaped their state machines to accommodate the large number of economic ministries which had evolved under the Soviet system. At the same time the Soviet pattern was also copied in the non-economic sector. Armies appeared in Soviet-style uniforms, studying military manuals copied from the Red Army; culture was subordinated to political needs and creativity therefore made way for socialist realism; the legal system was redesigned on Soviet lines; education was reshaped in emulation of the motherland of socialism; even fashion had to ape the proletarian east rather than the chic salons of Paris, London, or New York.

The theoretical framework

The communist takeovers, or, to use their terminology, the socialist revolutions, had brought the working class to power. However, that class was seldom in the majority and so, according to marxist laws, it had to establish the means for consolidating and perpetuating its authority: the socialist state. During the first stage of post-revolutionary development, namely the dictatorship of the proletariat, the class struggle would intensify as the last vestiges of bourgeois rule were eliminated. In this process the working class would be guided and led by its vanguard: the communist party. This was, of course, the pattern set in the Soviet Union, but eastern Europe differed somewhat from the Soviet Union where it had been a civil war which had finally placed the working class, or rather its vanguard, in power. This slight embarrassment was rapidly overcome by its being decided that the Red Army's presence in eastern Europe secured a relatively peaceful transition from capitalist to socialist rule and therefore obviated the need for a civil war. What emerged in eastern Europe, therefore, was what László Rajk referred to as 'a dictatorship of the proletariat without the Soviet form'. At this stage the state was usually called a 'people's democracy'.

As the dictatorship of the proletariat progressed, the non-proletarian social groups would be removed and a unified society would appear. From the dictatorship of the proletariat would emerge the socialist state of the whole nation under the leadership of the working class, a change which would be signified by a change of name, the state usually becoming a 'socialist' or 'people's republic'. The next stage would be to develop an advanced, or mature, socialist society in which state and non-state forms of social organisation would combine in what would be the first step in the creation of that communist society to which all human society was inevitably moving. In theory this was entirely logical, since it was a basic marxist tenet that the state is the mechanism which one class uses to exercise domination over another; if society has become unified, i.e. classless, there can be no domination of one class over another and therefore there is no need for a state; it can, in the classic phrase, 'wither away'. This was the message which the compulsory and hugely unpopular instruction in marxism-leninism drummed into all pupils. There were indications that some leaders also took it seriously; Khrushchev's programme for the Communist Party of the Soviet Union in 1961 certainly spoke confidently of the first stages of communism being reached by the 1980s, whilst the Yugoslav party theorist, Edvard Kardelj, saw his country's self-management system as a means by which communism could be built. At other times leaders appeared much less convinced by the ideology which they preached and in which every policy decision was dressed: Khrushchev, despite his 1961 programme, told the Romanians in the same year that he could not understand why they wished to press ahead with the collectivisation of agriculture when it had been a patent failure everywhere else; Todor Zhivkov of Bulgaria, according to a close associate, frequently gave vent to such exasperated feelings as, 'Ah, what were we playing at when we destroyed private property? What have we put in its place? We can't find a substitute for it.'[1]

There were few theoretical provisions for the withering away of the party; rather the contrary in Romania where it was said the state would 'blend' with the party, which might be construed as an admission that the problem of the state's withering away would simply be swept under the all-covering carpet of party power. The Bulgarian party made it clear that it did not see historical evolution as leading to the disappearance of the party:

> The gradual transition of our state into a state of the entire nation and the extension of socialist democracy are unthinkable without the further consolidation of the hegemonic role of the working class, and without enhancing the leading role of the communist party in the entire system of public life.[2]

Rather, as the state changed from the state of the proletariat to the state of the whole nation, so the party would evolve from the party of the working class into a party of and for the whole nation. In this process, it was presumed, ethnic differences would become less and less important as the state restructured on the basis of one, homogeneous social group; ethnic 'nationalities' would merge into the unified, socialist 'nation'.

The party: structure and membership

At the centre of the political system in eastern Europe from the communist takeovers to the revolutions of 1989–90 was the communist party; its leading role was an absolute political rule, in normal times a no-go area of political discussion.

Marx and Engels had said little on the precise nature of the party, other than that it would be the vanguard of the working class. It was Lenin who had translated this algebra into arithmetic, shaping a party which was able to seize power, not least because he had persuaded it to accept an extraordinary degree of discipline. Stalin developed this further and fashioned a party which, thanks largely to its burgeoning security organisations, would blindly apply the decisions of its leaders.

This was the party mentality that the stalinist purges of the 1930s had preserved but the east European parties differed organisationally from the CPSU in that most were technically coalitions. Only in Bulgaria and Czechoslovakia, and after 1965 in Romania, were there ruling parties which called themselves communist. The others were the Socialist Unity Party (SED) in the GDR, the Albanian Party of Labour (APL), the Romanian Workers' Party (RWP), the Hungarian Workers' Party (HWP) – after 1956 the Hungarian Socialist Workers' Party (HSWP) – and the Polish United Workers' Party (PUWP); in Yugoslavia the communist party, in order to mark its differentiation from its former associates, was to rename itself the League of Communists of Yugoslavia (LCY) in 1952. In some states other parties were allowed to exist but for the most part their only real function was to legitimise the existence of a national front or some similar umbrella organisation; all such parties acknowledged the communist party as the leading force in society and the state.

Whatever the name of the ruling party they all, like the CPSU, were based on the principle of 'democratic centralism'; centralism, be it noted, was the substantive. This meant in effect, that decisions taken at the centre could not be questioned by subordinate party organisations; theoretically there could be discussion before an issue was decided but once a decision was taken acceptance of it had to be absolute. Nor would the party tolerate the formation of distinct groups within its ranks, at whatever level, be they groups formed around a person or around a policy or a principle. Such 'factionalism' had been disallowed by the bolsheviks since 1921 and all communist parties were thereafter conjoined to be on their guard against it.

The organisation of the party was based on the 'territorial-production' principle. This meant that the lowest level unit, the primary party organisation, could be based either in an area or in a place of work. Above the basic level, organisation was territorial into districts, towns, regions, and states. Each level had its own committees, bureaux, and secretariat, the lowest level probably having no more than an unpaid, part-time secretary. Each level of the party elected from its own members its representatives at the next highest level up to the national party congress in which resided supreme power within the party.

Congresses met every five years, frequently not long after the Soviet party had held its congress and set the pattern for future developments. Emergency congresses could be called by decision of the central committee or in some cases by petition of a set percentage of party members. The congress heard a report from the central committee's general secretary, the party boss, and passed resolutions for implementation during the coming five years. It could also endorse new party programmes which mapped out policy over a longer period. The congress elected the central committee to exercise power on its behalf in the interlude between congresses. Attendance at party congresses was frequently given as a reward for long service at a lower level, though this might have been considered less a reward than a punishment given the length and content of some of the speeches. The vivacity of discussion tended to vary inversely with the degree of political stability inside the party or the country, with intense and passionate debate only really occurring in times of crisis.

In addition to national congresses parties sometimes held national conferences. These were called to discuss specific issues, and were attended not only by party members but also by non-party experts who were qualified to comment upon the matter under discussion. Party meetings below national level were also known as conferences.

The central committee usually met in full, or plenary, session two or three times per year. It discussed major policy issues and, most importantly, elected the highest body of the party, the politburo or praesidium. The central committee also elected the party secretariat. This numbered about 15–20 senior party officials, each of whom was in charge of a department of the party secretariat. These departments were either party 'shadows' of the governmental departments – agriculture, foreign affairs, education, etc. – or party-specific institutions such as that in charge of cadres, or personnel, or the party control commission which investigated any alleged infringements of party discipline. The secretariat was in effect a party civil service or bureaucracy providing it with information and also supervising the application of party policy in government. Because of the enormous patronage at its disposal the central committee became the crucial party organ in the distribution of power; its senior official, the first or general secretary, became the most powerful figure in the party.

Once elected, the party leader exercised his day-to-day authority through the politburo or praesidium. This varied in size but generally had 10–15 full members and a smaller number of candidate, or non-voting members drawn from the secretariat as well as the ordinary sections of the upper echelons of the party. In Romania, after the mid-1960s there was no politburo as such but a political executive committee from which party leader Nicolae Ceauşescu nominated a small permanent bureau consisting of himself, his wife, and four or five other members. The degree of debate which took place in the politburo depended greatly on the power and personality of its dominant figure; Ceauşescu faced little if any opposition, whilst in Bulgaria Zhivkov could take massively important decisions, such as that to force Bulgarian names on Bulgaria's ethnic Turks, without full discussion in the politburo. In general it could be said that the power of a first secretary, as long as he was in good health, increased with his period in office; new leaders frequently assumed their posts with assurances that they would follow the correct practice of 'collective leadership', but that idea seldom survived for more than a few years. Although the politburo was for the most part the decisive party body, there were cases where non-party members could attend. The leader of the Bulgarian Agrarian National Union was present when important agricultural matters were to be discussed, whilst in all countries the Soviet ambassador could and did attend and advise. He usually did so by invitation, but not always: in October 1956 Khrushchev and a number of other members of the Soviet leadership arrived unannounced in Warsaw with the intention of preventing the election of Gomułka as first secretary of the Polish party.

The party over which the politburo held sway was a select group; in accordance with leninist tradition it was a cadre rather than a mass party, with membership as a proportion of the population varying from as low as 3 per cent in Albania to a maximum of 13 or 14 per cent in Czechoslovakia; the average was around 10 per cent. Entry was not easy, particularly in the early years, and a period of probation had to be served before full membership was conferred. Individuals had to accept total obedience to the party. 'A communist', said a believer from the PUWP,

> is someone who has absolute faith in the party, which means that his faith in it is uncritical at every stage, no matter what the party is saying. It is a person with the ability to adapt his mentality and his conscience in such a way that he can unreservedly accept the dogma that the party is never wrong, even though it is wrong all the time.[3]

An ex-believer from the Yugoslav party saw the obverse of the coin: 'If you belong to the communist party it cannot be long before you have to sacrifice your beliefs and castrate your conscience.'[4] There could be no allegiances other than to the party, which to the fanatic could apply even to personal relationships. József Révai wrote in the early 1950s that a communist

> can fall in love with a non-communist, but with a real communist the two feelings of love and devotion to the party cannot run parallel. One can only love a person who shares one's thoughts and ideals and who, if not today, then tomorrow, can become one's partner not only in love but also in the struggle for the new world.[5]

Obedience to this exacting master was expected and conduct was monitored by local party organisations. All members had a party card or book in which were recorded attendance at meetings, service to the party, and any deviation from proper party conduct. Periodically these cards would be inspected; this was usually a prelude to a culling, or purge, of those considered undesirable or insufficiently committed to the cause.

The vanguard of the proletariat which attracted such messianic faith was by no means always a predominantly working class organisation. The Polish party saw its proportion of working class members fall from around 60 per cent in 1952 to 40 per cent in 1975, despite efforts by the leadership to increase the proletarian content. By the second half of the 1970s the proportion of industrial workers in the other parties were: Albania 37.5 per cent (1976); Bulgaria 41.8 per cent (1978); Czechoslovakia 45.0 per cent (1978); GDR 56.9 per cent (1979); Hungary 59.0 per cent (1979); and Romania 50.0 per cent (1978).

For those who did secure membership and who set out to make a career working in or for the party, the rewards were considerable. The party rapidly developed an elaborate and intensely hierarchical system of privileges. Special shops, with lower prices and a much greater range of goods, were available for party officials, as was privileged access to special schools, holiday facilities, hospitals, cinemas, cars, homes, furniture, and even works of art. In most countries official cars were given white plates with black numbers, whilst privately owned vehicles had black plates with white numbers, so that the police and ordinary motorists could show due deference to those who were working so hard on their behalf. Envelopes containing wads of banknotes, sometimes of hard currency, were not infrequently passed out to 'deserving' officials or to politburo members themselves. In the late 1940s, when the population at large was enduring swingeing austerity, members of the Hungarian politburo had cheque books with which they could draw unlimited sums from the national bank; at the same time the chief of the Hungarian army, Mihály Farkas, refused to accept a villa until its swimming pool had been equipped with underwater illumination.

The party had a good deal of patronage to dispense in terms of real estate and valuable objects because these had been confiscated from the former rulers. Bulgarian party bosses, for example, had use of former royal palaces in Evksinograd and Chamkoriya, whilst the 60,000 hectare hunting estate around Arlamów, the Red Principate, in eastern Poland had been confiscated from local Ukrainian villagers: as a repentant Yugoslav communist noted later, 'Taking over property, moving from residence to residence, remodelling our offices, expropriating *objects d'art*, and commissioning specially designed furniture assumed the proportions of a comfortable disease.'[6] Thus was socialism to be built and the working class to awake to a new dawn.

The leading role of the party

The communist parties of eastern Europe were not political parties in the western sense. They were apparatuses for running states and controlling societies; they did not represent sectional interests, they imposed them. This was recognised in the east European constitutions which allotted to the relevant party its leading role.

The leading role meant the subjugation of the state and society to the party. The executive branch in the stalinist period generally united the top posts in state and party in the same person. After Stalin's death, practice varied but even where the head of state was a different figure from the party chief there was never any pretence that executive authority rested anywhere other than in the party's highest organs. Institutions of state such as the armed forces were all under party domination; few officers above the rank of captain were not party members and all had to spend a period of training with the Soviet forces.

The legislature was similarly constrained. Parliaments were still elected but they seldom met for more than a few days per year, and their function was to give legitimacy to policies already decided upon by the politburo or the central committee. In Czechoslovakia, in the late 1940s and early 1950s, parliament was of such little consequence that dozens of deputies were recalled or appointed without reference to, or the knowledge of, their electors; that the building housing the parliament was located between a theatre and a museum seemed entirely appropriate. In Bulgaria, after elections early in 1989, five of the successful candidates were found to be dead. The party simply decided who would serve in the assembly, a seat often being the reward for faithful service to the party. Much the same happened with local elections. A Hungarian reporter in the early 1950s attended a local election in which one candidate was declared elected after the count of the votes had revealed a clear majority for an opponent;

when the reporter queried the procedures, the returning officer simply replied, 'I am sorry, comrade, these were my instructions.'[7]

The party's power was equally strong in the judiciary. Trial by jury was replaced by the Soviet system of tribunals in which a professional judge was helped by two lay assessors, the latter, of course, being entirely dependable from the party point of view. The party also made sure that professional lawyers understood party policy and how it should be enacted in the courts; even as late as 1988 in Hungary the 120 justices of Budapest had to attend a meeting every six months to hear lectures from high-ranking party officials on the latest evolutions in party thinking.

The official economy was entirely controlled by the party. The economic plans were administered, as was the whole of the economy itself, through the vast planning and economic ministries in the capital, all of which were in the hands of party members or those upon whom the party could depend. The same was true of collective and state farms, machine tractor stations, enterprises, and factories.

Within the wider social context all mass organisations were under the control of the party. Many of these, such as the Soviet friendship societies, the komsomol and their juniors, the pioneers, or the national fronts, were creations of the party itself, and those which had predated party rule, such as the trade unions or the universities, were restructured to ensure they fell under party domination. Given that most people of intelligence or initiative belonged to at least one such group, professional or recreational, almost everyone was brought under the direct or indirect control of the party.

In the arts and newspapers the party-approved censors exercised strict control, at least in the early years, and after the abolition of preliminary censorship editors were faced with the often more difficult process of self-censorship. One Hungarian intellectual in the 1950s described writers as being divided into five categories: there were 'Those who were forbidden to write, like myself. Then there were those who dared to write, who dared not to write, who did not dare to write and, finally, those who did not dare not to write.'[8] At the height of the stalinist period even the weather forecasts were changed if they had the temerity to suggest that the sun might not shine on 1 May, and under Ceauşescu they were doctored so that the temperatures were not seen to rise above or to fall below the levels which dictated that work must stop for the comfort and safety of the workforce.

The mechanisms by which the party exercised and maintained its leading role were intricate but two were of overarching importance. The first was the police apparatus. This might be termed the 'active' representation of party power and was primarily concerned with defending the party's political monopoly; it served to deter opposition and to contain it should it appear. The political police were in fact the core of the system. Their names and initials are synonymous with raw power and the threat of violent retribution should the individual become active against the collective: the Sigurimi in Albania, the State Security (DS) in

Bulgaria, the stasi in the GDR, the StB in Czechoslovakia, the AVO/AVH in Hungary, the UB in Poland, the Securitate in Romania, and the UDBa in Yugoslavia. In general the profile of the secret police declined after 1953 and except in rare intervals of tension it became less a means to instil terror than to preserve the existing distribution of political power; the secret police in effect became reactive rather than proactive. The exceptions were the régimes of Hoxha and Ceauşescu. The latter was reported to have dreamed of establishing an electronic monitoring system so complex that every family in the land would be subject to periodic, and if necessary constant, surveillance; Ceauşescu told the scientists involved in the project:

> it is too bad that we cannot tell our working people how the communist party is looking out for [sic] them, comrades. Wouldn't the miners go out and dig more coal, if they could just be sure that the party knew exactly what their wives were doing every single instant? They would, comrades, but we cannot talk about our system today. The western press might accuse us of being a police state.[9]

The security organs were all formed in the early days of the régime and control of them was vital to the survival of a party chief. Police containment and repression also became the norm, the established mechanism for securing control, once more showing that force is usually the first resort of the ideologue. Inevitably so valuable an organism assumed enormous powers of its own, and even after it had ceased to be an offensive weapon the secret police apparatus was still in many countries the real repository of power.

The party sought domination as well as total political control. In its early years the socialist state in eastern Europe was very much a state which discriminated in favour of the working class. Citizens were classified by social origin, the standard categories being: worker; peasant; intelligentsia; petty employee; others; and class enemies, the dreaded 'X' category. The intelligentsia was an important group because its social function did not determine its political attitude and it could therefore have allegiances either to the bourgeois past or the socialist future. Yet a compliant intelligentsia was essential to the construction of socialism and therefore the new régimes set out to create one to serve their needs. For this reason the children of class enemies were restricted to no more than primary education whilst those of the fourth and fifth categories would find it difficult to enter university; children of working-class and peasant parents, on the other hand, were favoured and were encouraged to enter higher education. Even the criminal code could be graded on a class basis; that of 1961 in Czechoslovakia insisted that the class origin of the convicted person should determine how dangerous to society his or her crime had been.

The need for such discrimination slackened after the first, harsh years of socialist rule; thereafter the party relied more on passive control through the second and more subtle of its two main levers of power: the 'nomenklatura' system. Each party office, at whatever level, had amongst the papers in its safe two lists: the cadre list and the nomenklatura list. The latter contained all those posts within that party organisation's area of jurisdiction which were considered critical to the smooth application of party policy; at the state level they would embrace all posts giving domination over the social organisations, the government machine, the armed forces, and the party itself, whilst at the municipal level they would include directors of local enterprises, editors of local newspapers, headteachers, rectors of any university in the area, ranking legal officers, garrison commanders, bank managers, and so forth. In Czechoslovakia after 1968 the nomenklatura lists were thought to involve 100,000 posts, whilst in Poland the number has been estimated as two or even three times higher.

The names of those whom the party considered trustworthy enough to occupy a nomenklatura post were entered on the cadre list. The endless information fed in by the police or by trusted observers in relevant party organisations ensured that the cadre lists were replete and up-to-date. It was not essential to be a party member to secure most of the nomenklatura posts, but any sign of unconventional behaviour would mean exclusion even from consideration for such posts. In effect anyone with aspirations to an influential or rewarding job, or with ambitions for promotion, had to be conformist.

Such was the party's mentality that any organisation, no matter what its function, had to be observable by the local party authorities; the party had to know what was going on in order to ensure that a seemingly innocuous group was not being used as a cover for conspiracy. The party therefore insisted that party members or persons trusted by the party had control of innocent organis- ations such as committees running blocks of flats or sporting associations.

The nomenklatura offered the privileges of office to those who met the party's requirements but even more importantly it provided a relatively simple yet enormously effective means of ensuring almost total social control for the party at all levels. There were few able and intelligent people who were prepared to endure the unrewarding, lonely, and deprived lives which exclusion from the system entailed; whilst the secret police ensured vertical or political control, the nomenklatura system guaranteed horizontal or social mastery.

The consequences of the leading role of the party

The domination of all aspects of economic and social life by the party was secured at considerable cost. In the first place the party bosses had extensive, almost baronial powers over their fiefdoms, being able to take major decisions in judicial, economic, social, and cultural affairs. But if the system resembled feudalism in the power it entrusted to the local chieftains there was no similarity between the feudal and communist systems in the relationship between the centre and the periphery. Democratic centralism seldom allowed any socialist baron to challenge the central authorities, nor would it tolerate any effective cohesion between local party organisations. Any sign of links between party bodies on the same level was forbidden; 'horizontalism' contradicted the leninist doctrine of

249

democratic centralism and was as much a sin as factionalism. This inevitably meant that the quality of party administration and leadership depended greatly upon the leaders concerned, and it was not the least of the contradictions of marxism-leninism that though its ideology down-played or even denied the role of the individual in the historical process, that ideology's practical application made the individual enormously influential.

Total power of course meant absolute responsibility. Even though initial difficulties could be blamed on bourgeois saboteurs or spies, and although some later problems, such as the need to adapt to the latest developments in computer technology or fibre optics, were thrust upon the communist régimes from outside, most of the difficulties of the communist rulers were home made, and many of them were a direct result of the inflexibility of the system by which they maintained themselves in power.

The socialist economic system

That inflexibility was nowhere more harmful than in the economic sector. The fact that Stalin's boundless brutality during the industrialisation and collectivisation drives of the early 1930s had meant that the Soviet Union was able to achieve economic growth in a period of savage economic depression in the rest of the world had confirmed planning in many people's minds as the infallible means to secure economic health. Thus, the east European economies were forced into the stalinist strait-jacket. All economic activity was to be governed by the five-year plans, which were themselves divided into yearly, quarterly, and even monthly segments. The primary, and frequently the sole, object of economic activity was to achieve plan-production targets; it did not much matter if there were no obvious market for the goods concerned as long as the plan targets were fulfilled; and the effect on the environment was never considered at all. There was little coordination between separate production units so that, for example, cars would be produced without any attempt to provide service stations or even build suitable roads, and a brand new hospital could stand empty in Warsaw for at least four years during the 1980s because the planners had not arranged for the production of the equipment to put into it. Nevertheless, the political objective of the economic activities involved had been achieved: the propagandists could boast of increased vehicle production and the completion of another new hospital. The planning system was hopelessly bureaucratic. An army of planners deluged enterprises with forms and production targets; Bulgarian farms in the 1950s had at least six hundred different plan fulfilment figures to meet.

The chief defect of the economic system was its absolute subjection to political requirements. At the level of strategic planning this meant that throughout the communist period, and more especially at the beginning, there was an over-emphasis on heavy industry and a neglect of light industry which supplied consumer goods. The building of socialism, the Soviet comrades had proved, needed a dictatorship of the proletariat but there was hardly a proletariat in eastern Europe; to create one, heavy industry had to be built. Heavy industry meant power generation, infrastructural projects in communications, mineral extraction, and steel production. The fact that each country set out to copy the Soviet model produced needless duplication and at times grotesque follies. Every country, even Albania, built steel mills, even if they lacked the necessary resources of energy and mineral ores; the Hungarian project at Sztálinváros (Dunapentele) relied on Hungarian coal and Yugoslav iron-ore, a distinct problem when economic ties with Yugoslavia were frozen after 1948. The massive Bulgarian metallurgical plant at Kremikovtsi, constructed in the 1960s, was built despite expert advice that local ores were inadequate for steel production, the result being that ore had to be imported from the USSR and carried over two hundred miles from the port at Burgas. An aluminium smelting plant at Zvornik in Bosnia-Hercegovina was proudly displayed by the Yugoslav authorities as the largest in Europe, but it never made a cent of profit. And the waste was prodigious; a list drawn up by Solidarity of equipment rusting to uselessness at the Ursus tractor factory in Warsaw in 1980 ran to fifty-two pages.

If the strategic decisions were frequently flawed by the need to conform to grand ideological designs, the local application of policy was impaired by the party's determination to keep all power and responsibility within its own control. Factory managers and foremen could hold their posts only if they were cleared under the nomenklatura system; not infrequently they were not the best people for the job. Even if they were capable managers they were constrained by political considerations which ran counter to the dictates of good management; as a Yugoslav factory director remarked, 'Politics are so dominant over the economy that the simplest economic logic is denied.'[10] The socialist economic system was probably the only one which could have made a broken light bulb an item of value: in the late 1980s, in a number of east European countries, light bulbs were unavailable in the shops; they could be found only in offices, factories, schools, etc., but to take them from there one had to have a replacement; hence the broken light bulb was invested with market value.

For the individual worker, more especially in the early years of socialist control, the need to meet production targets meant severe discipline. Work was arranged on the pattern of 'norms', with sanctions for non-fulfilment. The norm-system was little more than a structural inducement to inefficiency because, though there were sanctions against those who failed to produce their allotted norm, over-production was merely an encouragement to management to increase the norm. The piece-work system introduced in the late 1940s and early 1950s was, in Marx's view, the worst known form of exploitation and was later largely abandoned. Greater effort was encouraged by highlighting the achievements of particularly successful workers or work brigades, the stakhanovite system, and by introducing 'shock workers' into plants to show the others how much could be done. There were also campaigns, usually named after the Soviet worker who was reputed to have invented them, which were aimed at decreasing costs and boosting production. They had little effect and workers were generally much more conscious of the 'Lenin shifts' or 'Lenin Saturdays' when extra time was worked for no pay; even worse, in the early 1950s, were the 'voluntary loans' to the government. To refuse to participate was ill-advised and perhaps the workers would have accepted the need for them if they had been called what they really were: wage-reducing increases in taxation.

Whilst the masses bore the brunt of the drive to increase production it was they who suffered most from the economic shortages which the system produced; party officials safely and happily used the privileged, well-stocked, and exclusive stores provided for them.

This inevitably undermined moral respect for the party, as did the fact that the party-dominated system spawned corruption. Jobs, promotions, contracts, and favours could usually be secured by showing political obedience or by performing services for those who had the necessary political power or connections to secure the favour desired. Those who had no political connections could offer only money or goods, especially if the latter were *defitsitni* – a Russian word, appropriately, meaning difficult to procure. The lack of consumer goods encouraged the black market, which was often supplied by goods stolen from the public sector; as a Czechoslovak saying of the 1950s had it, 'If you do not steal from the state you are robbing your own family.' This was hardly a sound moral basis on which to construct socialism.

Lobbies and opposition

The shortcomings of the system were obvious to many but there were few individuals in a position to challenge the power of the ruling party. There were occasional gestures. One was Jan Palach's self-immolation in January 1969 in Prague; this was repeated by Romas Kalanta in Kaunas on 14 May 1972, and three other such incidents occurred in Lithuania shortly afterwards. Public anger could burst out spontaneously at sporting events; Czechoslovak teams playing in other east European countries in and after 1968 were loudly cheered, whilst the Czechoslovak victory over the Soviet Union in an ice-hockey game in 1969 sparked off violent attacks on Soviet buildings in Czechoslovakia.

Individual or spontaneous protest was ineffective as long as the régimes retained both the power and the will to impose order. Until these dissipated in the late 1980s, effective protest and action could be expected only from institutions. Occasionally churches might dig in their heels on issues such as abortion or mount propaganda campaigns on disarmament, whilst academies of science might come to the aid of a notable dissident, but the régimes concerned were not much affected. They would have been threatened, of course, had the army become politically active. In times of crisis the army could be crucial. It was the Polish army which constrained its Polish-Russian commander, marshal Konstantin Rokossovsky, in 1956; it was the rapid defection of Pál Maléter and the Hungarian army in the same year which gave initial success to the revolution in Budapest, just as the defection of the Romanian army was the decisive event in the toppling of Ceauşescu in 1989. In these cases the army commanders were following rather than leading mass action. There were occasions on which army officers took the lead. In 1965 the Bulgarian army attempted to seize power, in 1968 general Jan Šejna plotted against reformers in the Czechoslovak leadership, and in 1983 there was an attempted military coup in Romania.

There is a fine line in authoritarian systems between opposition and lobbying. The economic establishment was never a source of outright opposition but it could exert pressure for a relaxation of the political dogmas that were ruining the economy. In Czechoslovakia in the mid-1960s Ota Šik's ideas for economic restructuring were an important impulse towards the political reform movement which came to fruition in 1968. After 1968, however, not even the designers and practitioners of Hungary's economic reforms dared to say openly that their New Economic Mechanism (NEM) should become an engine for political as well as economic reform.

Policies could be affected by regional interests. The development of the socialist system in Yugoslavia was determined by this factor more than by any other and even in Czechoslovakia, especially when the grip of the centre was relaxed, the Slovaks mounted a powerful lobby.

Different social institutions could at times make their presence felt. The party's need for a compliant intelligentsia could give that group some leverage in more indulgent times, whilst their defection could inflict considerable damage. The loss of figures such as Leszek Kołakowski and Ladislav Mňačko were severe blows to the Polish and Czechoslovak régimes respectively. After 1968 the Prague government relentlessly pursued the dissident playwright Václav Havel, whilst the Romanian secret police made sure that prominent dissident intellectuals such as Doina Cornea were silenced, as was Milovan Djilas in Yugoslavia. The Bulgarian *émigré* writer, Georgi Markov payed with his life for his disclosures of *la dolce vita* amongst the priviligentsia of his home country, and his co-exile Vladimir Kostov only narrowly escaped the same fate. That the régimes were prepared to face the international adverse publicity which these repressive measures brought about is an indication of how much the voice of the dissident intellectual was feared.

The largest of all social groups in eastern Europe, the peasantry, was tamed by collectivisation in all countries except Poland and Yugoslavia, but it was still capable of resistance. It spontaneously rejected collectivisation in Poland and Hungary in 1956 and in some areas in Bulgaria and Romania had resisted it by force in the preceding years. The working class in whose name the party ruled had even more political muscle. Industrial workers gave vent to their frustrations in 1953 in a tobacco workers' strike in Plovdiv, in demonstrations in Plzeň, and above all in the rising in east Berlin. They also precipitated the vital changes in the Polish leadership in 1956 and provided the backbone of the forces which fought the Red Army in Hungary in the same year. Their power was shown persistently in Poland in 1970, 1976, and 1980–1; and in most countries it was their participation in the demonstrations of 1989 and 1990 which was critical in bringing about the end of the system.

In many instances the family had provided a bastion against the power of the communists. The party attempted to weaken an institution which it frequently found difficult to penetrate. Holidays ceased to be family events for most families outside the higher party circles; instead holidays were arranged for parents, often separately, through trade unions or other work-oriented, party-dominated bodies, whilst children went to camps run by the pioneers or the komsomol. During collectivisation the natural working unit of the family was divided by sending members to different brigades, whilst in the cities workers frequently found that they had to travel long distances to work and had to attend party, trade union, or other meetings at their workplaces; in many cases workers also ate at their workplaces, not least because these were better provided with food than the shops. These facts, together with the need to spend sometimes hours per day in queues, eroded the time available for family life. Nevertheless the family survived, and in many cases resisted the ideological and social pressures of the system. It was inside the family that the former traditions, values, and standards were preserved, to reappear with astonishing rapidity after the revolutions of 1989–90. Some of those old values, not least the nationalist passions which bedevilled eastern Europe in the inter-war period, were to pose as many problems as they solved, but they did and still do bear testimony to the failure of the party to create a new mentality, a *Homo sovieticus*.

Finally, an institution which posed a considerable threat to the party bosses was the party itself. Its arrogance and its overt privileges deprived it of the right to respect from the nation as a whole. Its structure also created an internal division between the general membership and the inner core of full-time officials. If only 10 per cent of the population belonged to the party, only 10 per cent of the party belonged to its inner group, and within that inner group real power rested with the few figures who controlled the politburo, the secretariat, and the central committee. Just as the party ceased to be a device for representing working class interests, so the party leadership came to represent the interests not of the party as a whole but of the party apparatus; the party was, in the words of Adam Michnik, the Polish dissident, 'a trades union for the rulers'.[11] Incumbent leaders had to exercise constant vigilance, usually through the security chiefs, lest an ambitious figure within the party's upper echelons made a bid for power.

If instability were to occur at the top then those other disenchanted elements in the party or society at large might shake off their fears and become active opponents of the régime. The same applied at the international party level. Just as a national party would tolerate no threat to its leading role in the state and society, or a national leader no rival to his power, so the Soviet party could not countenance any questioning of its leading role in the international socialist movement. This was made dramatically apparent in 1948.

15

EAST EUROPEAN STALINISM, 1948–53

THE YUGOSLAV-SOVIET SPLIT

The origins of Yugoslav-Soviet disagreements

The Prague coup of February 1948 appeared to have given Stalin mastery over an eastern Europe which, against the background of the intensifying cold war, was being refashioned on the Soviet model. Yet, as the events of the summer were to show, Stalin already felt his monopoly of power threatened, but threatened from within as much as from without, from the heretic as much as from the infidel. On 28 June 1948 the Yugoslav Communist Party was expelled from Cominform.

Beneath the surface there had always been tension between the Yugoslav communists and Moscow. This could be said for almost any east European communist party but the CPY, thanks to its war record and to the fact that all its leaders had spent the war in Yugoslavia and not in Moscow, felt more self-confident and independent. Moreover, as a victor power Yugoslavia did not have to play host to an Allied Control Commission which might limit the local government's freedom of action. Yugoslav leaders were consequently amongst the few who voiced their frustration with 'Grandfather' Stalin.

Many of the sources of frustration first appeared during the war itself. The communist partisans had expected at least some military assistance from the Soviet Union, no matter how hard pressed the latter might have been. They were to a large degree disappointed; at one point an exasperated Tito had telegraphed to Stalin: 'If you cannot help us, then please do not hinder us.'

After the war Stalin made disparaging remarks about the partisans, the pride of the Yugoslav party, comparing them unfavourably with the Bulgarian army which, said the Soviet leader, had a 'proper' officer cadre and a general staff. More pointedly, in the latter months of the war, when disputes arose between the partisans and the Bulgarian military who were fighting alongside them, Stalin intervened in favour of the Bulgarians.

For his part Stalin was alarmed by what he considered Yugoslav partisan excesses. He had been concerned by the creation of the first proletarian brigade in 1941 and by the ferocious policies that were frequently imposed by the partisans on areas under their control in late 1941 and early 1942, policies which included the execution of alleged kulaks, the desecration of churches, and the enforced collectivisation of the land. These policies were soon disavowed as 'left errors' but Stalin continued to fret at overt signs of communist affiliation in the partisan movement, such as the wearing of the red star as a cap badge; added to these concerns was the diplomatic embarrassment caused by the second AVNOJ conference on the eve of the Tehran conference.

After the war there were differences over the fate of the exiled king, and Stalin criticised the blatant communist domination of the National Front of Yugoslavia. In other east European states, Stalin argued, the popular front provided a means through which the communists, whilst remaining a relatively small party, could discredit and eliminate their political opponents and sharpen social and political consciences to the degree necessary for the social transformation which was to follow. In Yugoslavia, Stalin argued, this was not possible. The Yugoslav partisans, by insisting upon carrying out a social revolution during the war, had had to recruit far larger numbers than would have been necessary for the smaller type of resistance movement which merely prepared the ground militarily for the allied liberation; and because, in an under-developed society such as Yugoslavia, the vast majority of those recruited had to be peasants, the CPY had allowed the true bearers of the socialist revolution, the urban proletariat, to be swamped by petty-bourgeois elements, an allegation supported by Tito's statement that 'the peasant is the most stable foundation of the Yugoslav state'. The argument was false. The CPY was firmly under the control of marxist intellectuals and the partisan military establishment, neither of which could be accused of 'peasantist' or 'petty-bourgeois' mentalities.

That the CPY's drive towards socialism had not been impeded by petty-bourgeois elements was seen in the economic policies it pursued after the war. Arguing that Yugoslavia was well provided with raw materials but that these had previously been exploited by foreign capital, the CPY set out to build a heavy industrial base. The five-year plan of April 1947 earmarked huge proportions of the national product for investment; as only 8 per cent of this investment was to go to agriculture it meant that there would have to be widespread belt-tightening by the population. Consumption was to be greatly restricted. This was exemplary stalinism.

Not all Yugoslav leaders were convinced that these policies were correct. Andrija Hebrang, a Croat and former minister of industry who was still president of the federal planning commission, and Sreten Žujović, the minister of finance, had their doubts. So too did the Soviets, who soon made it clear to the CPY that its assumption that the Soviet Union would help to find the capital for Yugoslav economic development was misplaced; the Soviets needed all the capital and technicians they could find for their own reconstruction and for the arms race; for the time being, therefore, they expected Yugoslavia to concentrate primarily on agricultural production. They also expected Yugoslavia to accept

Soviet economic domination, if not exploitation. When discussions were held on the setting up of a joint Yugoslav-Soviet bank Moscow wanted it to have a Soviet director and to be able to carry out normal commercial banking; had it been able to do so it would have wielded enormous power within the Yugoslav economy. Under the trade treaties concluded immediately after the war Yugoslavia had to sell to the Soviet Union at low prices goods such as non-ferrous ores and hemp which in an open market would have fetched high prices in hard currency. The Soviets also persuaded the Yugoslavs to create two joint stock companies, JUSTA to run all external air services, and JUSPAD to control shipping on the Danube. Both companies gave the USSR access to hard currency earnings which were generated in Yugoslavia, but, even worse, Yugoslavia's input into the two companies was assessed at 1938 prices, that of the Soviet Union at the much higher 1945–6 prices. In March 1947, after vigorous Yugoslav complaint, Stalin agreed to abolish the two companies; such institutions, he admitted, were designed for defeated enemy states.

The Soviets were also excessively dominant and patronising in the cultural sphere, an attitude epitomised when Andrei Zhdanov, then the Soviet party's cultural supremo, enquired of one senior CPY member, 'Do you have opera in Yugoslavia?' The Soviets insisted that there should be an increase in the numbers of Russian plays put on in Yugoslav theatres, of Russian films screened in Yugoslav cinemas, of Russian songs sung on Yugoslav radio, and of Russian books published by Yugoslav publishers. The CPY was more than happy to present its people with good quality Soviet material, but it saw no purpose in foisting on them some of the rubbish which arrived from the motherland of socialism, often at exorbitant prices; the Yugoslavs had to pay twenty thousand dollars for the dubious pleasure of screening *Exploits of a Soviet Intelligence Officer*, whereas the wicked capitalist west had asked only two thousand dollars for Olivier's *Hamlet*.

Whilst Moscow attempted to dictate the nature of Yugoslav economic development and to dominate Yugoslav culture, Stalin was assiduously placing his agents throughout the country's party and state structures. Many of these agents arrived as army officers attached to the Yugoslav forces or as technical assistants in engineering projects. They were deeply resented. In the upper echelons of the CPY there was puzzlement that Moscow should think it necessary to place agents in a party which felt itself to be utterly loyal. For ordinary Yugoslavs the Soviet advisers and officers limited promotion opportunities. Great resentment was felt at the Soviet insistence that Red Army officers on secondment be paid three or four times more than their Yugoslav equivalents. The latter also sneered at the visitors' insistence that they have orderlies, which were unknown in the partisan army.

Moscow, in its assumptions of economic and cultural dominance, and in its efforts to infiltrate its agents into the CPY, was assuming that it should treat Yugoslavia no differently from the other east European states and parties. This Tito and his associates were not prepared to tolerate. They insisted that though their path towards socialism might be different from that of Stalin and the CPSU it was nevertheless equally valid. As tensions between Moscow and Belgrade increased the Yugoslav leadership elaborated its own position. They began to criticise stalinism as a phenomenon

> in which the abolition of capitalist private property did not mean the taking over the means of production by the workers themselves, but their exploitation by a new privileged social group, whose bureaucratic domination was based on ideological mystification, the abolition of political liberties and the most enormous police apparatus in history.[1]

The assumption that the Yugoslav comrades could be treated similarly to others in eastern Europe became critical in the field of foreign affairs. Here Tito's confidence that he could make his own policy caused real fears in the Kremlin that Yugoslav exuberance could provoke the west into anti-communist action precisely when Stalin needed tranquillity and time to consolidate his authority, at home and in eastern Europe, and to move the USSR rapidly towards nuclear capability. There was no doubting Tito's audacity. His troops had occupied Trieste at the end of the war and showed no disposition to leave it; Stalin had to order the Yugoslavs out, on the grounds that he was not prepared to make it the cause of a third world war. Nor was there support for Tito in August 1946 when his forces shot down two US transport aircraft overflying Yugoslav territory. Tito had no choice but to apologise and pay compensation. In Greece the Yugoslavs continued to help the communist forces despite Moscow's disapproval, and the Kremlin was equally disapproving of Tito's talk of a Balkan federation.

For his part Tito showed no signs of being willing to buckle to Soviet authority. After being ordered out of Trieste he made a speech in Ljubljana in May 1945 in which he stated that Yugoslavia would not be dependent upon anyone in its foreign policy. 'We do not want to be small change; we do not want to be involved in any spheres of influence,' he said; the Soviet ambassador in Belgrade thought the speech 'an act of hostility towards the Soviet Union'. The extension of Tito's speech could be that if Yugoslavia did not become part of any sphere of influence, it could become an independent factor in world affairs. And in communist affairs too. Given Tito's insistence that the Yugoslav version of socialist construction was of equal validity to that of the Soviet Union there was the danger that other east European leaders could find the Yugoslav model more attractive and more relevant than the Soviet, especially because they, like the CPY, had just emerged from depression, right-wing government, war, and foreign occupation. This danger seemed to be heightened by Tito's travels in 1946–7. The partisan war record had made him almost a legend and his visits to Warsaw, Prague, Sofia, Budapest, and Bucharest took on the appearance of a triumphal tour.

In July 1947 the Yugoslavs and Bulgarians concluded the Bled agreement in which there was reference to federation and a Bulgarian commitment to a new policy in Pirin Macedonia. The Greek communists misinterpreted the Bled agreement as an indication that Stalin was now prepared for a more forward policy and therefore they declared a provisional government and mobilised all forces under their control for an all-out offensive. Also, in November 1947, Nako Spiru, a pro-Moscow member of the Albanian politburo, committed suicide in protest against what he considered to be a virtual Yugoslav takeover of his country. Tito seemed to be dominating the Balkans and to be pursuing policies entirely of his own making; given his proven record of intransigence, and the widespread but fallacious assumption in the west that he was acting under Moscow's guidance, the dangers of western retaliation were increased. Tito had to be reined in or destroyed.

The expulsion of Yugoslavia from the Cominform

Stalin decided 'to overturn the Yugoslav Balkan policy by enticing it into overdrive'.[2] A Yugoslav delegation was called to Moscow and encouraged to absorb Albania, as a result of which Tito asked for a military base near Korcë; meanwhile the Bulgarian leader, Dimitrov, talked enthusiastically in Bucharest of a Balkan federation which would include communist Greece. Then came the cold douche. *Pravda* disagreed with Dimitrov, after which Yugoslavia and Bulgaria were invited to send delegations to Moscow; Tito refused to go and sent Edvard Kardelj, his ideological expert. On 10 February Stalin raged at the two delegations, insisting that the Bled agreement had been concluded without the Soviets being informed of its contents and that a Yugoslav entry into Albania would give the Americans an excuse to act in the Balkans. Stalin then insisted that the Greek revolt be closed down and that in future Yugoslavia should consult Moscow in all foreign policy questions. Finally, the Soviet leader demanded an immediate Bulgarian-Yugoslav federation of two equal units; he ruled out both the larger federation of all Balkan states and the Yugoslav concept of a Yugoslav-Bulgarian federation of seven units: the six republics of Yugoslavia plus Bulgaria. Belgrade rejected Stalin's proposed federation as a Bulgarian/Soviet trojan horse. In retaliation the Soviet Union turned down renewed requests for economic assistance put forward by the Yugoslavs.

Relations deteriorated rapidly. On 18 March Soviet advisers were withdrawn from Yugoslavia and on 27 March, the anniversary of the 1941 coup, Stalin sent his first letter to the CPY. Further exchanges produced a Soviet proposal to refer the matters at issue between the two parties to Cominform, but this the CPY would not accept. Tito stood firm but Soviet propaganda scored points off the CPY's decision in May to arrest Hebrang and Žujović. By now the Hungarian party, at the Kremlin's request, had joined in the criticism of the CPY; this was the beginning of a deep and bitter hatred which Tito felt for Rákosi who had himself once complained to Tito of Moscow's overbearing policies. By the end of May a settlement had become all but impossible and Cominform made its final preparations for expulsion of the CPY on 28 June.

Stalin's underlying fear had been of an uncontrollable element in the communist camp. This had been compounded by the rapid deterioration in east-west relations which followed the Prague coup of February 1948 and the five-nation Brussels treaty, the forerunner of NATO, which was signed a few weeks later. Stalin was also aware of the situation in the far east where the Chinese Communist Party was advancing rapidly towards victory. Mao Tse-tung's forces, like Tito's, had fought their own battles against the foreign occupier without help from Stalin; their Long March was comparable to the partisans' trek to Bosnia in 1941; and the Chinese, like the partisans, imposed a rural-based revolution on the territory they occupied. If Stalin were to remain unchallenged leader of the socialist world, he had to show that the Soviet system would prevail over such heretical revolutions.

The assumption in Moscow was that once it was known that he had lost Soviet approval Tito would collapse: 'I will shake my little finger and there will be no more Tito,' Stalin remarked. However, as Khrushchev was reported to have said, 'Stalin could shake his little finger, or any other part of his anatomy he liked, but it made no difference to Tito.' Yet Tito's survival was not guaranteed. In an extraordinary party congress, which was called in July, he allowed an open debate and a free and secret vote on the split; in addition, to the amazement of the other Cominform parties, he sanctioned publication of all correspondence between the CPY and Moscow. The Yugoslav party leader criticised neither Stalin nor the Soviet Union; his quarrel, he insisted, was with Cominform. Once the initial debate had been aired, however, Tito took severe measures against any 'cominformists' within the CPY, the more so after August when a senior general, Arso Jovanović, had been shot whilst trying to cross the border into Romania where, it was assumed, he would either prepare for the invasion of Yugoslavia or become head of a pro-Soviet government in exile. A number of cominformists were murdered, some went into exile, and many thousands were interned in a fearsome concentration camp established on the island of Goli Otok. Because of continuing Soviet intimidation Tito did not relax his grip until the early 1950s.

By then Stalin had been humbled. To save some prestige he attempted to utilise the split with Tito as an excuse for the collapse of the Greek communist cause which, he argued, had been sabotaged by the Yugoslavs. Much more sinister however, was the fact that Zhdanov at one point during the dispute of 1948 had told Cominform that the Soviets had proof that the CPY leadership had been penetrated by British spies. Although the accusation was not included in the official documentation, Zhdanov had conjured up the awful spectre of the purges of the 1930s. That ghost was soon to terrify all of eastern Europe. The charge of 'Titoism' was to be used to cleanse the east European parties of any potential threats to Stalin's authority or to the Soviet monopoly of the world communist movement.

THE PURGES OF THE LATE 1940s AND EARLY 1950s

The process

In the month when Yugoslavia's expulsion from Cominform was made known, the Albanian central committee launched a campaign against right-wing nationalism; in September Koçi Xoxe lost his post as minister of the interior because of his support for Tito. That the Albanians should align with the enemies of the Yugoslavs was hardly surprising, the recent friendship between the two having been the exception rather than the rule. There had also been moves in another Balkan capital, Bucharest, where Lucreţiu Pătrăşcanu, who has been described as the 'the only genuine nationalist'[3] in the Romanian party, was removed from office at the founding congress of the Romanian Workers' Party (RWP). Such developments were not confined to the Balkans. On 3 August, in Budapest, László Rajk was moved from his post as minister of the interior to become minister of foreign affairs, a move which could only be regarded as demotion. In Poland the central committee of the PUWP heard criticism of Gomułka's alleged right-wing nationalist deviations, and on 3 September removed him from the politburo and from his post as its secretary general, though as yet he remained in the central committee. The year ended with Gheorghi Dimitrov telling the fifth congress of the BCP that, 'It doesn't matter what someone's services and merits might have been in the past. We shall expel from the party and punish anyone who deserves it, no matter who he might have been once upon a time.'[4]

The following months and years were to show that Dimitrov was as good as his word, and that he was speaking not merely for the BCP. In Bulgaria itself in March 1949 Traicho Kostov, a relatively popular communist who was both deputy minister president and chairman of the politburo's influential economic and financial secretariat, lost these prestigious posts to find himself director of the national library; knowledge is not always power. Soon after that he was arrested. So too was László Rajk. The purges were under way.

In Tiranë events were a little more advanced and showed the destination as well as the direction in which they were moving; in June 1949, whilst Kostov and Rajk were accustoming themselves to the prison cell, Xoxe made his way to the scaffold. In September the accumulating drama burst into the sensational when Rajk, a lifelong communist and veteran of the Spanish civil war and the underground resistance in Hungary during the second world war, was put in the dock charged with having been an informer for the Horthyite police, a traitor to his comrades in Spain, a spy for the American and French intelligence services, and a co-conspirator of Tito's in a plot to overthrow the régime and restore capitalism. Even more sensational was the fact that Rajk lamely admitted guilt on all accounts; less than a month later, on 15 October, he was executed. In December Kostov went on trial charged with equally grave and absurd crimes. He, however, retracted a previous confession and to general consternation refused to admit his guilt; the public broadcast of the trial went silent and the simultaneous translations provided for foreign journalists developed immediate technical difficulties. To save further embarrassment the court decided to proceed without the accused who, on the basis of his previous, written confession, was sentenced to death and executed immediately.

There had been less dramatic events in Poland where in November the central committee held a 'vigilance plenum' to strengthen its stance against the nationalist heresy. In Czechoslovakia the ninth congress of the CPCS extracted self-criticism from leading Slovaks such as Ladislav Novomeský, Vladimír Clementis and Gustáv Husák; they were later to be arrested. In the GDR the purge was delayed until the summer of 1950 and then it was relatively mild in form; long-standing party members such as Paul Merker and Willi Kreikemeyer lost their top party posts in the third SED congress in July and were arrested in August, though they were not put on trial.

Any thoughts that the relatively mild treatment handed out to Merker, Kreikemeyer, and their associates heralded a general scaling down of the purges were soon dispelled. A number of arrests took place in Brno in October 1950, the main victim being Oto Šling, the chief of the Moravian party. On 31 July Gomuľka was taken into custody, though his captors subjected him to nothing more than house arrest. That was far from the fate of Rudolf Slánský, the deputy prime minister and secretary general of the CPCS, who was arrested on 24 November. Despite the experience gained it took a year to 'prepare' his trial which began on 20 November 1952. Slánský and his thirteen co-defendants were accused of being 'Trotskyist-zionist-titoist-bourgeois-nationalist traitors, spies and saboteurs, enemies of the Czechoslovak nation, of its people's democratic order, and of socialism'. They all confessed. Eleven were executed and their ashes mixed with material being used to fill roads on the outskirts of Prague. After the trials the property of the victims was sold off cheaply to surviving prominenti; the wife of a future leader of the party, Antonín Novotný, bought the china and the bedclothes of Clementis.

The Slánský case was the high-water mark of the show trials but the purges of top officials were not yet completed. Further arrests and executions followed in Czechoslovakia and in Romania, where the prominent communists, Ana Pauker and Vasile Luca, had been arrested in 1952; Pătrăşcanu, although arrested in 1948, was not put to death until 1954.

The arrest and public humiliation of prominent party officials was but the tip of the iceberg. With the arrest of each senior party member scores and sometimes hundreds of lesser figures were taken into custody, some of them to provide witnesses in the show trials which were being prepared, others because they were suspected of deviation from the strict stalinist line now being enforced throughout eastern Europe. General estimates indicate that in Bulgaria the party declined from around 500,000 members in December 1948 to 300,000 in 1951, a fall of some 40 per cent. In Czechoslovakia, where the purges began later and lasted longer, the party fell from around two million in December 1948 to 1.4 million six years later, a drop of about 30 per cent. In percentage terms the decline in the Hungarian party was similar, its membership being 1.2 million in June 1948 and 0.85 million in February 1951. The Romanian party lost about a third of its membership between 1948 and 1951. In Poland the PUWP had 1.5 million members at its formation in 1948 but only 1.15 million in 1952, a drop of just under 25 per cent. The extent of the purge is more strikingly illustrated by the fact that probably one in every four communist party members suffered some form of persecution during the years 1948–53, and without doubt more communists died at the hands of the communist governments of eastern Europe than under their inter-war predecessors.

Certain groups were particularly at risk. Anyone with a western connection was immediately vulnerable. This included those who had spent the war years in exile in the west, a category which was particularly large in Czechoslovakia; in Hungary there was the so-called 'Swiss group' from their place of exile. Many veterans of the Spanish civil war followed Rajk into the dungeons or the hands of the hangman because they were tainted by their western experiences. A western wife was another marker for persecution. Connections with Tito and Yugoslavia were equally if not more dangerous in that all the show trials went out of their way to 'prove' that the accused were working for the renegade in Belgrade.

Members of those parties which had joined with the communists in the fusion process were also at risk, as were party members from a non-working class background; Slánský's opening sentence in his confession included the phrase, 'I came into the workers' movement as a man of bourgeois origin.'

The political purges, especially at the higher level, were instigated and to a degree orchestrated by the Kremlin, with Stalin himself playing a leading role in the process. Nine copies of all reports, confessions, and other documents in all countries were prepared, signed and circulated to the Soviet and the satellite leaders. Stalin's emissary, colonel Bielkin of the NKVD, discussed with Rákosi and the Hungarian secret police chief, Gábor Péter, who was to be the star of the Hungarian show trials, the candidates being Imre Nagy, János Kádár, and László Rajk. And Bielkin personally interrogated many of those who were to appear as witnesses in the show trials, though he left the torturing to the locals. It was Soviet agents who kidnapped István Stolte near Munich and it was Bielkin who brought him back from NKVD headquarters at Baden bei Wien to Budapest, so that he might give false witness against Rajk; and it was also the Soviets who tricked the American religious charity worker, Noel Field, into going to Prague where he was detained and then shipped to Budapest, to be sentenced to fifteen years' imprisonment for organising espionage activities against the socialist governments. In Bulgaria it was the Soviet general Chernov who 'advised' the local police authorities, and after Kostov had been executed the leaders in Sofia sent a telegram of thanks to Stalin for his help in uncovering the danger in their midst.

The Czechoslovaks were more of a problem. The Rajk trial had been orchestrated to indicate that the conspiracy was not confined to Hungary. After the trial the Soviets put increasing pressure on the Czechoslovak leadership, insisting that enemy agents had penetrated high into the apparatus of both party and state and that a conspiracy trial was necessary to uncover them or at least to cow them into ineffectiveness. Gottwald and Slánský were puzzled and asked for Soviet advisers who arrived in the form of Likhachev and Makarov, aides of Bielkin. They did much to coordinate the preparation of the subsequent trials. Even in Poland, where the local leadership resisted Soviet pressure for show trials, the Soviets demanded the construction of more prisons, one of which was to contain a special wing for high-ranking party members.

The methods used during the show trials were similar throughout eastern Europe and were again largely the result of Soviet advice. Confessions for the show trials and 'evidence' from leading witnesses could be extracted by any means, even by threatening to torture the victims' wives and children; and generally speaking the higher the rank of the arrested party member the more vicious was the torture inflicted. Let one example serve for many. The original source for this quotation was the victim himself, János Kádár.

> Kádár had denied the charges.
>
> Mihály Farkas' son, Vladimir, who was a colonel of the AVO and a bald, tired young man of thirty, had questioned him. Vladimir had but one argument: blows. They had begun to beat Kádár. They had smeared his body with mercury to prevent his pores from breathing. He had been writhing on the floor when a newcomer had arrived. The newcomer was Vladimir's father, Mihály Farkas.
>
> Kádár was raised from the ground. Vladimir stepped close. Two henchmen pried Kádár's teeth apart, and the colonel, negligently, as if this were the most natural thing in the world, urinated into his mouth.[5]

For those who were not executed, degradation and humiliation continued after the trials with long years in appalling prisons or labour camps; mail from nearest relatives was not allowed, and even the last letters of those about to die remained undelivered. Years after their release some victims were compensated but in Czechoslovakia the authorities deducted a sizeable amount from this meagre sum to cover the costs of the prisoners' upkeep whilst in detention.

In the intimacy of the interrogation room the inquisitors made no pretence at seeking real evidence. The 'truth' had already been decided upon and it merely remained to convince those involved of it. In some cases the notion that a person *might* have become a spy, or a saboteur, or an opponent of the party, or a supporter of Tito was enough; this was 'essentially' guilt and ought to be admitted. A number of dedicated party members accepted the argument that they could perform one last service to the party by allowing themselves to be convicted of crimes which they had not committed. In Rajk's case, as in many others, this was made part of a deal in which the victim was promised that, although the public sentence would be death, there would be no execution and the prisoner would be reunited with his family. What was required of him was not his death but his 'moral suicide'. For a person whose life had been constructed around the party, and whose whole system of values and beliefs had been founded on the infallibility of the party, such a deal made sense and to refuse its last, macabre order would have negated all previous actions. Even when the authorities reneged on the deal, some of the victims clung to their faith. Rajk's last words were reputed to be 'Long live the party'; it seems, said one of those who was sentenced in the same trial, that 'his dilemma was decided by his loyalty to the cause, his loyalty to his own past and to the idealised communist party, and not to the hope that they might spare his life'.[6] Kostov highlighted this topsy-turvy moral world even more sharply. After he had withdrawn his confession he was asked by the presiding judge why he had given false evidence; Kostov replied, 'My party consciousness does not permit me to tell the truth.'[7]

Between 1948 and 1953 eastern Europe lived through monstrous terror. Inevitably in this kafkaesque world, where established reason and logic were abandoned in the name of a higher good, there were absurdities. George Paloczi-Horváth's interrogators squirmed with pleasure when they discovered the real depth of his deceit: 'We knew all the time – we have it here in writing – that you met professor Szentgyörgyi not in Istanbul, but in Constantinople.'[8] Another victim of the Hungarian secret police was condemned on the basis of a document showing him to have been an accomplice of the Nazis; the document had been taken from a glass cabinet in the Institute of the Working Class Movement where it had been displayed as an example of a Gestapo forgery calumniating a true servant of the workers' cause.

The trials themselves were, in the true sense of the word, 'shows'. Each had a script which all participants had to learn and which was rehearsed numerous times before the public performance; in the Slánský trial the judge skipped one of the scripted questions but the old trooper Slánský was better rehearsed and answered the one which should have been asked.

If there was an overall similarity in the methodology of the purges, there were also many variations. Neither in Poland nor in Hungary, nor even in the first round of purges in Romania, was there any overt sign of anti-semitism. By the time of the Slánský trial, however, Moscow was arguing that Israel had, like Tito's Yugoslavia, bitten the Soviet hand that fed it, and thus anti-semitism was a prominent feature of that trial; eleven of the fourteen accused with Slánský were Jewish, as were the two prominent communists arrested in Romania in 1952, Pauker and Luca.

The intensity of the political purges varied from country to country, as did their timing. In parties which were large, well entrenched, and reasonably popular the purges were more thorough in their impact on the mass of party members, Bulgaria and Czechoslovakia fitting into this category; in Slovakia local nationalism made the purges even more fierce. In Poland, Romania, and the GDR, where the party was less well established, the purges were lighter. In the well established parties local leaderships were stronger, and the cadres better versed in marxist-leninist theory; they were hit harder because it was feared that they might be more likely to question or resist unpopular decisions and to make a stand in support of local and national interests. It also has to be noted that in Bulgaria and Czechoslovakia there was no Red Army presence. The exception to this pattern was Hungary, where there were Soviet garrisons, where the party did not have deep roots or a sizeable, entrenched local apparatus, but where the purges were particularly severe. That fact cannot be dissociated from what was to happen in the country in 1956.

The purge in Poland was distinctive for its mildness. Gomułka, though to a lesser degree than Tito, had established his reputation during the war as the product of local forces and local decisions; the arrest of his predecessor had forced a leadership election even though, at the time, events in the military sector made it impossible to communicate with Moscow. Even if his forces were not as large or as prestigious as Tito's, Gomułka was clearly a national communist. He continued as such. He accepted entirely the Soviet Union's right, as the first socialist state, to play the leading role in the international working class movement, and he did not quarrel with Moscow over such sensitive national issues as the Nazi-Soviet pact, the Soviet invasion of 17 September 1939, the Katyn massacres, or the Warsaw uprising. On the other hand, he did exhibit strong nationalist feelings over the new western territories and the dispute with Czechoslovakia over Teschen, a dispute which in the immediate post-war months caused severe tension between Warsaw and Prague. Furthermore, Gomułka accepted collectivisation as strategically correct but suggested that it was tactically not advisable; it was an objective towards which Poland should evolve carefully and gradually. To this heresy Gomułka added a willingness to live with the Roman Catholic church without persecuting it; even worse, as far as Moscow was concerned, was that at the Szklarska Poręba meeting he had opposed the formation of Cominform.

In such circumstances it was not surprising that Gomułka was denounced for right-wing deviationism. What is surprising is that he, and many Polish communists who sympathised with him, escaped with their lives, despite pressure from Moscow. We do not know why the Soviets were so indulgent. It could be that memories of the war of 1919–21 and more recently of the Poles' willingness to fight against insuperable odds in 1944 made the Kremlin reluctant to push the Poles into an outright confrontation. It could also be that with the continuing fierce, and yet to us still shadowy, war with the anti-communist resistance the Soviets were unwilling to do anything which might destabilise the Polish communist régime. Be that as it may, the fact remains that Gomułka, the most overtly Titoist leader in eastern Europe, survived the anti-nationalist purges. That too was to have profound consequences in 1956.

The social purges

It was not only the communists who suffered in the late 1940s and early 1950s. The culling of their ranks may be termed a political purge but it was the prelude to a general and wide-ranging social purge which was aimed with equal or even greater ferocity at all ranks of society. No one was safe. Denunciations were rife, the definitions of crime were all-embracing – the possession of an item in short supply could be construed as hoarding – and, most importantly, responsibilities for administering the purges were cunningly integrated into the everyday lives of all citizens.

> This was achieved by a simple device: a factory, a local government department, a professional organisation was given a quota of people to be weeded out, which might mean sacking, sending to the mines or handing over to the security police as class enemies under the accusation of whatever happened to be the fashionable crime. The steering committee of the organisation, or the man responsible for personnel matters, knew that if they did not comply they would themselves be the victims. So they did comply, telling everybody that they saved ninety-eight good people by selecting two sacrificial lambs who were anyhow 'not much good', were spoiling things for everybody by working too hard, drinking too much or too little, were odd because they refused to sleep with the right person, or simply, and this was always a safe argument, were Jews.[9]

This was terror. And it was meant to be seen as such. In Budapest the vans set out at 2 a.m. on Mondays, Wednesdays, and Fridays to bring in the latest batch of victims, who by 1953 numbered somewhere in the region of 700,000, of whom 98,000 were branded as spies and saboteurs; 5,000 of them were executed. In Czechoslovakia between 1948 and 1954 there were around 150,000 prisoners, and similar proportions of the population suffered in the other states.

The social purges provided the context for swingeing attacks upon the régimes' domestic opponents, actual or potential, real or supposed. Once again any institution with western connections was particularly vulnerable. East European branches of organisations such as the boy scouts, the girl guides, and the international federation of professional and business women, were closed; even esperantists were persecuted. The churches were subjected to yet another attack. The Uniate church in Ruthenia and the Ukraine had been suppressed by Stalin in 1946, and in 1948 it was liquidated in Romania too, being forcibly merged with the Romanian Orthodox church; henceforth the Romanian communists would have to deal with only one religious body and one with no foreign connections. In Bulgaria in 1949 the government refused to allow a newly appointed papal delegate to take up his diplomatic post in Sofia, and even before Kostov appeared in court fifteen Protestant pastors were arrested, tried, and sentenced to heavy terms of imprisonment. The Roman Catholic church suffered in Hungary with the arrest of cardinal Mindszenty, whilst in Czechoslovakia's prison camps in the early 1950s there were over 8,000 monks and nuns. Even in Poland the authorities felt secure enough in 1953 to detain cardinal Wyszyński.

Another institution which was liable to the attentions of the modern witch-hunters was the army. In the summer of 1951, when Gomułka was finally arrested, the Polish authorities began to remove unreliable officers from their army, and in Hungary a similar pattern developed after the arrest and show trial of lieutenant-general György Pálffy. In a speech to Cominform in 1949 Slánský, still then amongst the purgers rather than the purged, noted that 'It is still a weakness in our party that the mass of the membership underestimates the resistance of the class enemy . . . Experience teaches us that, with a few exceptions, we need new men to replace the entire officer corps.'[10]

Universities and other educational institutions suffered similar fates. In the cultural sector, rigid adherence to socialist realism had to be enforced; even so renowned a scholar as György Lukács had to conform because

> The dislike of 'socialist realism' that he betrayed corresponded to the belief, prevalent in the first years after the second world war, that in the people's democracies the science of Marx and Engels would blaze new paths, unknown in Russia. Because Lukács expressed this belief in his books, the Party had no course but to stigmatise him.[11]

Those who were given an 'X' for their social category, that is former class enemies, were never safe, but in many cases former class allies were equally at risk. Those who had been in the non-communist leftist parties were regarded with great suspicion and any independent spirits in the trade union movement soon found themselves in the hands of the security police. In effect the régime used the purges and the terror to strike at all of its former enemies and at anyone thought likely to oppose it in the future: landowners, army officers, entrepreneurs, the unconverted intelligentsia, unrepentant peasants, and those who clung ostentatiously to a religious faith. Scarcely a family remained untouched.

The function of the purges

The purges, both political and social, were justified theoretically by Stalin's doctrine that the class struggle intensifies in the immediate aftermath of the socialist revolution and in the first stages of the construction of socialism. Not even in the developed states, says this doctrine, does the industrial working class form the majority. Bourgeois and petty-bourgeois attitudes abound, the more so when the switch to socialist construction and planning moves investment from the consumer market to capital projects. This, more plainly put, means that the inevitable shortages will force people to rely on home production, the black market, and other now illegal manifestations of the natural human instinct to improve the quality of life.

To the internal dangers posed by the persistence of petty-bourgeois activities had to be added the external dangers generated by the cold war. The capitalist west, said Moscow, had driven the communists out of the coalition governments in France and Italy and extra vigilance would be required to ensure that they did not do the same east of the Elbe. An age-old stratagem of the enemy was, of course, to divide and rule, and it was the imperialists' intention to do that in eastern Europe; they had already tricked the Yugoslav comrades into breaking with Moscow by dangling before Belgrade the concept of individual roads to socialism or national communism. This, of course, would be popular with the masses, and therefore vigilance was needed to prevent other régimes from falling into this alluring trap and thereby further weakening the socialist camp and opening the way to a restoration of capitalism. A dedication to socialism must, by this formula, mean devotion to the Soviet Union and its leader. Thus, Vûlko Chervenkov, who was to step over Kostov's body into Dimitrov's chair as boss of the Bulgarian party, could declare that 'There cannot be true love for one's fatherland if that love is in one way or another opposed to the love of the Soviet Union.' Similarly, a Hungarian newspaper could pronounce in July 1949:

> Only he who deeply loves the Soviet Union, the great protector of the world's peoples, the powerful and invincible vanguard of progress and peace, is a good Hungarian patriot. Only he is a good Hungarian patriot who reveres and loves our great teacher, generalissimo Stalin, who successfully leads the struggle of the peoples for a lasting peace and the triumph of freedom in the entire world.[12]

Thus, again in Hungary, the director of the National Theatre could produce a version of *Macbeth* in which the villainous king was revealed as none other than Tito himself.

The fact that the purges set out to eradicate local nationalism and to inculcate a sense of Soviet patriotism has sometimes led to their being represented as the elimination of 'home' communists by 'Moscow' communists. It is true that Stalin wanted reliable men and that that usually meant those over whom he could exercise the direct control which would have been established had the communists in question spent some years in the USSR. On the other hand, if a communist had never been in Moscow and if he had been in his own country during the war, when communication with Moscow was difficult and when decisions had perforce to be taken on the spot, he might have become habituated to self-reliance; he would be conditioned to think and act on his own. It is indeed the case that many victims of the purges were communists who had not been in Moscow during the 1930s or the war: Rajk, Gomułka, Kostov, Clementis, Pǎtrǎşcanu, Kreikemeyer, and Merker had all been active in the resistance movements, whilst Rákosi, Gottwald, and Dimitrov had been in Moscow and had become totally dependent on Stalin and the Kremlin clique. It was also the case that the Slovak party, which was very heavily purged, had been founded in 1939, and had never been brought fully under Moscow's domination, as its independence in helping to stage the rising of 1944 had shown. But the equation that purge victim equalled home communist is not that simple. The Romanian party leader Gheorghiu-Dej had never been to the Soviet Union before 1944 whilst two of his most famous victims, Pauker and Luca, had been and were so pro-Soviet that they had advocated Soviet occupation rather than an indigenous coup in 1944. And there was no more rabid anti-Titoist than Albanian party boss,

Enver Hoxha, who had been educated in France and Belgium and had spent the war in the Albanian mountains.

Albania's traditional suspicions of Yugoslav intentions may explain Hoxha's motivation but the Czechoslovak case is more anomalous. The first purges had been of Slovak nationalists such as Husák and Novomeský who had been in Slovakia and in the Slovak resistance during the war, and these purges therefore conformed to the anti-nationalist, anti-titoist pattern. Slánský had played a prominent part in carrying out these purges. When he himself became a victim, the home versus Moscow communist division broke down. He had spent most of his exiled years in the Soviet Union, although he had also served with the Ukrainian partisans. In fact the evolution of the terror in Czechoslovakia, like much of its history between 1948 and 1989, was a function of the late takeover by the communists. As the purges were gathering momentum in Hungary and to a lesser extent in Poland, Czechoslovakia was only beginning to adapt to the takeover and the concentration was therefore on immediate political and economic changes rather than on cleansing the party. In so far as there were political purges in Czechoslovakia in the late 1940s, they were directed against members of the former opposition parties rather than suspect groups within the CPCS, besides which Gottwald said in 1949 that in a party which had had a legal existence and in which there was an established tradition of accountability between the leadership and the membership there was no need for purges.

The CPCS leader was treading on dangerous ground. At a time when Stalin was showing an almost paranoic desire for unity and uniformity, Gottwald was saying that the Czechoslovak party was different. His stance excited jealousy and suspicion elsewhere in eastern Europe. Czechoslovakia, in addition to the strongest democratic traditions, had the best developed and the least damaged economic infrastructure in central Europe, and it should therefore in theory have been the best placed to move towards the construction of socialism. But Gottwald seemed to be intimating that, if it did so, the socialism that would emerge would not be of the Soviet variety. Furthermore, the Czechoslovaks had well established trading links with the west, and it was not host to any Red Army units. Could it be relied upon to remain loyal to its new socialist allies? The reluctance of Prague to accept the lessons of the Rajk trial could only intensify these unpleasant suspicions and increase pressure from Budapest, Warsaw, and Moscow to take action, the Soviets being particularly insistent that the more advanced the society the higher up the party apparatus the conspiracy had penetrated. Gottwald eventually gave way, sacrificing first the Slovaks, then Šling and the Moravians, and finally Slánský. In so doing he allowed the Stalinist juggernaut to flatten what was left of Czechoslovakia's liberal democratic traditions, and to iron out the economic advantages the country had previously enjoyed *vis-à-vis* its partners in the socialist bloc. Socialist unity had been secured but much to the long-term disadvantage of the Czechoslovak citizen and economy.

The purges were inseparable from the economic context in which they were conducted. As conditions deteriorated because of the switch to capital investment and also because of the dislocation caused by the purges themselves, the victims were held up as those responsible for the worsening of living standards; after all, a communist government could not but work for the good of the masses, so if things were going wrong it must be the fault of saboteurs within the system. In most countries of eastern Europe the purges coincided with the introduction of the first of the ambitious five-year plans and with the beginnings of collectivisation. Their objectives were absurd but the plans were holy writ and if they were not fulfilled then scapegoats had to be found. Workers who failed to fulfil targets were obvious candidates. Action against them would help to instil the discipline which would be needed to meet the new tasks required of the workforce, whilst at the same time ultimate responsibility for the general shortcomings could be pinned on the prominent victims of the political purge; in Romania Gheorghiu-Dej admitted that 80,000 peasants had been accused of siding with the class enemy because they resisted collectivisation, and he blamed Ana Pauker for this 'distortion'.

There was a deeper and more important function for the purges to play. This question was bound up with the kernel of marxist-leninist power: the reliability of the party itself.

In the past the leninist parties had thrived and survived through discipline: as the Polish stalinist, Stefan Staszewski, remarked, 'the party always has to have an enemy in order to consolidate its ranks. If the external enemy is crushed it will find its own internal one'.[13] By the early 1950s there was only one potential internal enemy: the communist party. All other political organisations and social groups had been either eliminated or rendered harmless, with the result that only the communist party remained as a functioning political body. At the same time it was known that the massive social and economic changes about to be introduced under the industrialisation and collectivisation programmes would cause enormous upheaval and deprivation. Inevitably resentment would be felt and discontent engendered amongst the mass of the population. Because of the neutralisation of all alternative forces, that discontent had no other point for effective coalescence than the communist parties. And old party members were, after all, steeped in the business of responding to mass discontent, particularly clandestinely. Could the leadership trust the party in such circumstances? Did the party have the resolution and will to inflict upon its natural constituency the hardships that the construction of socialism would involve? The risk was too great to take. The party had, in appropriate terminology, to be steeled to its stalinist task of industrialisation and collectivisation. Those, and they were the majority of the old party ranks, who believed that the function of the party was to defend and advance the interests of the masses, had therefore to be removed or terrified into obedience. And to eliminate the mighty amongst the party, men such as Kostov, Rajk, and Slánský, would show all party members that, as Dimitrov had warned in December 1948, no one was exempt from the duty to obey and conform. A worker imprisoned with Paloczi-Horváth told him:

The Rajk trial probably served many purposes: one was the anti-Tito drive. And also it introduced the period of full terrorism. In this Rajk case they eliminated those important communists who were blind idealists like yourself, who could have been suspected of elementary decency. The dictators got rid of all the political parties, the communist party included. To the cliques of murderous bastards ruling in Moscow and in the various slave-states, convinced communists are just as dangerous or perhaps more dangerous than social-democrats or liberals.[14]

The effects of the purges

If the purges managed to contain immediate dissatisfaction, they had devastating long-term effects. The economy was severely dislocated. Huge construction projects had been launched with insufficient capital and therefore unpaid prisoners had to serve in the place of modern equipment, although Marx had condemned slavery as the most inefficient form of labour. Equally damaging was the wholesale elimination of trained administrative and management élites. As a contemporary remarked in Czechoslovakia:

The highly qualified professional people are laying roads, building bridges and operating machines, and the dumb clots – whose fathers used to dig, sweep or bricklay – are on top, telling the others where to lay the roads, what to produce and how to spend the country's money. The consequence is the roads look like ploughed fields, we make things we can't sell and the bridges can't be used for traffic.... Then they wonder why the economy is going downhill like a ten-ton lorry with the brakes off.[15]

To this had to be added the cost of the vast apparatus created to initiate and sustain the purge: 'Almost a million adults, 90 per cent of whom would have been capable of productive work, were employed to record, control, calculate, indoctrinate, spy on, and sometimes kill Hungarians actually accomplishing the productive work.'[16] Hence the joke of the 1950s: 'What is the difference between capitalism and socialism? Capitalism is the exploitation of man by man: socialism is the opposite.' There would be some who would argue that the socialist economies never recovered.

Largely as a result of the purges, so many people were dismissed from the established professions that they had to be replaced by hastily trained younger people whose class origins were above reproach. Not only was it difficult for a 25-year old legal officer, whose qualifications were nothing more than a six-week crash course in basic law, to win public confidence but also the age profile of many occupations was totally distorted. Those now thrust into high office would remain there, as long as they retained the confidence of the local party bosses, for thirty or more years; succeeding generations would find the path to promotion hopelessly blocked and their morale would suffer accordingly.

The purges attained their immediate goals. Socialist unity and stalinist conformity were preserved; the party, in the conception of many of its original members, was tamed if not destroyed. But at tremendous cost. The condemnation of national communism by the party invited condemnation of the communist party by the nation. Yet the nation had no obvious prospect, as it did under Nazi occupation, of war bringing an end to its tribulations and morale accordingly fell, a process intensified by the endless double-speak of official propaganda which could present debilitating wage cuts as 'blows in the face of imperialism', and forced loans as 'voluntary contributions to building socialism'.

The purges had entrenched the political police to such an extent that the entire apparatus of both state and party was penetrated by a network of agents who were responsible only to the local police chiefs. The attainment and retention of power at any level, even the very highest, depended on a workable relationship with the local security officers. If the party were the élite within the country and the state, the political police were the élite of the élite, a state within and above the state, a party within and above the party.

The purges destroyed the moral base on which the party had operated. That morality was founded in the leninist notion that anything which is beneficial to the working class is moral; but it was the party which decided what was beneficial for the working class. Unfortunately for the party, after the death of Stalin it had to admit that it had made mistakes, that the execution of many of the purge victims had harmed the cause of the international working class. By the leninist canon, therefore, these acts could no longer be regarded as moral, and so the party itself had abrogated its claim to moral infallibility. Anyone searching for a faith, and for the secure system of moral values which a viable faith carries with it, would no longer look towards the Soviet variant of socialism. With faith thus dissipated, all that remained to compel loyalty and obedience amongst existing party members was fear, the fear engendered by the ubiquitous police apparatus. New members would henceforth not be drawn to the party by belief but would have to be attracted by the offer of power and privilege. The party therefore had now to rely on a mixture of fear and cynicism; in accepting Stalin's purges it had in the long run undermined its own legitimacy.

When the nightmare ended after the death of Stalin and the camps were emptied, the effect upon many was devastating. The returning prisoners told of the sufferings inflicted upon them not by a foreign occupier, not by sadistic Nazis, not by barbaric Soviets from the east, but by their own countrymen. The nation outside the party was revolted, but for the party rank and file the effect was even worse; the beatings, the tortures, the forced labour, and the endless humiliations had been handed out in the name of the party of which they were members. The party leaders in desperation blamed Stalin and stalinism, but it was too late. The crusade against national communism had made Soviet internationalism intolerable. Amongst the older generation of party activists the disillusion had penetrated too deeply. At the same time, younger party cadres, many of them trained in Moscow, had also concluded that the Soviet system was not necessarily the blueprint for everyone's future.

> Most of the young communists who studied in Soviet universities in the first half of the 1950s returned home with their ideological faith shaken. . . . for most of us a fundamental article of that faith had been shaken: we no longer believed that the USSR was the embodiment of our ideals, that it was a model we were bound to follow without reservations.[17]

The purges had worked too well. Is it too mischievous to suggest that the inner contradictions of marxism–leninism–stalinism were to be seen in the purges and that the seeds of its destruction were sown in the process of its consolidation?

16

THE RETREAT FROM STALINISM, 1953–6

THE ATTEMPTED 'NEW COURSE': EASTERN EUROPE, 1953–6

The emergence of the Yugoslav model

Whilst the east European communist lands were savaged by the 'anti-titoist' purges Yugoslavia's communists sought their own road to socialism.

The split of 1948 had forced destalinisation upon them, but for the next three or four years Tito, acting through his security chief, Aleksandar Ranković, felt it necessary to maintain police controls against the cominformists. The Cominform gave him good reason to do so. The Soviet Union's anti-Yugoslav propaganda continued remorselessly and Yugoslavia was intimidated in numerous ways; Soviet planes, for example, flew fifty or more flights per day across Yugoslav territory from bases in Albania to Bulgaria and other pro-Moscow countries. In August 1949 severe pressure was put on the Yugoslavs to return a number of White Russian refugees who had subsequently been recruited by the NKVD. When the Yugoslavs refused, troops were concentrated on the Romanian-Yugoslav border. Only then did Tito begin to relax his attitudes towards the west, accepting US aid in September 1949.

After the outbreak of the Korean war in June 1950 Yugoslav ties with the west increased because of Tito's fear that Stalin would permit in the Balkans what he had already sanctioned in the far east, namely forward action by a Moscow-backed communist state. At the height of the international tension in the early 1950s Belgrade moved close to a Balkan pact with Turkey and Greece, both members of NATO. But the treaty of friendship and cooperation signed in Ankara in February 1953 and the subsequent military agreement concluded at Bled in August 1954 faded into insignificance as the international climate changed. By the mid-1950s Tito had established much closer links with India, Indonesia, and Egypt in what came to be called the non-aligned bloc.

The relaxation of attitudes towards the west brought relief to the Yugoslav economy. Until then Yugoslavia, ostracised by both east and west, had found its trading patterns disrupted and its investment strategies shattered. For most Yugoslavs this had meant severe austerity.

The re-establishment of political relations with the west did not bring a return to capitalism. Tito was determined to preserve socialism in Yugoslavia but to give it a Yugoslav stamp. To that end the party was renamed the League of Communists of Yugoslavia (LCY) to differentiate it from the other east European parties. The collectivisation drive was also ended, though some limitations remained on the amount of land that an individual might own. Most important, however, was the prominence given to the workers' councils which were to be responsible for the running of enterprises. They also became part of the political structure, with one house of the bicameral local councils and then one chamber of the federal parliament being elected by the workers' councils. This made it possible for the Yugoslav ideologists, led by Kardelj, to argue that Yugoslav socialism had passed responsibility and power to the workers and was not therefore to be confused with state or police socialism of the Soviet or stalinist variety. Workers' self-management would create local, communal, working-class democracy, and would form the vehicle for evolution towards a classless society and eventually to communism.

The early 1950s was a period of relative stability in relations between the constituent ethnic groups of Yugoslavia, partly, no doubt, because of the need to hold together in face of the Cominform threat. The official doctrine of the party still upheld 'Yugoslavism' but there were extensive rights for each of the 'nations', or major ethnic groups, as well as for the 'nationalities' who formed the minorities to be found in all republics. Even Serbs and Croats found it possible to cooperate. In the Novi Sad agreement of 1954 the writers' unions of Serbia and Croatia expressed a willingness to cooperate in literary and linguistic questions; in many ways it was the high-point of good relations between the two peoples.

The strains and contradictions of early destalinisation

Under democratic centralism's hierarchical organisation instability and uncertainty at the top would cause destabilisation throughout the system. This was as true of the communist system as a whole as it was of any individual party. The death of Stalin on 5 March 1953 produced such dislocation in the Kremlin and therefore in all east European parties and states.

Stalin left no clear successor and his death initiated a long struggle for power in the Kremlin in which the first apparent victors were Gheorghi Malenkov and the secret police chief, Lavrenti Beria. They were the proponents of the so-called 'new course' which offered a more relaxed form of socialism with less emphasis on heavy industry and more on consumer goods, together with a reduction in the role of the police, the substitution of collective rule for 'the cult of personality' and, as a consequence of the latter, a separation of state and party, at least at the uppermost level.

Hints of an improvement in living standards sharpened consciousness of existing hardships whilst the more relaxed political atmosphere removed some of restraints against expressing dissatisfaction with those hardships. In May 1953 the tobacco workers in Plovdiv, traditionally one of the most reliable bastions of support for the BCP, came out on strike against high work norms and low wages. On Saturday 31 May the Czechoslovak government announced a currency reform which meant an instant and substantial rise in food prices and an effective 12 per cent cut in wages. Those most affected by what was described officially as a 'crushing blow against the former capitalists' were the workers in heavy industry who had done well out of the communist system and they reacted strongly. The political temperature rose as rapidly as the cost of living index and there were widespread demonstrations and strikes, the most serious being that by 20,000 workers in the Škoda plant at Plzeň who attacked portraits of Gottwald and Stalin and the Soviet flag. Only by enrolling the subservient trade unions could the party restore order. In Hungary in the following months there were similar outbreaks by workers in the Mátyás Rákosi steel works in Csepel and in factories in Odz and Diósgyör, as well as amongst the farmers of the great plain. It was, however, in the GDR that the troubles assumed their most serious aspect.

The East German rising of June 1953

In May 1952 Stalin, alarmed at Federal Germany's pending full integration into NATO, had approached the west with suggestions for the settlement of the German problem on the basis of unification and neutrality. After the west rejected this approach eastern Germany had to be built fully into the Soviet world; to achieve this it had to become as socialist as the rest of the bloc.

On 9–12 July 1952 the SED held its second conference at which it determined upon the 'systematic construction of socialism': more sectors of trade and industry would be taken into the people's ownership; more investment would be directed towards heavy industry and less to the consumer sector; more land would be collectivised; the five historic provinces would be abolished and replaced by fourteen districts with greatly reduced powers; and, ominously, the strength of the Vopos would be increased in order to cope with the intensification of the class struggle which the construction of socialism would bring. There were also the by now ritualistic attacks upon Tito and Gomułka.

The GDR was unique in the Soviet bloc in that the populace still had an effective vote, albeit one which had to be exercised with their feet rather than their pens. Small manufacturers whose workshops faced nationalisation, small traders whose livelihoods would disappear or be absorbed into a government agency, qualified people who feared that they would be able to exercise their profession only through the goodwill of local party agencies, and independent farmers whose land would be collectivised, all joined the politically disaffected in seeking refuge in the west, usually via Berlin. And despite the fact that, from the middle of 1952, the GDR régime placed more and more obstacles in the way of those of its citizens who wished to cross into west Berlin, the number doing so rose from an average of 60,000 per annum in 1949–51 to 129,000 in 1952 and 297,000 in 1953. The exodus intensified existing shortages of goods and services, whilst in agriculture the situation was approaching crisis point. Many farmers had left and most of those who remained were disinclined to do more than produce for their own needs because fixed procurement prices meant little profit, and conspicuous production invited hasty inclusion in a collective or state farm.

In April 1953 the East German authorities turned to Moscow for help, suggesting that they be allowed to end compulsory deliveries for farmers, and that the economic situation would be further eased if the Soviet Union renounced the war debt payments it was exacting from the GDR. The request from the East Germans came at a time when the new course had just been formulated. The response from Moscow was hardly what party leader Walter Ulbricht and his associates could have expected; they were told that they should back-pedal on socialism and introduce their own new course. There were also indications that the new Kremlin had not forgotten Stalin's ideas for a unified but neutral Germany. This caused divisions in the east German leadership, with the proposed shift of direction being resisted by Ulbricht and being supported primarily by Rudolf Herrnstadt, the editor of the party newspaper, *Neues Deutschland*, and by the head of state security, Wilhelm Zaisser.

On 9 June it seemed that the reformist faction had prevailed. The party admitted to 'aberrations in the past' and announced that in future there would be less concentration of investment in heavy industry, and that there would be less pressure on the churches, less interference in cultural matters, fewer restrictions on inter-German trade and traffic, and a diminution of the class struggle. There were also decreases in delivery quotas for farmers and in general taxation levels, and some private enterprises would be allowed to take out state loans. *Neues Deutschland* justified the changes on the grounds that they would further the cause of German unification. The SED, it seemed, was to become an all national party, and because it was to be an all nation party it could not be a one class party; if it were to have any chance of performing well in a future all-German election it would have to attract some votes from the bourgeoisie.

The 9 June declaration, however, did not announce the abolition of a 10 per cent increase in work norms which had been promulgated in May. The leadership could not swallow so obvious a reversal of policy and on 16 June the trade union newspaper, *Tribüne*, confirmed that the increases were to stay and to have immediate effect. Many workers were enraged; with essential supplies frequently unobtainable, the increased norms meant more work for no increase in the standard of living: the increased norms were in effect a pay cut. Angry building workers on the huge construction sites on the Stalinallee took to the streets; they were joined by others in a march to the trade union headquarters where no one would speak to them. At 2 p.m. a government spokesman conceded that the increases in norms would be withdrawn but by then the demonstrators' demands had escalated and become political. They now wanted the resignation of the government and free elections, threatening a general strike if these were not granted.

At the end of the working day most of the demonstrators went home but news of the strike spread throughout the country, not least because so many east Germans listened to news bulletins from western radio stations, though these stations were careful not to advise extreme action.

On 17 June east Germany was in ferment. Strikes were recorded in 317 locations and they involved approximately 400,000 workers. They were spread throughout the GDR but were particularly strong in former citadels of the pre-1933 German Social Democratic Party such as Magdeburg, Halle, Merseberg, and Bitterfeld. The strikes were remarkably similar in style and content. They were overwhelmingly working class events and they were mostly led by local trade union officials; few if any intellectuals involved themselves and there was reluctance even on the part of the technical élite in the factories. The strikers generally spent the morning in meetings where they elected strike committees, which in turn organised orderly marches into the nearby town centre. It was here that the traditional German working class discipline was diluted by the admixture of other elements, which prompted the looting, the arson, and the random attacks on party officials which then took place. The chief objectives of the arsonists were party buildings, though some prisons were also attacked and their inmates released. In Berlin the red flag was torn from atop the Brandenburg gate and Ulbricht thought it wise to leave town.

That the increases in work norms should be rescinded remained on the strikers' agenda, but the list of political demands had lengthened since the previous day. Added to the calls for the resignation of the government and for free elections was one for the disbanding of the army; in a parody of Goering's famous phrase there were slogans reading, 'Wir wollen keine Volksarmee; wir wollen Butter' (We don't want a national army; we want butter). There were also a few calls for German reunification but this did not play a prominent part in what remained overwhelmingly a working class and socialist outburst: Bonn was attacked as much as Berlin, and when protesters invaded SED headquarters in Leipzig they burned every portrait they found except that of Marx.

The Soviet response was surprisingly restrained. The first priority was the restoration of order but on 16 June the Soviets had refused to allow the east Berlin police chief freedom of action. During the night some important buildings in the major towns were taken over by Red Army soldiers and at noon on 17 June a state of emergency was declared. Action began some hours later when the tanks rolled on to the streets but even then it was less an immediate onslaught on the strikers than a gradual pressure against them. But bloodshed could not be avoided. Twenty-one deaths were officially acknowledged, with the real figure probably being in the region of 3,000. There were also forty executions and some 20,000 arrests.

The most prominent casualty of the events of 17 June was not in Berlin but in Moscow where Beria was arrested on 26 June. His new course was too dangerous for use in Germany. This had always been Ulbricht's view, and it was he who profited from the uprising which gave him the chance to remove the 'Herrnstadt-Zaisser faction' from the party leadership. There was also a purge of the party administration in which one-third of the central committee, two-thirds of the regional officials, and almost three-quarters of trade union officers were dismissed. In April 1954, at its fourth congress, the SED reaffirmed most of the 1952 decisions in muted form but the 10 per cent increase in work norms was dropped and there was no more braggadocio on the systematic construction of socialism. Instead the GDR would outpace the Federal Republic in the production of consumer goods and achieve a higher standard of living. To help it in this endeavour the Soviet Union, in August 1953, had renounced reparations, cancelled war debts, decreased the occupation costs it charged to the east Germans, transferred to German control enterprises on German soil which were under Soviet supervision, promised the delivery of various commodities from the Soviet Union, advanced a loan of 485 million roubles, and agreed to the establishing of full diplomatic representation at ambassadorial level between the USSR and the GDR.

These concessions, and more especially the last, underlined the fact that the post-Beria Kremlin would no longer treat the GDR as a *Handelsobjekt*, a counter in its diplomatic tradings with the west. East Germany was now a full partner, considered worthy of being built up into a strong, socialist state. It was, it seemed at the time and for many years after, the end of any realistic hope of German reunification, and for that reason the Federal Republic nominated 17 June as a public holiday in the name of German unity. The scathing experience of 17 June, the first time that Soviet tanks had shown their might in the containment of public unrest in eastern Europe, also meant that when much of the region was convulsed in 1956 the GDR remained tranquil.

From Berlin to Budapest: Eastern Europe 1953–6

In the long run the events of 1953 strengthened the authoritarian nature of communist party rule. The experimentation in relaxation which the new course represented had produced destabilisation, which could only make more difficult the tasks facing subsequent would-be reformers. In the short term, however, the east German storm was ridden with apparent ease.

After the death of Stalin the east European leaders were expected to follow and replicate changes in Moscow. No one did so more assiduously than the Czechoslovak party boss, Klement Gottwald. Although by no means always the most conspicuous of stalinists, he redeemed all past shortcomings by following Stalin in his very last act, dying on 14 March to be succeeded by a troika of Antonín Zápotocký, Antonín Novotný, and Viliam Široký. Such sacrifice was not expected of all leaders, but all were required to espouse the new course. Hungary did so in June, Romania in August, Bulgaria and Czechoslovakia in

September, and Poland in October. In some cases, however, commitment to the new course was minimal, being little more than lip-service to the new canons preached in the Kremlin. In this there was more than a modicum of wisdom because the power constellation in Moscow was not yet securely established. In June 1953 Beria had been arrested and in January 1955 Malenkov, who until then had seemed to be the dominant figure, was pushed aside by the new top dog, Nikita Khrushchev.

The issue which Khrushchev used to defeat Malenkov was that of investment policy, Khrushchev favouring a move closer to the old orthodoxy of concentration on heavy industry. The dislocation which this switch of policy caused was easily absorbed in Czechoslovakia and the GDR, where industry was sufficiently developed to be able to cope with the change, and it made little difference in Albania, Bulgaria, and Romania, where industry was not developed enough to be much affected. In Poland and Hungary, which were mid-way through the transition to reconstruction or industrialisation, the effects were more disruptive.

Khrushchev's switch back towards more traditional, stalinist economics was balanced by a move towards political relaxation. He urged each socialist state and party to be more independent, and sought to retain the cohesion of the socialist bloc through regulated economic, military, and ideological agreements; it was in the mid-1950s that Comecon began to assume a real role in the economic life of eastern Europe, and it was in 1955 that the WTO was established.

Khrushchev was attempting to grasp the nettle of destalinisation, a necessary process if eastern Europe were to be revivified and the socialist states to make any real economic and political progress. But so strong had been the bonds of stalinism that their loosening inevitably caused instability in the ruling parties; in Poland these instabilities spilled over into serious disturbances, whilst in Hungary they brought outright revolution.

Khrushchev's desire was to equip the east European parties with leaders who were popular in the party and the nation. This would inevitably mean having figures who were more in tune with national feelings and who would include national interests in the equation when determining policy. This would in turn imply that the Yugoslav communists had had a point, and it would therefore demand a relaxation of the ideological war against Tito and titoism.

Quiet overtures had gone out from the Kremlin to Belgrade when Stalin was still warm in his grave and these led in June 1955 to a rumbustious visit to the Yugoslav capital by Khrushchev and Bulganin, the Soviet prime minister. In one of the few moments when the alcoholic haze had cleared, the Belgrade declaration of 2 June was pronounced. It pledged the two governments to observe 'mutual respect and non-interference in one another's internal affairs'. This was by no means the end of differences between Moscow and Belgrade, not least because Khrushchev believed that, once the Kremlin had in effect admitted that it was wrong in 1948, the Yugoslavs would change their stance and accept Moscow's line for the good of the socialist bloc which, Khrushchev genuinely believed, was threatened by western imperialism.

This virtual rehabilitation of Tito may have had a limited effect in Moscow and Belgrade, but its impact on the other east European capitals and parties was explosive. The parties concerned had torn themselves apart, had sacrificed many of their best leaders, had savaged their cadres, and had hobbled their economies in order to extirpate the evils of titoism. It is not going too far to say that for most of the east European régimes anti-titoism was their legitimising factor; it was the chief justification for the methods they had used to maintain their authority against their own nations and their own parties. Now they were being told that Tito was a good boy after all; if what remained of the faith of the rank and file of the parties had been tested by the return of the prisoners, the already disturbed confidence of the leaders was devastated by the reconciliation between Moscow and Belgrade.

Hardly had this shock been administered when Khrushchev delivered another. In his second speech to the twentieth congress of the CPSU in February 1956 he dwelt upon Stalin's 'mistakes' which were said to have included the unjust persecution of 'honest comrades'. There must, said Khrushchev, be an end to the cult of personality and a return to socialist legality. This was necessary for the global strategy which Khrushchev unfolded. Atomic weapons and a general advance in civilisation had made redundant Zhdanov's notion of inevitable conflict – Cominform was to be abolished in April 1956 – and the contest between socialism and imperialism would henceforth be fought out under the conditions of 'peaceful coexistence'. Peaceful coexistence meant political competition, not least for the allegiance of the peoples now beginning to emerge from colonialism. In this competition the communists would have to cooperate with other parties of the left; it was back to the Popular Front, with the road to socialism lying through elections and parliamentary coalitions. For this the communists would have to be *Koalitionsfähig*, worthy of inclusion in a coalition, and to achieve this they would have to adapt their policies and attitudes to local conditions. Were African or Asian statesmen to look to eastern Europe the picture would not be very encouraging and it therefore followed that the east European parties would have to change and make themselves more responsive to local, national conditions.

Not only was Tito himself to be rehabilitated but also those who had previously reviled him were to be required to follow his example. Stalinism had demanded anti-titoism at home and complete subservience to Moscow in foreign policy; now the second requirement was to insist on the abandonment of the first. Here, for the committed, was the inner contradiction of destalinisation: the wildly unpopular stalinist régimes of eastern Europe, whose very existence was predicated upon their obedience to the Moscow which had created them, were to be forced to destalinise by Moscow itself; the intensely unpopular obedience to Moscow was to bring about the intensely popular policy of destalinisation. But if the new Kremlin policies were disorienting to the remaining believers they were welcomed by the vast majority of the population, both within and without the party.

The excitements of the mid-1950s were preparing a powerful mix which in 1956 was to boil over into a revolt which was in origin one *within* rather than *against* the party. The mix had five ingredients. The first was the disorientation of the parties, both leaders and led, which was common to all countries of the imperium. The four others were a dissatisfied intelligentsia; a working class and peasantry disgruntled by declining living standards; an alternative party leadership waiting in the wings; and a nationalism burning with resentment at Soviet domination and fuelled by a deep-seated anti-russianism. Of the last four factors none was to be discerned in Albania; in Bulgaria the first and second could be found, although intellectuals, workers, and peasants were all kept on a tight rein; Czechoslovakia had its dissatisfied intelligentsia and momentary working class discontent in 1953; the GDR was in a similar position, added to which its population was more anti-Russian than that in Czechoslovakia; Romania could compete with all-comers in anti-russianism but, apart from that, had only a diluted form of peasant and working class discontent. Only in Hungary and Poland were all four factors to be found. Both parties had heard Khrushchev redress wrongs done to their forebears, as he rehabilitated Béla Kun and admitted that Stalin's liquidation of the Polish Communist Party in 1938 had been based on false evidence. Of the two countries Hungary had suffered more in the recent past. Its leadership had taken part, with relish it seemed to many, in the vilification of Tito, and the purges there had far outstripped those in Poland in intensity, extent, and bestiality. Hungary also had borders with Yugoslavia and with Austria which in 1955 had become neutral and had seen the departure of all occupying troops, including those of the Red Army; inevitably this was seen by many Hungarians as a model for their own future. In contrast to this, all of Poland's land borders were with other socialist states. Poland was also forced into reliance on the Soviet Union for defence of its western border which the FRG had not yet recognised. Hungary, on the other hand, had twice allied with Germany and had an historical affinity with a country which had enabled it to wrest such favourable terms from Vienna in 1867.

THE UPHEAVALS OF 1956: POLAND

The origins of the 'Polish October'

Amongst the long term causes of the 'Polish October' of 1956 national resentment ranks amongst the most important. After the communist takeover memories of the lost territories to the east, of the Warsaw uprising, and above all of Katyn, were ever-present but never mentioned publicly. National sentiments were further offended by the very public presence of Soviet and Russian influences in all aspects of national life; the minister of war, Rokossovsky, spoke very poor Polish and made a vain attempt to persuade the Poles to alter their form of address and drop the courtly, but hardly comradely, 'pan' (sir) for 'wy' which sounded more Russian.

Economic hardship was a further long term contributory factor. Immediately after the war few had expected to see consumer goods in abundance and austerity was tolerable whilst the country's basic infrastructure was recreated; for such causes privation was comprehensible and acceptable. Yet in the early 1950s conditions were becoming worse rather than better; in 1951 food rationing was introduced, there were price increases in 1953, and by 1955 real earnings were 36 per cent below their 1949 levels. The Poles were told that these continuing sacrifices were for the sake of constructing socialism or staving off rapacious imperialism, and that in any case workers in the west were much worse off; this the Poles seldom believed, not least because so many of them had relatives in the west with whom, particularly after political relaxation in 1953, they could correspond or visit.

To an increasing degree in the first half of the 1950s Poland's intelligentsia began to sense and then to articulate the deepening national mood of frustration and anger. The faith with which the new régime had been welcomed by many was beginning to weaken as the promises held out by Moscow, of cooperating to build a new world based on proletarian justice and equality, wore ever thinner. By the summer of 1956 the intelligentsia was primed for full discussion of new ideas, many of which sought not the rejection but the perfection of socialism, but of socialism with a Polish face. These ideas were thoroughly explored in discussion groups such as the national centre for intellectual cooperation, *Krzywe Kolo* (Crooked Circle), and the centre of clubs for young intellectuals.

The youth in particular had been excited by the post-1953 relaxation of censorship which allowed the publication of Adam Ważyk's poem, *Poemat dla Dorosłych* (Poem for Adults), and of western writers such as Hemingway and Faulkner. By 1955 a questioning of the established order was already apparent in the popularity of blue jeans, jazz, and a witty, satirical student theatre movement. The authorities did not react, indeed they encouraged openness and diversity so as to impress the delegates to the world youth festival which convened in Warsaw in 1955. Many of the ideas of this younger and less inhibited generation found their way into *Po Prostu* (Frankly Speaking), the weekly journal which was to play an influential role in the fermentation of the 1956 crisis.

Whilst social forces became more vocal and critical, Poland's political masters became less and less secure. They had dutifully adopted the new course but in 1954 they were seriously embarrassed by the defection of Józef Światło. A former operative in the state security system, Światło not only escaped to the west but also proceeded to spill his multifarious beans in propaganda broadcasts beamed to Poland; even worse, he hinted that Gomułka would make a better leader for the country. His broadcasts did much to undermine any thoughts that the new course had brought back real freedom or full national sovereignty to Poland.

Insecurity was worse confounded by Khrushchev's speech to the twentieth congress, which triggered anti-Soviet demonstrations in Warsaw. It was all too much for the party leader, Bierut. He died in February, and there were rumours that he had committed suicide. He was succeeded by Edvard Ochab.

The new Polish leadership now took the destalinising thrusts of Khrushchev's speech to considerable lengths. The sejm was encouraged to be more independent, as a result of which Catholic deputies voted against an abortion bill and, in a tilt at the party's leading role, demanded the setting up of a Catholic youth organisation. In April an amnesty was declared which emptied the detention camps of 30–40,000 persons, many of them ex-AK men; Ochab admitted that releasing these prisoners was a risk.

The Soviets were now beginning to become concerned at the speed of Poland's destalinisation. What most angered them was the fate of Khrushchev's speech in Poland. The speech had never been published in the Soviet Union, though it was circulated to party organisations. In Poland the procedure was similar but three of the copies made for members of the central committee went missing; the Poles also arranged officially for the printing of 3,000 copies, though unofficially the printers were told to run off five times that number and no doubt in reality printed even more. Within days the text had reached western newspapers and was on sale on the Polish blackmarket. The Kremlin was furious. The Polish leadership had lost the confidence of the Soviet comrades as well as that of the majority of the Polish people. The Kremlin was not convinced that the Poles could manage the social crisis which seemed imminent.

From Poznań to Warsaw, July to September 1956

The dam broke in Poznań. Workers at the Stalin, formerly the Ciegelski railway shops, who were renowned for their reliability and stability, had been suffering declining real wages because of increases in taxes and work norms. On 28 June 1956 they struck and marched into town with banners demanding 'Bread and Freedom', the release of cardinal Wyszyński, and 'Russians Go Home'; the social, political, and national character of the Polish revolt had been explicitly stated at its very outset. The march was an orderly affair – there was even a loudspeaker van telling the marchers not to walk on the grass – but, once in the town, events escaped the control of the march's organisers and the local police alike. The marchers became convinced that they had been betrayed and that some of their number who had been negotiating with the local authorities had been arrested. The crowd attacked the prison and shooting broke out. Over fifty marchers were killed. Poles had killed Poles. Although this had happened in the past many Poles nevertheless regarded such a tragedy as unthinkable; Poles, they felt, could not kill Poles and therefore it could only mean that those wielding the guns were working for a foreign power and not for Poland. The national aspect of the revolt had assumed a higher profile than the social or the political.

The party, like the nation, was thrown into a deep state of shock. The seventh plenum, which met in July, rushed through further concessions, but they were made as much from fear and shame as from conviction. There was to be more decentralisation in industry and less investment in its heavy sector, wages were to be increased, collectivisation was to be slowed down, the party bureaucracy was to be slimmed and the size of the nomenklatura trimmed, AK men were no longer to be discriminated against, and Gomułka's exclusion from the party was ended. He was readmitted in August. The respite gained by these concessions was short-lived. In September workers at the Zerań car factory near Warsaw, acting on the advice of the *Po Prostu* group, began forming workers' councils. The example spread and it was a severe threat to the régime in that it endangered the party's leading role and could all too easily lead to horizontal affiliations. More immediately, however, the councils were demanding that Gomułka be readmitted not only to the party but also to its leadership.

The October crisis

This question dominated the eighth central committee plenum which was to meet on 19 October. The Soviets, with one eye on Poland and the other on Hungary, were so frightened that Khrushchev asked for the plenum to be postponed. Ochab refused, as a result of which beleaguered stalinists in the Polish party apparatus staged an abortive *putsch* aimed at keeping Gomułka and his supporters away from the meeting. Gomułka attended. So too did Khrushchev and some of his colleagues who had arrived uninvited and unannounced that morning. Khrushchev seemed in no mood for compromise in his view that Gomułka should be kept out of office, lecturing his Polish colleagues even on the airport tarmac, and scoffing when Ochab asked what would be the CPSU's reaction if the Polish party attempted to give it advice as to whom it should include in its ruling bodies. To back his bluster Khrushchev had sanctioned the movement of Soviet troops towards Warsaw and Soviet ships sailed into Gdańsk. In response the Poles also put their forces on alert. After tense debate and secret consultation with the Chinese, Khrushchev accepted the Polish argument that the readmission of Gomułka would strengthen rather than weaken socialism in Poland, and would not affect the country's links with the Warsaw Pact. Gomułka was therefore re-elected as party leader on 21 October.

Three days after his appointment Gomułka addressed a huge crowd in the centre of Warsaw. Events in Hungary had by this time raised anti-Soviet feelings to a fever pitch but Gomułka's fears that there would be anti-Soviet disorders in Poland were unfounded. There was, however, still a strong demand for the release of cardinal Wyszyński. To this Gomułka acceded on 28 October, and there were further concessions to the church with the release of other clerics and with the ending of government control over ecclesiastical appointments. Poland's corner had been turned – just. There were anti-Soviet outbursts early in November when the Hungarian tragedy was at its most intense but enough concessions had been made to Polish nationalism to enable Gomułka to contain the wave of anti-russianism. On 14 November he and his prime minister, Cyrankiewicz, went to Moscow to sign a new agreement with the Soviets. The latter promised that they would not interfere in Poland's internal affairs and agreed to more favourable trading terms for Poland, and to the recall of Soviet advisers, including the despised Rokossovsky.

The Polish October had shown what a nationalist communist régime could achieve without stepping outside the WTO security system or the Comecon trading bloc. Gomułka had been restrained by his conviction that Poland needed Soviet protection, the more so as the FRG had still not recognised the Oder-Neisse line; he was further restrained by the fear that any further adventurism would lead to a Soviet occupation, a fear soon to be confirmed by events in Hungary. He was also guided by his communist convictions, believing that mild revisionism was preferable to the only apparent alternative: an all out attack on the party. For the Polish people too the fear of Soviet intervention was a powerful restraining factor, and one which was stressed by the church as well as by the party. That the Polish nation did not take its dislike of communism and the Russians any further in 1956 was also due to the fact that, despite the enormous social influence of the church, there was no other organised political force in the country beyond the PUWP. Throughout 1956 in Poland the main struggle, apart from the demand for the relaxation of restrictions on the church and the clergy, was for rather than against the party. The ideas formulated by the intelligentsia were mostly born inside the party and were for the reformation of the party, not for its replacement. And, since the church refused to see itself as a political factor, the working class, whose discontent put a match to the fire, had no leaders and no organisations outside the party.

The gains that were made by the Poles in 1956 seemed impressive, but many of them were soon eroded. The workers' councils remained but they rapidly fell under the domination of the party establishment and lost their vitality; wage increases were negated by inflation; the economy was not rejuvenated; most of the freedom gained in the cultural sphere had largely disappeared by the early 1960s; and Gomułka himself became more authoritarian. On the other hand, in two fundamental ways Poland had been changed and was henceforth even more distinct from the other states of eastern Europe. The Polish party never again undertook a serious offensive against the Roman Catholic church whose intellectuals, particularly those associated with the Cracow journal Znak (Sign), enjoyed a freedom which was unparalleled in eastern Europe. Even if the church determinedly avoided presenting itself as an alternative political organisation, it did provide an alternative ideological refuge and it broke the PUWP's monopoly in non-political areas such as culture and education; Poland alone in eastern Europe had a Catholic university. The second fundamental change was that collectivisation was never reintroduced. The Polish party permitted the survival of the petty bourgeoisie in the countryside.

THE UPHEAVALS OF 1956: HUNGARY

The origins of the Hungarian revolution

The causes which brought about the Hungarian revolution of 1956 were similar to those which produced the crisis in Poland: an affronted nationalism; an economy in which all effort was directed towards infrastructure and heavy industry with little thought for the consumer; a challenging intelligentsia; and a ruling party which was more and more divided and disoriented at all levels. In Hungary it is also possible to detect a process of frustrated or aborted relaxation, a phenomenon which satisfied few and infuriated many.

The sense of affronted nationalism underlay everything. Each and every discontent and discomfort the Hungarians, usually with justice, ascribed to the Russians and to the system which they had imposed on the country. Furthermore, many of the key events leading to the revolution of 1956 drip with historical symbolism, especially that of 1848–9 when Poles helped Hungarians in their valiant but vain fight against a Russian army sent to suppress Hungarian national liberties. Just as the Poles smarted at the presence and prominence of Rokossovsky, so the Hungarians bitterly resented the fact that their soldiers had to wear the red star rather than the Kossuth coat of arms in their caps, and that their uniforms were not of the traditional Hungarian pattern but Soviet-style with the tunic worn outside the trousers, which to the Hungarians was ever the mark of an unsophisticated Balkan peasant. The brusque, coarse, and arrogant demeanour of top party officials was seen as a legacy of their Moscow days and was felt to be demeaning as well as offensive in a society where 'polished courtesy and smooth manners had been the rule'.[1]

The increasing drabness of life and the dearth of consumer goods, including foodstuffs, was the result of new economic policies and attitudes. And as more information became available after 1953 the extent of the devastation of the economy became ever clearer. Trading patterns had been skewed to favour the Soviet Union; Hungarians were outraged to learn after 1953 that the 'bauxite' from near Pécs, all of which went to the Soviet Union, was in fact uranium which would have fetched high prices on the world market. Industrialisation had been launched according to the Soviet pattern and work practices, too, followed those pioneered in the USSR. Compulsory deliveries at fixed prices and then collectivisation drove many peasants from the land. For those independent farmers who remained conditions deteriorated rapidly. After delivery quotas had been met there was little grain left for household use and it had to be purchased on the black market where prices were three or four times higher than for the grain that the household had been legally required to sell to the state purchasing agency. Party zealots in agriculture insisted on the introduction of Soviet-style machinery and crops which were frequently unsuitable: the heavy ploughs, for example, damaged the humus in the sub-soil; Soviet animal strains did not always combine well with local ones; and crops such as cotton, a particular favourite of Khrushchev's, did not thrive in Hungary. The results were often tragic and at times farcical. The state fruit purchasing agency, Gyümert, purchased good quality apples at a fixed price and then sent them for export or to privileged consumers; the only apples that found their way on to the domestic market were poor quality, but here the shortages were so great that even these apples fetched five times more than the good ones sold under fixed prices. The result was that the growers did all they could to produce poor quality apples from which they would make much greater profits than from the good quality apples they would have had to sell to Gyümert. And as the productivity of Hungarian agriculture declined under the assault of socialism, so the socialist authorities, following Moscow's orders, insisted that more food be sent abroad either to earn hard currency or, in 1953, to make good the damage the threat of socialism had caused in the GDR.

Whilst life for most Hungarians became more difficult and less rewarding, two factors grated ceaselessly on their already frayed nerves, at least until 1953. The first was that everyone was convinced that the evils of the day could be laid at the Russians' door; the second was that no one could say so with impunity. If they spoke out they would in all probability fall into the hands of the AVH, whose ubiquitous operatives, the public soon learned to its horror, were paid anything up to sixteen times the average worker's wage.

To this general social unrest the new Soviet leadership now added uncertainty at the apex of the political system. Hungarian party leader and head of government, Mátyás Rákosi, had been one of Stalin's most faithful pupils. After Stalin's death he was summoned to the Kremlin, told that he had ruined Hungarian agriculture by collectivising too rapidly, and that, in conformity with the new ideas now prevailing, he must relinquish one of his two top positions. He chose to remain party leader and he agreed that the prime ministership should go to Imre Nagy.

Nagy was an identikit version of new course man. His communist faith seemed above reproach; he spoke excellent Russian, and had been in Moscow during the war. But if he was by this definition a 'Moscow communist' he was by no means a stalinist. He had questioned the pace of industrialisation and collectivisation and he had not been associated with the purges of 1949–53. He appeared to be more a philosopher than a fighter and he was thoroughly disliked by Rákosi and his stalinist entourage. Furthermore, he was a gentile and not a Jew, a fact which counted both in the Kremlin and in Hungary; Rákosi and a number of his closest colleagues, especially in the uppermost echelons of the AVH, were Jewish.

The changes impending in Hungary were outlined in a central committee plenum at the end of June 1953. Two of the worst practitioners of terror, József Révai and Mihály Farkas, were sacked as Hungary moved into what Nagy described as a new stage of socialism. This promised both greater personal liberty and a more consumer-oriented economy. Law and order were to be restored in the party and in the country, political prisoners were to be released, party members who had been wrongfully convicted were to be rehabilitated, and there was to be no further government or party interference in religion. In the economic sphere the ambitious industrialisation programme would be abandoned and future industrial strategy would pay much more attention to light industry and the consumer; there was also to be considerable relaxation in the countryside where pressures towards further collectivisation were to be lessened. Nagy also promised better food supplies to the non-privileged consumer. The latter promise was carried out immediately and within days the shops were full of items such as pork and butter which had until then been extremely scarce.

The Rákosi versus Nagy duel, 1953–6

Hungary had taken a massive stride away from the hard-line policies of Rákosi, but the move had not been as complete as originally planned. It had been intended that the June plenum of 1953 should include a public denunciation of stalinism in general and of its Hungarian form in particular, but events in Berlin had questioned the advisability of being so out-spoken, and on the second day of the plenum came news of Beria's arrest; with the political atmosphere in Moscow unclear, Nagy and his allies had to tread with greater circumspection. He therefore dropped his plans to announce a judicial guarantee of civil rights and the setting up of a constitutional court. Also, in August, he had to accept the return of Mihály Farkas to the central committee secretariat. This was not to be the last time that Hungary's progress towards liberalisation had been interrupted or even reversed.

Such developments encouraged Rákosi; a deadly duel between himself and Nagy had begun. In January 1954 Rákosi was again called to Moscow, this time to be ordered to end his opposition to the new course. Knowing that he had considerable support amongst the upper ranks of the party he was not disposed to give up the fight against Nagy and he therefore changed tactics, concentrating his attack upon Nagy's economic policies where the prime minister was vulnerable to charges of creating inflation and unemployment.

Nagy, knowing his support lay in the lower echelons of the party and in the public at large, courted these elements with price cuts, increases in food supplies, and concessions which allowed workers to use state machinery for private work after hours. Nagy also sought to create a new political power base in which these elements would be represented; Nagy was attempting to turn the body of the party and the nation against Rákosi. The third congress of the Hungarian Workers' Party (HWP) was due to meet in May 1954 and shortly before then Nagy tried to revive the moribund Independent People's Front under the name of the Patriotic People's Front (PPF). Nagy wanted bodies such as DISz, the youth organisation, to be involved, but he also wanted individual membership, that is private citizens joining without having to belong to any of the corporate institutions affiliated to the PPF; in this way Nagy could capitalise on his support amongst the general, non-party public. He also wanted the PPF to be led by a prominent figure from one of the pre-1949 non-communist parties, and he approached, unsuccessfully, both Béla Kovács of the Smallholders Party and Anna Kéthly of the social democrats. In outlining his plans for the PPF Nagy made no mention of the leading role of the party. His aim of having the PPF functioning before the May congress failed but the organisation, which he called 'the conscience of the nation', was brought back to life in October 1954.

The May 1954 congress saw a skirmish between Nagy and Rákosi, with the former emphasising the new course and the dangers which arise when the party interferes too closely in the day-to-day running of state and public concerns. Rákosi flexed his muscles over the problems of inflation and the decline in economic production. Those issues were much more fiercely debated in December 1954 at a central committee plenum which saw virtually open warfare between the Nagy and Rákosi camps.

The economic problems arising from the new course were to provide the excuse for Nagy's removal. Nagy's economic management did, by marxist-leninist standards, leave much to be desired, but the real reason for his fall was that his Moscow patron, Malenkov, had lost out in a power struggle with Khrushchev. Nagy was told that he had beggared the Hungarian economy; he was then removed from the premiership, which went to a Rákosiite stooge, András Hegedüs. Nagy was later to be removed from the politburo, from the PPF, and from the party. He then became seriously ill, a fact which Rákosi exploited to the full. Unlike Malenkov, however, Nagy refused to recant and admit his mistakes. Had he done so he would have lost the confidence of the public; because he did not do so he remained a credible alternative leader who was kept out of office only because of the machinations of the Soviets and their semi-stalinist sycophants in Hungary. He had become Hungary's Gomułka.

The fall of Nagy meant that Hungary's progress to destalinisation had once more been interrupted and frustrated. Rákosi, despite warnings from Moscow that there was to be no return to his previous practices, increased restrictions on the media, limited cultural freedoms, and slowed down the release of political prisoners.

Yet Rákosi was swimming against the tide. His ultimate power base had always been his mastery of the secret police but Moscow would not allow a return to full police control and the chief of the AVH, Gábor Péter, had been arrested; even more damaging to Rákosi was the fact that the secret police networks of eastern Europe had been disrupted by the removal of Beria.

Other developments further weakened Rákosi's hold in 1955. In April the Bandung conference on colonialism endorsed five principles: national independence; sovereignty; equality; non-interference in internal affairs; and self-determination. A few months later the Soviet Union pledged itself to observe these five principles. The more cynical of observers might have considered this ironical, but in May the signature of the Austrian state treaty seemed to indicate that Soviet policy did recognise such notions, and in June the Belgrade declaration seemed proof of a change in Soviet attitudes towards other communist régimes.

By mid-1955 there was also a greater degree of interchange between Hungary and the west, especially Austria, than at any time since at least 1949, and what Hungarians learned of conditions in the west intensified the anger and frustration they felt with their own lot.

Rákosi was in an increasingly enfeebled position. Sensing this, he again attempted to tighten police controls but at the same time handed out some concessions in the arts or other supposedly neutral areas. This tactic failed entirely. The attempted repressions increased public discontents without containing them, and the concessions were interpreted, correctly, as a sign of weakness. And, unlike during the years of stalinism, the Hungarians had now had the experience of the Nagy premiership to show them that HWP rule did not have to be 'concentration camp communism'. As a young refugee from the 1956 revolution explained:

> People say we live behind the Iron Curtain. . . . This is not quite true. We lived in a tin. As long as a tin is hermetically closed, it's all right. But then during Imre Nagy's first premiership they pierced the tin and let in a little bit of fresh air. You know what happens to a tin when a little fresh air gets into it? . . . Everything inside gets rotten.[2]

The Kremlin vainly suggested to Rákosi that he resign and retire to the Soviet Union.

Nagy, whilst excluded from political power, was himself undergoing ideological change. He had found the switch from stalinism to the new course easy but now he underwent the more exacting transformation to full-blooded national communism of the titoist variety. In a long essay which he was secretly preparing, and which was later published as *On Communism*, he made little mention of the dictatorship of the proletariat and when dealing with the Yugoslav question dwelt on the peaceful coexistence of the two systems within socialism; that other parties could not enjoy such peaceful coexistence was due to one factor only: Soviet domination. Not only was Nagy now generally seen as a potential Gomuł- ka but he himself seemed to be willing to play that role.

The fall of Rákosi, summer 1956

In 1955 Nagy had lost power but not legitimacy. In 1956 Rákosi lost both. As elsewhere in eastern Europe Khrushchev's speech had a profound effect in Hungary. It did not receive such wide circulation as in Poland but reports of it were gleaned from western broadcasts and Magyar texts were sent into Hungary in balloons launched from the west. Soviet criticism of Stalin's mistakes inevitably reflected on Rákosi and increased popular support for Nagy. In early 1956 a further factor also sapped Rákosi's legitimacy. Tito took advantage of his better relations with Moscow to humiliate Rákosi, one manifestation of this being the eighty-five million dollars which Tito extracted from Hungary in compensation for breach of contract after 1948. Tito then added insult to injury when he travelled to Moscow via Romania rather than taking the direct route which would mean having to set foot in Rákosi's Hungary. In Moscow Tito persuaded Khrushchev to send a communist party mission to investigate the situation in Hungary. It was one of Rákosi's fatal miscalculations in 1956 to underestimate the influence Tito wielded in Moscow.

Rákosi could not help but sense the dangers accumulating around him. He attempted to buy support with some concessions to national feeling, including giving permission for the performance of a new composition by Zoltán Kodály. This was always a special occasion in Hungarian musical life but this time it was even more so because the work was based on the seventeenth century appeal of count Zrinyi with its great refrain, 'Leave the Magyars alone'. But Rákosi, having made this concession, lost any credit that he might have gained by not allowing any further national broadcasts of the piece.

In what Rákosi had seen as a minor concession in March 1956 he had allowed the formation within DISz of a debating club, the Petöfi circle, named after a nineteenth century poet and nationalist who had died fighting the Russians in 1849. By the summer the Petöfi circle had become in effect an alternative, non-legislating parliament, discussing with much more openness than would ever be allowed to a communist assembly all the major issues of the day, and attracting audiences of as many as 6,000; it was 'The intellectual prelude of the revolution'.[3]

A concession which made an immediate impact was the rehabilitation of Rajk, announced on 28 March. Rákosi had justified the purges and the repression which followed them on the grounds of Rajk's guilt; now to admit his innocence destroyed Rákosi's legitimacy. The rehabilitation speech had been subdued and had been delivered in Eger, a small provincial city, but it had an instantaneous nationwide effect. On the following day the writers' union denounced Rákosi as a 'Judas' and a few days later, when he appeared at a party meeting in a working-class district of the capital, a young teacher, György Litvan, boldly walked on to the podium and told him that he had lost the confidence of the people and should retire.

Rákosi attempted to retrieve some standing by dismantling the elaborate defences along the border with Austria and by admitting he had himself made mistakes during the period of the cult of personality. It did him little good. Popular opinion was flowing ever more strongly in Nagy's direction, as was shown on 19 June when his sixtieth birthday brought an avalanche of cards, telegrams, phone calls, and other forms of greeting. The final assault on Rákosi was being launched and he was about to suffer defeat. It was inflicted 'at the hands of those he feared and detested most, the Hungarian intelligentsia'.[4]

After the revelations of the returning prisoners the intelligentsia was smarting not only because so many of its members had suffered during the purges but also because so many others had given moral support to the murderous régime which carried them out, a feeling encapsulated in a famous contemporary admission: 'It was my crime to have believed in yours.' In November 1955 fifty-nine members of the communist party organisation within the writers' union, many of them distinguished names in Hungarian letters, addressed a memorandum to the central committee recalling with pleasure the decisions of the June 1953 plenum and the third congress of May 1954, but lamenting that 'certain organs and officials of the party apply more and more frequently the harmful and forceful methods repeatedly condemned by the central committee and by the congress'.[5]

By the summer of 1956 the intelligentsia were pushing forward the limits of toleration in journals such as that of the writers' union, *Irodalmi Ujság* (Literary Gazette), and in the published debates of the Petöfi circle. In June Gyula Hay wrote an article in *Iroldami Ujság* urging virtual freedom of the press. Rákosi ordered condemnation of the article but after a day or so the press revolted and turned not on Hay but on Rákosi. To make matters worse, the Hay incident came a few days before the writers' congress opened in Budapest; at the congress most of the party nominees for leading positions were rejected. The intelligentsia had challenged the leading role of the party.

Then the Petöfi circle became involved. On 27 June it held a debate on the press and censorship. People began crowding into the hall at 3 p.m. for a debate which was due to begin at 7 p.m. and when it did begin there was a huge overspill audience in the streets outside. The most dramatic moment in a highly charged debate came when Rajk's widow stood up to announce that the rehabilitation of her husband was not enough: she demanded vengeance. Two days later came the news of the clashes in Poznań.

Rákosi made his last stand. He closed the Petöfi circle, which did not meet again until October, and, gambling that the Poznań events would dispose the Kremlin to a reassertion of order in eastern Europe, he prepared the ground for a purge of Nagy and some 400 of his associates. Moscow in fact refused permission for the purge. At a politburo meeting on 17 July Atanas Mikoyan, a member of the Soviet leadership with special responsibilities for overseeing relations with east European parties, appeared demanding that Rákosi resign. Rákosi questioned Mikoyan's right to speak on behalf of the Soviet praesidium and telephoned Khrushchev for support. Khrushchev confirmed Mikoyan's message and on 18 July Rákosi resigned. A few days later he left for Moscow, taking with him from the country he done so much to impoverish three wagon loads of personal belongings.

The Gerö 'interregnum'

Of the two obvious successors to Rákosi, János Kádár was unacceptable to the Hungarians because he had been involved in tricking Rajk into a confession, whilst Nagy was unacceptable to the Soviets because he had been dismissed from the party and was feared to be too much of a titoist for comfort. The leadership therefore passed to Ernö Gerö. Gerö had been a close associate of Rákosi since 1948 and was therefore fully implicated in the purges, breakneck industrialisation, and collectivisation; as a former colonel in the Red Army he was also an insult to Hungarian nationalist sentiment. Furthermore, in stark contrast to what was soon to happen in Poland, the Hungarian party leader had been changed in accordance with Soviet wishes and not in opposition to them. As far as the Hungarians were concerned it was old wine in old bottles. Unlike in Poland, where the party was seen to be moving closer to national feeling, the Hungarian party was moving in the opposite direction, and once again it seemed to have aborted its move to liberalisation and by so doing had inflamed yet further popular resentment and anger.

In the articulation of such resentment and anger it was once again the intelligentsia which set the pace. At a writers' general meeting in Budapest on 17 September the supporters of Nagy had been so triumphant and the stalinists so roundly defeated that some of the latter left the room in tears. There were more tears at the Kerepesi cemetery in Budapest on 6 October. On that day, the anniversary of the execution by the Russians of thirteen Hungarian generals in 1849, up to 250,000 people assembled in what was the first unofficial demonstration since the communist assumption of power. It took place in front of a monument and mausoleum for the hero of 1848, László Kossuth, and the crowd listened to a former political prisoner whose speech made no mention of the communist party or of socialism. The occasion was the reburial of what were said to be the remains of László Rajk and three other victims of the purges.

The question which the reburial itself raised was that of culpability. There was no doubting the extent of the crimes committed under Rákosi, what was surprising was that so few criminals had been identified. One figure who had certainly not been implicated in the purges was Nagy, and the reburial heightened public consciousness of this because it produced the first newspaper photograph of him since his dismissal in January 1955. The party itself had discussed the readmission of Nagy, who was known to be Tito's preferred candidate for the leadership of the Hungarian party and who had established contacts with the Soviet ambassador in Budapest, Yuri Andropov. On 13 October, against a background of rising tension in Poland, Nagy was readmitted to the party without having to make any recantation or public self-criticism. He was again following in Gomułka's footsteps.

The October revolution

Nagy's readmission to the party did little to contain the discontent. On 16 October students in Szeged decided to disassociate from DISz; the Szeged students had flagrantly disavowed the leading role of the party and others followed their example. By 22 October a free youth association under the name of an extinct student organisation, MEFESz, had been formed; the rejection of the party had become national rather than local. With the rising tension in Poland, Red Army troops in Hungary and the rest of eastern Europe had been put on the alert on 18 October. This did nothing to deter the protesters, a number of whom now began to draw up lists of demands very much on the pattern of the revolutionaries of 1848. The most important were drawn up on 22 October by students at the Technological University in Budapest who had been inspired by Gomułka's victory in Warsaw. Along with the by now standard demands for political freedom, fundamental economic reform, the rule of law, and a proper relationship between Hungary and the USSR, they demanded that Nagy be made prime minister, that Soviet troops withdraw from the country, that Stalin's statue in Budapest be removed, that the Kossuth coat of arms be restored as the national emblem, and that as a gesture of solidarity with Poland a wreath be laid at Budapest's statue of general Bem, who had fought against the Russians in Poland in 1830 and in Hungary in 1849. It was also decided that the last demand would be implemented with a march to the statue on 23 October. The authorities banned the march but then relented. Unbeknown to all participants, the Hungarian revolution had begun.

The march to the statue was without event. The crowd carried slogans expressing support for the Poles and condemnation of Rákosi and it chanted Petöfi's treasured line, 'We will never again be slaves'. After the wreath had been laid the crowd split, some crossing the bridges to Parliament Square, others making their way to the Stalin statue. In the revolution's first act of violence the statue was torn down; the statue, which was built on the site of a bombed church and made of the bronze from melted down statues of Hungarian kings and queens, was one of the most blatant and hated symbols of Hungary's subjugation. If the actions of this section of the crowd pointed to one of the main causes of the discontent, the behaviour of the other indicated the objectives of the protesters: it gathered outside the parliament building and demanded that Nagy be made premier.

Nagy eventually appeared and spoke from a balcony. Oratory had never been his strong suit and on this occasion his speech verged on the disastrous; he began by addressing the crowd as 'comrades', only to be met with angry cries of 'We are not comrades'. Nagy switched to a non-communist form of address and ended by leading the crowd in singing the long-banned national hymn, 'God bless Hungary'. This was seen by many as a symbolic repudiation of the party.

At 8 p.m. Gerö addressed the nation on the radio. His speech, a mixture of cliché and denigration of the protesters, inflamed many of his listeners, a large number of whom marched on the radio station. Now the slogans had become significantly more aggressive and included 'Russians go Home', 'Death to Gerö', and 'Death to the AVH'. The radio station has been described as Hungary's Bastille, but unlike the French king's prison Budapest's radio station had strategic as well as symbolic significance. Radio was still by far the most important medium of public communication and the building was therefore regarded as the chief purveyor of government lies; and after Gerö's appalling speech the protesters insisted that their views be broadcast to the nation. The response to these demands was a hail of small arms fire from AVH men stationed on the roof. Within hours the regular police and the army had joined the protesters.

By the morning of 24 October Budapest was in a state of civil war between, on the one side, the AVH and the Red Army, and on the other the 'freedom fighters' who had been armed both by workers from the city's many arms factories and by the army.

The central committee met and agreed that Nagy should be made prime minister and that Kádár become party leader; Gerö left for an unknown fate in the USSR. Mikoyan and the Soviet ideology boss, Mikhail Suslov, flew in from Moscow to approve these changes. That evening Nagy went on the radio to address the nation. Some reports insist that he spoke with a Soviet revolver at his head, which may explain the most important point of the speech: he did not deny that he had asked for help from the Red Army. Nagy had disappointed nationalist expectations; he could no longer be regarded as Hungary's Gomułka. That being so, it meant that the HWP had no one who could, as Gomułka had done, contain the unrest and keep it within party control. On its first day the Hungarian revolution had reached a major turning point and had become essentially different from that in Poland.

The anti-party nature of the revolution was reflected in the nation-wide and spontaneous formation of revolutionary or national councils, or, as they were sometimes called, 'anti-Soviet soviets'. In some cases their origin was practical, as in Györ in western Hungary where a council was formed to organise food supplies for Budapest. The composition of the councils was as varied as the manner of their formation but by 30 October all of Hungary was under their control, with powerful regional councils emerging in places such as Debrecen and Györ. These councils, especially the latter under the leadership of Attila Szigeti, exerted enormous pressure for reform and were prominent in pressing radical demands such as election by secret ballot, the release of cardinal Mindszenty, a multi-party system, the withdrawal of the Red Army, and Hungary's disengagement from the Warsaw pact. The national council of Transdanubia, that based in Györ, threatened at one point to march on Budapest if more reforms were not enacted by Nagy. They were.

During 25 October the capital saw heavy fighting between Soviet tanks and the insurgents. Almost the whole of the Hungarian army had now gone over to the freedom fighters, and soldiers were 'ripping the red star insignia from their caps like scabs'.[6] On 26 October the central committee issued a declaration which referred to fratricidal strife, but did not call the freedom fighters fascists, and which promised that the government would correct its past mistakes and crimes; the latter was a word never before used by the party to describe its own actions. The declaration also promised that the government would negotiate with the Soviet Union 'on the basis of independence, complete equality, and noninterference in one another's internal affairs'. It also announced that the government approved of the formation of the national councils. On the following day, 27 October, Nagy formed a new government of the Patriotic People's Front. It was not a great advance on previous cabinets in that some of its 'new' faces were discredited renegades or covert communists such as Erdei and Ferenc Münnich, but it did have Zoltán Tildy as minister of state and Béla Kovács as minister of agriculture.

The destruction of communist authority

The situation appeared to change radically on 28 October. The government began negotiations with the freedom fighters, the HWP central committee dissolved itself, the freedom fighters constituted themselves as the national guard, and the Soviets agreed to withdraw their forces from the country. On 29 October the AVH was abolished; many of its agents had already been done to death in the streets. It seemed that Hungary had scored a great victory, but that victory was not Nagy's, nor did he control the forces which had driven out the Soviets; he had refused to order the Hungarian army to fight the Russians, leaving the decision to local commanders, and it was therefore they, and above all Pál Maléter in Budapest, who had earned the glory and accumulated the authority. And outside the capital it was the national councils not the government ministries which exercised power.

Nagy's PPF government was rejected on 30 October by the national revolutionary committee. The latter was the mouthpiece of the freedom fighters and specifically of one of their most determined leaders, József Dudás. Nagy, who was also under pressure from Szigeti in Györ who threatened a general strike if Soviet troops were not withdrawn, saw Dudás and agreed that a coalition government must be formed and that a multi-party system must be introduced. The government made the historic announcement that 'In the interests of further democratisation of the country's life, the cabinet abolishes the one-party system and places the country's government on the basis of democratic cooperation between the coalition parties as they existed in 1945.' The government also gave formal recognition to 'the democratic organs of local autonomy which have been brought into existence by the revolution', and admitted 'that it relies on them and asks for their support'. The formation of a revolutionary committee of the armed forces, which combined what was left of the army with the national guard, indicated that there were attempts to build the freedom fighters as well as the national councils into the state apparatus.

At the international level 30 October brought Mikoyan and Suslov once more to Budapest where they sanctioned the formation of a coalition government as long as capitalism was not restored and Hungary did not become a base for anti-Soviet forces. The Soviet Union also reiterated its promise to withdraw its troops from Hungary and issued a declaration, 'On the principles of the development and further strengthening of friendship and cooperation between the Soviet Union and other socialist states', which talked of 'the socialist commonwealth', though it also repeated that the WTO must remain the basis of relations between socialist states. On the same day Anglo-French forces attacked Egypt.

The freedoms promised on 30 October were the high-water mark of the revolution. They were acted upon with dispatch. The army freed cardinal

Mindszenty from house arrest and brought him to Budapest. The former political parties re-established themselves with remarkable rapidity, the first one to do so being the Smallholders Party which was closely followed by the Social Democratic Party; the National Peasant Party re-emerged as the Petöfi Party. In a further proof of Hungary's political vitality entirely new parties also appeared, including the Catholic Party, the Christian Democratic Party, and the Democratic People's Party. The HWP meanwhile was fragmenting, with the stalinists retreating to Moscow, the centrists grouping around Kádár, the revisionists following Nagy, and the liberals, who wanted an end to marxism-leninism and a democratic party in a democratic society, around Géza Losonczy and Ferenc Donáth. To support this new political plurality Budapest saw at least twenty-five new newspapers.

The revolution crushed

In its domestic political life Hungary had broken with communism; the leading role of the party had been destroyed. In its external affairs it was still a member of the socialist community, but the pressure for declaring neutrality on the Austrian model was growing rapidly, especially in the provincial councils. Hungary's new freedoms were by courtesy of the Soviet leadership, and that leadership was growing ever more dubious as to the wisdom of its generosity. On 31 October the Soviet praesidium decided to intervene to restore socialist order in Hungary.

Moscow could not afford to allow the contagion to spread and to destroy the leading role of the party in the other east European states because this would strip the USSR of its security cover against an attack from the west, something which many Soviet leaders still believed possible; in Hungary itself Kádár had visions of western intervention making of Hungary a European Korea in which the two systems would confront each other across the Danube or the Tisza. Khrushchev was also under very heavy pressure from his army, whose leaders had no confidence that a Hungary which had twice fought with the Germans could remain neutral. The Soviet leader was also sensible of the fact that he, as a nominal destaliniser, had to show the hard-liners that he too could take tough decisions and knew where to draw the line against the revisionists. Further pressure was exerted by the Chinese who insisted that the Polish events were still under party control but those in Hungary had gone far beyond it. As good marxist-leninists the Chinese were appalled at Hungary's return to the political situation of 1945; if history were allowed to go backwards in this fashion the whole basis of marxism would be called into question. Finally Khrushchev's doubts were dispelled by the Anglo-French action in Suez. This angered the United States, where preoccupations with the forthcoming presidential election had already lessened the probability of Washington taking any risks in retaliation against Soviet action in Hungary. However, the leader of the 'peace camp' would almost certainly have used its army to suppress the Hungarian revolt, even if

Britain and France had not made it easier for it to do so by providing 'a precedent for making war'.[7]

The impending cloud could be discerned in Budapest on 1 November. Intelligence reports spoke of Soviet tanks massing in Romania and Ruthenia and those still in Hungary assumed more aggressive positions. Five times that day Nagy spoke to ambassador Andropov, at whom Kádár screamed that same day, 'I am a Hungarian and if necessary I will fight your tanks with my bare hands.' Mikoyan and Suslov had meanwhile left for Moscow, whilst Khrushchev began a lightning series of talks with party leaders in Poland, Romania, Bulgaria, and finally Yugoslavia. In Budapest communist leaders, seeing that major changes were imminent, abandoned the coalition government and attempted to form one of their own; they also dissolved the HWP and formed a new party, the Hungarian Socialist Workers' Party. Kádár then disappeared for a week. In the provinces there were moves to coordinate resistance, with the council for Transdanubia in Györ establishing links with the national council in Debrecen and the eastern Hungarian national council at Miskolc. At 7 p.m. on 1 November Nagy announced on the radio that Hungary would leave the Warsaw pact and would become a neutral state. He also appealed to the United Nations for help.

Nagy had declared neutrality because he knew his country was being invaded. The Soviets used that declaration of neutrality to justify their invasion, just as they used public killings of AVH men to show that 'fascists' were murdering 'good communists'. The highpoint of Soviet cynicism, however, was on 2 November when Andropov requested that two delegates be sent to him to discuss the details of the Soviet withdrawal from Hungary. When those two delegates arrived on the following day they were arrested; one of them was Pál Maléter. On 4 November over 6,000 Soviet tanks moved into Hungary; Nagy and forty-one of his colleagues took refuge in the Yugoslav embassy. On 7 November, the anniversary of the bolshevik revolution, Kádár arrived at party headquarters in an armoured car to begin the political reconstruction of communist rule in Hungary.

Kádár still faced resistance. The workers in Budapest and elsewhere struck, in the provinces the national councils attempted to create an alternative government, and in the streets fighting continued until 14 November when the ammunition ran out. By then the revolution was broken and one of its inspirators, Tito, had betrayed it in a speech at Pula on 11 November in which he condemned the first Soviet intervention on 24 October but condoned the second in November. On 23 November Nagy, having been promised safe passage outside Hungary, left the Yugoslav embassy and was immediately arrested by Soviet troops; he was to be executed two years later. The last act of mass defiance in 1956 came on 4 December when thousands of women dressed in mourning defied Soviet troops and marched silently to the tomb of the unknown warrior in Budapest. Sporadic and uncoordinated acts of resistance were recorded into January 1957 but thereafter the work of restoring communist rule was unopposed.

In this task Kádár had wanted to use soft methods but early in December

Malenkov arrived from Moscow with instructions that controls must be tightened; as a result, 2–2,500 Hungarians were subjected to summary trial and execution. Up to 200,000 had in the meanwhile fled to sanctuary in the west.

The significance of the 1956 revolution

It is surprising that although discontent had been seething in Hungary ever since 1953, although communist repression in that country had been particularly vicious, and although the build up to the outburst of October had been slow and very public, there was nevertheless no indication whatever that the revolution and the deposition of the communist régime had been planned. The revolution was entirely unpremeditated and spontaneous.

The spontaneity and brevity of the revolution make it difficult to assess the goals and objectives of the revolutionaries. The passions which guided them were first and foremost national. The revolution was also anti-totalitarian and pro-democracy, demanding those freedoms which marxists had for long derided as 'formal' but which were still at the top of the reformists' shopping list, as they were to be again in 1989. Yet, if the demand for democratic liberties was intense, there was no indication, as there was to be in 1989, of a desire to return to capitalism. The workers who dominated the councils of such industrial districts as Csepel did not demand that their factories should be denationalised or that they should be taken out of state supervision; they asked rather that the internal organisation of the factories, the fixing of work norms, and the imposition of discipline should be the responsibility of elected workers' councils on the Yugoslav model. Nor did the speakers at the Petöfi debates call for the dissolution of the communist party; their main concern was that Nagy should be readmitted to its ranks. And Soviet propaganda claims that the revolution was a Horthyite, fascist conspiracy were nonsense. A few right-wing groups did emerge towards the end of the revolution, some of which placed their hopes for political leadership in cardinal Mindszenty, but there were no fascists; no one raised the name of Gömbös, whilst the man whom the Soviets portrayed as a fascist, Dudás, was a fanatical national communist. If the drive of the revolution in the cities seemed to be for communism of a national variety, there were some signs of outright anti-communism in the countryside where about 2,000 of the 3,950 collective or state farms dissolved themselves in 1956, despite the difficulties which a division of livestock and implements involved. Unlike in Poland, the dissolution of the collectives was not lasting.

The results of the revolution are as clear as its objectives were obscure. In the first place Hungary lost at least 3,000 citizens who were killed and over 200,000 who fled as refugees, in addition to which the Soviets deported unknown numbers, mainly of young men, in the months immediately after the second intervention. Many of those who escaped to the west were trained specialists, especially engineers, who were essential to the industrialisation programme upon which Hungary had embarked. Workers also joined the exodus; an estimated 40 per cent of Hungary's miners were amongst those who found their way across the border into Austria. The impact of these losses upon the Hungarian economy was considerable, as was the damage caused by the fighting and the strike of November–December, the cost of which has been estimated at twenty billion florints or a fifth of the yearly national income. Further damage was inflicted by the purges which followed November 1956. All officers suspected of collaboration with the insurgents were court-martialled, and the Soviets confiscated most Hungarian heavy armour and the entire bomber force.

The revolution also showed the fragility of the communist system. Dora Scarlett, a British communist resident in Hungary, later recalled that 'The astonishing thing to us who lived through the next two weeks in Budapest was the suddenness with which the established order fell apart.'[8] An aspect of this sudden collapse, which gave serious cause for concern amongst communist rulers, was that the two groups most dedicated to the revolution were the working class and the youth. It may have been the intelligentsia who destabilised the régime but it was predominantly workers and young people who took to the streets to fight the Soviet tanks. And both of these groups were amongst the most favoured in the communist system. The disaffection of the younger generation was particularly disturbing because it was they who had emerged from an insecure and hungry childhood towards the end of the war to be given education, recreation, and security by the communists. The loyalty which the communists expected in return had been denied them.

The revolution dictated some of the future strategy of the communist movement, particularly in eastern Europe. Given the power of nationalism, there had to be endorsement of polycentrism, the notion of separate roads to socialism; the Polish October showed that it could work, whilst the Hungarian November illustrated what would happen if it were frustrated. Yet there were limits. The suppression of the 1956 revolt in Hungary enabled Gomułka to persuade the Polish people that it was impossible to depart any further from sovietism than the installation of a nationalist communist leader. And there could be no abandoning the leading role of the party. In Hungary Kádár was made head of government as well as party leader; after 1956 the urge to separate party and government declined. Furthermore, polycentrism was to be confined to domestic policies. In the immediate aftermath of 1956 there could be no freedom of choice in major foreign policy issues such as the middle east and, above all, membership of the Warsaw pact. So great was the fear of neutrality that to advocate it became a capital offence under the Romanian penal code of 1958.

In global terms the Hungarian revolution showed that, no matter the lengths to which communism's opponents might go, the Soviet Union would intervene to protect what it considered its strategic interests. In 1956 it was hoped, vainly, that those interests would be construed only in terms of international relations and adherence to the Warsaw pact, and not in terms of domestic affairs and concern over the leading role of the party. A further consequence of 1956 in eastern Europe itself was that, because of the extraordinary lack of information made available by the official media, more people listened to the western radio stations which had brought them Światło's revelations and had then kept them informed on events in Poland and Hungary. But if east European malcontents looked to the west for information they no longer had any hopes of deliverance from that quarter. Events in 1956 had shown that, whatever lengths the opposition went to and whatever heroism they displayed, the west, Dulles' braggadocio of 'roll back' notwithstanding, would not intervene on their behalf.

The upheavals of 1956 had shown that the west would not intervene and that the Soviet Union would not allow the east European states to slip the leash. If the system could not be removed then it would have to be revised from within. Revisionism was to last until the summer of 1980.

Part III

REVISIONISM

17

EASTERN EUROPE, 1956–68

The period between the Hungarian revolution of 1956 and the Czechoslovak 'events' of 1968 was a difficult one for the rulers of eastern Europe. The Soviet Union, despite its technological achievements in space, suffered a number of major setbacks; so too did Moscow's east European allies. There were serious defeats for Soviet foreign policy in central and western Africa, in the six day war of 1967, and above all in the humiliation of Khrushchev during the Cuban missile crisis of 1962. At the same time there were ideological discomforts. Despite the marxist-leninist prediction that the capitalist states would inevitably fly at each others' throats and would equally inevitably impoverish their working classes, western Europe moved towards a significantly higher level of economic and political cooperation and enjoyed a seemingly unbreakable rise in living standards in all levels of society, whilst the Japanese showed that recovery from the devastation of war could be achieved outside the framework of marxism-leninism. And it was the communist world which was fragmenting, most dramatically with the Sino-Soviet split.

In eastern Europe the Hungarian revolution had shown that political experimentation could all too easily get out of hand. Gradual economic restructuring was a much safer option and it was one which received encouragement from Moscow where in 1961, after Khrushchev had indulged in a second and far more vehement denunciation of Stalin, the CPSU adopted a new programme based on the assumption of rapid economic expansion. In 1962 articles by professor Libermann in *Pravda* outlined a series of measures which were aimed at decentralising economic decision making. Economic rethinking was also prompted by the fact that for most states the first stage of socialist construction was well on the road to completion if it were not actually finished. Agriculture was by and large collectivised, urbanisation was proceeding apace, and massive heavy industrial complexes were either functioning or being built. However, the economic reforms which were enacted were generated from above, from within the party/state apparatus, and they involved primarily the reorganising of economic administration.

Upheavals such as those of 1956 inevitably demanded some examination of relations between Moscow and the east European communist parties and govern-

307

ments. A limited form of polycentrism in domestic policy was henceforth to be allowed, and in intra-bloc relations there was the binding force of the Warsaw pact of 1955. After 1956 the Soviet leaders were given to talking of 'supra-nationalism' and this notion fed into new plans to give more purpose and strength to Comecon, which in 1962 published *The Basic Principles of the International Socialist Division of Labour*. Although supra-nationalism was ruled out and member states were left with the right of veto, the plan was for separate east European states to specialise in designated economic sectors. The impulse towards such specialisation was strengthened by the building of the Berlin Wall in August 1961. Thereafter there was an increased determination to develop the GDR as a worthy socialist competitor of the Federal Republic, for which considerable investment was necessary. It was argued that, now that the basis of the socialist system had been constructed, it would be more in keeping with socialism's cooperative ethic for states to cooperate and coordinate their economic policies for the general good of the socialist community. Such a policy would also be cheaper and, in practical terms, would enable the USSR to direct sufficient funds into building up the GDR. This policy ran counter to the decentralising, polycentrist trends allowed after 1956 and not surprisingly provoked a fierce reaction. The contradictions between the two forces were never solved.

Yugoslavia

Polycentrism had been taken furthest by the Yugoslavs who continued in their determination to be socialist but not soviet. In foreign policy neutralism remained the guiding principle, with Belgrade hosting the 1961 conference of non-aligned nations; Yugoslavia was the only European state to be represented.

There was little dissent from the policy of non-alignment but there was much debate on the nature of domestic policy. The results of the change of direction in the early 1950s were not entirely encouraging. The workers' councils were not producing an economic miracle. Frequently they insisted on over-equalisation of wages which acted as a disincentive to skilled workers and, having achieved this, left real authority with the managers. Many of the latter had joined the partisans and were still young and uneducated; only two-fifths of even Slovene factory managers in the mid-1960s had anything more than a primary education, a condition which could only intensify the frustration of the better educated generation behind them. The incumbent managers were also bastions of the party. This was the Yugoslav form of the leading role of the party.

A further problem was an unresolved tension between the micro-economic drift towards local autonomy through the workers' councils and macro-economic strategies which still left the state in control of investment policies, the banks, foreign trade, and other major sectors of the economy.

On a political level the momentum towards the further decentralisation of power to the republics contrasted with the concept of Yugoslavism which was still officially upheld in both party and government; many suspected Yugoslavism of being a disguised form of resurgent Serbian nationalism, the more so when the extreme 'Yugoslavists' at the seventh party congress in 1958 called for the abolition of the republics.

Such extreme opinions had little impact and in the long struggle between conservatives and liberals which dominated the LCY in the 1950s and early 1960s it was the latter who emerged victorious, not entirely with the approval of Tito. In 1962 state planning of the economy was virtually abolished and in 1963 self-management was extended to the health service and education, thereby adding social self-management to worker self-management. In the same year Yugoslav citizens were allowed to travel freely to the west. The massive migration of labour which followed meant that by the end of the decade one adult worker in six was outside the country. Their remissions formed a valuable addition to the economy, as were the rising earnings from western tourists, but both tourists and the returning workers brought new ideas and new expectations as well as their deutschmarks and dollars.

The liberal movement gathered pace, with more decentralisation in banking and with a series of over thirty laws in 1965 which were generally known in Yugoslavia as 'the Reform'. The Reform was intended to provide the legal framework for 'market socialism' and to help Yugoslavia to integrate itself into the world economy. Amongst its more important provisions were: some limited private employment, with entrepreneurs being able to engage three workers and those in small workshops five; the abolition of most price controls together with an increase of 30 per cent where they were retained in food, clothing, and raw materials; and permission for enterprises to deal directly with foreign trading partners, with foreign currency allocations to such enterprises varying with their export earnings. In 1967 foreign investment was allowed up to a maximum of 49 per cent of the total capital, and foreign investors were allowed to export their profits.

The Reform was a huge step towards the market economy and it brought pain as well as profit. Small enterprises did flourish but the removal of many state subsidies and controls meant rises in unemployment, in prices, and in foreign indebtedness.

The liberals had had to fight for almost a decade before they registered their major success in the Reform. They had a similar wait in the political arena. The seventh party congress in 1958 had been dominated by the attack upon Milovan Djilas, who had criticised the party from within its uppermost echelons, castigating bureaucratisation, authoritarianism, and other ills. Djilas was condemned and the party reaffirmed its right to a leading role in society and in the struggle to construct socialism. By 1963, however, the reformists had seized the initiative. A new constitution in April of that year, although it made Yugoslavia a 'Socialist' as opposed to a 'People's' Federal Republic, also banned the simultaneous holding of state and party office, Tito being the one exception. The constitution also contained provisions to enforce the rotation of political office, whilst its remodelling of the federal assembly entrenched the position of the self-managing institutions in the state structure. Almost as a symbol of the more open political atmosphere an influential dissident marxist group appeared late in 1964, based on the journal *Praxis*.

One of the strongest arguments deployed by the reformers in favour of decentralisation was that it would nip nascent nationalism in the bud. They were wrong. The devolution of some economic responsibility whetted the appetite for more, and there was particular resentment at the fact that individual republics still had to deposit a fixed percentage of their foreign currency earnings in the National Bank of Yugoslavia in Belgrade.

As always in Yugoslavia discontent, whether economic or political, soon became linked to the national problem. The richer, northern republics were angered that they had to sacrifice their hard currency and other earnings to subsidise the less developed and, they would have said, the less hard-working republics of Serbia, Bosnia-Hercegovina, Montenegro, and Macedonia. This persistence of Yugoslavism was still seen by many in the northern republics as one example of surreptitious Serbian nationalism, others being: the fact that the federal capital was also the Serbian capital; that, as in the inter-war period, the apparatus of both the party and the state were dominated by Serbs; and that nowhere was this more true than in the security forces, the UDBa.

The chief of the UDBa, Aleksandar Ranković, seemed to many the personification of Serbian domination. Conservative, authoritarian, centralist, and Serbian, he had been minister of the interior since 1945, and organisation secretary of the LCY since 1957; in 1964 the new office of vice-president of the republic had been created for him in a gesture which seemed to nominate him as heir apparent to Tito. In 1966, however, Tito was informed that UDBa men under Ranković had bugged the offices and homes of leading party members, even those of Tito himself; typically, the sins of Ranković had been uncovered by military intelligence in which Ranković had little influence because it was under the control of a Croat, general Ivan Gošnjak. Ranković was sacked from all of his posts and disgraced, though he was not imprisoned.

The fall of Ranković was the most dramatic single political development in Yugoslavia since the breach with Moscow. It was interpreted by non-Serbs as an important victory. Nowhere was the departure of Ranković more warmly greeted than in Kosovo. During the war Kosovo had been attached to Italian-dominated Albania and its reintegration into Yugoslavia had occasioned resistance from the Kosovans. Ranković's police machine was therefore deployed in great strength in the area. After his ouster there were a number of demonstrations calling for greater recognition of Albanian rights in Kosovo. In Croatia, too, there were moves to demand more separation from Belgrade. In 1967 the Croats renounced the Novi Sad agreement of 1954 and national tensions increased as, in retaliation, the Serbs in Croatia demanded that all official documents be written in cyrillic. In both Croatia and Kosovo old-fashioned nationalism was rising rapidly to the forefront of politics; its progress was only temporarily halted by developments in Czechoslovakia in 1968.

The mid-1960s saw a significant weakening in the authority of the LCY. The Reform deprived the federal party of much of its economic muscle whilst the disgrace surrounding Ranković damaged its image. At republican levels the LCY still exercised great influence, though even here there was some loss of power to the state; in Slovenia, for example, the government actually resigned after it had been defeated in the republic's parliament.

Albania

The advent of polycentrism had given Yugoslavia a much greater sense of security. But one state's polycentrism was another's revisionism. The APL did not welcome Soviet efforts to re-establish contacts with Tito, and resisted all attempts to make it follow the same path. By the beginning of the 1960s discussion of supra-nationalism and the possible specialisation of labour had pushed the APL even further away from the Soviet bloc. The fourth congress of the APL in February 1961 heard party leader Enver Hoxha and prime minister Mehmet Shehu expound the 'dual adversary theory' according to which marxism-leninism was equally threatened by imperialism and revisionism. At the end of the year Albania broke off relations with the USSR and expelled the Soviet navy from its Adriatic bases.

This audacious step would have been impossible had not Tiranë been able to take advantage of the growing differences between Moscow and Peking, differences which were well known in leading party circles by the end of the 1950s. The Chinese, whose prestige amongst orthodox marxist-leninists had increased greatly after their resolute stand over Hungary in 1956, welcomed Albania's breach with Moscow as an opportunity to establish a toe-hold in Europe. The Chinese were able to help the Albanians to weather the consequences of the withdrawal of Soviet aid and advisors, and then in later years to equip the Albanian armed forces. For their part the Albanians continued to plough their own furrow. Although they called their massive campaign in the mid-1960s against increasing bureaucracy the 'ideological and cultural revolution' it was by no means a copy of the Chinese version. As with all Hoxha's policies, one of its functions was to promote national unity and it was with this end in view that in 1967 he banned religion, Albania becoming the world's first avowedly atheist state.

Romania

Romania did not go as far as Albania in its rejection of Soviet influence but between 1956 and 1968 the ties between the Romanians and the remainder of the bloc underwent considerable change.

Georghiu-Dej appeared a stalinist, but he was only a stalinist in domestic affairs; he was a stalinist at home and a titoist abroad. His position in the party had been strengthened when he eliminated his main opponents, some of whom could have been regarded as Moscow communists. His repressive policies had, he believed, been vindicated by the Hungarian emergency which illustrated the dangers of too much relaxation of party control. In 1956 the Romanian authorities had been determined that their own Hungarian minority should neither be infected with the revolutionary virus nor be allowed to provide any effective help to their co-nationals across the border; the Romanian party even agreed that Imre Nagy and his associates should be kept in Romania before their 'trial' and execution in Budapest.

Most of Romania's Magyar minority lived in the Hungarian autonomous district, established in 1952 and having a population which was 77 per cent Hungarian. After 1956 the minority was less favoured. In 1959 the Hungarian university in Cluj was merged with, or rather submerged by, its Romanian counterpart and in 1960 the boundaries of the autonomous district were redrawn so that its population was now only 62 per cent Magyar; its name was changed to the Mureş-Hungarian autonomous district.

The fact that the Romanians had been so ruthless in 1956 in preventing any contact between their Hungarians and those in Hungary persuaded the Soviets that the Romanians were reliable and dependable upholders of the system, and the Red Army was therefore withdrawn from Romania in 1958. This was an essential precondition for the assertions of Romanian separateness which were soon to follow. Those assertions were considerably encouraged by the Cuban crisis of 1962 which brought home to Georghiu-Dej, who was visiting Moscow at the time, how easily Soviet irresponsibility might involve Romania in an unwanted conflict.

Indications of Romanian separateness were to be seen in the neutral stance Bucharest adopted in the Sino-Soviet dispute and in the fact that, after a short break, diplomatic relations with Albania were resumed in 1963. But the major issue at stake between the Romanian and Soviet leaderships was the latter's plans for Comecon specialisation. Under the 1962 plan Romania was to concentrate on the extraction of raw materials and the production of agricultural goods. When Bucharest demurred at this prospect Khrushchev responded with suggestions of supra-national economic organisations which would limit the sovereignty of individual states, especially in the field of economic planning. The Romanians feared that if they were now to switch and concentrate on the areas suggested for them their economy and planning mechanisms would be thrown into chaos; what would become, for example, of the massive metallurgical complex then under construction at Galaţi?

There were deeper and more long-term difficulties. The Romanian communists did not have a very creditable record on nationalist issues; the party in the inter-war years had been dominated by non-Romanians, it had even supported Soviet claims to Bessarabia, and after the war many Romanians understandably assumed that a party with fewer than 1,000 members could not have risen to such power without the backing of the Red Army and the Soviet Union. The Soviet exploitation of Romania in the years immediately after the war merely confirmed many suspicions that the Romanian communists were puppets whose strings were pulled in Moscow. The Comecon plan of 1962 seemed to many to provide for the renewal of the Soviet exploitation of Romania. At the same time it would condemn Romania to becoming little more than a 'vegetable garden', preventing the development of the 'many-sided industrialisation' which the party had promoted since 1945, inhibiting the growth of a native working class, and retarding Romania's progression through socialism to 'communism. This offended both Georghiu-Dej's stalinism and his nationalism; besides which, the Comecon plan seemed to be asking Romania's communists to follow an economic policy which had been rejected even by Romania's pre-war liberals. Romania was in a strong position to resist. It could, and did, exploit the Sino-Soviet dispute, but in addition to that Romania was the second largest state in eastern Europe and was one of the richest in terms of mineral resources. If Romania wanted to go it alone towards industrialisation it had as good a chance as anyone else of succeeding.

Georghiu-Dej was in effect being asked to choose between the Soviet Union and what had been the Soviet model. He opted for the latter. The outcome was 'A Statement on the Stand of the Romanian Workers' Party concerning the Problems of the World Communist and Working Class Movement', published in April 1964. The 'Statement' contained a classic expression of the rights of individual parties *vis-à-vis* the Soviet:

> Bearing in mind the diversity of the conditions of socialist construction, there are not, nor can there be, any unique patterns and recipes; no one can decide what is and what is not correct for other countries and parties. It is up to every marxist-leninist party, it is a sovereign right of each socialist state to elaborate, choose or change the forms and methods of socialist construction.
>
> There does not and cannot exist a 'parent' and a 'son' party, or 'superior' parties and 'subordinate' parties . . . No party has, or can have, a privileged place, or can impose its line and opinions on other parties.

From 1964 Romania struck out on its own path. It did not repudiate either Comecon or the WTO but it ceased to play a significant role in either. To underline its disapproval of Moscow's hegemonism the Romanian party in 1964 permitted the publication of *Notes on the Romanians*, a recently discovered piece by Marx which attacked Russian encroachments upon Romania and the annexation of Bessarabia in 1812; it was published by a Romanian and a Polish scholar.

Georghiu-Dej died in March 1965. His successor, Nicolae Ceaușescu, pushed even further in the direction of Romanian separateness. His continued resistance forced the Soviets to abandon plans for more centralisation in the Warsaw Pact; in May 1966 he attacked Comintern for its interference in the internal affairs of the Romanian party and for foisting foreign leaders upon it between the wars; and in 1967 he was the only east European leader not to follow Moscow in refusing to re-establish diplomatic relations with Israel after the six day war. In the same year Romania became the first east European state to establish such relations with the Federal Republic of Germany.

In domestic affairs Ceauşescu was equally nationalist. The teaching of Russian in Romanian schools was greatly reduced and much greater attention was paid to Romanian cultural identity. In 1965 a new constitution was adopted which allotted the party, now renamed the Romanian Communist Party (RCP), the leading role in society and which declared Romania a socialist state rather than a people's republic. The inference was that whilst Georghiu-Dej had been responsible for creating the latter there was now a new era to be associated with the new leader. In 1967 Ceauşescu became president and therefore head of state as well as party leader.

The 1965 constitution had described Romania as a unitary state; this was a warning to the minorities, above all to the Hungarians. In 1968 the reintroduction of traditional local government units, the *judeţe*, in place of the Soviet-style regions, meant the disappearance of the Mureş-Hungarian autonomous district and a large reduction in the number of local government areas with Hungarian majorities.

This assertive form of national socialism was backed by new interpretations of the marxist canons. Ceauşescu argued that it was only after the disappearance of the exploiting classes that a nation could grow and coalesce, that 'It is only under socialism that the real community of economic interests, the common socialist culture of all citizens who live on the same territory, can fully express themselves.' Socialist culture, the argument continued, was the synthesis of national experience and socialist values, which meant that socialism combined national and class cultures and was therefore socialist in form but national in content. Socialist construction was thus the task of the working class of the nation, not of any international form of working class organisation.

Bulgaria

The Comecon scheme of 1962 had unearthed the great fault line running between the northern and southern socialist states of Europe. South of the line three of those states, Yugoslavia, Albania, and Romania, refused to have anything to do with the Soviet-sponsored notion of the specialisation of labour. The fourth, Bulgaria, accepted it.

With destalinisation in 1954 Bulgaria's 'little Stalin', Chervenkov, had relinquished the leadership of the party and had remained prime minister. Todor Zhivkov was appointed first secretary. In April 1956 the party laid down its 'April line' which rejected the cult of personality, granted amnesty to some exiles, and rehabilitated a number of communist purge victims. Anton Yugov was made prime minister in place of Chervenkov. The 'April line' was to provide the basis of BCP policy until 1987, but whatever buds of liberalisation appeared in April 1956 withered in the heat of the reaction against the Hungarian revolution. By mid-1957 the labour camps were full of the 'Hungarian prisoners', any hint of a thaw in culture had vanished, and the drive to complete collectivisation was under way.

In the late 1950s the leadership launched an adventurous economic plan known as Bulgaria's great leap forward, though its content was derived more from Khrushchev than from Mao. The great leap forward achieved few of its grandiose aims and its failure intensified a power struggle which was already in progress between Zhivkov and Yugov. Zhivkov came out the winner, but mainly thanks to ostentatious backing from Khrushchev; in the middle of a vital central committee plenum in November 1962 Zhivkov flew to Moscow for assurances of Soviet support. One who was so beholden to the Soviet leader was in no position to break ranks in the way that Georghiu-Dej was to do, and after Khrushchev was ousted in October 1964 Zhivkov remained as obsequious to Brezhnev as he had been to Khrushchev. Bulgaria was also in a much weaker position than Romania; it had little in the way of raw materials and very few reserves of fossil fuel for which it was dependent on the Soviet Union. It was equally dependent on the Soviet Union as a source of capital and as a trading partner, added to which were the supposedly strong, but usually exaggerated, cultural ties between the Bulgarians and the Russians.

The logic of close Bulgarian-Soviet friendship was not clear to all, however. In 1965 an abortive military coup led to the arrest and later execution of general Ivan Todorov-Gorunya. Details of the plot are still obscure but it seems probable that the conspirators were angry at what seemed to be Bulgaria's total subservience to the USSR and wished to adopt a more independent yet still socialist stance on the lines of Romania or perhaps Yugoslavia. Their failure left Zhivkov unchallenged.

Zhivkov nevertheless remained cautious and a promising economic reform programme introduced in the mid-1960s was abandoned as soon as events in Czechoslovakia began to show where such reforms could lead.

The GDR

After the construction of the Berlin wall the GDR was, in political terms, as subservient to the USSR as was Bulgaria, but the east Germans had more freedom in the economic field. As one of the most developed economies in the bloc the GDR was not surprisingly in the vanguard of economic reform in the early 1960s. The New Economic System of 1963 relaxed a number of central controls, but its underlying strategy was to harness new technologies. As a developed economy the GDR needed to move rapidly from extensive to intensive development, the more so if it were to prove itself a credible competitor of the FRG. This policy produced some tension. Technology was so much the centre of the new strategy that '*Mutatis mutandis*, the technocrats became for the GDR what the officer corps had been for Imperial Germany'.[1] The working class, still suspicious after what it considered the attempt to exploit it in 1953, became restive and in 1965 the reformists' wings were clipped. The new system was confined to a few areas of the economy and was reformulated as 'the Economic System of Socialism'.

Hungary

Of all of the east European states Hungary went through the greatest transformation in the years 1956–68. In the initial five years the party's first priority was to entrench its power. The new Hungarian Socialist Workers' Party (HSWP), under the leadership of János Kádár, naturally did not include any reformers but nor was there any place in it for leading stalinists such as Rákosi. Nevertheless, Kádár steadily eradicated all vestiges of the 1956 revolution; the workers' councils, which could have competed with the party for the allegiance of the working class, were dissolved in February 1957 to be replaced by a workers' militia firmly under the control of the secret police. Dissident bodies such as the writers' and journalists' unions were dissolved and many of their members fled to the west; most of those who did not joined the other former activists in labour camps and gaols.

In January 1959, after intense debate and considerable pressure from the Soviets, it was decided to reimpose collectivisation. By 1962 75 per cent of the land had been recollectivised but this time the pressure on the peasants was in the main fiscal rather than physical. Also, the cooperative farms were to be autonomous and not subject to day-to-day state and party interference; the Soviet system of paying labour by the day, irrespective of the quantity or quality of the work performed, was abandoned, and under the new system the régime was far more indulgent to the personal or private plots. The net result was that Hungarian agriculture emerged from recollectivisation as a much more productive force than its 1950s forebear.

The more understanding attitude towards the peasant was indicative of a relaxation of party control in the early 1960s. Kádár remained ultimately dependent upon the Soviets and the Red Army but Moscow had a vested interest in allowing him to consolidate his position. It was far better for the Soviets to have a reformist Kádár than a conservative whose orthodoxy drove the Hungarians once again to rebellion; and Kádár's excellent personal relationship with Khrushchev enabled him to drive this point home.

Another sign of relaxation came in the 1961 reform of the criminal code. Under the new regulations it was no longer obligatory to inform on relatives, penalties for attempted escape from the country were reduced, torture was made illegal, internal exile without trial was ended, and the number of labour camps was drastically reduced. In a speech in December 1961 Kádár summarised the new atmosphere with the famous phrase: 'Whereas the Rákosiites used to say that those who are not with us are against us, we say that those who are not against us are with us.' By the end of 1961 Hungarian stalinism was dead; it was buried in the following year.

In August 1962 most of those arrested in 1956–7 and still in detention were released; in August Rákosi, Gerö, and other leading stalinists were finally expelled from the party, and in November the eighth congress saw Kádár moving his own supporters into pivotal positions. The party ended its prohibition on 'former exploiters' and dispensed with its call for vigilance against the 'class enemy'. It also moved towards greater internal democracy, introducing secret ballots in party elections and encouraging debate before binding decisions were taken. Having ditched the terminology of the class war the HSWP was able to relax its grip on social power. It was prepared, for the sake of economic improvement, to employ non-party specialists and political reliability became progressively less important as a criterion for employment or promotion, whilst in 1962 Kádár said that he did not regard social origin as an important factor for university entrance.

By the mid-1960s the new mood was apparent in constitutional changes. In 1967 the end of single-list voting and the introduction of constituencies made it at least theoretically possible for more than one candidate to stand in an election, and in the same year the Hungarian parliament was encouraged to stage more rigorous debates on the budget, on the reform of the labour code, and on revision of the law on cooperative farms.

These items of legislation were all part of the most dramatic change introduced into Hungary, the New Economic Mechanism (NEM). In December 1963 the minister of finance, Rezsö Nyers, had been told to draw up plans for the reform of the economy. His report was published in November 1965, was approved by the central committee in May 1966, and became operative on 1 January 1968. The objectives of the NEM were: to bring about a more rational allocation of capital; to improve the economy to such an extent that Hungary could become part of the international economic order, eastern and western; to link enterprise effort to reward; and, by breaking the 'feudal' powers of the party-dominated enterprise managers, to fashion a system flexible enough to respond to consumer needs. To achieve these goals the power of the central planning agencies was to be greatly reduced, with the plans now serving as indicators rather than directives; private enterprise was to be encouraged, especially in the service industries and agriculture; and private producers were to be allowed to employ a small number of workers. Enterprises were to have much greater freedom to find their own supplies and markets, and they were also at liberty to compete for labour. The price structure was to be radically restructured.

The NEM was the boldest step yet taken in economic reform in eastern Europe, Yugoslavia excluded. It was at times to be under pressure but it was never revoked and remained at the core of Hungarian policy virtually until the end of communist rule. The real, if limited, economic reform embodied in the NEM put Hungary on the road from 'gulag' to 'golas' communism and would have been impossible without the dilution of the party's leading role which had begun in the eighth congress in 1962.

Poland

By 1968 it was possible to think that Hungary had lost the war of 1956 but had won the peace. In Poland the opposite was the case. The grand expectations of economic progress, national liberation, and greater individual liberty faded gradually but inexorably. For the reformists the new régime that was ushered in by the Polish October started encouragingly. The stalinists were swept away by Gomułka's more mild form of socialism; agriculture was not re-collectivised, the Catholic church continued to enjoy a position allowed to no other religious organisation anywhere else in eastern Europe, and Poland's intellectuals were given latitude enough to humanise marxism-leninism, thus aligning it with Polish traditions and bringing it closer to western patterns of thought. Yet Gomułka's instincts and his policies remained essentially authoritarian and he lost support as this became more and more apparent to his erstwhile admirers.

For some their complaint against Gomułka was his unwillingness to grant further relaxation in the political system. To others, for example general Mieczysław Moczar, even Gomułka's nationalist brand of communism was not nationalist enough. In the 1960s Moczar founded the veterans' association which attempted to bring together former fighters from both the communist resistance and the AK. Though still a communist, Moczar was quite prepared to criticise the Soviets over issues such as the Katyn massacres, and, at a lower level, he did not scruple to excite anti-semitism as a means to gather support. At the same time he had no truck with those who were calling for further relaxation; he was an authoritarian through and through, not least because he seemed to think that most dissidents were Jews.

The rise of Moczar and the veterans' association was but one sign of the restlessness affecting Poland in the mid-1960s. Another came with the celebration in 1966 of the millennium of the Christian church in Poland, a celebration which produced a head-on clash between party and church when the Polish bishops addressed a letter to their German colleagues saying that they were willing to forgive and to be forgiven. This was a mistake on the part of the church because it allowed the party to upstage it as the defender of national interests; the party did not see any reason why Poles should seek pardon from Germans, and in this most Poles agreed with their political bosses. Nor did the latter want reconciliation with the Germans, particularly those in the Federal Republic, not least because fear of German revanchism was still the only thing which could legitimise Poland's close ties with Moscow.

The party did not reap any lasting benefit from the church's gaffe. In 1967 the six day war provided the mass of the population with another chance to tweak the party's nose; thousands of Poles placed candles in their windows to commemorate the Israeli victories, not so much for love of Israel but because the Arabs were sponsored by the Soviets.

In January 1968 a Warsaw theatre staged a production of *Dziady* (The Forefathers) by the great nineteenth-century Polish poet and dramatist, Adam Mickiewicz. The play contained scenes which patronised or criticised the Russians and all the twelve performances which the authorities tolerated were sell-outs, some of them provoking spontaneous anti-Russian outbursts. Taken with contemporary developments in Czechoslovakia the play galvanised the student population of Poland. In March the police took to the offensive and allowed thugs to break up a student meeting in Warsaw. For weeks the students and the police were in continuous confrontation and it seemed that the ageing Gomułka was losing all control. There were many who were convinced that only Moczar could restore order. In fact Gomułka pinched many of Moczar's policies. Using a mixture of crude anti-intellectualism and even cruder anti-semitism, he managed to keep the workers and the intelligentsia apart.

His anti-semitism reached pogrom-like intensity and led to the sacking of most Jews in leading posts, one of the most prominent victims being Adam Rapacki, the foreign minister who had proposed disarmament and neutrality in a central European nuclear-free zone. Thousands of other Polish Jews fled the country, and so too did a number of distinguished Polish intellectuals.

Gomułka's political standing had been gravely weakened by the events of March 1968. That he continued to receive Soviet backing was mainly because the Kremlin, with its gaze fixed on Prague, did not want instability in another east European state.

Czechoslovakia

Whilst the expectations of Polish reformers declined, those of their Czechoslovak counterparts rose. In November 1957 Zápotocký died and was replaced by Antonín Novotný. It was not an encouraging start for would-be reformers. During the war Novotný had been a kapo in Mauthausen concentration camp, and after 1945 he worked his way up the party administration in Prague. Unadventurous, unimaginative, and unbending in his dogged marxist-leninist orthodoxy, he abandoned few of Stalin's policies and thus forced Czechoslovakia to 'suffer personality cult without the personality'.[2] In the 1950s he could defend his conservatism on the grounds that the Czechoslovak economy was doing well, but there was another reason: destalinisation would mean rehabilitation of the purge victims and this Novotný, who had been deeply implicated in the purges, could not survive. Furthermore, the purges in Czechoslovakia had involved a fierce assault upon Slovak nationalism, and destalinisation would mean concessions to the Slovaks, something which Novotný feared would let loose an uncontrollable wave of nationalism.

In 1961 Novotný was forced into some measures of relaxation by Khrushchev's second denunciation of Stalin. Characteristically, however, Novotný simply used this occasion to remove his rival Rudolf Barák, the ambitious minister of the interior and a member of the praesidium; but it was not enough. In September further pressure from the Soviets and from the intelligentsia at home forced Novotný to agree to the formation of a commission under Drahomír Kolder to enquire into the trials of 1949–54. This at last betokened a real move away from stalinism, as did the removal of Gottwald from his mausoleum and the blowing up of the huge statue of Stalin in Prague, the largest in Europe and, outside Tiranë, the only one remaining in a European capital. The tone had been set for the party's twelfth congress which met on 2–8 December 1962 and which marked 'an inconspicuous but extremely important turning point in the history of communist Czechoslovakia'.[3] In April 1963 a central committee plenum removed a number of compromised, old-guard stalinists from the leadership in both the Czechoslovak and the Slovak parties. A new atmosphere had been created and it was to dominate the mid-1960s. It allowed an immediate and rigorous examination of the problems of the nations and the parties, past and present.

For two of the most disaffected segments of the Czechoslovak state and party, the intelligentsia and the Slovaks, the area which most demanded attention was that of the purges. The report of the Kolder commission was shown to the party leadership in November 1962 but was not discussed in any detail by the December congress, and when it was finally presented to the central committee in April 1963 it had undergone considerable dilution. Slánský, it agreed, had not been guilty as charged but he, and others, had still acted in breach of party statutes. For most of the victims of the 1949–54 purges, rehabilitation was grudging and incomplete.

This partial concession fed discontent in much the same way as interrupted liberalisation had nourished the opponents of Rákosi in Hungary a decade before. As censorship relaxed the journalists, historians, economists, and philosophers moved on to the offensive. In *Plamen* (flame), a journal of the writers' union, Jiří Hájek challenged the party to undertake full destalinisation, whilst Karel Kosík's *Dialectics of the Concrete* and Ladislav Mňačko's *Delayed Reportage*, published in 1963 in Slovakia, added more fuel to the growing revisionist fire, particularly because they raised questions about responsibility for the purges.

Any examination of the repressions of the late 1940s and early 1950s inevitably opened Slovak wounds. These were inflicted not only by the repression of the purges; the Slovaks were dissatisfied with the basic structure of the state and the party. The 'asymmetrical model' meant that whilst there were separate party and state institutions for the Slovaks there were none for the Czechs. Czech interests were looked after in the Czechoslovak institutions, and Slovaks inevitably feared that it was much easier for Czechs than for Slovaks to make their voices heard in these federal state and party bodies. The new constitution of 1960 made worse of a bad job. Slovakia was divided into three regions, which meant that there was no central authority for Slovakia as a whole; the Slovak national council and the board of commissioners ceased to have any meaning and by 1964 had all but disappeared. And in party affairs the central committee in Prague dominated the party organs which were based in Bratislava.

This domination was checked in May 1963 with what was for Novotný a major reversal; for the first time his preferred candidate for a senior party post was not approved, and instead the Slovak first secretaryship passed to a Russian educated, inconspicuous party careerist who had been a member of the Kolder commission and who was himself too young to have been involved in the purges: Alexander Dubček.

Intellectual and Slovak dissatisfaction were not the only problems which Novotný had to face. Even more obvious and pressing was the state of the economy, now in sad contrast to its relative health of the 1950s. By the middle of 1962 economic growth was measured at 6.7 per cent, rather than the 9.4 per cent projected in the current five year plan. In August 1962, in what was a severe blow to Novotný's prestige, the plan was abandoned and a new seven year plan was put in its place. There was little immediate improvement and in 1963 there was virtually no growth at all in production, whilst the supply side was so dislocated that one day a week – Thursday – was made 'meatless'. The Czechoslovak party was soon to be forced to the galling admission that living standards in the country were lower than in Poland and Hungary, which in the inter-war years had been regarded as poor neighbours. The explanations offered were: the costs of the 1961 Berlin crisis; the need to subsidise Cuba; the undeniably ferocious winter of 1962–3; the collapse of trade with China; and the failure of the Soviet Union to provide the food supplies, the railway equipment, and the credits they were believed to have promised. It was also admitted that poor planning was in part responsible.

To find solutions for the economic problems a group of experts was established in the Institute for Economics at the Czechoslovak Academy of Sciences and was placed under the chairmanship of Ota Šik. Šik's recommendations, like those of Nyers in Hungary, were radical. He saw the root of the problem in the fact that demand was determined by centralised bureaucratic bodies which had little understanding of the market; the consumer should have much more say. In 1965 a major industrial reorganisation took place. Enterprises were to be grouped vertically into 'associations' and horizontally into 'trusts', and they were to enjoy much greater independence than heretofore. So too were factories, which were to assess demand for their products and to seek their own sources of raw materials. They were also to keep most of their profits, which could either be shared out amongst the workers or re-invested. On the other hand, subsidies were much more difficult to obtain, with factories being required to pay their way or close; about 1,300 did so in 1966. The reforms even allowed a certain amount of private economic activity in some parts of the service sector. Wages for those in the socialised industries could fluctuate with the quality of the produce but in general were controlled centrally, as were all but about 8 per cent of the prices of industrial goods. Despite these limitations, the Šik reforms were the most adventurous undertaken in Czechoslovakia since 1948.

The reforms were accompanied by changes in social policies which intensified the pace of and the appetite for restructuring. In the administration of the health services patients were to have some freedom to choose their doctor whilst in education many of the Russian and Soviet practices adopted after 1948 were abandoned. The 'brigades' and 'production work', to which young people were sometimes required to devote up to four months per year, were abolished; teaching in the humanities was increased; and gymnasia were reintroduced for those destined for university; other pupils would go to technical schools. In 1963 the revision of some textbooks was undertaken. Examinations for university entrance were also reintroduced and all entrants had to have completed secondary education, thus excluding the 'preparatory students', or woefully under-qualified and inappropriate party activists who since the communist takeover had enjoyed privileged access to higher education.

In 1965 there was an appreciable lightening of the censor's hand in the official media. Radio news in particular became less hidebound, adulation of the Soviet Union was toned down in all media, popular American television programmes such as 'Dr Kildare' were transmitted, and there was a much more open debate on a wide range of issues. New legislation made it possible to challenge the censor in a court of law but the former still had wide and loosely defined authority, being able to restrict any material which might endanger the security of the state or the stability of society. Nevertheless, the Czechoslovak media enjoyed a freedom which had not been experienced since February 1948.

The intellectuals made full use of this laxity. In May 1963 Eduard Goldstücker had organised a symposium on Kafka, and by 1965 relaxation had proceeded far enough for a Prague theatre to stage 'The Memorandum', a satire on bureaucracy by the young Czech playwright, Václav Havel; in the same year the party newspaper, Rudé Pravo, printed an article by Josef Smrkovský admitting that the Americans could have liberated Prague in 1945 but were prevented from doing so by fanatical communists, of whom he had been one.

A most significant feature of the relaxation of the mid-1960s, though it was one which was given only limited publicity, was the easing of restrictions on religion. A number of imprisoned clerics were released on condition that they went into retirement. There was no hiding another major relaxation: that on travel. In 1963 47,000 Czechoslovaks had made visits to the west; in 1965 154,000 did so, and in 1967 the figure was 258,000.

There were also steps in the direction of political reform. As early as 1964 the national assembly was showing an uncharacteristic liveliness for a communist parliament, even sending back to the government for redrafting bills on health and university reform. In 1964 Zdeněk Mlynář had argued that pressure groups should be allowed to influence the state machinery; this was an early call for what in the late 1980s became known as 'civil society', and it was Mlynář who was chosen by the CPCS's thirteenth congress in 1966 to head a team which was to prepare draft political reforms. In 1967 there were changes in the electoral law which allowed greater freedom in the nomination of candidates and even opened the way for the nomination of more candidates than places to be filled. Nor were the Slovaks forgotten. In the mid-1960s the influence of their local institutions was increased and the board of commissioners re-invigorated.

The two main questions to which the reforms and the 'Mlynář team' were directed were the nature of Czechoslovakia's place in the socialist community and the position of the communist party within the country. These questions had been raised implicitly in the new constitution of 1960 but the implications could not be discussed until after 1963 and the beginning of gradual liberalisation. The 1960 constitution had declared that Czechoslovakia had moved into the socialist stage of its development. Class differences had been removed and the dictatorship of the proletariat had been completed. Since the party had always been described as the instrument of that dictatorship, what was its role now that that dictatorship had ended? Furthermore, what was to be nature of the new, one-class society?

The Institute of Philosophy at the Czechoslovak Academy of Sciences had begun serious debate on these issues in 1963 and this was to be fundamental to the evolution of the country in the period up to the Soviet invasion of August 1968. One question frequently posed was on the precise nature of differences between various groups in a one-class society. The reformers argued that the Czechoslovak state was under no danger from within because only hostile classes could pose such a threat and now that socialism had been achieved there were no hostile classes. But, it was argued, if classes had disappeared, interest groups remained; furthermore, the objectives of these interest groups would run counter to one another, and harmonisation would not be automatic. The state or the party or both had to provide the means by which these conflicting objectives could be reconciled. The interest groups which were to play the leading part in formulating the demands that led to the reforms of 1968 were the intellectuals, the writers, the Slovaks, and the students.

All these groups were alarmed by the more repressive attitudes adopted by Novotný and the conservatives after the six day war in May 1967. This was made dramatically clear at the writers' congress held in the following month. Ludvík Vaculík electrified the congress by denouncing the constitution because it still guaranteed the leading role of the communist party which, said the writer, was no longer necessary or justified. The party, he said, had failed miserably to solve a number of social problems, particularly housing, and its interference in cultural affairs he condemned as totalitarian. This was too much for Novotný and his supporters, who attempted to use old-style methods to take over the writers' union from within and place it in the hands of their own trusties. This attempt was predictable, but the result was not: they could find no one who would do their dirty work for them.

Even more dramatic than Vaculík's outburst was the announcement from Vienna in August 1967 that Mňačko would not return to Czechoslovakia. He said he would stay abroad until Czechoslovakia recognised Israel and ceased to be so subservient to the Soviet Union in foreign affairs; in the meantime he would go to Israel. Mňačko's statement was amazing. He was not Jewish, and his career seemed a mirror of the party's own evolution; he had been an active partisan, an enthusiastic communist intellectual even during the purges, and finally a pioneer of relaxation when the dictatorship of the proletariat had ended.

His defection highlighted the cynical use that the conservatives had made of the Arab-Israeli conflict, and indicated that the party leadership had parted company with some of its most valuable supporters amongst the intelligentsia.

Mňačko's very public defection gravely embarrassed Novotný who now compounded his difficulties by his staggeringly inept and insensitive treatment of another major interest group, the Slovaks. The Slovaks were still resentful at the incomplete rehabilitation of the purge victims and they wished to see the restoration of more authority to Bratislava. This desire had been sharpened by the effects of the economic reforms because, just as after the first world war, the rationalisation of industry and the elimination of the weaker brethren amongst the enterprises hit Slovakia harder than the Czech lands. Here was confirmation of Slovak feelings that discrimination against them would continue, irrespective of the nature of the régime, as long as policies were decided in Prague. In August 1967 *Matica Slovenská* celebrated its one hundred and fiftieth anniversary. Novotný went to Turčanský Svätý Martin for the celebrations. The Slovak party, though led since 1963 by Dubček, had a sizeable conservative wing which Novotný could have won over with a few concessions to their Slovak sensibilities. Instead he behaved with boorish chauvinism. He forgot to take back to Prague the gift he had been given, and he enraged the arch-conservative Slovak Vasil Bil'ak by suggesting that the archives of *Matica Slovenská* should be sent to Prague. The Slovaks, including the most conservative amongst them, now realised that they had nothing to gain from supporting Novotný against his critics. And the Slovaks, unlike dissident intellectuals, had a voice where it mattered most: in the highest echelons of the party.

That voice was heard more loudly than ever before during a flash confrontation between Novotný and Dubček at a central committee plenum at the end of October. Dubček criticised investment allocations for Slovakia and an enraged and nonplussed Novotný replied that if Slovakia so wished it could become part of a federal structure and find its own capital for investment. Dubček, however, attracted support from a number of dissatisfied elements, Czech as well as Slovak; there were murmurings of too much power being accumulated in too few hands, and when the committee came to debate Novotný's 'Theses' on the role of the party in the socialist state, there was an unprecedented failure by the leadership to secure unanimous approval. Discussions were postponed until the next plenum in December.

On the last day of the October plenum violent discontent had broken out amongst the students of Prague. There was already general resentment at the régime's refusal to allow genuine democratisation of the party's youth organisations and to this was now added mounting anger at the poor living conditions in the capital's student hostels; not least among the complaints was that concerning the frequent interruptions in the electricity supply, even at the time of the annual examinations. The students therefore invited journalists to inspect the Strahov hostel, the largest in Prague. The arrival of the journalists coincided with yet another power cut, at which the students decided to march into the city. They were interrupted by the police who suggested that the marchers appoint spokespersons to articulate their demands. When the students refused, the police reverted to their traditional instruments of persuasion: the truncheon, the tear gas canister, and the water cannon. Thereafter student protest meetings became more and more frequent and they voiced ever more radical demands.

The clash between the students and the police had been an ugly one and together with the disarray in the central committee plenum showed that the Novotný régime was in deep trouble; a Yugoslav journalist believed that the power vacuum at the top had now become so great that the security forces would stage a *coup d'état* to reimpose party control.

It was not the security forces which stepped into the vacuum but Soviet party leader Leonid Brezhnev, who, at the invitation of Novotný, appeared at a central committee plenum on 8 December. What was decisive was not what he did but what he did not do: he did not give open support to Novotný; instead he stated that the leadership of the Czechoslovak party was a question for the Czechs and Slovaks themselves. This was 'tantamount to a death sentence on the political leadership of Novotný'.[4] At a further plenum on 5 January 1968 Novotný was removed as first secretary.

Czechoslovakia and eastern Europe had entered a new and decisive stage of their history. It was one in which the hopes for reform and an evolution away from totalitarianism, hopes gradually accumulated during the 1960s, were to be swept away for ever.

18

CZECHOSLOVAKIA, 1968–9

The consolidation of the Dubček régime: January to April 1968

The man appointed to succeed Novotný as leader of the Czechoslovak communist party in January 1968 was the one person to whom nobody was violently opposed: Alexander Dubček.

Dubček had been a member of the Czechoslovak party praesidium since 1962 and he now became the first Slovak ever to hold the senior post in the party. He was a pragmatic party apparatchik rather than an intellectual. He was not a naturally dominant personality, and was always more a follower than a leader. This made him the ideal man for his times. And so did other aspects of his character and his beliefs. At the party school in Moscow in 1955–8 he, like his fellow student Mikhail Gorbachev, had been much impressed by Khrushchev's speech to the twentieth congress and equally impressed when he returned to Bratislava by how little effect that speech had had on his own party. In 1961, when already a member of the Slovak central committee, he had encapsulated his moderate but contemporary views thus: 'The revolutionary aims of society can only be realised when the mass of the people support them. But this support and its resulting impetus . . . must be organised and led by the communist party.'[1] As first secretary of the Slovak party after April 1963, Dubček had not been on close terms with Novotný – that would have been personally distasteful and politically dangerous; but nor did he associate too closely with the Slovak dissidents – that would have brought down upon his head the wrath of Prague. Instead he sought genuine popular support as the basis of his power: and in general he found it. As a journalist had noted in 1962 when Dubček courageously attended the funeral of Karol Šmidke, a disgraced communist: 'This man Dubček is remarkable for his innocent honesty. He may reach the top of the party, but he is much more likely to find himself in prison. His ingenuousness is ridiculous, but astonishing and refreshing.'[2]

His few months as party leader in 1968 certainly produced astonishing and refreshing changes in Czechoslovakia, though the depth of these changes was not immediately apparent. Dubček himself was anxious to show his loyalty to the communist movement and went to Moscow at the end of January to assure the Soviet comrades that Czechoslovakia remained committed to socialism and to the Warsaw pact. Yet his first major public speech, on 1 February, to a congress of collective farmers, must have furrowed a few brows in the Kremlin. Dubček told the farmers that they should decide what crops should be grown as they knew better than bureaucrats in Prague what best suited the local conditions. The party, it seemed, was willing to scale down its leading role in agriculture.

The Kremlin also looked askance at the burgeoning of pressure groups in Czechoslovakia. From January until early in April, when the party published its new programme, a host of groups in Czechoslovakia were exploring and articulating their objectives. The Slovaks had a clear and easily formulated goal: an end to the asymmetrical model and federation in both state and party. The writers and the creative intelligentsia continued to press for full rehabilitation of the purge victims and now carried this further by demanding an inquiry into how such things could have been allowed to happen. This produced an extraordinary and intense discussion in the national media where there was also debate on why every social organisation, however insignificant, had to be controlled by the party. There were also demands that measures be taken to prevent a recurrence of past evils, that the militia should therefore wear identification numbers, that the secret police be abolished or greatly restricted, that the party be confined to the political arena and leave civil societies to organise themselves, and, most importantly, that all state and party officials abide by and be accountable to the law.

The Czechoslovak national motto, taken from the Husite reformers of the fifteenth century, is 'Truth will Prevail'. In their search for the truth the Czechoslovak intelligentsia in the early months of 1968 unearthed and made public shocking details of the communist past. In their demand for explanations of these events the enquirers produced what was a virtual inventory of the Soviet system as applied in Czechoslovakia. The effect of this was similar to the stories of the released political prisoners in Hungary before 1956.

Inevitably the search for truth alarmed the Czechoslovak old guard which made a last attempt to retrieve power by means of a military coup. The central figure in the plot was general Jan Šejna, a corrupt, loose-living friend of the Novotný family. He began plotting in December 1967 but found little support. At the end of February 1968 he was accused of embezzlement and deprived of his immunity as a parliamentary deputy. These accusations proved a test case for the Czechoslovak press which was still technically subject to censorship, as laid down in the 1967 law, but which had been operating since January 1968 with ever greater confidence and adventurousness; the revelations of corruption and high living which surrounded the Šejna case were too juicy to forgo, either by writer or reader; newspaper circulation in Prague, which had been 118,000 at the beginning of January was 557,000 in the second half of March, and at the beginning of that month the party had in effect abandoned censorship.

Šejna himself had meanwhile managed to escape via Hungary to the United

States. In so doing he became the highest ranking WTO officer then known to have defected to the west and he had done so because his own government and party had become too liberal for comfort. This was not an irony which Novotný could enjoy. After the Šejna revelations 4,500 letters and petitions were addressed to the party leadership in Prague demanding that Novotný step down as president. He did so on 21 March, the date which is generally accounted the first day of spring. His successor was Ludvík Svoboda, a former general who had commanded the Czechoslovak forces which fought with the Red Army and whose surname means 'freedom'. His first public act as president was to visit the grave of Tomáš Masaryk.

The accession of Svoboda was only one of a number of changes in the leading bodies of both state and party precipitated by the Šejna affair. In the middle of March the Slovak national council had removed its chairman, Michal Chudík, and further changes in personnel in that month and early in April saw Novotnýites being replaced by reformers in the central committee and in the state apparatus; 'In less than three months after Dubček's initial victory, the Novotný machine had disintegrated, thanks largely to general Šejna'.[3]

The April Programme

These changes in personnel were accompanied by another major turning point when, on 5 April, the party published its Action Programme.[4] Drawn up by enlightened marxists, it pointed to the way in which enlightened socialism was to be created in Czechoslovakia. It recognised that Czechoslovakia's path towards mature socialism would be individual and would be determined in part by the country's 'relatively advanced material base, uncommonly high level of education, and undeniable democratic traditions'. In the economic sector the Programme suggested that the competence of the government be confined to general economic policy, to long-term planning, and to protecting the consumers' not the producers' interests. There was to be much greater freedom for industrial enterprises and agricultural cooperatives in finding markets; there was a call for full equality in economic relations between Czechoslovakia and the Soviet Union and for the withdrawal of the remaining Soviet advisors. The critical questions of price control and wage regulation were funked.

In addressing the question of individual liberties the Programme showed no sign of evading difficult questions; it defined what later became known as 'socialism with a human face'. The Programme promised complete freedom of speech, debate, travel, and association, together with an end to arbitrary arrest. It also called for the transfer of many of the powers at present located in the ministry of the interior, including control of the prisons and what was left of censorship; the security organs were to be made accountable to parliament; and the courts were to have greater authority, though they were still not to be made completely independent.

In foreign affairs the Programme was largely orthodox, although it did call for the recognition of Israel and a cut in arms deliveries to Egypt and Nigeria, the Slovaks perhaps sensing a common cause with the Biafrans.

In internal party organisation there had already been considerable pressure for change, with demands that lower party organisations be provided with more information on policy and be allowed a greater influence in decision making. There were also calls for real elections for party officials, with campaigns, secret ballots, multi-candidate polls, and electoral commissions which were chosen openly and not nominated by their predecessors. The Programme accepted these ideas but it insisted nevertheless that decisions, once taken, were binding. Democratic centralism was to be recast but party discipline was to remain.

Of the two largest issues facing the reformers, namely Slovakia and the leading role of the party, the first was relatively easily dealt with. The Programme admitted that the asymmetrical system had caused injustices to Slovakia and that federation should be adopted, with the Slovak national council as the legislative body and the Slovak council of ministers as the executive authority in Bratislava. But, in what was a major concession to the Slovaks, federation was to apply also to the social organisations and to the party. It was, however, intimated that Slovakia would have to catch up economically with the Czech lands before it could enjoy the full benefit of federalisation.

On the other dominant issue, the nature of the party's leading role, a solution was much less obvious. The Programme argued that the party's leading role must be retained but should be redefined to remove the 'distortions' which arose from 'the false thesis that the party is the instrument of the dictatorship of the proletariat'; had that thesis not been declared false the party would have no function or purpose now that the dictatorship of the proletariat had ended. But in the new circumstances the party, at all levels, was to be much more responsive to pressure from below, and also to the feelings of society as a whole. In effect the party was to retain its leading role but this was to be regarded not as a permanent but as a renewable contract which had constantly to be justified. As an indicator of the party's retention of its leading role, the Programme still saw the trade unions performing their traditional task of 'orienting workers and employers toward a positive solution of the problems of socialist construction'.

Despite such traditionalist edges the central sections of the Programme called for a great deal more openness in the party and in society as a whole. The issue which now divided the party was whether the Action Programme was, as the radicals hoped, the beginning of the reforming process, or, as the conservatives desperately wished, the end. This question dominated Czechoslovakia from the April Programme to the invasion in August.

The liberalisation of Czechoslovakia, April to August 1968

Until the middle of July it seemed that the radicals would have their way. Although there had as yet been no legal guarantee of the freedom of association, numerous interest groups felt free enough to emerge into the open and to organise without fear of domination by the communists. By the middle of June about 250,000 individuals had joined the farmers' unions which sprang up throughout the Czech lands, despite conservative fears that they presaged the recreation of the post-1945 peasants' union or, even worse, the pre-war agrarian party. Veterans who had fought in the west and who had previously been persecuted by the official union of anti-fascist fighters formed their own association of soldiers who fought abroad, and they marched proudly in the May Day parade. Here they were joined by groups identifying themselves as former legionaries from the first world war, veterans of the Spanish civil war, associations of former political prisoners, and a group of small landowners and artisans in the traditional costumes of their guilds; there were even American and Israeli flags.

The revitalisation of religious life was another important development. Much greater contact was allowed between the Catholic church in Czechoslovakia and Rome and for its part the church was more flexible on the vexed question of ecclesiastic boundaries, giving up its long-standing resistance to changes which would remove some Slovak villages from Hungarian bishoprics. The government also agreed that, with effect from the academic year beginning in 1968, the church could take charge of religious education; further concessions included permission for the church to open a second theological college to cope with the rising number of would-be seminarists, the release of about 100 jailed priests, and the abolition of the 'stooge' organisation, the Peace Movement of the Catholic Clergy. The government was willing to see the re-emergence of religious youth organisations such as the Catholic boy scouts, and *Orel*, the Catholic gymnastic society. The Protestants, meanwhile, were allowed to reconstitute the YMCA and YWCA. Most surprising of all was the new attitude to the Uniate church, abolished in Czechoslovakia in 1950. In April 1968 clergy from the church met in Košice and resolved to seek relegalisation. To this the government agreed on 13 June 1968, much to the consternation of the Orthodox church in Slovakia which had inherited much of the Uniates' property. The Prague authorities, however, did not go as far as to relegalise religious sects such as the Mormons or the Jehovah's Witnesses which were totally dependent upon the west. The Freemasons also remained under interdict.

National minorities also received institutionalised recognition. There were plans to establish a Hungarian farmers' union and there were demands for separate status from Slovak, Hungarian, Polish, and Ukrainian youth groups. In general the Hungarians sought federalism *vis-à-vis* the Slovaks on the model of that which the Slovaks demanded from Prague, but there was not time to legislate on so complex an issue. After the invasion of 20–1 August a national minorities bill was passed but it was restricted to social and cultural associations.

The students who had been so vociferous in the months leading up to the fall of Novotný rapidly abandoned the official youth organisations which by the mid-summer of 1968 were moribund. They had been replaced by new and mostly decentralised associations, such as that for the students of Bohemia and Moravia which was established at Olomouc in May 1968. Youth rejection of established institutions was a central European as well as a western phenomenon in that heady year.

Two important and influential associations had appeared: K231, a club for former political prisoners detained under article 231 of the penal code, and KAN, the Club for Committed Non-Party Members. The latter had been established by 144 individuals, mostly from the Czechoslovak Academy of Sciences. They intended to seek representation in the national assembly.

KAN was one of a number of groups which was pressing strongly for much greater freedom to form political parties. This was an extremely popular demand which was supported in a May 1968 opinion poll by 90 per cent of the population but by only 55.5 per cent of party members. The government was willing to go some way in this direction, accepting that the shadow parties in the National Front should be allowed an independent existence; from April artificial limits on their numbers were removed and the parties were given the right to establish local branches. The sticking point came over demands for the re-establishing of the Social Democratic Party which had fused with the communists in 1948. Demands for its restoration had been voiced since March and were enthusiastically endorsed by KAN. In May the CPCS praesidium rejected the idea, not least because of the hostility towards it in other east European parties. The communists also feared that if their party were exposed to competition from another party of the working class, and one untainted by the sins of the recent past, the CPCS would become a rump of diehard stalinists and apparatchiks. After discussions with the SDP would-be leaders it was decided to leave the question until the next CPCS congress.

Though economic reforms did not feature prominently they continued during 1968. Šik had admitted privately in 1967 that the economic changes so far introduced represented only a quarter of what was needed, but, he said, the reformers had had to be pragmatic. Now there were fewer constraints and serious consideration was given to some form of association with the International Monetary Fund and other western financial institutions; on 17 August the prime minister, Oldřich Černík, admitted that the country was considering raising loans with the IMF and with some western firms.

The continuation of the economic reforms was not welcomed wholeheartedly by the industrial workers who faced relocation if their enterprises were not efficient enough to survive. Many workers were further angered by the shift away from wage equalisation caused by the reforms. To make sure that those for whom the communist movement was supposed to exist did not become completely alienated from the intelligentsia which was now in control of the party, strike action was legalised in May; some strikes did take place, almost all of them on parochial, economic issues, and many of them had the support of the local communist party organisation. A more significant development was the establishment throughout Czechoslovak industry of workers' councils. The councils came into legal existence on 1 July 1968, their form, composition, and power varying from industry to industry and factory to factory.

The creation of the workers' councils owed something to the revisionist experiences of Yugoslavia and of Poland in 1956. Further respect for Tito was seen in the fact that, in the international communist arena, the new Czechoslovakia refused to accept the anti-Yugoslav sections of Soviet declarations issued in 1957 and 1960; on the other hand, the Czechoslovak reformers always insisted that they would not allow their party to be cast out of the international socialist community as Yugoslavia had been, and partly for this reason they refused to join Romania in seeking some reservations on the nuclear non-proliferation agreements.

As the spring and summer progressed the reforming brush swept in wider and wider arcs until it seemed that no corner would be left untouched, not even the party itself. Reform of the party was a delicate issue: radicalism would insense conservatives at home and abroad; caution would convince sceptics outside the party that it would never alter, let alone abandon, the bases of its power. That dilemma had been palpable in the Action Programme, but by May the reformers were more confident and at a plenum at the end of the month they secured the concession that the next congress, scheduled for the spring of 1969, should be brought forward to September 1968. Thereafter the reformers concentrated upon preparing new party statutes to put before the congress and upon campaigning inside the party for the election of reform-minded delegates. The elections were held in June and July; four-fifths of those elected were pro-reform.

The new draft statutes were published on 10 August. They far outran the Action Programme in radicalism. Even in their vocabulary they stood far apart from similar documents from the past. Words such as 'humanitarian' and 'democratic' peppered the text and the substantive proposals were hardly less innovative. All party elections were to be by secret ballot, no party or state office could be held for more than two periods except in exceptional circumstances, party and state offices were to be separated, and punishments, including expulsion from the party, could be decided upon only by local party organisations. The federalisation of the party also went further under the new draft statutes than under the Action Programme.

The draft statutes seemed at last to have tackled the question which underlay so much of Czechoslovak development since 1963 and even more so during the debates of the so-called 'Prague Spring': that of the role of the party after the dictatorship of the proletariat. In *Rudé Pravo* on 13 January 1968 Mlynář had developed his argument that the party's function in future was to mediate between interest groups with conflicting aims, but there was increasing pressure to remove the party from all social debate. On 20 March a leader of the Prague students openly declared that if the party could not find an answer to the students' problems then they would have to search for other means to reach a solution. In April the tough-minded and liberal chairman of the national assembly, Josef Smrkovský, expounded the view that the leading role of the party should be expressed by the influence exercised in state bodies by communist delegates and deputies who were freely elected in real elections; they would operate like caucuses or interest groups in any open society. Dubček, in the same month, stated that the best defence for democracy was a high degree of public participation, but he was not yet ready to sacrifice the party's leading role. When debating the question of whether to relegalise the SDP he stated:

In our country there is no alternative to socialism than the marxist programme of socialist development which our party upholds. Nor is there any other political force, loyal to revolutionary traditions, which would be a guarantee of the socialist process of democratisation. That is why we are righteously defending the leading role of the party in society.[5]

In its actions as well as its theory the party moved a great distance from its former, stalinist concepts. The relaxation of central control over the economy, the accommodation with the church, the virtual abolition of censorship, and the increase in the independence of parliament were only four examples of its willingness to dilute its leading role, and in June 1968, despite the Action Programme, Dubček promised a meeting of the trades union congress that they need fear no interference from party or state. There were even moves in the middle of the summer to break the party's control over the appointment and promotion of army officers.

External concern over the reforms

All of this was too much for the conservatives, and if those in Prague and Bratislava had retired to lick their wounds, their allies in Berlin, Warsaw, Sofia, and Budapest were still keeping a watchful eye on developments in Czechoslovakia. Even as early as 1965, in a closed meeting of party chiefs, Walter Ulbricht had criticised the relaxation of party control in Czechoslovakia. In February 1968 Brezhnev, in Prague to celebrate the twentieth anniversary of the communist accession to power, threatened to go back to Moscow before the ceremony if Dubček did not change the speech he had prepared. This warning to the Czechoslovak leader was followed next month by a summons to Dresden. Here the assembled party bosses of the Soviet empire expressed concern at the pace and direction of the reforms in Czechoslovakia and, more ominously, Soviet troops were offered should Dubček feel that they were necessary to preserve his party's authority. Relations between Prague and the other east European capitals became much worse in May. On 4 May Dubček was in Moscow seeking a loan and reassuring the Soviets of his loyalty, but he was vehemently attacked for giving western propaganda so much to feed upon, and for allegedly breaking a promise given to Brezhnev earlier in the year that old comrades would not be removed from the leadership. The Soviets also increased noticeably their broadcasting output in Czech and Slovak and there were rumours of Soviet tanks and armour moving towards the Czechoslovak border from the Cracow region. On 9 May, the anniversary of Prague's liberation from Nazi rule, the *Berliner Zeitung* published reports of US tanks operating in the forests of

Bohemia; they were true – a film was being made there of the battle for the Remagen bridge in 1945. There were also rumours that the Soviets had drawn up an invasion plan. These rumours were also true: the text of the plan was published in Bulgaria in 1990.[6]

As a measure of good faith the Czechoslovak leadership, despite its previous resistance to such an idea, proposed in May that Warsaw pact manoeuvres should be held on Czechoslovak territory. The WTO accepted the plan. From now on Dubček and his colleagues were trapped in a vicious circle of their own making. To allay external concerns they made concessions to Moscow and its conservative allies, but these concessions heightened domestic fears that the government was double-dealing, fears that could be stilled only by further reforms at home, which, of course, reawoke the concerns of the conservatives.

On 26 June the national assembly abolished preliminary censorship. The following day a number of leading Czechoslovak newspapers published '2,000 Words' by Vaculík. His manifesto was meant to influence voters in the elections to the party congress but it had also been prompted by his distaste for rising anti-semitism, especially in Slovakia, and by the increasing mention in the mainly foreign, conservative press of anti-socialist forces at work in Czechoslovakia. '2,000 Words', though moderate and practical in tone, was dynamite. Not only did it expound, with impeccable marxist-leninist orthodoxy, the case for reform and democratisation but it also hinted that there was a danger of invasion by the WTO and suggested that in such circumstances the Czechs and Slovaks must defend themselves. Such 'action from below' would finally destroy the leading role of the party. The praesidium went into immediate emergency session and condemned the document for fear of the effect it would have in Moscow and the other east European capitals. This only served to highlight and further popularise the document at home and petitions of support came flooding in not only from intelligentsia-based groups but also from many workers' councils. In response the Soviets delayed the withdrawal of the Red Army troops who had been on manoeuvre in Czechoslovakia. The radicals were unintimidated. Eugen Loebl, who had been imprisoned in the 1950s, declared that the USSR had ruined the Czechoslovak economy by blocking reforms and jailing the best economists; the philosopher Ivan Sviták denounced socialist aid to semi-fascist Arab governments, and the press embarrassed the Soviets with revelations on the execution of Imre Nagy and the actions taken against Tito.

The conservatives returned to the attack. On 14 July the leaders of Poland, the Soviet Union, the GDR, Hungary, and Bulgaria assembled in Warsaw to consider the Czechoslovak situation. Out of this meeting came the Warsaw letter of 16 July to the leaders of the CPCS, condemning and demanding an immediate reversal of the reform programme; 'Not since Stalin's quarrel with Yugoslavia had the communist world seen such a document. Appropriately enough, the Yugoslav press printed the letter under the title "Cominform 1968".'[7] Two days later Dubček replied, justifying his policies and refusing to change them; on the same day, in a masterly television address to his people, he assured them that his commitment to the process of democratisation was undiminished but also reminded them that this process demanded 'a conscious civil discipline that requires statesmanlike wisdom of all citizens'. One prominent citizen who in the leaders' eyes did not exercise statesmanlike restraint was general Václav Prchlík. He it was who had warned Dubček of the Šejna plot and on 15 July he had condemned the WTO powers for breaching their own treaty agreements by failing to withdraw their troops from Czechoslovakia. Prchlík also suggested that the security agencies should be placed in state rather than party hands and that there was no reason why the WTO senior command should consist solely of Soviet officers. Here was an intimation that the spirit of reform might spill out from Czechoslovakia and affect other communist states or institutions. On 25 July the government removed him by closing the central committee's eighth department which oversaw security matters and of which he was head; this achieved Prchlík's objective of shifting control of the security services into state hands, but it was also the first occasion on which anyone had been removed from office on account of their reformist views.

None of this satisfied the Soviets who demanded that Dubček come to Moscow for negotiations. Dubček refused, insisting that he would talk only on Czechoslovak territory. From 29 July to 1 August the two sides met in an atmosphere of extreme tension at the frontier town of Čierná-nad-Tisou. The Soviet delegation was shunted across the border each day in an armoured train whilst the Czechoslovaks, knowing that their telephones were tapped, had to smuggle in helicopters with messengers bearing the latest news from Prague. The Soviets attacked with enormous ferocity, asserting that the Czechoslovak leadership had sacrificed all that the socialist movement had achieved since 1948; when they also declared that the Czechoslovaks were inciting the Ruthenians to demand secession from the Soviet Union Dubček walked out, refusing to talk further with anyone who could utter such drivel. Eventually Brezhnev moderated his tone and it was agreed to hold a further meeting on Czechoslovak soil in the near future.

The second round of talks took place in Bratislava on 3 August. The result was a declaration which was couched in terms of extreme ideological orthodoxy. It stated, *inter alia*, that

> Our fraternal parties oppose (with great vigilance and unshakeable solidarity) all plots of imperialism and other anti-communist forces which aim at weakening the leading role of the working class and the communist parties. We will never permit anyone to undermine the bases of the socialist régime. The various tasks necessary to build a socialist society in our respective countries are more easily resolved with mutual aid and support.[8]

After the Bratislava meeting there was considerable distrust amongst Czechoslovak reformers as to what Dubček had promised his allies. It was possible for the reformers to take some solace from the visit of Tito on 9–11 August and of Ceauşescu on 15–17 August, but Ulbricht also came on 12–13 August, there

335

were ominous meetings of east German and Soviet defence chiefs, and there was a series of minatory newspaper articles such as that in *Pravda* on 18 August on 'Loyalty to International Duty'. On 20 August *Neues Deutschland* stated that socialist internationalism included a readiness to seek help from fellow socialist states, and by implication a duty to provide such help.

The WTO invasion and the 'normalisation' of Czechoslovakia

'Help' reached Czechoslovakia on the night of 20–1 August in the form of what was at the time the largest military operation in Europe since the second world war; 'international proletarian solidarity' brought twenty-nine divisions, 7,500 tanks, and over 1,000 aircraft pouring into a defenceless allied country which had not even mobilised. The forces used were twice as large as those deployed in Hungary in 1956 and this time the Soviet army was accompanied by small contingents from the GDR, Poland, Hungary, and Bulgaria. The Czechs and Slovaks chose not to resist with arms but did all that they could to frustrate the invaders by denying them food and water, by removing road signs, and by arguing with the tank crews. Inevitably occasional skirmishes and accidents occurred and 80–200 lives were lost. The entire executive committee of the praesidium was taken to Moscow.

The military side of the operation had been carried out with precision but in political terms it was a shambles. The invasion had been timed to prevent the meeting of the new congresses elected in June and July, that in Slovakia being due to convene on 26 August and the Czechoslovak on 9 September; once those congresses met, the conservatives would be removed from the party offices they still retained and the Soviets would have no one on whom they could rely within the party apparatus. The executive committee of the praesidium would meet on 20 August for the last time before the Slovak congress and the invasion was timed to seize the members of that committee whilst it was in session. The assumption was that the Soviets would then find 'loyal comrades' who would form a new administration on traditional lines. But none came forth; there was no Kádár or Quisling, nor was there a Hácha figure who would surrender as had happened in 1939. The invasion could not even prevent the meeting of the fourteenth congress which was brought forward to 22 August and met in a factory in the Vysočany suburb of Prague; despite the disruption of the communications network, over 12,000 delegates, more than two-thirds of the total, managed to reach the congress which condemned the invasion and elected a totally reformist central committee. The population also remained solidly behind the reformers, an opinion poll of 14–16 September showing 94.6 per cent in favour and only 0.6 per cent against the policies pursued since January.

The failure to find a collaborationist leader forced the Soviets to negotiate with Dubček and his colleagues. Brezhnev bullied them mercilessly. Cheap anti-semitism was used against Jewish and some non-Jewish members of the delegation, and the Soviet leader even threatened to incorporate Slovakia into the

USSR and to make Bohemia and Moravia autonomous regions under Soviet administration – a Protectorate, perhaps? The outcome of the 'negotiations' was the Moscow protocol of 26 August, the day on which the Czechoslovak delegation returned to Prague. The protocol made no mention of the Action Programme, and banned all parties outside the National Front as well as any organisation which violated socialist principles. By the middle of September the government, the national assembly, and the party's central committee had all endorsed the protocol and a new censorship law had been passed. Dubček and his colleagues had returned from Moscow promising that they would continue the process of reform and that they would move as rapidly as possible to the 'normalisation' which would ensure the removal of foreign troops. On 16 October a treaty was signed 'On the conditions for the temporary stationing of Soviet troops on ČSSR territory'.

After the invasion a remarkable solidarity, news of which reached the leaders in Moscow via a telephone call from president Svoboda's wife, had enabled Dubček and his associates to prevent the imposition of harsher terms, but the prospects for long term resistance were not good. The Czechoslovak leadership failed to appeal to communist parties in the non-WTO states, a move which would have rattled a Moscow anxious to convene a conference of world communist parties later that year. There was no attempt by Dubček and his associates to declare a general strike or to delay signing the Moscow protocol for a few more days, a manoeuvre which might have complicated Soviet-American relations and endangered the forthcoming SALT talks.

At home, despite initial national solidarity against the invaders, the reformist lobby was far from united, a fact which enabled its opponents to apply a new form of salami tactics. They attempted in particular to exploit the differences between Czech and Slovak. State, but not party, federalisation was enacted on independence day, 28 October, but a more significant development had been the nomination of Gustáv Husák as Slovak party boss on 28 August; his intense nationalism made him acceptable in Slovakia and could be exploited to complicate relations between Bratislava and Prague; it would be relatively easy to see whether the Slovaks were more committed to federalism than to reform. Husák, like Svoboda, was also known for his intense sense of pragmatism which could enable the Soviets to open gaps between these two and the dogmatic reformers. The Soviets also had an important echelon on whom they could rely: those who 'feared the loss of positions gained by their zeal at the time of show trials'.[9] The stalinist spectre would haunt Czechoslovakia even after 1968.

The Soviets, however, moved with caution. The rehabilitation of purge victims continued, albeit more slowly, and the reformists were not immediately removed from office. But long term Soviet aspirations were clear; 'normalisation' was to mean the restoration of full party domination. At the turn of the year Husák persuaded his colleagues that the leading positions in party and state should be shared equally between Czechs and Slovaks, a device which enabled him to remove Smrkovský. It was in protest against this move that Jan Palach burned

337

himself to death in Prague's Wenceslas Square on 16 January 1969. On 21 and 28 March the Czechoslovak ice-hockey team beat the Soviets in world cup games which were transferred from Prague to Stockholm. The team manager received telegrams of congratulation from Dubček and other leaders whilst at home delirious crowds daubed graffiti such as 'Long Live the Victory of Athens over Sparta' and attacked Aeroflot offices and other Soviet institutions. There were suspicions that the crowds had been provoked in order to give the conservatives an excuse to demand more repression. In any event the incidents were so exploited; the Soviet defence minister arrived, declaring that the situation was more dangerous than in 1968, and on 17 April Dubček was replaced as first secretary by Husák. There were further confrontations on the streets on the first anniversary of the invasion, with four people being killed in Brno, but no further action was taken against Dubček until December when he was packed off to Ankara as ambassador; he was not allowed to take his children with him. On 9 May 1970, liberation day, a new agreement with Moscow made permanent the stationing of Soviet troops in Czechoslovakia, and in the following month Dubček was recalled and sacked. He was also expelled from the party, the first and the most prominent victim of a savage purge soon to be unleashed upon the CPCS; normalisation was all but complete.

The consequences of the invasion

The invasion had been justified by what became known as the 'Brezhnev doctrine'. This modified polycentrism by stating that if socialism were threatened in any state then other socialist governments had an obligation to intervene to preserve it.

The reasons for the invasion of 20–1 August are to be found to some degree in Kremlin politics. Whilst Czechoslovakia in the 1960s had been moving away from stalinism to a more liberal form of socialism, Brezhnev's Soviet Union was heading in the opposite direction. Brezhnev, like Khrushchev in 1956, also had some reason to fear the military; he had assured them that the removal of Novotný would calm the Czechs and Slovaks; when it did not, the Czechoslovak crisis became entangled with the party versus military tussle in Moscow.

There were, however, other, more complicated and more varied motives for the five-power invasion. There was some fear of western expansionism in general and west German revanchism in particular. The former had been fed by the Vietnam conflict, the six day war, and the Greek coup, whilst the second was sharpened because it was believed that Dubček had transgressed guidelines had been laid down in 1967 for the establishment of diplomatic relations with Bonn. Czechoslovakia was also the only state with borders with both the FRG and the USSR, a contemporary describing it as 'poised like a dagger aimed at the heart of the Soviet Union'.[10] Gomułka, already alarmed by events in Poland in March, feared that a vacuum would develop in Czechoslovakia into which German influence would inevitably be drawn. Ulbricht was even more alarmed by the new freedoms in the Czechoslovak Socialist Republic: he was in no position to allow such licence because it would lead to demands for union with the federal republic. Furthermore, the lax travel regulations in the new Czechoslovakia allowed many east Europeans to slip across the border into the west; this seemed to the east German and Soviet régimes to negate the economic and diplomatic difficulties which were endured as a result of the construction of the Berlin Wall. At the same time there was some alarm in Moscow and Kiev that the restoration of the Uniate church in Czechoslovakia would excite the population of the western Ukraine, whilst federalisation was seen as an implicit criticism of Soviet nationalities policies.

There was some concern that a new communist bloc could appear in Europe with Czechoslovakia, Yugoslavia, and Romania coming together in a reconstruction of the little entente; this would weaken Moscow's control over central and eastern Europe and its position *vis-à-vis* NATO. But such fears were exaggerated; economic relations between Prague and Bucharest were bad and a lasting association of reformist Czechoslovakia and Ceauşescu's régime was unlikely, whilst the Soviet Union, which had withstood Hitler's onslaught, could never be seriously threatened by an alliance of small communist states.

Another concern was that Czechoslovakia might move away from the east European trading community. Should Prague develop links with the west it would, as was its stated wish in 1968, move towards convertibility for the Czechoslovak crown and if this were to be achieved the finishing processes which Czechoslovak industry performed for other east European economies would become impossibly expensive. But again such fears had little substance; socialism had done a reasonably good job of wrecking the Czechoslovak economy and convertibility was a distant prospect if not a dream.

In fact external questions, political or economic, were of little importance in 1968. Despite the occasional scare story over German revanchism, the Soviets never claimed that Czechoslovakia was seeking neutrality or that the west intended to move its forces into the country; what the Soviets feared was that internal Czechoslovak political developments might lead to a situation where neutrality or a conversion to the western camp would become possible. The invasion was therefore as much a form of political prophylaxis as a surgical operation to remove a contaminated organ. Yet socialism was in no danger in Dubček's Czechoslovakia. The economic programme did not seek to imitate western consumerism; an enquiry carried out on the day of the invasion itself revealed that no more than 5 per cent of the population would have welcomed a return to capitalism; not one agricultural collective was dissolved in 1968; and the enormously popular manifesto which was issued by playwright Pavel Kohout at the time of the Čierná meeting listed as its demands, in this order: 'socialism, alliance, sovereignty, freedom'. Nor did the Soviets have to fear the sort of traditional anti-Russianism which complicated their position in Poland, Hungary, and Romania.

The only thing threatened in 1968 was Soviet-style socialism outside the

Soviet Union. The end of the dictatorship of the proletariat meant the transition from extensive to intensive economic development, in which the leading role would be played not by manual labour but by the scientific and technological revolution; control of the means of production would pass essentially from the traditional working class to the intelligentsia. Under the Soviet system the traditional working class had been controlled by the party bureaucracy; the intelligentsia was unlikely to be so compliant. This was complicated by national factors. The Czechs and Slovaks were hoping to follow polycentrism and to adapt socialism to their own historic traditions; in Russia socialism had combined with the historic tradition of absolutism to form stalinism, in Czechoslovakia it was to combine, as the Action Programme intimated, with the Czech traditions of humanism and tolerance to form democratic socialism. In economic terms the Czechoslovak reformers argued in the mid-1960s that their problems derived from the imposition of Soviet methods on to an advanced rather than a backward economy; if the west were to be converted to socialism it should therefore be of the Czechoslovak rather than the Soviet variety. Smrkovský told a youth meeting on 20 March 1968, 'Many of us, I think, realise that our country may be able to become a type of socialist state that would have a lot to say to the people of the developed countries of the European west.'[11] The Soviets therefore feared that the Czechoslovak experiment might threaten their domination of the world communist movement as well as their security cordon in central Europe.

The Soviet Union and the world communist movement were to pay a huge price for Moscow's determination to preserve its hegemonistic position in central Europe. The invasion had been staged to preserve a Soviet system which was based upon the leading role of the party, yet it had happened at a time when the Czechoslovak party was enjoying unprecedented popularity. If popular communism could not be equated with Soviet power, pro-communists would cease to look to the USSR for inspiration or support. In this sense, Czechoslovakia 1968 was one of the progenitors of eurocommunism.

Inside Czechoslovakia itself an immediate casualty of the invasion was the century-long tradition of russophilia; there were too many parallels between 1938–9 and 1968 for it to survive.

The damage caused by the invasion was, however, far more extensive than the questioning of Soviet primacy in the European communist world or the destruction of Czech russophilia. The Czechoslovak reforms had attempted to modernise the Soviet model and to adapt it to a more advanced, more liberal environment; Moscow's unwillingness to accept such an adaption

> proved something most Czechoslovak reformers ... did not even dare to believe at the time, namely, that the established marxist-leninist theory is incompatible with a genuine, modern, democratic, economic and political system and, what is more, that it is not even open to reform.[12]

The implication of this is that it is not stalinism which caused the invasion but leninism; the causation is thus pushed back from the alleged distorter to the founder of the Soviet system.

It was more than the hope for future change which died in 1968. For many the Prague spring had meant a rebirth of faith and had erased even the bitter memories of the purges; the reforms meant the overcoming of past disillusionment. The second disenchantment was permanent; 1989 was not to be another 1968, revisionism was finished and had given way to rejectionism. Socialism with a human face was 'the last attempt to rejuvenate communism in central Europe';[13] after 1968, said Kołakowski, communism 'ceased to be an intellectual problem and became merely a question of power'.[14] If communism was now nothing more than a question of power, logically its final defender must be that ultimate repository of power, the barrel of a gun. That communism depended upon the army was eventually to be proved in Poland.

Part IV

THE DECLINE OF SOCIALISM

19

EASTERN EUROPE, 1969–80

The Soviet reaction to the emergence of reformism within the CPCS prompted a general tightening of party reins in eastern Europe which persisted until the mid-1970s. At the same time most east European parties announced that they had moved from the stage of socialist construction into 'real existing', 'developed' or 'mature socialism'. Party programmes and state constitutions appropriate to this new stage of historical development were adopted. The socialist stage was in theory one in which material provision would increase rapidly; consumer goods and services would become ever cheaper and more widely available. But if the years 1956–68 ended with the bankruptcy of ideological communism, the years 1968–80 ended with the failure of consumer communism.

If the east European economies were to provide improved living standards they would have to be modernised and geared to intensive rather than extensive development. Such a transition would be difficult for a variety of reasons. The labour force had never been educated or trained to appreciate the importance of the quality rather than the quantity of production; capital could not be generated in sufficient volume to invest in the newest technologies, and those that were adopted were earmarked primarily for the military; besides which, it is doubtful whether any planned system could have coped with technological innovations as profound, as frequent, and as rapid as those of the 1970s and 1980s. One avenue of escape from the dearth of capital and from socialism's increasingly disadvantaged position in the technology race was to import or to steal know-how and equipment from the west.

If technology were to be imported there had to be an easier relationship, political and economic, with the western powers and above all the United States. Political détente was achieved in the Helsinki agreements of the summer of 1975. Closer economic links had been developing in the early 1970s when a number of east European states had decided to borrow from the west in order to finance domestic modernisation. Initially this had been easy as the western banks were eager to lend, interest rates were low, and trade was sufficiently buoyant to suppose that the loans could be serviced from exports. The great oil price increase of 1973 transformed the situation. Credit became much more difficult to find, interest rates rose, and trade contracted. To make matters worse, the Soviets were forced to bring their oil prices more into line with world market levels, which placed a huge extra burden on many east European states; all too often they borrowed to service existing debt and by 1981 the east European and Soviet debt to the United States and western Europe was fifteen times greater than in 1970. East European borrowers were left with the stark choice of defaulting, allowing their debts to mount until they became crippling, or depriving the home market in order to export what they could to pay off their debt.

Whichever course was chosen would cause enormous difficulties and the problems posed for the communist régimes in the mid-1970s were never in fact solved. The longed-for modernisation was never achieved; the communist states had hobbled themselves in a vain attempt to close the technology gap with the west. Scientific socialism just could not cope with science.

The problem was even more profound. Borrowing from the west enabled the régimes of eastern Europe to avoid fundamental restructuring. By holding out this hope of a short-cut to modernisation, western capital in fact allowed the inner contradictions of socialism time in which to mature and to wreck the system.

Czechoslovakia

One of Husák's first priorities after becoming first secretary was to purge the CPCS of reformists and revisionists. The process began in 1970 and was to last for four years. By the end of it 327,000 party members had lost their party cards and a further 150,000 had resigned voluntarily; the party had been cut by one-third. The purge was less rigorous in Slovakia but was particularly vicious amongst the main architects of the reforms, the intelligentsia. Two out of three members of the writers' union lost their jobs, 900 university teachers were sacked, and twenty-one academic institutions were closed; between 1969 and 1971, for the first time since 1821, not one literary journal was published in Bohemia and Moravia.

The main effects of the purge were to remove any potential opposition to the '69ers', and to create a virtual party-in-waiting, one which was far more able and much more respected than the one in office. It is one of the more remarkable features of post-1968 Czechoslovak history that this group had such little effect on the country; its lack of impact showed both its own demoralisation and the extent to which all communists were now discredited in the popular mind. When opposition to Husák's régime did appear, it was outside rather than inside the party, whether ruling or in the wings. Communism was now seen more than ever as a foreign imposition.

As the party was purged so too were state and local government institutions, whilst in Slovakia the new authorities took advantage of the clampdown to take their revenge on the Catholic church. The reimposition of party authority meant that the organs of public control burgeoned. The precise numbers of the police force were not revealed but it was known that they increased and that 70 per cent of police officers were party members, as were 90 per cent of the 120,000 strong people's militia, a virtual private army of the party which was equipped with heavy machine guns and light artillery. There were also an estimated 10,000 emergency police and 23,000 auxiliary police, in addition to which, of course, there was the Czechoslovak army and airforce, and a Red Army presence numbering some 70,000. Whereas five years after the Hungarian revolution Kádár had made his famous 'those who are not against us are with us' declaration, five years after the Czechoslovak reforms Husák promulgated a new criminal code 'especially designed to facilitate swift persecution of political and ideological deviance'.[1] In the following year a new law gave the police almost unlimited powers of search.

In May 1971 the 'official' fourteenth party congress met, Dubček having been forced in September 1968 to declare the Vysočany version illegal. The congress abolished the Action Programme and elected a new 137-member central committee, only twenty-six of whom had been in that body in 1968. In effect all of the reforms of 1968 had been dismantled, with the exception of state federalisation. Czechoslovakia had been 'normalised' and was ready to move into 'real socialism'.

The intensity of the purges and repression of the early 1970s owed something to the fact that at the beginning of the decade Poland had again been simmering with revolt but even when that danger had clearly passed the Czechoslovak authorities showed little disposition to relax. Instead they sought to buy their way to legitimacy with material provisions, a policy which has been analysed as 'coercion, consumerism, and circuses'.[2]

Consumerism was in general promoted with relative ease in the early 1970s, but Husák had the additional advantage that the Kremlin, in order to make his task easier, allowed him a temporary reduction in military spending and in aid to Cuba, Vietnam, and various Arab states. Czechoslovak citizens not only found their disposable income increasing but also, more surprisingly, found goods and services on which to spend it. Between 1970 and 1978 private consumption rose by 36.5 per cent, country cottages became popular status symbols, and whereas in 1971 there was one car for every seventeen Czechoslovaks, by 1979 the figure was one for every eight. Circuses were provided in the form of new and more adventurous television soaps, the publication of more books, and more imported western films and music, as long as they were not too subversive.

Not all Czechs and Slovaks could be bought off with dachas and soap operas. Much encouraged by the Helsinki declaration, a number of intellectuals met in December 1976 to form Citizens' Initiative, the main purpose of which was to demand the observance of those individual rights which Czechoslovak law itself guaranteed. Their manifesto, dated 1 January 1977, gave the group the name by which it later became renowned: Charter '77. The founders of the movement included Jiří Hájek, who had been Dubček's foreign minister, Václav Havel, and the philosopher Jan Patočka who was later to die after an eleven-hour interrogation by the Prague police. There were 241 original signatories to the Charter and by 1980 their number had grown to around 1,000; few of them were Slovak and fewer still were Hungarians, the majority being from the Prague and Brno intelligentsia.

The power of the police apparatus in Czechoslovakia and the widespread sense of disillusionment, especially amongst the Czechs, meant that Charter '77 never became the mass movement that Solidarity in Poland was to be, but that was never its intention. Its aim was not the creation of a political or a social movement; it did not call for the overthrow of the party or the government; instead it saw itself as a 'moral challenge' to the cynicism of officials, to the apathy of the public, and to the empty materialism of both. It asked little more than that the Czechoslovak authorities respect their own laws, and it provided documented cases of where they did not. Also, through its 600 or so samizdat publications, Charter '77 provided information on a whole range of issues. In later years it was to offer a nexus between Czechoslovak reformers and their sympathisers in the west.

Charter '77 was not the only unofficial organisation in Czechoslovakia. Much of its information on judicial malpractice, for example, was provided by the committee for the defence of the unjustly persecuted, which was set up in 1978. In the late 1970s the jazz section of the musicians' union also appeared as an identifiable group importing jazz and other forms of western music, though it had to fight a continuous battle with the authorities who looked with great suspicion on phenomena such as rock 'n' roll and punk. In 1979 the jazz section managed to affiliate to the International Jazz Federation, a body sponsored by UNESCO, and its bulletin, Rock 2000, was regarded as one of the world's most authoritative bibliographic compendium on the subject.

At the end of the 1970s, however, the unofficial groups posed little threat to a party so ruthlessly re-established at the beginning of the decade.

Hungary

Developments in Czechoslovakia made it seem as if Hungary had set out upon its course of economic reform, the NEM, at the least propitious moment. The new climate of 'counter reform' of the early 1970s did indeed bring some hedging of the reform process but, perhaps because its economic reforms had followed a process of gradual political relaxation rather than being seen as a prelude to it, Hungary weathered the reactionary pressures of the 1970s more easily than the other countries of the Soviet bloc.

It is arguable that there would have been some retrenchment in the NEM even without the Soviet pressure which followed August 1968. The loosening of central controls and the tentative move towards market forces had inevitably produced social tensions as wages for the working class failed to keep pace with rising prices; even as early as 1972 7 per cent of the Hungarian workforce was said to have more than one job. There was also the threat of dislocation, a euphemism for unemployment, as government subsidies to uneconomic concerns were cut. In addition to this there were growing disparities of wealth, with a raw, new-rich element making its appearance. To idealists who still retained a belief in equality this was offensive; to party conservatives a new élite based on wealth rather than power was threatening.

In a central committee plenum in November 1972 the opponents of the NEM, a coalition of managers of large enterprises, state and party bureaucrats, and trade unionists, scored a number of victories: the architect of the NEM, Nyers, was dropped from the party secretariat; wage increases were ordered for over a million workers, a step which was to be repeated in 1973; and fifty large corporations were placed under the direct control of the council of ministers. Other dilutions of the NEM followed with restrictions on profits and with tax concessions cast in a marxist-leninist mould. The NEM had been all but suspended.

When Nyers was removed from the secretariat so too was György Aczél. Aczél had been in charge of cultural affairs and his removal signified that the reimposition of greater economic control was to be accompanied by a tightening of the political reins. In 1974 a number of prominent writers and scholars associated with the so-called 'Budapest School', were deprived of their jobs and their party membership, the most notable victims being András Hegedüs, who had been prime minister for a short while in 1956, György Konrád, Miklós Haraszti, Agnes Heller, Ivan Szelényi and Ferenc Fehér.

This was not, of course, a purge in any way comparable to that in Czechoslovakia and many of those who were sacked in Hungary were allowed to find new careers in the west. In fact, the clampdown of 1974 affected few outside the leading ranks of the academic world. For the majority of Hungarians the political relaxation begun in the 1960s was still more palpable than the slight restrictions imposed in the 1970s. Foreign travel was relatively easy, though subject to having the requisite hard currency; most exiles had no difficulty in returning to the country, though visits were rationed to one in every five years; and foreign literature was obtainable with little difficulty. Before the slight frost of 1972, Béla Biszku, a close associate of Kádár, had called for an increase in democracy inside the party which, he said, was 'a most vital step towards democracy throughout the country'. His statement presaged legislation in 1971 which allowed individuals or recognised groups to nominate candidates in local and parliamentary elections. Though all candidates had to be approved by the party-dominated Patriotic People's Front it was now possible, for the first time since 1947, to have multi-candidate parliamentary elections. It was the first major move towards political relaxation in eastern Europe since August 1968. In 1972 the Hungarian parliament went even further, passing a law granting full rights to all citizens, not just to those classed as workers. Plurality as well as equality had been embedded in the Hungarian social and political system.

In the second half of the 1970s the major preoccupation of Hungary's rulers was again with the economy. There were some positive achievements. Between 1972 and 1982 Hungary's increase in agricultural production was the second

349

highest in the world, a success made all the greater by the fact that it had been secured in a collectivised system which had not alienated the peasantry. Consumer goods were more available than elsewhere in eastern Europe and it was in the 1970s that gulas communism had its heyday. Yet there were dangerous developments too. Hungary was badly affected by the world recession which followed the oil price rise of 1973. The prices of raw materials and food, which had formed an important part of the export trade by which Hungary serviced its debts to the west, fell sharply; between 1973 and 1980 the price of aluminum fell by 40 per cent, that of bauxite by 10 per cent, and that of grain by 19 per cent. The Soviet decision to raise its oil prices towards world levels meant that from the beginning of 1975 Hungary was paying 120 per cent more for most of its energy.

The increasing difficulties which were experienced after 1973 compromised the dilution of the NEM imposed in 1972. By 1977 economic conservatism had been discredited and from then on the NEM was rehabilitated and applied with greater vigour, if not always with the desired results.

Yugoslavia

The wave of demonstrations and street action which had characterised 1968 in both socialist and non-socialist societies did not leave Yugoslavia untouched. The social impact of the Reform caused some disquiet, students taking to the streets of Belgrade in May 1968 to demand more rather than less socialism. Tito, always by inclination a leninist, intervened, showing considerable sympathy with many of the students' demands.

In November 1968 there were further student protests, this time in Priština, the chief city of Kosovo, and this time with nationalist rather than socialist demands. The university of Priština was at this point still a satellite of the university of Belgrade, with teaching almost solely in Serbo-Croat. The protesters demanded, and were granted, an independent, Albanian-language university. As inclusion in Hoxha's Albania was far from an attractive prospect, there were no calls for secession from Yugoslavia but there were demands for a separate republic of Kosovo within the federation. This was not granted but Kosovo was made a 'socialist autonomous province' of Serbia in 1968 and Kosovans were allowed to fly the black-eagled, red flag of Albania. Kosovo was also given much higher priority for investments. These concessions bought time but no long-term solution. There were neither enough textbooks nor trained Albanian-speakers for the new university, which therefore imported teaching materials from Albania. These included the writings of Enver Hoxha which insisted that at the end of the war Tito had said that Kosovo should be included in Albania. The new university of Priština also produced far more graduates than could be absorbed in Kosovo, and no other republic would employ Albanian-speakers. The unemployed intelligentsia, so vital an element in the composition of extreme nationalist movements during the inter-war years, had been recreated.

In the late 1960s and early 1970s, however, it was not in Kosovo but in Croatia that nationalism seemed to pose the greatest threat to the Yugoslav state. The Reform had made the banks rather than the federal state the main source of investment funding but the banks had not been decentralised, with the result that, to Croats, the Reform seemed to have increased rather diminished Belgrade's control over the economy. This problem was exacerbated by the fact that a set proportion of foreign currency earnings still had to be transferred to the federal bank in Belgrade, and the Croats, with their flourishing Dalmatian tourist industry, resented this drain on their funds; Croatian economists argued that the republic lost 45 per cent of its revenue to the central coffers. Whilst economists made these calculations, historians fuelled old-fashioned cultural nationalism with monographs on Serbian domination of Yugoslavia in the years before 1939 or even 1944. Such nationalism also received a powerful boost from *Matica Hrvatska*. This long-established organisation was by the 1960s receiving support and money from newly founded branches amongst Croats working in the west, particularly in the FRG, Sweden, and Australia.

Nationalism soon began to affect the Croatian party with the appearance of a new dominant trio of Mika Tripalo, Savka Dabčević-Kučar, and Pero Pirker, who, if not necessarily liberals, were definitely decentralisers. For this reason they took no action against the Zagreb student demonstrators of November 1971 who carried slogans such as 'End the Retention Quotas', 'Stop the Plunder of Croatia', and 'A Separate Seat for Croatia at the UN'. Signs of incipient separatism, plus the fact that nationalists inside the Croat party were allowing non-communist nationalists to take prominent positions in the social organisations and thereby threatening the leading role of the party, forced Tito into action. He called the Croat party leaders to a crisis conference on his island of Brioni, and, when they appeared reluctant to impose discipline, he announced on the radio that the Croat leaders had lost control. Ten days later, on 12 December 1971, he used the threat of force to persuade the Croatian central committee to remove the three leaders. This was followed by the arrest of some 400 Croat nationalists and by Tito's resumption of control over the secret police. The 'Croatian Spring' was over.

The Yugoslav emergency of 1971, the most serious since 1948, had ended all pretence of socialism making possible an evolution away from nationalism. It also discredited those reformers who had argued so strenuously that economic reform was essential to head off a recrudescence of old-fashioned nationalism. It had also shown that centralism remained strong in the party even if it had weakened in the federal state. As the purges spread out from the Croatian to the other Yugoslav parties, the liberals as well as the local nationalists found themselves the victims. The anti-liberal purges strengthened nationalism. A solid party member might easily accept the need for the dismissal of avowed nationalists, but the punishment of someone whose only mistake was to argue for economic decentralisation was less easily explained. To many, and especially to Serbian communists, this looked like federal interference in their own party's affairs and, what was worse, an interference which was precipitated by the misbehaviour of Croats. The response was to be more vigilant against any sign of such interference from the centre and in turn this made local nationalism in the party and outside it more acceptable.

If an increase in parochial feelings was a predictable result of the 1971 emergency so too was constitutional change. Even before the Croatian crisis had come to a head there had been an important constitutional amendment which granted to the six republics and the two provinces prime sovereignty in all rights of government which the constitution did not assign specifically to federal institutions. In 1974 came a completely new constitution; with its 406 clauses it was the longest in the world. It was also amongst the most complex. One of its most important provisions was to give the two provinces, Kosovo and the Vojvodina, equal rights of veto with the republics. In an attempt to combine representation from interest groups and territorial units, the federal assembly was to contain delegates who were elected from six categories: workers' councils in the social sector; peasants and farmers; the liberal professions; territorial constituencies; socio-political organisations; and, finally, state and party bodies and the army. In 1976 there was a further refinement of self-management. In an attempt to revivify worker involvement, the workers' councils were now to be located not in the enterprise, an arrangement which had made technocratic and managerial domination too easy, but in the basic organisation of associated labour; there were over 30,000 such units by the end of the decade. Self-management was also extended as far as possible into the state administration and all other bodies except the federal army.

In the mid-1970s Tito, who was now over 80, also insisted that provision be made for continuity in government after his death; a rotating presidency was therefore devised, to be shared out to each republic in turn.

These provisions seemed to bring some political stability in the years up to Tito's death in May 1980. As elsewhere in eastern Europe, however, there was no concomitant easing of economic anxieties. The increase in oil prices, rising interest charges on a growing hard-currency debt, and internal inflation were problems which continued to plague Yugoslavia in the late 1970s.

Bulgaria

In the mid-1960s Bulgaria had embarked on a moderate package of economic reform which included some concessions to the profit motive, some decentralisation, and a great deal of talk about 'planning from below'; but Zhivkov, with his finely tuned political nose, smelled danger even before the Soviet intervention in Czechoslovakia. In July 1968 the reform programme was scrapped, as calls went out for the imposition of 'iron discipline' within the party and for the subjection of all social groups to party control.

Economic experimentation was not entirely abandoned. In 1969 seven cooperative farms in the Vratsa area were merged into one unit which was also to have some processing industries. In April 1970 the politburo extended this experiment and the so-called agro-industrial complexes (AICs) spread throughout the country. This was itself a considerable extension of party and central control over the agricultural sector, but for a while the worst consequences of this monopolistic manoeuvre were not visible. Rather the contrary, because with each farm concentrating on three crops and one animal, yields improved, and the party congratulated itself on finding a mechanism which not only increased agricultural production but also stemmed urban drift and moved towards homogenising town and country into a new single, socialist society.

In 1971 the country adopted both a new constitution and a new party programme. According to the new constitution Bulgaria was now 'a socialist state of the working people in the town and the countryside headed by the working class'. The party was acknowledged as having a leading role in state and society and in the construction of socialism. A new body, the council of state, which replaced the former council of ministers, combined executive and legislative functions. Its chairman, not surprisingly, was Todor Zhivkov. The Bulgarian party programme of 1971, like a number of other new programmes introduced in this period, recognised that a unified socialist society had been built and, this being so, that the party had to redefine its functions for the next stage of social evolution: that through mature socialism towards the first stages of communism. Just as social revolution had enabled the east European parties to construct socialism, so mature socialism was to be built by the scientific-technological revolution which would engineer the intensive growth which was now necessary. To hurry along that growth there would also be increasing trade with the west as well as joint ventures and licensing agreements with western firms.

By the end of the decade the results were disappointing. Foreign indebtedness was rising, the quality of the few goods on the market was appalling, trade outlets in the west were elusive if not illusive, whilst social provision for most Bulgarians was improving only slowly. Even the AICs were no longer so effective, Zhivkov admitting to a meeting of the Bulgarian Agrarian National Union in 1977 that present agricultural policies had 'landed us in a pretty pickle'.

There were other disquieting factors for many Bulgarians. The 1970s had seen a growth in the power of the secret police, the DS, a force which was entirely subservient to the KGB. Subservience to Moscow seemed to be an intensifying trend in Bulgaria in the 1970s. Sofia hardly deviated from the Soviet line in foreign policy, except intermittently over Macedonia or some other Balkan issue, and in September 1973 Zhivkov declared that Bulgaria and the Soviet Union would 'act as a single body, breathing with the same lungs and nourished by the same blood stream'. He made a second attempt, the first having been a decade previously, to incorporate Bulgaria into the USSR.

Bulgaria's political subservience to the Soviet Union did have some economic advantages, more particularly in preferential treatment over oil, some of which Bulgaria could sell on at world prices. However, it damaged the country's international standing, as did a series of allegations of involvement in unsavoury activities, among them drug smuggling, arms sales to terrorists, and the murder in London of Georgi Markov who died after being impregnated with a poisoned pellet shot from an umbrella on Westminster Bridge in September 1978. Such incidents distressed many Bulgarians even more than their leader's fawning attitude towards Moscow. Even in docile Bulgaria, therefore, discontent was increasing and in 1977 Zhivkov admitted to the existence of 'dissidents', a word he had never used in public before.

Romania

There was hardly a greater contrast between Bulgarian foreign policy and that of Romania. Ceauşescu continued to parade his independence of Moscow. He condemned the invasion of Czechoslovakia and in 1971 he visited China and North Korea; apart from Enver Hoxha he was the first east European leader to go to China since the Sino-Soviet split had become public. The Soviets were so offended that they staged WTO manoeuvres on the Romanian border. At the end of the decade Ceauşescu condemned Soviet intervention in Afghanistan and the Vietnamese incursion into Cambodia. Such defiance of the Kremlin earned him in 1969 the reward, if it can be so construed, of a visit from President Nixon, the first time a US leader had set foot in communist eastern Europe. President Ford also went to Bucharest. In return, Ceauşescu and his egregious wife, Elena, visited the United States no less than three times: in December 1970, January 1973, and April 1978. In 1978, to the displeasure of the Queen, he was awarded the especial distinction of staying in Buckingham Palace when on a state visit to the United Kingdom.

More substantial gains came when Romania was granted most favoured nation status by the USA, and in 1971 when Romania was admitted to the GATT; in 1972 Romania became the first east European state to join the International Monetary Fund. Romanian trading patterns moved steadily away from dependence on the Soviet and east European markets and became more involved with those of the west and of the developing world. In the long run this was to prove a disaster.

At home the Ceauşescu régime talked not of mature socialism but of the 'multi-laterally developed socialist state', a concept which was codified in the RCP programme of 1974. It was argued that structural development in society could not alone produce a full socialist consciousness; this could come only if all citizens became aware of socialist values operating in all sectors of society. The agency by which they would be made so aware was the party. The party would merge state and society, the individual and the collective, and would promote 'the ever more organic participation of party members in the entire social life'. In 1972 Ceauşescu told a national party conference that he had in mind 'a certain blending of party and state activities . . . in the long run we shall witness an ever closer blending of the activities of the party, state, and other social bodies'. These ideas were implemented in a number of joint party-state structures, for example the council for socialist education and culture, which had no exact parallel in the other socialist states of eastern Europe; at the local government level, as in Poland, the party leader of the 'county' was ex officio its chief administrator. The RCP was also closely integrated into the trade unions.

Ceauşescu himself combined the headship of the RCP with the state presidency. That was only one feature of a stalinism which seemed to grow rapidly after the 1971 visit to China and more particularly to Kim Il Sung's fortress state. The adulation of the new *conducator* (leader) intensified, as did the powers of the secret police, the Securitate. Protest, individual or mass, became more difficult and more dangerous. A few voices within the party did speak out but to little effect. At the twelfth congress in 1979 84-year old Constantin Pîrvulescu said that Ceauşescu had put his personal interests before those of the party; Pîrvulescu's party credentials were withdrawn. In August 1977 over 30,000 miners in the Jiu valley struck for more pay and in protest against their working conditions. In imitation of the Polish strikers of 1970 (see pp. 359–60), they also demanded direct negotiations with the party leader, who appeared on the third day of the strike to be greeted, once again *à la polonaise*, with cries of 'Down with the red bourgeoisie'. A settlement was reached but within the next few years 4,000 miners had been sacked and a number of the strike leaders had died in road accidents or of premature disease; Securitate doctors were later reported to have administered five-minute chest X-rays to guarantee the eventual development of cancer. An attempt in 1979 to form an independent trade union was totally ineffective.

A particularly pernicious feature of the Ceauşescu dictatorship was its demographic policy. Ceauşescu seems to have had a genuine delusion that he could make Romania a great power and a major actor upon the world stage. But he knew he that could not do this if the population did not increase; artificial birth control was therefore proscribed in October 1966 and women of child-bearing age were required to undergo regular pregnancy tests, with severe penalties for anyone who was found to have terminated a pregnancy. The birth rate rose from 14.3 per thousand in 1966 to 27.4 per thousand in 1967; the rate fell later but there were still many personal tragedies. There were recorded cases of women dying rather than reveal the name of their abortionist – there were Securitate agents in all gynaecological wards – and many of the products of unwanted pregnancies found their way into the appalling orphanages which so moved the civilised world after the revolution of 1989.

Ceauşescu added a Balkan dimension to stalinism: nepotism. Partly because career officials were never regarded as entirely trustworthy, near and not so near relatives of both Ceauşescu and his wife were placed in a large number of senior party and state posts, and the Ceauşescus' loathsome son, Nicu, was groomed for the succession. Even by the end of the 1970s it was being said that in Romania they were building socialism in one family.

By that time Romania, like all east European states, was beginning to encounter real economic difficulties. The causes of these difficulties were in broad outline similar to those elsewhere in the region but they were exacerbated by particular, Romanian, factors. In the 1970s Ceauşescu's economic strategy had been to build up Romania's oil-refining capacity. The intention was to process relatively cheap crude, first from Romania's own resources and then, as these were depleted, from Iran, Iraq, and elsewhere. The processed oil would then be sold at a handsome profit on the Rotterdam spot market. To build up its refining capacity Romania borrowed from the west against the expected profits. This strategy was wrecked by a number of factors: fluctuations in the world price for crude, political upheaval in the middle east, and the cost of repairing the damage caused by the 1977 earthquake. By the beginning of the 1980s Romania owed huge sums to western creditors. The earthquake also triggered Ceauşescu's manic plans to reconstruct Bucharest.

Albania

Ceauşescu's only companion as an east European 'independent stalinist'[3] was Enver Hoxha who was at least his equal in paranoia and vindictiveness; his party's leading role was as intense; his secret police, the Sigurimi, were every bit as brutal as the Securitate; the cult of his personality was just as pervasive; and his economic policies were equally directed towards autarky.

Albania condemned Soviet intervention in Czechoslovakia and quit the WTO in September 1968, though not through any love for Czechoslovak revisionism but rather in protest against great power hegemonism. With Chinese encouragement the Albanian régime sought security through closer links with Yugoslavia and Greece. At the same time Tiranë looked for better trading outlets and some political connections in selected western countries and in the third world. The United States was still an ideological untouchable and Britain was still on the Albanian black list because of the dispute over the Corfu channel incident of 1946 and the subsequent seizure of Albanian gold reserves, but Tiranë could work more easily with new states such as the FRG or the neutrals such as Austria and Sweden and the semi-neutral France. Historic and geographic links also brought about some trade between Albania and Italy.

In addition to seeking more contact with the outer world in the early 1970s, Hoxha permitted some relaxation of domestic controls, particularly those on intellectuals and on the young. He did not like the results. By 1973 he had decided to reimpose discipline on both groups and those who had argued for the more relaxed line had been purged from the leadership. In October of the following year his heavy hand fell upon the military where he feared the growth of a powerful, professional officer class. From October 1974 to April 1980 prime minister Shehu assumed control of the ministry of war and purged the officer corps. A similar 'cleansing' was visited upon the economic bureaucracy which Hoxha blamed for the poor economic performance of the second half of the 1970s. The 1976 constitution was rigidly marxist-leninist, not only making the party the leading force in state and society but also limiting private property to wages, personal homes, and articles for personal or family use. It also forbade foreign loans.

The second half of the 1970s saw a rupture between Albania and China. The Albanians disapproved strongly of China's closer relations with the United States, epitomised by Nixon's visit to Peking in 1972. Nor had Hoxha been enthusiastic over China's advocacy of *rapprochement* with Yugoslavia. Even more damaging was China's inability to deliver on time promised machinery and other forms of aid; Peking, in fact, unilaterally cut the amount of aid agreed for the period 1976–80. Relations declined even more rapidly after the death of Mao Tse-tung and Zhou Enlai in 1976, and the Chinese invitation to Tito to visit China in 1977. In 1978 the Chinese suspended aid to Albania and relations between the two countries cooled considerably, though they were not broken off entirely.

The GDR

Developments in the GDR in this period, as in all others, were to a large degree functions of Soviet and western actions.

In the early 1970s the Soviet Union was anxious to dispel the bad image left by 1968 and to relax international tensions so as to halt the increase in defence spending. The advent of Brandt's socialist-liberal coalition in Bonn in 1969 indicated that the FRG might also be ready for détente. In August 1970 Brandt signed a treaty normalising relations between the FRG and the USSR and in December of the same year he made his famous visit to Poland, during which he signed an agreement recognising the German–Polish frontier. The signing of the west German–Polish agreement was a major step towards real détente in central Europe. An accommodation between the two German states would have been an even greater step. Prodded by Moscow the GDR did agree to two meetings in 1970 between Brandt and GDR prime minister Willi Stoph, first in Erfurt in the GDR on 19 March and then in Kassel in the FRG on 21 May. There was little progress, Stoph even asking for a hundred million marks in compensation for the damage done to the GDR economy before the building of the Berlin Wall.

Ulbricht was the main obstructive element and the Soviets therefore encouraged the east Germans to find an alternative leader. This they did in May 1971 when Ulbricht was kicked upstairs to the newly created post of chairman of the SED. The eighth party congress in May chose as his successor Erich Honecker, who had been born in Saarbrücken, survived ten years in Nazi gaols and labour camps, and then become prominent in the communist youth movement. He had also supervised the building of the Berlin Wall.

The Wall was the most obvious expression of the principle of differentiation, *Abgrenzung*, between east and west Germany. It was a principle which Honecker held dear. He rejected Brandt's idea of there being two German states but only one nation, insisting that an identifiable east German socialist culture and

nationality had evolved east of the Elbe; he believed that what the 1968 constitution had called 'the socialist state of the German nation' was now peopled by
a distinct socialist nation. *Abgrenzung* was also a departure from Ulbricht's thinking, which could never shed the notion of a united, socialist Germany. For
Honecker accommodation with Bonn was possible because it was yet another
recognition that east Germany was a separate entity. He had welcomed the four-
power agreement on Berlin in September 1971 and late in the following year
had signed the basic treaty, the *Grundvertrag*; these two agreements, together with
accords which were signed between the two German governments, meant that
the FRG had now recognised the GDR whilst the latter had accepted west
Berlin's claim to exist separately from the rest of the city. That being done, the
United States removed its prohibition on the GDR joining the United Nations,
which it did in September 1973, as did the FRG. In 1974, on the twenty-fifth
anniversary of the foundation of the state, the GDR parliament enacted an
amendment which removed from the constitution all references to unification
or the German nation. At the same time the titles of a number of state institutions
were changed so that, for example, the German Academy of Sciences became
the Academy of Sciences of the GDR. *Abgrenzung* was complete and the population should not think that reunification was any longer a political option.

Complete separation also meant more Soviet-style socialism. In the early 1970s
the economic reforms of the 1960s were modified and the central planning
apparatus given more power. Trade was even more closely linked to the Comecon
countries, with the GDR replacing Poland in 1970 as the Soviet Union's chief
trading partner. The SED, at its eighth congress in May 1971, accepted the
Soviet Union as the leading force in world socialism and looked forward to
the increasing integration of the socialist economies. In east German schools
there was to be more emphasis on the teaching of Marx and Lenin, usually at
the cost of classical German literature, and, much to the anger of the churches,
military training was also made part of the school curriculum. It was only one
of a number of ways in which east German society became more disciplined,
organised, and militarised in the first half of the 1970s.

If this were irksome to the east German citizen some solace might have been
found in the fact that in general the standard of living was rising. At the SED's
eighth congress Honecker had pledged the party to improved social provision,
especially in housing, and to an increase in the supply of consumer goods. At
the subsequent congress in May 1976 he felt that sufficient progress had been
achieved to declare that the party had chosen the right road and that 'It had all
been worthwhile'.

The mood of euphoria was neither widespread nor prolonged. Within a year
of the Helsinki accords and their promise of freer travel, over 100,000 east
Germans had applied for permission to leave the country. In 1976 there came a
sign of tightening of cultural controls when Wolf Biermann, a singer of mild
protest songs who was then on a tour of west Germany, was deprived of his
GDR citizenship. Other critics who ventured abroad were similarly treated and

some were 'sold' for substantial sums in deutschmarks. In 1979 a new law decreed that anyone publishing abroad material which was damaging to the GDR could be punished; until then many east German writers had published in the FRG rather than in their own country.

Economic difficulties grew whilst tolerance of criticism contracted. The higher oil prices which were charged by the Soviet Union from the beginning of 1975 hit the GDR very hard; by the end of the decade it had to export three times as much as in 1973 to pay for one ton of Soviet oil. Despite the indirect subsidies the GDR received from west Germany, its foreign debt increased from $1.4 billion in 1971 to $10.9 billion in 1979. Although the GDR's industries were technically advanced when compared with the rest of the Soviet bloc, they lagged far behind those to the west and machinery was frequently subjected to damaging over-use in an attempt to maintain or improve productivity levels.

Poland

In Poland party leader Gomułka had lost nearly all internal credibility by 1968 but had survived because his hawkish views on Czechoslovakia had been so welcome in the Kremlin. He did not survive long.

In 1970 the country was facing severe economic dislocation and, in an attempt to combat this, on Saturday 12 December an immediate increase in food prices was announced on the radio. The nation was outraged, the more so because the increases were announced just before the Christmas festivities. If the régime hoped that welcome for the recent German-Polish normalisation agreement would neutralise anger at the price rises it was to be disappointed. On 14 December workers in the Lenin shipyard in Gdańsk struck and marched into the centre of the city. On the following day nearby Gdynia was also strike-bound whilst in Gdańsk strikers attacked the party headquarters. On the same day a clash between strikers and the forces of law and order ended with at least 75 strikers being killed. The party attempted to cover up the details of the conflict but it failed and Poland by mid-December was once more on the verge of rebellion; strikers in Szczecin were calling for independent trade unions and the establishment of a parallel administration.

Gomułka had ordered the repression at Gdańsk and elsewhere and his inclination was for the use of more and greater force to contain the revolt. The Kremlin did not agree and intervened to urge the need for a political solution. For the nationalist communist Gomułka, Soviet dictation of internal Polish policies was too much; he became apoplectic, metaphorically and literally. On 20 December he was replaced as first secretary by Edvard Gierek, who had spent much of his childhood in the Polish mining communities in Belgium, and who had built a powerful political base amongst the miners of Silesia. Gierek had a much more open and relaxed style than his predecessor and in January he went to the Baltic ports to negotiate directly with the strikers, placating them with promises of greater involvement in future decision-making. In Łódź, however, the textile workers were not so pliable and because of their implacable opposition the price increases announced on 12 December were rescinded.

December 1970 was the first occasion in eastern or western Europe since the second world war when spontaneous action by workers had dislodged an incumbent ruler. It was also the first time in which an east European régime had engaged in direct talks with its disaffected citizens. It is true that those citizens had remained overtly socialist, the strikers and demonstrators carrying red flags and singing the 'Internationale', but the workers of Poland had shown that they could act on their own, since in 1970 the intelligentsia kept as distant from the workers' protests as the workers had from the intelligentsia's two years earlier. The workers had shown that they had tremendous political muscle, a muscle which they were prepared to use should their putative patrons in the party let them down. Furthermore, December 1970 disturbed the diarchic balance in Poland in which the party exercised political power while the church exercised spiritual authority and not a little social control. Gierek and his colleagues certainly felt the shock and promised both a 'renewal' of the party, which would henceforth be less intrusive in governmental affairs, and a boost in living standards for all.

Gierek was to dominate Polish affairs for a decade. The first half of that decade was preoccupied with economic reforms, and the second with the attempt to deal with the consequences of them. The stated objective of the reforms was to increase living standards; a less publicly attested motivation was the knowledge that, with prices fixed and with demand increasing, goods had to be put into circulation to avoid rampant inflation. To satiate demand, more consumer goods were imported whilst at home food production was to be stimulated through a series of concessions to the peasantry, including access to public health and welfare schemes and pensions. Investment plans were redesigned to allow greater allocation of funds to the consumer sector. There was to be considerable reorganisation in manufacturing industry, with the grouping of factories in one branch of production into large industrial organisations (LIOs). By 1975 the LIOs accounted for 67 per cent of industrial production in Poland.

Initially Gierek's reforms enjoyed spectacular success. Between 1971 and 1975 real wages rose by 40 per cent, Poland's economic growth rate was the third highest in the world, and there was even talk of revising plan targets upwards rather than in the usual direction.

On the other hand, the economic reforms were not accompanied by any attempts to change the political system and the major structural change in the economy, the introduction of the LIOs, was primarily administrative and was not entirely beneficial. The LIOs decreased already fading party control in the factories but replaced it not by rational market forces or genuine workers' control but by the state administration. Yet that administration, despite its increased authority in the factories, did not dare to control wages; the workers and management therefore stoked the inflationary fires by helping themselves to more money at the expense of the central exchequer.

Nor did the Gierek reforms end the drive towards the construction of heavy industry. Petro-chemicals and oil production were increased on the basis of the cheap Soviet crude available before 1975 and medium priced light oil from Saudi Arabia; steel, too, was not neglected.

> What was unique about Gierek's 'great leap forward' was its scale, [and] the breathtaking incompetence with which it was executed . . . Gierek's monument is the gigantic, unfinished 'Huta Katowice' steelworks, a huge economic white elephant for which the only rationale is political: it lies in the heart of his former Silesian fief, providing jobs for the boys; a specially built broad-gauge railway runs from its gates straight to the Soviet Union.[4]

The major weakness of Gierek's economic strategy, however, was its reliance on western markets and western credit. Gierek gambled that the new technology, together with Poland's low labour costs, could produce enough goods to satisfy home demand and to sell abroad to pay for the loans. In the meantime he would rely on coal, Poland's main export, the price of which was increasing more rapidly than that of imported goods. With Poland's low level of indebtedness, the west's surplus of capital, and the atmosphere of détente in the run-up to the Helsinki agreements, borrowing was easy and apparently painless. The Yom Kippur war and the oil price hike of 1973 wrecked Gierek's gamble. The increase in oil prices made all Poland's imports from the west more expensive whilst, at the same time, the recession in the west depressed demand for Poland's exports; by 1975 these exports could pay for only 60 per cent of imports. Agriculture also suffered. Imported fertilisers were now beyond the pocket of many farmers, state or private.

During the second half of the 1970s Poland's economy went from bad to worse to apparently irredeemable. The growing shortage of consumer goods was partly made up by purchasing in the GDR where some stores priced goods in złoties as well as ostmarks. Despite increasing shortages there was little restraint upon wages, especially in the LIOs, which meant in turn rapid inflation in the black market, which was frequently the only source of domestic supply. Nor was there any relenting in the government's 'success propaganda', despite the fact that an unprecedented number of Poles were travelling in the west – some four million in the early 1970s – and knowledge of the comparative state of Poland's economic performance was therefore widespread.

Added to mounting economic frustration was growing social discontent. The housing sector had been given a much-needed boost in the earlier years of the decade but it was soon clear that the promise given then to provide a home for all by 1990 could not be met; in rural areas there seemed little progress away from a situation where one-third of dwellings had no running water; there was little relief for students, many of whom, even if married, had to live in appalling, sexually segregated hostels. Poland's health service, poor even by east European standards, found it difficult to cope with the sudden extra burden placed upon it by the admittance of peasants to state health 'benefits'. Social deprivation was reflected in the dreadful figures for alcoholism; even the official statistics admitted to one million alcoholics by 1980 with 40 per cent of alcohol being consumed at the work place.

Social resentments were made much sharper by the knowledge of the widespread privileges enjoyed by the small number of the party and administrative élite. In 1980 there was immense anger at the revelation of a separate hospital building programme for the employees of the ministry of the interior, i.e. the police, whilst Nowa Huta, the vast industrial complex near Cracow, had to make do with one hospital with only 1,000 beds for its 200,000 inhabitants. It was yet another illustration of the widespread and corrosive system of privilege that stripped all legitimacy from a régime which constantly mouthed the platitudes of equality and social justice; a respondent to an influential inquiry wrote:

> Inequality and injustice are everywhere. There are hospitals that are so poorly supplied they do not even have cotton, and our relatives die in the corridors; but other hospitals are equipped with private rooms and full medical care for each room. We pay fines for traffic violations, but some people commit highway manslaughter while drunk and are let off with impunity. In some places there are better shops and superior vacation houses, with huge fenced-in grounds that ordinary people cannot enter.[5]

The political front did not offer much obvious relief from the gloom dominating the economic and social sectors. The free trade unions which had been conceded to the workers of Szczecin and elsewhere in 1970 had been subverted, their elected members corrupted by being bound into the prevailing world of privilege and power; a second round of elections to these unions never took place. In 1973 censorship was tightened whilst government overtures to the church produced little in the way of concessions. Yet the reluctance of the party to relax its established power reflected fear and uncertainty as much as confidence and arrogance.

The party was far from being in a strong position. In 1970 the normalisation of relations between Poland and west Germany, and the latter's *de facto* acceptance of the Oder-Neisse line as the Polish-German border, deprived the leadership of the long-standing argument that, like it or not, Poland needed the Soviet Union to protect it from German revanchism.

This was but one of the reasons for the decline in the Polish party's self-confidence and power in the 1970s. Even as early as 1970, when the party headquarters in Gdańsk had been restored, the building was given a flat roof for helicopter evacuation; a few years later, when the police banned a lecture organised by students in Cracow on 'Orwell's 1984 and Poland today', the students simply relocated in a church where it went ahead unimpeded. If such actions were unimaginable in Romania, Bulgaria, the GDR, or even Czechoslovakia, yet more inconceivable was a communist régime withdrawing two clauses from a draft constitution because of pressure from the church and the intelligentsia, but in the face of such pressure in 1975 the PUWP dropped from its proposed new constitution clauses on the precise nature of the party's leading role and on the Soviet-Polish alliance.

This indecision and lack of will characterised party policy over possible price rises in 1976. The 1975 harvest in Poland and the Soviet Union had been poor, forcing the Poles to import grain from the west, grain which would be paid for, the authorities believed, by exporting meat. But the home market was avid for meat, especially pork and ham, and the government therefore suggested to the sejm that the price of meat at home be increased to force it into the export trade. Even the suggestion of possible price rises was seen by many as an abrogation of the agreements negotiated in 1970 and it produced strikes throughout Poland. In Radom the party building was ransacked and its hoarded stocks, including those of ham and sausage, were handed out to the crowd which, having denounced the 'red bourgeoisie', torched the building. The price rises were once again withdrawn, with only a few token and short-term arrests to salvage the authorities' damaged prestige.

The humiliation of 1976 was the beginning of four years of increasing confusion and dislocation amongst Poland's leadership and in the ranks of the party. As its own sense of purpose decayed, so did the respect with which it was regarded by the population at large.

The economy remained the most obvious difficulty. The debt problem had become acute, foreign currency debts rising from $700 million in 1971 to $6,000 million in 1975. With the contraction in international trade and the rise in western commodity prices Poland was having to borrow to service its debt, with the result that by 1979 debt servicing absorbed 92 per cent of Poland's export earnings. A Poland which was supposedly led by nationalist communists had become dependent on western finance capitalists; from this the vast anti–communist majority might derive wry satisfaction, but for those within the party it probed nationalist nerves which had previously been left untroubled since 1956. Yet the party was too enfeebled to grapple with the issue. Economic rationality insisted that the industrial programme had to be geared to paying off the debt rather than to increasing living standards, but political pragmatism dictated the opposite; many workers did not believe the propaganda of gloom any more than they had previously believed that of success, and, even if they did, they were not prepared to tolerate any diminution in their living standards either by forgoing wage rises or by allowing price increases. Political constraints deprived the Polish communist régime of the means to solve its economic problem.

Gierek faced another difficulty in that the intelligentsia and the church were moving closer together because the intelligenstia not only approved of the radicalism of churchmen such as cardinal archbishop Wojtyła in Cracow but also realised that poor relations between it and the church had weakened opposition to the régime in 1970. In an effort to keep church and intelligentsia apart, Gierek made overtures to the former. He met both cardinal Wyszyński and Pope Paul VI, proclaiming thereafter that there were no differences between state and church.

In 1978 the party leader attempted to sweeten nationalist tempers by allowing the erection of a statue to marshal Piłsudski.

Whether Gierek's gestures to the church and the nation were in reality signs of generosity or weakness mattered little because they had scant effect. A mountainous tide of opposition to him and all that he stood for was forming. Even the peasants showed signs of political activity and cohesion, many of them taking part in the unofficial colleges or the 'flying university' organised by the still-united church and dissident intellectuals. The workers were even more hostile. Poland's industrial workforce was atypically young, about one-third of it was aged under 25, which accounts in part for its assertiveness and its articulateness. Throughout the late 1970s there were lightning strikes across a wide spectrum of Polish industry, and even if most of them were short, local and entirely economic, they nevertheless kept alive the vocabulary, the ideas, and the habits of confrontation.

Peasant and worker discontent were familiar features for Poland's leaders, but what was new in the late 1970s was the assistance given to them by the non-party intelligentsia. After the hostility of 1968 and 1970 the two were again at one. The prime reason for this was the committee for workers' defence, KOR, which was originally formed to collect funds for and to give legal assistance to the workers who had been arrested after the strikes and demonstrations of 1976. It was a cutting blow for the communists to have a civil organisation posing as the best defender of workers' rights. In the following year, 1977, KOR reformed itself into the committee for social self-defence, KSS/KOR. This indicated that the emphasis had now shifted from care for the individual to concern for the working class as a whole, which was an even fiercer condemnation of the PUWP's alleged ability to protect working class interests. At the same time the formation of KSS/KOR also marked a shift from *post facto* to *ante facto* defence of working class rights, from a defensive to an aggressive posture. The main figure in KSS/KOR, Jacek Kuroń, certainly seemed willing to live up to this adventurous image; he advocated finlandisation for Poland, telling his compatriots that there was no need to fear a Czechoslovak solution to any attempt by Poland to be more independent, and that Poles should therefore press ahead with the formation of social movements outside the party. KSS/KOR was the most important statement yet in eastern Europe of the growing power of 'civil society'.

Many other civil associations were already being formed in Poland and they were political as well as social in aspiration; in September 1976 the minister of the interior admitted that there were at least twenty-six 'anti-socialist' groups in the country, prominent amongst them being the overtly right-wing and nationalist Confederation for an Independent Poland led by Leszek Moczulski, who announced his party's intention to contest the 1979 elections to the sejm.

Further blows to the party's prestige came in 1977 with the publication in the west of censorship regulations and in October 1979 with the appearance of a report drawn up by 'Experience and the Future' (DiP). Based on work by over a hundred leading intellectuals from within and outside the party, the DiP report analysed and described the difficulties facing Poland and concluded that the fundamental problem was that the country had not found any acceptable rules for social life, that there was no consensus to bind the nation together; by extension, therefore, the régime rested upon the use or threat of force. The report contained a sustained if restrained attack upon privilege, corruption, and the rulers' lack of accountability to the ruled. It was an implicit and powerful criticism of the party and its leading role.

Similar enquiries would no doubt have produced similar results in any east European state, but only Poland had an alternative focus of loyalty in its strong Roman Catholic church. The leader of the Polish clergy, cardinal Wyszyński, still enjoyed enormous popularity because of his steadfast stand against the stalinists in the 1950s but, from the early 1960s and especially after the second Vatican council, new currents were coursing through Catholicism and stressing the social mission of the church. In Poland the personification of these currents was Karol Wojtyła, a professor at the Catholic university of Lublin and later archbishop of Cracow. Wojtyła, who had trained a whole generation of priests in Lublin, argued that exploitation deprived mankind of dignity; his lectures did not openly attack marxism, they went beyond it: 'Wojtyła subtly but deliberately injected the Polish resistance movement with a universal ethic and began to attract the intellectual, atheistic critics of the government.'[6] On 16 October 1978 he was elected pope. The political situation in Poland was immediately and irreversibly changed. For the majority of Poles the pope was a new national leader operating freely outside the confines of the foreign-dominated national territory, as had other national leaders after the rebellion of 1830 or the partition of 1939.

In June 1979 Wojtyła, now Pope John Paul II, paid a triumphal visit to his native land. Nothing could have illustrated more eloquently the bankruptcy of communist authority. Huge crowds, congregating entirely voluntarily, accompanied him wherever he went, and listened enraptured as he spoke to them in a clear, precise, and sensible Polish devoid of the officialese and the ideological gobbledegook which obfuscated all government and party statements. The control of the crowds was left entirely to the church authorities who carried out this task with admirable and unobtrusive efficiency. The visit showed clearly the power and the popularity of the church and its leader; it produced a nation united by enthusiasm not by fear: there could have been no more dramatic contrast between the power of the church and the steadily dissolving authority of the party, between the nation and the state. Indeed, 'For nine days the state virtually ceased to exist, except as a censor doctoring the television coverage. Everyone saw that Poland is not a communist country, just a communist state.'[7]

The party was only too conscious of its declining legitimacy. Under Gierek the PUWP had become more and more the party of the technocratic and white collar élite, with a considerable number of manual workers being purged during the 1970s. This young, technocratic, élitist body had expected steadily rising living standards, an expectation which could only be disappointed after 1976. Nevertheless, inside the party it was still generally held that it was individual socialists rather than socialism itself which had failed, that the workers were discontented not with the idea but with its deformation. The answer, therefore, was to find within the leading ranks of the party the reformers who could rescue the idea from its deformation, just as the nationalist communist Gomułka had originally rescued his party from over-reliance on the Soviet comrades.

The opportunity for change presented itself in February 1980 with the meeting of the eighth congress. Preliminary discussions were intense, with many would-be delegates stressing the need for a revision of the party statutes to allow for the rotation of jobs, free and open election of party officials, and measures to make the party hierarchy more responsive to the rank and file who were in touch with the populace. In his opening speech Gierek disarmingly accepted many of the criticisms which were being expressed. If the reformers had hoped that this presaged real change they were to be disappointed. The leadership soon became engrossed in the usual intrigues and plotting, which resulted in Gierek removing a number of potential rivals and securing the appointment as prime minister of Edvard Babiuch. It seemed that the leadership, having long since squandered whatever legitimacy it had once enjoyed amongst the general public, had now frittered away its support inside the party. The party was enfeebled from within and execrated from without. This was the party which in the summer of 1980 was to be presented with the greatest challenge yet faced by any ruling communist party in peacetime. Once again the troubles began over prices, particularly those of meat; by 1980, 'There was something irrational, even aggressive, about the carnivorous obsession that now gripped the Poles. . . . In an act of subconscious aggression, the population was literally eating away the foundations of the political structure.'[8]

20

THE SOLIDARITY CRISIS, POLAND 1980–1

The birth of Solidarity

The great crisis of 1980, like so many previous upheavals in communist Poland, was triggered by price increases. On 1 July a new pricing system for meat was introduced. Although it was not universally applied it had an immediate impact by provoking a rash of strikes, the first being in the Ursus tractor factory in Warsaw. The authorities rushed more meat into the shops, conceded a number of wage increases, and attempted to use censorship to prevent the spread of the unrest. These efforts failed in no small measure because of the influence of KSS/KOR; in July an eight-day general strike in Lublin paralysed the rail link between the Soviet Union and the Red Army garrisons in the GDR, and by the end of the first week of August there had been over 150 stoppages throughout the country. The focal point was Gdańsk.

The Baltic ports had great experience of recent industrial unrest. On 14 August workers in the Lenin shipyard in Gdańsk struck over the dismissal of a crane driver, Anna Walentynowicz. Gdynia and Szczecin were soon strikebound and Gierek flew back from his holidays hoping to contain the unrest, as in 1970, by holding face-to-face negotiations with the strikers. But this time his opponents were of a different ilk: they were far more disciplined; they were not committed to socialism or the party; they were determined not to be bought off with workers' councils which were open to party subversion; and they were artfully advised, though never dominated, by leading members of the intelligentsia, the most important of whom was Jacek Kuroń who had joined the Gdańsk strikers on 23 August. The strikers were also strengthened by the inter-factory strike committees (IFSCs) which had emerged in August to coordinate action and to maintain discipline and order. It was on the basis of the IFSCs that the strikers wished to build the free trade unions which they were now demanding.

The insistence on the formation of free trade unions was only one of the twenty-one demands put forward by the Gdańsk strikers. Others included: pay increases; a limitation upon censorship; work-free Saturdays; welfare equality with the police; the broadcasting of mass; the election of important factory managers; access to the media; and the erection of a memorial to those who had died in the confrontations of 1970. On 30 August the government capitulated. A compromise had been reached over the critical question of the relationship between the new, free trade unions and the party. The Gdańsk workers accepted the leading role of the party in the state, but not in the construction of socialism, and the trade unions also accepted that, in compliance with the constitution, they themselves would be socialist in character.

Gierek had little choice but to concede. The last thing the Polish economy could endure was a disruption of economic activity, yet the strikes were spreading rapidly and were becoming more radical in complexion; when Gierek's bastion in the Silesian coalfields fell, his authority was all but destroyed. There were also doubts as to whether he could any longer rely upon the forces of order; the Polish navy certainly let it be known that it would not turn its guns on its fellow Poles. Not even the church could persuade the strikers back to work, an appeal from Wyszyński on 26 August falling on deaf ears.

During the negotiations with the government the strikers' hand had been immeasurably strengthened by the strong regional links established through the local IFSCs. The communists, conditioned by democratic centralism, had hoped that once the initial concessions had been made the IFSCs would dissolve, and the party could then revert to its established pattern of dividing one local factory from another. But divide and rule no longer worked; the workers refused to be divided. Rather than withering away the IFSCs continued to flourish and expand, spreading along the Baltic coast and then to other areas. In September a meeting of IFSC representatives from all over Poland convened in Gdańsk and set up a national coordinating committee. This was the ruling body of the new force which dominated Poland: Solidarity. Its undisputed leader was an electrician from the Lenin shipyards in Gdańsk, Lech Wałęsa, whose driving passion in life was to secure proper recognition for the martyrs of 1970. The very name Solidarity served to emphasise the self-confidence of the new movement and to contrast its strength with the weakness of the divided party and government.

Solidarity was different from anything previously seen in eastern Europe. In the eyes of one observer it was Europe's 'first genuine workers' revolution since the Paris Commune of 1871',[1] but it was more than that. It was clearly a mass trade union movement, a social movement, and, however strongly some of its adherents may have protested, a political movement. Since it encompassed at its height almost half of the adult population of the country, it was also a national liberation movement. That the demand for free trade unions should become a national liberation movement was a product of the communist system. A trade union cannot function without the population being free to join it without fear; the population cannot do that if it does not live in an open, democratic society; Poland could not be an open democratic society as long as the country was in thraldom to the Soviet Union. But national liberation in Poland was spiritual as well as political; it was a process which could not be separated from the church which had for so long offered spiritual sanctuary for the oppressed. As a Warsaw Solidarity militant remarked:

The cross symbolised a set of spiritual values which define us as a nation. We have always wanted to be the subjects, the creators of our national life, and not just a labouring mass. The feeling of being treated like objects was crucial in bringing about what is happening now, and it was the church which made us conscious of that.[2]

The struggle for the legal registration of Solidarity, August to November 1980

The revolt on the Baltic coast severely discredited the party and completely demoralised its leader. On 6 September Gierek stepped down, Stanisław Kania becoming first secretary in his place. Kania promised 'renewal' of the party and a new social contract with the nation. These were well-tried phrases but Kania actually seemed to mean what he said. He moved swiftly in the difficult circumstances to remove the most discredited of party officials, over 500 of whom lost their jobs. But ditching discredited officials could not redeem the party in the nation's eyes; if Kania wanted a new social contract he had to come to an accommodation with Solidarity.

This was far from easy to attain. The two sides sparred over a number of issues. Solidarity protested at the slowness of changes in the censorship procedures and then staged a symbolic one-hour general strike on 3 October to secure a 12 per cent increase in the national wages fund, an inflationary measure which could only inflict further hurt on the impaired economy.

The strike showed Solidarity's muscle but such sparrings did not conceal the real fight which was over the question of Solidarity's legal registration. Only a recognised body had a legal 'personality' with its attendant rights to own property, to have proper bank accounts, to be represented in the legal processes, and so on. The authorities stonewalled, arguing that Solidarity's claim to operate nationally conflicted with its regionally based organisation, and that Solidarity's ban on PUWP members holding office and its failure to mention the party's leading role in its statutes were illegal. On 24 October a Warsaw court announced that it would register Solidarity but only after inserting into its statutes clauses stating that it did not wish to become a political party, that it recognised the leading role of the PUWP, and that it did not intend to undermine Poland's alliances. The court had no right to insert items into Solidarity's statutes and the action was seen by many Solidarity activists as a provocation aimed at forcing the union to fight a political battle over an issue of the party's choosing: the leading role of the PUWP.

Tension was running very high. An open air mass on All Saints' Day honoured the victims of Katyn as Solidarity called for a general strike. Kania and his prime minister, Jósef Pińkowski, were in Moscow trying to reassure the Soviet leaders; meanwhile Czechoslovakia and the GDR closed their borders with Poland. On top of this came the Narożniak affair. Jan Narożniak had been arrested after the police found classified documents in a Solidarity office in Warsaw. He was the first Solidarity activist to be arrested and his Warsaw colleagues threatened a general strike if he were not released within twenty-four hours. At the same time Zbigniew Bujak, rapidly rising to prominence in Solidarity's Warsaw organisation, made several demands: an investigation into the security forces; measures to defend the population against the police; a cut in the police budget; and an investigation into the killings of 1970 and 1976. Bujak had transformed the Narożniak affair into an assault on the first arm of the party's authority, the police. The crisis was broken on 10 November when the Warsaw court recognised Solidarity after the contentious clauses had been removed from the statutes and tucked away in an appendix.

The tender truce, November 1980 to March 1981

Though the confrontation between Wałęsa and Kania had been intense, both combatants had an instinct and a desire for compromise. In December Wałęsa was given his longed-for memorial to the dead of 1970 after which he had issued six 'commandments' which included the injunctions, 'keep peace and order ... respect all laws', 'show prudence and reflection in all action for the good of our fatherland', and 'be vigilant in the protection of our fatherland's safety and sovereignty'. Moderation on the part of Solidarity was also seen in its refusal to align itself with extreme forms of Polish nationalism or anti-sovietism; it refused, for example, to exploit the widespread passion over Katyn. Wałęsa was determined that Solidarity should be a 'self-limiting revolution'.

The impulses to compromise rather than confrontation were equally strong on the side of the party and government. In the first place the government had to take into account the continuing economic decline. The situation was far worse than anyone could have imagined, and in March 1981 Poland had to admit that it could no longer meet its foreign debt obligations. To force Solidarity to the extremes of further strikes would inflict horrendous, and avoidable, injury on the economy.

The church too exercised its power in favour of restraint; a call from the episcopate on 10–11 December for acceptance of Kania's 'social contract' was so conciliatory that some of the bishops objected and even the politburo was shocked.

One factor forcing all Poles towards conciliation was fear of a Soviet invasion. There were indications that this was imminent. During November and December 1980 there were ostentatious troop movements in the Ukraine and the Baltic states, whilst in the Kaliningrad region troops were camping out in tents despite the wintry conditions. At the same time a Soviet delegation visited Rome, reputedly for a confrontation with the pope, whilst in Moscow a conference of European communist parties offered the Polish party fraternal aid; there were few Poles, even in the communist party, who regarded this as a promise rather than a threat. The Americans had already warned of possible Soviet military action.

370

The Poles remained remarkably cool in the face of the Soviet danger. The Soviet presence was, after all, nothing new; Wałęsa, when once asked whether he feared a Soviet invasion, had replied, 'But they have been here since 1945'.[3] The Poles were also confident that the Soviets would find no quisling to form a government after an invasion, and indeed would be faced with the sort of resistance with which the Germans had had to cope during the second world war.

A further cause of moderation in the winter of 1980–1 was that Kania and Wałęsa had, to a degree, become dependent upon one another. Despite the widespread conviction that no quisling would appear, Kania was not entirely confident of the loyalty of the party; he could not dismiss the possibility that the Kremlin would find 'honest communists' who would invite it to restore 'normality', particularly as the upper ranks of the party, like that of Czechoslovakia in 1968, were far from united. There was also a widening gulf between the central core of the party and the *doly*: the former had retreated into its bunker, expecting nothing more than survival but hoping in the meantime that it could chip away at and eventually supplant the power of KOR/KSS and the church within Solidarity; the unprivileged *doly*, who formed two-thirds of the party membership, were deserting to Solidarity in alarming numbers.

The ultimate cause of the moderation which prevailed at the highest level of the party, however, did not derive from concern at the defections of the *doly*. It was far more sinister; in December 1980 and January 1981 plans were being laid for a military coup, the Soviets having let it be known that they would remain inactive only as long as they could be assured that the Poles were taking operational steps to impose order themselves.

This, of course, was unknown to Wałęsa. One of his main concerns at this juncture was to secure time in order to consolidate the gains made so far. Thus, he did not want further confrontation to give the most extreme elements in the movement the opportunity to push the union to a general strike or to other measures which would both inflict further damage on the economy and raise the bogey of the 'national tragedy', i.e. Soviet military intervention.

At the end of January 1981 the mood of grudging mutual tolerance was signified by the signing of the Warsaw agreement which allowed Solidarity greater access to the media and provided for three non-working Saturdays per month.

For the government the Warsaw agreement had been signed by Pińkowski. He was replaced as prime minister the following month by Wojciech Jaruzelski, one of the longest-serving members of the politburo, who retained his former post as minister of defence.

The relaxation of tension suggested by the Warsaw agreement did not last long. A new and fierce controversy was brewing over the demand for the registration of 'rural Solidarity'. Strongly backed by the church, rural Solidarity claimed to represent at least half of Poland's 3.2 million smallholders. On 10 February a court had decided that rural Solidarity could register as an association but not as a trade union. This was a totally unacceptable solution for the union because it did not confer the right to strike or to take part in collective bargaining. Rural Solidarity therefore staged a massive sit-in in Rzeszów, the centre of the movement. For the government and the party there was clearly an ideological problem: could it grant recognition to an association of petty bourgeois producers? To judge from events in Bydgoszcz on 19 March it seemed not. The municipal council was interrupted by some Solidarity members who wished to raise the question of rural Solidarity; the police burst in, claiming that the debate was illegal, which it was not, and when the regional Solidarity leader, Jan Rulewski, showed them the constitution to prove the point, he was beaten up. There was no doubt in anyone's mind that the incident was a deliberate provocation. It caused the most serious tension in the eighteen months of Solidarity's first life. Wałęsa cancelled a visit to France and announced that the movement would be finished if it backed down on this issue. A general strike was called for 31 March if the government did not hold an investigation into the Bydgoszcz affair. Poland stood on the brink of the abyss. At the eleventh hour, on 30 March, a provisional agreement was at last reached. Rural Solidarity was told to act as if it were a legal body, pending final registration. The general strike was cancelled. The compromise was a real one, as was proved by the fact that Wałęsa was severely criticised by the radicals in his own ranks, whilst Moscow, along with some of the basic organisations in the PUWP, condemned what they saw as the government's weakness. Rural Solidarity was finally recognised in May.

March 1981 was the height of Solidarity's power in the period August 1980 to December 1981. Its battles over recognition and its restrained use of the general strike threat had shown its strength in an arena which was predominantly political. Yet in this period there had been little institutional change in Poland; few of Solidarity's gains had received legal consolidation: whilst labour felt that it had greater freedom of action there was as yet no law guaranteeing the right to strike and, similarly, whilst there were few restrictions on publication there was no law banning or even limiting censorship. And the party's control over the forces of law and order was unimpaired.

The party and Solidarity congresses, March to September 1981

In the time from Bydgoszcz to its first congress in September 1981 Solidarity concentrated upon its schemes for self-management and the reform of factory administration. Although this was in effect an attack upon the leading role of the party, no one was anxious to conduct an open debate on that issue and political attention during the summer focused on developments within the PUWP.

On 14–20 July the party held its ninth congress, which had been postponed since March because of the crisis over rural Solidarity. Kania promised that the elections for the congress would be free and secret, a fact which appalled the Soviets. They had been equally affected by his tolerance of a conference in

April of 'horizontalists', or those who wished to see the party, in response to Solidarity's successful regionalism, reorganised with a much stronger local basis; in effect the 'horizontalists' wanted a fundamental reform, if not the abandonment of democratic centralism. The Soviet leadership expressed its displeasure by writing to some central committee members suggesting that in the forthcoming congress they should remove Kania and Jaruzelski from office, which no doubt did much to bolster the prestige of both. The Soviets, of course, knew that the congress would purge the leadership and make radical changes in personnel and organisation.

As expected the congress revealed the deep unease of the mass of the party. Four-fifths of the delegates were appearing at a congress for the first time and they voted in secret to change the leadership's agenda. Seven-eighths of the central committee elected by the congress had not been in the central committee before, and only four of the eleven members of the politburo were not new to that body. One new member of the politburo and one-fifth of the central committee were members of Solidarity, though in October these 'bigamists' were required to resign from either the union or the party. The congress enacted new party statutes decreeing that no one could hold party or state office for more than ten years, that nomination for office was to be free and ballots secret in all party elections, and that machinery allowing for the instant recall of leaders who had lost the confidence of the party would be introduced.

If the congress produced new faces at the upper levels, it did not find new minds. Most of those catapulted into the top positions were not from the critical intelligentsia within the party but from a lower stratum of leninist apparatchiki who were later to acquiesce in the saving of the system and its values, along with their privileges, by one of the few institutions which had not been affected by changes of personnel at the upper levels: the army.

For the party the changes in statutes and in personnel were daringly radical; in normal circumstances in a communist state they would have caused great and general excitement. In the Poland of 1981 they were treated almost with indifference. Of at least equal interest was the first Solidarity congress which was to convene in September in Gdańsk.

The Solidarity congress began with a mass celebrated by the new cardinal archbishop, Glemp, Wyszyński having died on 28 May. Of the 892 delegates some 200 were full-time Solidarity employees and the traditional trade union and working class elements were relatively weakly represented. There was a distinctly radical air to the congress. Resolutions were submitted and discussed which demanded that the nomenklatura system be abolished, that if the sejm did not organise a nation-wide referendum on self-management then Solidarity should, and that Solidarity should also publish books on Polish history and the Polish language. Some elements of the leadership were embarrassed by a resolution which informed the peoples of eastern Europe that Solidarity was trying to help the working class and would assist anyone in the area who had a similar objective. This statement sent cold shivers down official spines in Berlin, Sofia,

Prague, Tiranë, and elsewhere. The congress also endorsed a programme which called for a life free from 'poverty, exploitation, fear, and allies'. On the other hand, as a counter to such radicalism, Wałęsa warned against any action which might cause bloodshed, and insisted that Solidarity do nothing which suggested that it was seeking political power for itself or questioning Poland's membership of the Warsaw Pact.

Nevertheless, the assertiveness of the congress depressed Kania who was further disquieted by continuing fears that 'honest communists' might invite the Soviets to restore order, fears exacerbated by the appearance of fundamentalist marxist-leninist organisations such as the Grunwald Political Union and the Katowice Forum. On 18 October Kania stepped down as first secretary, a post which he bequeathed to Jaruzelski who had now amassed a formidable power base as minister of defence, prime minister, and first secretary of the central committee. Jaruzelski reiterated Kania's call for a 'front of national understanding', and gave substance to this by meeting Wałęsa and Glemp on 4 November.

The military coup of December 1981

In reality Jaruzelski had, of course, decided early in the year that Solidarity must be suppressed. His resolve was hardened by divisions within Solidarity over organisational issues and over the extent to which it should compromise in the sejm on self-management. His resolve was further hardened by growing extremism in Solidarity. Kuroń was now arguing that no deals should be made with the party because it would not keep them, and he advised setting up a separate party. Further signs of Solidarity extremism were calls in Wrocław for the wringing of the Reds' necks, and the increasingly frequent appearance of caricatures lampooning Soviet leaders, something which the inmates of the Kremlin had always found impossible to understand or tolerate. Even the moderate, centre factions of Solidarity were moving ahead on the path of reform. On 17 November the movement's leading council demanded the implementation of its ideas for self-management, greater access to the media for Solidarity, economic restructuring, free local elections, and reforms in the legal system. A further spur to action by the party leadership could have been the revelations of an opinion poll in November which asked respondents in which national institutions they had confidence: 95 per cent had confidence in Solidarity, 93 per cent in the church; 68 per cent in the army; and 7 per cent in the party. Of those polled 11 per cent were party members.

The most compelling reason for action, however, was the continuing message from Moscow that if the Polish authorities did not put their house in order, the Soviets would do it for them. Jaruzelski prepared his ground carefully. He introduced into the sejm an emergency powers bill which would have given the government the legal right to break strikes. The assembly threw out the bill but the authorities were now confident enough to take action against Solidarity vans and speakers in at least two of its most radical centres: Wrocław and Katowice.

There was also resolute action against any strike or other form of protest action which began after the 4 November meeting between Glemp, Jaruzelski, and Wałęsa. On 2 December riot police landed from helicopters on the roof of the fire officers' training school in Warsaw to break up a strike and to end the occupation of the building. It was the first time that the government had used force on this scale since Bydgoszcz, and it was the first time since August 1980 that force had been deployed against strikers.

Solidarity's leadership went into immediate and closed emergency session in Radom. Feelings were running extremely high. Rulewski urged the calling of an immediate general election, Kuroń was reported to have talked of overpowering the government, and there were calls for the setting up of a workers' militia. The militants, encouraged by signs of growing support for Solidarity in the army and the police, were convinced that the soldiers would never fire on them; they were talking the language of revolt.

Unfortunately for Solidarity, the meeting was bugged and the authorities made much use of doctored tapes which were smuggled out of Radom. A desperate Wałęsa had two meetings with Glemp in an effort to find an escape, but there seemed to be none. To make matters worse, the anniversary of the 1970 killings was approaching and with it the dedication of the new memorial. In an effort to calm the atmosphere, Solidarity on 12 December demanded a national referendum on the government's methods of rule.

It was not to take place. On the night of 13–14 December martial law was declared as units of the Polish army and the ZOMO, the riot police, sealed Poland's borders, isolated Poland's towns one from another, and rounded up all the strikers and leading Solidarity activists on whom they could lay their hands; as a gesture to anti-party feeling, Gierek and some of his associates were also interned. Political authority was passed to a new military council of national salvation; all civil rights were suspended, and workers in some public services, including transport, were placed under military discipline. All this was not achieved without resistance, especially in the mining areas of Silesia, but the odds against those who resisted were hopeless and by Christmas the army was in total control. In his speech to the nation on Christmas Eve Jaruzelski insisted that he had not staged a military coup and that regular government would be restored when the military council had reimposed law and order. In what was an obvious reference to the danger from the east he pleaded that it had been 'necessary to choose between a greater and a lesser evil'. The ultimate fear of Soviet intervention was invoked to justify the Polish army's military action against its own people.

In January 1982 a special meeting of the sejm confirmed the legality of martial rule and on 8 October the assembly formally dissolved Solidarity. The government attempted after December 1981 to ease food shortages by introducing rationing but United States sanctions made the process more difficult because they denied credit to Poland.

Solidarity had, it seemed, been defeated and liquidated, but the defeat of

Solidarity was also a defeat for the communist party. The PUWP could no longer lay claim to popular support or legitimacy; its reliance on the army made it, in the eyes of most of its subjects, little different from the régimes of Franco, the Greek colonels, or Pinochet, except, perhaps, that these dictatorships had a better economic record. Solidarity had shown the bankruptcy of east European communism because the bulk of communism's chosen people, the workers, had looked outside the party for redress of their social grievances. The suppression of Solidarity had underlined the lesson of 1968, that communist party power could be preserved only by military force; if, in the long term, even the use of the domestic military could not contain discontent then the marxist-leninist systems of eastern Europe would be entirely dependent on Soviet intervention to save them. If that were denied them they could not survive.

Part V

THE DEATH OF SOCIALISM

21

EASTERN EUROPE, 1980–9

The Soviet bloc did not weather the storm of Solidarity well. Deeply conscious of a deteriorating economic situation and of a technological inadequacy made all the more apparent by developments in the arms race, the communist states of eastern Europe were further disadvantaged by the gerontocracy which dominated the Kremlin for most of the first half of the 1980s. To make matters more difficult, the west changed after 1980; it adopted more right-wing policies and with them a more truculent tone. It no longer hesitated to deride the pathetic economic performance and the woeful social provision which socialism *à la russe* provided for itself and its outer empire in eastern Europe. Western powers were able to reassert their influence in Grenada and the Falkland Islands whilst the marxist presence in Africa crumbled and Afghanistan became a disaster for the Soviets. A new broom arrived in Moscow in 1985 but it was already too late. In each state communist power had weakened.

Poland

In Poland general Jaruzelski began to relax military rule by releasing Wałęsa from detention and suspending martial law in December 1982; it was abolished and the military council of national salvation dissolved in July 1983. A year later an amnesty was declared to celebrate the fortieth anniversary of the 1944 liberation.

There was, however, no permanent peace between the government and its opponents. In October 1984 most Poles were revolted by the kidnapping and subsequent murder of father Jerzy Popiełuszko, a priest whose anti-government sermons had earned him a large following in his Warsaw suburban parish. In January 1985 price rises again caused confrontation, the government eventually modifying the proposed increases after opposition from a newly resurgent, although still illegal, Solidarity. In October of the same year Solidarity called for a boycott of the parliamentary elections. The boycott may have been less effective than its organisers had hoped but it nevertheless did much to frustrate the government's attempt to recoup some legitimacy by allowing more than one candidate to stand for each seat. In February 1986 Wałęsa was arrested and put on trial for allegedly disputing the results of these elections, but the charges were subsequently dropped. In May 1986 the government claimed one success with the arrest of Bujak, who had been in hiding for five years.

This was the last success that Poland's communist rulers were to enjoy and even this was limited. It caused demonstrations in the streets and within a few months Bujak was again at liberty. And, notwithstanding Bujak's arrest, there were in 1986 still over six underground newspapers and Radio Solidarity was widely disseminated. By the end of the following year, Solidarity, though still underground, had once more become a major factor in Polish political life. The government had introduced hard-hitting economic reforms in October of that year but had linked to them some political relaxations; confident that the political concessions would persuade people to accept the economic constraints, the authorities made both the subject of a single referendum. The tactic of linking popular and unpopular reforms failed. Solidarity called for a boycott of the vote, and the reforms did not receive the requisite proportion of popular support. At the end of January 1988 Solidarity called for protests against further price rises, and by the spring of that year the illegal union had unleashed industrial guerilla warfare with a rash of strikes across the country. In August, following a stoppage by the coal miners, the government offered negotiations with the various labour groups. Soon after that the government resigned, following a vote of no confidence in the sejm, and was replaced by a more reformist cabinet under Mieczysław Rakowski. Sweeping changes in the party leadership came at the end of the year with no less than six members of the politburo deciding to step down.

When Rakowski became first secretary of the PUWP the wits of Warsaw quipped, with more prescience than they could possibly have imagined, that he would have done better to have called himself the last secretary.

Hungary

Mass action, in the form of demonstrations rather than strikes, was also a feature of Hungarian political life in the second half of the 1980s. In 1985 there were huge protests against the Gabčikovo-Nagymaros hydro-electric scheme on the Danube. On 15 March, the anniversary of the 1848 demand for legal separation from Austria, confrontations regularly took place between police and demonstrators, and there were massive protests in June 1988 against Ceauşescu's plans to destroy Hungarian villages in Transylvania as part of his 'systematisation' process. The thirtieth anniversary of the execution of Imre Nagy on 16 June 1958 provided another cause for popular outbursts in the streets.

Although the police frequently dealt roughly with such demonstrations for most of the 1980s, this did not mean that the party authorities were entirely deaf to voices demanding change. In 1983 a constitutional council had been introduced and in May 1985 a new electoral law had allowed independent candidates to fight party nominees in parliamentary elections. Although these 'independent' candidates had to be approved by the party-dominated Popular Patriotic Front, pluralism of a sort had been introduced into political affairs; the talk now was less of 'gulas communism' than of 'constitutional communism'. In the following year a group of academics and reformers within the party, led by Imre Pozsgay, drew up 'Change and Reform', a discussion document which suggested that Hungary should evolve towards a duopoly in which parliament as well as party could be seen as focal points of political power. In June 1987 the samizdat journal *Beszélö* (Speaker) went much further, proposing a new 'social contract' in which the party would have control over defence and foreign policy, the issues which concerned the Soviets, whilst in domestic affairs society would be left to rediscover its autonomy and to fashion its own democratic institutions; it was a variant of 'finlandisation' in which parliament would resume sovereignty, with the party exercising the power of veto like some east European House of Lords.

The reformists within the party seemed to have suffered a setback in April 1988 when four of them were expelled for their radicalism. They savoured revenge in the following month when a special HSWP conference removed János Kádár as head of the party and sacked him from the politburo. The new general secretary was Károly Grósz and reformers such as Pozsgay and Rezsö Nyers, the architect of the NEM, were brought into the politburo. By July 1988 the reformists had devised an economic programme which would bring austerity, devaluation, and unemployment but which would also strengthen market forces.

There was also significant political change. In 1988 no action was taken to contest the emergence either of the Hungarian Democratic Forum in September or of the Alliance of Free Democrats two months later. It seemed that political pluralism had arrived, though the communist party's reaction was as yet unclear.

The GDR

In the 1960s and 1970s the GDR had striven to delimit itself from the Federal Republic to the west. By 1980 it might have been thought that Honecker was now concentrating on *Abgrenzung* to the east. The GDR government had not welcomed the deployment on its territory of SS20s, not least because it made less credible its incessant propaganda against west German militarism. In addition to this, since the late 1970s the Protestant churches in east Germany had been running an increasingly powerful 'peace movement'; the SS20s focused that peace movement on the GDR more than Honecker would have liked.

Gorbachev's *perestroika* also posed problems. The east German economy, thanks in large measure to disguised subsidies from the west, was amongst the most successful, or least unsuccessful, in eastern Europe, but it still had foreign debts of $12 billion by 1981. And even if it was in better shape than that of its Comecon colleagues it certainly could not compete with that of the FRG, with which it was usually compared. But if reform were needed there could not be too much retreat from the principles of state socialism lest this deprive the socialist state of its *raison d'être*. Economic reform in the GDR was therefore limited, and political change virtually non-existent, with the east German authorities even censoring some material translated from the Soviet media.

Other leaders in eastern Europe, when looking for additional sources of legitimacy, had fallen back on nationalism. In the GDR this was a complex process. It was easy to force-feed athletes, perhaps with banned substances, in order to give the state a high profile at international sporting gatherings, but this had more impact abroad than at home where, as in the rest of eastern Europe, the pampered and privileged few of the sporting world were exceedingly unpopular. To win over the domestic constituency, and particularly the young, much more was needed. *Abgrenzung* had been based on the argument that socialism had created its own national consciousness; socialism was not doing too well and therefore the 1980s saw the east German régime making efforts to present itself as the heir of previous German national heroes. In 1983 Honecker himself took charge of organising the celebrations to mark the five hundredth anniversary of Luther's birth; Luther was duly presented as a revolutionary figure and little was said of his views on peasants or Jews. The statue of Frederick the Great reappeared in Berlin and even Bismarck, the embodiment of aristocratic paternalism and Prussian conservatism, was treated with some sympathy by the east German historian Ernst Engelberg.

Such gestures had little effect and by the end of the 1980s Honecker was if anything less popular and secure than a decade before. Living standards were not rising, he had little support from Moscow and even less from the majority of his own people.

Bulgaria

As economic problems intensified in the late 1970s the Zhivkov régime instituted yet another series of reforms in agriculture, this time edging towards what it called 'market socialism' and greater responsibility for the basic labour organisations, the brigades. The results were encouraging and in 1982 were extended to the rest of the economy under the guise of the 'New Economic Mechanism' (NEM). The initial promise was not fulfilled. This was in part due to natural factors such as a harsh winter, severe droughts in mid-decade, and a destructive earthquake near Strazhitsa in 1986, but it was also due to the poor quality of Bulgarian production, a point which Zhivkov rammed home in a specially convened national party conference in Varna in 1984. In 1986 the leadership announced a fundamental reform with a massive shift from bureaucratic to economic planning. In March 1987 Zhivkov told another national party conference that 'In the future it will be exceptionally important not to permit individual party and state figures or organs, whose power is strong, to interfere in economic activities.' 'Self-management' was to be the order of the day and was to be the basis for a restructuring which would be 'revolutionary in essence'. The new approach was codified in the 'July Concept', promulgated at a central committee plenum in

July 1987; the new doctrine replaced the so-called 'April Line' which had guided the party since 1956.

By the second half of the 1980s Zhivkov's leadership was in disarray. At home the reforms amounted to little more than a tinkering with economic administration; the leading role of the party was protected and was now to be that of explaining the new principles to the nation; moreover, the reforms were enacted with such rapidity that they produced serious dislocation both in administration and in production. Even worse for Zhivkov, what had always been for him the fount of all wisdom, the CPSU, was now speaking with a forked tongue; Zhivkov tried desperately to argue that his reforms showed that Bulgaria already had *perestroika* and that there was no need for *glasnost*. To an increasing degree his views were disregarded. By the end of the decade there were signs of organised protest in Sofia university, amongst the large number of Bulgarians concerned at environmental degradation, and not least amongst the hard-pressed Turkish minority.

The conservative factions of the BCP made their last, despairing gamble over the Turkish issue. In the late 1970s Zhivkov's daughter, Liudmila, had risen rapidly to dominance in the cultural sector, eventually securing a seat in the politburo. She was an interesting and unusual figure. She was fascinated by mysticism; she dabbled in alternative medicine; and above all she insisted upon the value, the individuality, and the separateness, even from the Russian, of Bulgarian culture. This the Russians did not like, but it was popular with sections of the Bulgarian intelligentsia. Liudmila, however, died at the age of 38 in 1981. Her father was deeply grieved by her loss. He had perhaps noticed, however, how popular her emphasis on Bulgarian individuality had been. To play the nationalist card might deflect opinion from disappointing economic results and provide the régime with some legitimacy.

This was one of the principal causes of the so-called 'regenerative process' initiated in 1984. It was decided that the Turks in Bulgaria were not in fact Turks at all but Bulgarians who had been forcibly converted to Islam and had then lost their Bulgarian national characteristics; the new policy would allow them to rediscover their true national affinity. Severe restrictions has been gradually introduced on Muslim rites such as circumcision, washing the dead, and the *hadj*, but now all Muslims were to be required to assume Bulgarian rather than Turkish names and there were proscriptions against the public use of the Turkish language. All broadcasting, teaching, and publication in Turkish was abolished. The enforced name-changes were so bitterly resisted that the Bulgarian army had to be called in to carry out what was in fact its biggest operation since the end of the second world war. Similar policies, though with less extravagant methods, had been applied in previous decades to the Gypsies and the *Pomaks*, Bulgarian-speaking Muslims, but those groups had been smaller in number and could not be linked to any supposed external threat to Bulgarian sovereignty or integrity. The Turkish minority could. It already formed around 10 per cent of the total population, a percentage which was likely to rise because the Turks had higher birth rates than the Bulgarians; and there were fears of Turkish autonomous zones being formed and then annexed by Turkey in the fashion of northern Cyprus.

The regenerative process further damaged Bulgaria's external image, which was still tarnished following the accusations of the 1970s. The anti-Turkish outbursts were condemned by bodies as diverse as the Islamic Conference Organisation, the European Court of Justice and the United Nations. The regenerative process also offended a brave section of the Bulgarian intelligentsia who gradually rallied to the unpopular cause of defending the embattled Turks.

By the end of the 1980s Zhivkov had few defenders at home or abroad, in the party or outside it.

Czechoslovakia

On the surface political life in Czechoslovakia in the 1980s seemed no less glacial than in the 1970s. Gorbachev's reforming spirit was hardly welcome to a leadership whose authority stemmed directly from Soviet action in 1968, action which the new Soviet leader pointedly refrained from endorsing when he visited Prague in April 1987. The Czechoslovak police remained as vigilant and brutal as ever. They suppressed demonstrations, such as that in Prague to mark the twentieth anniversary of the invasion; they had done the same even to a peaceful, candle-lit vigil which was held in Bratislava to demand greater religious freedom and more respect for human rights.

Despite the intimidating atmosphere, Charter '77 continued its advocacy of proper respect for civil rights as laid down in Czechoslovak law. In the 1980s it developed more contact with western sympathisers and added a few more hundred names to its list of signatories.

Czechoslovakia in the 1980s did, however, see some changes, albeit not dramatic ones. Although at the seventeenth party congress in 1986 Husák remained adamantly opposed to any compromise with market forces, he did hint at reform in the shape of some decentralisation of economic planning, and by 1987 Czechoslovakia was seeking western credits and wider trading links with the capitalist world. Husák resigned as general secretary in December 1987, but his replacement, Miloš Jakeš, was of the same mould and had been one of the chief organisers of the purge of the early 1970s.

One of the most notable developments in Czechoslovakia in the 1980s was the growing strength of the Roman Catholic church. Although weakened by the large number of vacancies both at parish and episcopal level, the church grew greatly in assertiveness. Its leader, the octogenarian cardinal Tomášek, undoubtedly enlivened by the advent of the east European pope, adopted a much more aggressive attitude to *Pacem in Terris*, a pro-régime organisation of clergy. He made little progress against this strong opponent but he did succeed in raising his own prestige and with it that of the church. The church, of course, had always been stronger in Slovakia than in the Czech lands but even its established power did not lead many to expect the strength of religious feeling which broke out in 1985 on the 1,100th anniversary of the death of Saint Methodius, who was supposedly buried in Slovakia. Nor had modern Czechoslovak history seen many figures like the Moravian peasant Antonín Navrátil, who in 1988 organised a petition calling for more religious freedom and less state interference in church affairs. The fact that over 400,000 people, not all of them Catholics, signed Navrátil's petition showed that beneath the glacial surface of official Czecho-slovakia there was still life and movement.

Romania

Ceauşescu's propagandists promised the Romanian people that multi-laterally developed socialism would bring them a 'golden age'. In fact the 1980s were years of intensified police terror and of privation worse even than the second world war.

Police informers were everywhere, with some estimates putting their number at one in three of the adult population. Contact with foreigners was permitted only within designated, public rooms; all typewriters had to be registered each year, with their owners submitting a set text to the police for checking against any samizdat literature which might appear, whilst typewriters in offices had to be padlocked out of office hours.

Opposition to the Ceauşescus continued to be rare and dangerous. In 1982 Virgil Trofil's censure from within the party brought down upon him such retribution as to drive him to suicide. Conspiracies were equally ineffective. In 1983 a group of army officers attempted to engineer a coup but were betrayed; their action subsequently led to the promotion within the ministry of defence of more relatives of the 'conducator'. There were still occasional and isolated outbursts of industrial unrest. In October 1981 there was further trouble in the Jiu valley coalfield, though not on the scale of 1977, and in September 1983 there were strikes in Maramureş. The most notable outbreak, however, was at Braşov in November 1987 when workers in the Red Star tractor plant struck for higher wages, moved into the city, and ransacked the local party headquarters. In December there were protests in Timişoara and other centres.

The Braşov and Timişoara outbursts began as old-fashioned hunger riots. The economic strategy of the early 1970s had gone disastrously wrong. Romania had borrowed from the west to build a refining capacity in order to process cheap crude bought in the middle east, but by the end of the decade both the price of crude and the cost of borrowing had risen. Then, in the early 1980s, when Romania was in a position to export refined petrol, prices began to fall. Romanians were now trapped between the anvil of the world market and the hammer of Ceauşescu's demonic ego. Ceauşescu was determined to make Romania a major factor in international politics, and knowing that a debtor nation cannot be strong, he asked for a rescheduling of the external debt and determined that it would be paid off, almost at whatever cost. Imports were reduced to the absolute minimum and almost everything that could be sold abroad was exported. Food became scarce and fuel was so strictly rationed that households were allotted only one forty-watt bulb per room, cooking was frequently possible only in the middle of the night, and at times even the traffic lights ceased to function. Perhaps the Romanians might have borne this austerity with less resentment had the régime not, at the same time, boasted of its lending to third world nations and embarked upon grandiose and hugely expensive projects such as the reconstruction of the centre of Bucharest.

By the mid-1980s Ceauşescu's domestic supporters were virtually confined to the praetorian guard of the Securitate. His international standing had fallen because the Gorbachev-inspired détente between east and west made his individual foreign policy pointless. As the west became more conscious of what his domestic policies entailed his stock fell even further. The 'systematisation' programme, by which ancient villages were to be bulldozed and their inhabitants concentrated in 'agro-towns', had been condemned by prominent figures such as the Prince of Wales. In fact, the systematisation programme was largely confined to a small area around Bucharest but it was one of a number of factors which alerted the outside world to the horrors of life in Ceauşescu's Romania.

By 1989 Ceauşescu had in fact succeeded in paying off almost all of Romania' foreign debt, but it had been at terrible cost.

Yugoslavia

In December 1985 Tito's luxurious yacht was sold for much-needed hard currency, and his island retreat on Brioni was turned into a national park. These changes were symbolic of the fall in Tito's stature which had taken place since the LCY had proclaimed shortly after his death: 'After Tito: Tito'.

The first to question his legacy were historians who in the early 1980s produced new evidence on casualties during the second world war and who brought to light previously unknown or unmentionable facts, such as the conversations Tito had had with the Germans in March 1943.

Whilst Tito's reputation was being questioned the titoist system was becoming less appropriate as a mechanism for dealing with the problems of contemporary Yugoslavia, problems which in many respects were the product of that system. In the first place, even more than was the case with Ceauşescu, Tito's allegedly neutralist stance in the east-west confrontation was rendered nugatory by Gorbachev's dash for détente. At the same time the Yugoslav economy was heading with equal rapidity for crisis. Self-management had produced little more than rampant borrowing and a chronically inefficient labour force, and the foreign debt, expected to be $6 billion, turned out to be $21 billion. Austerity drives were imposed on the country but their impact was largely vitiated by the collapse of the Bosnian-based Agrokomerc enterprise which was shown to have issued promissory notes without collateral to the tune of $500 million.

The effects of this gigantic economic scandal were profound. In the first place, what faith was left in the country's institutions, political as well as financial, was severely tested if not entirely destroyed; whilst the unprivileged were being asked to endure austerity the privileged, it seemed, were descending ever deeper into the pit of corruption. General austerity and the Agrokomerc scandal were two important causes of the widespread strikes for higher wages in late 1987 and in June 1988, and of violence such as the workers' invasion of the federal assembly in July of the same year. More importantly, the Agrokomerc affair questioned the efficacy of the economic strategy that had been pursued since the early 1970s. Since then, in response to the persistent and all-pervasive pressures of particularism, the drift of Yugoslav policy had been towards decentralisation or rather polycentrism, economic and political. With economic stagnation and decline, together with scandals such as the Agrokomerc case, it became obvious that decentralisation did not offer a way out of the country's difficulties. For some, usually Serbs, the response was that there had been too much decentralisation; for others, usually non-Serbs, the conclusion was that there had not been enough.

As ever, Yugoslav politics were immensely complicated by the national question. The Croats still resented the suppression of the 'Croatian spring' but the most active opponents of Belgrade in the 1980s were the Albanians of Kosovo, and particularly its numerous unemployed intelligentsia, almost all of them graduates of Priština university. That university was the origin of the riots of March 1981, at that point the worst violence seen in Yugoslavia since the second world war. There were further disturbances in December 1985, after which relations between Serbs and Albanians deteriorated rapidly. Emergency security measures were introduced in October 1987 but they had little effect. In November 1988 100,000 Albanians massed in Priština to protest against the arrest of two Kosovo party leaders; in response a crowd estimated at a million protested in Belgrade against alleged discrimination against Serbs in Kosovo.

This protest was but one indication of the mounting backlash against what the Serbs saw as discrimination against them. The most cogent expression of this feeling had come in a draft memorandum prepared by the Serbian Academy of Sciences in 1985. The memorandum claimed that the Yugoslav federation had an inbuilt bias in favour of the richer republics of Slovenia and Croatia which was the result of the anti-Serb sentiments of the predominantly non-Serb inter-war communists who had designed the federation. The memorandum also pointed to the fact that these non-Serbs had detached eastern Slavonia from Serbia and that 'genocide' had been practised against Serbs in Croatia. There were also complaints that the 1974 constitution allowed the Vojvodina and Kosovo, although they were part of the Serbian republic, to deal directly with the central, federal authorities. As for affairs in Kosovo itself the memorandum, which was drawn up before the worst of the confrontations, criticised the other republics for supporting the anti-Serb elements in the area to such a degree that many Serbs were being forced to flee. The memorandum confirmed many populist Serb suspicions that the Yugoslav federation was a trick played on them by the half-Croat, half-Slovene Tito and his mainly non-Serb gang.

From the mid-1980s Yugoslavia was in deep crisis. The decade of devolution had failed to satisfy non-Serbian national desires and had sharpened those of the Serbs. For the non-Serbs the conclusion was that devolution had failed because of the communist system; for the Serbs it seemed easier to think that the communist system had failed because of devolution; thus, whilst the non-Serbs wanted to ditch the system in order to preserve devolution, the Serbs wanted to ditch devolution to save the system. Thus, Serbian nationalism entered into its unholy alliance with the communist party apparat. From the creation of an independent Yugoslav state in 1918 to the *sporazum* of 1939 the Serbs, especially those of Serbia, had dominated the political system. During the second world war it had been the Serbs of Bosnia and Croatia who rose to dominance within the partisan movement. After the war Serbia remained the dominant republic, the location of the capital, the state bank, and other institutions of central government, whilst in the non-Serb republics the local Serbs enjoyed a disproportionate share of influential positions in the administration, the banks, the army, and above all the party. With the death of Tito in 1980 the system began to crumble. By the end of the decade the Serbs of Serbia had lost their empire without finding a role whilst the Serbs of Croatia and Bosnia, and even more so those of Kosovo, were frightened that the disintegration of the federation would rob them of their positions of power and privilege. It was a logical move to link the ailing, communist, nationalist Serbian party to the cause of the threatened Serbs outside Serbia. They were more than ready to play this game, and they were in a good position to do so, because it had been the *prečani* Serbs of Bosnia and Croatia who had dominated the communist parties of those republics since the days of the second world war; in Croatia in 1982 the local Serbs formed 15 per cent of the population but 24 per cent of the membership of the Croatian party; 11.6 per cent of *prečani* Serbs in Croatia were party members as opposed to 7 per cent of Croats. Initially that meant a contest for power within the existing republics of the federation but if the federation were to collapse entirely the Serbs would feel free to redefine their state boundaries so as to include in it as many as possible of the *prečani* Serbs. Fearing for the balance of power the Croats would be anxious to do the same.

The death of Tito had left a huge gap in the leadership. The rotating presidency which followed him was a sensible device for defusing regional jealousies but it did so primarily by weakening the centre, with the result that federal power could not contest republican power. Should a republican leader become over-assertive there would be little that the central political authority could do to restrain him. Should the Serbian nationalist-communist alliance find a competent leader there would be nothing in the federal structure capable of resisting it. In 1986 Slobodan Milošević was elected head of the Serbian League of Communists; in 1987 he visited Kosovo and promised the local Serbs that they would no longer be harassed. In May 1989 he became president of Serbia.

Albania

Although the APL maintained connections with only three ruling communist parties, those of Vietnam, Laos, and North Korea, in the 1980s the Albanian state gradually returned to a wider and more rational, as well as a more regional, international orientation. In July 1980 a commercial agreement had been signed with Yugoslavia, which had already replaced China as Albania's main trading partner. The Kosovo riots of 1981 had blocked any further progress to closer political relations with the ancient enemy but in May 1981 Albania did establish some links with another old foe, Greece. In 1984 Franz-Josef Strauss visited the country and relations would probably have been established with the FRG had it not been for an Albanian demand for four million deutschmarks in compensation for war damage.

The first half of the 1980s witnessed a major sensation in Albanian politics. On 18 December 1981 it was announced that the prime minister, Mehmet Shehu, a long-time associate of Enver Hoxha, had killed himself. Hoxha denounced his former comrade as an agent working for the British, the Yugoslav, the American, and the Soviet secret services; there were few in Albania who did not believe that he had been murdered and many who were convinced that he had been killed during a politburo meeting.

If the death of Shehu was the most dramatic development in Albania in the 1980s the most important was the death of Hoxha himself in April 1985. His successor was the head of state, Ramiz Alia, who, unlike Hoxha, was a Gheg. Alia held fast to Hoxha's firm internal line and continued his cautious movement towards the outside world. In 1987 full diplomatic relations were established with Greece for the first time since before the second world war and in the same year official links were finally set up with Bonn.

There was, however, no sympathy for the new revisionists in Moscow or for the reforming ideas they were spreading. But, in the end, not even Albania could hold out against the sweeping changes affecting Europe's communist states.

EASTERN EUROPE BORDERS AS AT JUNE 1993

* Proposed official name
of the former Yugoslav
Republic of Macedonia
not yet universally recognised

22

THE REVOLUTIONS OF 1989–91

In the late summer and early autumn of 1989 waves of reform and revolution crashed upon eastern Europe's communist régimes with such force that within two years the entire system had been swept away. Some of the forces which accumulated into these cleansing waves were to be found in all the affected states, others were peculiar to only one or a few of them.

The reforming and revolutionary processes were discernible first in Poland and Hungary. In Poland the movement was driven by forces outside the system, whilst in Hungary, though popular protest was by no means absent, the party itself instituted many radical changes. The Hungarian party was also to play a significant role in destabilising the east German state and in opening the Berlin Wall, the event which both symbolised the failure of east European socialism and precipitated the collapse of its remaining socialist governments and parties.

Poland

The changes in personnel at the end of 1988 made it easier for the Polish party to bite the bullet and talk directly with Solidarity. On 18 January 1989 the central committee, urged on by Jaruzelski, agreed to begin negotiations on the relegalisation of the union. This in turn opened the way for the round table talks between the government and its opponents which began on 6 February with the non-governmental groups being led by Wałęsa. The Polish authorities and their opponents had set a precedent which was to be followed in almost all east European states. Equally unwittingly, the Polish communist government had taken the first step to the dismantling of its power and in so doing had begun the revolution of 1989; the nature of this step determined that that revolution would by and large be peaceful. Only in Romania, where the leadership refused to acknowledge, let alone talk to its critics did the revolution have to assume violent form.

The beginning of the round table talks immediately changed the political atmosphere in Warsaw and in March the government was able to state officially that it held the Soviet Union responsible for the Katyn massacres. This was only one of many about-turns which the Polish and other communist authorities were to make in the following months.

In Poland itself the final outcome of the round table talks, which was announced at the conclusion of the discussions on 5 April, seemed sensational enough. Solidarity was to be relegalised, there were to be wide-ranging economic reforms, and, most exhilarating of all, elections were to be held in the summer in which half the seats in parliament were to be freely contested. Further reform introduced a bicameral legislature and gave the Roman Catholic church full legal status in Poland; symbolically the May Day parade in Warsaw was cancelled. The elections of June provided the greatest surprise of all, not so much in the fact as in the scale of Solidarity's victory. Despite its lack of electoral experience and back-up in terms of offices, telephones, and so on, it won 99 per cent of the freely elected seats; even more astonishing was that only two of the thirty-five pro-government candidates in uncontested seats secured the 50 per cent of the votes of the eligible electorate necessary for their return to parliament. Most surprising of all, the government and the PUWP accepted this humiliation.

The new sejm met on 4 July. One of its first acts was to restore diplomatic relations between Poland and the Vatican but constitutional issues were not so easily resolved. There was, first, the problem of the presidency. It had been a matter of common consent that Jaruzelski would remain head of state, his removal perhaps causing too much alarm in the army or in the Soviet Union. In the new sejm, however, a majority could not be guaranteed for a communist leader. In the end, a number of Solidarity deputies arranged a discreet absence and Jaruzelski was voted president by a majority of one. He remained head of state and commander in chief of the army, but it was quite clear to all to whom he owed these positions. In a significant gesture towards the separation of party and state Jaruzelski then resigned from the central committee, the politburo, and from the leadership of the party.

Wałęsa, the unquestioned victor of the election, refused to take Solidarity into a coalition government but, after almost two months of haggling, it was agreed that the union would back an administration formed by Tadeusz Mazowiecki, a journalist and Solidarity activist. Under its new prime minister Poland witnessed the dismantling of the communist system. On 29 December 1989 parliament sanctioned constitutional amendments which abolished the leading role of the party, renamed the state 'The Republic of Poland', and restored the pre-war flag and coat of arms. At the same time it endorsed Leszek Balcerowicz's 'big bang' economic reform package which was designed to restore the market system. Poland had ceased to be a socialist state; marxism-leninism had been jettisoned; and the party itself was to wither away.

Hungary

In December 1988 and January 1989 the Hungarian parliament had passed legislation allowing the rights of association and assembly. In February came laws permitting a multi-party system, and on 20 February the central committee of the HSWP voted to abandon the leading role of the party.

There was also a series of concessions to popular misgivings over the past. In January 1989 the party announced that it was to establish a commission of enquiry into the 1956 'popular uprising against the existing state power'. This was an explosive statement. Until then the party had been adamant that the events of 1956 had been a counter-revolution, the suppression of which had been the historic duty of the Hungarian party; but if 1956 had not been a heinous counter-revolution the Hungarian party had had no right to suppress it, and therefore its legitimacy was severely undermined. The party did not deny it, and in March denounced the errors of the thirty-two years of Kádár's rule. In April the communist youth organisation, DISz, dissolved itself, re-emerging as FIDESz, which had no links with the communist party. In May a cabinet reshuffle strengthened the reformist group, but even more important was the HSWP's decision that henceforth the cabinet should be responsible not to it but to parliament. It was also decided that round table talks should begin with opposition groups to determine further constitutional reform.

Any doubts that communist rule in Hungary was dissolving were set aside on 16 June 1989. On that day the now rehabilitated Imre Nagy and four other victims of repression were taken from their ignominious and theoretically anonymous graves and reburied in a style and place befitting national heroes. Over 300,000 Hungarians lined the streets and multitudes watched the ceremony on television; an English observer noted, 'This is not the funeral of Imre Nagy. It is his resurrection, and the funeral of János Kádár.'[1]

Kádár died on 6 July. By then the round table talks had begun and shortly after his death a by-election produced the first genuine opposition deputy to sit in the Hungarian diet since 1947. By the end of September there were seven of them and they were able to form a parliamentary group. In the following month a two-day congress saw the majority of the HSWP split away to form the Hungarian Socialist Party. Later in October all party cells in the workplace were abolished, as was the communist-run workers' militia. This gave substance to the earlier vote in parliament; the leading role of the party was no more.

As the party's power dissolved, new institutions and mechanisms were prepared to replace it. The round table had finished its discussions in the middle of September. These charted the way to a new and entirely open electoral system, the abolition of the presidential council, the direct election of the president, the establishment of a constitutional court, and the renaming of the state as the Hungarian Republic. This last recommendation was applied by the national assembly on 23 October 1989, thirty-three years to the day since the students of Budapest had begun their historic march to the Stalin statue.

The GDR

The round tables had enabled Poland and Hungary to move relatively gradually towards the dissolution of communist power. In Berlin events moved more rapidly, not least because of a decision by the Hungarian government on 10 September to open its frontier to Austria, thus releasing into the west thousands of east Germans who had been accumulating on the border ever since Hungary announced on 3 August that it was considering offering asylum to citizens of the GDR. On 11 September 125,000 crossed into Austria and when access to Hungary became difficult frustrated east Germans began besieging west German diplomatic missions in Prague and Warsaw. Inevitably pressure was exercised from Bonn and by the end of September Honecker's régime had been embarrassed and shamed into ferrying its defecting citizens across its own territory in sealed trains.

Massive pressures were now acting on that régime, but it was not yet to be moved. On 21 September it refused recognition to Neues Forum, a grouping of critical intellectuals, but it was powerless to prevent a series of meetings each Monday in Leipzig, meetings which had begun at the end of September after a complaint from religious leaders in the city that eleven demonstrators had been beaten by police. Shortly after the first Leipzig meeting an even greater embarrassment was suffered by Honecker and his colleagues when Gorbachev visited the GDR in the first week of October. The occasion was supposedly one of celebration and self-congratulation for the régime: the fortieth anniversary of its foundation. But it proved to be Honecker's humiliation rather than his apogee. On the day of the great parade in Berlin the crowd chanted 'Gorbi, Gorbi', whilst Gorbachev himself studiously refused Honecker the customary comradely embrace and made meaningful remarks on the fate awaiting those who refuse to adapt in time. Honecker seemed uncowed. On 10 October, with church leaders throughout the country calling for a round table or some form of dialogue, Honecker received a high Chinese dignitary and referred to the similarities between the 'counter revolution' in Peking and the surge of unrest in the GDR. He then made plans to suppress the next Leipzig meeting, using methods not much different from those used by the Chinese a few months earlier. He was overruled by his politburo and resigned, to be replaced as party leader by Egon Krenz.

Krenz, a Sorb by origin, was to be one of a number of communist officials whose period in office was brief but important because it spanned the political transition to post-totalitarianism. On 8 November Krenz called a meeting of the central committee which began sensationally with the resignation of the entire politburo. On the following evening came the much greater sensation of the opening of the Wall. The east German party was fatally undermined; once opened, the Wall could not be closed and thus the intensifying movement for fundamental political change and real liberalisation was immeasurably strengthened. The party and the government were bemused. A new party action programme, promising reform and economic restructuring, was endorsed by a party congress, and on 17 November Hans Modrow, the moderate and respected party boss of Dresden, formed a new administration, one of the first acts of which was to sanction meetings by the now-recognised Neues Forum.

These major changes did not bring stability. East Germany was swamped both by revelations of its former leaders' corruption and by the sophisticated, and elated, political practitioners from the FRG. On 3 December the entire politburo once again resigned and this time the central committee went with it; five days later Gregor Gysi was elected leader of the party, which also renamed itself the Party of Democratic Socialism.

Round table discussions with Neues Forum had begun the previous day and, as in Poland, they charted the way to free elections. In the GDR elections on 18 March 1990, however, there were no reserved seats for the communists and the results were perhaps as astounding as those in Poland. To the consternation of all of the pollsters, the pro-unification parties secured a clear majority. The GDR had voted for self-liquidation, a process which began with the introduction of the deutschmark in July and was completed with formal reunification on 3 October 1990.

Bulgaria

One day after the opening of the Berlin Wall an older, if less prominent, communist landmark disappeared when Todor Zhivkov was ousted as Bulgaria's *numero uno*.

Already angered by the anti-Turkish campaign and the further tarnishing of Bulgaria's image, and emboldened by Gorbachev's new spirit, elements within the intelligentsia formed an Independent Association for the Defence of Human Rights in Bulgaria in February 1988. Though only one of a number of emerging independent groups it spearheaded the campaign against the regenerative process. In May 1989 the campaign reached its peak with widespread strikes and demonstrations in the Turkish communities, especially in north-eastern Bulgaria. Police repression coincided with the CSCE meeting in Paris and once more Zhivkov's image was damaged. Greater damage was to follow in the summer when over 300,000 ethnic Turks left Bulgaria for Turkey; though many were later to return, the impact of this 'brawn drain' was so severe that part of the civilian population had to be mobilised to replace the lost labour force.

After the summer there were few who would have given the Zhivkov régime a prolonged life-expectancy. In October police repression of an ecologists' demonstration precipitated action by a cabal of oppositionists within the leadership. An emergency meeting of the central committee was called and on 10 November 1989 Zhivkov was deposed.

In 1989 Bulgaria experienced a palace coup rather than a popular revolution, and 'people power' was more the consequence than the cause of the change of leadership. After Zhivkov's fall huge demonstrations were staged to hasten the process of reform, though the streets were also used by chauvinist elements who had approved of the regenerative process and wanted to prevent its reversal. In its first weeks of office the new administration under Petûr Mladenov diluted police .power, released political prisoners, and allowed the formation of non-communist political associations. On 7 December a number of these came together in the Union of Democratic Forces (UDF) which, under the leadership of Zhelyu Zhelev, was to provide the main opposition to the communists in the coming months. In the middle of December a party congress, followed immediately by a session of the national assembly, sanctioned political pluralism and encouraged the separation of party and state. It also took the first steps in the process which was to lead early in 1990 to the abolition of Article 1 of the 1971 constitution under which the communist party had been guaranteed the leading role in the state and in society.

The initial demand of the UDF was for round table discussions, and in this they were backed by large demonstrations and strike action by *Podkrepa* (Support), an independent trade union founded in February. The discussions did not begin until 22 January 1990. On 29 December the government had decreed full rights and equality for all Muslims and Turks, a concession which sparked off noisy demonstrations and a week of great tension until a social council was established to guarantee that the decree would be implemented and that no organisation would be allowed to advocate breaking up the unity of the Bulgarian state. It was the danger from the unreconstructed, chauvinist elements which persuaded the authorities that direct negotiations with the UDF were essential to safeguard the reform process. From the social council emerged Bulgaria's version of the round table.

The chief function of the round table in Bulgaria, as elsewhere, was to prepare the country for free elections. Agreement was reached in mid-March that a grand national, or constituent, assembly (GNA) should be elected in mid-June. Before the elections were held the Bulgarian Communist Party metamorphosed, shedding its old image – many said that it was simply its outer skin – so as to appear in the election campaign as a new force, allegedly having no connections with the old régime. At its fourteenth, extraordinary congress the party's structure was changed, Mladenov announced he could not be head of state and leader of the party and the latter post was assumed by Aleksandûr Lilov. On 3 April 1990 the party changed its name to the Bulgarian Socialist Party (BSP).

The BSP had enormous advantages in the electoral campaign. Its opponents lacked basic electoral capital, such as typewriters, telephones, and offices, whereas the BCP/BSP apparatus was virtually intact, especially in the countryside where it waged an effective whispering campaign suggesting that the radicals of the UDF, who were predominantly urban intellectuals, would abolish pensions and discriminate against the countryside.

The elections gave the BSP a majority in the GNA but the party found it difficult to impose its authority. There were allegations of electoral fraud and in July Mladenov was fatally compromised by a video-recording of a December

1989 protest meeting in which he was seen to suggest using tanks against demonstrators. He resigned on 6 July, to be replaced by Zhelev. Social and political tension mounted as the BSP insisted that there must be a coalition government; it argued that the economic measures which had to be taken were so severe that all parties should be involved in enacting them. The opposition, on the other hand, insisted that as the mess was of the communists' making and therefore that their successors in the BSP must clear it up. A BSP government was eventually formed under Andrei Lukanov, but it was driven from office in November by a combination of student protests and strike action by the trade unions.

The next administration, led by Dimitûr Popov, delicately engineered compromises both on the social front and in the political arena. Economic managers, the trade unions, and the government were brought into a tripartite agreement, while progress was at last made towards defining a new constitution which was adopted in July 1991. In October of the same year elections produced a hung parliament; a UDF administration was formed with the backing of the Movement for Rights and Freedom (MRF), a mainly Turkish party which held the balance in the assembly. For the first time since 1944 there were no communists in the government.

Czechoslovakia

In Czechoslovakia, 1989 opened with demonstrations to commemorate the twentieth anniversary of Palach's self-immolation. As a result Havel and thirteen other Charter '77 activists were arrested. The police were again in action on May Day, suppressing marchers in the traditional parade who dared to suggest that their human rights were being infringed. In May, however, there was also the first sign of relaxation when Havel was released from detention.

There were further indications of a softening of official attitudes in August when the police scarcely intervened in demonstrations to mark the Soviet invasion of 1968. The authorities responded similarly to a large gathering on 28 October, the anniversary of the foundation of the Czechoslovak state and, until communist rule, the country's national day. But if the Jakeš régime had decided to permit some public acknowledgement of and solidarity with the changes in Poland and Hungary, it had not moved over to a positively reformist stance. The only significant concession made by that régime before it too became engulfed in the tide of change was its announcement on 15 November that exit visas would no longer be needed for travel to the west.

That concession came two days before the police savagely attacked an officially sanctioned student demonstration in Prague. The coincidence of the concession and the seemingly contradictory police action of two days later has led some to believe that the final collapse of the Jakeš régime was part of a plot by Czech and Soviet reformist communists to lever into power a Gorbachev-type administration. This theory is supported by the fact that immediately after the demonstration the police spread rumours that their action had led to the death of a student; that this was similar to the events of October 1939, when the Germans had used Jan Opletal's death as the excuse for a clampdown on the Czech intelligentsia, strengthened the suspicion that the crowds in Prague were being manipulated from behind the scenes. The reported death of the student was later disproved but not before the rumours had provoked very large anti-government demonstrations on 20 November, which did much to undermine the Jakeš' authority. On 21 November the government began discussions with two recently formed civil organisations, Civic Forum, which was based in Prague, and its Slovak counterpart, Public Against Violence (PAV).

If reformist communists had conspired to dislodge Jakeš, their plot had released forces which they could not contain. Once initiated, progress towards change could not be halted. On 24 November the entire praesidium of the party resigned, Jakeš being replaced as party leader by Karel Urbanek. Urbanek, like Rakowski, Krenz, and Mladenov, was to have little more than his allotted fifteen minutes of fame. On 26 November Czechoslovakia's past seemed to join its present and, many hoped, its future. A huge crowd of a quarter of a million was addressed in Wenceslas Square by prime minister Ladislav Adamec, Václav Havel, and Alexander Dubček. On the following day there were yet more demonstrations, together this time with a two-hour general strike. On 28 November Civic Forum and PAV were officially registered and on the following day the federal assembly abolished the constitutional provisions guaranteeing the party its leading role.

Within two weeks of the student demonstrations of 17 November, the Czechoslovak communist system seemed to have voted itself out of existence. But the exhilarated crowds were not yet satisfied. Civic Forum, backed by an exceedingly vocal popular opinion, rejected the government proposed by Adamec on 3 December, and on the following day the crowds once more gathered in Wenceslas Square. This time they were further encouraged by the Malta summit conference, with its moves to even greater détente between east and west, and by the announcement from Moscow that the five Warsaw Pact powers which had taken part in the 1968 invasion of Czechoslovakia were about to renounce that action. Since Urbanek, Adamec, and what was left of the Husák clique derived their power and their legitimacy from that invasion, the Moscow announcement was perhaps the final nail in the coffin of Czechoslovak communism. Changes in the government seemed to confirm that analysis. On 7 December Adamec resigned. His successor, Marian Čalfa, was a Slovak whose cabinet, announced on 10 December, had a majority of non-communists. On the same day Husák resigned as president.

There were some, particularly in the west, who wondered whether Dubček might be his successor, but, however sweet such revenge might have been, Dubček was more a part of the past than the future. He was not, however, to be left without a role and on 28 December was elected chairman, or speaker, of the federal assembly. On 29 December Havel was elected president.

Czechoslovakia now moved rapidly towards restructuring and the dissolution of the communist system. On New Year's Day Havel granted amnesty to over 16,000 political prisoners and on 2 January 1990 the secret police were officially disbanded. The National Front soon followed them and in March new laws were enacted guaranteeing freedom of association and of the press. Exiles were allowed, indeed encouraged, to return and major constitutional reform at the end of March at last granted the Slovaks their long-desired equality of status; Czechoslovakia ceased to exist and became the Czech and Slovak Federative Republic. A further break with the past came with the rigidly monetarist finance minister, Václav Klaus, who attempted to swing the Czechoslovak economy away from its centralised, planned past towards capitalism and the free market. In June a general election secured a majority for Civic Forum/PAV, although the communists won a surprising 13 per cent of the vote. They alone of the major parties, however, were not included in the new government.

Romania

Up to the end of November 1989 Ceauşescu was conscious but still contemptuous of the pressures swirling around him. When American criticism became too irksome he unilaterally scrapped the most favoured nation treaty status with the United States; inside the socialist bloc he placed himself at the head of the movement to contain reformist pressure, using the WTO conference in Bucharest in July 1989 in a vain attempt to call for intervention in Poland. Outwardly neither Ceauşescu nor his system seemed damaged by the maelstrom of discontent in eastern Europe. In November the party held its fourteenth congress, at which Ceauşescu received no fewer than sixty-seven standing ovations. In the middle of December he left for a visit to Iran.

Meanwhile in Timişoara László Tökés, a young Protestant pastor, had breached regulations by allowing three students to recite poetry during a service in his church. Tökés came under police pressure and his bishop decided to transfer him to a remote country parish. Tökés was not disposed to go, and in this he was supported not only by his parishioners but also by many of the citizens of Timişoara, Hungarians and Romanians alike. On 15 December a vigil began outside his church. On 16 December the vigil turned into a demonstration against the régime and on the following day the army turned its guns on the demonstrators. The army was again in action on 21 December, this time in Bucharest when Ceauşescu, back from Iran, was heckled whilst addressing a crowd from the balcony of the party headquarters. On 22 December he again addressed the crowds from party headquarters but this time he found no defenders and was forced to flee by helicopter from the roof of the building. In the next few traumatic hours everything hinged on the attitude of the army which, after initial hesitation, finally sided with the demonstrators. The protest had turned into a full-scale revolution whose fate seemed to depend on the battle then raging around the television studios to the north of the city centre. After furious exchanges of fire with fanatical Securitate forces a shadowy body calling itself the National Salvation Front (NSF) established control of the building. For two days, however, fighting continued in the centre of Bucharest and other cities. Only after the Ceauşescus had been captured and shot on Christmas Day did the Securitate give up the struggle, staging a final and fruitless assault on the TV station on 27 December.

The NSF was drawn mainly from reformist elements within the communist apparat and its leader, Ion Iliescu, was a student colleague of Gorbachev. Iliescu became president of 'Romania', as the country was to be called after 28 December, and a new government was formed under Petre Roman. On 1 January 1990 the Securitate was abolished but hopes for a smooth transition to a non-totalitarian system received a setback when the NSF reneged on its promise that it would not contest the elections to be held in May 1990. A further cause for concern was increasing tension between the Romanians and Hungarians in Transylvania, a tension which exploded in ugly clashes between supporters of the Hungarian Democratic Union of Romania and the ultra-nationalist Romanian group, Vatra Românescâ, in Tîrgu Mureş on 19 March. When the elections were held in May the NSF won two-thirds of the seats in both houses and Iliescu had an easy victory in the concurrent presidential election.

It is not yet certain that the basis of the one-party state has been dismantled in Romania. Much of the old bureaucracy remains intact and despite some privatisation, mainly in the service sector, economic reform has not advanced greatly. Even more dispiriting was Iliescu's use of the miners against protesting students in June 1990. The tide was perhaps turned in February 1992 when the first multi-party local elections since 1945 registered, compared to the national elections of 1990, a substantial swing away from the NSF and towards the Democratic Convention, an alliance of democratic parties. In March 1992 the NSF group in parliament split, which gave even more hope that the national poll which was scheduled for June would at last produce free and open elections. The poll, which was held eventually in September 1992, returned Iliescu to power and, though not a model of the representative process, was not marred by serious irregularities.

Yugoslavia

If in Romania the Ceauşescu system was overthrown in a sudden, violent spasm which was followed by a long and unsteady truce between the ex-communists and their opponents, the reverse was true in Yugoslavia. Here the titoist edifice crumbled slowly, producing an unsteady truce which finally dissolved into woeful and prolonged violence. The truce began to fracture in Kosovo.

The unrest which had led to the temporary arrest in November 1988 of two prominent communists, one of them Azem Vlasi, the Kosovo party leader, surfaced again in February 1989 when troops were deployed in the area and a curfew was imposed in Priština; shortly afterwards the LCY sacked Vlasi, who was arrested again with other leaders of the Kosovo party organisation in March. He was released in April but this did not presage reconciliation. Milošević had already announced that the Serbian ministry of internal affairs would be taking over responsibility for security in Kosovo from its federal namesake, and on 26 June the Kosovo assembly was suspended and its powers assumed by that in Serbia. On 5 July the Serbian assembly voted for the permanent dissolution of the Kosovo body. This was confirmed in the new Serbian constitution of September 1989 which incorporated into the Serbian republic both the Vojvodina and Kosovo. The Albanians of Kosovo refused to accept the legitimacy of the new constitution, insisting that their loyalty was to the autonomous Kosovo republic proclaimed when 114 deputies from the Kosovo assembly had met in secret on 2 July.

Milošević exploited the Kosovo issue to the full. It was not the least reason why he was able in November 1989 to secure a majority for his communist party, soon to be renamed the Serbian Socialist Party, in Serbia's first direct and secret ballot since 1945. But the policies of Milošević transgressed one of the fundamental principles of federal Yugoslavia: that one unit did not interfere in the affairs of another; and if it did then the awful dangers of simultaneous wars of expansion by Serbia and Croatia would arise. Despite the dangers this is precisely what Milošević did, not only in Kosovo but also in the Vojvodina, and he even went as far as to pronounce Macedonian a dialect of Serbian and to raise the question of the Serbs in Croatia and Bosnia. Such policies could only fan fears of Serbian hegemonism and therefore strengthen the decentralising camps in the non-Serb republics. Milošević and the republics were now engaged in a struggle in which, wittingly or unwittingly, most of the factors capable of preserving the unity of the Yugoslav federation were destroyed or discredited.

The pace was set in Ljubljana. In September 1989 the Slovene assembly reasserted the sovereignty of the Slovene republic and proclaimed its right to secede from the federation. By the end of the year Serbia and Slovenia had declared virtual economic war on one another. At the fourteenth, extraordinary congress of the LCY, the Slovene communists argued that the eight constituent parties should become completely independent and that the leading role of the party should be excised from the constitution. When the latter proposal was accepted but the former roundly rejected, the Slovenes walked out, rendering the congress useless. It was postponed but was never to reconvene. At the end of March the absence of the Slovene delegates meant that the central commit-tee of the LCY could not secure a quorum. In effect the LCY, the architect of the federation, had been made impotent.

The effects of these developments were soon felt. On 8 March the Slovene assembly dropped the word 'socialist' from the republic's title; in April a centre-right alliance, Demos, won a majority in elections to the Slovene assembly; in Croatia victory in elections to its assembly in May went to the Croatian Demo-cratic Union (CnDU). The CnDU leader, Franjo Tudjman, was elected president of Croatia, though in Slovenia the presidency went to Milan Kučan, a member of the reformed communist party. In December a referendum in Slovenia showed an even greater majority in favour of full independence.

In Croatia the new government took a number of steps which could not fail to antagonise the local Serbs, for example the downgrading of the status of the cyrillic alphabet. The Serbs retaliated by forming their own associations and in August by conducting a referendum as a result of which a Serbian national council was formed which proclaimed autonomy for the Serb-dominated Krajina area centred on Knin. In October Croatian police units were withdrawn from Serb areas. The Serbs in Croatia received constant support from Milošević whose domestic position was bolstered by presidential elections in December which gave him 65 per cent of the votes cast.

By the end of 1990 all six republics had conducted elections and three of them, Serbia, Slovenia, and Croatia, had adopted new constitutions. How those constitutions might fit into a federal structure had not been decided and a conference to discuss this question opened in January 1991. It was the first of a number of such meetings, all of them fruitless.

Before the January constitutional discussions convened, Yugoslavia had been rocked by another damaging economic scandal. In December 1990 it was revealed that the Serbian National Bank had secretly issued 18,300 million dinars ($1,400 million) of new money in order to make a loan to the Serbian government which then used the money, in good socialist fashion, to subsidise loss-making enterprises. The note issue did not have the sanction of the federal National Bank of Yugoslavia and critically undermined the painful economic reforms which had recently been drawn up by federal prime minister, Ante Marković, as a condition for the IMF's sanctioning of a nine-year rescheduling of Yugoslavia's massive foreign debt. To many non-Serbs, and especially to the non-socialist economic reformists in Croatia and Slovenia, it seemed that Milošević was ready to debauch the federal currency in an illegal attempt to prop up his ailing socialist Serbia. The currency, like the party, was now useless as a force for holding together the federation.

In February the Slovene assembly restored to the republic all rights which had previously been vested in the federal authorities and called for a separate Slovene currency, banking system, and tax structure, whilst the Croats put Croat law above federal law and set out the conditions on which they would remain in the federation. This was an interesting switch, in that the Croats were now stating their conditions for remaining in the federation rather than saying what might eventually drive them out of it.

In March 1991 another federal institution was compromised. Boris Jović, a pro-Milošević Serb, resigned as chairman of the rotating state presidency, i.e. head of state, because the council had refused to sanction his proposal that the army be allowed to take unspecified emergency measures. The head of state was also commander in chief of the armed forces. Jović, who in any case would have come to the end of his term in office in May, was replaced by his deputy, an anti-communist Croat, Stipe Mesić. The succession, however, was frustrated by the withdrawal of the delegates from Montenegro and the Vojvodina, together with the sacking of Kosovo's representative. Jović withdrew his resignation later in the month but there were few who did not believe that the whole episode had been managed by Milošević in an effort to seize control of the army. In any event the crisis had compromised the state presidency and had sharpened fears in Croatia and Slovenia of possible military action by the Serb-dominated Yugoslav National Army (JNA).

Concern at possible military action was not new. The Croats had already established a force which was armed with light weapons bought from the disbanded Hungarian workers' militia, a force which the Croats had demobilised in face of threats from the JNA. On 7 March the Slovene assembly had enacted a law allowing Slovene conscripts to perform their military service with the local territorial defence force rather than in the JNA.

There was little left to hold Yugoslavia together beyond the naked force of the JNA. On 19 May a referendum in Croatia produced a 93 per cent vote in favour of leaving the federation. On 25 June the assemblies of Croatia and Slovenia declared full independence. The JNA went into action the following day. Its strategy seemed to be to strike first at Slovenia and then turn on Croatia, but it failed to secure its anticipated easy victory. The JNA was soon to abandon Slovenia and after fearful fighting in Croatia, especially around Vukovar, a truce was eventually brokered. Then the battle turned to Bosnia where, at the time of writing, it rages still.

Albania

So great were the upheavals of 1989 that not even isolated Albania could remain untouched by them. Indication of a softening of official attitudes was visible in November 1989 when some political prisoners were included in a general amnesty but the concession seemed to sharpen rather than satiate the appetite for reform. In December 1989 and January 1990 there were anti-government riots in Shkodër, with troops being deployed on the latter occasion. In March an outburst of hooliganism amongst football supporters in Kavajë, which rapidly turned into an anti-government demonstration, was only one of a number of such incidents. At a central committee plenum in April the APL showed that it was ready to grant economic reforms and to move away from isolationism in foreign affairs; party leader Ramiz Alia announced that relations would be restored with both the USSR and the USA. In May the national assembly went further, adopting a series of measures which allowed foreign investment in Albania and which brought the first real liberalisation in domestic affairs; the penal code was considerably relaxed and religious rights were restored.

Once again concession inflamed rather than dampened the demand for change. There was more rioting in Tiranë at the beginning of July, after which desperate Albanians adopted a modified form of the tactics used by east Germans in the previous summer. Foreign embassies were swamped with would-be emigrants,

5,000 of whom were eventually allowed to leave the country. The communist authorities suffered a further blow in October when their favourite literary son, Ismail Kadare, requested political asylum in France.

On 11 November 1990, at Shkodër cathedral, thousands attended the first public mass to be celebrated in the country since 1967 but this did not bring any permanent decrease in political dissatisfaction. In December students at the Enver Hoxha University in Tiranë launched two days of demonstrations demanding further political reform and a change in the name of their university. They were soon to be gratified on both accounts. On 11 December a party plenum agreed to the legalisation of opposition parties. On the following day the Democratic Party of Albania (DPA) was founded. Now that they had opposition parties the dissidents wanted free elections and, as had happened elsewhere in eastern Europe, the dismantling of the communist party's leading role. Demonstrations to support these demands were held throughout the country and were made more forceful by the general economic dislocation then affecting all Albanians.

The pace of change was accelerating. Hoxha's widow, Nexhmije, was replaced as head of the Democratic Front and on 26 December an extraordinary conference of the APL outlined a series of economic and constitutional reforms. Five days later a draft constitution was published which guaranteed multi-party democracy and wide-reaching economic liberalisation. Further pressure from the opposition elements secured the postponement of the general election until March 1991, the opposition wanting more time to organise and prepare their campaign.

The extra time did not bring them victory. The APL won some 60 per cent of the votes, and opposition suspicions of unfair practice burst out in further riots, with four people dying in Shkodër in what were the most serious disturbances yet seen in Albania. Social unrest was added to political discontent. New trade unions had been acquiring considerable support amongst a populace increasingly affected by hunger, unemployment, and uncertainty. This increasing economic dislocation forced the government to make further political concessions, such as: the interim constitutional law of 29 April by which Albania ceased to be officially a 'Socialist' republic; the formation in June of a new 'government of national solidarity' which included opposition supporters; and the change in the name of the APL which in June became the Socialist Party of Albania (SPA).

These concessions had little effect in the face of the huge economic and social dislocation now being endured. Once again these tensions were expressed most dramatically in flight, this time in an exodus by sea in August of thousands of Albanians. At the end of the month there was another rash of the rioting which was to continue sporadically throughout the remainder of the year.

Much of the discontent remained economic, particularly in September and October when serious food shortages were experienced. However, there were also clearly formulated political demands, especially for the end of socialist party control over the media and for the abolition of the secret police. The Albanian reformists were following those in the rest of eastern Europe in demanding the dismantling of the old communist apparat. By November the government had to admit that parts of the country were out of its control and so, in an attempt to appease discontent, it agreed that the next general election should be brought forward from May/June to 1 March 1992. The government of national solidarity had presided over virtual national disintegration and it resigned on 14 December, with a new administration being formed under a non-party intellectual, Vilson Ahmeti.

The elections of March 1992 produced a sweeping victory for the DPA, after which the new assembly elected the DPA leader, Sali Berisha, president; an overwhelmingly DPA cabinet was then formed under Aleksander Meksi. The communists/socialists had finally been dislodged from power but the problems facing the new government were daunting even by east European standards.

The Baltic states

The new atmosphere created by Gorbachev inside the Soviet Union had encouraged the non-Russians of Estonia, Latvia, and Lithuania to extend the degree to which they could assert their national identity and make decisions at a local level. In December 1987 the Estonian Heritage Society had been established to look after churches and other national monuments. By 1988 the banned Estonian national flag was appearing once more and in June the legal prohibition against its use was lifted. In Latvia in March 1988, in a step which would have been impossibly audacious a year or so earlier, the creative unions organised a demonstration to mark the anniversary of the mass deportations of 1949. Significant moves towards a loosening of ties with Moscow came in Lithuania in November with a law making Lithuanian the official language of the republic and restoring the pre-war flag and national anthem. In January 1989 the Estonian supreme soviet passed a law making Estonian the official language and allowing a four-year period of grace for non-Estonian speaking bureaucrats to learn it.

The increasingly emboldened decentralisers had by the end of 1988 channelled their support into quasi-political bodies. The most vocal was Sajudis (movement) in Lithuania, but both Estonia and Latvia had well-organised and effective people's fronts. Equally importantly, by the end of 1988 reformists had taken over most if not all posts in the state and party leaderships. In 1989 Estonia and, even more so, Lithuania edged towards a break with Moscow.

On 18 May the supreme soviet in Vilnius adopted a declaration of economic and political sovereignty for Lithuania; six months later, on 6 December, the same body abolished the CPSU's authority in Lithuania and allowed the formation of non-communist political parties; Lithuania had become the first Soviet republic to establish a multi-party system. On 19 December the Lithuanian Communist Party detached itself from the CPSU.

Estonia and Latvia moved more cautiously, not least because the percentage of the population which was 'non-local' was much higher than in Lithuania: 39 per cent of Estonians and 48 per cent of Latvians came into this category whereas in Lithuania the figure was 20 per cent. In August the Estonian franchise regulations were modified to exclude from the vote those who had been resident in a constituency for less than two years or in Estonia for less than five, the object being to disenfranchise the large Soviet garrisons and those Russians who had recently settled in the republic. Estonia, like the other two Baltic republics, was much affected by the fiftieth anniversary of the Nazi-Soviet pact, an event which was marked spectacularly by a human chain which stretched almost unbroken through the three countries. The Estonian government daily, *Rahva Hääl*, also published the full text of the pact. On 11 November 1989 the Estonian supreme soviet declared that the Soviet annexation of the country had been a 'military occupation' and was therefore illegitimate; the Estonian party leader, Vaino Väljas, then engineered a skilful declaration *about* rather than *of* sovereignty. In December the Estonians set up their own national bank and announced that they would issue their own currency.

The Soviet leadership in general and Gorbachev in particular did not really know how to deal with the rising secessionist movement in the Baltic states. In July 1989 Moscow conceded virtual economic independence but in political terms Moscow always seemed prepared to offer only what Tallinn, Riga, and Vilnius had already rejected as insufficient. Nevertheless, the December 1989 declaration by the supreme soviet of the USSR that the Nazi-Soviet pact had been illegal was a concession of enormous significance because it destroyed the basis of all Soviet claims to legitimacy in the three republics.

The Soviet concession strengthened the nationalist groups who emerged as the strongest parties in elections which were held in all three republics early in 1990. Again Lithuania took the lead in pressing further along the road to separation. On 11 March the Lithuanian supreme soviet renamed itself the supreme council and declared the country once more an independent state which was to be known by its former name, the Republic of Lithuania. Estonia declared its transition to independence on 30 March and Latvia on 28 July. On 12 May the presidents of the three republics had met in Tallinn and had reconstituted the Baltic entente of 1934 and the council of Baltic states which provided for regular consultation between the three leaders.

The Kremlin, spurred on by its own dissident Russian populists, now felt that it had been pushed too far. In response to the declaration of Lithuanian independence Moscow imposed a fuel embargo on the republic, which was forced in the summer of 1990 to 'suspend' its independence. In January 1991 outright violence was used, thirteen people being killed when Soviet troops stormed the television station in Vilnius; in Riga four died when Soviet troops occupied government buildings later in the month. The Lithuanians responded by organising a referendum, which showed that nine out of ten of those who voted were in favour of complete independence. At the end of July eight more Lithuanians were killed, this time when Soviet forces of the ministry of the interior attacked a Lithuanian border post. The attack had been an attempt to torpedo the forthcoming union treaty which would have greatly loosened the ties between the centre and the constituent republics. The abortive coup of 19 August 1991 in Moscow was a further attempt to block this union treaty. The failure of the coup removed all obstacles to the full independence of Estonia, Latvia, and Lithuania which Moscow recognised on 4 September 1991.

Some observations on the end of communist power in eastern Europe

Between 1989 and 1991 the world witnessed a unique event: the peacetime dissolution of a multi-national great power and its empire. It was a transformation which was all the more remarkable in that a system based so ruthlessly on the use of force and naked power had been reconstructed with the communist party still in control of the media, the judiciary, the army, the police, and the secret police. Communist power in eastern Europe was not destroyed, it abdicated. And, Romania and Yugoslavia excepted, it was by and large a peaceful process. The very names given to the transformation showed an unspoken pride in its peaceful nature, the Bulgarians talking of their 'gentle revolution', the Czechs and Slovaks of the 'velvet revolution', and, because of the role played by national music, the Estonians of the 'singing revolution'. In Poland and Hungary the changes were so gentle and so gradual that Timothy Garton Ash saw them as less than revolution but more than reform, dubbing them therefore 'refolutions'. Whether refolutions or revolutions the events of 1989–91, whilst differing from state to state, did share some common features.

Hopes for reform and liberalisation had been encouraged by the Helsinki agreements, not least because signatories had pledged themselves to examine 'both the security of states and the security of peoples'.[2] This raised the possibility of piecemeal, gradual reform, the permanence of which would depend on the ultimate bosses of communist Europe, the CPSU and the Red Army. It is no coincidence that the régimes which were least reliant on Moscow, those of Bucharest, Belgrade, and Tiranë, put up the toughest resistance to the dissolution of the system. Understandably, in the more repressive régimes, in Albania, Romania, the GDR, Czechoslovakia, Serbia, and to a lesser degree Bulgaria, the population welcomed or even idolised Gorbachev whilst the rulers treated him with suspicion and reserve; in the more open systems of Poland and Hungary the leaders welcomed Gorbachev, who was confirming their own policies, and it was the population, which wished to go even further, which tended towards suspicion and reserve.

As soon as Gorbachev had become general secretary in March 1985 he had filled the CPSU posts which dealt with the European socialist states with a fresh team of administrators who had been studying Soviet–east European relations for years and who had new, radical ideas. They were to tell Gorbachev that eastern Europe was no longer a strategic necessity, that it was a costly economic burden, and that it was a source of political embarrassment because it tied a modernising Soviet Union to socialist dinosaurs such as Husák, Honecker, and Zhivkov. In 1987 Yegor Ligachev, later to become the personification of circumspection in the Soviet politburo, told Hungarian television viewers that 'Every nation has a right to its own way'.[3] Gorbachev, in his November 1987 speech on the anniversary of the bolshevik revolution announced that 'unity does not mean uniformity... There is no model of socialism to be imitated by all' and that the principles which guided relations between socialist states were 'complete and full equality'. In September 1988 a senior Soviet foreign policy adviser said in Italy, 'We have given up the Brezhnev principle of limited sovereignty',[4] and in December Gorbachev himself told the United Nations general assembly that 'freedom of choice is a universal principle which allows no exception'. Early in July 1989, *after* the humiliation of the Polish communists, Gorbachev went even further. On 5 July in Paris he said, 'democracy affects all countries nowadays. What the Poles and Hungarians decide is their affair, but we will respect their decision whatever it is.' On 6 July he told the Council of Europe in Strasbourg that it was 'the sovereign right of each people to choose their social system at their own discretion'; he went on to say that 'the very possibility of the use or threat of force, above all military force, by an alliance against another alliance, inside alliances or wherever it may be, is totally unacceptable.' On 8 July, at the end of a cantankerous and chaotic conference of the WTO in Bucharest, Gorbachev told the delegates that 'there is a new spirit within the Warsaw treaty, with moves towards independent solutions of national problems. We recognise the specifics of our parties and peoples on their path towards socialist democracy.' Within four days the Soviet leader had told the world, and the peoples of eastern Europe, that they had complete freedom, that force would not be used against them, and that they could pursue socialist democracy rather than democratic socialism. And this was after the Polish elections had shown what freedom of choice could produce and after Tiananmen Square had shown what a communist party bent on using force to preserve its power could do.

The east European communist leaders had been abandoned. The Soviet experience in Afghanistan had convinced the politburo in Moscow that investment in an unpopular communist régime did not pay, and that it created more problems than it solved. Also, it is worth noting that the two pace-setters in the east European changes, Poland and Hungary, had shown, in 1944 and 1956, that they were prepared to fight against all odds for the sake of their national freedom.

If the Red Army was not to be used against anti-communist dissidents there remained the national armies of the individual states, but experience had already shown that these were not entirely reliable. In 1953 Czechoslovak military leaders had refused to bring out the tanks against strikers in Plzeň and in the same year some east German units had refused to leave their barracks during the rising of June; the Hungarian army had joined the revolutionaries at a very early stage in 1956; and in Poland in the same year the authorities were forced to rely more on the secret security forces than on the regular army, whilst the suppression of resistance to the 1981 military coup was as much the work of the riot police as the army. Moscow could not rely on local forces and it was unwilling to use its own. The east European régimes were defenceless.

The change in Soviet military thinking came not merely because of Afghanistan and the dubious reliance of the east European armies. In the summer of 1987 the central committee of the CPSU began a serious examination of military thinking which brought about a shift from an offensive to a defensive strategy. This made it possible for Gorbachev to negotiate seriously on troop withdrawals from eastern Europe. The development of long-range missiles obviated the need for the strategic buffer zone which eastern Europe had previously formed; furthermore, because conventional war in Europe could lead to an impossibly destructive nuclear conflict, conventional warfare itself was ruled out, and if there were to be no conventional war, the USSR had no need of buffer states in eastern Europe. Security would be achieved not through confrontation but through cooperation within what Gorbachev now liked to refer to as 'the common European home'. Moreover, the rising cost of the arms race, particularly with US development of 'Star Wars' and the stealth bomber, was wrecking all attempts to modernise and improve the Soviet economy; even Ligachev admitted that, having seen the true costs, 'I became convinced that without reductions of military expenditures, there could be no *perestroika*, no renewal of socialism.'[5] As the example of Japan had shown, the future belonged to those states which used their wealth and technology for economic not military purposes. The Soviet Union's great power posture and especially its presence in eastern Europe was enfeebling it and impairing its efforts to make itself the economic equal of the western states; therefore 'Gorbachev realised that the Europeanisation of the Soviet Union could not proceed without the de-Sovietisation of eastern Europe'.[6]

The economic factor was critical not only in the redefinition of Soviet policy but also in precipitating the demand for change in eastern Europe. Initially Gorbachev had believed that the declining economic situation in the socialist countries was a crisis of performance rather than of structure. But the very persistence and universality of the decline proved the contrary. Decline had begun in the mid-1970s but in many cases had been masked by western loans; after 1980 these were increasingly difficult to come by and all east European states suffered accordingly. Official statistics for the rate of growth in per capita living standards for the years 1970-5 and 1980-5 are shown in Table 22.1. These figures, however, leave out inflation on the black market, often the only source of some goods, even necessities, and the inescapable conclusion is that the 1980s saw a general decline in living standards. Between 1980 and 1986 real wages in Poland declined by 17 per cent and in Hungary the introduction of income tax in 1988 lowered them by 15 per cent; the Hungarians complained of Swiss taxes being imposed on Ethiopian wages. In Yugoslavia between 1979 and 1985 the fall in real wages was 24.9 per cent. Meanwhile the Romanians suffered more than anyone.

There were many reasons for this economic decline. The rigidity of the planned system meant that it could not cope with the rapidity of technological change, particularly in the 1980s with the intensifying pace of computerisation. Nor could it respond to the cheap production flowing in from the far east; the

Table 22.1 Percentage growth in per capita living standards, 1970–85

	1970–5	1980–5
Bulgaria	3.6	2.0
Czechoslovakia	2.5	1.4
GDR	4.9	1.6
Hungary	3.1	0.6
Poland	4.6	0.5
Romania	4.0	1.2

Source: Charles Gati, The Bloc that Failed: Soviet-East European Relations in Transition, London, Taurus, 1990, p. 108.

east European states, like the Soviet Union, were locked into the habits of the five-year plan and continued to pour out steel, concrete, and other products which no one wanted at prices few could afford. In fact industry was positively damaging:

> Antiquated, labour-intensive mines produce coal, at a loss, which has to be made up by subsidies out of the state budget. The coal is transported by rail to highly inefficient power stations, which produce a little energy, a lot of pollution and further losses which also have to be made up out of the state budget. The energy goes to a huge steel works which produces the metal, which goes to make the trucks, which transport the coal, which produces the energy, which goes to the steelworks, which produces the metal, which etc . . . [7]

Oil prices were another cause of the economic crisis. In the Brezhnev era Soviet oil production and world oil prices had both been increasing and if Moscow was short of hard currency for itself or its Comecon partners it could always sell a few billion extra barrels. At the same time the USSR could afford to sell cheaply to its allies; the opportunity cost was worth it in terms of political loyalty and for the propaganda value of being able to say that the socialist economies could offer stable energy prices. By the mid-1980s the picture was very different. Soviet production had levelled off and world prices were falling. Oil could no longer be used to raise quick hard-currency funds and the Soviet Union's own problems were forcing it to charge market prices even to its east European partners. The effect was devastating. The Comecon trading system was conducted through barter and whereas in 1974 Hungary could 'buy' a million tons of Soviet oil by exporting 800 Ikarus buses, in 1981 the number was 2,300 and in 1988 over 4,000. All east European states suffered in a similar manner.

The economic decline helped to undermine the régimes' claim to legitimacy. Socialism was a materialist philosophy which promised plenty for all. It was literally failing to deliver the goods. The raising of living standards which had once been so prominent a feature of communist propaganda now caused embarrassment, with experience flatly contradicting ideology to such a degree that

Marx's theory of the pauperisation of the workers seemed a far more fitting description of socialism than of capitalism.

The impact of the economic decline was made greater by the fact that information concerning conditions in the west was far more widely disseminated than it had been a generation before. In most of eastern Europe the jamming of radio stations had ceased and the BBC, Deutsche Welle, Voice of America, and Radio Vatican were extremely popular. Television, either through direct relay or the video-cassette, was even more influential. It was not merely east Germans who could watch western television; Estonians could watch, and understand, Finnish TV, Czechs and Slovaks watched output from western Germany and Austria, the Albanians watched programmes from Italy, and many Bulgarian Turks watched those from the Turkish republic; Bulgarian television relayed one Soviet channel which, after 1985, became increasingly subversive of the Zhivkov régime. For the Romanians any foreign stations had offerings better than their own, and various parts of the country could receive Bulgarian, Yugoslav, Russian, and Hungarian programmes; it was Hungarian TV which first popularised László Tökés, just as it had been the Polish media which had awakened Lithuanians to the dangers from Chernobyl.

Travel also expanded knowledge and experience of the west. By 1988 there were few restrictions, other than financial ones, for citizens of Poland, Hungary, or Bulgaria; there were none for Yugoslavs, and even east Germans were more free to cross into the west: whilst in 1985 66,000 GDR citizens of working age had been granted visas for such travel, in 1987 the number was 1,200,000. For Romanians and Soviets movement was much more difficult, and for Albanians virtually impossible.

For the young who made up a large number of the travellers the west offered diversity, colour, individuality, and freedom. Pop music embodied much of what they admired in the west and this they brought back in audio and video cassettes. Initially the authorities tried to restrict their importation but it was a hopeless task and, however painful it might be to persons with a true musical sensibility, the ghastly pop music which pervades so much of western life was, on the other side of the Iron Curtain, a liberalising force.

The revolutions of 1989, like most revolutions, were very much the work of the younger generation. Even in 1989 four of the six east European party leaders had been born in or before 1917 and had been in office for at least twenty-five years. They were, to say the least, superannuated, all the more so when set alongside Gorbachev; they had nothing to offer the younger generations. In 1989 eastern Europeans who were under 40 years of age had had no negative experiences of western-style capitalism. For them the depression and fascism were part of history, and usually a history which they did not believe because it was part of official propaganda. Alienation for this generation meant alienation from socialism. Not surprisingly, therefore, the younger generation were frequently instrumental in the formation of the unofficial groups which sprang up in the 1980s. In previous decades the authorities would have been much more

411

vigilant against any grouping outside the official youth organisations, but there was by the 1980s a deepening desire and determination to form such groups. These unofficial, frequently informal associations of young people were amongst the first representations of 'civil society'. Other groups were soon to follow such as heritage societies, societies to commemorate the victims of oppression, religious bodies and environmental associations.

Concern at environmental degradation did much to undermine communist legitimacy, not least amongst the younger generation. In many cases concern over pollution proved the vital link between the intelligentsia and the masses, and the issue on which the latter could be mobilised, especially in the more closed systems of Bulgaria, the GDR and, most particularly, the Baltic states. The Chernobyl disaster did more than any single event to raise environmental consciousness but there were many other environmental issues at stake. Some of the earliest large-scale demonstrations in Hungary were against the Gabčikovo-Nagymaros project, by which the Danube would be partially re-routed at enormous cost to the ecology of the surrounding area. In January 1988 ecological groups in the GDR began to coalesce in the 'Ark-Green Movement' which was one of that country's first examples of civil society and which by November of that year had over 150 constituent groups; it also made an influential film about the appalling pollution in and near Bitterfeld. In Bulgaria too it was the environment which prompted the formation of one of the earliest civil groups, Ecoglasnost. Here the crystallising factor was the suffering of the north-eastern city of Russé which was periodically poisoned by gas leaking from a malfunctioning chemical plant across the Danube in Romania: in Russé the incidence of lung disease rose from 965 per 100,000 in 1975 to 17,386 per 100,000 a decade later; the Bulgarian writers' union, not usually an organisation to make difficulties for the régime, described Russé as 'the touchstone of the nation's conscience'.[8] The environmental factor was even more influential in the Baltic states. Serious medical problems were reported in the Kohtla-Järve oil-shale mining areas and around the uranium extraction town of Sillamäe in Estonia. In Ventspils in Latvia schools issued gas masks and gave instruction in the use of them, while journalists were forbidden to mention the pollution caused by the local petro-chemical complexes; in Riga a resident professor of medicine likened the city to a disaster zone where as many as one in four babies were reported to be born defective. Estonia was the first state to register protest action when demonstrations were staged in 1985 against a decision, taken in Moscow, to extend open face phosphate mining in the north east of the republic. In 1986 there were complaints, even in the official Estonian communist youth journal, at the conscription of Estonians for clearing-up work at Chernobyl. Lithuania had its own green movement, formed in February 1988 to protest against the nuclear power station at Ignalina. An important constituent group in the Latvian People's Front, which was formed in June 1988, was EPC, the Latvian Environmental Protection Club. The EPC had been founded in 1986 to combat plans to construct a hydro-electric dam on the Daugava. In 1987 the EPC had been further politicised by organising protests against a plan for an underground railway system in Riga which would have lowered the local water table to the point where the foundations of historic buildings would have been undermined. After that it turned its attention to the atomic power station at Leipaja and to the problem of coastal pollution which was so bad that the holiday beaches at Jurmala had to be closed in the summer of 1988. The president of National Front acknowledged that 'In Latvia everything began with the movement to save the environment'.[9] Even in Belorussia, where political consciousness was less developed, the Chernobyl disaster, which contaminated one-fifth of the republic's total arable area, made ecology 'a painful and hotly debated issue'.[10]

The environmental protest in the Baltic states was important not only because it raised consciousness but also because it achieved results. In 1986 popular pressure had ended drilling for oil off the Lithuanian coast, and in August 1988 the council of ministers in Vilnius suspended financial support for the Ignalina reactor until completion of an enquiry into its safety; 'This act in defiance of the central ministries [in Moscow] was unprecedented.'[11] The plans to construct a hydro-electric scheme on the Daugava were also scrapped, this time by Moscow in November 1987; 'For the first time in nearly half a century, Latvians savoured a collective success.'[12] The Estonians saw it as a major victory when demonstrations in the spring of 1987 persuaded Moscow to abandon its plan to extend the phosphate mines. But such victories could not eradicate the growing feeling that environmental degradation was a product of the communist system and that the ultimate answer to the question of the ecology, as to many others, was to escape from that system. The myriad hurts inflicted on the environment were, for many, 'powerful testimonies to the fact that the Soviet system does not work'.[13] In municipal elections in autumn 1989 environmentalists in Ventspils argued, 'We are for an independent Latvia; we can improve Ventspils when we are free from Moscow.'[14]

The green issue throughout eastern Europe was a singular one. Many, particularly amongst the younger generation, 'saw environmentalism as an expression of spiritual values'.[15] Given the general collapse of the official ideology, environmentalism could therefore offer an alternative both to the official marxist creed and to the nationalist or chauvinist sentiments which the more cynical members of the apparat were enlisting to replace 'scientific socialism'. The environmentalists in fact undermined the materialism which was at the base of marxist socialism, at least as practised in the Soviet bloc, because what argument was there against the assertion that if economic expansion through the medium of industrial production was poisoning the planet, it should be stopped? A Bulgarian ecologist writing in 1988 warned of an impending catastrophe in the Black Sea and identified its causes as mismanagement 'and the absurd human ambition to subdue nature in the name of industrial growth'.[16] The ecologists' attack was difficult for the establishment to parry because its instigators could not be written off as acting in the interests of any class, or at the behest of any 'obscurantist' or 'reactionary' church or religion.

Another factor eating away at the vitals of the communist system was a desire for a fair and accurate interpretation of the national past, a desire which was fed to a considerable degree by the patently ridiculous stories that were handed out by the official propagandists. Katyn had been an enormously emotive issue in Poland, the more so because it had for so long been officially unmentionable. As early as 1966 a Hungarian intellectual wrote that 'The touchstone for genuine national feeling in Hungary is still, and will remain for a long time to come, the attitude towards the revolution of 1956',[17] a statement more than justified by the reaction to Pozsgay's statement in January 1989 that the events of 1956 had indeed been a revolution. In April 1989 Zhelyu Zhelev, then prominent in dissident circles, told a British visitor that the first desideratum of the critical intelligentsia in Bulgaria was 'the true history of our country since 1944'.[18] For the Baltic states the thirst for knowledge about the 1939 pact and also about the deportations of the 1940s was insatiable. There were few more emotional moments in eastern Europe in 1988 than that on 23 August when a huge crowd in Vilnius listened to a tape recorded by Juozas Urbsys, the minister of foreign affairs in 1939 and the sole survivor of the last independent Lithuanian government; he was too ill to travel from his home in Kaunus. The grim excavations begun in the summer of 1988 in the Kuropaty forest, where an estimated 300,000 Belorussians are buried, ranked with Chernobyl as a causal factor in the rise, albeit slow, of Belorussian national consciousness. Gorbachev's *glasnost* had allowed open enquiry into all of these horrors but in so doing it had become yet another factor undermining communist legitimacy in the Soviet Union and in eastern Europe.

In addition to allowing the discussion of previously taboo issues, liberalisation *à la Gorbachev* allowed more room for manoeuvre for institutions previously tolerated on sufferance. Religious life underwent considerable revival in the second half of the 1980s. In Czechoslovakia this was attested both by Navrátil's petition and by the St Methodius celebrations which the government would not allow the pope to attend; the village of Medjugorje in Hercegovina continued to be the place of pilgrimage it had been for many Catholics since the alleged appearance of the Virgin Mary in 1981, whilst the restoration of the national cathedral in Vilnius in February 1989 was a recognition of the power of Catholicism in Lithuania and a huge stimulus to the development of Lithuanians' determination to break away from the Soviet Union. In Estonia in 1989 a Protestant pastor in the south of the country, in conversation with this author, described the last year as one of miracles in which baptisms had increased tenfold and in which enough money had been contributed to rebuild the organ and re-roof the church, and his experiences were not singular. In Bulgaria too church attendances increased noticeably in the late 1980s; in the church of the Mantle of the Holy Virgin in Sofia baptisms rose from 129 in 1986 to 280 in 1988. In Hungary in 1985 three priests were elected to parliament, though they would not have been able to stand for election without the approval of the Popular

Patriotic Front. Religion for many provided continuity with the national past and an escape from the corrupt present.

By the mid-1980s, when Gorbachev set out to renew socialism, east Europeans wanted not its renewal but its abandonment. Socialism had lost credibility. At the same time the west had changed its attitudes. In addition to an assertive, charismatic, and east European pope, there had been Reagan and Thatcher, whose advent had suggested a shift away from the basically consensual attitudes of the 1960s and 1970s, an abandonment of the unspoken assumption that east and west were going in the same direction but at a different pace and in different vehicles. The denunciation of 'the evil empire' may have shocked western liberals but it showed east Europeans that they were not forgotten, and that their plight was understood; it indicated that there was an alternative to Soviet domination, that socialism was not an historical inevitability; it emphasised that the planned, centralised economy in a totalitarian, one-party state was not ineluctable. The market operating within a multi-party democracy had reasserted itself. The revolutionaries of 1989 have been criticised for not producing new ideas. They did not need to do so. They believed the west had shown them the solution to their problems.

Their guiding principle was the rejection of a binding ideology; they wished to disengage the state from ideology. They had decided that in eastern Europe the twentieth century had run its course.

Part VI

AFTER THE TWENTIETH CENTURY – AND AFTER EASTERN EUROPE?

23

SEPARATE ROADS TO DEMOCRACY – AND ELSEWHERE

When they emerged from totalitarianism the states of the former Soviet bloc faced the task of redefining their political systems, their economies, and their individual places in the international community.

Redefinition in the international sense was easy. The binding institutions of the old Soviet system collapsed under the impact of the political changes in eastern Europe. At a meeting in Paris in November 1990 leaders of NATO and the WTO signed a treaty on conventional armed forces in Europe and announced the inauguration of a 'new era of democracy, peace and unity in Europe'. In February 1991 in Budapest the member states agreed to liquidate the Warsaw pact with effect from 31 March 1991. In June 1991 Comecon, which had been atrophying since early 1990, was formally disbanded. Thus, even before the Soviet Union itself ceased to exist, the institutional links which bound east European states to it had disappeared.

Immediately after the collapse of communism it was widely believed that eastern Europe would now be left free to determine its own future without external interference. Tragically that was not to be the case in Bosnia. Elsewhere a new form of influence was rapidly established. Governments needed no convincing that they had to adopt political pluralism and the market economy; but to create the latter they needed financial help. The international financial institutions (IFIs) were the only available source of such help. They were happy to extend loans or in some cases to make donations, but whether as a loan or a gift the money came with a price tag. The IFIs insisted on rigid budgetary control, privatisation, and the ending of state subsidies to loss-making enterprises.

The conditions the IFIs laid down were in general accepted. The new governments of eastern Europe were committed to the market economy and all of them expressed a wish to draw near to, or eventually become, a member of the European Union (EU). They were saying in effect that they did not wish to remain east European. Full membership of the EU would depend on rigid economic judgements but entry into the political institutions of western Europe was less difficult and most former totalitarian states were soon admitted to organisations such as the Council of Europe and the Organisation for Security and Cooperation in Europe (OSCE). In strategic terms most east European states expressed an interest in joining NATO. This raised delicate questions and the west, not wishing to tread too heavily on Russian toes, was guarded in its response. It did, however, welcome the former WTO states into the partnership for peace scheme when that was introduced in 1994, and joint exercises with NATO and east European forces became commonplace.

In some cases the state itself could not bear the strain of transition, though the strains which caused the break up of an existing state were not economic but national; sometimes the consequences were appalling. The Baltic states did manage to slip unharmed from a moribund Soviet Union, and the Czechs and Slovaks contrived a peaceful 'velvet divorce', but in the Caucasus and Yugoslavia there was barbarism of second world war proportions.

Where the state remained intact, internal redefinition and restructuring, or transition, was a three-stage process. The first, and easiest, was the abolition of the apparatus of totalitarianism. This meant the limitation or elimination of the secret police, the dissolution of the primary party organisations in the workplace, the revocation of those constitutional provisions guaranteeing the party's leading role, and the end of party domination over the social bodies, particularly the trade unions. The end of monopoly in the political sphere produced a proliferation of parties, some of them recreations of historic organisations, others entirely new. With party pluralism came a free press and, a little later, the easing or ending of political control over radio and television.

The second phase of domestic redefinition was the construction of the apparatus of democracy. Once again this was generally accomplished with impressive ease and efficiency. Parliaments, usually elected on a sophisticated variant of proportional representation, were installed, constitutions enacted, civil liberties assured, and new institutions such as the constitutional court introduced.

With this achieved the east European states entered the third and most difficult phase of the transition: the working of the institutions of democracy. In a minority of states this was hampered by the persistence of traditions of authoritarianism. In some the process of transition was frustrated by the corrosive effects of corruption which in certain cases reached gargantuan proportions.

Transition could be made more difficult and less attractive to those involved in it by the social costs it exacted. In the first place, most east European states suffered economically because their trading patterns, previously involving the USSR and Comecon, were disrupted. More importantly, the conditions laid down by the IFIs meant the closing of many enterprises and simultaneous control of the welfare budget; whilst the demand for welfare funds rose, the supply remained static or contracted. The result was falling standards of living, especially for those out of work or on fixed incomes. Amongst the latter, the pensioners were prominent because most east European states had low birth rates.

The resulting social tensions increased political support for those who wished to slow the pace of reform. This was reflected in the 'velvet restoration', the electoral success of a number of former communist parties, usually at the second or third round of post-totalitarian general elections. The former communist parties also profited from the decay and dissolution of the anti-communist alliances which had led the struggle against the old régime. These were essentially one-objective movements and when that objective, the toppling of communist rule, had been attained, they generally fell apart.

By the second half of 1996, however, the pendulum appeared to be swinging once more in the opposite direction. Former communist governments had not lived up to the expectations held of them and suffered a series of defeats. Parliamentary elections in Lithuania and Romania returned anti-socialist majorities; presidential elections in Romania and Bulgaria nominated non-socialist heads of state; in elections to the Slovene assembly the right performed far better than expected; and in Serbia's municipal elections the socialists lost their majority in many of the larger towns.

At least in bringing about change via the ballot box eastern Europe had joined the democratic camp. In economic terms the picture was less uniform with states in the north and centre moving relatively rapidly and successfully into the market economy, whilst those in the Balkans remained far behind.

ALBANIA

For the first two years after the election of President Berisha, Albania made considerable progress towards integration into the new, post-totalitarian world. In the sphere of foreign policy a number of fences were mended. In May 1992 Tiranë admitted responsibility for the Corfu channel incident of 1946, and in February 1994 Albania joined the partnership for peace scheme. In July 1995 it was admitted to the Council of Europe.

In its Balkan policy Tiranë played a careful hand. It gave full official support to United Nations sanctions against Serbia and Montenegro, though in reality it was impossible to stop smuggling over the border. Relations with Serbia were inevitably clouded by tensions in Kosovo, whilst the problem of the Albanian minority also complicated relations between Albania and Macedonia, which Albania had recognised as the Former Yugoslav Republic of Macedonia (FYROM) in April 1993.

Albania's most difficult Balkan relationship was that with Greece. Tension was at its worst in 1994. In April two Albanian recruits were killed during a raid on an Albanian army training camp; in August five ethnic Greeks were sentenced to between five and eight years in prison for the attack. The Greek government recalled its ambassador, closed the border with Albania, and ejected seventy thousand hapless Albanian economic migrants. German diplomatic pressure and a weakening of Berisha's internal political prestige led to some relaxation of tension, a process encouraged by the release of the 'Tiranë Five' in December 1994 and February 1995. Thereafter relations gradually returned to normal and in March 1996 an Albanian–Greek treaty of friendship was signed.

Albania's increasingly close relations with the west enabled it to receive substantial financial help from the IFIs, as a condition of which the Albanians moved towards a market economy. In April 1992 Meksi's government enacted a series of economic reforms with the result that by March 1996 the private sector embraced 65 per cent of all enterprises.

Economic reform helped Albania escape from the social crisis threatening it when Berisha and Meksi came to power in March 1992. Food shortages in the first quarter of the year had led to attacks on shops and the situation did not really ease until the first harvests under privatised agriculture were gathered in the spring of 1993.

With the easing of social tensions, developments in the political sector were thrown into greater relief. From the very beginning of his period in office Berisha made plain his implacable enmity for the communists. In July 1992 parties loyal to Enver Hoxha were banned, and Hoxha's successor, Ramiz Alia, was placed under house arrest. In January 1993 Hoxha's widow, Nexhimije, was jailed for nine years, her sentence being increased to eleven years on appeal. Alia was moved from house arrest to gaol in August and other leading members of the old communist régime were also incarcerated.

It was not merely unreconstructed former communists whom Berisha had in his sights. In July 1993 Fatos Nano, the leader of the SPA, the reformed communists, was arrested for mishandling Italian aid money, whilst in the following month the post-communist prime minister Vilson Ahmeti was jailed for abuse of power. The institutions as well as the practitioners of political debate were threatened. In the beginning of 1994 a long-running battle began between Berisha and the independent newspaper, *Koha Jonë* (Our Way), founded in 1991.

Later in 1994 the political situation in Albania was transformed. On 6 November, at Berisha's insistence a referendum was held on a proposed new constitution which would significantly increase presidential powers. Berisha argued that the changes were necessary to escape communism, to draw closer to Europe, and to attract investment. He lost. His defeat seemed to strengthen his determination to neutralise his opponents.

He was soon at odds with the judiciary in the personage of the president of the supreme court, Zef Brozi. Brozi had been appointed by Berisha to combat corruption but had incurred popular and presidential displeasure by his willingness to release the 'Tiranë Five'. In May and July he fought off parliamentary efforts to extend ministerial influence over the courts by controlling their budgets, but in September his parliamentary immunity was withdrawn. He left for the United States thanks to a Fulbright Award.

In September 1995 the genocide and the verification laws dealt a savage blow against the political opposition. The first act excluded from public life until 2002 all those who had held office under the communists. The second established a commission to examine the former secret police files on all candidates for public office; anyone found to have had any links with the former secret police would also be banned from public life until 2002. The main effect of this legislation was to disqualify 139 candidates, almost all from the SPA and the Social Democratic Party, from the elections of May 1996.

Those elections, in the words of a United States State Department spokesperson, 'cast a shadow on the prospects for democracy in Albania'. The elections saw the culmination of a long and persistent government campaign to restrict its opponents. Since the end of 1995 pressure on the opposition press had been increased. In February the electoral law was modified, reducing the number of parliamentary deputies to be chosen by proportional representation from forty to twenty-five, a measure which would benefit only the ruling DPA. In April the electoral commission announced that the DPA would be allotted as much broadcasting time as all the other parties combined. Opposition meetings were subject to frequent disruption and on polling day, 26 May, there was intimidation inside the voting booths. The final result gave the DPA 122 seats, the SPA 10, the Republican Party 3, the Greek Party for the Defence of Human Rights and Freedoms 3, and Balli Kombëtar 2.

Few outside the government ranks pretended that the elections were fair. Monitors from the OSCE reported that thirty-two of the seventy-nine articles of Albania's electoral law had been infringed, and the Council of Europe, together with other international organisations, called for new elections. By the mid-summer of 1996 Berisha had shown no sign of conceding to such a demand.

THE BALTIC STATES

General

Extrication from Soviet domination was more complicated for the Baltic states than for the other states of eastern Europe. The Baltic states had been integrated, albeit unwillingly, into the USSR. They had no separate currencies, their economies were massively dependent on the remainder of the Union for supplies and markets, they had had to absorb large numbers of Russian settlers, and there were no renegotiable international treaties regulating the presence and activities of the Red Army. The assertion of national autonomy in the Baltic States and then the disintegration of the Soviet Union in 1991 therefore caused chaos in the Baltic states. Trading patterns were disrupted as markets and supplies were cut off; tariff regulations were unpredictable and at times non-existent; the number of currencies increased without any reliable regulation of where they were valid; and the banking system was in disarray. Some order was restored to the latter; the International Monetary Fund (IMF) provided advice and western banks, including the Bank of England, returned the gold the Baltic states had in their accounts in 1940. Currencies, too, soon began to regulate themselves, but the Baltic states could not assert full control over their own economies until they could establish full control over their own borders.

This inevitably raised the question of the Red Army, the presence of which was also a deterrent to western investment in the Baltic states. Individual states had to negotiate their own terms, and inevitably Moscow tried to use discussions on the fate of the Russian armed forces to secure concessions for the Russian minorities.

Russian pressure over the minority issue varied in intensity but the rise of the populist right in Russia, with its chauvinist rhetoric and its reference to the Baltic states as part of the 'near abroad', intensified the desire on the part of those states to seek security through closer association with the west, and above all NATO. In March 1992 the secretary general of that organisation, Manfred Wörner, paid a visit to the Baltic states, all three of which were quick to sign the partnership for peace programme in 1994. They also declared their intention to bring the quality of their own armed forces up to NATO standards. In September 1994 a number of NATO countries helped the Baltic states form a 600-strong peace-keeping battalion and in the same year troops from the three nations took part in NATO exercises in the Netherlands.

A corollary of wishing to join NATO was to become part of the EU, particularly after the accession of Sweden and Finland which had close links with the Baltic states. The latter argued that their individual markets, or even all three combined, were too small to attract the foreign investment or to sustain the level of economic activity necessary for full-scale reform and national prosperity. Brussels made comforting noises but little was done until July 1994 when an agreement on trade in industrial goods was signed. By the middle of 1996 there had been further progress and all three states had signed association agreements with the EU, and had submitted formal applications for full membership.

Closer association with the EU would also strengthen the Baltic states vis-à-vis their large eastern neighbour. This objective could also be pursued through regional associations. The Baltic states were rapidly admitted to organisations such as the council of Baltic sea states, and the Baltic parliamentary conference. There was also cooperation on the level of the three states themselves. Meetings of heads of state and of parliamentarians became regular and could be used to emphasise local interests. In December 1993, for example, a Baltic summit in Tallinn declared that the three states would defend their democratic systems, whatever Zhirinovksy and his ilk might say.

Notwithstanding examples of concord such as this there were also differences between the states. Latvia had maritime border disputes with both its neighbours, and although that with Estonia was regulated by an agreement of May 1996, that with Lithuania, which involved oil, proved more intractable.

Despite these tensions, and despite tendencies towards public corruption and banking instability, in the five years following the collapse of the Soviet Union all three Baltic states made considerable progress in both the economic and the political sphere.

Estonia

One of the most important tasks facing the new Estonia was to regulate the status of its Russian minority; the Russians and Ukrainians together made up a third of the total population. For most Estonians, for whom memories of the deportations were constant and omnipresent, the Russians were colonisers whose loyalty was primarily to another state. In a citizenship law of February 1992 it was enacted that two years' residence was necessary to secure Estonian citizenship, but counting towards these two years was to begin only from March 1990 which would effectively exclude many Russians from the forthcoming elections; all applicants for citizenship were required to have a knowledge of Estonian and to swear an oath of allegiance to the Estonian republic. This was less draconian than many Russians had feared, the more so as considerable help in learning Estonian was provided, if desired. The Estonian government also made concessions to Red Army pensioners resident in Estonia. These people posed a particular problem. They were mainly Russians who, during their time of service in Estonia, had come to enjoy a higher standard of living than that available in Russia, and had therefore settled in Estonia and had no home or base outside it.

The law of February 1992 did not mean the end to dispute between the Estonians and the Russian minority. In July 1993 the Russians of Narva and Sillimäe, who were in a majority in those areas, held unauthorised referenda to express their desire for autonomy. The Estonian government refused to be panicked into counter-reaction and by October, when nation-wide local elections were held, the question had receded into the background. In November Estonia enacted a law similar to the famous legislation of 1925 giving virtual autonomy in cultural affairs to all ethnic minorities.

The Estonians had been subject to constant but gentle pressure from western Europe over the minority question. They were also subject to constant but brutal pressure from Moscow during negotiations for the withdrawal of Russian forces. These talks had begun as soon as Estonia left the Soviet Union, but it was not until 31 August 1994 that the garrisons were emptied of Russian troops; and even then the Russians retained until the end of September 1995 the nuclear submarine training facility at Pildiski on the Estonian coast.

After the withdrawal of the Russian forces the main question at issue between Estonia and Russia was the border. In June 1994 Russia announced that it would regard the existing border as definitive, despite Estonian arguments that it should be determined by the treaty of 1920 signed by the Estonian government and the bolsheviks. The nub of the dispute was the Petseri district which the 1920 agreement had included in Estonia. President Yeltsin underlined Russian attitudes to the issue when, during a visit to the Petseri area, he declared that 'not an inch' of Russian territory would be given away.

After the enactment of the citizenship law in February 1992 preparations were advanced for the first general election in post-Soviet Estonia which took place in September of that year. The Popular Front which had coordinated the struggle against Soviet power was by now divided and weakened, and after the poll the centre of political gravity in the assembly lay with the right. A government was formed under the leadership of Mart Laar whilst in a simultaneous poll the electorate chose Lennart Meri as president; both men were from the Fatherland

Election Alliance. Tension between president and prime minister appeared, not least because Laar's enthusiasm for Thatcherite economics was not shared by all his countrymen. In 1993 it became clear that he had profited from the illegal sale of roubles when they were replaced by the new Estonian kroon. He resigned in September 1994 to be succeeded by Andras Tarrand. In March 1995 Estonia's second general election brought about a new governing coalition which was more centrist than its predecessor; its leader was Tiit Vähi. In October his administration was severely shaken by the disclosure that the minister of the interior, Edgar Savisaar, had illegally tapped the phones of political opponents. Vähi resigned but was able to form a new cabinet when the pro-market Reform Party pledged its support.

By this time the market was already well established in Estonia, which had been the most adventurous of the Baltic states as far as economic reform was concerned. In June 1992 it had left the rouble zone and introduced the kroon which was to be pegged to within three per cent of the Deutschmark. Shortly afterwards, it had embarked on privatisation, eschewing, however, the mass sale of enterprises through a voucher system and setting up instead the Estonian Privatisation Company, a centralised body which decided to seek only foreign capital. Foreign investors were further encouraged by legislation in the following year which allowed them to buy land subject to governmental approval. These policies paid dividends. By 1995 Estonia was top of the east European league for foreign direct investment as a percentage of gross national product and in 1996 *The Economist* could point to the Estonian economy as one of the success stories of eastern Europe.

Latvia

Latvia, even more than Estonia, had need to regulate the position of its Russian minority which, together with Ukrainians and Belorussians, made up over two-fifths of the population. In its first appearance in June 1994 the Latvian citizenship bill provoked outrage in Russia whilst the CSCE and the Council of Europe both expressed their reservations over it. The bill stated that citizenship was a necessary requirement for the franchise and for the ownership of property. Citizenship was to be awarded only on the successful completion of an examination in the Latvian language, and was to be denied to former Red Army personnel and to all those who supported 'chauvinism, nationalism or fascism'. There were to be quotas which would exclude over half a million residents, mainly non-Latvians; further admission to citizenship would begin only after the year 2000 and then at the rate of 0.1 per cent of the existing number of citizens, in effect between two and three thousand new citizens per year. The government itself disowned the bill and asked the president to return it to the assembly for revision. This he did and the assembly then diluted the quota arrangements whilst retaining the language test and the ban on former military personnel. The amendments softened criticism from western Europe but Russians, including President Yeltsin, still complained loudly and bitterly.

Despite the unsettled question of citizenship the Russians had agreed in 1993 to withdraw the remainder of their forces from Latvia by the end of August 1994, retaining only the early-warning radar station at Skrunda until May 1995; after the Russians had left the facility it was demolished in a huge 'peace explosion'.

The destruction of this symbol of Russian occupation did not end disputes between Latvia and Russia. Latvia continued to claim the Abrene district of Russia, and to be concerned at the rhetoric of the Russian right, whilst the Russians retained their anxieties over the position of the Russian minority in Latvia. Both sides, however, saw the need to regulate their frontiers, and agreements on border crossings were signed in 1995 and 1996.

The first general election after the separation from the Soviet Union was held in June 1993. True to its inter-war traditions, Latvia produced a large number of parties. The result of the vote favoured the right-of-centre elements and a government was formed with the backing of Latvian Way (LW) and the Farmers' Union; it was led by Valdis Birkavs of LW. The parliament elected as president Guntis Ulmanis. Birkavs' government was gravely weakened in May 1994 by the revelation that five deputies, including the minister for foreign affairs, had worked as informers for the KGB. The cabinet limped on until September when Maris Gailis, also of LW, took over as prime minister. Gailis' government altered the electoral law so that parties had to secure five rather than four per cent of the national vote to be represented in the saeima. Elections under these new regulations took place on 30 September–1 October 1995 and resulted in a more or less clean split between the rightist forces and their opponents. So complex had the process of cabinet formation now become in Latvia, that it was not until 7 December that a workable coalition could be found. It consisted of no less than eight separate parties; a new government was then formed under the non-party Andris Skele.

Like Estonia, Latvia made considerable progress in the economic sector during the first five years of the post-Soviet period. Privatisation had begun in 1992, though here it was by the voucher system, and was to progress particularly rapidly in agriculture. In 1992 the Latvian rouble was declared the only legal currency; it was replaced by the lat in March 1993. The only threat to Latvia's steady economic advance seemed to come from instability in its banking sector, the problem being highlighted in 1995 with the failure of the Baltija Bank in which one in five Latvians had deposits. The government managed the crisis in a mature fashion and it was not considered sufficient impediment to Latvia's submitting in October 1995 a formal application for EU membership. Latvian finances, like those of Estonia, had been kept on a tight rein in order to comply with the demands of the IFIs whose loans had become so important to the country's financial stability.

Lithuania

Lithuania, where Russians and Belorussians formed no more than 12 per cent of the population, was not as threatened by the minority problem as were Estonia and Latvia. Not surprisingly, therefore, Lithuania was the first of the Baltic states to enact a citizenship law. It was relatively generous to the minority groups and caused few difficulties. A further indication of the relaxed nature of relations between Vilnius and Moscow was the agreement in 1992 that all former Red Army soldiers would leave Lithuania by 31 August 1993. The evacuation proceeded according to plan, despite a sudden suspension of troop withdrawals in the spring of 1993. By the middle of the 1990s the major issue at dispute between Russia and Lithuania was neither the minority question nor the Red Army but gas supplies; in early 1996 Russia carried out a previous threat to reduce supplies of gas to Lithuania because of unpaid debts to the Russian oil company, Gasprom, but in February a settlement on this problem appeared to have been reached.

Post-Soviet Lithuania's first general election was held in October 1992. As in Estonia, the alliance which had eased the country out of the Soviet orbit, Sajudis, was already weakening, and its decline was furthered by the realisation that its leader, Vytautas Lansbergis, had little taste or capacity for the introduction of the economic reforms which the IFIs were now insisting upon and which alone could bring Lithuania nearer to its avowed goal of closer association with the rest of Europe. The party which emerged in first place was the Lithuanian Democratic Labour Party (LDLP), the former communists led by Algirdas Brazauskas. Brazauskas, even as a communist, had proved his sensitivity and willingness for consensus, and these traits were revealed again when his cabinet included only four of his former comrades in the ex-communist party. Brazauskas soon went on to be elected president, his place as prime minister being taken by Bronislovas Lubys. In February 1993 Lubys was replaced by Adolfas Slezevicius, also of the LDLP but with a greater commitment to market reforms. The LDLP continued to maintain relatively good relations with Russia and seemed little troubled by internal opposition until December 1995. In that month the Lithuanian Incorporated Innovation Bank, the largest commercial bank in the country, suspended operations, as did the Litimpeks Bank in January 1996. The crisis became politically explosive when it was revealed that two days before the first bank closed prime minister Slezevicius had withdrawn $30,000 from his account to buy his wife a new car. Slezevicius refused to be moved either by mounting public criticism or by a direct order from the president to resign. He was finally forced out on 8 February when parliament approved a presidential decree removing him from office. He was succeeded by Laurynas Mindaugas Stankevicius of the LDLP.

He did not survive the year in office. The elections of October and November 1996 inflicted a heavy defeat on the LDLP and gave victory to the parties of the right and centre. LDLP representation in the 141-seat seimas fell from 73 to

12; the Homeland Union (Conservatives of Lithuania) had 70 seats and their allies, the Christian Democrats, had 16, giving these two right-wing parties secure control of parliament.

BOSNIA AND HERCEGOVINA

Unlike the independent Croat and Slovene states a separate Bosnia was more a consequence than a cause of Yugoslavia's demise. During the years of communist domination Bosnia and Hercegovina had shown little sign of the restiveness seen in Slovenia and, more markedly, in Croatia. In 1961 the Muslims of Bosnia had been recognised as a separate nation within Yugoslavia and 'Muslim' became an accepted category for ethnic identity in the census of 1971. These moves gratified local Muslims and enhanced Yugoslavia's image in the non-aligned world, but there were critics who regretted that it was only the Muslims of Bosnia who had been given separate national status; it was argued that to make religious affiliation a condition of nationality was peculiar in a socialist state, and it was pointed out that Bosnian identity derived not from religious loyalties which were in any case weak but from a common political culture, a political culture shared equally by Muslims, Catholics, Orthodox, atheists, and agnostics, be they Croats or Serbs.

Outside Bosnia and Hercegovina the nationalists of Croatia and Serbia had never given up their designs on the republic. Bosnia had considerable economic value. Over four-fifths of Yugoslavia's iron-ore, a fifth of its coal reserves, 28 per cent of its hydroelectric potential, and 30 per cent of its timber resources were to be found in Bosnia. More significantly, the republic contained a number of important weapons-producing plants and military bases, all placed there because of all the Yugoslav republics Bosnia was the least accessible to any invader. The suppression of the Croat nationalists in the early 1970s meant there was little public discussion of Croat aspirations in Bosnia and Hercegovina for a decade, but debate was renewed after Tito's death in 1980 and voices were soon raised insisting that western Hercegovina, at least, was an integral part of Croatia. The response of the Serb nationalists to such arguments was not to come to the defence of Hercegovinian integrity but to stake out their own claim for the eastern half of the territory. Furthermore, extremists such as the then little-known Radovan Karadžić were insisting that Bosnian Serbian families had title to as much as 64 per cent of the land in Bosnia and that this should become Serbian territory. The implication was that such territory should be joined to the Serbian republic and as the federation based on Belgrade began to weaken Serb activists in Serbia and in Bosnia moved from words to deeds. The Serbian secret police were at work in Bosnia in 1989 after Milošević's victories in Kosovo, the Vojvodina, and Montenegro. Furthermore, the JNA in Bosnia was already cooperating with and arming local Serbs.

The Bosnian political scene was dominated by the Party of Democratic Action (PDA) led by Alia Izetbegović. Izetbegović had come to prominence in 1983 when he was sentenced to thirteen years' imprisonment for 'hostile and counter-revolutionary acts derived from Muslim nationalism', the main evidence against him being a relatively mild pamphlet published in 1970 under the title, 'The Islamic Declaration'. He was released in 1988 and in May 1990 founded the PDA.

The PDA was predominantly though not exclusively a Muslim party and it could never win the allegiance of the irreconcilable Croats and Serbs. The latter moved rapidly. In April 1991 Serbs in the Drvar area declared autonomy. Serbs in other areas followed suit and by September there were four distinct autonomous regions. The Serbs were also increasingly well-armed. When it withdrew from much of Bosnia in May the JNA passed most of its heavy weaponry to the local Serbian territorial defence forces, and in the summer and autumn some federal troops returned in response to a call from local Serbs for protection. Relations between the Sarajevo government and the Serb extremists were decaying rapidly and when the Bosnian parliament began seriously to discuss a declaration of Bosnian sovereignty the Serb deputies, led by Radovan Karadžić, walked out. A few days later the Serbs established what was to all intents and purposes an alternative Serb state and parliament in Banja Luka.

During the first months of 1991 the western powers' attention had been focused on the Persian Gulf; in the summer there was preoccupation with developments in the Soviet Union. The mounting Yugoslav crisis was one in which the United States had no real interest and Washington was therefore content to leave Europe to play the major role. In December 1991 Europe, or part of it, was heady with self-confidence, the integrationist tendencies of Maastricht leading some to believe that Yugoslavia provided Europe with its first chance to deploy a common foreign policy and prove its effectiveness on the international scene. Slovenia and Croatia were recognised and this, it seemed to some, produced an apparent end to the fighting in the latter. Other potential successor states were therefore invited to apply for recognition, provided that they were adjudged to have complied with certain standards. Bosnia, together with Kosovo and Macedonia, made such an application.

The head of the EU's arbitration commission for Bosnia, Robert Badinter, had recommended that any state seeking recognition should hold a referendum to secure popular endorsement of its request. The Bosnian poll was held on 29 February–1 March 1992 but it was boycotted by most of the Serbian population. A declaration of Bosnian independence followed on 3 March but it was not recognised by the Serbs and within days fighting had been reported from several areas. On 22 April Sarajevo came under artillery fire; its long, agonising, and utterly avoidable agony had begun. On 20 June the Bosnian government declared a state of war against the JNA and the Serbs.

The Bosnian war was to last for three and a half years and was the worst fighting seen in Europe since 1945, excelling even the Greek civil war in brutality. It was characterised by instability in the alliances between the various factions, by 'ethnic cleansing', and by the ineffectiveness of the international organisations which became involved.

On the surface there were three main factors in the fighting: the Bosnian government; the Croats; and the Serbs. The latter were the strongest. Well-equipped, largely by the JNA and then by Milošević's Serbia, the Serbs strove to secure and retain corridors between their various enclaves in Bosnia and Hercegovina. The Croats were also reasonably well-supplied with war material, their chief objective being to preserve Croat domination of western Hercegovina. The Bosnian government, whose forces were not solely comprised of Muslims, were the least well-equipped, their lack of heavy artillery and air power being particularly telling.

In that the Serbs with their autonomous regions, or krajinas, were a threat to both Bosnia and Croatia, and given the fact that the Serb forces were by far the best equipped, political and military strategy seemed to dictate the need for anti-Serb coalition between the Croats and Muslims. For much of the war this in fact did exist, but it was neither constantly nor universally applicable. In June 1992 the Croatian and Bosnian governments signed an agreement on military cooperation but this did not prevent the formation in the following month of a new Croat political unit, Herceg-Bosna, in western Hercegovina. By the end of the year, after much heavy fighting, Croat troops were in effective control of much of western Hercegovina and central Bosnia. In the following year clashes between Croat and Bosnian forces produced some of the most intense fighting of the war, one casualty being the famous sixteenth century bridge in Mostar which was wrecked by Croat gunfire. In 1994 Mostar had to be placed under European Union administration, so great were the differences between Bosnia and Croatia over this question.

In the north of Bosnia there was collaboration for a while between Serbs and the local Muslim freebooter, Fikret Abdić, who had become infamous in the 1980s as the man responsible for the Agrokomerc scandal. Abdić denounced Izetbegović's domineering rule and criticised him for not being more flexible in peace negotiations; in September 1993 his supporters set up 'the autonomous province of western Bosnia' based in Abdić's stronghold of Bihać. From then until the middle of 1995 Abdić's forces cooperated with local Serbs in Bosnia and in the neighbouring krajina in Croatia.

'Ethnic cleansing' soon came to dominate much of the external press reporting from the Bosnian war. The only new thing about ethnic cleansing was the name. The practice of forcing out or destroying opposing national groups was a well-established feature of twentieth-century Balkan, east European, and indeed world history. In Bosnia all sides indulged in this depressing practice, but for the Serbs in particular it served vital political purposes. In the first place the persecution of differing ethnic groups helped destroy the credibility of the multi-ethnic idea incorporated both in the former Yugoslav federation and in the political culture of the new Bosnia. The fact that the Bosnian Serb media, especially the television, gloried in the 'achievements' of the butchers and rapists indicates that there was

431

a deliberate policy of building up ethnic cleansing as a praiseworthy policy and denigrating the multi-ethnic attitudes of the opponents.

Such propaganda was aimed not only at the opposing communities. Most of the atrocities carried out in Bosnia were the work of small, irregular groups recruited in the slums of the towns and cities. They were constrained neither by the communal inter-relationships bred in mixed villages nor by the codes of professional honour nurtured by regular military units. The propaganda praising such elements served to convince the remaining majority of the ethnic group that they should choose the extremists' side, not least because they could only expect retribution should their home area fall to opposing troops. This led to a considerable degree of voluntary ethnic cleansing, particularly amongst Serbs, when whole communities fled 'to avoid imagined future dangers that Serbian leaders planted in their minds'.[1]

The excesses of ethnic cleansing and the maltreatment of prisoners of war impelled outside groups to concern themselves with the Bosnian question. For a long while this created more problems than it solved. Armed intervention was demanded by many observers both within and outside Bosnia but military action could not be seriously contemplated without a clearly defined political objective. And neither the Bosnian factions themselves nor the external operators found it easy to agree upon a political solution for the region. A plan worked out jointly by the United Nations and the European Union, the Vance-Owen plan, so called after the chief negotiators Cyrus Vance and Lord David Owen, was rejected by the Bosnian Serbs in March 1993, whilst a scheme produced in Geneva later in that year, which replaced the ten-fold division proposed by Vance-Owen with a tripartite system, was rejected by the Muslims.

International action was further weakened by divisions amongst the powers and the conflicting claims of the international agencies. The EU was soon shown to be a busted flush and by the middle of May 1992 had given way to the United Nations (UN) as the main external organisation concerned with Bosnia. Unfortunately, the United Nations command structure was unwieldy and though troops from many lands were deployed for months and even longer, they could do little more than ensure the safe delivery of aid, though this was an appreciable service to the beleaguered Bosnians, especially in Sarajevo. Russia believed its historic links with the Serbs entitled it to a part in any international exercise to restore peace to the region. In 1994 the Contact Group of Russia, Britain, France, Germany, and the United States was established to incorporate Russia into the diplomatic process.

For a considerable time divisions between the United States and its allies meant that NATO could not be used as an effective strike force in the conflict. Washington argued for the delivery of heavy weapons to the Muslims, a view rejected by other capitals on the grounds that such a policy would provoke an all-out Serbian offensive before the weapons could be delivered into Muslim hands. Others believed that Washington's stance increased Muslim reluctance to concede, the Sarajevo government wanting to hang on until the USA got its way and weapons were supplied.

International involvement was not without result, however, both political and military. The sanctions imposed on Serbia and Montenegro under UN auspices in May 1992 did much to bring the Milošević régime to a more accommodating attitude. The schemes proposed for a political settlement also eventually produced some result. In February 1994 the Bosnian and Croatian governments signed a military cooperation agreement in Zagreb. In the same month talks began in Washington which were to lead to a political accord signed in the US capital in March and ratified in Geneva on 14 May. The agreement created a new 'Bosnian Federation of Muslims and Croats' which had a Croat president and a Muslim prime minister; the federation was divided into eight cantons, four with Muslim majorities, two with Croat majorities, and two, Travnik and Mostar, where no group enjoyed an overall majority. In July the Contact Group put forward a plan under which the original Bosnia-Hercegovina was to be divided between the Muslim–Croat federation (51 per cent) and the Serbs (49 per cent). After much debate the Muslims and Croats accepted the plan but the Bosnian Serbian leadership, now established in Pale just outside Sarajevo, rejected it. Despite this, for the first time since the outbreak of the war in April 1992, there was the outline of a political solution which military action, if agreed upon, could be used to bring about.

There had already been some attempts to exercise international power. At the end of 1992 a 'no-fly' zone had been declared over Bosnia. In February 1993, after 68 had been killed by a single shell fired into a Sarajevo market place, NATO announced that it had set up an exclusion zone around the Bosnian capital and it demanded the removal of all heavy weapons from that area. In the same month, four Serbian planes were shot down in the first action taken to enforce the no-fly zone. It was also the first time that a force operating under NATO auspices had fired a shot in anger. It was not to be the last.

The instability of the Croat–Muslim alliance and the apparent ineffectiveness of external factors helped the Serbs. By May 1993 Serb advances had been recorded in many areas and under the prompting of US secretary of state, Warren Christopher, safe areas for Muslims guarded by UN troops were established in Goražde, Žepa, and Šrebrenica. Nevertheless, in August 1993 the Serbs enjoyed further military success on Mount Igmen, south of Sarajevo. In late 1994 and early 1995 the Serbs, together with Abdić's forces, halted and then repulsed a Muslim advance from Bihać and in May 1995 even Sarajevo was under renewed threat from the Serbs. Yet a number of factors were eating away at the Serbs' strength.

The February 1994 agreement in Zagreb between the Croats and Muslims had put an end to the debilitating divisions between the two anti-Serb factions, as had the political accord ratified in Geneva in May. The Pale leadership's rejection of the Contact Group's 51–49 split in Bosnia had not been opposed by the Serbs of Bosnia but it did produce one very important shift in the political balance. Milošević and the Belgrade Serbs, weakened by UN sanctions, accepted the plan and in August 1994 the Belgrade administration went as far as to say that it would impose sanctions on the Pale Serbs if they did not prove more conciliatory. It was the first major split between Karadžić's Serbs and Milošević and it could only weaken the former. Now isolated from almost all outside support, or restraint, Karadžić's forces seemed to move from excess to excess. For this they were to pay a heavy price. In May 1995 Serbian gunners fired phosphorus shells in a bombardment of Sarajevo. The use of these illegal weapons finally persuaded the UN representative, Yakushi Akashi, to lift his veto on further air-strikes by NATO. In retaliation the Serbs took some 370 soldiers hostage which led Britain, France, and the Netherlands to establish a 'Mobile Theatre Reserve' or rapid reaction force. Pointedly, in July French troops deployed in regular battle camouflage rather than the UN white.

The war was now nearing its fearsome climax. In July Bosnian Serb forces began an assault on the safe areas of Žepa and Šrebrenica. The fall of the latter resulted in the disappearance of some seven thousand Muslim men whose fate could not be proved but could be all too easily imagined. After the fall of the two safe areas the Contact Group convened a conference in London, the one positive result of which was to decrease the UN's power to veto NATO action in Bosnia. In August the position of the Serbs weakened dramatically. In Croatia government forces routed those of the krajina Serbs around Knin; tens of thousands of refugees fled from Croatia. On 28 August a Bosnian Serb shell killed 37 civilians in the Markale market in Sarajevo, despite NATO rulings on the exclusion zone. The reaction was swift and massive. 'Operation Deliberate Force' unleashed the greatest show of force yet used by NATO which blasted Bosnian Serb gun-emplacements, ammunition stores, and communications facilities. It was made clear that strikes of such magnitude would continue if the Serbs repeated their bombardment of Sarajevo.

Operation Deliberate Force and the collapse of the Serb position in Croatia broke Serbian morale. Pale was at last susceptible to a diplomatic approach and this came when President Clinton's special envoy, Richard Holbrooke, set out on a mission to bring the warring factions to the negotiating table. The parties met eventually in a hangar at the Wright-Paterson airbase in Dayton, Ohio, where a peace agreement was initialled on 21 November. It was signed formally in Versailles on 14 December 1995.

The Dayton agreement was an optimistic document. Under it Bosnia was defined as one state with two entities, the larger Muslim–Croat federation covering 51 per cent of the territory; the other, the Serbian Republic (*Republika Srbska* or RS), was to occupy the remaining 49 per cent. The presidency was to consist of a Bosnian and a Croat both elected by the federation and a Serb elected by the RS. The state was to have a council of ministers, a bicameral assembly, a constitutional court, and a central bank, but the powers of the Bosnian government were not to include exclusive control over military affairs, the right to establish a unified taxation system, or a common judiciary. There was to be binding arbitration in the event of inter-entity disputes, and an independent commission sitting in Sarajevo was to organise the return of displaced persons and refugees. A high representative was to be responsible for the general overseeing of the implementation of the agreement and any UN Security Council decisions affecting Bosnia. The former Swedish prime minister, Carl Bildt, was appointed to this task. The main mechanism for the maintenance of peace and order was to be the 60,000 strong UN Implementation Force (IFOR). Elections were scheduled for 14 September 1996.

Despite considerable difficulties the elections took place as scheduled. Voting was for the federal presidency and for the assemblies of the federation and both its constituent entities. International observers reported a series of irregularities but pronounced that these did not materially affect the outcome of the poll, though the irregularities did lead to the postponement of municipal elections due to be held in November. In the September 1996 vote Izetbegović emerged with a clear majority in the presidential race whilst in the three assemblies the distribution of seats reflected very closely the ethnic composition of the areas represented.

Izetbegović was installed as president of Bosnia and, after a hesitant start, meetings of the new three-person presidency began in October.

BULGARIA

When Filip Dimitrov became prime minister in October 1991 it seemed that he was in a strong position to push through the anti-communist and reformist policies upon which he and the UDF had campaigned. MRF support seemed to assure a majority in the sŭbranie, and Dimitrov's position appeared to strengthen when the BSP fell to post-electoral squabbling, a split in the party being narrowly avoided at the December 1991 conference which elected the 34 year old Zhan Videnov as leader. A further apparent strengthening of Dimitrov's position came in January 1992 when the former UDF leader Zheliu Zhelev was elected president in a nation-wide poll.

Dimitrov's government never realised its potential. It did push through some economic reforms which allowed both the return of property sequestrated by the communists and the privatisation of land. But progress was painfully slow and the government spent much of its time fighting with the opposition over such issues as the fate of secret police files.

Dimitrov's government was further weakened by the decay of the anti-communist alliance. In May 1992 the government parted company with Dimitûr Ludjev, the first civilian minister of defence since 1934 and a close ally of president Zhelev. Relations between president and prime minister were to decline rapidly. On 30 August virtual open warfare broke out when, in a television interview, Zhelev accused the government of needlessly sharpening national divisions. One such division had been in the Bulgarian Orthodox Church where the incumbent patriarch had been deposed on the grounds that his election under the communists had been irregular. It had, but the constitutional court decided that the government had no right to interfere in Church affairs.

As threatening for the prime minister as the loss of presidential confidence was the increasing dissatisfaction of the MRF, upon whom Dimitrov depended for his parliamentary majority. The Turks complained at high levels of unemployment in their communities and of a bias against them in the land privatisation act. When, in October, the MRF refused to support the government in a vote of confidence Dimitrov's days were numbered; he resigned on 20 November 1992.

It took a month before a new government could be formed; its leader was Liuben Berov, who had been sponsored by the MRF and who was Zhelev's economic advisor. He appointed a cabinet of non-party experts.

Berov produced a few grandiose sounding schemes, promised to accelerate privatisation, and made noises pleasing to the IFIs which were lending heavily to Bulgaria. But, once again, little happened. Berov's disadvantages were that he had no mandate to govern, he had no secure base in parliament, and his own health was far from good. In March 1994 he underwent heart surgery and in September he resigned.

After Berov's resignation Bulgaria was ruled by an interim cabinet under Reneta Indjova, Bulgaria's first woman prime minister. Her main task was to oversee the elections which took place on 18 December.

The elections gave the BSP an overall majority in the sûbranie, the first enjoyed by any party since 1991. The BSP benefited from popular disappointment with declining living standards and also from the UDF's chronic lack of cohesion. There had been mounting tension between the larger and smaller members of the coalition and shortly before the elections two of the largest groups defected to form the Popular Union. Both the Popular Union and the Bulgarian Business Bloc took enough votes, many of them from the UDF, to secure representation in the new parliament.

In January 1995 the victorious BSP leader, Videnov, formed an administration most of whose members were fellow socialists, but it was soon apparent that the new régime was no more effective than its predecessors. There was continued conflict between prime minister and president, particularly over proposed amendments to the land law and over a bill, introduced by Berov, which confined the upper ranks of the judiciary to those with at least five years' experience, i.e. to those who had been trained before 1989. The petty-mindedness and party parochialism of local politicians seemed to many Bulgarians to contrast sharply with the energy, commitment, and ability of King Simeon II who in June 1996 paid a hugely successful three-week visit to his native land.

By the time of the King's visit, however, the country was descending into its most serious post-totalitarian crisis. The crisis had begun in May. The root of the problem was the weakness of government since 1989. This had allowed the emergence of powerful commercial conglomerates which made fortunes out of manipulating the subsidies given to loss-making state enterprises. The conglomerates used their mighty influence against any attempt to end the subsidy system, and, it was rumoured, exercised at least as much influence as Videnov within the BSP parlimentary faction, which meant that, even had he wanted to, Videnov could not use his parliamentary majority against the conglomerates. Their influence also meant that banks were persuaded into lending to loss-making enterprises, a practice which eventually led to the realisation that the banks were being ruined and so precipitated in May a collapse of confidence in the banks and in the Bulgarian currency.

In July the IMF stepped in to help but insisted that if further loans were to be granted to Bulgaria 64 loss-making enterprises must be closed, a further 70 'isolated' from further government hand-outs, and the banking system drastically reformed. By August, when an IMF inspection team visited the country, almost nothing had been done and the second tranche of an IMF stand-by loan was cancelled.

By November the IMF was stating baldly that the July agreement had been wrecked; if Bulgaria were to receive further help it would have to set up a currency board which would fix exchange rates and allow changes in the money supply only in response to movements in foreign currency. The IMF would also have to be allowed to appoint senior officials in the National Bank.

Bulgaria was on the verge of bankruptcy and its problems were intensified by a continuing crime wave. Petty crime had risen as respect for the police had fallen, but large-scale criminal operations had also flourished when sanctions-busting into Yugoslavia became so profitable. Here was another source of wealth for the conglomerates. And when the former prime minister, Andrei Lukanov, was murdered outside his Sofia home on 2 October 1996 it was immediately assumed that he had been killed because he had threatened to spill the beans over the conglomerates and their activities.

The catastrophic ineptitude of the BSP government was the main reason why the UDF candidate, Petûr Stoyanov, emerged the victor from the two-stage presidential elections of October–November 1996.

Against the severe internal failings of all its post-1989 administrations, Bulgaria's creditable foreign policy record counted for little. But Bulgaria had been the first country to recognise the Macedonian state, though not the Macedonian nation, and it was widely believed that Zhelev had in effect vetoed Greek–Serbian plans for a Greek–Bulgarian–Serbian partition of Macedonia and had thereby prevented yet another Balkan crisis.

CROATIA

Croatian affairs in the half decade after independence were naturally dominated by the conflict with the Serbs both in Croatia itself and in Bosnia. Any hope harboured by the indigenous Serbs that the JNA intervention of June 1991 would be to their benefit was dispelled when a ceasefire was signed in October. The Croatian Serbs, it seemed at this point, would have to look to their own defences. By the spring of 1992 they had established a number of autonomous krajinas, the largest of which were those around Knin in south-west Croatia and in eastern Slavonia in the north-east. Both krajinas expressed the intention to unite with the Serbian state.

The Serbs had been alarmed by what they considered Croat triumphalism. Many Serbs had lost their jobs, the latin alphabet had been made compulsory in all public transactions, and Croatia had adopted as its state emblem the flag used by the Croatian state during the second world war. Fear of a return to the excesses of that time drove some Serbs to seek separation from Croatia. Separatism was far more common amongst rural Serbs than amongst those in the cities; in the latter it was generally only the most impoverished of Serbs who supported extreme causes, with many other Serbs being integrated into Croatian life. In the Knin and Slavonian krajinas, however, special factors applied. In both areas a large proportion of the Serbian population were relative newcomers and had not had time to establish traditions of cooperation with other ethnic groups. Many Slavonian Serbs had been moved in after 1945 and had taken possession of the abandoned farms and properties of Germans, Hungarians, and alleged collaborators; many of the immigrants had come from the Knin area where their place had been taken by Serbs from eastern Hercegovina and Montenegro.

The Knin area was at the heartland of the impoverished karst region; its relative poverty and backwardness were as prominent after 1945 as before the second world war. Also, the region had seen intense and hideous conflict between Serbs and Croats during the war, and had been one of the few areas outside Serbia itself where the Serbs had rallied to the chetniks rather than the partisans. The memories of those bitter conflicts were easily invoked both amongst the Serbs who had remained in the Knin region and amongst those who had migrated to Slavonia.

The under-equipped Croatian army could not restore Croatian authority in the krajinas. On the other hand Serbian forces, which now had support from the JNA, were equally unable to establish themselves on the Adriatic, despite the shelling of Dubrovnik. The stalemate thus produced and the prospect of continued and more bitter fighting brought about international intervention. In the autumn the European Community had vainly attempted to construct an all-Yugoslav solution to the region's problems but in December 1991 Germany insisted upon the recognition of both Slovenia and Croatia as independent states. At the same time, the United Nations had become involved though its presence was military as well as diplomatic. Troops of the UN Protection Force (UNPROFOR) were being deployed in Croatia by January 1992 and in April had established four UN protected areas (UNPAs) in eastern and western Slavonia and along the borders of north-western Bosnia.

The UN forces prevented a major confrontation between Serbs and Croats but they could not prevent almost constant small-scale fighting. Nor could they extinguish Croat determination to retrieve all territories lost to the krajinas and to the UNPAs. In January 1993 the Croatians made their first foray into Serb controlled areas when they retook the Maslenica bridge; two years later, in April 1995, with the UN bogged down in Bosnia, the Croats launched a successful offensive against western Slavonia and then in June took Mount Dinara near the border with Bosnia in south-west Croatia, enormously strengthening their strategic position against the Serbs of the Knin region. On 4 August 1995 the Croats unleashed Operation Storm which in four days gave them complete control of the Knin krajina; 150,000 Serbs trudged into exile. Triumph in the Knin area was followed by success in eastern Slavonia where, under UN auspices, an agreement was concluded to establish a transitional administration to prepare for elections and the restoration of Croatian rule. By the end of 1995 Croatia seemed almost to have achieved its goal of re-establishing the borders of 1990.

Croatian domestic politics during this period had been dominated by Franjo Tudjman, the leader of the Croatian Democratic Union (CnDU). Tudjman had joined the partisans in 1941 and after the war had had careers as a 'desk officer' on the general staff and subsequently as an academic historian. He had made useful contributions to the scholarship of the second world war before becoming increasingly involved with Croat nationalism. In the early 1970s and the early 1980s he served short terms in prison after which he continued his activity in Croat nationalist politics and propaganda. In May 1990 he was elected president of Croatia, a position he retained after the presidential election of 2 August 1992. In the parliamentary poll on the same day the CnDU was the largest party returned but neither then nor in a further election held after the military triumphs of 1995 did it secure the two-thirds majority necessary to enact constitutional changes.

Preoccupation with military affairs and the disruptive effects of the war no doubt slowed the pace of economic reform in Croatia. These factors were also seen by some Croats as justification for political restrictions. Laws on pornography and the manipulation of tax regulations were used in attempts to limit the activities of opposition newspapers, particularly those in Dalmatia and Istria where regional opposition to Zagreb's centralist tendencies was apparent. Croatia enacted laws against defaming the president or senior officials; the judiciary were subject to political pressure; and Tudjman refused to accept the mayor elected by the Zagreb city council after local elections had produced an opposition majority.

The restrictions placed on non-CnDU activists were the main reason why, when Croatia was finally admitted to the Council of Europe in April 1996, strong reservations were expressed in the parliamentary assembly of the Council over the human rights situation in the country.

CZECHOSLOVAKIA

After the velvet revolution of 1989 Czechoslovakia moved rapidly to consolidate its democratic gains. In June 1990 Václav Havel was elected president for a further two years whilst parliamentary elections gave victory to the Civic Forum/

PVA reformist alliance. Reforms enacted by the new régime included the abolition of the secret police, a requirement that the communist party finance itself solely from membership contributions, and an agreement with Moscow that the remaining 75,000 Red Army troops would leave Czechoslovakia by July 1991. The return of the country to the democratic fold was celebrated by a string of distinguished western visitors, who in 1990 included President Bush, Mrs Thatcher, Chancellor Kohl, President Mitterrand, and the Pope, and by the admission of Czechoslovakia as a full member of the Council of Europe in 1991.

There was also rapid progress towards economic restructuring. Legislation in 1990 provided for the restitution of over 70,000 properties expropriated by the communists and for the sale in 1991 of over 100,000 small businesses. Shares in large state enterprises were also to be sold, either to local or foreign investors, and Czechoslovak citizens would be offered at a nominal price vouchers which they could, if they wished, convert into shares. In January 1991 price controls were lifted and strict management of the budget ensured that inflation, after an initial rise, was contained and that the currency remained stable. By the end of 1991 over 3,000 joint ventures with foreign companies had been established, the most notable being Volkswagen's decision to modernise the Škoda car plant.

Restructuring and reform in Czechoslovakia inevitably meant addressing the question of the federal structure of the country, and here progress was much less easy than on the general political and economic fronts. The creation in March 1990 of the Federative Republic had pleased all Slovaks, but there were many who considered it as the first rather than the last step towards full devolution. After the elections of June 1990 the federal parliament was instructed to draw up new Czech, Slovak, and federal constitutions. At the end of the year a great deal of administrative power was devolved to the Czech and Slovak republics. In 1991 there were long debates and eventual agreement upon an inter-republic treaty which defined the distribution of powers and which was to be signed before the new constitutions were to be enacted. The Czechs, however, saw the document as one produced by the two republican assemblies whilst the Slovaks insisted that it enjoyed at least the same juridical validity as the federal constitution itself. In July 1991 the federal assembly, having agreed to hold a referendum on the constitution, then found it impossible to decide what questions to ask.

Elections in June 1992 produced a federal assembly in which the divisions were even more entrenched. A series of meetings confirmed what everyone feared: that there was no prospect of compromise and the Czech and Slovak leaders agreed that the only solution was to dissolve the federation. On 20 July the Slovak parliament passed a declaration of sovereignty and then in effect blocked the re-election of Havel as federal president. On 25 November 1992 the federal assembly adopted a law dissolving the federation with effect from 1 January 1993; a series of agreements on the division of state properties and other questions was then enacted, the politicians of Prague and Bratislava being determined that the collapse of their federation should not lead to the violence already breaking out in Yugoslavia and the Caucasus. The 'velvet divorce' had followed the velvet revolution.

THE CZECH REPUBLIC

The Czech republic, like Czechoslovakia after the first world war, soon established itself as an enviable bastion of order and stability in a disorderly and unstable environment. The new state was rapidly accepted into the international community, becoming a member not only of the UN and the CSCE but also of the World Bank, the IMF, and GATT in 1993; in 1995 it became the first post-communist member of the OECD and on 23 January 1996 formally submitted an application to become a member of the EU.

Two figures dominated the political life of the new republic. The first was Václav Havel who remained president, being re-elected by the Czech parliament in January 1993. The second was Václav Klaus, who retained the prime minister's chair to which he had been elected in 1990.

Klaus had risen to power as a dominant figure within Civic Forum and became the architect of the Czechs' apparently successful transition towards a market economy. Civic Forum, however, could not long outlive the collapse of communism. Even in 1990 separate factions were becoming apparent and in 1991 the alliance split into the Civic Democratic Party (CDP) led by Klaus, the Civic Movement (CM), and the Czech Social Democratic Party (CSDP).

The elections of June 1992 produced a predominantly right-wing assembly giving Klaus the secure majority he needed to continue with his economic reforms. In 1993 the second round of privatisation began and by the end of the year 60 per cent of Czech companies were in private hands and unemployment had been kept to an enviable 3.4 per cent, although inflation refused, despite strenuous budgetary control, to drop below 20 per cent. By the end of 1994 the Czech government declared the process of privatisation to be complete; the year had also seen an increase of 3 per cent in GDP, inflation had fallen to 11 per cent, unemployment was still under 4 per cent, and for the first time since 1989 there had been an increase in industrial production; in the following year the Czech crown was made convertible.

Governmental stability, economic progress, and general international approbation did not mean that the Czech republic was free of internal problems. Plans to restore the property of the Roman Catholic Church were not welcomed by the less right wing sections of the coalition and there was enough opposition in parliament on this question to prevent definitive legislation. There was also a long-running debate over the question of a second chamber. The constitution called for the setting-up of a senate but a draft law submitted to the assembly by the government in February 1994 was rejected, the decisive vote coming from the ruling coalition's junior members who thought the proposed scheme would give too much power to the CDP. In 1995 the coalition partners at last agreed that the second chamber should consist of 81 members, but then Klaus and his partners disagreed on when those 81 senators should be chosen, Klaus arguing unsuccessfully for simultaneous elections for both houses of the assembly. After Havel's intervention, Klaus reluctantly conceded separate elections. The constitution had also called for a decentralisation of power in the Czech republic but progress towards this goal was even slower than with the senate. In 1994 a plan to divide the country into 17 regions was rejected because it was believed the resulting authorities would be too weak to withstand centralising pressures which would once more strengthen the power of the ruling party or parties. As in inter-war Czechoslovakia much of the politics of the Czech republic revolved around the distribution of power within the constitution and within the various political coalitions.

In the sector of foreign affairs the Czech republic had some disagreements with Germany, largely over the question of the Sudeten Germans. Havel had admitted in 1990 that too much force had been used during the post-war expulsions, but no Czech politician was prepared to go further towards meeting the demands of the émigré organisations in Germany. The Czech republic also distanced itself from the other members of the Višegrad four: Slovakia, Hungary, and Poland. Czech policy was aimed at early admission to NATO and the EU and too close an association with its former partners in the Višegrad four might frustrate that process; Prague therefore showed little enthusiasm for military cooperation with Bratislava, Budapest, and Warsaw, and sought to keep trading relations within the framework of the Central European Free Trade Agreement.

That Klaus' domestic and external policies had stimulated opposition was shown by the elections to the lower house of the assembly in May 1996 which deprived Klaus of his secure majority. His CDP lost a number of seats whilst the CSDP increased its representation four-fold. Klaus decided to continue in office at the head of a minority government whose existence would depend to a considerable degree on the goodwill of the CSDP.

HUNGARY

Hungary had moved quietly and peacefully out of totalitarianism in 1989 and at the beginning of the new decade found itself in something of a vacuum in that the communists were totally discredited but no-one else had a mandate to govern and to enact the reforms which everyone knew to be necessary. The general election in March–April 1990 was intended to put an end to this state of inertia.

The most successful group in the elections was the Hungarian Democratic Forum (HDF) whose leader, József Antall, formed a coalition with the Small-holders' Party (SHP) and the Christian Democrats. In the immediate post-election months the dominant mood of the nation was consensus. The opposition and government agreed on the appointment as president of a Free Democrat, Arpád Göncz, and the opposition also allowed the government a period of grace in which to prepare a programme of social and economic reform.

Little came of this exercise, and inactivity and inertia continued to dominate Hungarian political life. In part this was due to fear. In October 1990 threatened increases in the price of petrol had enraged the taxi drivers of Budapest who blocked roads and bridges in protest; their action was immediately followed throughout the country and the government was forced to compromise on the question of petrol prices. Inaction was also partly a result of divisions within the ruling coalition. The SHP had complicated the privatisation process by insisting that all land be restored to those who owned it in 1947, a demand which everyone outside the SHP knew to be impracticable. Furthermore, Antall was a historian by training and was unwilling to commit himself on the complex issue of economic restructuring; when action eventually came, therefore, it was half-hearted. A reform scheme put forward by the minister of finance in February 1991 was not fully implemented, and when privatisation was announced it was to be brought about only by direct purchase; there was to be no Czechoslovak-style voucher scheme which would involve the entire nation.

The Antall government was further disabled by continuing and increasing divisions within the ruling coalition and the HDF itself. In 1992 the SHP split, whilst within the HDF a vociferous populist group under the leadership of István Csurka was making itself felt. Csurka attacked the party leadership and the government for being too soft on the opposition, the former communists, and the media. Csurka also had strong nationalist views and was by no means a stranger to anti-semitism; his populist demands, if implemented, would have meant the end of democracy in post-communist Hungary. In 1993 his faction was expelled from the HDF and formed a separate group, Hungarian Justice, in parliament. At the end of that year, with all political minds concentrating on the general elections to be held in 1994, Antall died at the age of 61; he was succeeded by Péter Boross.

The Antall coalition had done little to further economic reform. Its fear of social upheaval was undiminished; to avoid rising unemployment it continued to pump money into loss-making enterprises, a policy which also helped to preserve extensive powers of government patronage.

The coalition showed more energy in dealing with the media. Despite its anti-communist credentials the Antall government did not seem able to realise that a free press must also be free to criticise an incumbent government. The government was particularly anxious to control the electronic media; in 1992 it suspended the head of Hungarian television for alleged incompetence and subordinated the budget for both television and radio directly to the prime minister's office; in 1993 the head of television was sacked and increasing pressure was put upon journalists who found it more and more difficult to make programmes critical of the government.

The slow pace of economic reform and signs of authoritarianism in the government's dealings with the media offered the opposition useful propaganda material, but little was made of it. The anti-government camp remained uncoordinated, leaderless, and lacking in coherent strategy, especially in the critical area of the economy. Some opposition parties, notably the Alliance of Young Democrats (FIDESz) showed themselves capable of organisation and registered encouraging results in a series of public opinion polls; but it was the former communists of the Hungarian Socialist Party (HSP) who did best in by-elections.

This was to be repeated in the general election of 8 and 29 May 1994. The coalition parties of the centre-right lost heavily, the HDF dropping from over 40 per cent in 1990 to only 10 per cent. Victory went to the parties of the left with the HSP collecting an overall 54 per cent of the vote and the centre-left Alliance of Free Democrats (AFD) taking second place with 18 per cent.

The voters had punished the HDF for its inaction. They had also registered their disapproval of the corruption which had become increasingly apparent in the later stages of HDF rule. The left had also appeared a much more organised force, with the professionalism and organisational skills of the HSP contrasting sharply with the amateurish, bungling image of the HDF. The left inevitably benefited from the swing back towards what were believed to be the more stable years of *fin de régime* communism. Another cause of the left's victory was nationalism. The previous government's constant rhetoric over the position of the minorities abroad had begun to have an adverse effect; no-one questioned that the government had been right to show concern on this issue but many asked what, if anything, had been achieved, and some even seemed to think that the previous government had been more interested in Hungarians abroad than those at home, especially when the latter were having to cope with a declining standard of living. In this regard it was significant that the extreme nationalists of Csurka's party received only 1.3 per cent of the vote.

The leader of the HSP, Gyula Horn, could, had he wished, have formed a single-party administration. He did not, choosing instead to go into coalition with the AFD. This had two main advantages. It would enable Horn to enact economic reforms to which the left of his own party might take exception. Second, it would give Horn a two-thirds majority in the assembly and therefore enable him to enact constitutional changes, the latter being necessary as Hungary was still operating under the old, albeit much-amended communist text. A further and lesser advantage of a coalition was that it would reassure the west that Hungary was not solely in the hands of the former communists.

The new government's first priority was economic reform, and the reduction of Hungary's foreign debt which, in per capita terms, was the largest in Europe. The IMF in 1993 had issued a warning that reform must be introduced and in March 1995 the minister of finance, Lajos Bokros, laid a major reform scheme before parliament. This called for cuts in government spending, an increase in taxation, and a progressive devaluation of the forint.

The reforms almost wrecked the government. The left were aghast, some ministers resigning rather than vote for the Bokros package. When Horn tried to appease the left by promoting a leading trade union official to high government office this enraged the AFD which almost walked out of the cabinet. When Bokros proposed a reduction in the social security budget in February 1996 the government refused to endorse it and Bokros resigned. The lessons of caution, so rapidly absorbed by Antall, were not lost on Horn.

Hungary, which had been one of the pioneers of change in the late 1980s, was slow to move in the early 1990s. Despite this, and despite the impoverishment threatening so many Hungarians, the country enjoyed western confidence, and in some years attracted half of all the western investment into eastern Europe.

MACEDONIA

Macedonian communist leaders began liberalising their republic in the late 1980s and by 1989 had agreed to allow multi-party elections. In 1990 a number of parties were founded, including the Movement for All Macedonian Action (MAMA) and the more nationalist Internal Macedonian Revolutionary Organisation – Democratic Party of Macedonian National Unity. In January 1991 the sobranie, or republican assembly, elected Kiro Gligorov, a former communist, president.

In the same month the sobranie voted for a declaration of national sovereignty and in September 1991 a referendum showed a 95 per cent majority in favour of independence; the turnout had been 75 per cent. On 18 September the sobranie voted for full independence which was officially declared on 6 January 1992. In December 1991 Macedonia had responded positively to the EC invitation to seek recognition. The Badinter report gave Macedonia an entirely clean bill of political health which should have meant all-round immediate recognition by the states of the EC. Greece, however, objected.

The Greeks argued that 'Macedonia' was a purely geographic term and were a state to entitle itself 'Macedonia' that would imply a claim upon all the territory in the geographic area. In January 1992 the Macedonians altered their constitution to include an explicit statement that the republic had no territorial claims upon any other state, but it was not enough to calm Greek anxieties. Some Macedonian extremists had indeed made wild claims, and in 1989 signs had appeared in Skopje proclaiming 'Thessaloniki is ours', but such opinions were confined to a tiny minority and the Macedonian authorities denounced them in forthright fashion. Despite this the Greeks mounted a frenzied campaign against Macedonia. Goods destined for Macedonia via Greece were subjected to unconscionable delays, even including, in January 1992, a shipment of medicine and children's food intended to alleviate the effects of a severe flu epidemic in Macedonia.

In July 1992 the Macedonian government resigned after losing a vote of no confidence, largely because of its failure to make progress on the question of recognition. In August a new government was formed under Branko Crvenkovski; the new government was a coalition of Crvenkovski's Social Democratic Alliance and the ethnic Albanian Party of Democratic Prosperity (PDP). The cabinet included five Albanians and a Turk as well as Macedonians.

The new government continued its search for an accommodation with Greece.

In February 1993 international arbitration produced a compromise title of 'The Former Yugoslav Republic of Macedonia' (FYROM) to which the sobranie agreed in April. At least it prevented the implementation of the suggestion of one deputy who despairingly suggested that the republic should call itself 'Coca-Cola' as this would ensure the republic had a well-known symbol and might even bring some much-needed cash. The Greeks agreed to some discussions but no substantive progress was made. By the end of 1993 Greece was the only EU state not to have recognised Macedonia and when the USA and Russia both joined the European states the Greeks imposed trade sanctions in February 1994. They remained in force until an agreement engineered by Cyrus Vance was signed in New York in September 1995; for its part Macedonia agreed to remove from its flag the Star, or Sun, of Vergina, a symbol which the Greeks regarded as solely theirs. Talks on the name issue were to continue.

The long battle over the name question absorbed much of Macedonia's time and energy when other problems also needed urgent attention. The trade embargo imposed by Athens further complicated economic difficulties caused both by the sanctions on Yugoslavia to the north and by the influx of almost fifty thousand Albanian refugees from Kosovo.

The Albanians in Macedonia were already one of the new state's major difficulties. According to a census held in 1993 the Albanians formed 23 per cent of the population, though many regarded this as an under-estimate, not least because the census had not included the refugees from Kosovo. The real problem, however, was demographic. Albanian birth-rates were much higher than those of the Macedonian Slavs. The long-term prospects also held considerable dangers. The Albanians in the Balkans already numbered five and a half million, less than half of whom lived in the Albanian state; given present demographic trends the numbers of Albanians would double by 2030 and make the Albanians the most numerous people in the Balkans with the possible exception of the Turks. In such circumstances the existing state structure of the Balkans could scarcely survive.

The Macedonian government recognised the long-term dangers, this being one reason why the PDP was included in the governing coalition. But this did not prevent outbursts of unrest amongst the ethnic Albanians with rioting in Skopje in November 1992, and a year later after the arrest of ten Albanians, including the minister of defence, on charges of arms-smuggling. By the spring of 1994 the PDP split into accommodationist and irreconcilable wings, the latter being strengthened in 1995 when the authorities refused to allow the use of Albanian on passports and identity cards and also blocked efforts to establish an Albanian-language university in Tetovo. Such issues naturally strained relations between Macedonia and Albania.

There were also tensions between Macedonia and Serbia. There is a small Serbian minority in Macedonia and early in 1992 the Serbs around Kumanovo staged demonstrations and demanded the setting-up of an autonomous zone. More alarming from the Macedonian point of view was Milošević's open sympathy with Greece. The Serbian leader pointedly referred to Macedonia as 'Skopje', one of the terms used by Athens, and in March 1993 Gligorov told a Bulgarian newspaper that the Serbs and the Greeks had agreed to partition Macedonia. Other Serbs called not for partition but for the absorption of Macedonia into Serbia; Karadžić in Bosnia and Vuk Drašković in Serbia both argued that this was the only way in which the Macedonians could ensure that they would not be swamped by the Albanians.

The Macedonian state clearly faced many difficulties but it has so far contained the Albanian danger without resort to the extreme repressive measures used by the Serbs in Kosovo, and despite all the odds against it the Macedonian economy in 1996 earned glowing reports from western financial institutions.

POLAND

Poland, whose round table discussions had provided the methodology for the dismantling of totalitarian rule in the whole of eastern Europe, made steady progress towards the creation of a democratic and open society. During 1990 Mazowiecki's government enacted over fifty acts reforming the police forces, the judicial system, the media laws, and local government. There was little opposition from the supporters of the old régime. In January 1990 the PUWP dissolved itself, re-emerging as Social Democracy of the Polish Republic (SDPR) and then as the central force in the Democratic Left Alliance (DLA). Jaruzelski recognised that he had outlived his function as president and asked the sejm to limit his period in office. To this the assembly agreed and Jaruzelski stepped down in December 1990. The presidential election which this made necessary was the first serious political conflict in Poland since the collapse of communism; its vicious nature was only one of the many echoes soon to be heard of Polish politics in the early 1920s.

In one area, however, there were few if any parallels with the chaotic early years of the inter-war republic. On 1 January 1990 came 'the big bang'. The brain child of Leszek Balcerowicz, the finance minister, this set out to throw Poland's economy into the capitalist pool at the deep end. The big bang removed most price controls with immediate effect and prices shot up by anything from 30 to 600 per cent. State subsidies were drastically cut and in July came a privatisation law which provided for the transformation of 7,600 state enterprises into joint stock companies which were to be offered for sale to individuals, groups, or companies, including foreign ones. The costs of this bold policy were high. Inflation in 1990 was reckoned to be in the region of 550 per cent, although it fell significantly in subsequent years, standing at 43 per cent at the end of 1992 and 20 per cent in December 1995. The rapid restructuring of industry brought a fall in production of 3 per cent in 1990 and 13 per cent in the following year. The human side of this process was a steep rise in unemployment which reached 12 per cent by the end of 1991 and 15 per cent four years later. Whilst unemployment statistics moved inexorably upwards budget constraint

447

meant that welfare payments moved in the opposite direction; the unemployed and pensioners paid the price for Balcerowicz's big bang.

The costs of this policy were high and were immediately apparent. Its benefits were slower to materialise but were nevertheless considerable. The IFIs were impressed by Balcerowicz's boldness. In March 1991 the Paris Club wrote off half of Poland's inter-governmental debt and the USA lopped almost four-fifths off the $2.9 billion it was owed by Poland; France and Germany also reduced Poland's debt. At the end of 1991 an interim agreement with Brussels eased barriers against Polish exports into the EC. By the middle of the 1990s Poland was experiencing high growth rates and in the summer of 1996 President Chirac of France could speak in Warsaw of Polish accession to the EU in the year 2000.

The robust reforming policies of Balcerowicz had a further and perhaps more important advantage. The speedy nature of the change and the reasonably rapid response of the west locked Poland onto a reform course. Balcerowicz's successors did not abandon the main thrust of his policy and all maintained strict budgetary control, never letting the deficit rise above the 5 per cent limit which the IMF had decreed. This meant that when the reaction against the revolution of 1989 came and Poland veered back towards the left, the economy was already so much changed that there was no serious prospect of a return to anything like the old system. In effect the big bang did much to set the parameters of Polish political development after 1990 and placed a halter round the neck of those who might want to bolt back into the marxist stable.

These policies also helped Poland move towards its new foreign policy objectives of membership of NATO and the European Union. Relations with Germany were simplified by an agreement in April 1990 under which both parties accepted the Oder–Neisse line as their definitive frontier. In February 1994 Poland became a member of the partnership for peace programme and in April of the same year it was one of nine new associate members of the Western European Union (WEU). Relations with Russia were less easily regulated, though serious tensions were not apparent in the first half of the 1990s. In April 1990 Poles were gratified by Moscow's belated admission that the Katyn massacres had been the work of the Soviets, and in April 1995 presidents Yeltsin and Wałęsa attended the unveiling of a memorial at the site of the atrocity. By that time, the dissolution of the WTO and the collapse of the Soviet Union had meant that a major bone of contention had been removed from Russo–Polish relations with the withdrawal of Red Army garrisons from Polish territory, although Russia still retained and frequently expressed doubts about projected Polish membership of NATO.

In the domestic political arena the Solidarity-based alliance between Wałęsa and Mazowiecki soon began to show signs of strain. Mazowiecki's measured but far from slow approach to political change was not to Wałęsa's taste; he called for 'permanent war at the top' which would involve more rigorous attacks upon former communists and wider, deeper, and more rapid reforms. When Jaruzelski stepped down as president the two former Solidarity allies became the main contenders in the election of November 1990. Surprisingly, however, a third contender, a maverick Canadian businessman, Stanisław Tyminski, pushed Mazowiecki into third place and as Wałęsa had not received an absolute majority a second round took place on 9 December with Wałęsa securing 74.25 per cent of the votes cast. A new government was formed under a free-marketeer, Jan Krzysztof Bielecki.

The new administration did not have a secure base in the sejm, primarily because the assembly was still that elected in the semi-free election of 1989. Wałęsa, characteristically, was anxious to press ahead with elections after which a new constitution could be devised, but the old guard in the sejm resisted and there was widespread disagreement over the voting system to be used. This debate was not resolved until June 1991 when it was decided that the majority of deputies would be elected by PR with a few seats being reserved for those chosen from the national lists of the most successful parties. The poll took place in October and, in keeping with the traditions of the early 1920s, there were no fewer than 67 parties standing, of which 29 secured representation in the sejm. The largest was Mazowiecki's post-Solidarity Democratic Union (DU) but when a new prime minister was agreed upon in December it was not a member of the DU but Jan Olszewski of the Citizens' Central Alliance. He, however, never secured himself in power and in July 1992 was replaced by Hanna Suchocka of the DU.

Suchocka secured a pact with dissatisfied labour organisations, thus reassuring Poland's external financial supporters. She also presided over the introduction of the 'little constitution' in August 1992. The basic constitutional need was to define the relations between president and parliament and the little constitution went some way in this direction, but it did not end dispute between the two main political factions. The tensions between them increased after the elections of September 1993 which brought the DLA into office in alliance with the old pro-communist Peasants' Party which also provided the new prime minister, Waldemar Pawlak.

President and parliament fought a running battle during 1994 and 1995 with Wałęsa frequently using vocabulary reminiscent of Piłsudski. The two major points at issue were Wałęsa's largely ungrounded fear that the new administration wanted to turn the clock backwards, and the power of ministerial appointment. Whilst the sejm and the president squabbled the political parties regrouped and reformed much in the fashion of the early 1920s but the public, preoccupied with the tough new economic and social conditions, became ever more apathetic; in the elections of September 1993 the turnout was barely over 50 per cent.

Around two-thirds voted in the presidential elections of November 1995. This proved to be a major turning point in post-communist Poland. Wałęsa waged a belligerent and intemperate campaign against his main opponent, Aleksander Kwasniewski, the leader of the DLA. Kwasniewski was more restrained and insisted that he had rejected his former communist views and was now a social democrat or even what he called a 'socio-liberal'. He said nothing to frighten the IFIs. In the first round Kwasniewski took more of the votes than Wałęsa but without securing an overall majority. This he attained in the run-off on 19 November. Wałęsa took defeat badly, preferring to sulk in Gdańsk rather than attend Kwasniewski's inauguration ceremony.

The defeat of Wałęsa marked the end of an era, an era dominated by the man who had thrust one of the first nails into the coffin of Soviet-style communism. The summer of 1996 saw another totemic change when the Polish government announced that the former Lenin shipyard in Gdańsk was bankrupt and would close. In a development symbolic of the new Poland the profitable parts were to be formed into a new company which would absorb only half the labour force of the old industrial giant.

ROMANIA

The violent revolution of December 1989 passed power so rapidly and effectively to the former communists who dominated the National Salvation Front (NSF) that many believed the revolution had been provoked by reformist communists who then hi-jacked it before it could go too far. There was no doubt that the men who came to dominate Romania, above all president Ion Iliescu, came from reformist communist backgrounds and that after 1989 they retained some of the practices they had perfected in their previous careers.

This is not to say that they did not institute far-reaching changes. Civil liberties were granted, political pluralism became a reality, and previously proscribed bodies such as the Uniate Church were allowed to function anew. Economic reforms were also enacted. In April 1991 prime minister Petre Roman removed controls from all but twelve food commodities, whilst wages could only be increased by 60 per cent of the increased cost of food; living standards were further reduced by the introduction of income tax ranging from 6 to 20 per cent of earnings. In August a privatisation law was passed which allowed for 30 per cent of the assets of state enterprises to be passed to Romanian citizens in the form of fee vouchers; the remaining 70 per cent were available for purchase.

The economic reforms caused tensions. By the middle of 1992 GDP had fallen by 16.5 per cent, inflation was running at 200 per cent, and one in six families was said to be living below the poverty line. In September 1991 the miners of the Jiu valley, the very group whose brutality had saved Roman and Iliescu in 1990, returned to Bucharest. In a few days of savage violence a number of people lost their lives and Roman lost his job. He was replaced as prime minister by Theodor Stolojan, an economist.

Stolojan was more dedicated than Roman to the ideology of the free market which made it easy for him to form a coalition with the National Liberal Party (NLP). Stolojan, however, not being a professional politician, could not prevent a weakening of the NSF. In local elections in February 1992 its vote was only a half of that recorded in the general election of 1990, and in March the organisation split with Roman and the economic reformers divorcing themselves from the more numerous pro-Iliescu conservatives who now formed the Democratic National Salvation Front (DNSF). To the surprise of many the DNSF emerged as the most popular party in the elections of September 1992, with the oppositionist Democratic Convention of Romania (DCR) pushing Roman's NSF into third place. At the same time, in another surprising development, Iliescu was forced into a second round before securing victory in the presidential election.

After the elections Stolojan went off to a job with the World Bank and left another economist, Nicolae Vacaroiu, to head the Romanian government. The new government combined both non-party experts and a number of seasoned politicians from the DNSF. The hallmark of the new administration was gradualism. One reason for this was no doubt the fear that excessive zeal, at least on the economic front, would cause a repeat of the social unrest which had toppled Roman. The pace of economic reform and privatisation therefore slowed and the government continued to pour subsidies into loss-making enterprises in order to avoid further unemployment. By the end of 1994, although over a thousand enterprises were in private hands, the stated target of having 50 per cent of the economy in the private sector was nowhere near being achieved. The government also continued giving large subsidies to agriculture and tolerating a high level of inter-enterprise debt. These examples of economic conservatism, together with an unhealthy trade deficit, persuaded the IMF and the World Bank to withhold the issue of an agreed loan in the summer of 1995.

The September 1992 elections had not given Vacaroiu an absolute majority in parliament and he was therefore forced to resort to coalitions to ensure continuity in office. The easiest support was to be found amongst the nationalist or neo-communist groups such as the Party of Romanian National Unity (PRNU) and the Socialist Labour Party (SLP). To reassure the doubting, particularly those abroad, that the government had not fallen into unsavoury company, the NSDF changed its name in July 1993 to the Party of Social Democracy in Romania (PSDR). In January 1996 an agreement was signed with the SLP and the Greater Romania Party (GRP) but these two junior partners in the coalition did not embarrass Vacaroiu by seeking cabinet office, being content with junior government posts. The GRP did not last long as a coalition partner. Within months of the January agreement the GRP's newspaper was making extraordinary attacks on Iliescu accusing him of treason for allegedly running down the Romanian armed forces on instructions from NATO, of being a former collaborator with the KGB, and, typically for the GRP, of being involved in an anti-Romanian zionist conspiracy. In October the prosecutor-general's office began an investigation into the activities of the GRP leader, Corneliu Vadim Tudor.

Vacaroiu's hold on power was helped to a considerable degree by the weakness of the opposition. Despite general agreement on the main political issues, Roman and his NSF proved incapable of cooperating effectively with the DCR, a grouping of up to eighteen opposition factions.

One opposition group which did exhibit consistency, if not cohesion, was the Hungarian minority which numbered some 1.6 million. Confrontations similar

451

to that at Tîrgu Mureş in 1990 were not repeated but tensions remained. The election of the extreme nationalist, Gheorghe Funar, as mayor of Cluj in 1992 immediately raised the temperature, as did the decision in the same year to appoint Romanian prefects to the predominantly Hungarian counties of Covasna and Harghita. Funar not only removed a number of bilingual public signs but he also attempted, unsuccessfully, to remove the statue of the Hungarian King Martinus Corvinus from the centre of Cluj to allow for archaeological excavations. The Hungarian minority was also angered by laws reducing the use of Hungarian in the educational system, particularly at university level. Hungarian interests were stoutly defended by the Hungarian Democratic Union of Romania (HDUR). By 1995 it was demanding cultural autonomy and a large measure of independence in local government. In the summer of 1996 Romania and Hungary signed a state treaty in Timişoara but this failed to reassure Hungarian activists and angered many Romanian chauvinists.

The other major national issue in Romanian politics was Moldova. Here extreme caution was displayed by rulers in Bucharest. Initially, good relations between Iliescu and Gorbachev had prevented any Romanian pressure for the union of Soviet Moldavia with Romania and after the breakup of the USSR restraint continued. The authorities in Bucharest knew that Moldova contained a large Slav minority which would resist incorporation into Romania; the secession of that minority from Moldova in 1993 increased Romanian circumspection as did the Moldovan referendum of March 1994 which revealed a majority for independence rather than amalgamation with Romania. Thereafter, Moldova joined the Commonwealth of Independent States and all but the most extreme of Romanian chauvinists abandoned thought of reunion.

Romania's transition towards political pluralism and the market economy had been slow but Bucharest shared the general east European aspiration to join NATO and the EU. These aspirations were not helped by Romania's initial reluctance to conform with sanctions against Yugoslavia and close the Danube to traffic destined for Serbia. Nor was Romania aided by its record in human rights. There had been no thorough investigations into the activities of the Securitate or into the present whereabouts of its funds. In 1996 a decision by the lower house of the Romanian parliament to keep the legal ban on homosexuality caused the European parliament to seek Iliescu's intervention; a few weeks later it was agreed that homosexuality should only be illegal if it caused a public scandal.

The Romanian political scene underwent profound change a few months later in the elections of November 1996. Iliescu's PSDR suffered considerable losses at the expense primarily of the DCR and Petre Roman's Social Democratic Union. In an even greater turnaround Iliescu himself lost the presidential elections to Emil Constantinescu of the DCR. Romania, it seemed, had at last broken from the reformist communists who had assumed power immediately after the revolution of December 1989.

SLOVAKIA

The anti-communist coalition PAV split in March 1991 when the Slovak prime minister, Vladimir Mečiar, and his nationalist followers formed the Movement for Democratic Slovakia (MDS); other groups to emerge from the break-up of the alliance were the Civic Democratic Union, the Christian Democratic Party, and the small Democratic Party. Mečiar was succeeded as prime minister by the leader of the Christian Democrats, Jan Carnogurský. However, it was Mečiar who was to be the dominant figure in Slovak affairs in the coming half decade; he was to be out of office only from March 1991 to June 1992 and from February to December 1994.

PAV had split initially on nationalist lines and after the creation of the new Slovak state in January 1993 that division remained. It was also the case that, as in the inter-war years, Slovak political formations were soon characterised by instability. Parties divided and regrouped easily and relatively frequently, and government coalitions were hardly more coherent. In March 1993 the minister of foreign affairs was sacked because he had put himself at the head of a dissident group within the MDS; he immediately formed his own Alliance of Democrats. At the same time, the leader of the Slovak National Party (SNP), an important element in the ruling coalition, quit as minister for economics and led his party out of the coalition. The SNP returned to government in October, but in February 1994 it split and brought about the collapse of Mečiar's government. He was succeeded, after much coming and going, by Jozef Moravčik, a former foreign minister, who was more moderate on the nationalist front and more committed to economic reform. His great mistake was to persuade his coalition partners that a general election would strengthen their positions. The vote was held on 30 September and 1 October 1994 and led in December to Mečiar's return to power at the head of a coalition consisting of the MDS, the SNP, and the small Association of Workers of Slovakia.

Mečiar was a politician of the old school with a strong inclination towards authoritarianism. Even in 1992 he had threatened to punish any section of the media which criticised him or his government, at the same time replacing a large number of administrators in Slovak radio and television. After his return to office in December 1994 he instituted a thorough purge of opponents in state posts; by September 1995 4,000 of them had been sacked for political reasons. He strengthened his hand further in March 1996 by enacting a subversion law, which threatened with imprisonment anyone found guilty of disseminating abroad false information about Slovakia or anyone organising demonstrations which might undermine Slovakia's constitutional stability, territorial integrity, or defence capabilities.

Nationalism remained one of Mečiar's trusted warhorses. Before the velvet divorce there were real grievances to exploit. Slovak industry was weaker than that in Bohemia and Moravia; it was less well-developed; it was more dependent on the now collapsing Soviet market; and it was also more dependent on state concerns whose funding was less secure after the fall of communism. As after 1918, the effects of economic restructuring were much more sharply felt in Slovakia than in the Czech lands. There was also tension between the Slovaks and their Hungarian minority, tension which Mečiar exploited in 1992 by refusing to meet the Hungarians' leaders. After January 1993 Mečiar maintained his tough attitude towards minorities, Hungarian and Gypsy. In March 1995 a state treaty was agreed between Slovakia and Hungary but not only was ratification delayed for a year by the Slovak parliament, but in November 1995 the government, in an effort to appease the SNP, introduced a draft language law to which the Hungarian minority strongly objected. In 1993 Mečiar had refused to follow Council of Europe recommendations on minority policy, and in both 1994 and 1995 the EU warned Slovakia that it should mend its ways if it wanted closer relations with Brussels.

Nationalism could be expressed externally as well as internally. Mečiar remained officially committed to membership of NATO and the EU but he did not object when leaders of the other coalition parties spoke against such membership. In June 1995 Mečiar even felt confident enough to snub the international financiers by cancelling the second round of privatisation.

There was much opposition to Mečiar's rule but in parliament this was weakened by the instability within the parties and in the alliances between them. The head of state was a more formidable opponent. Michal Kováč had been elected president in February 1993 with the enthusiastic backing of his MDS party colleague, Mečiar. The two soon fell out and by 1995 were in a state of constitutional warfare with Mečiar failing by only eight votes to secure the three-fifths majority in parliament necessary to remove the president. Kováč was then weakened by a scandal which followed the kidnapping of his son in August 1995; as the affair dragged on it brought accusations of illegal exports and the involvement of the Slovak intelligence services.

Despite the robust nature of its political affairs, Slovakia by the mid-1990s had overcome its former economic difficulties. In the middle of 1995 GDP was 6.4 per cent higher than the previous year, inflation was down to 7.9 per cent, and the budget deficit was lower than anticipated.

SLOVENIA

Slovenia had set the pace in decentralising the Yugoslav federation. The Slovene party had walked out of the 14th congress in January 1990 and, like the Croat and Macedonian parties, had refused to attend the special plenum in March. In December a referendum showed a 95 per cent majority for secession if a satisfactory solution to the Yugoslav federal constitutional crisis had not been reached within six months; the favoured Slovene solution was confederation, but just in case this was not achieved the government had already arranged for the secret printing in Austria of a separate Slovene currency. In February 1991 the Slovene assembly passed a law allowing for the dissolution of the federation and on 25

June independence was declared. The JNA moved immediately to secure control of the federal frontiers. The JNA, however, fared ill. It suffered around six thousand desertions and over four thousand of its troops were captured by the enthusiastic and well-prepared Slovene territorial defence force units. Within ten days the JNA had withdrawn. At the end of 1991 Slovenia, like Croatia, benefited from German determination that the new states be recognised by the EC. Recognition was granted on 12 January 1992.

Slovenia proved to be the success story amongst the Yugoslav successor states. Its domestic politics remained relatively peaceful, its economy showed enviable capacity for growth, and its foreign relations were well-regulated. In January 1996 Slovenia became the first of the former Yugoslav republics to reach agreement with foreign creditors on repaying its share of the former Yugoslav foreign debt. In June 1996 Slovenia became an associate member of the WEU and, most importantly, earlier in the same month it signed an association agreement with the EU and applied officially for membership of that organisation.

Slovenia had a number of advantages. It did not have a significant minority population, its economy was already well-advanced in Yugoslav terms, and its ruling communists had themselves initiated gradual change and had resisted any centralising trends long before 1990. By that year civil society flourished in Slovenia with as many as a hundred organisations for homosexuals, feminists, ecologists, and many others; there were also a number of independent political parties. Public confidence in the former communists meant that Milan Kučan, who had led the Slovene communists since 1986, and who had been elected president in April 1990, was returned to office in December 1992 with a comfortable majority.

After independence gradualism and moderation continued to dominate Slovene political culture, albeit in a somewhat corporatist mould. In April 1990 the elections to the republican assembly produced a majority for Democratic Opposition in Slovenia (DEMOS), a coalition of six centre-right parties. Lojze Peterle became prime minister. By the spring of 1992 DEMOS had fulfilled its function of breaking Slovenia free of the federation and in April, after losing a vote of no confidence, it gave way to a coalition dominated by the Liberal Democratic Party (LPD) whose leader, Janez Drnovšek, became prime minister. After parliamentary elections in December 1992 a wider coalition was formed. Some left-wing groups, worried by the effect of economic reforms on the underprivileged and on weaker enterprises, left the government in January 1996, but when elections were held in November of that year it was the right rather than the left which benefited from discontent with the government. The LDP remained the most popular party but second in the polls was the Slovene People's Party, and other right-wing groups also made noticeable advances.

Although it enjoyed enough political and economic stability to be a serious contender for EU membership, Slovenia did have some difficulties. The Italians had frustrated Slovene European ambitions because the Slovenes refused to allow foreigners who had formerly been resident in their country to purchase land;

this affected many ethnic Italians driven out of the area after 1945, and only after the return of a centre-left government in Italy did relations between Ljubljana and Rome improve. There were also tensions with Croatia over the status of four villages in Istria, whilst Serbia in 1996 attempted to block the Slovene agreement with western financiers on the repayment of the Yugoslav foreign debt.

Internally, the corporatist atmosphere meant that the government exercised what some considered undue influence over the media, whilst the always sensitive issue of state–church relations surfaced when the Roman Catholic authorities, along with many others, reacted against government plans to privatise large tracts of forest land. There were also social tensions, with the early months of 1996 seeing a rash of strikes amongst professionals such as journalists, medics, and university teachers.

YUGOSLAVIA

The former Yugoslav federation had ceased to exist in real terms by the end of 1991; its complete demise was registered in April 1992 when only Serbian and Montenegrin delegates appeared at a Serbian-sponsored convention on Yugoslavia. Henceforth, the Yugoslav federation, in name as well as in effect, consisted only of Serbia and Montenegro.

The two republics had one important feature in common: alone of the constituent parts of the old Yugoslav federation they had elected communist-dominated parliaments as well as former communist presidents, Slobodan Milošević in Serbia and Momir Bulatović in Montenegro. Yet the relationship between the two was never easy. A referendum in Montenegro on 1 March 1992 registered a 96 per cent vote in favour of federation, but the ethnic minorities had boycotted the poll, and whilst the former communist Party of Democratic Socialists in Montenegro (PDSM) remained pro-Serb it wanted to revise the federation and it was criticised by increasingly strong forces which wanted more emphasis on Montenegrin cultural and economic individuality. Many Montenegrins were anxious that Serbia's desire to secure a naval base on the Adriatic would lead Belgrade to make concessions to Zagreb over the Prevlaka peninsula, a narrow strip of territory flanking the Bay of Kotor. In March 1993 the pro-Serb attitudes of the ruling party had become so unpopular that the purely PDSM cabinet gave way to a coalition, though the incumbent prime minister, Milo Djukanović, remained in office. In November those who wanted looser ties with Serbia were gratified when the Orthodox Church in Montenegro separated from that in Serbia.

In Serbia itself Kosovo remained at the centre of political affairs. In January 1990 twenty-one people had been killed in demonstrations demanding political reform; in February the JNA had been deployed in Kosovo. Milošević's responses were centralisation, liberalisation, and serbianisation; populist and popular policies which brought him victory in the Serbian presidential elections in December 1990. Thereafter he continued to pressurise the Albanians of Kosovo, suspending the Kosovo constitution in March 1992, replacing Albanians with Serbs in the police force and other public posts, declaring Serbian the only official language, and attempting, with very limited success, to colonise the province with Serbs, some of them refugees from Bosnia and Croatia. When the illegal Democratic League of Kosovo held clandestine elections and established a shadow-state, repression increased, particularly with the closing of Albanian schools and other educational institutions. In December 1992 Milošević had a relatively easy victory in the presidential elections.

The Kosovo conflict served to distract many Serbs from the economic tribulations which they faced. Before the collapse of the original federation Yugoslavia had faced rigorous demands from western financial institutions; in 1990 federal prime minister Ante Marković had met these with tough policies which introduced a new dinar pegged to the Deutschmark and which succeeded in containing inflation. His efforts were ruined by Milošević's illegal issue of currency to prop up loss-making enterprises, but these were minor problems compared to those created by international sanctions against Yugoslavia. In December 1991 the EC restricted the sanctions formerly imposed on all republics to Serbia and Montenegro as a punishment for their obstructionism in negotiations in the Hague. In May 1992 Serbian conduct in Bosnia was the reason for the imposition by the UN of full sanctions on Serbia and Montenegro, the critical commodity being oil. The sanctions hurt and by the end of 1993 the economy was in virtual free fall with inflation running at an estimated 2 per cent per hour. Only the introduction of another new dinar in January 1994 stopped the decline.

Economic privation was widely felt and was one reason why Milošević's SPS did not achieve an absolute majority in the elections to the Serbian skupshtina in December 1992. There were other reasons. Milošević had promised multi-party democracy but he used tremendous pressure against opposition groups. In March 1991 protests against Milošević's interference with the media led to confrontations so serious that it seemed possible Milošević might be deposed. A year later further demonstrations were staged over the same issue. They did little to soften Milošević's rule. In July 1993 there were yet more riots in Belgrade, this time against Milošević's sacking of the federal president, Dobrica Čosić; the leader of the opposition Serbian Renewal Movement, the poet Vuk Drašković, and his wife Danica, an actress, were imprisoned and severely beaten after the riots; and in September 1993, when a vote of no confidence in president Milošević was tabled in the federal assembly, Milošević simply dissolved the assembly.

Milošević's lack of an overall majority in the skupshtina had forced him into coalition with Vojislav Šešelj's Serbian Radical Party (SRP). As sanctions began to bite Milošević realised that alleviation could be secured only by some compromise in Bosnia. This was not to the liking of Šešelj. Disagreements over the Vance-Owen plan led Šešelj to leave the coalition in May 1993 and a year later Milošević's willingness to impose sanctions on the Bosnian Serbs caused a great deal of anger in extreme nationalist circles in Serbia. Milošević, however, stuck to his task. In 1995 he showed himself more pliant towards the UN, particularly after he had been embarrassed by accusations that Serbia was resupplying the Bosnian Serb forces near Šrebrenica; and Belgrade's official reaction to Croatian successes in the Knin krajina and in Slavonia were more muted than many nationalists would have liked.

Milošević's reward was to be the sole representative of the Serbs at the Dayton talks where he did secure some easing of the sanctions. They were not lifted, however, the USA insisting that this could not happen until after the Bosnian elections of September 1996 had been verified.

Despite this, Milošević's SPS secured an easy victory in the elections of November 1996, although the party's hold on local government was considerably weakened, especially in the large industrial centres which had suffered most as a result of sanctions. The government's declaration that these elections were invalid provoked massive demonstrations in Belgrade and other cities, demonstrations which at the time of writing are still continuing.

NOTES

PREFACE

1 Winston S. Churchill, *The World Crisis 1911–1918*, London, Four Square Books, 1960, p. 114.
2 Various authors, 'A Survey of Opinion on the East European Revolution', *East European Politics and Societies*, vol. 4, no. 2 (Spring 1990), pp. 153–207, see p. 156.
3 F. R. Bridge, *From Sadowa to Sarajevo: The Foreign Policy of Austria-Hungary, 1866–1914*, London and Boston, Mass., Routledge & Kegan Paul, 1972.
4 W. M. Fullerton, *Problems of Power: a Study of International Politics from Sadowa to Kirk Kilisse*, London, Constable, 1913.
5 The wording was chosen by Alan Palmer for an excellent introductory history of the area, *The Lands Between: A History of East-Central Europe since the Congress of Vienna*, London, Weidenfeld & Nicolson, 1970.
6 C. A. Macartney and A. W. Palmer, *Independent Eastern Europe*, London, Macmillan, 1966, is excellent for inter-state relations between the wars. There is also a wealth of scholarship on diplomatic history between 1938 and 1941. Of especial value on the late 1930s is Donald Cameron Watt, *How War Came; The Immediate Origins of the Second World War, 1938–1939*, London, Heinemann, 1989. During the war an independent foreign policy was difficult and it was scarcely much easier after 1945. Yugoslavia was forced into a separate stance but it was to be almost a generation before Albania and Romania went their own ways; Bulgaria and the northern tier states of the German Democratic Republic, Poland, Czechoslovakia, and Hungary never did so. The economic history of eastern Europe is splendidly catered for in M. C. Kaser (ed.) *The Economic History of Eastern Europe: 1919–1975*, 5 vols (three published to date), Oxford, the Clarendon Press, 1985–6. We still await a comprehensive study of culture in eastern Europe in the twentieth century.

1 BEFORE THE TWENTIETH CENTURY

1 Anne Applebaum, 'Simulated Birth of a Nation', *Spectator*, 29 February 1992.
2 Wiktor Sukiennicki, *East Central Europe during World War I: From Foreign Domination to National Independence*, edited by Maciej Sierkierski, preface by Czesław Miłosz, 2 vols, East European Monograph 99, New York and Boulder, Colo., Columbia University Press and East European Monographs, 1984, p. 108.
3 Piotr S. Wandycz, 'Poland's Place in Europe in the Concepts of Piłsudski and Dmowski', *East European Politics and Societies*, vol. 4, no. 3 (Fall 1990), pp. 451–68, see pp. 454–5.
4 C. J. C. Street, *Hungary and Democracy*, London, Unwin, 1923, pp. 59–62.

5 Ivo Banac, *The National Question in Yugoslavia: Origins, History, Politics*, Ithaca, N.Y., and London, Cornell University Press, 1984, p. 303.

2 THE INTER-WAR YEARS

1 Joseph Rothschild, *Return to Diversity: A Political History of East Central Europe since World War II*, New York and Oxford, Oxford University Press, 1990, p. 3.
2 H. Hessell Tiltman, *Peasant Europe*, London, Jarrolds, 1934, p. 68.
3 N. Momtchiloff, *Ten Years of Controlled Trade in South-Eastern Europe*, National Institute of Economic and Social Research, Occasional Paper 6, Cambridge, Cambridge University Press, 1944, p. 18.

3 POLAND, 1918–39

1 Norman Davies, *Heart of Europe: A Short History of Poland*, Oxford, Oxford University Press, 1986, p. 120.
2 A *numerus clausus* was intended to limit the participation of a particular group to a defined proportion of the total.
3 Quoted in Robert Machray, *Poland 1914–1931*, London, George Allen & Unwin, 1932, p. 359.
4 Olga A. Narkiewicz, *The Green Flag: Polish Populist Politics, 1867–1970*, London, Croom Helm, 1976, p. 203.
5 Ferdynand Zweig, *Poland between Two Wars: A Critical Study of Social and Economic Changes*, London, Secker & Warburg, 1944, p. 66.
6 Antony Polonsky, *Politics in Independent Poland, 1921–1939: The Crisis of Constitutional Government*, Oxford, Clarendon Press, 1972, p. 421.
7 Ibid., p. 428.
8 Ibid., p. 447.

4 CZECHOSLAVKIA, 1918–38

1 Quoted in Josef Korbel, *Twentieth-Century Czechoslovakia: The Meanings of Its History*, New York, Columbia University Press, 1977, p. 93.
2 Joseph A. Mikus, *Slovakia: A Political History; 1918–1950*, translated from the French by Kathryn Day Wyatt and Joseph A. Mikus, Milwaukee, Wis., Marquette University Press, 1963, p. 12.
3 Radomir Luža, *The Transfer of the Sudeten Germans: A Study of Czech-German Relations, 1933–1962*, London, Routledge & Kegan Paul, 1964, p. 30.
4 Edward Táborsky, *Czechoslovak Democracy at Work*, with a foreword by Sir Ernest Barker, London, George Allen & Unwin, 1945, p. 94.
5 Vera Olivová, *The Doomed Democracy: Czechoslovakia in a Disrupted Europe, 1914–38*, London, Sidgwick & Jackson, 1972, p. 111.
6 Táborsky, op. cit., p. 104.
7 Victor S. Mamatey, 'The Development of Czechoslovak Democracy, 1920–1938', in Victor S. Mamatey and Radomir Luža, *A History of the Czechoslovak Republic, 1918–1948*, Princeton, N.J., Princeton University Press, 1973, pp. 99–166, see p. 108.
8 Quoted in Josef Anderle, 'The First Republic, 1918–1938', in Hans Brisch and Ivan Volgyes (eds) *Czechoslovakia: The Heritage of Ages Past; Essays in Memory of Josef Korbel*, East European Monograph 51, New York and Boulder, Colo., Columbia University Press and East European Monographs, 1979, p. 97.
9 Quoted in Elizabeth Wiskemann, *Czechs and Germans: A Study of the Struggle in the*

Historic Provinces of Bohemia and Moravia, Oxford, Oxford University Press, 1938, p. 143.

10 Quoted in Jozef Lettrich, *History of Modern Slovakia*, New York, Praeger, 1955, pp. 76–7.

11 Quoted in Jörg K. Hoensch, *Dokumente zur Autonomiepolitik der Slowakischen Volkspartei Hlinkas*, Veröffentlichungen des Collegium Carolinum 44, Munich and Vienna, R. Oldenbourg, 1984, p. 51.

12 Quoted in C. A. Macartney, *Hungary and her Successors: The Treaty of Trianon and its Consequences, 1919–1937*, Oxford, Oxford University Press, 1937, p. 145.

5 HUNGARY, 1918–41

1 Stephen D. Kertesz, 'The Consequences of World War I: The Effects on East Central Europe', in Béla K. Király, Peter Pastor, and Ivan Sanders (eds) *Essays on World War I: Total War and Peacemaking; A Case Study on Trianon*, Brooklyn College Studies on Society in Change, East European Monograph 15, New York and Boulder, Colo., Columbia University Press and East European Monographs, 1982, pp. 39–57, see p. 52.

2 Peter Kenez, 'Coalition Politics in the Hungarian Soviet Republic', in Andrew C. Janos and William B. Slottman (eds) *Revolution in Perspective: Essays on the Hungarian Soviet Republic of 1919*, Berkeley, Los Angeles and London, University of California Press, 1971, pp. 61–84, see p. 74.

3 A *hold* was 0.576 hectares or 1.43 acres.

4 Richard Löwenthal, 'The Hungarian Soviet and International Communism', in Janos and Slottman (eds) op. cit., pp. 173–81, see p. 177.

5 Thomas L. Sakmyster, 'Great Britain and the Making of the Treaty of Trianon', in Király, Pastor, and Sanders (eds) op. cit., pp. 107–29, see p. 125.

6 C. A. Macartney, *October Fifteenth: A History of Modern Hungary, 1929–1945*, 2 vols, Edinburgh, Edinburgh University Press, 1956, vol. 1, p. 46.

7 Quoted in Andrew C. Janos, *The Politics of Backwardness in Hungary, 1825–1945*, Princeton, N.J., Princeton University Press, 1982, p. 229.

8 Quoted in Michael Károlyi, *Memoirs of Michael Károlyi: Faith Without Illusion*, London, Jonathan Cape, 1956, p. 374.

9 Thomas Karfunkel, 'The Impact of Trianon on the Jews of Hungary', in Király, Pastor, and Sanders (eds) op.. cit., pp. 457–77, see p. 463.

10 Janos, op. cit., p. 246–7.

11 George Mikes, *The Hungarian Revolution*, London, André Deutsch, 1957, p. 21.

12 Janos, op. cit., p. 261.

13 J. Erös, 'Hungary', in S. J. Woolf (ed.) *Fascism in Europe*, London and New York, Methuen, 1981, pp. 117–50, see p. 131.

6 THE BALTIC STATES, 1918–40

1 John Hiden and Patrick Salmon, *The Baltic Nations and Europe: Estonia, Latvia and Lithuania in the Twentieth Century*, London and New York, Longman, 1991, p. 38.

2 Georg von Rauch, *The Baltic States: The Years of Independence; Estonia, Latvia, Lithuania 1917–1940*, London, C. Hurst, 1974, p. 142.

3 Rolf Ahmann, 'Nazi German policy towards the Baltic states on the eve of the Second World War', in John Hiden and Thomas Lane (eds) *The Baltic and the Outbreak of the Second World War*, Cambridge, Cambridge University Press, 1992, pp. 50–72, see p. 67.

7 ROMANIA, 1918–41

1 See Mattei Dogan, 'Romania, 1919–1938', in Myron Weiner and Ergun Ozbuden (eds) *Competitive Elections in Developing Countries*, Durham, N.C., and London, Duke University Press, 1987, pp. 369–89. I am grateful to the author of this essay for bringing it to my notice and for providing me with a copy of it.

2 Nicholas M. Nagy-Talevara, *The Green Shirts and Others: A History of Fascism in Hungary and Romania*, Hoover Institution Publication 85, Stanford, Calif., Stanford University Press, 1970, p. 264.

3 Dietrich Orlow, *The Nazis in the Balkans: A Case Study of Totalitarian Politics*, Pittsburgh, PA., University of Pittsburgh Press, 1968, p. 101.

8 BULGARIA, 1918–41

1 Marshall Lee Miller, *Bulgaria during the Second World War*, Stanford, Calif., Stanford University Press, 1975, p. 1.

9 YUGOSLAVIA, 1918–41

1 A cadastral *yoke* was 0.58 hectares or 1.4 acres.

2 Professor Slobodan Jovanović, 'The Yugoslav Constitution', *Slavonic and East European Review*, vol. 3, no. 7 (June 1924), pp. 166–78, see p. 178.

3 Archibald Lyall, 'The Making of Modern Slovenia', *Slavonic and East European Review*, vol. 17, no. 50 (Jan. 1939), pp. 404–15, see p. 414.

4 S. K. Pavlowitch, *Yugoslavia*, London, Benn, 1971, p. 58.

5 The date, 28 June, St Vitus' Day – *Vidovdan* in Serbo-Croat – was a fateful one in Serbian history, since this was the day on which the medieval empire was defeated at the battle of Kosovo in 1389, and on which Franz Ferdinand met his violent end in Sarajevo in 1914. It was also to be the day on which Tito's Yugoslavia was to be expelled from the Cominform in 1948.

6 R. W. Seton Watson, 'The Background of the Yugoslav Dictatorship', *Slavonic and East European Review*, vol. 10, no. 29 (Dec. 1931), pp. 363–76, see p. 367.

7 Vladko Maček, *In the Struggle for Freedom*, translated by Elizabeth and Stjepan Gaxi, University Park, Pa, and London, Pennsylvania State University Press, 1957, p. 100.

8 'X——x', 'A Croat View of the Yugoslav Crisis', *Slavonic and East European Review*, vol. 7, no. 20 (Jan. 1929), pp. 304–10, see p. 309.

9 R. W. Seton Watson, 'Yugoslavia and the Croat Problem', *Slavonic and East European Review*, vol. 16, no. 46 (July 1937), pp. 102–12, see p. 102.

10 J. B. Hoptner, *Yugoslavia in Crisis*, New York and London, Columbia University Press, 1962, p. 288.

10 ALBANIA, 1918–39

1 Bernd Jürgen Fischer, *King Zog and the Struggle for Stability in Albania*, East European Monograph 159, New York and Boulder, Colo., Columbia University Press and East European Monographs, 1984, pp. 57–8.

2 Michael Schmidt-Neke, *Entstehung und Ausbau der Königsdiktatur in Albanien (1912–1939); Regierungsbildungen, Herrschaftsweise und Machteliten in einem jungen Balkanstaat*, Südosteuropäische Arbeiten 84, Munich, R. Oldenbourg, 1987, p. 119.

3 Ibid., p. 216.

11 IDEOLOGICAL CURRENTS IN THE INTER-WAR PERIOD

1 Hugh Seton Watson, *The Pattern of Communist Revolution: A Historical Analysis*, revised and enlarged edition, London, Methuen, 1960, p. 69.
2 Ibid., p. 73.
3 D. J. Hall, *Romanian Furrow*, with a foreword by R. H. Bruce Lockhart, London, Harrap, 1939, pp. 206–7.
4 István Deák, 'Hungary', in Hans Rogger and Eugen Weber, (eds) *The European Right*, second edition, Berkeley and Los Angeles, University of California Press, 1974, pp. 364–407, see p. 385.
5 Nicholas M. Nagy-Talavera, *The Green Shirts and Others: A History of Fascism in Hungary and Romania*, Hoover Institution Publication 85, Stanford, Calif., Stanford University Press, 1970, p. 99.
6 Paul Hayes, *Fascism*, London, George Allen & Unwin, 1973, p. 118.
7 Rogger and Weber, (eds) op. cit., p. 548.
8 Hayes, op. cit., p. 148.
9 Nagy-Talavera, op. cit., p. 270.
10 Romuald J. Misiunas, 'Fascist Tendencies in Lithuania', *Slavonic and East European Review*, vol. 48, no. 110 (1970), pp. 88–109, see p. 109.
11 Béla Vago, *The Shadow of the Swastika: the Rise of Fascism and Anti-Semitism in the Danube Basin, 1936–39*, published for the Institute of Jewish Affairs, London, Saxon House, 1975, p. 345.
12 Stephen Fischer-Galați, ' "Autocracy, Orthodoxy and Nationality" in the Twentieth Century: the Romanian Case', *East European Quarterly*, vol. 18, no. 1 (March 1984), pp. 25–34, see p. 28.
13 Ibid.
14 Nagy-Talavera, op. cit., p. 270.
15 Vago, op. cit., p. 298.
16 C. A. Macartney, *Hungary and her Successors: The Treaty of Trianon and its Consequences, 1919–1937*, Oxford, Oxford University Press, 1937 p. 287.
17 Asher Cohen, 'Some Socio-Political Aspects of the Arrow Cross Party in Hungary', *East European Quarterly*, vol. 21, no. 3 (Sept. 1987), pp. 369–84, see p. 375.
18 Zev Barbu, 'Romania', in S. J. Woolf (ed.) *Fascism in Europe*, London and New York, Methuen, 1981, pp. 151–70, see p. 153.
19 Macartney, op. cit., p. 290.
20 Ezra Mendelsohn, *The Jews of East Central Europe between the World Wars*, Bloomington, Ind., Indiana University Press, 1987, p. 6.
21 Ibid., p. 7.
22 There was occasional confusion in terminology even in the world of national politics. The Jewish Dr Czech, for example, was a leader of the German social democrats in Czechoslovakia, whereas in the Czechoslovak social democratic leadership was the Czech Antonín Nemec whose surname means 'German'.
23 Anonymous, *From Serfdom to Self Government: Memoirs of a Polish Village Mayor, 1842–1927*, translated from the Polish by William John Rose and with an Introduction by Stanisław Kot, London, Minerva, 1941, pp. 100–01.
24 Wiktor Sukiennicki, *East Central Europe during World War I: From Foreign Domination to National Independence*, edited by Maciej Sierkierski, preface by Czesław Miłosz, 2 vols, East European Monograph 99, New York and Boulder, Colo., Columbia University Press and East European Monographs, 1984, pp. 60–1.
25 Peter F. Sugar, 'Conclusion', in Peter F. Sugar (ed.) *Native Fascism in the Successor States, 1918–1945*, Santa Barbara, Calif., Clio, 1971, pp. 145–56, see p. 154.
26 Andrew C. Janos, *The Politics of Backwardness in Hungary, 1825–1945*, Princeton, N.J., Princeton University Press, 1982, p. 223.

27 Ivo Banac, *The National Question in Yugoslavia: Origins, History, Politics*, Ithaca, N.Y., and London, Cornell University Press, 1984, p. 409.
28 Nagy-Talavera, op. cit., p. 136.
29 Vago, op. cit., p. 322.

12 THE SECOND WORLD WAR IN EASTERN EUROPE

1 J. Child, 'The Ukraine under German Occupation', in Arnold Toynbee and Veronica M. Toynbee, *Hitler's Europe*, Survey of International Affairs 1939–1946, Oxford, Oxford University Press, 1954, pp. 632–47, see p. 636.
2 Ivor Porter, *Operation Autonomous: with S.O.E. in Wartime Romania*, London, Chatto & Windus, 1989, p. 31.
3 Nicholas Kállay, *Hungarian Premier: a Personal Account of a Nation's Struggle in the Second World War*, with a foreword by C. A. Macartney, Oxford, Oxford University Press, 1954, p. 283.
4 Dietrich Orlow, *The Nazis in the Balkans: A Case Study of Totalitarian Politics*, Pittsburgh, Pa., University of Pittsburgh Press, 1968, p. 173.
5 Lucy S. Dawidowicz, *The War against the Jews, 1933–45*, London, Penguin Books, 1987, pp. 260–1.
6 George Bárány, 'The Dragon's Teeth: The Roots of Hungarian Fascism', in Peter F. Sugar (ed.) *Native Fascism in the Successor States, 1918–1945*, Santa Barbara, Calif., Clio, 1971, pp. 73–82, see p. 79.
7 Eduard Beneš, *The Memoirs of Dr Eduard Beneš: From Munich to New War and New Victory*, translated by Godfrey Lias, reprint edition, Westport, Conn., Greenwood Press, 1978, p. 107.
8 Thomas Lane, 'The Soviet occupation of Poland through British eyes', in John Hiden and Thomas Lane (eds) *The Baltic and the Outbreak of the Second World War*, Cambridge, Cambridge University Press, 1992, pp. 142–64, see p. 151.
9 John Erickson, *The Road to Berlin*, London, Grafton Books, 1985, p. 210.
10 Ibid., p. 367.
11 Václav L. Beneš and Norman G. J. Pounds, *Poland*, London, Benn, 1970, p. 252.

13 THE COMMUNIST TAKEOVERS

1 Wolfgang Leonhard, *Child of the Revolution*, Chicago, Regnery, 1958, p. 381.
2 Elizabeth Kridl Valkenier, 'Stalinizing Polish Historiography: What Soviet Archives Disclose', *East European Politics and Societies*, vol. 7, no. 1 (Winter 1993), pp. 109–34, see p. 110.
3 Milovan Djilas, *Conversations with Stalin*, New York, Harcourt Brace Jovanovich, 1962, p. 114.
4 Norman Davies, *Heart of Europe: A Short History of Poland*, Oxford, Oxford University Press, 1986, p. 3.
5 Quoted in Fernando Claudin, *The Communist Movement; from Comintern to Cominform*, London, Penguin Books, 1975, p. 460.
6 Rober Lee Wolff, *The Balkans in our Time*, Cambridge, Mass., Harvard University Press, 1956, p. 241.
7 David Childs, *The GDR: Moscow's German Ally*, second edition, London, Unwin Hyman, 1988, p. 23.
8 This is the title Pavel Tigrid gives to his chapter on Czechoslovakia in Thomas T. Hammond (ed.) *The Anatomy of Communist Takeovers*, with a foreword by Cyril E. Black, New Haven, Conn., and London, Yale University Press, 1975, pp. 399–432.

14 THE COMMUNIST SYSTEM

1 Kostadin Chakûrov, *Vtoriya Etazh* (The Second Floor), Sofia, no publisher indicated, 1990, p. 99.

2 *Todor Zhivkov: Statesman and Builder of New Bulgaria*, edited by Robert Maxwell, second revised edition, Oxford, Pergamon Press, 1985, p. 207.

3 Teresa Toranska, *Oni: Stalin's Polish Puppets*, translated from the Polish by Agnieszka Kołakowska, with an introduction by Harry Willets, London, Collins/Harvill, 1987, p. 128.

4 Milovan Djilas, quoted in Nora Beloff, *Tito's Flawed Legacy; Yugoslavia and the West: 1939 to 1984*, London, Victor Gollancz, 1985, p. 157.

5 Tamás Aczel and Tibor Meray, *The Revolt of the Mind: A Case History of Intellectual Resistance behind the Iron Curtain*, London, Thames & Hudson, 1960, p. 112.

6 Milovan Djilas, *Tito: The Story from Inside*, translated by Vasilije Lolić and Richard Hayes, London, Weidenfeld & Nicolson, 1981, p. 100.

7 Aczel and Meray, op. cit., p. 278.

8 George Paloczy-Horváth, *The Undefeated*, London, Secker & Warburg, 1959, p. 268.

9 Ion Pacepa, *Red Horizons: The Extraordinary Memoirs of a Communist Spy Chief*, London, Heinemann, 1988, p. 138.

10 Harold Lydall, *Yugoslavia in Crisis*, Oxford, Clarendon Press, 1989, p. 218.

11 Quoted in Timothy Garton Ash, *The Polish Revolution: Solidarity 1980–82*, London, Jonathan Cape, 1983, p. 170.

15 EAST EUROPEAN STALINISM, 1948–53

1 Fernando Claudin, *The Communist Movement; from Comintern to Cominform*, London, Penguin Books, 1975, p. 389.

2 Ivo Banac, *With Stalin against Tito; Cominformist Splits in Yugoslav Communism*, Ithaca, N.Y., and London, Cornell University Press, 1988, p. 40.

3 Michael Shafir, *Romania: Politics, Economics and Society; Political Stagnation and Simulated Change*, London, Frances Pinter, 1985, p. 35.

4 Atanas Slavov, *With the Precision of Bats; the Sweet and Sour Story of Real Bulgaria during the Last Fifty Years or So*, no place of publication indicated, Occidental Press, 1986, p. 112.

5 Tamás Aczel and Tibor Meray, *The Revolt of the Mind: A Case History of Intellectual Resistance behind the Iron Curtain*, London, Thames & Hudson, 1960, p. 251.

6 Béla Szász, *Volunteers for the Gallows: Anatomy of a Show-Trial*, London, Chatto & Windus, 1971, p. 147.

7 Slavov, op. cit., pp. 129–30.

8 Quoted in George Paloczi-Horváth, *The Undefeated*, London, Secker & Warburg, 1959, p. 152.

9 A. H. Hermann, *A History of the Czechs*, London, Allen Lane, 1975, p. 300.

10 Jiří Pelikán (ed.) *The Czechoslovak Political Trials, 1950–1954; the Suppressed Report of the Dubček Government's Commission of Inquiry, 1968*, London, Macdonald, 1970, p. 50.

11 Czesław Miłosz, *The Captive Mind*, translated from the Polish by Jane Zielonko, London, Secker & Warburg, 1953, p. 214.

12 Szász, op. cit., p. 66.

13 Teresa Toranska, *Oni: Stalin's Polish Puppets*, translated from the Polish by Agnieszka Kołakowska, with an introduction by Harry Willets, London, Collins Harvill, 1987, p. 194.

14 Paloczi-Horváth, op. cit., p. 186.

15 Rosemary Kavan, *Freedom at a Price; an Englishwoman's Life in Czechoslovakia*, introduction by William Shawcross and an epilogue by Jan Kavan, London, Verso, 1985, p. 58.

16 Tamás Aczel, *Ten Years After; A Commemoration of the Tenth Anniversary of the Hungarian Revolution*, London, Macgibbon & Kee, 1966, p. 66.

17 Zdeněk Mlynář, *Night Frost in Prague: the End of Humane Socialism*, translated by Paul Wilson, Hurst, London 1980, p. 21.

16 THE RETREAT FROM STALINISM, 1953–6

1 Ferenc A. Vali, *Rift and Revolt in Hungary: Nationalism versus Communism*, Cambridge, Mass., Harvard University Press, 1961, p. 50.

2 Georg Mikes, *The Hungarian Revolution*, London, André Deutsch, 1957, p. 131.

3 Vali, op. cit., p. 220.

4 Ghiţa Ionescu, *The Break-Up of the Soviet Empire in Eastern Europe*, Westport, Conn., Greenwood Press, 1965, p. 74.

5 Tamás Aczel and Tibor Meray, *The Revolt of the Mind: A Case History of Intellectual Resistance behind the Iron Curtain*, London, Thames & Hudson, 1960, pp. 345–56.

6 David Irving, *Uprising; One Nation's Nightmare: Hungary 1956*, London, Hodder & Stoughton, 1981, p. 245.

7 Stephen Borsody, *The Tragedy of Central Europe: Nazi and Soviet Conquest and Aftermath*, revised with a new epilogue, Yale Russian and East European Publications, New Haven, Conn., Yale Concilium on International and Area Studies, 1980, p. 212.

8 Dora Scarlett, 'Window onto Hungary', in Bill Lomax (ed.) *Eyewitness in Hungary: The Soviet Invasion of 1956*, Nottingham, Spokesman, 1980, pp. 26–82, see p. 52.

17 EASTERN EUROPE, 1956–68

1 J. F. Brown, *Eastern Europe and Communist Rule*, Durham, N.C., and London, Duke University Press, 1988, p. 236. The second edition of this work is entitled *Surge to Freedom: The End of Communist Rule in Eastern Europe*, Durham, N.C., Duke University Press, 1991.

2 Z. A. B. Zeman, *Prague Spring: A Report on Czechoslovakia 1968*, London, Penguin Books, 1969, p. 22.

3 Galia Golan, *Reform Rule in Czechoslovakia; the Dubček Era, 1968–1969*, Cambridge, Cambridge University Press, 1973, p. 37.

4 Hans Renner, *A History of Czechoslovakia since 1945*, London and New York, Routledge, 1989, p. 45.

18 CZECHOSLOVAKIA, 1968–9

1 William Shawcross, *Dubček*, London, Weidenfeld & Nicolson, 1970, p. 72.

2 Ibid., p. 63.

3 Harry Schwartz, *Prague's 200 Days; the Struggle for Democracy in Czechoslovakia*, London, Pall Mall Press, 1969, p. 110.

4 The quotations used here are taken from the text of the Action Programme printed in *Dubček's Blueprint for Freedom*, London, William Kimber, 1968, pp. 123–212.

5 Galia Golan, *Reform Rule in Czechoslovakia; the Dubček Era, 1968–1969*, Cambridge, Cambridge University Press, 1973, p. 166

6 Kostadin Chakûrov, *Vtoriya Etazh* (The Second Floor), Sofia, no publisher indicated, 1990, pp. 119–23

7 Schwartz, op. cit., p. 182.

8 Quoted in Pavel Tigrid, *Why Dubček Fell*, London, Macdonald, 1969, p. 88.

9 Jiří Pelikán (ed.) *The Czechoslovak Political Trials, 1950–1954; the Suppressed Report of the Dubček Government's Commission of Inquiry, 1968*, London, Macdonald, 1970, p. 27.

10 Erazim Kohák, 'Making and Writing History', in Norman Stone and Eduard Strouhal, (eds) *Czechoslovakia: Crossroads and Crises, 1918–88*, London, Macmillan in association with the BBC World Service, 1989, pp. 183–206, see p. 187.

11 Z. A. B. Zeman, *Prague Spring: A Report on Czechoslovakia 1968*, London, Penguin Books, 1969, pp. 112–13.

12 Radoslav Selucký, *Czechoslovakia: The Plan that Failed*, with an introduction by Kamil Winter, London, Nelson, 1970, p. xii.

13 Jacques Rupnik, *The Other Europe*, London, Weidenfeld & Nicolson in association with Channel Four Television, 1988, p. 142.

14 Quoted in ibid., p. 227.

19 EASTERN EUROPE, 1969–80

1 Vladimir V. Kusin, 'Husák's Czechoslovakia and Economic Stagnation', *Problems of Communism*, vol. 31, no. 3 (May–June 1982), pp. 24–37, p. 26.

2 Ibid, p. 25.

3 Peter J. Wiles, 'East Central Europe as an Active Element in the Soviet Empire', in Milorad M. Drachkovitch (ed.) *East Central Europe: Yesterday = Today = Tomorrow*, Stanford, Calif., Hoover Institution Press, 1982, pp. 81–105, see p. 101.

4 Timothy Garton Ash, *The Polish Revolution: Solidarity 1980–82*, London, Jonathan Cape, 1983, p. 14–15.

5 Michael Vale (ed.) *Poland: The State of the Republic: Reports by the Experience and Future Discussion Group (DiP) Warsaw*, London, Pluto Press, 1981, pp. 62–3.

6 Alfred Bloch, 'Poland in the Present', in Alfred Bloch (ed.) *The Real Poland: An Anthology of National Self-Perception*, New York, Continuum, 1982, pp. 53–70, see p. 68.

7 Garton Ash, op. cit., p. 29.

8 Neal Ascherson, *The Polish August: the Self-Limiting Revolution*, London, Penguin Books, 1982, p. 117.

20 THE SOLIDARITY CRISIS, POLAND 1980–1

1 Jacques Rupnik, *The Other Europe*, London, Weidenfeld & Nicolson in association with Channel Four Television, 1988, p. 252.

2 Quoted in Alain Touraine, François Dubet, Michel Wieviorka and Jan Strzelecki, *Solidarity: Analysis of a Social Movement; Poland 1980–81*, translated by David Denby, Cambridge, Cambridge University Press, 1983, pp. 47–8.

3 Rupnik, op. cit., p. 35.

22 THE REVOLUTIONS OF 1989–91

1 Timothy Garton Ash, *We The People: The Revolution of '89 Witnessed in Warsaw, Budapest, Berlin and Prague*, Cambridge, Granta Books in association with Penguin Books, 1990, p. 53.

2 Karen Dawisha, *Eastern Europe, Gorbachev, and Reform: The Great Challenge*, Cambridge, Cambridge University Press, second edition, 1990, p. 34.

3 Ibid., p. 214.

4 Ibid., p. 88.

5 Robert Cullen, *Twilight of Empire: Inside the Crumbling Soviet Bloc*, London, Bodley Head, 1991, p. 288.

6 Dawisha, op. cit., p. 198.

7 Timothy Garton Ash, *The Independent*, London, 8 December 1989.

8 Richard Crampton, 'The Intelligentsia, the Ecology and the Opposition in Bulgaria', *The World Today*, vol. 46, no. 2 (February 1990), pp. 23–6, see p. 24.

9 Juris Dreifelds, 'Latvian National Rebirth', *Problems of Communism*, vol. 38, no. 4 (July-Aug. 1989), pp. 77–95, see pp. 81–2.

10 Jan Zaprudnik, 'Belorussian Reawakening', *Problems of Communism*, vol. 38, no. 4 (July-Aug. 1989), pp. 36–52, see p. 48.

11 V. Stanley Vardys 'Lithuanian National Politics', *Problems of Communism*, vol. 38, no. 4 (July-Aug. 1989), pp. 53–76, see p. 62.

12 Dreifelds, op. cit., p. 82.

13 Ibid., p. 89.

14 Quoted in Cullen, op. cit., p. 115.

15 Keith Sword (ed.) *The Times Guide to Eastern Europe; Inside the Other Europe, A Comprehensive Handbook*, London, Times Books, 1990, p. 203.

16 Crampton, op. cit., p. 26.

17 Tamás Aczel, *Ten Years After; A Commemoration of the Tenth Anniversary of the Hungarian Revolution*, London, Macgibbon & Kee, 1966, p. 149.

18 David Selbourne, *Death of the Dark Hero: Eastern Europe, 1987–90*, London, Jonathan Cape, 1990, p. 169.

23 SEPARATE ROADS TO DEMOCRACY – AND ELSEWHERE

1 Mark Almond, 'Learning from Our Mistakes and How to Make New Ones', in Sir Julian Bullard and Robert O'Neill (eds) *Lessons from Bosnia*, Summary Record of a seminar series of that title held in All Souls College, Oxford, Hilary Term 1996, private publication, pp. 24–8, see p. 25.

BIBLIOGRAPHY

GENERAL

Ackerman, Bruce A. *The Future of Liberal Revolution*, New Haven, Conn. and London, Yale University Press, 1992.

Aczel, Tamás and Merey, Tibor *The Revolt of the Mind: a Case History of Intellectual Resistance Behind the Iron Curtain*, London, Thames & Hudson, 1960.

Adam, Jan *Why did the Socialist System Collapse in Central and Eastern Europe? The Case of Poland, the Former Czechoslovakia and Hungary*, Basingstoke, Macmillan, 1996.

Aldcroft, Derek Howard *Economic Change in Eastern Europe Since 1918*, Aldershot, Edward Elgar, 1995.

Bahro, R. *The Alternative in Eastern Europe*, translated by David Fernbach, NLB, no place of publication indicated, 1978.

Balcerowicz, Leszek *Socialism, Capitalism, Transformation*, Budapest and London, Central European University Press, 1995.

Banac, Ivo (ed.) *Eastern Europe in Revolution*, Ithaca, N.Y. and London, Cornell University Press, 1992.

Batowski, Henryk 'Parliamentary and Multiparty Systems in Central Europe, 1918–1939/ 41', *East European Quarterly*, vol. 2, no. 3 (Sept. 1968), pp. 295–302.

Beamish, Tufton *Must Night Fall?*, World Affairs Book Club, London, 1950.

Beeson, T. *Discretion and Valour: Religious Conditions in Russia and Eastern Europe*, London, Fontana, 1974.

Berend, Ivan T. *The Crisis Zone of Europe: an Interpretation of East-Central European History in the First Half of the Twentieth Century*, translated by Adrienne Makkay-Chambers, Cambridge, Cambridge University Press, 1986.

Berend, Ivan T. *Central and Eastern Europe, 1944–1993: Detour from Periphery to Periphery*, Cambridge Studies in Modern Economic History, no. 1, Cambridge, Cambridge University Press, 1996.

Berend, Ivan T. and Ranki, G. *Economic Development in East Central Europe in the 19th and 20th Centuries*, New York, Columbia University Press, 1974.

Berglund, Sten and Dellenbrant, Jan Eke (eds) *The New Democracies in Eastern Europe: Party Systems and Political Cleavages*, Studies of Communism in Transition, Aldershot, Edward Elgar, 1991.

Beyme, Klaus von *Transition to Democracy in Eastern Europe*, Basingstoke, Macmillan, 1996.

Borsody, Stephen *The Tragedy of Central Europe: Nazi and Soviet Conquest and Aftermath*, revised with a new epilogue, Yale Russian and East European Publications, New Haven, Conn., Yale Concilium on International and Area Studies, 1980.

Bridge, F. R. *From Sadowa to Sarajevo: the Foreign Policy of Austria-Hungary, 1866–1914*, London and Boston, Mass., Routledge & Kegan Paul, 1972.

Brogan, Patrick *Eastern Europe 1939–1989: the Fifty Years War*, London, Bloomsbury, 1990.

Bromke, Adam *Eastern Europe in the Aftermath of Solidarity*, New York, Columbia University Press, 1985.

Bromke, Adam and Rakowska-Harmstone, Teresa (eds) *The Communist States in Disarray, 1965–1971*, Minneapolis, University of Minnesota Press, 1972.

Brown, A. and Gray, J. *Political Culture and Political Change in Communist States*, second edition, London, Macmillan, 1979.

Brown, J. F. *Surge to Freedom: the End of Communist Rule in Eastern Europe*, second edition, Durham, N.C., Duke University Press, 1991.

Brus, Wodzimierz and Laski, Kazimierz *From Marx to the Market: Socialism in Search of an Economic System*, Oxford, Clarendon Press, 1989.

Bryant, Christopher G. A. and Mokrzycki, Edmund (eds) *The New Great Transformation? Change and Continuity in East-Central Europe*, London, Routledge, 1994.

Brzezinski, Zbigniew K. *The Soviet Bloc: Unity and Conflict*, Cambridge, Mass., Harvard University Press, 1960.

Bugajski, Janusz *Ethnic Politics in Eastern Europe: a Guide to Nationality Policies, Organizations, and Parties*, Armonk, N.Y. and London, Sharpe, 1994.

Bugajski, Janusz *Nations in Turmoil: Conflict and Cooperation in Eastern Europe*, Boulder, Colo. and London, Westview Press, 1995.

Bugajski, Janusz and Pollack, Maxine *East European Fault Lines: Dissent, Opposition, and Social Activism*, Westview Special Studies on the Soviet Union and Eastern Europe, Boulder, Colo. and London, Westview Press, 1989.

Buford, Bill (ed.) 'New Europe', *Granta*, no. 30 (Winter 1990).

Carlton, David, Ingram, Paul and Tenaglia, Giancarlo (eds) *Rising Tension in Eastern Europe and the former Soviet Union*, Aldershot, Dartmouth Publishing Co., 1996.

Charlton, Michael *The Eagle and the Small Birds: Crisis in the Soviet Empire; from Yalta to Solidarity*, London, BBC, 1984.

Chirot, Daniel (ed.) *The Origins of Backwardness in Eastern Europe: Economics and Politics from the Middle Ages until the Early Twentieth Century*, Berkeley, University of California Press, 1991.

Chirot, Daniel 'What Happened in Eastern Europe in 1989?', in Daniel Chirot (ed.) *The Crisis of Leninism and the Decline of the Left*, Seattle, University of Washington Press, 1991.

Churchill, Winston S. *The World Crisis 1911–1918*, London, Four Square Books, 1960.

Claudin, Fernando *The Communist Movement: from Comintern to Cominform*, London, Penguin Books, 1975.

Clemens, D. S. *Yalta*, New York, Oxford University Press, 1970.

Clogg, Richard (ed.) *Balkan Society in the Age of Greek Independence*, London and Basingstoke, Macmillan, 1981.

Cornwall, M. *The Last Years of Austria-Hungary*, Exeter, Exeter University Press, 1990.

Cowen-Karp, Regina *Central and Eastern Europe: the Challenge of Transition*, Oxford, SIRPI and Oxford University Press, 1993.

Crampton, Richard and Crampton, Ben *Atlas of Eastern Europe in the Twentieth Century*, London, Routledge, 1996.

Crawford, Keith *East Central European Politics Today: From Chaos to Stability?*, Manchester and New York, Manchester University Press, 1996.

Cullen, Robert *Twilight of Empire: Inside the Crumbling Soviet Bloc*, London, The Bodley Head, 1991.

Cuthbertson, Ian M. and Leibowitz, Jan (eds) *Minorities: the New Europe's Old Issue*, Prague, Institute for East–West Studies, 1993.

Dahl, R. (ed.) *Régimes and Opposition*, New Haven, Conn. and London, Yale University Press, 1973.

Dahrendorf, Ralf *Reflections on the Revolution in Europe in a Letter intended to have been sent to a Gentleman in Warsaw*, London, Chatto & Windus, 1990.

Davy, Richard (ed.) *European Détente: a Reappraisal*, London, Sage, 1992.

Dawidowicz, Lucy S. *The War against the Jews, 1933–45*, London, Penguin Books, 1987.

Dawisha, Karen *Eastern Europe, Gorbachev, and Reform: the Great Challenge*, second edition, Cambridge, Cambridge University Press, 1990.

Dawisha, Karen and Hanson, Philip (eds) *Soviet–East European Dilemmas: Coercion, Competition, and Consent*, London, Heinemann for the Royal Institute of International Affairs, 1981.

Djilas, Milovan *Conversations with Stalin*, New York, Harcourt Brace Jovanovich, 1962.

Djilas, Milovan *The New Class: an Analysis of the Communist System*, with an introduction by Robert Conquest, London, Unwin, 1966.

Djilas, Milovan *The Imperfect Society: Beyond the New Class*, translated by Dorian Cooke, London, Unwin, 1972.

Drachkovitch, Milorad M. (ed.) *East Central Europe: Yesterday = Today = Tomorrow*, Stanford, Cal., Hoover Institution Press, 1982.

Drachkovitch, Milorad M. and Lazich, Branko (eds) *The Comintern: Historical Insights. Essays. Recollections. Documents*, New York, Praeger, 1966.

Elster, Jon *Rebuilding the Boat in the Open Sea: Constitution-Making in Eastern Europe*, Oxford, Nuffield College, Centre for European Studies, Discussion Paper no. 24, 1993.

Elster, Jon (ed.) *The Round Table Talks and the Breakdown of Communism*, Chicago and London, University of Chicago Press, 1996.

Erickson, John *The Road to Berlin*, London, Grafton Books, 1985.

Erickson, John *The Road to Stalingrad*, London, Grafton Books, 1985.

Evans, Grant 'The Accursed Problem: Communists and Peasants', *Peasant Studies*, vol. 15, no. 2 (Winter 1988), pp. 73–102.

Evans, Ifor L. 'Agrarian Reform in the Danubian Countries: I. Historical Introduction', *Slavonic and East European Review*, vol. 7, no. 21 (Mar. 1929), pp. 604–20.

Fehér, F. and Arato, A. (eds) *Crisis and Reform in Eastern Europe*, London, Transaction Books, 1991.

Fehér, F. and Heller, A. *From Yalta to Glasnost: the Dismantling of Stalin's Empire*, Oxford, Blackwell, 1990.

Fejtö, Francois *A History of the People's Democracies: Eastern Europe since Stalin*, translated by Daniel Weissbort, London, Pall Mall Press, 1971.

Fihir, Ferenc and Arato, Andrew (eds) *Crisis and Reform in Eastern Europe*, New Brunswick and London, Transaction Books, 1991.

Fischer-Galați, Stephen *The Communist Parties of Eastern Europe*, New York, Columbia University Press, 1979.

Fowkes, Ben *The Rise and Fall of Communism in Eastern Europe*, Basingstoke, Macmillan, 1995.

Frankland, M. *The Patriots' Revolution: How East Europe won its Freedom*, London, Sinclair-Stevenson, 1990.

Gafencu, Grigore *Prelude to the Russian Campaign: from the Moscow Pact (August 21st 1939) to the Opening of Hostilities in Russia (June 22nd 1941)*, London, Frederick Muller, 1945.

Garton Ash, Timothy *We The People: the Revolution of '89 Witnessed in Warsaw, Budapest, Berlin and Prague*, Cambridge, Granta Books in association with Penguin Books, 1990.

Garton Ash, Timothy *The Uses of Adversity: Essays on the Fate of Central Europe*, Cambridge, Granta Books in association with Penguin Books, 1991.

Garton Ash, Timothy *In Europe's Name: Germany and the Divided Continent*, Jonathan Cape, London, 1993.

Gati, Charles *The Bloc that Failed: Soviet–East European Relations in Transition*, London, Taurus, 1990.

Glenny, Misha *The Rebirth of History: Eastern Europe in the Age of Democracy*, London, Penguin Books, 1990.

Goldfarb, Jeffrey C. *After the Fall: the Pursuit of Democracy in Central Europe*, London, Basic Books and HarperCollins, 1992.

Gordon, L. *Eroding Europe: Western Relations with Eastern Europe*, Washington D.C., Brookings Institute, 1987.

Graubard, Stephen R. (ed.) *Eastern Europe . . . Central Europe . . . Europe*, Boulder, Colo., Westview Press, 1991.

Gros, Daniel and Steinherr, Alfred *Winds of Change: Economic Transition in Central and Eastern Europe*, London, Longman, 1995.

Gsovski, Vladimir and Grzybowski, Kazimierz *Government, Law and Courts in the Soviet Union and Eastern Europe*, 2 vols, London, Stevens and Sons, 1959.

György, Andrew *Governments of Danubian Europe*, reprint edition, Westport, Conn., Greenwood Press, 1978.

Hammond, T. (ed.) *The Anatomy of Communist Takeovers*, with a foreword by Cyril E. Black, New Haven, Conn., Yale University Press, 1975.

Hammond, T. (ed.) *Witnesses to the Origins of the Cold War*, Seattle, University of Washington Press, 1982.

Hankiss, Elemér *East European Alternatives*, Oxford, Clarendon Press, 1990.

Hausner, Jerzy, Jessop, Bob and Nielsen, Klaus *Strategic Choice and Path-Dependency in Post-Socialism: Institutional Dynamics in the Transformation Process*, Aldershot and Brookfield, Vt, Edward Elgar, 1995.

Havel, Václav *The Power of the Powerless: Citizens against the State in Central-Eastern Europe*, edited by John Keane, London, Hutchinson, 1985.

Havel, Václav *Living in Truth*, edited by Jan Vladislav, London, Faber & Faber, 1989.

Havel, Václav *Summer Meditations: on Politics, Morality and Civility in a Time of Transition*, London, Faber & Faber, 1992.

Hayes, Paul *Fascism*, London, George Allen & Unwin, 1973.

Held, Joseph (ed.) *The Columbia History of Eastern Europe in the Twentieth Century*, New York, Columbia University Press, 1992.

Held, Joseph (ed.) *Populism in Eastern Europe: Racism, Nationalism and Society*, East European Monographs, no. CDLX, New York and Boulder, Colo., Columbia University Press and East European Monographs, 1996.

472

Heller, Agnes and Fihir, Ferenc *From Yalta to Glasnost: the Dismantling of Stalin's Empire*, Oxford, Blackwell, 1990.

Hill, Ronald and Zielonka, Jan (eds) *Restructuring Eastern Europe: towards a New European Order*, Aldershot, Edward Elgar, 1990.

Hoensch, Jörg K. *Sowjetische Osteuropa-Politik, 1945–1975*, Düsseldorf, Droste, 1977.

Holmes, Leslie *The Political Process in the Communist States: Politics and Industrial Administration*, with a foreword by Roger E. Kanet, London, Sage, 1981.

Holmes, Leslie *The End of Communist Power: Anti-Corruption Campaigns and Legitimation Crisis*, Cambridge, Polity, 1993.

Holmes, Leslie (ed.) *The Withering Away of the State: Party and State under Communism*, London, Sage, 1981.

Howard, A. E. Dick (ed.) *Constitution Making in Eastern Europe*, Woodrow Wilson Center Special Studies, Washington D.C., Woodrow Wilson Center Press, 1993.

Hupchick, Dennis *Conflict and Chaos in Eastern Europe*, Basingstoke, Macmillan, 1995.

Ionescu, Ghiţa *The Break-Up of the Soviet Empire in Eastern Europe*, Westport, Conn., Greenwood Press, 1965.

Ionescu, Ghiţa *The Politics of the European Communist States*, London, Weidenfeld & Nicolson, 1967.

Jackson, George D., Jr *Comintern and Peasant in East Europe, 1919–1930*, New York and London, Columbia University Press, 1966.

Jowitt, Ken *New World Disorder: The Leninist Extinction*, Berkeley and Los Angeles, University of California Press, 1992.

Judt, Tony 'The Dilemmas of Dissidence: the Politics of Opposition in East-Central Europe', *East European Politics and Societies*, vol. 2, no. 2 (Spring 1988), pp. 185–240.

Kaldor, M. *The Imaginary War, Understanding the East–West Conflict*, Oxford, Blackwell, 1990.

Kann, Robert A. *A History of the Habsburg Empire, 1526–1918*, Berkeley, University of California Press, 1977.

Kaser, M. C. (ed.) *The Economic History of Eastern Europe; 1919–1975*, 5 vols, three published to date, Oxford, the Clarendon Press, 1985–6.

Keane, John (ed.) *Civil Society and the State: New European Perspectives*, London, Verso, 1988.

Kertész, Stephen D. 'The Consequences of World War I: the Effects on East Central Europe', in Béla K. Király, Peter Pastor and Ivan Sanders (eds), *Essays on World War I: Total War and Peacemaking. A Case Study on Trianon*, Brooklyn College Studies on Society in Change, East European Monographs, no. XV, New York and Boulder, Colo., Columbia University Press and East European Monographs, 1982, pp. 39–57.

Khrushchev, Nikita S. *Khrushchev Remembers*, translated and edited by Strobe Talbott with an introduction, commentary and notes by Edward Crankshaw, London, André Deutsch, 1971.

Khrushchev, Nikita S. *Khrushchev Remembers: the Last Testament*, translated and edited by Strobe Talbott with a foreword by Edward Crankshaw and an introduction by Jerrold L. Schecter, London, André Deutsch, 1974.

Kitschelt, Herbert *Party Systems in East Central Europe: Consolidation or Fluidity?*, Centre for the Study of Public Policy, University of Strathclyde, 1995.

Klein, G. and Reban, M. J. (eds) *Politics of Ethnicity in Eastern Europe*, East European Monographs, no. XCIII, New York and Boulder, Colo., Columbia University Press and East European Monographs, 1981.

Kołakowski, Leszek *Main Currents of Marxism: its Origins, Growth, and Dissolution*, translated by P. S. Falla, Oxford, Oxford University Press, 1981.

Konrad, G. and Szelenyi, I. *The Intellectuals on the Road to Class Power*, translated by Andrew Arato and Richard E. Allen, Brighton, Harvester Press, 1979.

Korbonski, Andrzej 'Leadership, Succession and Political Change in Eastern Europe', *Studies in Comparative Communism*, vol. 9, no. 1/2 (Spring/Summer 1976), pp. 3–26.

Korbonski, Andrzej and Graziano, Luigi *The Emergence of Pluralism in East Central Europe, Communist and Post-Communist Studies*, special issue, Oxford, Butterworth-Harman, 1993.

Kornai, János 'Socialist Transformation and Privatization: Shifting from a Socialist System', *East European Politics and Societies*, vol. 4, no. 2 (Spring 1990), pp. 255–304.

Kovrig, Bennett *Of Walls and Bridges: the United States and Eastern Europe*, New York, New York University Press, 1991.

Kriesberg, Louis and Segal, David R. (eds) *The Transformation of European Communist Societies*, Research in Social Movements, Conflicts and Change, no. 14, Greenwich, Conn., JAI Press, 1992.

Krooth, Richard and Vladimirovitz, Boris *Quest for Freedom: the Transformation of Eastern Europe in the 1990s*, Jefferson, N.C. and London, McFarland & Co., 1993.

Latawski, Paul (ed.) *Contemporary Nationalism in East Central Europe*, Basingstoke, Macmillan, 1994.

Lemke, Christiane and Marks, Gary (eds) *The Crisis of Socialism in Europe*, Durham, N.C. and London, Duke University Press, 1992.

Lendvai, Paul *Anti-Semitism in Eastern Europe*, London, Macdonald, 1971.

Lendvai, Paul *The Bureaucracy of Truth: How Communist Governments Manage the News*, London, Burnett Books, 1981.

Lewis, Paul G. *Central Europe since 1945*, London, Longman, 1994.

Lewis, Paul G. (ed.) *Party Structures and Organisation in East-Central Europe*, Studies of Communism in Transition, Cheltenham and Brookfield, Vt, Edward Elgar, 1996.

Lichtheim, George 'Social Democracy and Communism, 1918–1968', *Studies in Comparative Communism*, vol. 3, no. 1 (Jan. 1970), pp. 5–30.

London, Kurt (ed.) *Eastern Europe in Transition*, Baltimore, Md, The Johns Hopkins Press, 1966.

Longworth, Philip *The Making of Eastern Europe*, London and Basingstoke, Macmillan, 1992.

Loth, Wilfried *Die Teilung der Welt: Geschichte des kalten Krieges 1941–1955*, Munich, Deutscher Taschenbuch Verlag, 1982.

Lovenduski, Joni and Woodall, Jean *Politics and Society in Eastern Europe*, London and Basingstoke, Macmillan, 1987.

Lukacs, John A. *The Great Powers and Eastern Europe*, New York, American Book Company, 1953.

Macartney, C. A. *Hungary and her Successors: the Treaty of Trianon and its Consequences, 1919–1937*, Oxford, Oxford University Press, 1937.

Macartney, C. A. *The Habsburg Empire, 1790–1918*, New York, Macmillan, 1969.

Macartney, C. A. and Palmer, A. W. *Independent Eastern Europe*, London, Macmillan, 1966.

Machray, Robert *The Little Entente*, reprint edition, New York, Howard Fertig, 1970.

Magocsi, Paul Robert *Historical Atlas of East Central Europe*, A History of East Central Europe, vol. I, Seattle and London, University of Washington Press, 1993.

Magris, Claudio *Danube: a Sentimental Journey from the Source to the Black Sea*, London, Collins Harvill, 1989.

Mason, David S. *Revolution and Transition in East-Central Europe: the Rise and Fall of Communism and the Cold War*, Dilemmas in World History, Boulder, Colo., Westview Press, 1996.

Mastny, Vojtech *Russia's Road to the Cold War*, New York, Columbia University Press, 1979.

Mastny, Vojtech *Helsinki, Human Rights and European Security: Analysis and Documentation*, Durham, N.C., Duke University Press, 1986.

Mastny, Vojtech and Zielonka, Jan (eds) *Human Rights and Security: Europe on the Eve of a New Era*, Boulder, Colo., Westview Press, 1991.

May, Arthur J. *The Habsburg Monarchy, 1867–1914*, Cambridge, Mass., Harvard University Press, 1968.

McCauley, M. (ed.) *Communist Power in Europe, 1944–1949*, London, Macmillan for the School of Slavonic and East European Studies, 1977.

Mendelsohn, Ezra *The Jews of East Central Europe between the World Wars*, Bloomington, Indiana, Indiana University Press, 1987.

Michta, Andrew A. and Prizel, Ilya *Post-Communist Eastern Europe: Crisis and Reform*, New York, St. Martin's Press, 1992.

Mičunović, Veljko *Moscow Diary*, New York, Doubleday, 1980.

Miłosz, Czesław *The Captive Mind*, translated from the Polish by Jane Zielonko, London, Secker & Warburg, 1953.

Miłosz, Czesław *The Seizure of Power*, translated by Celina Wieniewska, reprinted London, Abacus, 1985.

Milyukov, Paul ' "Indivisible Peace" and the Two Blocks in Europe', *Slavonic and East European Review*, vol. 15, no. 45 (April 1937), pp. 577–87.

Mitrany, David *Marx against the Peasant: a Study in Social Dogmatism*, Chapel Hill, University of North Carolina Press, 1951.

Mlynář, Zdeněk *Night Frost in Prague: the End of Humane Socialism*, translated by Paul Wilson, London, Hurst, 1980.

Morris, L. P. *Eastern Europe since 1945*, London, Heinemann, 1984.

Morrison, J. (ed.) *Eastern Europe and the West*, Harrogate, St. Martin's Press, 1992.

Narkiewicz, Olga A. *Eastern Europe, 1968–1984*, London, Croom Helm, 1986.

Neuburg, Paul *The Hero's Children: the Post-War Generation in Eastern Europe*, London, Constable, 1972.

Newman, Bernard *Danger Spots of Europe*, London, The Right Book Club, 1939.

Nollau, Günther *International Communism and World Revolution: History and Methods*, with a foreword by Leonard Schapiro, London, Hollis & Carter, 1961.

Offe, Klaus *Variations of Transition: the Eastern Europe and the East German Experience*, Oxford, Blackwell, and Cambridge, Polity, 1996.

Okey, Robin *Eastern Europe, 1740–1980: Feudalism to Communism*, second edition, London, Hutchinson, 1986.

Oleszczuk, T. 'Dissident Marxism in Eastern Europe', *World Politics*, vol. 34, no. 4 (July 1982), pp. 527–47.

Olson, David M. and Norton, Philip (eds) *The New Parliaments of Central and Eastern Europe*, Frank Cass, London, 1996.

Palmer, Alan *The Lands Between: A History of East-Central Europe since the Congress of Vienna*, London, Weidenfeld & Nicolson, 1970.

Pearson, Raymond *National Minorities in Eastern Europe, 1848–1945*, London, Macmillan, 1983.

Pech, Stanley Z. 'Political Parties in Eastern Europe, 1848–1939: Comparisons and Continuities', *East Central Europe*, vol. 5, no. 1 (1978), pp. 1–38.

Pelly, M. E., Yasamee, H. J. and Hamilton, K. A. (eds) *Documents on British Policy Overseas*, series I, vol. VI, *Eastern Europe 1945–1946*, London, HMSO, 1991.

Piirainen, Timo (ed.) *Change and Continuity in Eastern Europe*, Aldershot, Dartmouth Press, 1994.

Plasser, Fritz and Pribersky, Andreas *Political Culture in East-Central Europe*, Aldershot and Brookfield, Vt, Avebury, 1996.

Polonsky, Antony *The Little Dictators: the History of Eastern Europe since 1918*, London, Routledge & Kegan Paul, 1975.

Pravda, Alex (ed.) *The End of the Outer Empire: Soviet–East European Relations in Transition, 1985–90*, London, Sage, 1992.

Pridham, Geoffrey and Lewis, Paul G. *Stabilising Fragile Democracies: Comparing New Party Systems in Southern and Eastern Europe*, London and New York, Routledge in association with the Centre for Mediterranean Studies, University of Bristol and the Economic Social Research Council, 1996.

Pridham, Geoffrey and Vanhanen, Tatu *Democratization in Eastern Europe: Domestic and International Perspectives*, London and New York, Routledge, 1994.

Prins, Gwyn (ed.) *Spring in Winter: the 1989 Revolutions*, with a preface by Václav Havel, Manchester, Manchester University Press, 1990.

Radice, Lisanne 'The Eastern Pact, 1933–1935: a Last Attempt at European Cooperation', *Slavonic and East European Review*, vol. 55, no. 1 (Jan. 1977), pp. 45–64.

Rakowska-Harmstone, T. and György, A. (eds) *Communism in Eastern Europe*, Bloomington, Indiana University Press, 1979.

Ramet, Pedro (ed.) *Cross and Commissar: the Politics of Religion in Eastern Europe and the USSR*, Bloomington, Indiana University Press, 1987.

Ramet, Sabrina P. *Social Currents in Eastern Europe: the Sources and Meaning of the Great Transformation*, Durham, N.C. and London, Duke University Press, 1991.

Ramet, Sabrina P. *Protestantism and Politics in Eastern Europe and Russia: the Communist and Postcommunist Eras*, Christianity Under Stress, vol. III, Durham, N.C. and London, Duke University Press, 1992.

Remington, Thomas F. (ed.) *Parliaments in Transition: the New Legislative Politics in the Former USSR and Eastern Europe*, Boulder, Colo. and Oxford, Westview Press, 1994.

Ringen, Stein and Wallace, Claire (eds) *Societies in Transition: East-Central Europe Today*, Prague Papers on Social Responses to Transformation, no. I, Prague, Central European University Press, 1993.

Rothschild, Joseph *East Central Europe between the Two World Wars*, A History of East Central Europe, vol. IX, Seattle, University of Washington Press, 1974.

Rothschild, Joseph *Return to Diversity: a Political History of East Central Europe since World War II*, New York and Oxford, Oxford University Press, 1990.

Rupnik, Jacques *The Other Europe*, London, Weidenfeld & Nicolson in association with Channel Four Television Company Limited, 1988.

Sanders, Irwin T. (ed.) *Collectivization of Agriculture in Eastern Europe*, Lexington, University of Kentucky Press, 1958.

Schöpflin, George *Politics in Eastern Europe, 1945–1992*, Blackwell, Oxford, 1993.

Schöpflin, George 'Post-Communism: Constructing New Democracies in Central Europe', *International Affairs*, vol. 67, no. 2 (April 1991), pp. 235–50.

Schöpflin, George and Wood, Nancy (eds) *In Search of Central Europe*, Cambridge, Polity, 1989.

Selbourne, David *Death of the Dark Hero: Eastern Europe, 1987–90*, London, Jonathan Cape, 1990.

Serafin, Joan (ed.) *East-Central Europe in the 1990s*, Boulder, Colo. and Oxford, Westview Press, 1994.

Seton-Watson, Hugh *Eastern Europe between the Wars, 1918–1941*, Cambridge, Cambridge University Press, 1946.

Seton-Watson, Hugh *The East European Revolution*, London, Methuen, 1950.

Seton-Watson, Hugh *The Pattern of Communist Revolution: a Historical Analysis*, revised and enlarged edition, London, Methuen, 1960.

Seton-Watson, Hugh *The Decline of Imperial Russia*, London, Methuen, 1966.

Seton-Watson, Hugh *The Russian Empire, 1801–1917*, Oxford, Clarendon Press, 1967.

Seton-Watson, Hugh *The Imperialist Revolutionaries: World Communism in the 1960s and 1970s*, London, Hutchinson, 1978.

Seton-Watson, Hugh and Seton-Watson, Christopher *The Making of the New Europe: R. W. Seton-Watson and the Last Years of Austria-Hungary*, London, Methuen, 1981.

Simons, Thomas W., Jr *Eastern Europe in the Post-War World*, New York, St. Martin's Press, 1991.

Sked, Alan *The Decline and Fall of the Habsburg Empire, 1815–1918*, London, Longman, 1989.

Skilling, H. Gordon *Communism National and International: Eastern Europe after Stalin*, Toronto, Toronto University Press, 1964.

Skilling, H. Gordon *Samizdat and an Independent Society in Central and Eastern Europe*, Basingstoke, Macmillan in association with St. Antony's College, Oxford, 1989.

Social Research vol. 55, nos 1–2 (Spring/Summer 1988) special issue on Central and Eastern Europe.

Staniszkis, Jadwiga 'Patterns of Change in Eastern Europe', *East European Politics and Societies*, vol. 4, no. 1 (Winter 1990), pp. 77–97.

Starr, Richard F. *Communist Régimes in Eastern Europe*, Stanford, Cal., Hoover Institution Press, 1977.

Stehle, Hansjakob *Eastern Politics of the Vatican, 1917–1979*, translated by Sandra Smith, Athens, Ohio, Ohio University Press, 1981.

Stokes, Gale *The Walls Came Tumbling Down: the Collapse of Communism in Eastern Europe*, New York and Oxford, Oxford University Press, 1993.

Stokes, Gale (ed.) *From Stalinism to Pluralism: a Documentary History of Eastern Europe since 1945*, New York and Oxford, Oxford University Press, 1991.

Stone, Norman *The Eastern Front, 1914–17*, London, Hodder & Stoughton, 1975.

Sugar, Peter F. 'Conclusion', in Peter F. Sugar (ed.) *Native Fascism in the Successor States, 1918–1945*, Santa Barbara, Calif., Clio, 1971, pp. 145–56.

Sugar, Peter F. and Lederer, Ivo J. *Nationalism in Eastern Europe*, Seattle and London, University of Washington Press, 1969.

Sukiennicki, Wiktor *East Central Europe during World War I: From Foreign Domination to National Independence*, edited by Maciej Sierkierski, preface by Czesław Miłosz, 2 vols, East European Monographs, no. CXIX, New York and Boulder, Colo., Columbia University Press and East European Monographs, 1984, p. 108.

Swain, Geoffrey and Swain, Nigel *Eastern Europe since 1945*, Basingstoke and London, Macmillan, 1993.

Sword, Keith (ed.) *The Times Guide to Eastern Europe: Inside the Other Europe, a Comprehensive Handbook*, London, Times Books, 1990.

Szacki, Jerzy *Liberalism after Communism*, Budapest, London and New York, Central European University Press, 1995.

Szász, Béla *Volunteers for the Gallows: Anatomy of a Show-Trial*, London, Chatto & Windus, 1971.

Thomas, Hugh *Armed Truce: the Beginnings of the Cold War 1945–46*, London, Hamish Hamilton, 1986.

Tiltman, Hessell H. *Peasant Europe*, London, Jarrolds, 1934.

Tismaneanu, Vladimir *Reinventing Politics: Eastern Europe from Stalin to Havel*, New York, Free Press, Toronto and London, Maxwell Macmillan International, 1992.

Tökés, Rudolf L. (ed.) *Opposition in Eastern Europe*, London, Macmillan in association with St. Antony's College, Oxford, 1979.

Tomaszewski, Jerzy *The Socialist Régimes of East Central Europe: Their Establishment and Consolidation, 1944–67*, translated by Jolanta Krauze, London, Routledge, 1989.

Toynbee, Arnold and Toynbee, Veronica M. (eds) *Hitler's Europe*, London, Oxford University Press, 1954.

Turczynski, Emanuel 'Nationalism and Religion in Eastern Europe', *East European Quarterly*, vol. 5, no. 4 (Jan. 1972), pp. 468–86.

Turnock, David *The Human Geography of Eastern Europe*, London, Routledge, 1989.

Vago, Béla *The Shadow of the Swastika: the Rise of Fascism and Anti-Semitism in the Danube Basin, 1936–39*, published for the Institute of Jewish Affairs, London, Saxon House, 1975.

Valenta, Jiří 'Eurocommunism in Eastern Europe', *Problems of Communism*, vol. 27, no. 2 (Mar–April 1978), pp. 41–54.

Valiani, Leo *The End of Austria-Hungary*, New York, Alfred A. Knopf, 1973.

Various authors 'A Survey of Opinion on the East European Revolution', *East European Politics and Societies*, vol. 4, no. 2 (Spring 1990), pp. 153–207.

Volgyes, Ivan *Political Socialisation in Eastern Europe: a Comparative Framework*, New York, Praeger, 1975.

Waller, Michael *The End of the Communist Power Monopoly*, Manchester, Manchester University Press, 1993.

Waller, Michael (ed.) *Party Politics in Eastern Europe*, special issue of *Party Politics*, vol. 1, no. 4, London, Sage, 1995.

Waller, Michael, Coppieters, Bruno and Deschouwer, Kris *Social Democracy in a Post-Communist Europe*, Ilford and Portland, Oregon, Frank Cass, 1994.

Waller, Michael and Myant, M. R. (eds) *Parties, Trade Unions and Society in East-Central Europe*, special issue of *Journal of Communist Studies*, vol. 9, no. 4, London, Cass, 1993.

Walters, Philip (ed.) *World Christianity: Eastern Europe*, with a foreword by Michael Bourdeaux, Eastbourne, MARC, 1988.

Wandycz, Piotr S. *The Price of Freedom: a History of East Central Europe from the Middle Ages to the Present*, London, Routledge, 1992.

Warriner, Doreen *Revolution in Eastern Europe*, London, Turnstile Press, 1950.

Warriner, Doreen 'The Population Question in Eastern Europe', *Slavonic and East European Review*, vol. 16, no. 48 (April 1938), pp. 629–37.

Watt, Donald Cameron *How War Came: the Immediate Origins of the Second World War, 1938–1939*, London, Heinemann, 1989.

White, S. *Communist and Postcommunist Political Systems: an Introduction*, London and Basingstoke, Macmillan, 1990.

White, S., Batt, J. and Lewis, Paul G. (eds) *Developments in East European Politics*, Basingstoke, Macmillan, 1993.

White, S., Gardiner, J. and Schöpflin, G. *Communist Political Systems: an Introduction*, London and Basingstoke, Macmillan, 1987.

Whitefield, Stephen (ed.) *The New Institutional Architecture of Eastern Europe*, Basingstoke, Macmillan, 1993.

Wiles, Peter J. 'East Central Europe as an Active Element in the Soviet Empire', in Milorad M. Drachkovitch (ed.) *East Central Europe: Yesterday = Today = Tomorrow*, Stanford, Cal., Hoover Institution Press, 1982, pp. 81–105.

Zagorov, S. D. *The Agrarian Economy of the Danubian Countries, 1935–1945*, Stanford, Cal., Stanford University Press, 1955.

Zeman, Z. A. B. *The Break-Up of the Habsburg Empire, 1914–1918: a Study in National and Social Revolution*, London, Oxford University Press, 1961.

Zeman, Z. A. B. *Pursued by a Bear: the Making of Eastern Europe*, London, Chatto & Windus, 1989; amended and republished as *The Making and Breaking of Communist Europe*, Oxford, Blackwell, 1991.

Zloch-Christy, Iliana *Eastern Europe in a Time of Change: Economic and Political Dimensions*, Westport, Conn., Praeger, 1994.

THE BALKANS

Barker, Elizabeth *British Policy in South-East Europe in the Second World War*, London and Basingstoke, Macmillan, 1976.

Carter, F. W. and Norris, H. T. (eds) *The Changing Shape of the Balkans*, London, University College London Press, 1996.

Crefeld, Martin van *Hitler's Strategy 1940–1941: the Balkan Clue*, Cambridge, Cambridge University Press, 1973.

Cviić, Christopher *Remaking the Balkans*, London, Pinter for the Royal Institute of International Affairs (Chatham House Papers), 1991.

Deakin, William, Barker, Elizabeth and Chadwick, Jonathan *British Political Strategy in Central, Eastern and Southern Europe in 1944*, London and Basingstoke, Macmillan, 1988.

Eyal, Jonathan (ed.) *The Warsaw Pact and the Balkans: Moscow's Southern Flank*, London and Basingstoke, Macmillan, 1989.

Hösch, Edgar *Geschichte der Balkanländer: von der Frühzeit bis zur Gegenwart*, Munich, C. H. Beck, 1988.

Jelavich, Barbara *History of the Balkans*, 2 vols, Cambridge, Cambridge University Press, 1983.

Jelavich, Charles and Jelavich, Barbara *The Establishment of the Balkan National States, 1804–1920*, A History of East Central Europe, vol. VIII, Seattle, University of Washington Press, 1977.

King, Robert R. *Minorities under Communism: Nationalities as a Source of Tension among Balkan Communist States*, Cambridge, Mass., Harvard University Press, 1973.

Lendvai, Paul *Eagles in Cobwebs: Nationalism and Communism in the Balkans*, London, Macdonald, 1969.

Momtchiloff, N. *Ten Years of Controlled Trade in South-Eastern Europe*, National Institute of Economic and Social Research, Occasional Papers no. VI, Cambridge, Cambridge University Press, 1944.

Orlow, Dietrich *The Nazis in the Balkans: a Case Study of Totalitarian Politics*, Pittsburgh, Penn., University of Pittsburgh Press, 1968.

Poulton, Hugh *The Balkans: Minorities and States in Conflict*, London, Minority Rights Publications, 1991.

Shoup, Paul S. and Hoffman, George W. *Problems of Balkan Security: Southeastern Europe in the 1990s*, Washington, D.C., The Wilson Center Press, 1990.

Stavrianos, S. *The Balkans since 1453*, Hinsdale, Ill., Dryden Press, 1958.

Stoianovich, Traian *Balkan Worlds: the First and the Last Europe*, Sources and Studies in World History, Armonk, N.Y. and London, M. E. Sharpe, 1994.

Sugar, Peter F. *Southeastern Europe under Ottoman Rule, 1354–1804*, A History of East Central Europe, vol. V, Seattle, University of Washington Press, 1977.

Todorov, Kosta *Balkan Firebrand: the Autobiography of a Rebel, Soldier, and Statesman*, Chicago, Ziff-Davis, 1943.

Troebst, Stefan *Mussolini, Makedonien und die Mächte, 1922–1930*, Cologne and Vienna, Böhlau, 1987.

Winnifrith, T. J. *The Vlachs: the History of a Balkan People*, London, Duckworth, 1987.

Wolff, Robert Lee *The Balkans in our Time*, Cambridge, Mass., Harvard University Press, 1956.

THE BALTIC STATES, AND BELORUSSIA

Ahmann, Rolf 'Nazi German policy towards the Baltic states on the eve of the Second World War', in John Hiden and Thomas Lane (eds) *The Baltic and the Outbreak of the Second World War*, Cambridge, Cambridge University Press, 1992, pp. 50–72.

Applebaum, Anne 'Simulated Birth of a Nation', *The Spectator*, 29 February 1992.

Child, J. 'The Ukraine under German Occupation', in Arnold Toynbee and Veronica M. Toynbee, *Hitler's Europe*, Survey of International Affairs 1939–1946, London, Oxford University Press, 1954, pp. 632–47.

Dreifels, Juris *Latvia in Transition*, Cambridge, Cambridge University Press, 1996.

Dreifels, Juris 'Latvian National Rebirth', *Problems of Communism*, vol. 38, no. 4 (July–Aug. 1989), pp. 77–95.

Hiden, John and Lane, Thomas (eds) *The Baltic and the Outbreak of the Second World War*, Cambridge, Cambridge University Press, 1992.

Hiden, John and Salmon, Patrick *The Baltic Nations and Europe: Estonia, Latvia and Lithuania in the Twentieth Century*, London and New York, Longman, 1991.

Kirby, D. G. *The Baltic World, 1772–1993: Europe's Northern Periphery in an Age of Change*, London, Longman, 1995.

Krivickas, V. 'The Polish Minority in Lithuania, 1918–26', *Slavonic and East European Review*, vol. 53, no. 130 (1970), pp. 67–87.

Lieven, Anatol *The Baltic Revolution: Latvia, Lithuania, Estonia and the Path to Independence*, New Haven and London, Yale University Press, 1993.

Misiunas, Romuald J. 'Fascist Tendencies in Lithuania', *Slavonic and East European Review*, vol. 48, no. 110 (1970), pp. 88–109.

Misiunas, Romuald J. and Taagepera, Rein *The Baltic States: Years of Dependence, 1940–1980*, London, Hurst, 1983.

Rauch, Georg von *The Baltic States: the Years of Independence: Estonia, Latvia, Lithuania 1917–1940*, London, Hurst, 1974.

Sakwa, George 'The Polish Ultimatum to Lithuania in March 1938', *Slavonic and East European Review*, vol. 55, no. 2 (April 1977), pp. 204–26.

Smith, Graham (ed.) *The Baltic States: the National Self-Determination of Estonia, Latvia, and Lithuania*, Basingstoke, Macmillan, 1996.

Stephens, David 'The German Problem in Memel', *Slavonic and East European Review*, vol. 14, no. 41 (Jan. 1936), pp. 321–31.

Swettenham, John Alexander *The Tragedy of the Baltic States: a Report Compiled from Official Documents and Eyewitnesses' Stories*, London, Hollis and Carter, 1952.

Taagepera, Rein *Estonia: Return to Independence*, Boulder, Colo. and Oxford, Westview Press, 1993.

Vardys, Stanley V. (ed.) *Lithuania under the Soviets: Portrait of a Nation, 1940–1965*, New York, Praeger, 1965.

Vardys, V. Stanley 'Lithuanian National Politics', *Problems of Communism*, vol. 38, no. 4 (July–Aug. 1989), pp. 53–76.

Zaprudnik, Jan 'Belorussian Reawakening', *Problems of Communism*, vol. 38, no. 4 (July–Aug. 1989), pp. 36–52.

ALBANIA

Bartl, Peter *Albanien vom Mittelalter bis zur Gegenwart*, Ost- und Südosteuropa, Geschichte der Länder und Völker, Regensburg and Munich, Verlag Friedrich Pustet with the Südosteuropa-Gesellschaft, 1995.

Fischer, Bernd Jürgen *King Zog and the Struggle for Stability in Albania*, East European

Monographs, no. CLIX, New York and Boulder, Colo., Columbia University Press and East European Monographs, 1984.

Fontana, Dorothy Grouse 'Recent Sino-Albanian Relations', *Survey*, vol. 21, no. 4 (97, Autumn 1975), pp. 121–44.

Gardiner, Leslie *The Eagle Spreads his Claws: a History of the Corfu Channel Dispute and of Albania's Relations with the West, 1945–1965*, Edinburgh and London, William Blackwood & Sons, 1966.

Halliday, J. *The Artful Albanian: the Memoirs of Enver Hoxha*, London, Chatto & Windus, 1986.

Hocevar, T. 'The Albanian Economy 1912–1944: a Survey', *Journal of European Economic History*, vol. 16, no. 3 (Winter 1987), pp. 561–8.

Logoreci, Anton *The Albanians: Europe's Forgotten Survivors*, London, Gollancz, 1977.

Pano, Nicholas C. *The People's Republic of Albania*, Baltimore, Md, Johns Hopkins University Press, 1968.

Pano, Nicholas C. 'The Albanian Cultural Revolution', *Problems of Communism*, vol. 23, no. 4 (July–Aug. 1974), pp. 44–57.

Pano, Nicholas C. 'Albania in the 1970s', *Problems of Communism*, vol. 26, no. 6 (Nov.–Dec. 1977), pp. 33–43.

Pollo, Stefanaq *The History of Albania from its Origins to the Present Day*, English translation by Carol Wiseman and Ginnie Hole, London, Routledge & Kegan Paul, 1981.

Prifti, Peter R. 'Albania and the Sino-Soviet Conflict', *Studies in Comparative Communism*, vol. 6, no. 3 (Autumn 1973), pp. 241–79.

Schmidt-Neke, Michael *Entstehung und Ausbau der Königsdiktatur in Albanien (1912–1939): Regierungsbildungen, Herrschaftsweise und Machteliten in einem jungen Balkanstaat*, Südosteuropäische Arbeiten no. 84, Munich, R. Oldenbourg, 1987.

Skendi, Stavro *The Albanian National Awakening, 1878–1912*, Princeton, N.J., Princeton University Press, 1967.

Skendi, Stavro (ed.) *Albania*, New York, Praeger, 1956.

Swire, J. *Albania, the Rise of a Kingdom*, London, Williams & Norgate, 1929.

Swire, J. *King Zog's Albania*, London, Rupert Hale, 1937.

Vickers, Miranda *The Albanians: a Modern History*, London, Tauris, 1995.

BULGARIA

Bell, John D. *Peasants in Power: Alexander Stamboliski and the Bulgarian Agrarian National Union, 1899–1923*, Princeton, N.J., Princeton University Press, 1977.

Bell, John D. *The Bulgarian Communist Party from Blagoev to Zhivkov*, Stanford, Cal., Hoover Institution Press, 1986.

Black, Cyril E. 'The Start of the Cold War in Bulgaria: a Personal View', *Review of Politics*, vol. XLI, no. 2 (1979), pp. 163–202.

Boll, Michael B. *Cold War in the Balkans: American Foreign Policy and the Emergence of Communist Bulgaria, 1943–1947*, Lexington, The University Press of Kentucky, 1984.

Boll, Michael B. (ed.) *The American Military Mission in the Allied Control Commission for Bulgaria, 1944–1947: History and Transcripts*, East European Monographs, no. CLXXVI, New York and Boulder, Colo., Columbia University Press and East European Monographs, 1985.

Boll, Michael B. 'Reality and Illusion: the Allied Control Commission for Bulgaria as a Cause of the Cold War', *East European Quarterly*, vol. 17, no. 4 (Winter 1983), pp. 417–36.

Boll, Michael B. 'Pro-Monarchist to Pro-Muscovite: the Transformation of the Bulgarian Army, 1944–1948', *East European Quarterly*, vol. 20, no. 4 (Jan. 1987), pp. 409–28.

Bristow, John A. *The Bulgarian Economy in Transition*, Studies of Communism in Transition, Cheltenham and Brookfield, Vt, Edward Elgar, 1996.

Brown, J. F. *Bulgaria under Communist Rule*, London, Pall Mall Press, 1970.

Chakûrov, Kostadin *Vtoriya Etazh* (The Second Floor), Sofia, no publisher indicated, 1990.

Chary, Frederick *The Bulgarian Jews and the Final Solution, 1940–1944*, Pittsburgh, Penn., University of Pittsburgh Press, 1972.

Chary, Frederick 'The Bulgarian Writers' Protest of 1940 against the Introduction of Anti-Semitic Legislation into the Kingdom of Bulgaria', *East European Quarterly*, vol. 4, no. 1 (Mar. 1970), pp. 88–93.

Crampton, Richard J. *Bulgaria 1878–1918: a History*, East European Monographs, no. CXXXVIII, New York and Boulder, Colo., Columbia University Press and East European Monographs, 1983.

Crampton, R. J. *A Short History of Modern Bulgaria*, Cambridge, Cambridge University Press, 1987.

Crampton, R. J. *A Concise History of Bulgaria*, Cambridge, Cambridge University Press, 1997.

Crampton, Richard J. ' "Stumbling and Dusting Off" or an Attempt to Pick a Path through the Thicket of Bulgaria's New Economic Mechanism', *East European Politics and Societies*, vol. 2, no. 2 (Spring 1988), pp. 333–95.

Crampton, R. J. 'The Intelligentsia, the Ecology and the Opposition in Bulgaria', *The World Today*, vol. 46, no. 2 (Feb. 1990), pp. 23–6.

Garson, Robert 'Churchill's Spheres of Interest: Bulgaria and Rumania', *Survey*, vol. 24, no. 3 (108, Summer 1979), pp. 143–58.

Grothusen, Klaus-Detlev (ed.) *Bulgarien*, Südosteuropa–Handbuch, vol. VI, Göttingen, Vandenhoeck & Ruprecht, 1990.

Groueff, Stephane *Crown of Thorns: the Reign of King Boris III of Bulgaria, 1918–1943*, Lanham, Md and London, Madison Books, 1987.

Horner, John E. 'The Ordeal of Nikola Petkov and the Consolidation of Communist Rule in Bulgaria', *Survey*, vol. 20, no. 1 (90, Winter 1974), pp. 75–83.

Horner, John E. 'Traicho Kostov: Stalinist Orthodoxy in Bulgaria', *Survey*, vol. 24, no. 3 (108, Summer 1979), pp. 135–42.

Lampe, John R. *The Bulgarian Economy in the Twentieth Century*, London, Croom Helm, 1986.

Markov, Georgi *The Truth that Killed*, translated by Liliana Brisby with an introduction by Annabel Markov, London, Weidenfeld & Nicolson, 1983.

Miller, Marshall Lee *Bulgaria during the Second World War*, Stanford, Cal., Stanford University Press, 1975.

Oren, Nissan *Bulgarian Communism: the Road to Power, 1934–1944*, New York and London, Columbia University Press, 1971.

Oren, Nissan *Revolution Administered: Agrarianism and Communism in Bulgaria*, Baltimore, Md, Johns Hopkins University Press, 1973.

Padev, Michael *Dimitrov Wastes No Bullets: the Inside Story of the Trial and Murder of Nikola Petkov (leader of the Bulgarian Agrarian Party)*, London, Eyre & Spottiswoode, 1948.

Rothschild, Joseph *The Communist Party of Bulgaria: Origins and Development, 1883–1936*, New York, Columbia University Press, 1959.

Simşir, Bilal N. *The Turks of Bulgaria (1878–1985)*, London, K. Rustem & Brother, 1988.

Slavov, Atanas *The 'Thaw' in Bulgarian Literature*, East European Monographs, no. XXIV, New York and Boulder, Colo., Columbia University Press and East European Monographs, 1981.

Slavov, Atanas *With the Precision of Bats: the Sweet and Sour Story of Real Bulgaria during the Last Fifty Years or So*, Washington, D.C., Occidental Press, 1986.

Swire, J. *Bulgarian Conspiracy*, London, Rupert Hale, 1939.

Todor Zhivkov: Statesman and Builder of New Bulgaria, edited by Robert Maxwell, second revised edition, Oxford, Pergamon Press, 1985.

Zloch-Christy, Iliana *Bulgaria in a Time of Change: Economic and Political Dimensions*, Aldershot and Brookfield, Vt, Ashgate Publishing, 1996.

CZECHOSLOVAKIA

'A German Bohemian Deputy' 'The German Minority in Czechoslovakia' *Slavonic and East European Review*, vol. 14, no. 41 (Jan. 1936), pp. 295–300.

Anderle, Josef 'The First Republic, 1918–1938', in Hans Brisch and Ivan Volgyes (eds) *Czechoslovakia: the Heritage of Ages Past; Essays in Memory of Josef Korbel*, East European Monographs, no. LI, New York and Boulder, Colo., Columbia University Press and East European Monographs, 1979.

Beneš, Eduard *The Memoirs of Dr Eduard Beneš: from Munich to New War and New Victory*, translated by Godfrey Lias, reprint edition, Westport, Conn., Greenwood Press, 1978.

Burks, R. V. 'The Decline of Communism in Czechoslovakia', *Studies in Comparative Communism*, vol. 2, no. 1 (Jan. 1969), pp. 21–49.

Čapek, Emanuel 'The Background of Political Parties in Czechoslovakia', *Slavonic and East European Review*, vol. 10, no. 28 (June 1931), pp. 90–104.

Čapek, Karel 'A Representative Czech: Antonin Svehla' *Slavonic and East European Review*, vol. 7, no. 20 (Jan. 1929), pp. 268–71.

Crane, J. O. 'Church and State in Czechoslovakia', *Slavonic and East European Review*, vol. 6, no. 17 (Dec. 1927), pp. 364–78.

Dubček's Blueprint for Freedom, London, William Kimber, 1968.

Duff, Sheila Grant *A German Protectorate: the Czechs under Nazi Rule*, reprint edition, London, Cass, 1970.

Golan, Galia *The Czechoslovak Reform Movement: Communism in Crisis, 1962–1968*, Cambridge, Cambridge University Press, 1971.

Golan, Galia *Reform Rule in Czechoslovakia: the Dubček Era, 1968–1969*, Cambridge, Cambridge University Press, 1973.

Golan, Galia 'Youth and Politics in Czechoslovakia', *Journal of Contemporary History*, vol. 5, no. 1 (Jan. 1970), pp. 3–22.

Hanak, H. (ed.) *T. G. Masaryk (1850–1937)*, 2 vols, London and Basingstoke, Macmillan, 1990.

Hermann, A. H. *A History of the Czechs*, London, Allen Lane, 1975.

Kaplan, Karel *The Short March: the Communist Takeover in Czechoslovakia 1945–1948*, London, Hurst, 1987.

Kaplan, Karel *Report on the Murder of the General Secretary*, translated by Karel Kovenda, London, Tauris, 1990.

Kavan, Rosemary *Freedom at a Price: an Englishwoman's Life in Czechoslovakia*, introduction by William Shawcross and an epilogue by Jan Kavan, London, Verso, 1985.

Klima, Ivan *The Spirit of Prague and Other Essays*, London, Granta in association with Penguin, 1994.

Kohák, Erazim 'Making and Writing History', in Norman Stone and Eduard Strouhal, *Czechoslovakia: Crossroads and Crises, 1918–88*, London, Macmillan in association with the BBC World Service, 1989, pp. 183–206.

Korbel, Josef *The Communist Subversion of Czechoslovakia, 1938–1948*, Princeton, N.J., Princeton University Press, 1959.

Korbel, Josef *Twentieth-Century Czechoslovakia: the Meanings of Its History*, New York, Columbia University Press, 1977.

Kraus, Michael 'The Thaw and Frost: the Prague Spring and Moscow Nights, Ten Years After', *East Central Europe*, vol. 6, no. 1 (1979), pp. 63–75.

Krejči, Jaroslav *Social Change and Stratification in Postwar Czechoslovakia*, London and Basingstoke, Macmillan, 1972.

Kusin, Vladimir V. *The Intellectual Origins of the Prague Spring: the Development of Reformist Ideas in Czechoslovakia*, Cambridge, Cambridge University Press, 1971.

Kusin, Vladimir V. *Political Grouping in the Czechoslovak Reform Movement*, London and Basingstoke, Macmillan, 1972.

Kusin, Vladimir V. *From Dubček to Charter 77: a Study of Normalisation in Czechoslovakia, 1968–1978*, Edinburgh, Q Press, 1978.

Kusin, Vladimir V. 'Husák's Czechoslovakia and Economic Stagnation', *Problems of Communism*, vol. 31, no. 3 (May–June 1982), pp. 24–37.

Loebl, Erzen and others 'A Symposium on Czechoslovakia', *Studies in Comparative Communism*, vol. 2, no. 2 (April 1969), pp. 74–94.

Luža, Radomir *The Transfer of the Sudeten Germans: a Study of Czech-German Relations, 1933–1962*, London, Routledge & Kegan Paul, 1964.

Maček, Josef 'Land Reform in Czechoslovakia', *Slavonic and East European Review*, vol. 1, no. 1 (June 1922), pp. 144–50.

Mamatey, Victor S. 'The Development of Czechoslovak Democracy, 1920–1938', in Victor S. Mamatey and Radomir Luža, *A History of the Czechoslovak Republic, 1918–1948*, Princeton, N.J., Princeton University Press, 1973, pp. 99–166.

Mamatey, Victor S. and Luža, Radomir *A History of the Czechoslovak Republic, 1918–1948*, Princeton, N.J., Princeton University Press, 1973

Mastny, Vojtech *The Czechs under Nazi Rule: the Failure of National Resistance, 1939–1942*, New York, Cambridge University Press, 1971.

Mňačko, Ladislav *The Seventh Night: a Personal Inside View of the First Week of the Occupation of Czechoslovakia – and of the Previous 30 Years*, with a foreword by Harry Schwarz, London, Dent, 1968.

Musil, Jiři *The End of Czechoslovakia*, Budapest and London, Central European University Press, 1995.

Myant, M. R. *Socialism and Democracy in Czechoslovakia, 1945–1948*, Cambridge, Cambridge University Press, 1981.

Nečas, Jaromir 'Economic and Social Problems in German-Bohemia', *Slavonic and East European Review*, vol. 15, no. 45 (April 1937), pp. 599–611.

Olivová, Vera *The Doomed Democracy: Czechoslovakia in a Disrupted Europe, 1914–38*, London, Sidgwick & Jackson, 1972.

Palaček, Anthony 'Antonin Svehla: Czech Peasant Statesman', *American Slavic and East European Review*, vol. 21, no. 4 (Dec. 1962), pp. 699–708.

Palaček, Anthony 'The Rise and Fall of the Czechoslovak Agrarian Party', *East European Quarterly*, vol. 5, no. 2 (June 1971), pp. 177–201.

Pelikán, Jiři *Socialist Opposition in Eastern Europe: the Czechoslovak Example*, translated by Marian Sling and V. and R. Tosek, London, Allison & Busby, 1976.

Pelikán, Jiři (ed.), *The Czechoslovak Political Trials, 1950–1954: the Suppressed Report of the Dubček Government's Commission of Inquiry, 1968*, London, Macdonald, 1970.

Renner, Hans *A History of Czechoslovakia since 1945*, London, Routledge, 1989.

Schwartz, Harry *Prague's 200 Days: the Struggle for Democracy in Czechoslovakia*, London, Pall Mall Press, 1969.

Schwarz, Karl-Peter *Tschechen und Slowaken: der lange Weg zur friedlichen Trennung*, Vienna, Europa Verlag, 1993.

Selucky, Radoslav *Czechoslovakia: the Plan that Failed*, with an introduction by Kamil Winter, London, Thomas Nelson & Sons, 1970.

Seton-Watson, R. W. *A History of the Czechs and Slovaks*, London, Hutchinson, 1943.

Shawcross, William *Dubček*, London, Weidenfeld & Nicolson, 1970.

Skilling, H. Gordon *Czechoslovakia's Interrupted Revolution*, Princeton, N.J., Princeton University Press, 1976.

Skilling, H. Gordon *Charter 77 and Human Rights in Czechoslovakia*, London, Allen & Unwin, 1981.

Skilling, H. Gordon 'Revolution and Continuity in Czechoslovakia, 1945–1946' *Journal of Central European Affairs*, vol. 20, no. 4 (Jan. 1961), pp. 357–77.

Smelser, Ronald M. *The Sudeten Problem 1933–1938: Volkstumpolitik and the Formulation of Nazi Foreign Policy*, Middletown, Conn., Wesleyan University Press, 1975.

Sobota, Emil 'Czechs and Germans: a Czech View', *Slavonic and East European Review*, vol. 14, no. 41 (Jan. 1936), pp. 301–20.

Stone, Norman and Stouhal, Eduard *Crossroads and Crises: Czechoslovakia 1918–1988*, London, Macmillan in association with the BBC World Service, 1989

Sviták, Ivan *The Czechoslovak Experiment, 1968–1969*, New York and London, Columbia University Press, 1971.

Szporluk, R. 'Masaryk's Idea of Democracy', *Slavonic and East European Review*, vol. 41, no. 96 (Dec. 1962), pp. 31–49.

Táborsky, Edward *Czechoslovak Democracy at Work*, with a foreword by Sir Ernest Barker, London, George Allen & Unwin, 1945.

Táborsky, Edward *Communism in Czechoslovakia, 1940–1960*, Princeton, N.J., Princeton University Press, 1961.

Táborsky, Edward *President Edvard Beneš: Between East and West, 1938–1948*, Stanford, Cal., Hoover Institution Press, 1981.

Táborsky, Edward 'Local Government in Czechoslovakia, 1918–1948', *American Slavic and East European Review*, vol. 10, no. 3 (1951), pp. 202–15.

Teichova, Alice *The Czechoslovak Economy 1918–1920*, London, Routledge, 1988.

Thomson, S. Harrison *Czechoslovakia in European History*, Princeton, N.J., Princeton University Press, 1943.

Tigrid, Pavel *Why Dubček Fell*, London, Macdonald, 1969.

Tigrid, Pavel 'Czechoslovakia: a Post Mortem; Part I', *Survey*, vol. 15, no. 73 (Autumn 1969), pp. 133–64.

Tigrid, Pavel 'Czechoslovakia: a Post Mortem; Part II', *Survey*, vol. 16, no. 74/5 (Winter/Spring 1970), pp. 112–42.

Ulc, O. *Politics in Czechoslovakia*, with a foreword by Jan F. Triska, San Francisco, W. H. Freeman, 1974.

Valenta, J. *Soviet Intervention in Czechoslovakia, 1968: Anatomy of a Decision*, Baltimore, Md, Johns Hopkins University Press, 1979.

Warren, W. Preston *Masaryk's Democracy: a Philosophy of Scientific and Moral Culture*, London, George Allen and Unwin, 1941.

Weiss, John 'Fascism in Czechoslovakia, 1919–1939', *East Central Europe*, vol. 4, no. 1 (1977), pp. 35–43.

Wightman, Gordon 'The Changing Role of the Central Party Institutions in Czechoslovakia, 1962–69', *Studies in Comparative Communism*, vol. 34, no. 4 (Oct. 1981), pp. 401–20.

Windsor, Philip and Roberts, Adam *Czechoslovakia 1968: Reform, Repression, and Resistance*, London, Chatto & Windus, 1969.

Wingfield, Nancy 'Czech, German or Jew: the Jewish Community of Prague during the Inter-war Period', in Morrison, John (ed.) *The Czech and Slovak Experience*, pp. 218–30.

Wiskemann, Elizabeth *Czechs and Germans: a Study of the Struggle in the Historic Provinces of Bohemia and Moravia*, London, Oxford University Press, 1938.

Zeman, Z. A. B. *Prague Spring: A Report on Czechoslovakia 1968*, London, Penguin Books, 1969.

Zeman, Zbenek *The Masaryks; the Making of Czechoslovakia*, London, Tauris, 1990.

Zinner, Paul E. *Communist Strategy and Tactics in Czechoslovakia, 1918–48*, London, Pall Mall Press, 1963.

Zorach, Jonathan 'The Nationality Problem in the Czechoslovak Army between the Two World Wars', *East Central Europe*, vol. 5, no. 2 (1978), p. 169.

THE GDR

Baring, A. *Uprising in East Germany*, translated by Gerald Onn, Ithaca, N.Y. and London, Cornell University Press, 1972.

Caracciolo, Lucio 'Der Untergang der Sozialdemokratie in der sowietischen Besatzungszone. Otto Grotewohl und die "Einheit der Arbeiterklasse" 1945/46', *Vierteljahresheft für Zeitgeschichte*, vol. 36, no. 2 (April 1968), pp. 281–318.

Cate, Curtis *The Ides of August: the Berlin Wall Crisis of 1961*, London, Weidenfeld & Nicolson, 1978.

Childs, David *The GDR: Moscow's German Ally*, second edition, London, Unwin Hyman, 1988.

Childs, David (ed.) *Honecker's Germany*, London, Allen & Unwin, 1985.

Croan, Melvin 'Régime, Society and Nation: the GDR after Thirty Years', *East Central Europe*, vol. 6, no. 2 (1979), pp. 137–51.

Glass, George A. 'Church–State Relations in East Germany: Expanding Dimensions of an Unresolved Problem', *East Central Europe*, vol. 6, no. 2 (1979), pp. 232–49.

Krisch, Henry 'Nation Building and Régime Stability in the DDR', *East Central Europe*, vol. 3, no. 1 (1976), pp. 15–29.

Krisch, Henry 'Politics in the German Democratic Republic', *Studies in Comparative Communism*, vol. 9, no. 4 (Winter 1976), pp. 389–419.

Leonhard, Wolfgang *Child of the Revolution*, Chicago, Regnery, 1958.

McCauley, Martin *The German Democratic Republic since 1945*, London, Macmillan in association with the School of Slavonic and East European Studies, 1983.

Meuschel, Sigrid 'The End of "East German Socialism" ', *Telos*, no. 82 (Winter 1989–90), pp. 3–26.

Naimark, Norman *The Russians in Germany: a History of the Soviet Zone of Occupation, 1945–1949*, Cambridge, Mass. and London, Harvard University Press, 1995.

Nettl, J. P. *The Eastern Zone and Soviet Policy in Germany 1945–50*, London, Oxford University Press, 1951.

Offe, Klaus *Variations of Transition: the Eastern Europe and the East German Experience*, Oxford, Blackwell, and Cambridge, Polity, 1996.

Sandford, Gregory W. *From Hitler to Ulbricht: the Communist Reconstruction of East Germany, 1945–46*, Princeton, N.J., Princeton University Press, 1983.

Sandford, J. *The Sword and the Ploughshare: Autonomous Peace Initiatives in East Germany*, London, Merlin Press/CND, 1983.

Schneider, Eberhard *The GDR: the History, Politics, Economy and Society of East Germany*, translated by Hannes Adomeit and Roger Clarke, London, Hurst, 1978.

Shears, David *The Ugly Frontier*, London, Chatto & Windus, 1970.

Staritz, Dieter *Die Gründung der DDR: von der soujetischen Besatzungsherrschaft zum sozialistischen Staat*, Munich, Deutscher Taschenbuch Verlag, 1984.

Steele, J. *Socialism with a German Face: the State that came in from the Cold*, London, Cape 1977.

Weber, H. *Die DDR: 1945–1986*, Munich, R. Oldenbourg, 1988.

Woods, R. *Opposition in the GDR under Honecker, 1971–85: an Introduction and Documentation*, London and Basingstoke, Macmillan, 1986.

Woods, Roger 'East German Intellectuals in Opposition', *Survey*, vol. 28, no. 3 (122, Autumn 1984), pp. 111–23.

Zimmermann, Hartmut 'The GDR in the 1970s', *Problems of Communism*, vol. 27, no. 2 (Mar–April 1978), pp. 1–40.

HUNGARY

Aczel, Tamás *Ten Years After: a Commemoration of the Tenth Anniversary of the Hungarian Revolution*, London, Macgibbon & Kee, 1966.

Argentieri, Frederigo and Gianotti, Lorenzo *'Ottobre Ungharese*, Rome, Valerio Levi, 1986.

Ballogh, Eva S. 'Romania and the Allied Involvement in the Hungarian *Coup d'Etat* of 1919', *East European Quarterly*, vol. 9, no. 3 (Fall 1975), pp. 296–314.

Barany, George 'The Dragon's Teeth: the Roots of Hungarian Fascism', in Peter F. Sugar (ed.) *Native Fascism in the Successor States, 1918–45*, Santa Barbara, Cal., Clio, 1971, pp. 73–82.

Bell, Peter D. *Peasants in Socialist Transition: Life in a Collectivized Hungarian Village*, Berkeley and Los Angeles, University of California Press, 1984.

Berend, I. T. *The Hungarian Economic Reforms, 1953–88*, Cambridge, Cambridge University Press, 1990.

Berend, I. T. and Ranki, G. *Hungary: a Century of Economic Development*, Newton Abbot, David & Charles, 1974.

Bozóki, András 'Post-Communist Transition: Political Tendencies in Hungary', *East European Politics and Societies*, vol. 4, no. 2 (Spring 1990), pp. 211–30.

Büky, Barnabas 'Hungary's NEM on a Treadmill', *Problems of Communism*, vol. 21, no. 5 (Sept.–Oct. 1972), pp. 31–9.

Cohen, Asher 'Some Socio-Political Aspects of the Arrow Cross Party in Hungary', *East European Quarterly*, vol. 21, no. 3 (Sept. 1987), pp. 369–84.

Deák, István 'Hungary', in Hans Rogger and Eugen Weber (eds) *The European Right*, second edition, Berkeley and Los Angeles, University of California Press, 1974, pp. 364–407.

Don, Yehuda 'The Economic Dimensions of Anti-Semitism and Anti-Jewish Legislation in Hungary, 1938–1944', *East European Quarterly*, vol. 20, no. 4 (Jan. 1987), pp. 447–65.

Eddie, S. M. 'The Changing Pattern of Land Ownership in Hungary, 1867–1914', *The Economic History Review*, second series, vol. 20, no. 2 (1967), pp. 293–310.

Erös, J. 'Hungary' in S. J. Woolf (ed.) *Fascism in Europe*, London and New York, Methuen, 1981, pp. 117–50.

Fehér, F. and Heller, A. *Hungary 1956 Revisited: the Message of a Revolution – a quarter of a Century After*, London, Allen & Unwin, 1983.

Fenyo, Mario D. *Hitler, Horthy, and Hungary: German–Hungarian Relations, 1941–44*, New Haven, Conn. and London, Yale University Press, 1972.

Fryer, Peter *Hungarian Tragedy*, reprint edition, London, New Park Publications, 1986.

Gati, Charles *Hungary and the Soviet Bloc*, Durham, N.C., Duke University Press, 1986.

Gati, Charles 'The Kádár Mystique', *Problems of Communism*, vol. 23, no. 3 (May–June 1974), pp. 23–35.

Grothusen, Klaus-Detlev (ed.) *Ungarn*, Südosteuropa-Handbuch, vol. V, Göttingen, Vandenhoeck & Ruprecht, 1986.

Haraszti, Miklós *A Worker in a Workers' State: Piece-Rates in Hungary*, translated by Michael Wright with an introduction by Heinrich Böll, London, Penguin Books, 1981.

Hare, P. J. and Wanless, P. T. 'Polish and Hungarian Economic Reforms: a Comparison' *Soviet Studies*, vol. 33, no. 4 (Oct. 1981), pp. 491–517.

Heinrich, Hans-Georg *Hungary: Politics, Economics and Society*, London, Pinter, 1986.

Hoensch, Jörg K. *A History of Modern Hungary: 1867–1986*, translated by Kim Traynor, London, Longman, 1984.

Horthy, Admiral Nicholas *Memoirs*, London, Hutchinson, 1956.

Irving, David *Uprising: One Nation's Nightmare: Hungary 1956*, London, Hodder & Stoughton, 1981.

Janos, Andrew C. *The Politics of Backwardness in Hungary, 1825–1945*, Princeton, N.J., Princeton University Press, 1982.

Janos, Andrew C. and Slottman, William B. (eds) *Revolution in Perspective: Essays on the Hungarian Soviet Republic of 1919*, Berkeley, Los Angeles and London, University of California Press, 1971.

Kállay, Nicholas *Hungarian Premier: a Personal Account of a Nation's Struggle in the Second World War*, with a foreword by C. A. Macartney, London, Oxford University Press, 1954.

Karfunkel, Thomas 'The Impact of Trianon on the Jews of Hungary', in Béla K. Király, Peter Pastor and Ivan Sanders (eds) *Essays on World War I: Total War and Peacemaking: a Case Study on Trianon*, Brooklyn College Studies on Society in Change, East European Monographs, no. XV, New York and Boulder, Colo., Columbia University Press and East European Monographs, 1982, pp. 457–77.

Karolyi, Michael *Memoirs of Michael Karolyi: Faith Without Illusion*, London, Jonathan Cape, 1956.

Kenez, Peter 'Coalition Politics in the Hungarian Soviet Republic', in Andrew C. Janos and William B. Slottman (eds) *Revolution in Perspective: Essays on the Hungarian Soviet Republic of 1919*, Berkeley, Los Angeles and London, University of California Press, 1971, pp. 61–84.

Kertész, Stephen D. *Between Russia and the West: Hungary and the Illusions of Peacemaking, 1945–1947*, Notre Dame, Ind. and London, Notre Dame University Press, 1986.

Király, Béla and Jónás, Paul *The Hungarian Revolution of 1956 in Retrospect*, East European Monographs, no. XL, New York and Boulder, Colo., Columbia University Press and East European Monographs, 1978.

Király, Béla K., Pastor, Peter and Sanders, Ivan (eds) *Essays on World War I: Total War and Peacemaking: a Case Study on Trianon*, Brooklyn College Studies on Society in Change, East European Monographs, no. XV, New York and Boulder, Colo., Columbia University Press and East European Monographs, 1982.

Klay, Andor 'Hungarian Counterfeit Francs: a Case of Post World War I Political Sabotage', *Slavic Review*, vol. 33, no. 1 (Mar. 1974), pp. 107–13.

Kornai, Janos *The Road to a Free Economy: Shifting from a Socialist System: the Example of Hungary*, New York, Norton, 1990.

Kovrig, Bennett *Communism in Hungary: From Kun to Kádár*, Stanford, Cal., Hoover Institution Press, 1979.

Lomax, Bill *Hungary 1956*, London, Allison & Busby, 1976.

Lomax, Bill (ed.) *Eyewitness in Hungary: the Soviet Invasion of 1956*, Nottingham, Spokesman, 1980.

Löwenthal, Richard 'The Hungarian Soviet and International Communism' in Andrew C. Janos and William B. Slottman (eds) *Revolution in Perspective: Essays on the Hungarian Soviet Republic of 1919*, Berkeley, Los Angeles, University of California Press, 1971, pp. 173–81.

Macartney, C. A. *October Fifteenth: a History of Modern Hungary, 1929–1945*, 2 vols, Edinburgh, Edinburgh University Press, 1956.

Mikes, George *The Hungarian Revolution*, London, André Deutsch, 1957.

Molnár, Miklós *From Béla Kun to János Kádár: Seventy Years of Hungarian Communism*, translated by Arnold J. Pomerans, Oxford, Berg, 1990.

Nagy, Ferenc *The Struggle behind the Iron Curtain*, translated by Stephen K. Swift, New York, Macmillan, 1948.

Nagy, Zsuzsa L. *The Liberal Opposition in Hungary, 1919–1945*, Budapest, Akadémiai Kaidó, 1983.

Nagy-Talevara, Nicholas M. *The Green Shirts and Others: a History of Fascism in Hungary and Romania*, Stanford, Cal., Stanford University Press, 1970.

Paloczy-Horváth, George *In Darkest Hungary*, London, Gollancz, 1944.

Paloczy-Horváth, George *The Undefeated*, London, Secker & Warburg, 1959.

Pastor, Peter 'The Vix Mission in Hungary, 1918–1919: a Reexamination', *Slavic Review*, vol. 29, no. 3 (Sept. 1970), pp. 481–98.

Radványi, János *Hungary and the Superpowers: the 1956 Revolution and Realpolitik*, Stanford, Cal., Hoover Institution Press, 1972.

Sakmyster, Thomas L. 'Great Britain and the Making of the Treaty of Trianon', in Béla K. Király, Peter Pastor and Ivan Sanders (eds) *Essays on World War I: Total War and Peacemaking: a Case Study on Trianon*, Brooklyn College Studies on Society in Change, East European Monographs, no. XV, New York and Boulder, Colo., Columbia University Press and East European Monographs, 1982, pp. 107–29.

Scarlett, Dora 'Window onto Hungary', in Bill Lomax (ed.) *Eyewitness in Hungary: the Soviet Invasion of 1956*, Nottingham, Spokesman, 1980, pp. 26–82.

Shawcross, William *Crime and Compromise: János Kádár and the Politics of Hungary since Revolution*, London, Weidenfeld & Nicolson, 1974.

Street, C. J. C. *Hungary and Democracy*, London, Unwin, 1923.

Sugar, P. (ed.) *A History of Hungary*, London, Tauris, 1990.

Szelenyi, Ivan 'Alternative Features for Eastern Europe: the Case for Hungary', *East European Politics and Societies*, vol. 4, no. 2 (Spring 1990), pp. 231–54.

Tökés, Rudolf L. *Béla Kun and the Hungarian Soviet Republic: the Origins and Role of the Communist Party of Hungary in the Revolutions of 1918–1919*, New York, Praeger, 1967.

Tökés, Rudolf L. *Hungary's Negotiated Revolution: Economic Reform, Social Change, and Political Succession, 1957–1990*, Cambridge Russian, Soviet and Post-Soviet Studies, no. CI, Cambridge, Cambridge University Press, 1996.

Tökés, Rudolf L. 'Polycentrism: Central European and Hungarian Origins', *Studies in Comparative Communism*, vol. 6, no. 4 (Winter 1973), pp. 414–28.

Tökés, Rudolf L. 'Hungarian Reform Imperatives', *Problems of Communism*, vol. 33, no. 5 (Sept.–Oct. 1984), pp. 1–23.

Tökés, Rudolf L. 'Hungary's New Political Elites: Adaptation to Change, 1989–90', *Problems of Communism*, vol. 39, no. 6 (Nov.–Dec. 1990), pp. 44–65.

Unwin, Peter *Voice in the Wilderness: Imre Nagy and the Hungarian Revolution*, with a foreword by the president of the Hungarian Republic, Arpád Göncz, London, Macdonald, 1991.

Vali, Ferenc A. *Rift and Revolt in Hungary: Nationalism versus Communism*, Cambridge, Mass., Harvard University Press, 1961.

Volgyes, Ivan *Hungary: a Nation of Contradictions*, Epping, Bowker, 1985.

Zinner, Paul E. *National Communism and Popular Revolt in Eastern Europe: a Selection of Documents on Events in Poland and Hungary, February–November 1956*, New York, Columbia University Press, 1956.

Zinner, Paul E. *Revolution in Hungary*, New York, Columbia University Press, 1962.

Zinner, Paul E. 'Revolution in Hungary: Reflections on the Vicissitudes of a Totalitarian System', *Journal of Politics*, vol. 21, no. 1 (Feb. 1959), pp. 3–36.

POLAND AND UKRAINE

Andrusiak, N. 'The Ukranian Movement in Galicia: I', *Slavonic and East European Review*, vol. 14, no. 40 (July 1935), pp. 163–75.

Andrusiak, N. 'The Ukranian Movement in Galicia: II', *Slavonic and East European Review*, vol. 14, no. 41 (Jan. 1936), pp. 372–9.

Anonymous, *From Serfdom to Self Government: Memoirs of a Polish Village Mayor, 1842–1927*, translated from the Polish by William John Rose and with an Introduction by Stanisław Kot, London, Minerva, 1941.

Ascherson, Neal *The Polish August: the Self-Limiting Revolution*, London, Penguin Books, 1982.

Ascherson, Neal *The Struggles for Poland*, London, Michael Joseph, 1987.

Benes, Václav and Pounds, Norman G. J. *Poland*, London, Benn, 1970.

Bethel, Nicholas *Gomułka: his Poland and his Communism*, London, Longman, 1969.

Blit, Lucjan *The Eastern Pretender: the Story of Boleslaw Piasecki*, London, Hutchinson, 1965.

Bloch, Alfred (ed.) *The Real Poland: an Anthology of National Self-Perception*, New York, Continuum, 1982.

Bloch, Alfred 'Poland in the Present', in Alfred Bloch (ed.) *The Real Poland: an Anthology of National Self-Perception*, New York, Continuum, 1982, pp. 53–70.

Boyes, Roger and Moody, John *The Priest who had to Die: the Tragedy of Father Jerzy Popiełuszko*, London, Gollancz, 1986.

Browning, Christopher R. 'Nazi Ghettoization in Poland, 1939–41', *Central European History*, vol. 19, no. 4 (Dec. 1987), pp. 343–68.

Bruce, George *The Warsaw Uprising, 1 August–2 October 1944*, London, Hart-Davis, 1972.

Ciechanowski, Jan M. *The Warsaw Rising of 1944*, Cambridge, Cambridge University Press, 1974.

Cienciala, Anna M. *Poland and the Western Powers, 1938–1939: a Study in the Interdependence of Eastern and Western Europe*, London, Routledge & Kegan Paul, 1968.

Cienciala, Anna M. and Komarnicki, Titus *From Versailles to Locarno: Keys to Polish Foreign Policy, 1919–1925*, Lawrence, Kansas, University Press of Kansas, 1984.

Coutouvidis, John and Reynolds, Jaimie *Poland: 1939–1947*, Leicester, Leicester University Press, 1986.

Davies, Norman *White Eagle, Red Star: the Polish-Soviet War, 1919–1920*, with a foreword by A. J. P. Taylor, London, Macdonald, 1972.

Davies, Norman *God's Playground: a History of Poland*, 2 vols, Oxford, Clarendon Press, 1981.

Davies, Norman *Heart of Europe: a Short History of Poland*, Oxford, Oxford University Press, 1986.

Dziewanowski, M. K. *Joseph Piłsudski: a European Federalist*, Stanford, Cal., Hoover Institution Press, 1969.

Dziewanowski, M. K. *Poland in the 20th Century*, New York, Columbia University Press, 1977.

Fountain, Alvin Marcus II *Roman Dmowski: Party, Tactics, Ideology 1895–1907*, East European Monographs no. X, New York and Boulder, Colo., Columbia University Press and East European Monographs, 1980.

Friszke, Andrzej 'The Polish Political Scene (1989)', *East European Politics and Societies*, vol. 4, no. 2 (Spring 1990), pp. 305–41.

Garlinski, Józef *Poland in the Second World War*, London and Basingstoke, Macmillan, 1985.

Garton Ash, Timothy *The Polish Revolution: Solidarity 1980–82*, London, Jonathan Cape, 1983.

Groth, Alexander J. 'Proportional Representation in Pre-War Poland', *American Slavic and East European Review*, vol. 23, no. 1 (Mar. 1964), pp. 102–16.

Groth, Alexander J. 'Polish Elections, 1919–1928', *Slavic Review*, vol. 24, no. 4 (Dec. 1965), pp. 653–65.

Groth, Alexander J. 'The Legacy of Three Crises: Parliament and Ethnic Issue In Pre-War Poland', *Slavic Review*, vol. 27, no. 4 (Dec. 1968), pp. 564–80.

Hahn, Werner *Democracy in a Communist Party: Poland's Experience since 1980*, New York, Columbia University Press, 1987.

Hare, P. J. and Wanless, P. T. 'Polish and Hungarian Economic Reforms: a Comparison' *Soviet Studies*, vol. 33, no. 4 (Oct. 1981), pp. 491–517.

Hayden, Jacqueline *Poles Apart: Solidarity and the New Poland*, Blackrock, Co. Dublin, Irish Academic Press, and London and Portland, Oregon, Frank Cass, 1994.

Heller, Celia Stopnicka *On the Edge of Destruction: the Jews of Poland between the Two World Wars*, New York, Columbia University Press, 1977.

Hiscocks, Richard *Poland: Bridge for the Abyss? An Interpretation of Developments in Post-War Poland*, London, Oxford University Press, 1963.

Kemp-Welch, A. (ed.) *The Birth of Solidarity*, Basingstoke, Macmillan in association with St. Antony's College, Oxford, 1991.

Korbel, Josef *Poland between East and West: Soviet and German Diplomacy towards Poland, 1919–1939*, Princeton, N.J., Princeton University Press, 1963.

Korbonski, Stefan *The Polish Underground State: a Guide to the Underground, 1939–1945*, translated by Marta Erdman, East European Monographs, no. XXXIX, New York and Boulder, Colo., Columbia University Press and East European Monographs, 1978.

Korzec, Pawel 'Polen und der Minderheitenschutzvertrag (1919–1934)', *Jahrbuch für Geschichte Osteuropas*, vol. 22, (1974), pp. 515–55.

Lane, David and Kolankiewicz, George (eds) *Social Groups in Polish Society*, London and Basingstoke, Macmillan, 1973.

Lane, Thomas 'The Soviet occupation of Poland through British eyes', in John Hiden and Thomas Lane (eds) *The Baltic and the Outbreak of the Second World War*, Cambridge, Cambridge University Press, 1992, pp. 142–64.

Leslie, R. F. (ed.) *A History of Poland since 1863*, Cambridge, Cambridge University Press, 1980.

Lipski, Jan Jósef *KOR: A History of the Workers' Defense Committee in Poland, 1976–1981*, translated by Olga Amsterdamska and Gene M. Moore, Berkeley and Los Angeles, University of California Press, 1985.

Los, Stanislas 'The Ukrainian Question in Poland', *Slavonic and East European Review*, vol. 10, no. 28 (June 1931), pp. 116–25.

Machray, Robert *Poland 1914–1931*, London, George Allen & Unwin, 1932.

McShane, Denis *Solidarity, Poland's Independent Trade Union*, Nottingham, Spokesman, 1981.

Michnik, Adam *Letters from Prison and Other Essays*, translated by Maya Latynski with a foreword by Czesław Miłosz and an introduction by Jonathan Schell, Berkeley, University of California Press, 1985.

Mikołajczyk, Stanisław *The Pattern of Soviet Domination*, London, Sampson Low, Marston, 1948.

Motyl, Alexander J. *Dilemmas of Independence: Ukraine after Totalitarianism*, New York, Council on Foreign Relations Press, 1993.

Motyl, Alexander J. 'Ukrainian Nationalist Political Violence in Inter-War Poland (1921–1939)', *East European Quarterly*, vol. 19, no. 1 (March 1985), pp. 45–55.

Myant, Martin *Poland: a Crisis for Socialism*, London, Lawrence & Wishart, 1982.

Narkiewicz, Olga A. *The Green Flag: Polish Populist Politics, 1867–1970*, London, Croom Helm, 1976.

Nowak, Jan *Courier from Warsaw*, with a foreword by Malcolm Muggeridge, London, Collins/Harvill, 1982.

Ost, D. *Solidarity: the Politics of Anti-Politics: Opposition and Reform in Poland since 1968*, Philadelphia, Penn., Temple University Press, 1990.

Polonsky, Antony *Politics in Independent Poland, 1921–1939: the Crisis of Constitutional Government*, Oxford, Clarendon Press, 1972.

Polonsky, A. and Drukier, B. (eds) *The Beginnings of Communist Rule in Poland*, London, Routledge & Kegan Paul, 1980.

Pomian-Srzednicki, M. *Religious Change in Contemporary Poland: Secularization and Politics*, London, Routledge & Kegan Paul, 1982.

Reddaway, W. F. *Marshall Piłsudski*, London, Routledge, 1939.

Rosenthal, Harry K. 'National Self Determination: the Example of Upper Silesia', *Journal of Contemporary History*, vol. 7, no. 3–4 (July–Oct. 1972), pp. 231–41.

Roszkowski, Wojciech 'Large Estates and Small Farms in the Polish Agrarian Economy between the Wars (1918–1939)', *Journal of European Economic History*, vol. 16, no. 1 (Spring 1987), pp. 75–88.

Rothschild, Joseph *Piłsudski's Coup D'Etat*, New York, Columbia University Press, 1966.

Ruane, Kevin *The Polish Challenge*, London, BBC, 1982.

Sakwa, George 'The Polish Ultimatum to Lithuania in March 1938', *Slavonic and East European Review*, vol. 55, no. 2 (April 1977), pp. 204–26.

Sandford, George *Polish Communism in Crisis*, London, Croom Helm, 1983.

Staniszkis, J. *Poland's Self-Limiting Revolution*, edited by Jan T. Gross, Princeton, N.J., Princeton University Press, 1984.

Subtelny, Orest *Ukraine: a History*, University of Toronto Press with the Canadian Institute of Ukrainian Studies, Toronto and London, 1994.

Szczypiorski, Andrzej *The Polish Ordeal: the View from Within*, translated by Celina Wieniewska, London, Croom Helm, 1982.

Taras, Ray *Ideology in a Socialist State: Poland 1956–1983*, Cambridge, Cambridge University Press, 1984.

Taras, Ray *Consolidating Democracy in Poland*, Boulder, Colo. and Oxford, Westview Press, 1995.

Toranska, Teresa *Oni: Stalin's Polish Puppets*, translated from the Polish by Agnieszka Kołakowska, with an introduction by Harry Willets, London, Collins/Harvill, 1987.

Touraine, Alain, Dubet, Francois, Wieviorka, Michel and Strzelecki, Jan *Solidarity: Analysis of a Social Movement: Poland 1980–81*, translated by David Denby, Cambridge, Cambridge University Press, 1983.

Vale, Michael (ed.) *Poland: the State of the Republic: Reports by the Experience and Future Discussion Group (DiP) Warsaw*, London, Pluto Press, 1981.

Valkenier, Elizabeth Kridl 'Stalinizing Polish Historiography: What Soviet Archives Disclose', *East European Politics and Societies*, vol. 7, no. 1 (Winter 1993), pp. 109–34.

Wałęsa, L. *A Path of Hope*, London, Collins/Harvill, 1987.

Wandycz, Piotr S. 'Poland's Place in Europe in the Concepts of Piłsudski and Dmowski', *Eastern European Politics and Societies*, vol. 4, no. 3 (Fall 1990), pp. 451–68.

Woodall, Jean (ed.) *Policy and Politics in Contemporary Poland: Reform, Failure, Crisis*, London, Pinter, 1982.

Wynot, Edward D., Jr ' "A Necessary Cruelty": The Emergence of Official Anti-Semitism in Poland, 1936–39', *American Historical Review*, vol. 76, no. 4 (Oct. 1971), pp. 1035–58.

Zajdlerowa, Zoë *The Dark Side of the Moon*, new edition edited by John Coutouvidis and Thomas Lane, London and New York, Harvester, 1989.

Zinner, Paul E. *National Communism and Popular Revolt in Eastern Europe: a Selection of Documents on Events in Poland and Hungary, February–November 1956*, New York, Columbia University Press, 1956.

Zweig, Ferdynand *Poland between Two Wars: a Critical Study of Social and Economic Changes,* London, Secker & Warburg, 1944.

ROMANIA

Barbu, Zev 'Romania', in S. J. Woolf (ed.) *Fascism in Europe,* London and New York, Methuen, 1981, pp. 151–70.

Behr, Edward '*Kiss the Hand You Cannot Bite': the Rise and Fall of the Ceauşescus,* London, Penguin Books, 1992.

Boia, Eugene *Romania's Diplomatic Relations with Yugoslavia in the Interwar Period, 1919–1941,* East European Monographs, no. CCCLVI, New York and Boulder, Colo., Columbia University Press and East European Monographs, 1993.

Bolitho, Hector *Roumania under King Carol,* London, Eyre & Spottiswoode, 1939.

Brucan, Silviu *The Wasted Generation: Memoirs of the Romanian Journey from Capitalism to Socialism and Back,* Boulder, Colo. and Oxford, Westview Press, 1993.

Deletant, Dennis *Ceauşescu and the Securitate: Coercion and Dissent in Romania, 1965–1969,* London, Hurst, 1996.

Dogan, Mattei 'Romania, 1919–1938', in Myron Weiner and Ergun Ozbuden (eds) *Competitive Elections in Developing Countries,* Durham, N.C. and London, Duke University Press, 1987, pp. 369–89.

Eidelberg, Philip Gabriel *The Great Rumanian Peasant Revolt of 1907: Origins of a Modern Jacquerie,* Leiden, E. J. Brill, 1974.

Evans, Ifor Leslie *The Agrarian Revolution in Roumania,* Cambridge, Cambridge University Press, 1924.

Fischer, Mary Ellen *Nicolae Ceauşescu: a Study in Political Leadership,* Boulder, Colo., Lynne Rienner, 1989.

Fischer-Galaţi, Stephen *The New Rumania: from People's Democracy to Socialist Republic,* Cambridge, Mass., MIT Press, 1967.

Fischer-Galaţi, Stephen *The Socialist Republic of Rumania,* Baltimore, Md, Johns Hopkins University Press, 1969.

Fischer-Galaţi, Stephen *Twentieth Century Romania,* second edition, New York, Columbia University Press, 1991.

Fischer-Galaţi, Stephen 'Myths in Romanian History', *East European Quarterly,* vol. 15, no. 3 (Fall 1981), pp. 327–34.

Fischer-Galaţi, Stephen ' "Autocracy, Orthodoxy and Nationality" in the Twentieth Century: the Romanian Case', *East European Quarterly,* vol. 18, no. 1 (March 1984), pp. 25–34.

Floyd, David *Rumania: Russia's Dissident Ally,* London, Pall Mall Press, 1965.

Gallagher, Tom *Romania after Ceauşescu: the Politics of Intolerance,* Edinburgh University Press, Edinburgh, 1995.

Galloway, George and Wylie, Bob *Downfall: the Ceauşescus and the Romanian Revolution,* London, Futura, 1991.

Garson, Robert 'Churchill's Spheres of Interest: Bulgaria and Rumania', *Survey,* vol. 24, no. 3 (108, Summer 1979), pp. 143–58.

Gilberg, Trond *Nationalism and Communism in Romania: the Rise and Fall of Ceauşescu's Personal Dictatorship,* Boulder, Colo., Westview Press, 1990.

Gill, Graeme J. 'Rumania: Background to Autonomy', *Survey,* vol. 21, no. 3 (96, Summer 1975), pp. 94–113.

Grothusen, Klaus-Detlev (ed.) *Rumänien,* Südosteuropa-Handbuch, vol. II, Göttingen, Vandenhoeck & Ruprecht, 1977.

Hale, Julian *Ceauşescu's Romania: a Political Documentary,* London, Harrap, 1971.

Hall, D. J. *Romanian Furrow*, with a foreword by R. H. Bruce Lockhart, London, George G. Harrap, 1939.

Hillgruber, A. *König Carol und Marschall Antonescu: die deutsch-rumänischen Beziehungen, 1938–1944*, Wiesbaden, Veröffentlichungen des Instituts für Europäische Geschichte, 1954.

Hitchins, Keith *Rumania 1866–1947*, Oxford, Clarendon Press, 1994.

Ionescu, Ghita *Communism in Rumania, 1944–1962*, London, Oxford University Press, 1964.

Jowitt, Kenneth 'Political Innovation in Rumania', *Survey*, vol. 20, no. 4 (93, Autumn 1974), pp. 132–51.

King, Robert R. *A History of the Rumanian Communist Party*, Stanford, Cal., Stanford University Press, 1980.

King, Robert R. 'The Blending of Party and State in Rumania', *East European Quarterly*, vol. 12, no. 4 (Winter 1978), pp. 489–500.

Kitch, Michael 'Constantin Dobrogeanu-Gherea and Rumanian Marxism', *Slavonic and East European Review*, vol. 55, no. 1 (Jan. 1977), pp. 65–89.

Lungu, Dov B. *Romania and the Great Powers 1933–1940*, Durham, N.C. and London, Duke University Press, 1989.

Mitrany, David *The Land and the Peasant in Rumania: the War and Agrarian Reform, 1917–21*, London, Oxford University Press, 1981.

Nagy-Talevara, Nicholas M. *The Green Shirts and Others: a History of Fascism in Hungary and Romania*, Stanford, Cal., Stanford University Press, 1970.

Nelson, Daniel N. (ed.) *Romania after Tyranny*, Boulder, Colo., Westview Press, 1992.

Nelson, Daniel N. 'Worker-Party Conflict in Romania', *Problems of Communism*, vol. 30, no. 5 (Sept.–Oct. 1981), pp. 40–9.

Pacepa, Ion *Red Horizons: the Extraordinary Memoirs of a Communist Spy Chief*, London, Heinemann, 1988.

Pearton, Maurice *Oil and the Romanian State, 1895–1948*, Oxford, Clarendon Press, 1971.

Porter, Ivor *Operation Autonomous: with S.O.E. in Wartime Romania*, London, Chatto & Windus, 1989.

Rady, Martyn *Romania in Turmoil: a Contemporary History*, London, Tauris, 1992.

Schöpflin, George 'Rumanian Nationalism', *Survey*, vol. 20, no. 1/2 (91/92, Spring/ Summer 1974), pp. 77–104.

Seton-Watson, R. W. *A History of the Romanians from Roman Times to the Completion of Unity*, Cambridge, Cambridge University Press, 1934.

Shafir, Michael *Romania: Politics, Economics and Society: Political Stagnation and Simulated Change*, London, Frances Pinter, 1985.

Turnock, David *The Romanian Economy in the Twentieth Century*, London, Croom Helm, 1986.

SLOVAKIA

Conway, John S. 'The Churches, the Slovak State and the Jews, 1939–1945', *Slavonic and East European Review*, vol. 52, no. 126 (Jan. 1974), pp. 85–112.

Hoensch, Jörg K. *Dokumente zur Autonomiepolitik der Slowakischen Volkspartei Hlinkas*, Veröffentlichungen des Collegium Carolinum no. 44, Munich and Vienna, R. Oldenbourg, 1984.

Jansak, Stefan 'The Land Question in Slovakia', *Slavonic and East European Review*, vol. 8, no. 24 (Mar. 1930), pp. 612–26.

Jansak, Stefan 'Land Reform in Slovakia (II)', *Slavonic and East European Review*, vol. 9, no. 25 (June 1930), pp. 177–86.

Jelinek, Yeshayahu A. *The Parish Republic: Hlinka's Slovak People's Party, 1939–1945*, East

European Monographs, no. XIV, New York and Boulder, Colo., Columbia University Press and East European Monographs, 1976.

Jelinek, Yeshayahu A. *Nationalism in Slovakia under the Communists, 1918–1948*, East European Monographs, no. CXXX, New York and Boulder, Colo., Columbia University Press and East European Monographs, 1983.

Jelinek, Yeshayahu A. 'Storm Troopers in Slovakia: the Rodobrana and the Hlinka Guard', *Journal of Contemporary History*, vol. 6, no. 31 (July 1971), pp. 97–119.

Jelinek, Yeshayahu A. 'The Slovak Right: Conservative or Radical? A Reappraisal', *East Central Europe*, vol. 4, no. 1 (1977), pp. 20–34.

Jelinek, Yeshayahu A. 'The Final Solution: the Slovak Version', *East Central Europe*, vol. 6, no. 1 (1979), pp. 76–84.

Kirschbaum, Stanislav J. *A History of Slovakia: the Struggle for Survival*, Basingstoke, Macmillan, 1995.

Lettrich, Jozef *History of Modern Slovakia*, New York, Praeger, 1955.

Mikus, Joseph A. *Slovakia: a Political History: 1918–1950*, translated from the French by Kathryn Day Wyatt and Joseph A. Mikus, Milwaukee, Wisc., Marquette University Press, 1963.

Seton-Watson, R. W. *A History of the Czechs and Slovaks*, London, Hutchinson, 1943.

Steiner, Eugen *The Slovak Dilemma*, Cambridge, Cambridge University Press, 1973.

YUGOSLAVIA AND ITS SUCCESSOR STATES

Akhavan, Payam and Howse, Robert (eds) *Yugoslavia: the Former and the Future: Reflections by Scholars from the Region*, Washington, D.C., The Brookings Institution, and Geneva, the United Nations Research Institute for Social Development, 1995.

Alexander, Stella *Church and State in Yugoslavia since 1945*, Cambridge, Cambridge University Press, 1979.

Almond, Mark *Europe's Backyard War: the War in the Balkans*, revised and updated edition, London, Mandarin, 1994.

Auty, Phyllis *Tito: a Biography*, London, Longman, 1970.

Banac, Ivo *The National Question in Yugoslavia: Origins, History, Politics*, Ithaca, N.Y. and London, Cornell University Press, 1984.

Banac, Ivo *With Stalin against Tito: Cominformist Splits in Yugoslav Communism*, Ithaca, N.Y. and London, Cornell University Press, 1988.

Baskin, Mark 'Crisis in Kosovo', *Problems of Communism*, vol. 32, no. 2 (Mar.–April 1983), pp. 61–74.

Beloff, Nora *Tito's Flawed Legacy: Yugoslavia and the West: 1939 to 1984*, London, Victor Gollancz, 1985.

Benderly, Jill and Kraft, Evan (eds) *Independent Slovenia: Origins, Movements, Perspectives*, Basingstoke, Macmillan, 1994.

Bennett, Christopher *Yugoslavia's Bloody Collapse: Causes, Course and Consequences*, Hurst, London, 1995.

Bertsch, Gary K. 'Currents in Yugoslavia: the Revival of Nationalisms', *Problems of Communism*, vol. 22, no. 6 (Nov.–Dec. 1973), pp. 1–15.

Biberaj, Ele 'The Conflict in Kosovo', *Survey*, vol. 28, no. 3 (122, Autumn 1984), pp. 39–57.

Bigelow, Bruce 'Centralization versus Decentralization in Interwar Yugoslavia' *Southeastern Europe*, vol. 1, no. 2 (1974), pp. 157–72.

Bullard, Sir Julian and O'Neill, Robert (eds) *Lessons from Bosnia*, summary record of a seminar series of that title held in All Souls College, Oxford, Hilary Term 1996, private publication, Oxford, All Souls College, 1996.

Carter, April *Democratic Reform in Yugoslavia: the Changing Role of the Party*, London, Frances Pinter, 1982.

Cigar, Norman *Genocide in Bosnia: the Policy of 'Ethnic Cleansing'*, College Station, Texas, Texas AandM University Press, 1995.

Clissold, S. (ed.) *A History of Yugoslavia from Early Times to 1966*, Cambridge, Cambridge University Press, 1966.

Cohen, Lenard J. *Broken Bonds: Yugoslavia's Disintegration and Balkan Politics in Transition*, Boulder, Colo. and Oxford, Westview Press, 1995.

Crnobrnja, Mihailo *The Yugoslav Drama*, London, Tauris, 1994.

Dedijer, Vladimir *Tito Speaks: His Self Portrait and Struggle with Stalin*, London, Weidenfeld & Nicolson, 1953.

Dedijer, Vladimir *The Battle Stalin Lost: Memoirs of Yugoslavia 1948–1953*, New York, Grosset & Dunlap, 1972.

Denitch, Bogdan *Ethnic Nationalism: the Tragic Death of Yugoslavia*, Minneapolis and London, University of Minnesota Press, 1994.

Djilas, Aleksa *The Contested Country: Yugoslav Unity and Communist Revolution, 1919–1953*, Cambridge, Mass. and London, Harvard University Press, Harvard Historical Studies, no. 108: Russian Research Center Studies, no. 85, 1991.

Djilas, Aleksa 'Communists and Yugoslavia', *Survey*, vol. 28, no. 3 (122, Autumn 1984), pp. 25–38.

Djilas, Milovan *Tito: the Story from Inside*, translated by Vasilije Lolić and Richard Hayes, London, Weidenfeld & Nicolson, 1981.

Djilas, Milovan 'Tito and Stalin', *Survey*, vol. 28, no. 3 (122, Autumn 1984), pp. 73–83.

Donia, Robert J. and Fine, John V. A., Jr *Bosnia and Hercegovina: A Tradition Betrayed*, Hurst, London, 1994.

Dragnich, Alex N. *Serbia, Nikola Pašić and Yugoslavia*, New Brunswick, N.J., Rutgers University Press, 1974.

Dragnich, Alex N. *Yugoslavia's Disintegration and the Struggle for Truth*, East European Monographs, no. CDXXXVI, New York and Boulder, Colo., Columbia University Press and East European Monographs, 1995.

Dyker, David A. 'The Ethnic Muslims of Bosnia – Some Basic Socio-Economic Data', *Slavonic and East European Review*, vol. 50, no. 119 (April 1972), pp. 238–56.

Glenny, Misha *The Fall of Yugoslavia: the Third Balkan War*, London, Penguin Books, 1992.

Grothusen, Klaus-Detlev (ed.) *Jugoslawien*, Südosteuropa-Handbuch, vol. I, Göttingen, Vandenhoeck & Ruprecht, 1975.

Heuser, Beatrice *Western 'Containment' Policies in the Cold War: the Yugoslav Case, 1948–1953*, London, Routledge, 1989.

Hoptner, J. B. *Yugoslavia in Crisis*, New York and London, Columbia University Press, 1962.

Jovanović, Professor Slobodan 'The Yugoslav Constitution', *Slavonic and East European Review*, vol. 3, no. 7 (June 1924), pp. 166–78.

Kardelj, Edvard *Reminiscences: the Struggle for Recognition and Independence: the New Yugoslavia, 1944–1957*, London, Blond & Briggs, 1982.

Lampe, John R. *Yugoslavia as History: Twice there was a Country*, Cambridge, Cambridge University Press, 1996.

Lees, Michael *The Rape of Serbia: the British Role in Tito's Grab for Power, 1943–1944*, San Diego, New York and London, Harcourt Brace Jovanovich, 1990.

Little, Allan and Silber, Laura *The Death of Yugoslavia*, revised edition, London, Penguin, 1996.

Lyall, Archibald 'The Making of Modern Slovenia', *Slavonic and East European Review*, vol. 17, no. 50 (Jan. 1939), pp. 404–15.

Lydall, Harold *Yugoslavia in Crisis*, Oxford, Clarendon Press, 1989.

Maček, Vladko *In the Struggle for Freedom*, translated by Elizabeth and Stjepan Gaxi, University Park and London, Pennsylvania State University Press, 1957.

Magaš, Branka *The Destruction of Yugoslavia: Tracking the Break-Up, 1980–92*, London and New York, Verso, 1993.

Malcolm, Noel *Bosnia: a Short History*, London, Macmillan, 1994.

Marković, Lazar 'The Yugoslav Constitutional Problem', *Slavonic and East European Review*, vol. 16, no. 47 (Jan. 1938), pp. 356–69.

Meier, Viktor 'Yugoslavia's National Question', *Problems of Communism*, vol. 32, no. 2 (Mar.–April 1983), pp. 47–60.

Mirković, Mijo 'The Land Question in Yugoslavia', *Slavonic and East European Review*, vol. 14, no. 41 (Jan. 1936), pp. 389–402.

Novak, Bogdan C. *Trieste 1941–1954: the Ethnic, Political, and Ideological Struggle*, with a foreword by William H. McNeill, Chicago and London, University of Chicago Press, 1970.

O'Ballance, Edgar *Civil War in Bosnia, 1992–94*, Basingstoke, Macmillan, 1995.

Owen, David *Balkan Odyssey*, London, Indigo, 1996.

Pavlowitch, S. K. *Yugoslavia*, London, Benn, 1971.

Pavlowitch, S. K. *The Improbable Survivor: Yugoslavia and its Problems, 1918–1988*, London, Hurst, 1988.

Pavlowitch, S. K. *Tito: Yugoslavia's Great Dictator: A Reassessment*, Hurst, London, 1992.

Petrovich, Michael Boro *A History of Modern Serbia, 1904–1918*, 2 vols, New York, Harcourt Brace Jovanovich, 1976.

Poulton, Hugh *Who are the Macedonians?*, Hurst, London, 1995.

Raditsa, Bogdan 'Yugoslav Nationalism Revisited: History and Dogma', *Journal of Central European Affairs*, vol. 21, no. 4 (Jan. 1962), pp. 477–84.

Ramet, Sabrina P. *Nationalism and Federalism in Yugoslavia, 1962–1991*, Bloomington, Indiana University Press, second edition, 1992.

Ramet, Sabrina P. *Balkan Babel: the Disintegration of Yugoslavia from the Death of Tito to Ethnic War*, Boulder, Colo. and Oxford, Westview Press, 1995.

Ramet, Sabrina Petra and Adamovich, Ljubiša S. (eds) *Beyond Yugoslavia: Politics, Economics, and Culture in a Shattered Community*, Eastern Europe after Communism, Boulder, Colo. and Oxford, Westview Press, 1995.

Ristić, Dragisa N. *Yugoslavia's Revolution of 1941*, University Park, Pennsylvania State University Press, 1966.

Rusinow, Dennison *The Yugoslav Experiment, 1948–1954*, London, Hurst, 1977.

Schöpflin, George 'The Ideology of Croat Nationalism', *Survey*, vol. 19, no. 4 (86, Winter 1973), pp. 123–46.

Schöpflin, George 'Nationality in Yugoslav Policies', *Survey*, vol. 25, no. 3 (112, Summer 1980), pp. 1–19.

Sells, Michael A. *The Bridge Betrayed: Religion and Genocide in Bosnia*, Berkeley, Los Angeles and London, University of California Press, 1996.

Seton-Watson, R. W. 'The Background of the Yugoslav Dictatorship', *Slavonic and East European Review*, vol. 10, no. 29 (Dec. 1931), pp. 363–76.

Seton-Watson, R. W. 'Yugoslavia and the Croat Problem', *Slavonic and East European Review*, vol. 16, no. 46 (July 1937), pp. 102–12.

Sharp, Samuel 'The Yugoslav Experiment in Self-Management: Soviet Criticism', *Studies in Comparative Communism*, vol. 4, no. 3/4 (July/Oct. 1971), pp. 169–78.

Shoup, P. *Communism and the Yugoslav National Question*, New York and London, Columbia University Press, 1968.

Singleton, Fred *A Short History of the Yugoslav Peoples*, Cambridge, Cambridge University Press, 1985.

Slijepcević, Pero 'Land Settlement in Yugoslav Macedonia', *Slavonic and East European Review,* vol. 9, no. 25 (June 1930), pp. 160–76.

Tochitch, Desimir 'Titoism without Tito', *Survey,* vol. 28, no. 3 (122, Autumn 1984), pp. 1–23.

Tomasevich, Jozo *Peasants, Politics and Economic Change in Yugoslavia,* Stanford, Cal., Stanford University Press, 1955.

Tomasevich, Jozo *War and Revolution in Yugoslavia, 1941–45: I. The Chetniks,* Stanford, Cal., Stanford University Press, 1975.

Ulam, Adam *Titoism and the Cominform,* Cambridge, Mass., Harvard University Press, 1952.

West, Richard *Tito and the Rise and Fall of Yugoslavia,* Sinclair-Stevenson, London, 1996.

Wilson, Duncan *Tito's Yugoslavia,* Cambridge, Cambridge University Press, 1979.

Woodward, Susan L. *Balkan Tragedy: Chaos and Dissolution after the Cold War,* Washington, D.C., The Brookings Institution, 1995.

Woodward, Susan L. *Socialist Unemployment: the Political Economy of Yugoslavia, 1945–1990,* Princeton, N.J., Princeton University Press, 1995.

'X——x', 'A Croat View of the Yugoslav Crisis', *Slavonic and East European Review,* vol. 7, no. 20 (Jan. 1929), pp. 304–10.

INDEX

Abdić, Fikret 431, 433
Abgrenzung (differentiation) 357–8, 381, 382
Abyssinia 150
Academy of Sciences (Czechoslovakia) 331; Institute for Economics 321; Institute of Philosophy 323
Academy of Sciences of the GDR 358
Academy of Sciences (Serbian), memorandum 387
Aczél, György 349
Adamec, Ladislav 398
Afghanistan 354, 379, 408, 409
Africa 307, 379
Agram trial 16, 17
Agrarian Party: Czechoslovak 13–14, 61, 62, 64–5, 68, 69, 71, 155; German 61, 68, 75; Serbian 135
agrarians 10, 11, 23–4, 45, 61, 64–5, 98, 152, 153, 166, 209, 217, 219, 228; Bulgarian *see* Bulgarian Agrarian National Union; Hungarian 61; Poland *see* Peasant Party; Polish Peasants' Party
Agrokomerc (Bosnia) 386–7, 431
Ahmeti, Vilson 405, 422
Aizsargi 101
AK *see Armia Krajowa*
Akashi, Yakushi 434
Alba Iulia 108, 112
Albania 7, 15, 144–51, 204, 356–7, 389, 403–5, 421–3; army 356; bureaucracy 148, 150, 356; and China 356, 357, 389; communism in 215, 244; and depression 35; economy 240, 251, 404, 422; education 148–9; factors for revolt 283; fascism in 159, 204; finanical aid 421–2; foreign policy 421; gendarmerie 147–8; genocide 422–3; and Germany

215; and Gorbachev 407; and Greece 356, 421; industry 281; intelligentsia 144, 147, 148; and Italy 23, 141–2, 148, 149–51, 179, 204, 356; and Kosovo 21, 180, 182, 310, 350, 401; land law 149; and Macedonia 446; as monarchy 33, 148–50; and nationalism 261; partition 144; political allies 356; political groups 145, 213; political sector developments 422–3; reformism 404–5; reforms of Zog 148–9; religion 144, 149, 311; and revisionism 311, 389; revolts 6, 20, 22–3; riots 403, 404; and Romania 312; secret police 247, 356, 404; and Soviet Union 275, 311, 356, 403; and television 411; and USA 403; verification 422–3; Yugoslav forces in 145; and Yugoslavia 259, 356, 357
Albanian Party of Democratic Prosperity (PDP) 445, 446
Albanian–Greek treaty of friendship (1996) 421
Albanians: in the Balkans 446; of Kosovo 20, 132, 387, 456; in Macedonia 446, 447
Alexander, King (earlier regent) of Yugoslavia 15, 22, 37, 91, 130, 136, 137, 138–9, 140–1, 159
Alexander of Battenberg, Prince of Bulgaria 26
Alexander III, Tsar 6
Alia, Ramiz 389, 403, 422
Alliance of Democrats (Slovakia) 453
Alliance of Free Democrats (Hungary) 381, 444
Alliance of Young Democrats (FIDESz) (Hungary) 393, 444